ANGELA AND ELKAN ALLAN

Elkan Allan could be said to have films in his blood: his grandfather ran the first cinema in East London, the Penny Palace, where his father used to turn the projector. Elkan Allan has worked in films, television and journalism, and he estimates that he has seen 10,000 films in a lifetime of viewing for both work and fun. He has written and produced many television documentaries, and some of his programmes, including *Freedom Road* and *Ready, Steady, Go!* have won national and international awards. He directed the movie *Love In Our Time*. For nine years, until 1978, he wrote the 'Critical Guide to the Week's Television' in *The Sunday Times,* before moving to *Now!* magazine in 1979.

Angela Allan was a show-business columnist before she married Elkan. The Allans live in a Victorian rectory in Suffolk with their two children, four cats, a dog and a donkey.

THE SUNDAY TIMES

GUIDE TO MOVIES ON TELEVISION

ANGELA and ELKAN ALLAN

Hamlyn Paperbacks

THE SUNDAY TIMES GUIDE TO MOVIES
ON TELEVISION
ISBN 0 600 20033 7

First published in Great Britain 1973
by Times Newspapers Ltd
This revised edition published by
Hamlyn Paperbacks 1980
Copyright © 1973, 1980 by Angela and Elkan Allan

Hamlyn Paperbacks are published by
The Hamlyn Publishing Group Ltd,
Astronaut House,
Feltham,
Middlesex, England

(Paperback Division: Hamlyn Paperbacks,
Banda House, Cambridge Grove,
Hammersmith, London W6 0LE)

Set, printed and bound in Great Britain by
Cox & Wyman Ltd, Reading

ACKNOWLEDGEMENTS

Among the many people we would like to thank for their help, encouragement and inspiration are the staff of the British Film Institute reference library, who originally checked the facts in the first edition; Harold Evans, Oscar Turnill, Alan Howden, Kevin O'Shea, Fred Zentner, and Leslie Halliwell in his dual capacity as ITV film buyer and reference book compiler. A special word of thanks to Derek Jewell of Times Newpapers for putting no obstacles in the way of republication, and, indeed, for his encouragement.

Inclusion of a film in this book does not guarantee that it has been or will be acquired for showing on television in Britain.

Some films have been distributed in the UK or US under different titles. An index of alternative titles will be found on page 359.

WHAT THE RATINGS MEAN

√ √ √	Cancel all other arrangements
√ √	Catch it if you can
√	If you've nothing better to do
×	Find something better to do
××	Don't waste your time
×××	Ring up and complain
(c)	Film in colour
(b/w)	Film in black and white

INTRODUCTION TO THE FIRST EDITION

The MGM lion . . . the Columbia lady . . . the man with the gong . . . the pleasure begins there for the real film fan. Then the swelling music, the opening credits, and we are swept into the magic world of the movie. Film as art, film as sociology, film as politics – all are superseded, at least while the movie lasts, by film as fun.

But which of the fifty or so films that every viewer is offered each month on TV is worth watching? You may recognise a few of the names; the rest is speculation. We hope that this book will make the choice easier by giving the facts about most of the movies that compete with each other and the rest of the programmes for your time. We have also given a critical opinion on each one – you may not agree with it, but at least it will give you some guide, if only to watch the film because we hate it.

These opinions and the tick-and-cross ratings are the fruit of many years of film-watching. When we haven't seen a film – or can't remember what we thought of it – we have fallen back on a critical consensus of never fewer than five contemporary reviews.

Over the next two years, even without the fourth channel coming into operation, about one thousand films will be shown on British television, taking into account the variations and duplications of the fifteen ITV programme areas. Most of them are summarised and criticised in this book, but inevitably there will be some we haven't covered – either because we don't know them to be available, or considered for TV showing, or because they have slipped through our net. There are more than 20,000 movies theoretically available, and we have cut out most foreign language films, made-for-TV efforts and such products as Walt Disney's bread-and-butter which are unlikely to be sold to TV.

Conversely, we must have included a large number that will not get a showing in the lifetime of this edition. Some have not yet been sold to television; other may not be available for many years, until their cinema box-office potential has been completely exhausted. Others may have been bought, but not yet scheduled in your area.

The viewer might be forgiven for wondering why so many bad old films are shown on television. Why don't those in charge choose only the best ones out of the 20,000-plus available to them? The answer is that the distributors who own the rights of the films force the TV companies and the BBC to buy the rotten ones along with the good. They sell in blocks of twenty to thirty; a typical 'package' contains two or three outstanding movies, half a dozen very bad ones, and a majority of in-betweens. In order to get the winners, the companies have to buy the losers. The question then is what to do with the bad ones? The overwhelming temptation, having paid for them, is to show them. Can one really plead with programme controllers not to succumb? In difficult financial times, probably not; but when the revenue is rolling in, it's cheap-skate of them to put out films that they must know are pretty awful – usually at periods when a large proportion of viewers is assured, as when the opposition is off the air or has scheduled something unappealing to the mass audience.

The art of scheduling is a complicated and expert one. While some programme controllers have been rumoured to sit down at the kitchen table with their friends and relatives and pick out the films that they personally would like to see again, the more painstaking station-heads will take the 'track record' of films on previous showings in other areas into account. Some ITV controllers rely on a forecasting system called TAPE that awards points to every available movie in terms of audience appeal – proven or speculative. For instance, Robert Mitchum rates 90 points, Henry Fonda 50, Judy Garland 10. A 'non-sadistic modern dress action' gets 70 points; but stories set in newspaper offices or the Deep South only 10, and so on. This is the creation of Mr Mike Firman who is an awfully nice chap personally, but an enemy of all film-lovers.

We decided against including the original lengths of films because the figures can be very misleading. Television shows films at the speed of 25 frames per second against the cinema's 24; thus all movies run just over 4 per cent faster. In addition, the calculation as to how many minutes a film will run on TV has to take into account the number and length of breaks that are inserted in it – for advertisements in the case of ITV, and for news bulletins in the case of longer films on BBC 2. We have indicated after each film whether it was originally made in colour (*c*) or black-and-white (*b/w*). But sometimes only a black-and-white print of a colour film is available for showing, so don't blame the TV people for that.

However, you can blame them for their reprehensible practice of cutting movies to fill a pre-ordained slot. Frank Capra, the veteran film director, speaking on *Film Night* in March 1973 expressed his feelings about this: 'I can't explain to you the horror of seeing a film mutilated . . . It's like destroying any work of art, like putting a moustache on a Picasso painting.'

The ITV answers are that it is done discriminatingly and that they have to time their programmes to fit into fixed slots because of the networking system. Is this a valid excuse for cutting 7½ minutes out of *The Ship That Died of Shame*, as Ulster Television did on 11 December 1972? Or for slashing whole crucial scenes out of *The Pumpkin Eater*, as London Weekend did? There may even be a case under the Trade Descriptions Act for insisting on the word 'Abridged' going in front of the title when the product is so substantially altered.

You may find this a highly opinionated book. It certainly would have been much easier merely to have listed the facts about each film, but we are out to stimulate and entertain as well as to suggest what may be worth watching – and missing. We couldn't claim to be unprejudiced. What is there about Humphrey Bogart or Hitchcock to make one overlook their faults? And Ingrid Bergman or Otto Preminger to make one seek out their weaknesses? But perhaps it's the other way round for you. You are entitled to your prejudices too, and there are no absolute standards of critical opinion. Putting your prejudices against ours will, we hope, be part of the fun.

Enjoy yourselves.

Angela and Elkan Allan
April 1973

INTRODUCTION TO THE SECOND EDITION

At one of the parties, or wakes, held to mark the cessation of publication of *The Times* and *The Sunday Times* at the end of 1978, Gail Rebuck of Hamlyn Paperbacks, our agent Hilary Rubinstein, and one of us all happened to be present. The talk turned, naturally enough, to how those who worked at the papers were going to occupy themselves in the coming weeks or months. Ms Rebuck, who had just done very well with Roy Pickard's *The Oscar Movies from A-Z,* asked why we didn't bring our TV movie guide up to date. So here it is.

In the seven years since the first edition, hundreds more movies have become available for showing on television. There are others we wrongly judged to have been too obscure, too violent, too old or too bad to have been shown on TV, but which popped up just the same. So altogether there are some 1,250 extra films in this edition. The five-year rule, which prevents virtually all commercial movies from being shown till that time has expired after their first British showing, still generally applies, so by including films that were released up to the end of 1975, we should have covered nearly all the films likely to be scheduled on TV up to 1981.

Doubtless there are a few errors. If you find one, please let us know so that we can correct it in the next edition. We are extremely grateful to everyone who did this for the first edition. In particular, we should have liked to thank by name Britain's No. 1 film buff, who went to the trouble of writing to *Films and Filming* to list a whole string of minor fluffs; he subsequently kindly responded to our invitation to look again and send us privately any more he could spot. But, with his usual modesty, he has asked us not to name him. Thanks, anyway, Dick!

Angela and Elkan Allan
November 1980

A

Aaron Slick From Punkin Crick ×× Dinah Shore trilling her way through creaky old stage comedy served up with a few weak songs; Robert Merrill is city lad trying to con her. Claude Binyon; 1952. (c)

Abbott and Costello . . . Meet the Killer, directed by Charles T. Barton (1950), **Meet the Invisible Man** (1951), **Meet Dr Jekyll and Mr Hyde** (1953), **Meet the Mummy** (1954), **in the Foreign Legion** (1950) all directed by Charles Lamont, **in Hollywood**, directed by S. Sylvan Simon (1945). Strictly for those with debased tastes or nostalgia addicts; the slapstick is crude, the gags ancient, the fun less furious than the discriminating viewer. (b/w)

Abbott and Costello Meet Franken-stein √ Remarkably successful blend of horror and comedy, with Dracula and the Wolfman thrown in for value. Lon Chaney and Bela Lugosi repeat their roles, but not Boris Karloff. Charles Barton; 1948. (b/w)

The ABC Murders ××Agatha Christie wrote a clever murder story; Frank Tashlin made a dreary, absurd film. Just imagine All-American funny guy Tony Randall made up as Hercule Poirot and you'll see the starting-point of the general ghastliness; 1966. (b/w)

The Abdication ×× Not Edward VIII's, but Queen Christina of Sweden's, the same butch lady Garbo portrayed 41 years before Liv Ullmann's 1974 version. This fanciful yarn is set mostly in Rome where she falls for Cardinal Peter Finch. Historically wrong in too many details, it is not much more satisfactory dramatically, and director Anthony Harvey seems to have been weighed down by all the expensive production details. (c)

The Abductors √ Andrew McLaglen directing his father Victor in based-on-real-life story of man robbing the grave of Abraham Lincoln; Fay Spain looks on helplessly; 1957. (b/w)

Abilene Town √ Sturdy Marshal Randolph Scott going from cattlemen to homesteaders (remember that battle from Shane?) and from dance hall girl Ann Dvorak to grocer's daughter Rhonda Fleming; Edward L. Marin made this above-average western in 1946. (b/w)

The Abominable Dr Phibes ×× Well, er, yes. One couldn't have put it much better. Abominable is a fair word for this horror of a movie about disfigured Vincent Price wreaking vengeance on the surgical team that failed to save his wife. The only way this stuff could have worked would have been with braggadocio in the direction. Instead, it got Robert Fuest; 1971. (c)

The Abominable Snowman √ Made in the dizzy heights of an English studio, this comes out quite well, thanks to Peter Cushing and Richard Wattis camping it up at the base camp. Val Guest seems to have enjoyed directing it in 1957. (b/w)

About Face ×× Tiresome All-American triple romance; Gordon MacRae and Eddie Bracken toothily warble. Directed by Roy del Ruth, from play, *Brother Rat*; 1952. (b/w)

About Mrs Leslie × Come back, little Sheba, all is forgiven. This is Shirley Booth and director Daniel Mann trying to recapture the dubious charms of their earlier hit; but this 1954 sudser, about her happy holidays with Robert Ryan before she found out he was married, never catches fire. (b/w)

Above and Beyond X Robert Taylor as husband chosen to drop first A-bomb and Eleanor Parker as his racked wife; Mel Frank and Norman Panama manage some interesting technical footage about preparations, however. More a whimper than a bang; 1952. (b/w)

Above Us the Waves √ John Mills, John Gregson, Donald Sinden prominent among the well-spoken young (it was shot in 1956, about war-time naval hunt) as the upper classes save Britain again. Sub crew stalks German warships; Ralph Thomas keeps up the excitement. (b/w)

The Absent-Minded Professor √ √ Fred MacMurray defying gravity and giving real pleasure all round; Robert Stevenson; 1961. (c)

Accident √ √ If you didn't see this Joseph Losey—Dirk Bogarde—Harold Pinter piece of cleverness in 1967 don't miss it now; if you did, you may be disappointed on second viewing at the dramatic flaws, the inadequacy of Jacqueline Sassard and the ultimate emptiness. (c)

Accidental Death × Routine Edgar Wallace whodunit about mutually-set death traps, with John Carson, Richard Vernon; Geoffrey Nethercott directed fitfully; 1963. (b/w)

Across 110th Street ✓✓ — that's where Harlem starts, and this neat, elliptically informative thriller about three blacks posing as cops to make a theft who are subsequently hunted by both an affronted police force (Anthony Quinn) and Mafia (Anthony Franciosa). Barry Shear directed, skilfully, in 1972. (c)

The Accused ✓ One of those maddening plots in which if the panicked hero (or, in this case heroine – Loretta Young) had only told the police the full story (she was being attacked by rape-minded student) there needn't be any film – or not this one, at any rate. Having said that, William Dieterle made a smashing job of on-the-run suspensing in this 1948 thriller; Wendell Corey is tec, Robert Cummings, Sam Jaffe, Sara Allgood support. (b/w)

Accused of Murder ✗ Vera Ralston is, but surely she didn't do it? Have faith, along with policeman. Joe Kane produced-directed from a W. R. Burnett story; 1956. (b/w)

Ace in the Hole ✓✓ Strong Billy Wilder attack on yellow journalism, through reporter Kirk Douglas's deliberate delaying of rescue so that story of trapped man makes him bigger and bigger headlines and meal-ticket. Made in 1951. Jan Sterling, Porter Hall support. (b/w)

Across the Bridge ✓ Ken Annakin directed this in 1957 from a Graham Greene story. Rod Steiger defaults with a wanted man's stolen identity. (b/w)

Across the Pacific ✓ Humphrey Bogart, Mary Astor, Sidney Greenstreet together again; John Huston didn't quite manage to make a *Maltese Falcon* out of this Second World War thriller in 1942, but its pot boils merrily enough. (b/w)

Across the Wide Missouri ✓ Under veteran William Wellman's seasoned direction, Clark Gable turned in routinely attractive performance as Flint Mitchell who led pioneers into Blackfoot territory in 1829. This 1951 effort has some fine photography and J. Carrol Naish. Unfortunately, it also has a yawnful script, John Hodiak and Adolphe Menjou. (c)

Action in the North Atlantic ✓ Made in 1943 by Lloyd Bacon as contribution to keeping up morale, this actioner tells how brave merchant seamen are. And they were. Humphrey Bogart, Raymond Massey, Alan Hale, Sam Levene score; Dane Clark takes too many chances. (b/w)

Action of the Tiger ✗ Terence Young directing Sean Connery, but years before James Bond – 1957, in fact. Dogged Van Johnson is the star and the story is something about escaping from Albania and those Un-American Reds; Herbert Lom, Martine Carrol keep it dragging. (c)

Act of Love ✓ Irwin Shaw turned this Albert Hayes novel of GI and near-tart in wartime Paris into an acceptable script in 1954, Anatole Litvak did his directorial best. Unfortunately the front office cast rugged Kirk Douglas as the man, Dany Robin as the girl, and chickened out on the *denouement*. (b/w)

Act of Murder ✓ Tentative 1965 attempt of TV director Alan Bridges to make a big-screen movie remained just too tethered to the more intimate medium but should play well on television. John Carson is man Justine Lord once had affair with, but now she's married to Anthony Bate. (b/w)

An Act of Murder ✓ Heavy, portentous drama about Fredric March as a judge euthanasing his wife. Director Michael Gordon indulged himself in appallingly ubiquitous music, which considerably detracts from the tension. Florence Eldridge, Geraldine Brooks do their best to compete with soundtrack; 1948. (b/w)

Act of Violence ✓✓ Exciting thriller about Van Heflin being chased by old army anti-chum Robert Ryan; Mary Astor is friendly tart; Janet Leigh love interest. Fred Zinnemann (*The Men, High Noon*) could certainly pack a punch in 1949. (b/w)

Act One ✗✗ Disastrous 1963 attempt by Dore Schary to convey the flavour of playwright Moss Hart's Broadway autobiography. Jason Robards' impersonation of George S. Kaufman isn't absolutely embarrassing, which George Hamilton's essay at Hart is. Stalwarts Jack Klugman, Eli Wallach, Sam Levene clomp unhappily around. (b/w)

The Actress ✓ Touching period piece set in the Twenties about author Ruth Gordon's own fight to get out of a small town and into Broadway. Jean Simmons does fine as the girl, while Anthony Perkins made his debut (it's 1953) as her beau. But Spencer Tracy dominates the film, as he did everything he was in, as her disapproving Dad. George Cukor obviously enjoyed himself directing; so did the cast. So will you. (b/w)

Ada XX Unfortunate attempt to turn Dean Martin into an actor founders less on his inadequacies than on director Daniel Mann's desperate effort to make an incredible story of Southern political manipulation stand up. Susan Hayward is cute where she should have been dangerous, Wilfrid Hyde White monumentally miscast; only Martin Balsam survives this 1961 disaster. *(c)*

Adam and Evelyn XX Sub-sub-Coward about gambler Stewart Granger and dead friend's daughter, Jean Simmons; 1949 Harold French production-direction all gloss and no substance. *(b/w)*

Adam Had Four Sons √ Take cover when you see Gregory Ratoff's name as director – it means that a film's going over the top emotionally. Susan Hayward, Warner Baxter, Fay Wray oblige in this one about brave Ingrid Bergman as governess looking after widowed Baxter's sons. Maybe you could get servants like her in 1941 – though it's doubtful. *(b/w)*

Adam's Rib √√ In his book *Tracy and Hepburn*, Garson Kanin tells how Katharine Hepburn made him build up litigious wife's part so that Judy Holliday would want to play it. Hepburn even refused to do a reaction shot in Holliday's introductory scene lest it distracted. But Judy Holliday almost refused part because she was called Fatso in the script. Altogether a delightful Tracy-Hepburn team job, playing husband-wife lawyers on opposing sides of wife *v.* husband case. Judy Holliday, Tom Ewell are warring spouses. Directed by George Cukor; 1949. *(b/w)*

The Adding Machine XX Ill-conceived attempt by writer-director-producer Jerome Epstein to bring Elmer Rice's seminal play to the screen, in 1969, 46 years after it was written and was topical. Compounding the error is the central casting of Milo O'Shea, who doesn't have the range or power the part demands. Made in Britain, with a valiant cast half-pretending to be American, it lacks the necessary assurance and stylisation. *(c)*

The Admirable Crichton √ Kenneth More as the perfect butler who becomes natural leader when family is shipwrecked; Barrie play adequately filmed by Lewis Gilbert in 1957 has Diane Cilento, Cecil Parker, Gerald Harper, Jack Watling, Martita Hunt, Sally Ann Howes. *(c)*

Adolf Hitler – My Part in His Downfall XX Jim Dale (aged 37) is as painfully miscast in the part of Spike Milligan aged 21 as the real Spike Milligan is in the role of his own father. Apart from never being able to surmount this, director Norman Cohen has allowed a batch of TV comics (Arthur Lowe, Bill Maynard, Windsor Davies) to do their set pieces when they were supposed to be portraying real people in Private Milligan's war service; 1972 *(c)*

Advance to the Rear XX The Civil War wasn't funny and nor is this 1964 attempt by George Marshall to make it so; Glenn Ford, Melvyn Douglas and Joan Blondell are lost in there somewhere. *(c)*

Adventure X Clark Gable's first film after air force service was this 1945 would-be comedy of torpedoed bo'sun who meets meek librarian, marries her, divorces her, and – well, you know the old story, Boy Meets Girl, Boy Loses Girl, Boy Gets Girl – the only plot in the movies, according to Joan Blondell in *Stand In*. Oddly enough, she's in this one, too, along with Thomas Mitchell; so it can't be all bad, despite Victor Fleming's tired direction. *(b/w)*

The Adventurers XXX Harold Robbins's ghastly epic novel is matched by Lewis Gilbert's and Michael Hastings's screenplay, and Gilbert's flaccid direction. The whole unbelievable mishmash of childhood traumas and South American revolutions includes such non-contributors as Candice Bergen, Ernest Borgnine, Charles Aznavour, Olivia de Havilland and John Ireland. For masochists only; 1970. *(c)*

Adventures of a Young Man XX If you've read the Ernest Hemingway short stories on which this 1962 hotchpotch directed by Martin Ritt is based, don't bother with the movie; don't bother with it anyway, unless you are a Paul Newman fan. Arthur Kennedy, Susan Strasberg do their limited best. In the main role, Richard Beymer does his worst – and that's pretty bad. *(c)*

The Adventures of Barry McKenzie √ Barry Humphries's *Private Eye* comic strip about his archetypal Aussie almost comes to life under Bruce Bereford's direction, but stays closer to cartoon than reality. A gaggle of his English mates – Peter Cook, Dennis Price, Julie Covington among them – enjoy themselves, but it is Edna Everedge, soon (after this 1972 effort) to engulf Humphries almost entirely, who sweeps regally away with the movie. (c)

Adventures of Don Juan √ A 1949 Errol Flynn swashbuckle; he strides a little slowly through Spanish court drama, fighting baddie Robert Douglas on a staircase watched by Queen Viveca Lindfors. Vincent Sherman makes it as easy for him as possible, and keeps the excitement going with Alan Hale, Raymond Burr – who actually walked quite springily in those days. (c)

Adventures of Gallant Bess X Should Cameron Mitchell choose the nag or the nagger? OK for kids who like watching horses. Lew Landers churned this one out in 1948. (c)

Adventures of Huckleberry Finn √(1) The old (1938) Mickey Rooney version; nice for the kids, and it sticks to the story. Richard Thorpe. (b/w)

The Adventures of Huckleberry Finn X (2) Don't expect more than a pretty picture-book illustration of Mark Twain's story from this 1960 attempt of Michael Curtiz; it's desperately short of real actors and even Tony Randall drowns. (c)

Adventures of Mark Twain √√ Probably the best of all its period's epics (1944), with Fredric March impersonating the grand old man with fire and devotion. Watch for the moment on his global tour when the camera pulls away to show the vast crowd listening to him at Allahabad. Irving Rapper never got the credit he deserved for this super-production; solid old Alan Hale, C. Aubrey Smith, Donald Crisp back up splendidly. (b/w)

The Adventures of Quentin Durward X Robert Taylor in drag wooing Kay Kendall under Richard Thorpe's direction; the general vulgarity is only slightly lightened by the presence of Robert Morley, Alec Clunes, Wilfrid Hyde White, Marius Goring, Ernest Thesiger; 1955. (c)

The Adventures of Robin Hood √ Despite all those Richard Todd repeats, this is the definitive version – with Errol Flynn, Olivia de Havilland, Basil Rathbone, Claude Rains, Eugene Pallette's Friar Tuck, Alan Hale's Little John. Directed by Michael Curtiz and William Keighley; 1938. (c)

Adventures of Sadie XXX Weak British attempt by Noel Langley to bring Norman Lindsay's naughty-naughty novel about three men and a girl

castaway to life. Doubtless Joan Collins, Kenneth More, George Cole, Hattie Jacques will blush in excruciating agony when it comes chattering out of the television set at them, reminding them of the things they did for money in 1953 when it was called *His Girl Friday*. (c)

The Adventures of Sherlock Holmes √√ Basil Rathbone and Nigel Bruce made such a hit with *The Hound of the Baskervilles* that they were quickly hurried into this remake of William Gillette's stage play *Sherlock Holmes* the same year, 1939. It has to do with Moriarty's attempt to steal the Crown jewels and is splendid. Director, Albert Werker. (b/w)

The Adventures of Tartu XX Robert Donat helping Czech resistance destroy chemical plant during Second World War. Predictably far-fetched, with Glynis Johns, Valerie Hobson, Walter Rilla acting cluelessly under Harold Bucquet's bottom-of-the-bucket direction; 1943. (b/w)

Advise and Consent √√ Lovely piece of hokum should have you fooled as to what Washington, DC is like. Henry Fonda, Don Murray, Franchot Tone as the President and, above all, Charles Laughton as conniving Southern senator, are great. Otto Preminger served up a steamy brew of scandal in 1962, and it still smells rancid. (b/w)

The Affair X And a pretty boring one it is. Crippled Natalie Wood, singer and songwriter, tries living with extrovert Robert Wagner but her neuroses make him run. The rest is turgid self-analysis which director Gilbert Cates compounds with arty-crafty shooting; 1973. (c)

Affair in Havana X John Cassavetes, Raymond Burr, Sara Shane are triangle involving songwriter, crippled man, revenge and murder; Laslo Benedek makes it all rather heavy weather, but there are always Cuban backgrounds to look at, fortunately; 1957. (b/w)

Affair in Monte Carlo XX It isn't worth trying to work up too much interest in this silly yarn of Merle Oberon, Richard Todd, Leo Genn in Monte Carlo; can the gambler give it up? Can you fail to? Victor Saville must have dozed in the Riviera sunshine – or did he just stay at home? 1952. (c)

Affair in Reno X Do they really have lady bodyguards in Arizona and Nevada? If they do, you can bet they don't look like Doris Singleton, who gets involved with her assignment, John Lund, R. G. Springsteen; 1957. (c)

Affair in Trinidad X Rita Hayworth's tawdry glamour can't quite save this post-*Casablanca* spy excitement from utter disbelief. Glenn Ford sleepwalks through, suggesting that director Vincent Sherman couldn't rouse enough enthusiasm in him to wake up; 1952. (b/w)

An Affair to Remember XX Much-flawed attempt to recreate McCarey's earlier Boyer-Dunne *Love Affair*, with Cary Grant and Deborah Kerr, made by Leo McCarey in 1957. Starts well, tails off. (c)

Affair With a Stranger √ Jean Simmons, Victor Mature plan divorce but adopt child; Jane Darwell does her usual service in making mush seem plausible; Roy Rowland; 1953. (b/w)

The African Queen √√√ Won 1951 Oscar for Bogart as tough riverboat captain and nomination for Katharine Hepburn as forbidding spinster. Her humour wasn't in C. S. Forester's novel nor screenplay by James Agee, John Collier and director John Huston; in fact the whole project was going stickily until Huston suggested that Hepburn play Rosie 'as Eleanor Roosevelt'. Then it really took off, and this journey down river to escape in 1915 has become a classic. Topped *The Sunday Times* poll for movie most wanted to be seen on TV. (c)

Africa Screams X 1950 Abbott and Costello floundering in the jungle with Clyde Beatty and Frank Buck, famous white hunters of the period (1950) or, to tell the truth, a bit before. Even the lions are long in the tooth and claw. Somehow Max and Buddy Baer, slapsy heavyweight boxers, are involved, too. Pity director Charles Barton. (b/w)

Africa Texas Style X Remember a terrible series called *Cowboy in Africa*? This was the 1967 original, with John Mills hiring cowboy Hugh O'Brian to help look after his animals in Kenya; director Andrew Marton. (c)

After the Ball XX If you like *The Good Old Days*, you'll love this prettied-up picture of Vesta Tilley's life and times; Pat Kirkwood's rendering is spirited if nothing else (and it's nothing else); Laurence Harvey, Clive Morton, Leonard Sachs, Eric Chitty pop in and out as stage door johnnies, lovable Cockneys and the like; 1957. (c)

After the Fox X Peter Sellers has clearly ignored director Vittorio de Sica and decided to play it for the broadest laughs possible. Alas, they don't come in this silly story of jailbird pretending to be film director to cover gold caper in Italy. A mystery is the provenance of this 1966 effort – a Neil Simon script. (c)

After the Thin Man √√ Neat 1936 follow-up to smash success of sophisticated detective hit, *The Thin Man*, with same stars Myrna Loy, William Powell, dog Asta, plus James Stewart, Elissa Landi. W. S. van Dyke II directed tale of several murders in San Francisco, with classic ending where all seven suspects are gathered for *denouement*. (b/w)

Against All Flags X If you like pirates, Errol Flynn, Anthony Quinn and Maureen O'Hara don't be put off by the sound of our yawns. George Sherman; 1952. (c)

Against the Wind X 1948 wartime adventure about training Belgian saboteurs in England and parachuting them back home. Sticky beginning leads to rip-roaring chase near the end, with director Charles Crichton pulling all the stops out. Benefits from presence of Simone Signoret. Stiff upper lips include those of Gordon Jackson, Jack Warner. (b/w)

Agent for H.A.R.M. XX For H.A.R.M. read U.N.C.L.E. with Mark Richman in the Robert Vaughn role and Wendell Cory as overseer. The one about saving a scientist from the Reds; Gerd Oswald, 1966. (c)

The Agony and the Ecstasy XX Much more of the former than the latter in this ill-conceived chunk of marble about Michelangelo and Pope Julius II. Carol Reed seems to have suffered a mental lapse in 1965 and considered that a documentary on the artist followed by bits of his life would so overawe us we wouldn't notice we weren't being entertained. On the contrary, we're overbored. Charlton Heston, Rex Harrison, Diane Cilento go along. (c)

Ain't Misbehavin' X Reginald Gardiner and Jack Carson do their experienced best to save this rich boy (Rory Calhoun) who loves chorus girl (Piper Laurie) yarn, but writer-director Edward Buzzell makes it tough going for the veterans; 1955. (c)

Air Force √ Exciting story of a bomber crew made in 1943 by Howard Hawks; William Faulkner helped write it, and John Garfield, Gig Young, Arthur

Kennedy, Harry Carey are outstanding. (b/w)

Airport √√ Impossible to knock this eminently-knockable entertainment without taking it seriously, which is fatal. A *Grand Hotel* of the airways, it gives all sorts of players (notably Burt Lancaster as the much-imposed-upon airport manager, George Kennedy, Maureen Stapleton) the chance for histrionics as a mad bomber (Van Heflin) is killed in the air. George Seaton directs with jumbo jet of tongue in his cheek; 1970. (c)

Airport 1975 X This time the plane is in danger because all the crew are killed in a mid-air crash, except stewardess Karen Black, who has to be taught by radio how to fly the 747. Among those popping up are Charlton Heston, George Kennedy, Helen Reddy, Gloria Swanson, Susan Clark, Linda Blair, Dana Andrews, Sid Caesar, Myrna Loy, Martha Scott, all given pretty awful dialogue to spout, so it's a grand night for star-spotters, if nobody else. (c)

Air Raid Wardens √ Awkward Laurel and Hardy wartime comedy (1943) about foiling saboteurs. Donald Meek, Edgar Kennedy grace the cast; Edward Sedgwick directed. (b/w)

Akenfield XX Prettification of Ronald Blythe's documentary record of a Suffolk village, mercilessly perpetrated by Peter Hall, in 1974. By grafting on a story-line he lost the integrity of the book and gained nothing except a trite and universal yarn about a lad leaving home. (c)

The Alamo √ John Wayne directed-produced-starred in this tribute to the 185 Americans who held off 7,000 Mexicans. He's Davy Crockett, Richard Widmark's Jim Bowie (of the knife). It's very long, very loud, and great entertainment, if you like super-westerns; 1961. (c)

Alaska Seas X Why Jan Sterling is supposed to prefer Brian Keith to Robert Ryan is as obscure as the rest of this fishy yarn is obvious. Documentary montage of salmon trawlers is splendid, though. Jerry Hopper; 1954. (b/w)

Albert RN √ PoW escape yarn about building a dummy to fool the Boche. Anthony Steel, Jack Warner, Robert Beatty show upper-class upper-lip under Lewis Gilbert; 1953; (b/w)

Al Capone √√ Remarkable and under-rated *tour de force* on the part of Rod Steiger as king of the underworld and Richard Wilson as director of the underworld. Made when gangster movies were out of fashion – in 1959 – it ranks with the earlier *Scarface* and later *Godfather* as convincing picture of the seamy side. Nehemiah Persoff is outstanding in strong supporting cast. (b/w)

Alexander's Ragtime Band X Slickly made (by Henry King in 1938) but extremely boring account of show biz from 1911-38 with 26 overrated Irving Berlin songs – pretty tunes but insipid lyrics, if you can bear to listen intently enough. All the Fox stable including Ty Power, Don Ameche, Alice Faye, Jack Haley. (b/w)

Alexander the Great √√ Or at least greater than the usual run of epics. This actually has a convincing script by director Robert Rossen and real acting by Richard Burton, Fredric March, Harry Andrews. They more than make up for Claire Bloom, Danielle Darrieux, Stanley Baker, Peter Cushing. The battle scenes are exciting; 1955. (c)

The Alf Garnett Saga XX Bitty attempt in 1972 to cash in on Warren Mitchell's TV persona with Adrienne Posta replacing television's Una Stubbs as his daughter. Director Bob Kellett clearly hoped that extreme sight gags – eating LSD by mistake, wetting his trousers, setting fire to his bed – would help. They didn't. (c)

Alfie √√ Michael Caine as Bill Naughton's Cockney Don Juan convinces remarkably; Shelley Winters, Millie Martin, Julia Foster, Jane Asher, Vivian Merchant, as some of his conquests, equally outstanding. Lewis Gilbert did a fine and, let's admit it, unexpected job in 1966. (c)

Alfie Darling XXX A soft-core *Confessions of a Truck Driver*, this rip-off of the competent 1966 morality-movie turned up in 1975 with a hopeless Alan Price thundering around in a 32-ton juggernaut while making advances to every girl in sight. Ken Hughes wrote the script, which claimed to have been 'inspired by the play *Alfie*', as well as the direction. Inspired it ain't. (c)

Alfred the Great X Well, not very. At least in this movie, which ends before his mature 'greatness', if he ever was. And nor could the string of banal clichés that issue from the mouths of a distinguished but not very happy supporting cast be called great; Clive Donner sets up some marvellous pictures and occasionally makes you feel what it must have been like in the ninth century, but in come the words again to wash all reality away. Nor is David Hemmings's playing of the cake-burner anything to savour; 1969. (c)

Alias John Preston XX What are the strange dreams that bother this young man on his way to success? They may be yours, as you doze in your armchair. Alexander Knox portentous, Christopher Lee puzzled. David MacDonald; 1955. (b/w)

Alias Nick Beal √√ Ray Milland was never better than in this 1949 reworking of the Faust legend, with Thomas Mitchell as his policitian-prey and Audrey Totter as his winsome accomplice. John Farrow (Mia's father) directed with distinction and understatement. (b/w)

Ali Baba and the Forty Thieves √ Jon Hall, vainly being built up as Universal's answer to Errol Flynn in 1943, played Robin Hood in curved sandals, with Maria Montez and Andy Devine; much of the lavish production was so spectacular that you'll see the same footage appearing in lots of later pix. Arthur Lubin. (c)

Alice Doesn't Live Here Anymore √ √ √ Beautifully-accomplished slice of near-life – warm, dramatic and funny – as Ellen Burstyn traipses the country in her efforts to support her son (a surprisingly endearing little boy, Billy Green Bush). Most of the action takes place in a diner which has Diane Ladd as one of the waitresses, memorably encapsulating all the tough, wisecracking broads that were ever on the screen, and adding reality in the shape of dirty dishes. As Alice's suitor, Kris Kristofferson is slightly more bearable than in his other movies. Budding stars Jodie Foster and Harvey Keitel pop up in small roles (it was made in 1974), and the whole film is orchestrated with brilliance by director Martin Scorsese. (c)

Alice's Adventures in Wonderland XX Poor effort by director William Starling and a bunch of well-known players who must have felt very sorry they agreed to appear when they saw the final, dispirited result. Fiona Fullerton (later one of the Angels in the BBC soap opera) made a prissy, dull little Alice. Among the bigger flops: Michael Crawford as the White Rabbit, Spike Milligan as the Gryphon, Peter Sellers as the March Hare; 1972. (c)

Alice's Restaurant √ Museum-piece of the dying Sixties (1969), with singer-composer Arlo Guthrie playing someone all too like himself, Pat Quinn as obliging Earth Mother, Alice, plus assorted drop-outs, hippies, flower-children and other non-conformists. Arthur Penn put it all together more competently than the random script and acting deserved. (c)

Alive and Kicking √ Kathleen Harrison and Sybil Thorndike abscond from old people's home; quite a jolly geriatric romp. Cyril Frankel; 1958. (b/w)

All About Eve √√ Highly literate Bette Davis vehicle, written and directed by Joseph L. Mankiewicz in 1950; she's marvellous as ageing stage star fighting to stay at the top, while newcomer (brilliant Anne Baxter) tries to claw her down. Neat ending. Applause, applause! (b/w)

The All-American X Tony Curtis in his younger days (1953) as football star – what could those rules be? – romancing Lori Nelson. Another later TV package star, Stuart Whitman hovers. Director Jesse Hibbs. (b/w)

All Ashore √ Lively musical about three sailors on shore leave (yes, again) which Richard Quine – so promising, so ultimately unfulfilled – directed in 1953. Mickey Rooney is lead, Dick Haymes croons along. (c)

All Coppers Are . . . XX Bastards is the word so genteely missing from the title. But on this showing they are something worse – dull. Martin Potter makes a posh policeman, and almost everyone (Julia Foster, Nicky Henson, Ian Hendry) is wrong for their parts. Sad that Allan Prior should have written this script; no surprise, though, that Sidney Hayers directed; 1971. (c)

All Fall Down √ Sincere attempt to reflect the problems of growing up which fails, admits director John Frankenheimer, because it wasn't all told from the boy's (Warren Beatty's) point of view, as was original James Leo Herlihy novel that William Inge wrote script from. Splendid performances from Karl Malden as potty father, Brandon de Wilde as kid brother, Angela Lansbury as over-mothering mother, Eva Marie Saint as loving suicide; 1962. (b/w)

All For Mary XX One of those dreadful genteel comedies Nigel Patrick specialised in. This time it's Kathleen Harrison making young couple happy in Switzerland. Wendy Toye; 1956. (c)

All Hands on Deck XX Mild fun and

19

games aboard a docked navy boat; strictly for lovers of Buddy Hackett and crooner Pat Boone, if any. Norman Taurog; 1961. (c)

All I Desire X Barbara Stanwyck goes the way of all flesh to return from a wicked career on the stage to see her daughter graduate. It was ludicrous enough in 1953 – what on earth will we make of it now? Douglas Sirk directed King of the Soapsuds, Ross Hunter's production. (b/w)

An Alligator Named Daisy XX There's this suitcase taken in mistake. And there's a real alligator in it. J. Lee Thompson propels archetypal 1955 cast of British cameo players – Diana Dors, Donald Sinden, Stanley Holloway, Roland Culver, Margaret Rutherford, Stephen Boyd – through subsequent complications. (c)

All in a Night's Work √ Comedy about death of tycoon, with Shirley MacLaine, Cliff Robertson, Dean Martin. Jack Weston, Jerome Cowan join in the fun and games under Joseph Anthony's 1961 direction. (c)

All Mine to Give √ Our own Glynis Johns turns up as pioneer lady with Cameron Mitchell in this hard slog of life on the frontier, sparely directed by Allen Reisner with considerable respect for the hardships of early Wisconsin; 1957. (c)

All My Sons √ Edward G. Robinson ruggedly plays profiteer father in Irving Reis' version of Arthur Miller award-winning play. Burt Lancaster. looking skinny in 1948, is son who finds out that Pop's defective aircraft part killed brother. (b/w)

All Night Long X Michael Relph and Basil Dearden did their double act of producing and directing this in 1961; a jazzed up version of Othello, it misses Shakespeare badly. Patrick McGoohan, Betsy Blair do their best; among those present who later made it big are Richard Harris, Keith Michell, Bernard Braden. (b/w)

All Quiet on the Western Front √√ One of the greats. Although 1930 dialogue from Maxwell Anderson is winceable and the sound primitive, its story of German schoolboys joining up and being slaughtered is as powerful a pacifist argument as ever. Lew Ayres was starred by director Lewis Milestone but Louis Wolheim steals the picture. Final minutes among most famous movie moments. (b/w)

All That Heaven Allows X Jane Wyman lowers herself to love a gardener; Rock Hudson elevates himself to love trees; whether you'll love either depends on how indulgent you're feeling; Agnes Moorehead wasted, as usual. Douglas Sirk; 1956. (c)

All the Brothers were Valiant X . . . if not particularly convincing. It's all to do with pearl-fishing, but you'll be lucky to find much to thrill you in this high-spirited, action-packed yarn, with MGM's second eleven – Robert Taylor, Stewart Granger, Keenan Wynn – slugging it out. Richard Thorpe; 1953. (c)

All the Fine Young Cannibals X One of those small-town Texan dramas that they used to force poor Natalie Wood through in 1960. Here she's involved with Robert Wagner and George Hamilton, and very boring it is, with Michael Anderson's nerveless direction. Even Pearl Bailey's singing doesn't help. (c)

All the King's Men √√ Triple Academy Award winner (Best Film of 1949, Best Actor, Broderick Crawford, Best Supporting Actress, Mercedes McCambridge). Story of Willie Stark, idealist turned corrupt politician, based on the career of Huey Long, the Louisiana Kingfish. Robert Rossen directed. (b/w)

All the Right Noises √ Triangle between Tom Bell, Judy Carne (from Rowan and Martin's Laugh-In) and Olivia Hussey (who is supposed to be only 15, although the actress was 18). Gerry O'Hara wrote-directed; 1969. (c)

All the Way Home X James Agee's very personal novel, A Death in the Family, can't be entirely brought down by Alex Segal's version of the Tad Mosel play based on it, but it's so poorly cast and minimally acted (Robert Preston, Jean Simmons, Michael Kearney are way out of their depth) that it fails to deliver; 1963. (b/w)

All the Way Up XX Crude and immoral fable about Warren Mitchell's clambering his way up the commercial ladder, using his daughter's charms as bargaining counters. Some accomplished comedy players (Richard Briers, Adrienne Posta) are put through unfortunate antics by Philip Mackie's adaptation of David Turner's play, Semi-Detached. The late James MacTaggart's direction does nothing to redeem the unpleasantness; 1970. (c)

All the Young Men XX Cheap attempt to cash in on liberal feelings towards 'negroes' in this 1960 Korea war-drama just embarrasses. Sidney Poitier is put in charge of platoon, aimid resentment from Alan Ladd. Luckily Mort Sahl is around, but even he has to mouth writer-producer-director Hall Bartlett's lines. (*b/w*)

All This and Heaven Too X Escape to 19th-century France with Charles Boyer in front of a roaring fire mouthing sentimental nuggets to eye-fluttering Bette Davis; Anatole Litvak was the chap to bring you something to look at and forget the reality of 1940 while doing it. It might perform the same function for you now, but your worries hadn't better be too pressing – it has lost a certain magic with the years. (*b/w*)

All Through the Night √ Humphrey Bogart lifts this otherwise routine (but nonetheless exciting) second world war counter-spy sleuthing in New York to a film worth an effort; Vincent Sherman packed it with other fine actors in 1942 – Conrad Veidt, Jane Darwell, Frank McHugh, Jackie Gleason, Phil Silvers and, above all, Peter Lorre. (*b/w*)

Alvarez Kelly √ Wild western based on supposedly true story of the two sides in the Civil War forcing a vast herd of cattle (owned by William Holden) to seesaw between their hungry forces. Richard Widmark, Patrick O'Neal; director, Edward Dmytryk; 1969. (*c*)

Aloma of the South Seas XX Jon Hall puts on clothes to leave Dorothy Lamour and his South Sea island to get some education in the US; but he comes back to thwart the baddies. Alfred Santell; 1941. (*c*)

Along Came Jones √ Incomparable Gary Cooper in case of mistaken identity – cowboy for killer. Only film he ever produced himself – in 1945. Director Stuart Heisler gets fine performance from Gary's old partner, Loretta Young. (*b/w*)

Along the Great Divide √ Kirk Douglas's first western (1951) and it's a wonder that his career survived all the clichés as well as the mechanical hazards the script provides, as he struggles to deliver prisoner to jail; Walter Brennan, Virginia Mayo play standard types; Raoul Walsh directed the traffic. (*b/w*)

Always a Bride XX Ronald Squire as man from the Treasury who gets caught with con-man via Peggy Cummins; Terence Morgan and James Hayter play it down, and Ralph Smart's direction isn't smart; 1954. (*b/w*)

The Amazing Mr Blunden √√ Superior junior-oriented story of two children going with their mother to live in what turns out to be a kindly ghost's house. They are taken back in time and foil a dastardly plot. Lynne Frederick did particularly well as the girl, in 1972, backed up by Laurence Naismith as the ghost and Diana Dors as a wicked old woman from the past. Director Lionel Jeffries managed it all beautifully. (*c*)

The Amazing Mrs Holliday XX Or the *Inn of the Eighth Sadness* as Deanna Durbin struggles with plot and lines to look after Chinese orphans; she sings dully, too. Barry Fitzgerald and Arthur Treacher are put through their usual paces by Bruce Manning; 1943. (*b/w*)

Ambassador's Daughter X Norman Krasna tried for pre-war sparkle in 1956 in tale of soldier picking up title-lady Olivia de Havilland but it doesn't quite come off, despite presence of Adolphe Menjou and Myrna Loy. (*c*)

Ambush X Wooden Robert Taylor as scout in Indian territory juts his pretty jaw into various bits of mild trouble; director Sam Wood obviously treated it all as routine for the 1950 MGM factory. (*b/w*)

Ambush at Tomahawk Gap √ Four released convicts looking for the fortune they stashed away in the Wild West. The Indians get three of them – who will be left alive? John Hodiak, who was being paid most for his name above the title, at a guess. Fred F. Sears directed; 1953. (*c*)

Ambush Bay X 1966 was a bit late to churn out a drama about war behind the Japanese lines, but then Mickey Rooney, Hugh O'Brian are old enough to remember it well. Director Ron Winston does his very best with creaky patrol story, but he can't do anything about James Mitchum as young soldier who learns the hard way. (*c*)

The Ambushers XX Childish and rather boring Matt Helm adventure, made extremely glossily by Henry Levin, but empty as a prop revolver. Janice Rule tries hard, but Dean Martin and Senta Berger shrug their way through a poor script, never even convincing themselves, let alone us. As for the man-killing bra, see *The Tenth Victim*; 1968. (*c*)

Ambush in Leopard Street XX Norman Rodway is only bright thing in this dull British story of diamond robbery directed by J. Henry Piperno; 1961. (b/w)

American Graffiti √ So beautifully mounted, set, dressed, observed and accompanied by period music is this 1973 nostalgia-trip to 1962 that the hollowness of the intertwining high school plots and the boringness of the characters is disguised. Ultimately, though, even the most dazzled viewer must wonder if it was all worthwhile. Star, Richard Dreyfuss; director, George Lucas. (c)

American Guerilla in the Philippines Fritz Lang's name as director should have meant a better film than this one (1950) about brave Ty Power doing his bit; Tom Ewell uncomfortable in non-comedy role. (c)

An American in Paris √√ Gershwin music ('Our Love Is Here To Stay', 'I Got Rhythm'); Gene Kelly, Leslie Caron; wry Oscar Levant; 17-minute climactic ballet; Alan Jay Lerner script; Vincente Minnelli direction (he knocked off another film, *Father's Little Dividend*, in the four weeks it took to rehearse the ballet), made this the outstanding musical of 1951 and an all-time favourite. (c)

The Americanization of Emily √√ What's a nice girl like Julie Andrews doing in a sharp, cynical movie like this one about American brass pushing James Garner around? Answer: rather well. This 1964 Paddy Chayevsky-scripted bitter comedy never got the response it deserved. Arthur Hiller. (b/w)

The Americano X Standard western that happens to take place in the Matto Grosso. A Southern, in fact. Otherwise, its the same old rustling and hustling, with Glenn Ford doing his pint-sized toughie bit and Cesar Romero adding local colour. William Castle; 1955. (c)

An American Romance √ Louis B. Mayer congratulated director King Vidor on 'the greatest picture our company ever made' at the 1944 preview. Alas, this over-long slog through the Americanisation of an immigrant couple received raspberries elsewhere, including the box office. Brian Donlevy, Ann Richards, Walter Abel starred. (c)

The Amorous Adventures of Moll Flanders XX Instead of some good honest Defoe-type pornography all Terence Young can serve up is titillations that don't tickle. In the part of Moll, Kim Novak is laughable, and

'supports' Richard Johnson, Angela Lansbury, Lilli Palmer, George Sanders, Leo McKern, Vittorio de Sica and Daniel Massey provide a gallery of failure. *Mrs Tom Jones*, it isn't; 1965. (c)

The Amorous Prawn X Super people – Dennis Price, Ian Carmichael, Cecil Parker, Joan Greenwood – manage to make this trifle about salmon-fishing money-making scheme mildly amusing; Anthony Kimmins; 1962. (b/w)

Amsterdam Affair XX Did William Marlowe kill his former mistress? Van der Valk (Wolfgang Kieling, sounding more like a Dutch Maigret than TV's Barry Foster) investigates; Gerry O'Hara directed on canal locations; 1968. (c)

Anastasia √√ Helen Hayes, as the dowager empress who questions whether Ingrid Bergman is real royal or pretend princess, is outstanding; everyone else is just a little hammy – but then what else do you expect from La Bergman (*pace* her Oscar for it), Akim Tamiroff, Yul Brynner? Anatole Litvak keeps the guessworks going merrily enough, however, and it's a nice hour or two's look; 1956. (c)

The Anatolian Smile √ Elia Kazan's biography/autobiography of Greek immigrant not quite making it; he has put so much of his own emotions in that it's beastly to remain unmoved; 1963. (b/w)

The Anatomist √ Alastair Sim and George Cole in a rather grim account of Burke-and-Harey grave-robbings; Jill Bennett suitably frightened; Leonard William; 1961. (b/w)

Anatomy of a Murder √√ Otto Preminger's 1959 detailed murder trial with James Stewart splendid as defence lawyer, Lee Remick as equivocal rapee, Ben Gazzara as client. (b/w)

Anchors Aweigh √ Sinatra and Kelly on the town in Hollywood, sailors on leave in 1945, with Tom and Jerry to dance with, and Kathryn Grayson to sing to. Director, George Sidney. (c)

And Baby Makes Three X The bride faints at the altar. She's pregnant! If that sounds like the start of a wicked Preston Sturges comedy, you'll be disappointed. This is Harry Levin and she was safely married to first husband when conceiving. She's Barbara Hale and wants to stay married to Robert Young; lucky Robert Hutton; 1950. (b/w)

The Anderson Tapes √√ Refreshingly

original caper-yarn with the emphasis less on the conspirators and their robbery but the way they are all being independently tape-recorded, bugged and put under surveillance by various people and governmental agencies. The satirical theme brought out the best in director Sidney Lumet and his players, notably Sean Connery, Martin Balsam, Dyan Cannon and Alan King; 1971. (c)

And Now Miguel √ Slow but seductive open-air adventure of young shepherd attempting to prove himself; Guy Stockwell does well. James Clark directed; 1966. (c)

And Now Tomorrow X Little Alan Ladd climbs on a chair to cure Loretta Young of deafness and then – of course – falls in lurve with her; Irving Pichel made this one for the dying handkerchief trade in 1944. (b/w)

Androcles and the Lion X Photographed theatre by the man who screwed up so many G.B.S. plays in the cinema, Gabriel Pascal. He somehow talked the old man into letting him have near-monopoly, and the result – as in this artificial, unconvincing case – is fatty ham. Dreadful casting shows the level of his taste: Alan Young, Victor Mature, Robert Newton, Maurice Evans. Pity poor Jean Simmons who must have thought this was going to give her career a boost in 1953. Charles Erskine. (b/w)

The Andromeda Strain √ Heavy going 1970-shot sci-fi adventure in which all the details piled on to impress us with authenticity, squeeze the tension out of the plot. Arthur Hill makes a concerned scientist, sacrificing his life for humanity. Director Robert Wise appears to have had insufficient respect for author Michael Crichton's built-in suspense. A pity Crichton didn't direct it himself, as he did *Westworld* a year later. (c)

And Soon the Darkness XX This tepid little tale of rape and murder in the French countryside was the first fruit of Bryan Forbes's disastrous attempt to set Elstree on its feet in 1970. Pamela Franklin and Michele Dotrice are nurses on a cycling trip; one is murdered, the other just escapes. Which of the suspicious strangers is the villain? A question in which one loses interest. (c)

And Then There Were None √√ Of the three versions of Agatha Christie's *Ten Little Niggers*, this is easily the best, directed by René Clair and featuring Barry Fitzgerald, Walter Huston, Roland Young, Mischa Auer, Judith Anderson among the victims – or so it seems; 1945. (b/w)

And the Same to You XX British boxing comedy with Brian Rix, William Hartnell, Tommy Cooper, Sid James, Shirley Ann Field; director George Pollock; 1959. (b/w)

And Women Shall Weep XXX Embarrassing 1960 piffle about Ruth Dunning handing over her son to face murder charge. Pull the other one, John Lemont. (b/w)

Angela XX Dennis O'Keefe falling in love with Mara Lane and over the body of her employer. He directed it, too; Rossano Brazzi and lots of Italians are there, because that's where it was made in 1955. (b/w)

Angel and the Badman √ Don't be put off by the title, this is an unusual western with Gail Russell playing a Quaker girl who gradually turns John Wayne away from his wicked path; Harry Carey, Bruce Cabot support strongly, and James Edwards Grant fords problems derivatively. (b/w)

Angel Baby √ A pity that George Hamilton was cast as post-Elmer Gantry character. Salome Jens as deaf-mute he may have cured, Mercedes McCambridge, Joan Blondell, Burt Reynolds all act him off the screen despite Paul Wendkos's best efforts; 1963. (b/w)

Angel Face X Otto Preminger going all pretentious about psychology in 1953, but ending up with as phoney a movie as he ever turned out (even more so than usual, in fact). Robert Mitchum does his moody bit as chauffeur, but looks as though he's as baffled as we are by what homicidal Jean Simmons, Daddy Herbert Marshall, wicked stepmother Barbara O'Neil are up to. (b/w)

The Angel Levine √ How does the idea of Harry Belafonte as a Jewish angel grab you? Zero Mostel finds it equally hard to credit, but until he accepts the fat, is wife, Ida Kaminska, won't get well again. Director Jan Kadar didn't do enough to make it all credible, but Mostel was always worth watching; 1970. (c)

Angels One Five √ A 1952 stiff upper-lipper that launched Jack Hawkins into a thousand such roles. Among his fellow-fliers in this rigid RAF drama are Michael Denison, Cyril Raymond, Humphrey Lestocq, John Gregson. Director, George More O'Ferrall. (b/w)

The Angel Who Pawned Her Harp X
A rather similar East End excursion to
A Kid for Two Farthings, which was
made in the same year, 1954. Alan
Bromly and Sidney Cole had Diane
Cilento, Felix Aylmer and Robert
Eddison trying to suggest something of
what the place was really like. (b/w)

The Angel With The Trumpet XX
Could you care about the lives of an
Austrian family of piano-makers from
1888 to the day the Second World War
ends and they decide to start all over
again? If so, Anthony Bushell is the
director for you – he leaves nothing out
and plods deliberately through it all.
To help, he has Eileen Herlie growing
old, plus Maria Schell, Andrew
Cruickshank, Wilfrid Hyde White,
Norman Woland, Basil Sydney; 1950.
(b/w)

Angels With Dirty Faces √ James
Cagney and Pat O'Brien as two East
Side kids who grow up as gangster and
priest, but bound together by friendship. Cagney is idol of the Dead End
Kids who spun off into series of own
films; Humphrey Bogart is double-
crossing racketeer, Ann Sheridan
girlfriend. Sadly, this 1938 blockbuster
survives largely as museum-piece,
mainly due to a risible sentimental
ending and heavenly choir. Michael
Curtiz delivered the product Warner
Bros wanted. (b/w)

The Angel Wore Red √ Fascinating
cop-out attempt to tell the story of a
whore and a priest in love during
Spanish Civil War. Dirk Bogarde and
Ava Gardner make excellent attempts
at authenticity, but Nunnally Johnson
made too many concessions to 1960
Hollywood. Strong supports include
Joseph Cotten, Vittorio de Sica, Finlay
Currie. (b/w)

The Angry Hills X Stanley Baker,
Theodore Bikel, lovely Gia Scala and
authentic Greek scenery are plusses;
Robert Mitchum as American involved
with guerrillas, Raymond Stross's
typical tasteless production, Robert
Aldrich's attitudinising direction are
minuses; 1959. (b/w)

The Angry Red Planet XX It's Mars as
imagined by a poor comic-strip artist,
realised on the cheap by American
International Pictures, with unknowns
(Jack Kruschen is only little name
around) playing comic and serious
explorers with a girl along. Lauritz
Melchior's son, Ib, takes the blame –
and the profit; 1959. (c)

The Angry Silence √ A rather nasty
film about Richard Attenborough
refusing to join an unofficial strike and
being persecuted by his fellow-
workers; it pretends to stand up for
individualism, but is in fact a sneaky
way of knocking men with grievances
who have been forced to turn to their
ultimate weapon, the right to withhold
their labour; Guy Green should be Sir
Guy if the Tories looked after their
own property. Bernard Lee created the
archetype shop steward (still, since this
was made in 1960, the popular
caricature of the man who gives his
spare time to his mates) and Alfred
Burke must be a bit ashamed of the on-
the-phone-to-Moscow organiser he
played so well. (b/w)

Animal Crackers √√ Marx Brothers'
second film, made in 1930. It's hooray
for Captain Spaulding, the big-game
hunter, who wrecks Margaret
Dumont's party. Director, Victor
Heerman. (b/w)

Animal Farm X This 1954 effort is one
of the few full-length cartoons made in
England; it should have been great,
given the possibilities of Orwell's
savage novel, but Halas and Batchelor
gooed it all up and it stands as neither
satirical nor even entertaining for
children. (c)

Anna and the King of Siam √√ 1946
original of later musical *The King and
I*, with Rex Harrison as the King,
Irene Dunne the governess, plus
Linda Darnell, Lee J. Cobb. John
Cromwell did sumptuous job of
direction. (b/w)

Anna Karenina X None of the 13
filmings begin to measure up to the
magnificence of the novel; in 1935
Basil Rathbone was merely sinister as
the husband in Garbo's; Ralph Richardson merely Ralph Richardson in
Vivien Leigh's (1947). We await a good
version. (b/w)

Anna Lucasta XX It's a toss-up who is
more embarrassingly awful, Eartha
Kitt as the whore with a good heart or
Sammy Davis Jr. as a brash, money-
spending sailor. Arnold Laven doesn't
do much to help his black cast; 1958.
(b/w)

Anne of the Thousand Days XX A real
stinker of a history lesson, using the
legend of Anne Boleyn dully told (by
Maxwell Anderson, helped by others),
leadenly directed (Charles Jarrott) and
indifferently acted (Richard Burton a
bellowing Henry VIII, Genevieve
Bujold a simpering Anne) with a
second eleven of theatrical worthies

backing them up amid unconvincing set; 1969. (c)

Anne of the Indies X Suspend your disbelief, if you can, and accept Jean Peters as pirate captain; starting from this pantomime premise you won't be surprised when she spares Louis Jourdan. Debra Paget, Herbert Marshall and bluff, boring James Robertson Justice muck in. Jacques Tourneur; 1951. (c)

Annie Get Your Gun √ Betty Hutton bulldozes her way into the spirit of her action as gun-slinging Annie Oakley, eventually making it with a Howard Keel who hates bossy women. Based on the Irving Berlin Broadway hit, directed by George Sidney, the production numbers still seem stage-starched, but the songs are fine ('Anything You Can Do', 'Doin' What Comes Naturally') and the pathos tender; 1950. (c)

The Anniversary X Black comedy from Bill MacIlwraith's play about highly possessive mother gives Bette Davis in an eye-patch a field day; Sheila Hancock as daughter-in-law and James Cossins as transvestite son outstanding; rest of the cast a bit weak, and Roy Baker's direction decidedly so; 1968. (c)

Another Dawn XX Arab ambushes and a triangular love affair (Errol Flynn, Kay Francis, Ian Hunter) in an east of Suez melo bogged down in the sand by director William Dieterle, 1937. (b/w)

Another Man's Poison X Val Guest must take the blame for dreadful script about lady doing in her husband, sussed out by a vet. Director Irving Rapper doesn't help, but Bette Davis and Emlyn Williams almost made this 1952 British pic worth watching. (b/w)

Another Part of the Forest √ About the Hubbard family who appear in Lillian Hellman's other film, *The Little Foxes*, only set twenty years earlier; Fredric March, Edmond O'Brien, Florence Eldridge, Betsy Blair shine; Michael Gordon doesn't quite make it much more than photographed stage play; 1948. (b/w)

Another Thin Man √√ William Powell and Myrna Loy sort out the threats to life of C. Aubrey Smith, particularly from Sheldon Leonard (who later – this was 1939 – himself produced *I Spy, My World and Welcome to It*, etc.). Otto Kruger, Ruth Hussey, Nat Pendleton, Marjorie Main add to the pleasures. W. S. Van Dyke directed as usual. (b/w)

Another Time, Another Place X Another woman, and just another movie. Cast of second-line stars (Lana Turner, Glynis Johns, Sean Connery, Barry Sullivan, Sid James) can't do much with this 1957 weepie about a man in love with two women, nor can director Lewis Allen. (b/w)

Antony and Cleopatra XX Poorly cast – unsubtle Charlton Heston and unsympathetic Hildegard Neil in the title role. Heston directed, as well, with an insensitivity that allowed even Shakespeare's best moments to go for nothing. Heston was unfortunate in having ATV's brilliant TV version of the RSC staging with Janet Suzman coming so soon after his; 1972. (c)

Any Number Can Play X You don't have to be ashamed of your father just because he's a big-time gambler. That's the stirring message of this 1949 'woman's picture', as they used to call 'em. Clark Gable is Dad, Alexis Smith Mum, Darryl Hickman his little lad. Luckily, Mervyn Le Roy has Wendell Corey, Frank Morgan, Mary Astor, Marjorie Rambeau and the rest of the MGM stock company along to keep you awake. (b/w)

Anything Goes √ Bing Crosby made this twice; in 1936 and this 1956 version (with Donald O'Connor, director Robert Lewis). Only the Cole Porter songs are memorable, but they are superb: 'I Get a Kick Out of You'; 'You're the Tops'; 'It's De-lovely'. (c)

Any Wednesday √ Called *Bachelor Girl Apartment* when first released here in 1967, this sophisticated comedy has Jason Robards as businessman who puts Jane Fonda down on his expenses; his wife gets suspicious, and it's all quite good fun, not exactly clean, but not actually dirty; directed by Robert Ellis Miller. (c)

Apache X Burt Lancaster as lone crusading Indian fighting against both US Cavalry and Charles Bronson (when he was still called Buchinsky); director, Robert Aldrich; 1954. (c)

Apache Rifles X If you think you've seen this one about Audie Murphy rounding up naughty braves before, you may be right; it uses chunks of other westerns liberally. What a swizz! Stand in the corner, William Witney; 1964. (c)

Apache Territory X Rory Calhoun defeating the entire tribe all alone. Pull the other one, Ray Nazarro; 1958. (c)

Apache Uprising X 1966 Cowboys v.

Injuns has array of earlier stars – Rory Calhoun, Corinne Calvet, Lon Chaney Jr, Richard Arlen, Jean Parker, and same old story too. R. G. Springsteen. (c)

Apache Warrior X Made 1957, before Hollywood committed itself to the virtues of the Red Indians; here they are the baddies, as they always used to be, a starless cast routinely directed by Elmo Williams. (c)

Apache War Smoke X Gilbert Roland as heavy redeeming himself when the Indians attack; others in lonely frontier fort are Glenda Farrell, Robert Horton, Gene Lockhart, Henry Morgan, Douglass Dumbrille. Directed by Harold F. Kress; 1953. (b/w)

Apache Woman √ Lloyd Bridges proving that the Red Indians aren't the villains; other baddies want to get the old wars going again. Lively western directed by Roger Corman; 1955. (c)

The Apartment √√√ The great Billy Wilder comedy from his own and I.A.L. Diamond script about the office schnook who lends his flat to his bosses in return for advancement. Shirley MacLaine just right as the girl who gets left behind. It's funny, tender, sharply-observed and unbeatable entertainment. 1960 Oscar-winner. (b/w)

Apartment for Peggy X William Holden's a returned GI, Jeanne Crain's preggers, and this is a simple story of their solvable problems; but Edmund Gwenn and Gene Lockhart lift the film away from them with a small smile of experience; writer-director George Seaton just gives up and lets them; 1949. (c)

The Appointment X Omar Sharif as a lawyer falling in love with dangerous Anouk Aimée. Lotte Lenya is around the Italian locations; Sidney Lumet; 1969. (c)

Appointment in Honduras X Suffers from jungle fever as Ann Sheridan oomphs her way (Glenn Ford staggers manfully alongside) through a steamy bit of the RKO lot, supposedly in the middle of a South American revolution. Zachary Scott and a handful of convicts glumly join in. Jacques Tourneur; 1953. (c)

Appointment in London √ Dirk Bogarde, Ian Hunter make this routine bomber yarn (set 1943, made 1952), culminating in raid, rather more meaningful than it deserves. Philip Leacock. (b/w)

Appointment With a Shadow X Hard-drinking reporter is marked as murder victim; not much to write home about (or in his paper either). George Nader, Virginia Field; Joseph Pevney churned it out; 1956. (b/w)

Appointment With Venus XX Coy, heavy-handed war pic about rescuing a cow. Ralph Thomas lumbered it along in 1951; David Niven, Kenneth More, Glynis Johns perk it up. (b/w)

The Apprenticeship of Duddy Kravitz √√ High-spirited and entertaining comedy from Canada with a serious undercurrent. By Mordecai Richler from his novel, it is extravagantly directed by Ted Kotcheff, with Richard Dreyfuss in his *Portnoy* mood. Some strong back-ups were imported in 1974, including Jack Warden, Joseph Wiseman, Denholm Elliott. (c)

The April Fools √ Jack Lemmon alone earns this dated (1969) comedy its tick, as the dog-in-a-manger who finally meets the right bitch (Catherine Deneuve). Despite some splendid troupers – Peter Lawford, Jack Weston, Myrna Loy, Charles Boyer, Sally Kellerman – director Stuart Rosenberg simply could not get the film out of a rut of New York parties and expense-account fripperies. (c)

April in Paris √ Doris Day, as always, makes this a watchable experience, although the story (she's a chorus girl invited to Paris by mistake – it should have been Ethel Barrymore at the cultural conference) is dismal and everyone (even British revue veteran Herbert Farjeon) except Ray Bolger, who can dance, pretty awful. Even the songs are substandard Sammy Cahn. But David Butler makes a silly script zing and you'll forgive it all for Miss Day; 1952. (c)

April Love XX Dull little effort about Kentucky and a horse that's ill; Henry Levin works hard to put some life into it, but is defeated by pleasant but weak Pat Boone, Shirley Jones; 1957. (c)

April Showers √ Minor backstage musical with the peppy team of Jack Carson and Ann Sothern rowing and Cuddles Sakall picking up the pieces; James V. (not Jerome) Kern directed; 1948. (b/w)

Arabesque √√ Delightful concoction of nonsense involving Gregory Peck as linguistics expert forced to do some deciphering with the help of Sophia Loren, doing what she does nicely. Alan Badel makes a splendid heavy and Stanley Donen makes it all move, particularly the final chase; 1966. (c)

Arabian Nights X Whatever happened to the great desert cycle? Here it is at its height (1942) with Jon Hall leading revolt against caliph, Maria Montez urging him on in harem bra like they never wore and Billy Gilbert milking laughs from being fat and camp; John Rawlins directed. (c)

Arena √ Rodeo yarn that throws you more with its plot clichés than bucking broncos. Have you ever wondered how they get them to buck? This film won't tell you but it's pretty disgusting. This is all about Gig Young's rotten marriage with Polly Bergen, extra fun and games with Barbara Lawrence. Richard Fleischer; 1953. (c)

Are You With It? X Not really, we're afraid. Donald O'Connor tries too hard as maths whizz-kid who joins the carnival and sings, too. But Jack Hively didn't have much else going for this picture in 1948. (b/w)

Arise My Love √ Charles Brackett and Billy Wilder wrote this one about reporter Claudette Colbert in love with flyer Ray Milland in Civil War Spain, but you wouldn't know it. 1940 was a hack year for them, and Mitchell Leisen, Paramount's top comedy director, did a neat, self-effacing job on their scripts. (b/w)

Arizona Bushwackers X Howard Keel brings order to Cotton, Arizona, and much-needed cash to some ageing stars in 1967. Among them: Yvonne de Carlo, John Ireland, Marilyn Maxwell, Brian Donlevy, Barton MacLane. Director, Lesley Salander. (c)

Arizona Mission X James Arness, Harry Carey and the girl who was later to prove herself an actress (but not here) Angie Dickinson in revenge-for-being-left-to-die plot. Andrew McLaglen shot from the hip. 1956. (b/w)

Armored Attack √ The changing political allegiances of America towards Russia made this account of USSR being defended against the Nazis change script in mid-1943. The result is a mess, but an interesting one, with Erich von Stroheim v Walter Huston and wife Ann Harding being tortured; Jane Withers, Anne Baxter strongly supporting. But it's all too much for Lewis Milestone. (b/w)

Armored Car Robbery √ One of those familiar movies (since *Rififi*) of a caper that goes wrong; here a policeman is killed. But Richard Fleischer did superior job in 1950 with virtual unknowns to add authenticity. (b/w)

Armored Command X Tedious, improbable wartime stuff about Tina Louise being exposed as spy by Howard Keel, having already exposed herself (but not too much – this was made in pre-permissive 1961) for the troops. Byron Haskin is the man to blame – or pity for having to direct such a script. (b/w)

Around the World in 80 Days √√ Lightly based on Jules Verne novel, with lovely aerial shots and a galaxy of stars making cameo appearances around David Niven as globe-encircling Phileas Fogg. One point each for spotting Robert Newton, Shirley MacLaine, Charles Boyer, Ronald Colman, Noel Coward, Marlene Dietrich, Trevor Howard, Buster Keaton, Peter Lorre, Victor McLaglen, John Mills, Robert Morley, Jack Oakie, George Raft, 1956. Michael Anderson directed. (c)

Around the World Under the Sea XX Sorry little attempt to do a major sci-fi undersea spectacular on a shoestring and a diving bootlace; non-stars Lloyd Bridges, David McCallum, Shirley Eaton squabble in a sub. Andrew Marton directs-produces-boobs; 1966. (c)

The Arrangement XX Self-pitying mishmash by Elia Kazan, thrusting an inadequate Kirk Douglas centre-stage as ad-man who is driven to attempt suicide by feelings of inadequacy (quite justified, one would think) and the rejection of his mistress, Faye Dunaway. She keeps coming back to him, for some reason, with and without the cooperation of wifey, Deborah Kerr; 1969. (c)

Arrowhead X Goody cavalry (Charlton Heston) v nasty Indians (Jack Palance), with moody Katy Jurado in the middle. Strictly simplistic and before (it's 1953) many enlightened westerns came on the scene. Director Charles Marquis Warren is the real heavy. (c)

Arrow in the Dust X American Civil War deserter takes on commander's identity and finds himself having to lead wagon train defence against Indians; Sterling Hayden may be sterling but he's also dull; Lesley Selander's brisk direction helps; 1954. (c)

Arsenic and Old Lace √ Frantic 1944 version of hit play about two old ladies who see nothing wrong in poisoning their guests' elderberry wine. Frank Capra directed this wholesome black comedy so that Cary Grant appears pottier than the old girls. (b/w)

Artists and Models X One of those Dean Martin-Jerry Lewis not-nearly-so-funny-as-they-ought-to-be's with Shirley MacLaine, Dorothy Malone as the luscious neighbours; it's even got a 1955 model parade to make you laugh at the corny fashions. Frank Tashlin directed-co-wrote. (b/w)

The Art of Love X Comedy based on the unfunny premise that only dead artists sell well, so Americans in Paris James Garner, Dick Van Dyke fake a suicide. A Norman Jewison flop, 1965. (c)

Ask Any Girl √ Delightful David Niven trying to pair dependable Gig Young off with Shirley MacLaine, for some reason, like that's what it says in the script. Of course, she fancies Niven. Charles Walters wisely lets the male stars keep the fun going; 1959. (c)

As Long as They're Happy XX A grisly Jack Buchanan comedy (director J. Lee Thompson) made in 1955 about a Johnnie Ray-type singer invited to a nice English home with Jeanette Scott, Diana Dors. (c)

The Asphalt Jungle √√ One of the great thrillers; an unpretentious masterpiece by John Huston in 1950. Sam Jaffe is brains behind jewel caper, but accomplices Sterling Hayden and Louis Calhern could screw him up. Also noteworthy for brilliant brief major debut by the unique Marilyn Monroe. Sam Jaffe's final scene makes you want to stand up and cheer. (b/w)

Assassin √ Slick, time-passing spy thriller, with Ian Hendry stalking Frank Windsor on Edward Judd's instructions. Unfortunately, too many twists in the plot were clearly there just to keep things going, and Peter Crane's direction is horribly flashy; 1973. (c)

The Assassin X The scenery is Venice and real; the actors are English and phoney. It really was a nerve to cast such weakies as Richard Todd, Eva Bartock, John Gregson in roles that cry out for real acting. Ralph Thomas's tension isn't very tense, either; 1953. (b/w)

The Assassination Bureau XX Strained and tedious Man-Who-Was-Thursday type plot about head of international Murder Inc organisation (Oliver Reed) who accepts assignment to kill himself; Diana Rigg as reporter who falls in love with him, Kenneth Griffith, Clive Revill are to be pitied for having to go through this nonsense with a smile on their lips; Basil

Dearden directs energetically; 1969. (c)

The Assassination of Trotsky XX Agonisingly slow, dull narrative of Alain Delon killing Richard Burton with an icepick. Despite the trappings, there is no sense of politics, purpose or place, and director Joseph Losey seems to have had very little understanding of what was going on; 1972. (c)

Assault √ Frank Finlay hunting for rapist killer, Suzy Kendall a schoolmistress bravely risking own life. Workaday director Sidney Hayers competently pushes it along to surprise denouement. Lesley-Anne Down plays a victim (a 16-year-old in 1971). (c)

Assault on a Queen √ Despite the regally-rapist come-on of the title, it's about Frank Sinatra leading band of adventurers to invade bank vaults of the good ship Queen Mary. Directed by Jack Donohue; 1966. (c)

Assignment K XX Rubbishy spy story with absurdly over-complicated plot but some nice skiing locations; what Michael Redgrave, Leo McKern, Jeremy Kemp were doing in it must be as big a mystery to them as it will be to you, even after it's over (if you wait that long). Val Guest directs somnambulistically; 1968. (c)

Assignment Paris X Dana Andrews is reporter saving the West from the Reds, with George Sanders as spy chief; French location shooting lifts it a little above usual run and Robert Parrish does conscientious job of direction. Marta Hari - sorry, Toren - is Delilahesque; 1952. (b/w)

The Astonished Heart XX Noel Coward wrote (it was one of the 'Tonight at 8.30 plays') and even acts in this disappointing version of psychiatrist who can't solve his own problem - wife, Celia Johnson, or her friend, Margaret Leighton? Terence Fisher and Antony Darnborough somehow shared the direction - perhaps by telephone from the Bahamas? 1949. (b/w)

As Young As You Feel √√ Monty Woolley proving that a retiring age of 65 is all wrong, trying to get his old job back by impersonating company president; Marilyn Monroe delightful, as always, as his secretary; strong aid from Thelma Ritter, Constance Bennett, Allyn Joslyn. Harmon Jones made this one of the pleasant trifles of 1951. (b/w)

At Gunpoint √ Look here, mister, I'm a peaceful citizen and don't want no gunplay, but if you and your band of hooligans speak to this lady like that I'm going to be forced to do something about it. That's Fred MacMurray's line in this well-made (by Alfred L. Werker), 1955 western. Dorothy Malone is the lady, Walter Brennan does his ornery old cowpoke act. (c)

Athena X Crazy family comedy about lawyer and singer falling for two granddaughters of weight-lifting nut crank and stargazing wife. Richard Thorpe has to work hard to keep the fun going, but has some yeomen helpers in Jane Powell, Debbie Reynolds, Louis Calhern; as suitors, Edmund Purdom and Vic Damone are so-so; 1954. (c)

At Long Last Love X Love in real life must outweigh even screen love when Peter Bogdanovich created this entire musical in 1975 to show off his ladyfriend Cybill Shepherd. Tragically, she is not up to the dancing and singing – nor is co-star Burt Reynolds, who looks grotesque lumbering about in fancy suits. The music is De-Lovely Cole Porter, but you've heard it all before – and much better sung. (c)

Atomic City X Kidnap at Los Alamos to influence nuclear scientist; Gene Barry puckers his brow, otherwise it's capably acted and directed, by Jerry Hopper; 1952. (b/w)

At Sword's Point X Three-Musketeer-type swordplay at the French court; Maureen O'Hara queens it, Cornel Wilde leads goodies; Lewis Allen should have known better by 1952. (c)

Attack! √ Robert Aldrich's taut 1956 war film about a cowardly officer's actions causing the death of his troops was un-American enough to cause a US ambassador to walk out of the Venice Film Festival. Well cast with Jack Palance, Eddie Albert, Lee Marvin. (b/w)

Attack of the Crab Monsters √ Roger Corman yarn about scientists eaten by 25-ft. crustaceans, who assume their personalities! Nobody you ever heard of is in it; 1957. (b/w)

Attack on the Iron Coast √ Neat, economical war film about a suicide mission which characterises German defenders particularly well. Paul Wendkos gets almost believable portraits from Lloyd Bridges and Sue Lloyd, which is pretty clever; 1968. (c)

At the Stroke of Nine XX Stephen Murray and Patricia Dainton in low-budgeter about kidnapping of girl reporter by revengeful pianist; Lance Comfort; 1957. (b/w)

At War With the Army X Strictly for fans of Dean Martin and mugging Jerry Lewis, this 1951 assembly-line job had Hal Walker as director, but both their characters are so tedious that you'll hate 'em unless you love 'em. (b/w)

Aunt Clara X Margaret Rutherford inherits pub, greyhounds, fairground sideshow and brothel (a bit vague this last one, as you can imagine in a 1954 family comedy) and gradually and amusingly cleans them up. Anthony Kimmins has marvellous cast to help him: Ronald Shiner, A. E. Matthews, Fay Compton, Nigel Stock, Jill Bennett, Sid James. (b/w)

Auntie Mame √ Rosalind Russell in high-spirited camp comedy based on novel and play about wacky lady and nephew who appeals to her hidden sentimental side; Morton Da Costa lets her get away with anything she wants; 1958. (c)

The Autobiography of Miss Jane Pittman √ Worthy, over-praised biopic of an aged black lady who was once a slave. The bravura performance of Cicely Tyson in 1973 made critics overlook the pedestrian direction of John Korty. The moving moments should look better on the small screen, for which it was originally made. (c)

Autumn Leaves √ If you can suspend your disbelief and imagine Joan Crawford making her disturbed husband (Cliff Robertson) well again by exposing roots of his mental trouble (Vera Miles, first wife; Lorne Greene, father), you'll enjoy this 1956 weepie directed by Robert Aldrich. She's marvellous, of course. (b/w)

Avanti! √ Mild comedy about a rather nasty Jack Lemmon trying to hush up the disgrace of his father's death in a car accident with his paramour, mother of Juliet Mills. They meet on romantic Ischia, and the result is a foregone conclusion. Surprisingly, the co-writer and director is the usually mordant Billy Wilder (1973 vintage, past his great years). (c)

Away All Boats X Turn the sound down if walls are thin as guns blast away incessantly in this dreadfully heroic action 1956 naval war movie. Lex Barker (ex-Tarzan) swims, Jeff Chandler fights, Japanese kamikazes commit hari-kari, Joseph Peveny directs. (c)

The Awful Truth √√ Classic comedy

with Irene Dunne and Cary Grant divorcing-making up, was written-directed-produced by Leo McCarey and it won him 1937 Oscar. Ray Milland and Jane Wyman remade it as *Let's Do It Again*. (b/w)

B

Babes in Arms √√ First Mickey Rooney-Judy Garland partnership musical under the great choreographer and here director Busby Berkeley; Rooney dominates even the old-timers like Charles Winninger and Guy Kibbee, but ultimately the success is due to Rodgers & Hart's and others' 'Lady Is a Tramp', ' Where or When', 'You Are My Lucky Star', 'I Cried for You', 'I'm Just Wild About Harry', etc., etc.; 1939. (b/w)

Baby Doll √√ It's a bit sad that all that's passed into the mythology about this smashing evocation of poor-white South are Carroll Baker's nightdress and thumb-sucking; there's much else to admire, not least Tennessee Williams' cunning script and Elia Kazan's steamy direction; Eli Wallach as fast-talking stranger seducing Baby Doll is every city slicker, and Karl Malden was never better; 1956; (b/w)

Baby Love √ Sexploitation thriller with Ann Lynn involved in lesbian affair with nymphet Linda Hayden. Keith Barron is husband, once the lover of girl's mother, Diana Dors. Alastair Reid directs somewhat chop-lickingly; 1968. (c)

Baby, The Rain Must Fall √√ Steve McQueen as a man just released from prison with all the uncertainties of the future . . . Lee Remick as his wife, coming to him with the daughter he has never seen . . . Don Murray as the solid deputy he grew up with . . . the flat, desolate landscape of Texas. A beautiful start for a distinguished film by Robert Mulligan, produced by him and Alan J. Pakula in 1965. Perhaps we could see the full version? It was shortened by 12 minutes for British distribution. (b/w)

The Baby and the Battleship √ Happy cast of jolly tars enjoy themselves in this harmless comedy about a child smuggled aboard; John Mills, Richard Attenborough, Bryan Forbes, Lionel Jeffries, Gordon Jackson, Michael Hordern, Kenneth Griffith sent up conventional naval heroics under Jay Lewis; 1956. (b/w)

Baby Face Nelson √√ Mickey Rooney remarkably convincing under Don Siegel's direction as Public Enemy No 1. Exciting stuff, using some authentic facts; 1957. (b/w)

Bachelor Flat XX Sure is. Flat. Terry-Thomas finds that grinning and grimacing isn't enough to get him by in Hollywood; Celeste Holm as fiancée and Tuesday Weld as her daughter waltz rings round him as visiting archaeologist in southern California. Frank Tashlin directed and co-wrote in his usual slap-happy way; 1962. (c)

Bachelor in Paradise X Bob Hope as writer living out a kind of Peyton Place existence to provide him with copy. Lana Turner decorative; Paula Prentiss, Janis Paige, Agnes Moorehead among married ladies on hand. Jack Arnold directed; 1961. (c)

Bachelor Mother √√ Ginger Rogers finds a baby, and employer Charles Coburn gives her back her sacked job in sympathy, thinking she's the mum. From then on, complications proliferate as David Niven falls for her. This 1939 riot, directed by Garson Kanin, was later remade, less successfully, as *Bundle of Joy*. (b/w)

Bachelor of Hearts XX Wolf Rilla's mild May Ball goings-on with Sylvia Syms and Hardy Kruger; 1958. (b/w)

Bachelor Party √√ In the wake of *Marty*'s success, Hollywood thought that every Paddy Chayevsky teleplay would be a goldmine if opened out on the big screen. Alas, this 1957 version, also directed by *Marty*'s Delbert Mann, didn't deliver at the box office, but was still a superior fiction, with Don Murray accepting marriage in the course of his stag party. Carolyn Jones turned in a fine performance as a philosophising kook. The British censor cut scene showing men's reactions to stag movie – maybe TV could put it back, please? (b/w)

Back Door to Hell X Supposedly about conflicts among three American soldiers and between them and Philippino guerrilla leader during second world war, it may also by implication be about conflicts in Viet Nam; directed by Monte Hellman on tiny budget; 1965. (b/w)

Back from Eternity X Plane crash in jungle picture with Robert Ryan, Rod Steiger, Anita Ekberg, Gene Barry,

Fred Clark among quarrelling, loving stranded; John Farrow; 1956. (*b/w*)

Background XX Stilted drama of effects on children of marriage breakdown, steeped in the values of 1953. Janette Scott, Mandy Miller, Jeremy Spenser (trying to kill new Dad with airgun) are the moppets; Valerie Hobson is distressed, genteel Mum. Director, Daniel Birt. (*b/w*)

Background to Danger √ Peter Lorre and Sidney Greenstreet in Raoul Walsh-directed yarn of intrigue in Turkey during the Second World War. George Raft and Brenda Marshall seem to have wandered in from another flick but bemusedly join the chases; 1943. (*b/w*)

Backlash X Richard Widmark hunting his father's murderer in western which gets superior John Sturges treatment, but is let down by Donna Reed as widow he tangles with; 1956. (*c*)

Back Street X Fannie Hurst's archetypal soap-opera story about the 'other woman' has been filmed three times: (1) 1932, with John Boles and Irene Dunne, director John M. Stahl; (2) 1941, with Charles Boyer and Margaret Sullavan, director Robert Stevenson; (3) 1961, with John Gavin and Susan Hayward, director David Miller. Pity the only one that's likely to bathe your small screen in tears is No 3. (*c*)

Back to Bataan X John Wayne winning the war again, this time in the Pacific, leading the guerrilla band he forms to help the Yanks; Anthony Quinn adds his clumsy two-cents-worth; Edward Dmytryk proving his patriotism in 1945. (*b/w*)

Back to God's Country X Steve Cochran trying to murder Rock Hudson for his wife Marcia Henderson and cargo of furs; can brave dog Wapi stop him? Joseph Pevney churned this out in 1953. (*b/w*)

The Bad and the Beautiful √ One of those movies that pretend to take the lid off the movie-world but really keep it tightly on. Kirk Douglas is supposed to be producer who's a shit, and Vincente Minnelli has surrounded him with a splendid cast of haters: Lana Turner, Walter Pidgeon, Dick Powell, Gloria Grahame. But, despite Charles Schnee's acerbic script it just doesn't gel. It won a lot of Oscars in 1952 (best support – Grahame; script; photography; art direction; costumes) but if it had been truer to life, would Hollywood have voted for it? (*b/w*)

Bad Day at Black Rock √√ Why the hostility when Spencer Tracy gets off the train at this God-forsaken western town to deliver a medal? The answer is chilling, exciting, suspenseful; besides the superb Tracy, John Sturges's 1954 cast included Ernest Borgnine, Lee Marvin, Robert Ryan, Walter Brennan. (*c*)

Bad for Each Other X In what must have been very strange 1953 partnership Irving (*Carpetbaggers*) Wallace and Horace (*They Shoot Horses, Don't They?*) McCoy came up with this light exposé of the risks run by society doctors when they forget their Hippo oaths. Unfortunately, neither Charlton Heston as the hero nor Lizabeth Scott as society gal, can do more than look pretty; only Ray Collins gives it the real acid and director Irving Rapper lets it fall through his fingers. (*b/w*)

Badge 373 √ Brave, misunderstood New York detective shoots Puerto Rican drug hassler. This slick, routine offering, directed by Howard Koch in 1973, has a claim to authenticity – it used the services of Eddie Egan, the cop who inspired *The French Connection* as source and small-part actor (playing hero Robert Duvall's superior). (*c*)

The Badlanders X Alan Ladd and Ernest Borgnine get their own back on horrid rancher Kent Smith by robbing him of his gold and his girl, Claire Kelly; Delmer Daves directed from W. R. Burnett novel, the moral of which seems to be that old Hollywood morality – it's OK to steal if your victim is a baddie; 1958. (*c*)

Badlands √√√ Beautifully-made (writer-producer-director: Terrence Malick) crime odyssey, illuminated by Sissy Spacek's performance as a 15-year-old who goes with Martin Sheen on a cross-country crime spree, having first disposed of her father (Warren Oates). There is a satisfactory ending; 1973. (*c*)

Bad Lord Byron XX They said it – sure is, bad. The poet on his death bed remembers his life – well, what David Macdonald insists it was, anyway. The biographies tell it differently. Dennis Price miscast, Joan Greenwood camps her way through it, Mai Zetterling limps along with old clubfoot; 1949. (*b/w*)

Bad Man's River XXX One of those terrible westerns with more plot than it can handle, and ageing stars (James Mason, Gina Lollobrigida) trapped in

31

the hands of a maladroit director (Gene Martin); 1971. (c)

Badman's Territory X Randolph Scott forcing law and order on tough town; Tim Whelan; 1946. (b/w)

The Bad Seed X Enough to send all environmental-influence believers wailing into the night, this shocker's thesis is that some kids (this one especially) are Born Bad. Such unscientific rubbish enables director-producer Mervyn LeRoy to have apparently sweet little Patty McCormack wreak havoc all round her. You won't believe the ending, but if you've got any sense you won't believe the beginning, either; 1956. (b/w)

The Balcony √√ Very X-y version of the Genet play, set in brothel during a revolution. Fantastic is a literal description for once. Shelley Winters is the Madame, Peter Falk the Police Chief, Leonard Nimoy leader of the revolutionaries. Directed by Joseph Strick; 1962. (b/w)

Ballad in Blue X Not content with a blind star, Ray Charles, Paul Henreid has a blind boy (Piers Bishop, only acting), to make it difficult for you to turn a blind eye. Mary Peach and Tom Bell play parents who are brought together again by Ray Charles' friendship with their son. It's all a bit tearful, but the songs are good; 1965. (b/w)

The Ballad of Cable Hogue √ Less than satisfactory western fable with Jason Robards making what he can of a thin character who sets up as water-seller in the western desert. David Warner, Stella Stevens wander in and out, but director Sam Peckinpah rarely seems at home with such fey material; 1970. (c)

The Ballad of Joe Hill √ Sentimentalised, poorly-cast account by Swedish director Bo Widerberg of American folk hero that misses too much of the grit of the unions and labour that he became canonised for helping to organise. Even the song is badly sung; 1969. (c)

The Ballad of Josie √ Doris Day puts the sheep among the cattle in 1890 Wyoming. George Kennedy, Peter Graves play up to her under Andrew V. MacLaglen's flatfooted direction; 1968. (c)

Ball of Fire √√ If this lark about dancer Barbara Stanwyck moving in with eight professors, including Gary Cooper, reminds you of Snow White, the resemblance isn't coincidental. Excuse is, he's studying slang. Howard Hawks at his zingiest; 1941. (b/w)

Bananas √ Woody Allen goes to wonderfully-absurd lengths to woo Louise Lasser, including taking over a South American republic. More than a little strained, but mostly fun; 1971. (c)

Bandido √ Robert Mitchum in Butch Cassidy country, trying to make a bit on the side out of the 1916 Mexican revolution; Richard Fleischer directs with a sense of fun; 1956. (c)

The Bandit of Zhobe XX Victor Mature as an unlikely Indian tribal chief is duped into fighting the British – or nearly; Anthony Newley, Walter Gotell, Norman Wooland go through the motions under John Gilling's automatic direction; 1959. (c)

Band of Angels X Comic-strip values make this attempt at showing life during the Civil War into a strictly two-dimensional flop, despite presence of Clark Gable. Yvonne de Carlo as once-rich high yaller gal is sold into slavery. Raoul Walsh permits all kind of excesses except the interesting ones, and Sidney Poitier's educated slave is just embarrassing. A long way from the Robert Penn Warren novel; 1957. (c)

Bandolero! √ Superior western with James Stewart beginning by impersonating the official hang-man in order to free his brother (Dean Martin) and gang; George Kennedy is sheriff, Raquel Welch decorative but dispiriting love interest; Andrew McLagen and several of the others who worked on the earlier Shenandoah were reunited for this 1968 show. (c)

Band Waggon XX Nostalgia for the 1939 radio show starring Arthur Askey and Dickie Murdoch is the only reason to glance at this soppy spy story; Marcel Varnel directed in 1939. (b/w)

The Band Wagon √ Made in 1953 by Vincente Minnelli at his most energetic, this teaming of Fred Astaire and Jack Buchanan in a backstage musical was a critics' delight, but never got off the ground at the box-office. Hard to see why, as it also had Cyd Charisse, whose legs dazzle. (c)

Bang! You're Dead √ Little boy with passion for guns mistakenly kills; crime is blamed on man. Jack Warner, Gordon Harker in surprisingly sensitive period piece (1953), directed by Lance Comfort. (b/w)

Bang, Bang, You're Dead XX Basically British spy movie shot partly in Morocco with American Tony Randall to make it palatable to Stateside audiences, but it would take more than even his charming manner. Producer Harry Alan Towers collected a cast of well-known if inferior talents (Senta Berger, Herbert Lom, Terry-Thomas) but director Don Sharp couldn't make Peter Yeldham's frantic chase script work; 1966. (c)

The Bank Dick √ √ Often cited as W. C. Fields's best movie, it's the one where he is made a guard after capturing a bank robber accidentally. In the opening, he tears the American family myth apart, and there's a splendid chase up a mountain. Made in 1941 by Eddie Cline; four years later, Fields was dead. (b/w)

Bank Shot √ Comedy thriller with George C. Scott as a master criminal who has the bright idea of towing away a whole bank to rob it at leisure. The fun wears a bit thin under Gower Champion's direction; 1974. (c)

Banning X This eponymously-titled drama has the unusual setting of a golf course as Robert Wagner tries to win the tournament and pick the right girl among those smuggling themselves into his golf-bag. Jill St John naturally loses to the less obvious Anjanette Comer; Ron Winston directs James Lee's untidy script neatly; 1967. (c)

Barabbas XX Long, heavy, ultimately off-putting speculation as to what might have been the life of the thief saved from the cross when Jesus was crucified. In the end, he's crucified anyway. Anthony Quinn seems to be enjoying all the flagellation under the moans and groans, and Silvano Mangano, Arthur Kennedy, Jack Palance, Ernest Borgnine appear to be under delusion they are partaking in an Important Picture. Alas, despite the deeply-buried respectable origins (Pär Lagerkvist's novel) director Richard Fleischer drowns in a load of tomato-ketchup gore; 1962. (c)

Barbarella √ Sexy comic strip heroine provocatively brought to life by Jane Fonda under Roger Vadim's hand; great fun; 1968. (c)

The Barbarian and the Geisha X If you tried really hard you couldn't find an actor less fitted to play the man who opened up Japan to the rest of the world, the first American consul, Townsend Harris, than – you'll never guess – John Wayne. Quite why John Huston allowed his otherwise beautiful picture to be made ludicrous by this casting probably lies buried in one of Hollywood's many skeleton-cupboards; 1958. (c)

The Barber of Stamford Hill X John Bennett fails to grip as Jewish romancer and Megs Jenkins is too far from Wales in this parochial fable which Ronald Harwood adapted from his TV play and Casper Wrede directed sparsely; 1962. (b/w)

The Barefoot Contessa √ Flashbacking biography of beautiful (if you like the type) movie star played by Ava Gardner, cynically promoted by producer Humphrey Bogart and press agent Edmond O'Brien (he won an Oscar for this), but still remaining the simple, barefoot girl they found dancing in Spain (oh yeah?). 1953 location shooting had another star around, who wasn't in the picture but was in love with Ava – Frank Sinatra. Joseph L. Mankiewicz turned in pro job, but there's no real heart there. (c)

The Barefoot Executive X Chimpanzee is a mastermind and helps owner Kurt Russell in his job as TV executive; Bob Butler directed for Walt Disney Productions, 1971. (c)

Barefoot in the Park √ Some very funny moments, linked together with a thin story line about newly-weds in walk-up apartment, from Neil Simon play. Robert Redford, Jane Fonda, Mildred Natwick are all treats; Gene Saks hasn't directed the funniest film ever, but it's good enough for a few laughs, so don't complain; 1966. (c)

The Barkleys of Broadway X Fred Astaire and Ginger Rogers teamed up again in 1949 after ten years apart to make this mild behind-the-scenes musical with a relatively undistinguished Harry Warren score; they play double-act that splits up only to find that ... well, you know. Oscar Levant, Billie Burke hover around. Charles Walters unobtrusively directed. (c)

Barnacle Bill √ Called *All at Sea* in America. Neat little 1957 time-filler for Alec Guinness as seasick sailor who buys a pier; T. E. B. Clarke script and Charles Frend direction are impeccable if slightly old-fashioned. Maurice Denham among strong supports. (b/w)

The Baron of Arizona √ Vincent Price as land-grabbing heavy in slightly out-of-the-rut western directed by latter-day cult figure Samuel Fuller; Beulah Bondi; 1950. (b/w)

The Barretts of Wimpole Street √ (1) 1934 version starred Charles Laughton as father, Norma Shearer as Elizabeth, Fredric March as Robert Browning, directed by Sidney Franklin, was a wild success. (b/w)

The Barretts of Wimpole Street XX (2) 1957 version with John Gielgud, Jennifer Jones, Bill Travers was dismal flop (unsurprising, seeing who was playing the young lovers), although Sidney Franklin was still in there pitching. (c)

Bartleby √ Self-consciously symbolic about drop-outs, Anthony Friedmann's adaptation of the Herman Melville story fails to convince. Nevertheless, the way John McEnery refuses to do any work or even move out of the office to go home, and Paul Scofield's involvement with him, just about carry the viewer along; 1970. (c)

The Bat X Agnes Moorehead, least appreciated great actress of the American screen, goes all-too-competently through the motions as lady terrified by masked prowler. Could it be Vincent Price? Gavin Gordon? John Sutton? Richard Nixon? Crane Wilbur directed; 1959. (b/w)

Bataan X Routine 1943 war story with Robert Taylor and the American army bravely running away; Senator George Murphy, millionaire Desi Arnez among them. Tay Garnett manfully directed. (b/w)

Bathing Beauty XX Awful musical about Esther Williams pursued by jilted husband enrolling at her girls' school. Pity Basil Rathbone. George Sidney shows his embarrassment in directing it fluffily; 1944. (c)

Batman √ Caped crusader Adam West and his little buddy Robin from the TV series in full-length feature, introducing all the favourite villains - Catwoman Lee Meriweather, Joker Cesar Romero, Penguin Burgess Meredith, Riddler Frank Gorshin; director, Leslie H. Martinson; 1965. (c)

Battle at Apache Pass XX Western about Cochise (Jeff Chandler) vainly trying to keep the Red Indians tame; George Sherman directed, possibly with his eyes shut, in 1952. (c)

Battle Beneath the Earth XXX Tripe about the Red Chinese burrowing underground to invade America; Viviane Ventura and Kerwin Matthews are directed by Montgomery Tully in a daze; 1968. (c)

Battle Circus X Humphrey Bogart fought many a tough scrap in his screen life, but none more taxing than this one with dreadful script and a downright embarrassing performance by cutie June Allyson as his nurse girlfriend. It's all about a medical unit in Korea; Richard Brooks directed his own

wordy script reverently but it's hollow stuff; 1953. (b/w)

Battle Cry X The cry concerned being 'tell it to the Marines!' That tough, hard-drinking, hard-swearing outfit of professionals must laugh when they see sentimental cliché versions of their lives like this one by Raoul Walsh, from Leon (*Exodus*) Uris' script. It purports to follow careers from rookies to battle-hardened veterans, with interludes with girlfriends Dorothy Malone (Tab Hunter's) and Nancy Olson (Aldo Ray's), 1955. (c)

The Battle for Anzio X Just another war picture, tricked out with the pretence that it's about Robert Mitchum's search for why men risk death for their country; Edward Dmytryk was, perhaps, kidding himself. He won't kid you; 1968. (c)

Battle for the Planet of the Apes XX Clapped-out series ended its film career in 1973 with this dull film of what started out as an intriguing colony of humanoid monkeys. It was followed the next year by the TV series which died the death. Those trapped into watching J. Lee Thompson's antics could pass the time by spotting Roddy McDowall, Lew Ayres, France Nuyen, John Huston. (c)

Battleground X Somebody must like war pictures - if you're among them this is for you: Van Johnson and John Hodiak fighting their way through France, set in 1944, made five years later; director William Wellman. (b/w)

Battle Hymn XX Real Flying Parson Colonel Dean Hess is made the object of a panegyric positively Victorian in its sentimental prettifying. He certainly did great work for Korean orphans in between making them orphans, but director Douglas Sirk and stalwart Rock Hudson combine to turn him into improbable perfection; 1957. (c)

Battle of Britain X Considering the resources and the cast (Olivier, Michael Caine, Trevor Howard, Redgrave, Richardson, Robert Shaw *et al*), Guy Hamilton came up with the stinker of 1969. Blame partly the feeble script, partly lack of imagination in the air sequences. (c)

Battle of Rogue River X Action-starved western about Oregon seeking statehood in 1850 but needing Indian truce first; only George Montgomery really wants sincere peace. William Castle; 1954. (c)

Battle of the Bulge X Or rather, one small incident in it, involving Henry

Fonda, Robert Shaw, Robert Ryan, Dana Andrews. Ken Annakin made it all very old-fashioned for 1965, and any deeper message has been allowed to remain buried. (c)

Battle of the Coral Sea X Cliff Robertson as submarine commander caught by the Japs escaping with enough info to help the freedom-lovers to win the eponymous battle; Paul Wendkos: 1959. (b/w)

The Battle of the River Plate X Rather dull for a war picture: how the British Navy won a much-needed victory in the early days of the Second World War. Peter Finch is captain of the *Graf Spee*, pride of the German navy; Anthony Quayle, John Gregson, Bernard Lee and a cast of other rather obvious stalwarts hunt him down. Writer-directors, Michael Powell-Emeric Pressburger, 1956. (c)

Battle of the Sexes √ One of Peter Sellers' best films; he had Charles Crichton directing him in this 1960 story of American business efficiency expert, Constance Cummings, invading the tweed firm where he works, driving him to thoughts of murder. Plus Robert Morley, Ernest Thesiger, Donald Pleasence, William Mervyn. (b/w)

Battle of the V1 XXX Nasty novelettish 1958 reconstruction of Polish underground wink-tipping to England that Germans are making flying bombs there. Pretends it's factual, but isn't. Vernon Sewell directs Michael Rennie, Patricia Medina. (b/w)

The Battle of the Villa Fiorita XX One of those sickly dramas about children of divorcing couple screwing up the proceedings. Delmer Daves directed Maureen O'Hara, Rossano Brazzi, Richard Todd, Phyllis Calvert in 1965. (c)

Battle on the Beach X Japanese attack on the Philippines seems important mainly because it makes up the mind of Dolores Michaels whether she prefers her American husband or local guerrilla leader; Audie Murphy, Gary Crosby pick their way through the battle lines and script lines, both equally fatal; Herbert Coleman; 1961. (c)

Baxter! √√ Director Lionel Jeffries makes a sympathetic job of presenting a 12-year-old fighting his psychological disabilities, including a lisp. They grow worse as various disasters (his first girlfriend moves away, a model – Britt Ekland - he is pally with is killed)

compound his state. As the boy, Scott Jacoby is almost convincing; Reginald Rose's script provides Jeffries with the opportunity to make a watchable film; 1972. (c)

The Beachcomber √ (1) 1938 version was notable for superb performance by Charles Laughton as lotus-eater and his wife Elsa Lanchester as missionary; Erich Pommer directed. (b/w)

The Beachcomber (Vessel of Wrath) XX (2) 1955 saw ham-fisted attempt by Sidney and Muriel Box to improve on the original, with swaying Robert Newton in the Laughton part and Glynis Johns the plum-and-prune reformer; Donald Pleasence, who played a small part, would have been better lead. (c)

Beachhead X Tony Curtis and Frank Lovejoy as two American soldiers outwitting Japanese in wartime Hawaii to get vital info to HQ. Unfortunately for the action they get mixed up with Mary Murphy as French planter's daughter and her 'lovable character' of a father. Stuart Heisler should have known better; 1954. (c)

Beach Party √ 1964 musical that started a fashion for teenage fun and passes time agreeably enough. Bob Cummings, Dorothy Malone play the adults; Frankie Avalon, Harvey Lembeck stand out among the kids; director, William Asher. (c)

Beach Red X Too obvious anti-war pic, earnestly directed by Cornel Wilde, about 1943 war in the Pacific, made in 1967, with himself and Rip Torn. (c)

Bearheart of the Great Northwest X Denver Pyle in rugged yarn of dog who tracks down killers in Canadian timber-land; director, Rand Brooks, 1964. (c)

The Beast from 20,000 Fathoms √ 1953 classic of science-fiction film-making, allegedly based on Ray Bradbury's story, *The Foghorn*, but the poignant idea of foghorn and sea monster communicating has gone and only King-Kongruous 'Loch Lomond Monster' (sic) remains. Super effects from Ray Harryhausen helped director Eugene Lourie's skimped budget. (b/w)

Beast With Five Fingers √ The idea of a hand, unjoined to human body, with a life of its own is pretty horrifying, and Robert Florey's 1947 invention packs a powerful charge. Peter Lorre watches it play Bach, wriggle across the floor, disarrange a bookshelf. In the climax, he vainly attempts to nail it to a table, then the most awful thing of all happens . . . Florey had intended to show it was all in Lorre's imagination, but Jack Warner cut all the 'flim-flam' out. (b/w)

Beat the Devil √ Thoroughly indulgent spoof of con-men after uranium; the joke is supposed to be that nobody – not even scriptwriter Truman Capote and director John Huston? – knows what's going on. Throwing all attempt at coherence to the winds, Humphrey Bogart, Robert Morley, Peter Lorre, Gina Lollobrigida enjoy themselves. Jennifer Jones seems to have wandered in from a more dramatic picture. But somehow it's amusing, if you enjoy other people's clever home movies; 1954. (b/w)

Beau Brummell XX Highly embarrassing for all concerned – Stewart Granger as Beau, Elizabeth Taylor as his belle, Peter Ustinov as fat Prinny, Robert Morley, Rosemary Harris. Director Curtis Bernhardt presumably wasn't upset; after all, it's his baby, although Karl Tunberg must take the blame for the dreadful script; 1954. (c)

Beau Chumps √ Laurel and Hardy in the Foreign Legion; 1931. (b/w)

Beau Geste √ (1) 1939 remake of Ronald Colman classic has Gary Cooper, Ray Milland, Robert Preston as Foreign Legion brothers up against tough sergeant Brian Donlevy and desert hordes.

Beau Geste X (2) 1965 director-writer Douglas Heyes has ignored the possibilities in original P. C. Wren book of asking when should a man rebel and settled for a routine adventure; unfortunately, he hasn't even managed that very well, and the result is a bit of a bore with Telly Savalas, Guy Stockwell and others playing a caricature Foreign Legion yarn that hasn't even got the virtue of satire. (c)

Beau James X Poor attempt to retell New York mayor Jimmy Walker's story with Bob Hope, Paul Douglas, Alexis Smith, directed by Mel Shavelson; 1957. (c)

The Beautiful Blonde from Bashful Bend X Preston Sturges disappointment, meant to be satire on western musicals but let down by flabby Betty Grable as Annie Oakley-type character. Cesar Romero, Rudy Vallee; 1949. (c)

Beautiful Stranger X Ginger Rogers upsetting Stanley Baker on the Riviera by falling in love with Jacques Bergerac (real-life husband); David

Miller doesn't really rise to his star and the occasion; 1953. (b/w)

Because of You X Loretta Young conceals her (not very terrible) past from husband Jeff Chandler, who reels around as though she's admitted to being Eva Braun, escaped from Hitler's bunker. Joseph Pevney directs with a desperate pretence that it all makes sense; 1952. (b/w)

Becket √ Don't expect to see the epic spectacular the posters (and perhaps the trailers TV may still run ahead of it) promised, although with Peter O'Toole and Richard Burton starring you might expect it. This is an extended chat between weak Henry II and Burton's correct Archbishop of Canterbury, often witty, beautifully by Peter Glenville who rather lets the stars get on with their own ideas. From Jean Anouilh's play, not the historical records; 1964. (c)

Bedazzled X *Faust* retold as a comedy with Pete and Dud encountering Lust (Racquel Welch), Sloth (Howard Goonery), Envy (Barry Humphries), and the rest in fitfully funny script directed by Stanley Donen, out of his home country and his element. Michael Bates, as those who saw his Inspector in the stage production of *Loot* will know, was the funniest cop around; 1967. (c)

Bedevilled X Paris locations lift this out of its deep rut of silly plot about night club singer (Anne Baxter) fleeing scene of murder helped by postulant (Steve Forrest), but not far enough. Mitchell Leisen, subject of some cult worship, directs; 1955. (c)

The Bedford Incident √ Magazine reporter Sidney Poitier nearly screws up wartime mission in which destroyer commander Richard Widmark hunts German sub with Ahab-like determination. Apart from plot extravagances, this is well-directed by producer James B. Harris with claustrophobic strength; Martin Balsam turns in particularly unlikeable but convincing portrayal of ship's doctor; 1965. (b/w)

The Bed Sitting Room XX No story, no sense and very few laughs, despite the presence of several comics, including author Spike Milligan. Or maybe because of it. Director Dick Lester tried too hard; 1969. (c)

Bedtime for Bonzo XX Long-time Presidential candidate Ronald Reagan was still earning his bread as an actor back in 1951. Unfortunately for him, a chimp stole this one; Bonzo, played brainy proof of Prof. Reagan's theories. Frederick de Cordova directed. (b/w)

Bedtime Story √ Tasteless but funny con-men comedy with Marlon Brando and David Niven out-smarting each other on the Riviera; Ralph Levy; 1964. (c)

Before Winter Comes X Padded story of multilingual would-be defector (Topol) in 1945 Displaced Persons' camp; with David Niven and John Hurt as British representatives and Anna Karina as dragged-in love interest. J. Lee Thompson fails to make it matter; 1969. (c)

The Beggar's Opera X Olivier is Macheath in Peter Brook's first major film, 1953. Lacks the confidence of his later work, and Stanley Holloway, Dorothy Tutin, George Devine can't turn it into more than tuppenny opera. (b/w)

The Beguiled √√ Clint Eastwood as a Unionist soldier holed up in a girls' seminary full of repressed ladies. The mood changes from adventure to black comedy to tragedy. While our hero looks increasingly ill at ease, Geraldine Page, Elizabeth Hartman and Jo Ann Harris enjoy themselves. The mixed brew finally coheres, thanks to director Don Siegel's mastery of the medium; 1970. (c)

Behind the Mask X Surgeon's, that is; Michael Redgrave and Niall McGinnis as opposing surgeons, Tony Britton as honest young doctor; Vanessa Redgrave in small part (it was made in 1958); director Brian Desmond Hurst is more fascinated by the details of a heart operation than all viewers will be. (c)

Behemoth The Sea Monster X If only a bit more trouble and expense had been taken over the model of the 'monster' this sci-fi of London threatened by Thames-cruising bit of prehistory might have been really exciting. As it is, Gene Evans and André Morell seem to be excited over a largely imaginary fear; directors Douglas Hickox and E. Lourie; 1959. (b/w)

Behold A Pale Horse √ Gregory Peck as former Spanish Republican fighter and Anthony Quinn as civil guard captain for Franco are well-matched in this Basquerade; unfortunately, Fred Zinnemann has let the milky ideological chit-chat get in the way of the action; 1964. (b/w)

Believe in Me XX An Awful Warning in 1971 against the dangers of 'speed' and other drugs, acted stiffly by Michael Sarrazin and woodenly by the lovely but untalented Jacqueline Bisset. As a pusher, Allen Garfield provides some professionalism, but director Stuart Hagmann's use of his camera is too lurid to make the statement that needs to be delivered about drugs. (c)

Bell, Book and Candle √ James Stewart, Jack Lemmon, Ernie Kovacs, Elsa Lanchester, Hermione Gingold carry miscast Kim Novak as modern witch in a funny 1958 version of John van Druten play. Richard Quine does his best as director. (c)

The Bellboy X Jerry Lewis is writer-producer-director-star of this collection of short sketches about Miami's ghastly Fountain Blue (they spell it Fontainebleau) Hotel. Despite occasional sniggers, he misses the chance to satirise the awfulness of the place; 1960. (b/w)

The Belle of New York X The old operetta about life in the nineties doesn't make a very inspiring vehicle for Fred Astaire (already 53 in 1952) and Vera-Ellen, who had to have her songs dubbed by Anita Ellis. He's playboy, she's Salvation Army-type, you're yawning. Charles Walters does his very best to put some zing in it, but he's defeated by the material of most of the cast. (c)

The Belles of St Trinian's √ Alastair Sim in double role of headmistress and bookie; George Cole, Joyce Grenfell plus younger versions of Beryl Reid, Joan Sims, Hermione Baddeley (it was made in 1954) as Searle's schoolteachers. Director, part writer-producer, Frank Launder. (b/w)

Belles on Their Toes √ Sequel to *Cheaper by the Dozen* lacks Clifton Webb; instead, Myrna Loy is working widow bringing up the brood, coping with love-affairs and sundry domestic dramas, but not stepping outside the never-never land of the studio re-creation of turn of the century middle America. Jeanne Crain, Debra Paget are insipid Belles; Edward Arnold is surrogate father figure. Director Henry Levin; 1952. (c)

Belle Starr √ Riproaring post-Civil War excitement, with Gene Tierney helping guerrilla Southerner Randolph Scott. Director, Irving Cummings; 1941. (c)

A Bell for Adano X Sentimental stuff about nice kind Americans finding church bell for war-torn Italian village; William Bendix. Directed by Henry King, 1945, when it was much praised. (b/w)

The Bells are Ringing √ Judy Holliday carries this slight musical comedy about a girl who runs a telephone answering service and organises the lives of her clients, especially Dean Martin (terrible in his part). Saved by Vincente Minnelli's briskness as director, two songs ('Just in Time', 'The Party's Over') and the incomparable, much-mourned Judy, whose final film (1960, five years before her death) this was. (c)

The Bells of St Mary's X Sickly affair with Ingrid Bergman as chirpy nun out-cloying even Bing Crosby's priest in their joint efforts to raise money for school. Even (particularly?) Irish Catholics will find it too much. Leo McCarey produced and directed, doubtless laughing all the way to the church; 1945. (b/w)

Beloved Infidel XX Sheilah Graham's side of the last years of Scott Fitzgerald, mawkishly screened in 1959 by a running-scared (of the facts, the screenplay and Cinema-Scope) Henry King, and starring a self-conscious Gregory Peck and Deborah Kerr. It starts on note of high comedy with the Marquis of Donegal, 'her fiancé', waving sadly goodbye on the dock, but soon stumbles. Oh, if only Scott could write his version. (c)

The Belstone Fox X Despite painstaking and sometimes beautiful animal photography, this poor effort by James Hill has an unconvincing plot (clever fox chums up with hound and leads a pack to destruction under a train). Eric Porter and Rachel Roberts seem understandably ill at ease; 1973. (c)

Be My Guest X 1965 pop scene comedies tend to be as depressing as yesterday's mashed potatoes, but this one, directed-produced by Lance Comfort with David Hemmings as newspaper-reporter-cum-musician, might just stand up. (b/w)

Ben X Sequel to *Willard,* a saga of a rat-pack, which has destroyed its trainer. The rats terrorise the city, but King Rat Ben makes friends with a boy (Lee Harcourt Montgomery) who has to decide whether to reveal the pack's whereabouts to the authorities. Nasty stuff: sentimental but powerful. Director, Phil Karlson; 1972. (c)

Bend of the River √ James Stewart and Arthur Kennedy make splendid sparring partners in this superior western about the battles between miners and farmers. ITV film editors looking for cuts, please excise the intrusive, degrading scenes where Stepin' Fetchit libels his own race. Otherwise, Anthony Mann makes an impeccable, exciting job; 1952. (c)

Beneath the Planet of the Apes √ The smudginess that afflicts many sequels is present in this one; a shame in this case, because the first movie (1968) was really quite superior. Follow-on director Ted Post lacks Franklin Schaffner's style; and actors Charlton Heston, James Fransiscus, Maurice Evans are lost without it. However, sequels that came later were even worse; 1969. (c)

Beneath the Twelve-Mile Reef XX Sponge-fishermen fight between themselves off Florida, and it's hard to get involved. Pallid romance between boy (Robert Wagner) of one and girl (Terry Moore) of other, doesn't help. Only J. Carrol Naish and underwater filming flicks the interest in otherwise poor show by Robert D. Webb; 1953. (c)

Bengal Rifles X Rock Hudson in Lancer (Bengal division) territory, fighting both rotten officers and the Rajah; Laslo Benedek; 1953. (c)

The Benny Goodman Story X Boring biopic of bandleader, sketchily impersonated by Steve Allen. The music's good to listen to, if that's your era. Writer-director Valentine Davies settles for shots and lines he (and we) have seen too often before; 1956. (c)

Bequest to the Nation X 'It's the worst over-acting I've ever committed' admitted Glenda Jackson after seeing her strident Lady Hamilton. Peter Finch's Nelson wasn't much better. Director James Cellan Jones did his best with a less than riveting biography of the great sailor and lover from Terence Rattigan. There are some watchable moments, mostly involving Margaret Leighton and Nigel Stock, but the rest of the cast is too lost in theatricalism; 1973. (c)

Best Foot Forward √ June Allyson's 1943 debut as high school kid, also Nancy Walker's as the ugly girl, when Lucille Ball as film star accepts boy's invitation to graduation dance; Edward Buzzell made it buzz. (c)

The Best House in London XX A really dreadful attempt to squeeze some humorous mileage out of the idea that 19th century whores weren't driven to it by unspeakable social conditions but because they were really nympho-maniacs. One David Hemmings in this sort of nonsense is bad enough, but he plays a double role, which is much too much. Philip Saville has cast badly all through (except Joanna Pettet, in a thankless role), and there is no point in listing the rather inferior players who turn in decidedly inferior perform-ances. Denis Norden is credited with the script, which is surprising; 1969. (c)

The Best Man √√ Gripping battle between Henry Fonda and Cliff Robertson for presidential nomination makes gorgeous 'in' movie from Gore Vidal's play. Franklin Schaffner's cast is impressive – Edie Adams, Margaret Leighton, Shelley Berman, Lee Tracy, Ann Sothern, Gene Raymond, Rich-ard Arlen, Mahalia Jackson – and proved, in 1964, that the old-timers could more than hold their own. (b/w)

The Best Pair of Legs in Business √ A light year away from the awfulness of the star's usual appearances in *The Rag Trade* and *On the Buses,* this extended TV play by Kevin Laffan gives Reg Varney the opportunity of playing a better if faintly embarrassing part – the run-down comic with a load of worries. Despite a tendency of director Chris Hodson to dissipate this by *Carry On* vignettes, Varney manages to excite real pity in the audience as his wife is unfaithful and his son is embarrassed by his behaviour at a vicar's tea-party; 1972. (c)

The Best of Enemies √ Underrated anti-war movie using comic battle between British commander David Niven and Italian opposite number Alberto Sordi to point out ironies. Harry Andrews strong support in Guy Hamilton's slightly soft direction of Jack Pulman's script; 1962. (b/w)

Best of the Badmen X Ex-Union officer becomes outlaw: Robert Ryan in grimly strong performance matched by Claire Trevor, Walter Brennan in William Russell's 1951 actioner. (c)

The Best Things in Life Are Free √ Biopic of songwriters of 'Sonny Boy', 'Button Up Your Overcoat', 'Sunny Side Up', 'If I had a Talking Picture of Yoo-oo' played decorously by Ernest Borgnine, Dan Dailey, Gordon Macrae; director Michael Curtiz makes it pleasing entertainment; 1956. (c)

Betrayed X Can you care whether Lana Turner as improbable Dutch resist-ance worker was a two-timer? Clark Gable has to, in this dull plot, and looks suitably fed up with having to go through the motions. It suits Victor Mature's solid style of unimaginative acting much better. He's American liberator – rah, rah, rah. Gottfried Reinhardt provides some nice loca-tions in Holland to look at; 1954. (c)

Between Heaven and Hell X War film about sergeant under neurotic officer, Robert Wagner, Broderick Crawford, Frank Gorshin; director Richard Fleischer at least makes the battle scenes fairly exciting; 1956. (c)

Beyond a Reasonable Doubt √ Dana Andrews as newspaperman making the mistake of setting himself up as innocent victim of miscarriage of justice so that he can prove inefficiency of the system; instead, as you can guess, it's his alibi that goes wrong; Fritz Lang makes it almost credible and very exciting, with help from Joan Fontaine, Sidney Blackmer; 1956. (b/w)

Beyond the Curtain XX Eva Bartok unconvincingly searching for brother in East Germany; Richard Greene, Marius Goring, Andree Melly uncom-fortably involved. Compton Bennett; 1961. (b/w)

Beyond the Forest √ Bette Davis in apotheosis of a part as small-town wife of worthy Joseph Cotten who kicks over the traces and follows a discourag-ing David Brian to Chicago, where terrible fates await her. She is marvellous, far larger than life but lighting up the whole screen with her erotic vitality. King Vidor was content to give her the chances, knowing that she'd take them – and how; 1949. (b/w)

Beyond this Place XX Van Johnson in England trying to prove father's innocence; Vera Miles, Emlyn Wil-liams, Bernard Lee; directed by former top cameraman Jack Cardiff; 1958. (b/w)

Bhowani Junction √ Stewart Granger as British colonel loves unsuitable Ava Gardner as the riots explode in British withdrawal from India - filmed in Pakistan; George Cukor uncomfort-ably emphasises more questionable aspects of John Masters novel; 1956. (c)

The Bible . . . In the Beginning X John Huston only managed to get to the 23rd chapter of Genesis before quit-ting, and that took him 174 minutes in the cinema. You may not wait so long. It has all the faults of the epic. Portentous, picture-book script by Christopher Fry; fancy-dress performances from Richard Harris, Stephen Boyd, George C. Scott, Peter O'Toole and Huston himself. The original's better and quicker; 1965. (c)

The Bigamist √ Ida Lupino directs/ acts in this serious soaper as bigamous wife of Edmond O'Brien, trapped into marrying her out of compassion because she's pregnant; Joan Fontaine real wife; 1953. (b/w)

Big Bad Mama X . . . is a big bad movie. Producer Roger Corman has cynically taken Angie Dickinson and William Shatner, two previously respected players, and bundled them into bed (nude) and on an assortment of heists, some of them mildly thrilling. Episodic and half-hearted, it is all directed with misplaced enthusiasm by Steve Carver; 1974. (c)

The Big Bankroll XX One of Diana Dors' ghastly Hollywood films – gangsters and politicians in the twenties, directed by Joseph Newman, with Jack Carson and David Janssen; 1961. (b/w)

The Big Bounce X Well, not very big. Ryan O'Neal is a pawn in the hands of Leigh Taylor-Young, who tries to get him to rob her boyfriend, James Daly. All a bit hysterical; director, Alex March; 1968. (c)

The Big Caper √ Starts well, with Rory Calhoun and Mary Costa posing as man and wife while casing small town for dynamiting and pay-or-else threat, but goes to pieces when the friendliness of the townspeople softens their hearts and they want to switch. Robert Stevens fails to lift it directorially; 1957. (b/w)

The Big Circus X Five-ringed circus extravaganza with real acts stealing the show from frowsty old plot about bankruptcy and lions turned loose by rival. Climax of wire-walk attempt over Niagara Falls is well-directed by Joseph M. Newman, however. But Victor Mature, Red Buttons are weak, Vincent Price, Gilbert Roland adequate; 1959. (c)

The Big Clock √√ When Charles Laughton as the head of a huge publishing empire murders his mistress, he is forced to track down the only witness, a man glimpsed on a stairway. But Ray Milland, picked for the job of tracking the witness down, is himself his prey. Wonderfully conceived, imaginatively shot by John Farrow, and full of the ironies of power, this makes an unusual, almost expressionist film to come out of America; 1948. (b/w)

The Big Combo X For some reason police lootenant Cornel Wilde and gangster Richard Conte are both potty about the limpid Jean Wallace; director Joseph Lewis does his best to make it exciting, but you get the feeling that all concerned know it's just fatty ham; 1955. (b/w)

The Big Country √√ 'There are better westerns, but it is difficult to think of many which have been more enjoyable', say Michael Parkinson and Clyde Jeavons in their *Pictorial History of Westerns.* Burl Ives won 1958 Oscar for his performance as cattle baron; Gregory Peck, Carroll Baker, Charlton Heston, Jean Simmons blossomed under William Wyler's direction. (c)

Big Deal at Dodge City √√ Poker movie in the style of *The Cincinnati Kid,* this time with Henry Fonda as compulsive gambler disregarding his little kid's plea not to risk all his money in a compulsive (for us) game with Paul Ford, Jason Robards, Charles Bickford, Kevin McCarthy *et al.* Joanne Woodward, Burgess Meredith, Chester Conklin, contribute to the excitement, and director-producer Fielder Cook has pulled off what should be even better on TV than the big screen; 1965. (c)

The Big Gamble X Three would-be but never-were stars, Stephen Boyd, Juliette Greco, David Wayne, in a routine man-against-the-jungle epic which Richard Fleischer does his best to make exciting. But you feel that this was just one more excuse in 1961 for producer Darryl F. Zanuck to take La Greco on safari. (c)

A Bigger Splash √√ Intriguing dramatised quasi-documentary with some real people (David Hockney, Ossie Clark, Celia Birtwell) playing out some gay relationships and the painting of several Hockneys. Director Jack Hazan manages a difficult genre with assurance; 1974. (c)

Bigger Than Life √ Unwarranted attack on cortisone, taken from *New Yorker* article; James Mason needs it to keep going and he takes too much of it, thus upsetting his body and his family. Nicholas Ray later (it was made in 1956) admitted that he made a big mistake in naming the drug; he had meant to make the point that people accept 'miracle cures' too easily. (c)

The Biggest Bundle of Them All X Edward G. Robinson, Robert Wagner, Godfrey Cambridge wasted in Ken Annakin's failure to put some zip into a story of three capers; Vittorio de Sica and Raquel Welch are about right weight (very light) for this rather self-indulgent comedy-thriller which fast editing fails to save; 1968. (*c*)

The Big Gundown √ Superior European-made western about Lee Van Cleef chasing the wrong suspect to a rape and murder. Sergio Sollima makes this consistently worth watching; 1969. (*c*)

The Big Heat √ Corruption in police force, Glenn Ford exposing with Gloria Grahame's aid. Lee Marvin as sadist is encouraged by director Fritz Lang into all sorts of gratuitous violence, including throwing scalding coffee in girl's face. Made in 1953, as old Hollywood codes started breaking down. (*b/w*)

Big House, USA √ Ralph Meeker demands ransom for missing boy, is caught, jailed, pursued by Broderick Crawford and bloodthirsty convicts; Howard W. Koch made two pictures here in effect, neither specially impressive; 1955. (*b/w*)

Big Jim McLain XX John Wayne on his Save-America kick in 1952, prefaces this spy-ring stuff in Hawaii with a solemn dedication to the Un-American Activities Committee who are 'undaunted by the slander against them'. God should have preserved them from their friends, like Wayne and his director Edward Ludwig. (*b/w*)

The Big Job √ Less suggestive than the *Carry-Ons*, this is a jolly romp about some crooks (Sid James, Dick Emery) trying to get at some loot they have stashed in a tree – now in the police station garden, they find when they get out of jail. Joan Sims is a grasping landlady, Deryck Guyler a police sgt. Gerald Thomas directed; 1965. (*b/w*)

The Big Knife √ Jack Palance is only inadequate player in very low-down on Hollywood drama written by Clifford Odets, who was there and should have known. Rest of the cast: wife Ida Lupino, studio boss Rod Steiger, cover-up publicist Wendell Corey, Jean Hagen, Shelley Winters, Everett Sloane, Ilka Chase all super. But Robert Aldrich never makes it really convincing; 1955. (*b/w*)

The Big Lift X Misguided attempt to salute American flyers who airlifted supplies to Berlin during blockade, has miscast Montgomery Clift falling for German girl Cornell Borchers; Paul Douglas just hates Germans. Writer-director George Seaton can't quite pull it off; 1950. (*b/w*)

Big Money XX Ian Carmichael as fumbling scion of a crooked family; adequate fun, with Robert Helpmann, Kathleen Harrison; directed by John Paddy Carstairs; 1957. (*c*)

The Big Operator X Union drama with Mickey Rooney trying to take it over and honest Steve Cochran trying to stop him; Charles Haas must be kidding; 1959. (*b/w*)

The Big Show X Cliff Robertson goes to prison for father Nehemiah Persoff's negligence, emerges to find brother Robert Vaughn conniving to oust him from circus heritage. It should have been taut, exciting, but somehow even the acts seem dull; James B. Clark must accept the blame; 1961. (*c*)

The Big Sky √ Fur-trappers go up the Missouri in a keel-boat, scrapping along the way. Producer-director Howard Hawks does usual superior job, and has A. B. Guthrie's fine novel, *The Big Star*, as basis. Arthur Hunnicutt out-acts Kirk Douglas (not difficult); 1952. (*b/w*)

The Big Sleep √√ 'Neither the author (Raymond Chandler), the writer (William Faulkner), nor myself (Howard Hawkes) knew who had killed whom,' admitted the director of this muddled but otherwise marvellously atmospheric 1946 thriller of society girls (Lauren Bacall, Martha Vickers), drug addicted nymphomaniac (Dorothy Malone, when brunette) and, above all, detective (Humphrey Bogart). (*b/w*)

The Big Store √ Margaret Dumont: 'I'm afraid after we've been married a while a beautiful young girl will come along and you'll forget all about me.' Groucho. 'Don't be silly – I'll write to you twice a week.' . . . The greatest detective since Sherlock Holmes and his assistants foil a plan to murder the heir to the store . . . Charles Riesner; 1941. (*b/w*)

The Big Trees √ Kirk Douglas only slightly less wooden than the Californian redwoods he's so keen to grab for himself in turn-of-the-century California. Felix Feist provides some spectacular shots of the trees, but the rest is strictly splinters; 1952. (*c*)

Billie √ Nearly a good film, as Patty Duke who won a minor award for this best juvenile performance of 1965, embarrass male supremacist politician father by beating all the high school boys athletically; Jim Backus an asset as Pop; producer-director Don

41

Weiss does highly competent job. (c)

Billion-Dollar Brain √ Disappointing Harry Palmer (Michael Caine), ex-Len Deighton, thriller, set in Finland and Texas, with the bespectacled owl agent taking on Karl Malden and Ed Begley. Ken Russell self-indulgently used it as chance to show off some over-bloated effects; 1967. (c)

Billy Budd √√ Outstanding sea drama based on Melville's novel of slow-wit sailor (Terence Stamp, with blond rinse, in his best-ever part) v. evil master-at-arms (Robert Ryan), with Peter Ustinov taking on just a little too much as director-producer as well as actor – it's his part as captain that suffers, badly needing either another director to sharpen him up or another actor for him to look at more objectively; 1962. (b/w)

Billy Jack XX Naïve curiosity directed by Tom Laughlin who also plays the young half-breed who is the defiant hero. A weak 'youth' action film, it was cleverly promoted to become a box office blockbuster in America, in 1971. (c)

Billy Liar √√ More than just a marvellous comedy of frustrated adolescence; an all-too-true picture of urban society being sold down the river of false hopes. Only the size of TV screens and the shopping precincts have improved since 1963. John Schlesinger got cracking performances from Mona Washbourne, Helen Fraser, Leonard Rossiter, Wilfred Pickles – and, of course, Tom Courtenay in the title role. Julie Christie as understanding heroine is just too twee, perhaps the fault of Schlesinger who retreated into toothpaste commercials whenever she appeared. (b/w)

Billy the Kid √ How to make a psychopath into a hero, with wooden Robert Taylor as likeable killer; Brian Donlevy, Gene Lockhart grimace along under David Miller's direction; 1941. (b/w)

Billy Two Hats √ British-made western, actually shot in Israel, with Ted Kotcheff directing Gregory Peck as a wounded outlaw chased by Sheriff Jack Warden. There are racial overtones, as Warden expounds his hatred for Peck's friendship with the other outlaw on the run, a Red Indian (Desi Arnez Jr); 1973. (c)

Birdman of Alcatraz √√ Compelling, often touching, 1962 study from John Frankenheimer of Robert Stroud, who became world-famous birdlife autho-

rity while serving time for murder. One of Burt Lancaster's best as extraordinary Stroud. (b/w)

The Birds √√√ If you think the idea of the bird population turning on us humans is far fetched, know that Daphne du Maurier based her fantasy on a real-life story. A real director's film, with the acting (Tippi Hedren, Rod Taylor) adequate, but all the tricks of angles, editing, perspective, soundtrack, and above all the *trompe l'œil* that the birds really are attacking. Hitchcock at his best; 1963. (c)

The Birds and the Bees XX Pretty awful Jeanette MacDonald musical made in 1948, in which her daughter has to make an emotional adjustment to her remarriage. Jane Powell leads the brats. Edward Arnold chunters around. Fred M. Wilcox directed. (c)

The Birds and the Bees √ Mitzi Gaynor as con girl, plus David Niven as her father, make a set at George Gobel (TV funnyman, although you wouldn't know it); if this sounds familiar, it's because you've seen it not only in dozens of other movies but specifically in *The Lady Eve* (1941) when Barbara Stanwyck, Charles Coburn, Henry Fonda played the parts. This 1956 Norman Taurog version just isn't in the same class. (c)

Birds of Prey √ Exciting helicopter chase drama with David Janssen first as hunter then, when his plane conks out, as hunted; director, William Graham; 1973. (c)

The Birthday Party √ Inadequate literal filming of the Pinter play. The two hours drag as the lack of understandable plot and plethora of jaunty or menacing small talk make themselves increasingly obvious. That said, Dandy Nichols, Robert Shaw, Sidney Tafler, Patrick Magee come up shining; director William Friedkin is out of his country and his league, and shows it; 1968. (c)

Birthday Present √ Tony Britton makes the mistake of trying a little bit of smuggling for wifey Sylvia Syms in this pleasant low-budgeter directed by Pat Jackson; 1957. (b/w)

Birth of the Blues √ Slight plot of younger (1941) Bing Crosby trying to form Dixieland band in early New Orleans is good enough vehicle for 'St Louis Blues', 'St James Infirmary', 'Melancholy Baby'; with Mary Martin and high note from Jack Teagarden. Victor Schertzinger directs. (b/w)

The Bishop's Wife √ Cary Grant as

angel sent to help Bishop David Niven (odd casting) and especially his wife, Loretta Young; strong supports: Gladys Cooper, James Gleason, Monty Woolley, Elsa Lanchester; Henry Koster; 1947. (*b/w*)

Bite the Bullet √ A 700-mile horse race across the West provides a colourful background to a story of camaraderie (Gene Hackman, James Coburn) and escape (Candice Bergen trying to get husband out of chain gang), with undertones of portentousness from ranch-owner Paul Stewart. Producer-writer-director Richard Brooks failed to show any clear line through all this, however, in 1975 and it grips less than intended. (*c*)

Bitter Harvest X Janet Munro longs for the Big City, but there's tragedy waiting; John Stride, Alan Badel are waiting, too. Peter Graham Scott; 1963. (*c*)

Bitter Sweet √ Doubtless this will be remade, and better than this sweeter rather than bitter version of Noel Coward operetta with the arch Jeanette MacDonald trilling and Nelson Eddy hohumming; Ian Hunter, George Sanders looking grave but gay, weak but strong, paradoxical but obvious. You'll see it again, never fear. And it won't take much to improve on Woody van Dyke's 1941 version. (*c*)

Bitter Victory √ Stiff Curt Jurgens awarded medal he didn't earn in raid on Rommel's HQ; Richard Burton had affair with his wife, Ruth Roman. Nicholas Ray's direction (set in 1942, made 1957) disappoints, perhaps because it was made in French and dubbed. But surely Burton & Co spoke English originally? Confusing, like the plot. (*b/w*)

The Black Arrow XX Poor version of Stevenson's adventure yarn, with Louis Hayward at 39 (in 1948) too old for the part of youthful hero, and a changed ending. Janet Blair is the ward of nasty George Macready. Director, Hollywood maid-of-all-work, Gordon Douglas, brought no excitement with him. (*b/w*)

Blackbeard the Pirate X Hammy Robert Newton captures, pallid Richard Egan frees, simpering Linda Darnell in Raoul Walsh's 1952 swasher. (*c*)

Black Beauty √ Based more securely on Anna Sewell's original (and including a character called Anna Sewell who rescues the horse in old age) than the TV rip-off, this unpretentious child-

oriented sentimentality works well enough. Mark Lester, Patrick Mower and director James Hill add professionalism; 1971. (*c*)

The Blackboard Jungle √ A shocker in its day, this exposure of violent conditions in New York schools now looks as dated as its theme-music, 'Rock Around the Clock'. Richard Brooks got sincere performances from Glenn Ford, Anne Francis in 1955; an absurd sub-sub-Brando one from Vic Morrow. (*b/w*)

The Black Castle √ Not very horror movie with Boris Karloff and Lon Chaney the reasons for Richard Greene's pals going missing on hunting trip. So he goes on the next one. Nathan Juran directed fitfully; 1952. (*b/w*)

The Black Cat √√ Classic horror movie, in which devil-worshipper Boris Karloff faces Dr Bela Lugosi, was beautifully shot, designed and directed by Edgar G. Ulmer in 1934. (*b/w*)

The Black Dakotas X Gary Merrill getting his nasty hands on gold sent by Abe Lincoln to Indians as peace offering; Ray Nazzaro helmed routine western; 1954. (*c*)

Black Devils of Kali XX Lex Barker in 1955 hokum about human sacrifices in India; Ralph Murphy did his best; 1955. (*b/w*)

Black Flowers for the Bride X There is so much that is wrong with this black comedy (mostly traceable to the heavy hand of director Harold Prince, who should have stuck to Broadway musicals), that its small virtues of some funny scenes are easy to overlook. Michael York gains control of everyone (except a lady who forces him to marry her at the end), thanks to a combination of sexual potency and ruthlessness of character which are both familiar and hard to swallow – really you can't believe in him for a moment. However, there are some compensations, of whom an outrageously-camp Angela Lansbury is not one; 1970. (*c*)

Black Gold XX Sickening story of brave Indian Anthony Quinn adopting Chinese boy, and his faithful horse that he loves; Phil Karlson; 1947. (*b/w*)

Black Horse Canyon √ Joel McCrea hunting big black stallion and Mari Blanchard; Jesse Hibbs made it move; 1953. (*c*)

Blackjack Ketchum, Desperado X Victor Jory's familiar heavy is only compensation in this yarn of badman trying to become goodman but having to fight one last battle first; Earl Bellamy; 1956. (c)

The Black Knight X Alan Ladd's only a common smithy like you and me, but in this Camelot he disguises himself as a knight to protect King Arthur from the baddies. If you can't guess the ending, go to the bottom of the class. Tay Garnett keeps it moving and happily makes us overlook the awful script. Peter Cushing, Harry Andrews, Patricia Medina; 1954. (c)

Black Magic √ Orson Welles turns this heavy-handed Italian spectacle into watchable melo with his usual larger-than-life performance, here as Cagliostro. But what a waste this Gregory Ratoff-directed 1947 hokum was of his talents. (b/w)

Blackmail √√ (1) 1929 Hitchcock, first talking picture made in England, still marvellously exciting, particularly in classic breadknife scene with Anny Ondra.

Blackmail √ (2) 1939 Edward G. Robinson melo about escapee blackmailed by Gene Lockhart; directed H. C. Potter.

Blackmail XX (3) 1947 Ricardo Cortez B-pic about tycoon and blackmailing girlfriend. (all b/w).

Black Narcissus √ If you can take nuns building mission school in the Himalayas, this is your film. Deborah Kerr, Jean Simmons head finely-handled (by directors Michael Powell and Emeric Pressburger) cast, and it was way ahead of its time (in 1947) by admitting that some nuns went off their rockers due to sex repression. Won Oscars for photography and art direction; Miss Kerr won New York Critics' best actress award. (c)

The Black Orchid X Poorly developed soaper about two threatened marriages: Papa Anthony Quinn's to gangster's widow Sophia Loren; daughter Ina Balin's detemination that he shouldn't and subsequent up-screwing of her own engagement. Director Martin Ritt seems to have accepted Sophia's spouse Carlo Ponti's production values – a grim mistake; 1959. (b/w)

Blackout X (1) Maxwell Reed as blind ex-serviceman solving murder when eyesight restored. 1950. Robert S. Baker and Monty Berman; (b/w)

Blackout X (2) Dana Clark, broke, accepts job that leads him to murder, with Belinda Lee, Betty Ann Davies,

director Terence Fisher; 1954. (b/w)

Black Patch XX Poor western about sheriff trying to clear name; George Montgomery falsely accused of murder and hiding loot, stands rightly accused of appearing in rotten picture. Allen H. Miner; 1957. (b/w)

The Black Rose √ Henry Hathaway's 1950 romp set in mediaeval Orient. Orson Welles' enthusiastic hamming nearly overbalances Tyrone Power's handsome underplaying as Saxon hero. Not to be taken seriously, but the action scenes are special. (c)

The Black Shield of Falworth X Costume nonsense about rightful earls and trials by combat, with Tony Curtis appearing only slightly more out of place than Janet Leigh. Rudolph Maté's direction looks as though he once read Walter Scott at school a very long time ago; 1954. (c)

The Black Swan √ Tyrone Power v. George Sanders in 17th-century Jamaica, with Laird Cregar camping it up as the Governor; finely designed and bawdily written by Ben Hecht and Seton I. Miller, it received less than its due from director Henry King, who seemed bored with the whole thing; 1942. (c)

The Black Tent XX The love of a simple Arab girl for Eighth Army officer Anthony Steel makes for a dull actioner; Brian Desmond Hurst; 1957. (c)

The Black Torment X Heather Sears, Ann Lynn in chiller about conspirators trying to scare widower by Robert Hartford-Davis; 1965. (c)

Black Tuesday √ Edward G. Robinson as king of the gangsters, escaped from prison and tracked to warehouse. Surprise is it was made as late as 1955, by Hugo Fregonese. (b/w)

Black Widow √ Who kills nasty little Peggy Ann Garner? Well, she's so infuriating that anyone might, but the list of suspects is down to five: Van Heflin as Broadway producer, Ginger Rogers, Gene Tierney, George Raft or Reginald Gardiner. Writer-producer-director Nunnally Johnson cooks a steamy brew; 1954. (c)

The Black Windmill X British-made thriller by master craftsman Don Siegel which received a general critical pasting, but easily stands comparison with television spy serials and is much better directed and cast. Michael Caine is a framed, beleaguered secret service-man whose son is brutally kidnapped; Janet Suzman is his anguished wife.

On the run, he has to prove who the real villain is: Donald Pleasence, his boss? Joseph O'Conor, head of MI5? Joss Ackland of Scotland Yard? 1974. (c)

Black Zoo XX Lovely people (Michael Gough, Jerome Cowan, Elisha Cook) in lousy film about killer loose in zoo; Robert Gordon; 1963. (b/w)

Blaze of Noon √ The men who fly and the women who wait for them to crash in the setting of early air mail planes. William Holden, Howard da Silva outstanding; Anne Baxter among wives; also William Bendix, Sonny Tufts (Sonny Tufts?). John Farrow; 1947. (b/w)

The Blazing Forest X John Payne, Agnes Moorehead, William Demarest, Richard Arlen in old-timers' benefit-night logging yarn with heart and brain of wood. Edward Ludwig; 1952. (c)

Blazing Saddles √ Fitfully-funny western by Mel Brooks (himself in two roles) that pushed Gene Wilder into stardom in 1974. There are some marvellous moments but they never add up to more than squibs among repetitive would-be belly-laughs that soon pall. However, Wilder, Madeline Kahn, and Harvey Korman work and ride hard. (c)

Bleak Moments √ Those familiar with Mike Leigh's later television work – notably the viciously funny *Abigail's Party* and *Nuts In May* – may need reminding that in 1971 he was unsmilingly putting the world to rights. This group of unhappy, disparate typists, hippies and mental defectives failed to communicate as powerfully. However, when they did they were touchingly comic; Anne Raitt was particularly good as an attractive girl who is bowed down by having to look after her retarded sister, Sarah Stephenson. (c)

Blindfold XX Rock Hudson is unbelievable psychologist in this even more incredible yarn about two governments in tug-o'-war for scientist's mind; Claudia Cardinale is scientist's draggy sister. Philip Dunne wrote-directed; 1966. (c)

Blind Terror √ Garish thriller, hyped up by Richard Fleischer's direction of hokum-expert Brian Clemens's flashy script. Mia Farrow makes her heroine put-upon by a psychopathic killer as believable as possible; 1971. (c)

The Bliss of Mrs Blossom XX Desperately embarrassing attempt to make inflatable dreams of bra-maker's wife funny; Shirley MacLaine, Richard Attenborough, James Booth play a triangle that seems to be a contest for tastelessness. Joe McGrath, director, must take a large part of the blame; 1968. (c)

Blithe Spirit √√ Absolutely delicious Noel Coward comedy; Margaret Rutherford making Madame Acarti the happiest medium, Rex Harrison as harassed husband. Constance Cummings and Kay Hammond as real and ghostly wives are absolutely divine. David Lean could do no wrong in 1945. (c)

The Blob √ In 1958, before he made it big, Steve McQueen was involved in ridding mankind of fungus from falling star. Irwin S. Yeaworth made it highly watchable, even without seeing the youthful Steve doing his bit. (c)

Blood Alley X John Wayne saving the world from communism again, this time one whole Chinese village and Lauren Bacall as doctor's orphan daughter. William Wellman makes it all moderately exciting if you can bear 'The Duke' and his mission; 1955. (c)

Blood and Sand √√ Superb colour and careful, loving direction by Rouben Mamoulian lifted this bullfight story out of the sensational into a higher bracket. Despite inadequate casting, he made even Tyrone Power, Linda Darnell, Rita Hayworth and Anthony Quinn seem impressive, and the bullfighting shots are delicately yet excitingly filmed; 1941. (c)

Blood from the Mummy's Tomb √ Reincarnation of Egyptian princess is attempted by Andrew Keir and James Villiers under the superior direction of Seth Holt; 1971. (c)

Blood of Dracula's Castle XX Laboured reworking of the usual stuff, with only John Carradine's butler managing to evoke any authentic shivers. Director Al Adamson was working with inferior human and scripted material; 1969. (c)

Blood of the Vampire XX Donald Wolfit forcing doctor to get the bad blood out of his veins. Director Henry Cass doesn't seem to believe it either; 1958. (b/w)

Blood on the Arrow X Dale Robertson, lone survivor of Indian massacre, helps Wendell Cory and Martha Hyer get back their child, held captive by redskins; Sidney Salkow; 1964. (c)

Blood on the Moon √ Roberts Mitchum and Preston fall out over underhanded scheme to rob old Walter

45

Brennan and Barbara Bel Geddes; Robert Wise; 1948. (b/w)

Blood on the Sun √ James Cagney sniffs out Japan's plans for world conquest in 1928 (made 1945). Frank Lloyd directs. (b/w)

Blood Sisters √ Director-author Brian De Palma was to become a cult director on his own terms. This early (1972) thriller about twin sisters, one of them homicidal, should send shivers down your back, even if the music (Bernard Herrman) and several of the devices are like set questions for a Hitchcock buff's examination; Margot Kidder plays the sisters. (c)

Bloody Mama √ Powerful and gory, Roger Corman's account of Ma Barker's forays into violent crime in the mid-Thirties works as long as the action keeps up. If it finally alienates, it is because Corman pushes it too far over the top into incest and mass death. Shelley Winters plays the matriarch; Robert De Niro, Bruce Dern, Pat Hingle, Diane Varsi excel; 1970. (c)

Blossoms in the Dust X A lovely cry, ever since 1941. Greer Garson founds a home for illegitimate children. The shamelessly sentimental script is, astonishingly, by Anita Loos, who wrote *Gentlemen Prefer Blondes*. Director: Mervyn LeRoy. (c)

Blowing Wild √ You've seen it all before – rough-tough oil-man (Gary Cooper), his tough-rough pal (Anthony Quinn), the heart-of-gold wife (Barbara Stanwyck), the gushers, the explosions, the fires, the disappointments, the triumphs, the bandits. Don't let us stop you if you want to see it again – Hugo Fregonese makes it all very watchable; 1953. (b/w)

Blow up √√ Antonioni's British picture, 1967, had David Hemmings earnestly letting down an otherwise sparkling overlay of Italian conjecture on the swinging London scene. Condemnation of a photographer's uninvolvement with his subjects is brilliantly implied; the episodes each dazzle individually, even if the totality is disappointing. (c)

Blue √ Terence Stamp in a pretentious cowboy movie that manages to carry its pretensions about being existentialist and significant remarkably well. Director Silvio Narizzano tells the story of the ruthless orphan who ends up leading the goodies against his pals in too moody a way and without sufficient technical care; but Karl Malden and Ricardo Montalban are encouraged to give fine performances. Stamp just looks menacing and doesn't even speak for the first forty minutes; 1968. (c)

The Blue Angel √ (1) Famous 1930 German melo about professor (Emil Jannings) squandering All for nightclub singer (Marlene Dietrich) was made in both German and English, and the song 'Falling In Love Again' established Dietrich internationally. Trickily directed by Joseph von Sternberg. (b/w)

The Blue Angel XX (2) The awful 1959 remake by Edward Dmytryk with Curt Jurgens and May Britt even had a happy ending. (c)

Bluebeard XX John Carradine murdering every girl who poses for him in Paris; Edward Ulmer; 1945. (b/w)

Bluebeard's Ten Honeymoons XX Same plot as Chaplin's *Monsieur Verdoux* – both are based on the career of bride-murderer Landru. But here it's George Sanders, playing it for real, or as near-real as lightweight director W. Lee Wilder can get. Parade of British lady has-beens (only one can act, but you won't get us naming her) provide the victims; 1960. (b/w)

Blue Blood XX A lurid working-over of *The Servant*, with Oliver Reed fitting well in the role of boorish, villainous butler, while Derek Jacobi is unhappy as the weak aristocrat who submits to his titular servant. There is a lot of rubbish about siring heirs by three different women – Fiona Lewis, Meg Wynn Owen, Anna Gael – and unconvincing orgies of various kinds. Director Andrew Sinclair allows the whole enterprise to go well over the top; 1973. (c)

The Blue Dahlia √√ Who killed Alan Ladd's unfaithful wife? Was it the little chap himself? His pal, William Bendix, with blank periods due to war wound? Smoothie Howard da Silva? George Marshall keeps the suspense going. Writer Raymond Chandler had to change the ending due to official pressure and was also fed up with the female lead, whom he called Moronica Lake; 1946. (b/w)

The Blue Gardenia √ Anne Baxter arrested on say-so of smart reporter Richard Conte, who then decides she's innocent; as heavy Raymond Burr (later reformed as Ironside) is around, maybe there's a clue there? However, Fritz Lang's direction lifts above the banal; 1953. (b/w)

Blue Hawaii XX Fourteen Elvis Presley songs and a travel-poster Honolulu will either turn you on or put you off, so that's all you need to know. Norman Taurog's homage to Presley happened also to be the top-grossing motion picture in the US; 1962. (c)

The Blue Knight √ Originally four hours long (less commercial time) and shown over four nights on American TV, Robert Butler's standard yarn of a cop (William Holden) acting on his own in solving the murder of a whore trims down handily. If it contains no surprises, it is at least viewable; 1973. (c)

The Blue Lagoon X Soppy, slow-moving but ultimately pleasant idyll on desert isle as kids grow up into lovers; Jean Simmons, Donald Houston; directed earnestly by Frank Launder; 1949. (c)

The Blue Lamp X Have a glance at it to see just how soft, sentimental and indulgent we were in 1950. Ted Willis' script and Basil Dearden's direction will embarrass anyone who watched *Softly, Softly* or even *Z Cars*. Dirk Bogarde is the nasty who kills PC Dixon, only to rise again, the Messiah of Dock Green. (b/w)

The Blue Max √ Spectacularly shot and directed (John Guillermin) re-creation of a German fighter squadron in First World War, with flyers George Peppard, Jeremy Kemp (marvellous) vying for honour of shooting down 20 planes and thus winning title medal; James Mason cynical CO. Unfortunately, the ground action is severely tethered to *terra firma*; 1965. (c)

Blue Murder at St Trinian's √ Made in 1958, it has Sabrina among the girls; Terry-Thomas, George Cole, Joyce Grenfell, Alastair Sim, Lionel Jeffries make absurd story of crook hiding out there and army called in more than watchable, actually enjoyable. (b/w)

The Blue Peter XXX Not the great success of BBC children's television, but wooden Kieron Moore rediscovering himself as instructor to Outward Bounders. John Pudney helped script. Wolf Rilla directed; 1954. (c)

Blueprint for Murder √ Is Jean Peters planning to murder Joseph Cotten's nephew, having already done in brother and niece? Good suspenser, written and directed by Andrew Stone; 1953. (b/w)

Blue Skies X Fred Astaire in a little nothing of a musical with familiar but dull Irving Berlin songs; Bing Crosby, Billy de Wolfe come out best. Stuart Heisler; 1946. (c)

Blume in Love XX Heavy-handed comedy about George Segal mooning after his divorced wife Susan Anspach. Writer - producer - director Paul Mazursky slogs towards a happy ending when they fall into each other's arms in Venice, where Segal has been remembering their unlikely and rather unpleasant history over some doubtless very expensive coffee outside Florians. Kris Kristofferson, Shelley Winters, Marsha Mason add to the general air of disbelief; 1973. (c)

The Boatniks X Accident-prone coast-guard Robert Morse tries to catch jewel thief Phil Silvers. Stefanie Powers and old-timer Don Ameche join in strained Disney live-action fun under director Norman Tokar; 1970. (c)

Bob and Carol and Ted and Alice √ Titillating comedy in which Robert Culp and Natalie Wood and Elliott Gould and Dyan Cannon shed their inhibitions and go to bed together, but only literally. And then nothing. It's a period piece of the Swinging 1969s, and Paul Mazursky's cop-out script and direction (co-written with producer Larry White) don't deliver what they claim. (c)

Bobbikins XXX Shirley Jones, Billie Whitelaw in tepid comedy about 14-month-old who talks like adult and gives stock exchange tips. For some reason, Robert Day cast Max Bygraves in it; 1960. (c)

Body and Soul √√ The classic boxing picture, directed in 1947 by Robert Rossen, with Robert Aldrich as first assistant, James Wong Howe, cameraman. John Garfield was golden boy, Lilli Palmer romantic interest. (b/w)

The Body Snatcher √ Boris Karloff and producer Val Lewton got together for the first time in this 1945 version of the Burke and Hare saga. Bela Lugosi haunts the Edinburgh streets for young girls. The end is guaranteed to chill; director Robert Wise. (b/w)

The Body Stealers XX Cheaply-made, weak sci-fi about parachuters disappearing. Nobody around seems to believe in what they are doing, including George Sanders, Hilary Dwyer or director Gerry Levy; 1969. (c)

Boeing-Boeing X Silly, embarrassing 'comedy' about swinger Tony Curtis keeping three airhostess girlfriends on the go while Jerry Lewis drools. John Rich seemed under the impression that if everybody walked even faster and talked louder than stage version, they would be funnier, too; 1965. (c)

The Bofors Gun √√ Tight, prim David Warner and wild Irish gunner Nicol Williamson play out a lethal game on guard duty in Germany, with Ian Holm and John Thaw drawn in. Jack Gold makes this a vivid and unnerving piece of theatre, and almost an outstanding film; 1968. (c

Bond Street XX Individual performances pop up like rockets in this episodic and on the whole dreadful film directed by Gordon Parry. Cripple girl and twister husband – Patricia Plunkett and Kenneth Griffith – steal the show; 1947. (b/w)

Bonjour Tristesse X Miscasting (Jean Seberg, Deborah Kerr, David Niven, Juliette Greco) sinks this adaptation of Sagan novel about father and daughter relationship on the Riviera; Otto Preminger hokes it up, to no avail; 1957. (c)

Bonnie and Clyde √√√ Warren Beatty and Faye Dunaway in influential blockbuster, which does not seem as gratuitously violent as it did in 1967 – a lot of blood has run under the bridge since then. Michael J. Pollard, Gene Hackman, Estelle Parsons, Gene Wilder all superb; in case you didn't know, the eponymous couple are bankrobbers in it for kicks as well as money and there's a gruesome shootup at the end; Arthur Penn. (c)

The Bonnie Parker Story √ Made nine years before Bonnie and Clyde – in 1958 – this tells the lady's fall from waitress to gangster rather more conventionally. Dorothy Provine essays her under William Witney's unambitious direction. (b/w)

Bonnie Scotland √√ Classic 1935 Laurel and Hardy ribtickler (as they used to say). Director Jimmy Horne managed to keep some sort of story about Stan being disappointed over a Scottish legacy going, but all that matters is interplay between the divine couple in India. (b/w)

Boom! X How could Elizabeth Taylor, Richard Burton, Noel Coward acting a Tennessee Williams script for Joseph Losey, photographed by Douglas Slocombe, come up with an almighty flop? If it doesn't seem possible, here is the evidence – self-indulgence and (one suspects) the sin of hubris all round. Of course, there are marvellous bits in this tale of the poet and the 'older woman', but watching is a disheartening experience; 1969. (c)

Boomerang √√ First of the socially-conscious thrillers that blossomed in 1947 Hollywood, only to be killed soon after by McCarthy era; Elia Kazan directed Dana Andrews as politically-motivated DA. Exciting, brilliantly-made, true-life story. (b/w)

Boom Town √ Clark Gable and Spencer Tracy as oil wildcatters. Need to know more? How about Claudette Colbert as Tracy's wife, Hedy Lamarr as Gable's girlfriend. Plus gushers, fires and the rest of the oil movie excitements. Jack Conway; 1940. (b/w)

Borderlines √ Joan Crawford (harsh) v. Robert Stack (gentle) battle out approaches to the mentally sick; Polly Bergen cracks up, Janis Page is a whore. It once had a postscript by President Kennedy; also gone are two scenes with Miss Bergen – one where she's nearly raped by the men's ward and one showing her shock treatment. Hal Bartlett produced-directed; 1963. (b/w)

Border River X Confed Joel McCrea gets arms and a girlfriend Yvonne de Carlo from Pedro Armendariz; George Sherman; 1953. (b/w)

The Borgia Stick √ Excitingly filmed entirely on location in New York, this 1967 actioner by David Lowell Rich shows how the Mafia is going into legit business. Don Murray and Inger Stevens take them on. (c)

Born Free √ First and best of long inferior series of wild animal epics starring Virginia McKenna and Bill Travers, based on more or less true story of lion-rearer Joy Adamson; 1964 direction by James Hill. (c)

Born to be Bad X Or not very good, anyway. Joan Fontaine is tough girl on the make – she makes rich man Zachary Scott, writer Robert Ryan, artist Mel Ferrer, but is shown up to be what she is – and no better. Nicholas Ray doesn't even try to turn this hokum into the believable; 1950. (b/w)

Born to Dance √√ Cole Porter wrote 'Easy to Love' and 'I've Got You Under My Skin' in 1936 for this sailors - in - New - York type extravaganza. James Stewart and Sid Silvers are the gobs; Eleanor Powell and Virginia Bruce the gals. Other pleasures to watch are Una Merkel, Frances Langford, Raymond Walburn and Roy del Ruth's confident direction. (b/w)

Born to Win √ George Segal drags Karen Black into heroin addiction in this unlikely comedy directed by Ivan Passer in 1971. Robert de Niro, Paula

Prentiss figure in strong cast list. (c)

Born Yesterday √√ Outstanding comedy that won 1950 Oscar for Judy Holliday, as dumbest blonde, after she desperately slimmed for film of her Broadway success. William Holden as her Professor Higgins and Broderick Crawford fine supports. George Cukor directed from script covertly supplied by play's writer, Garson Kanin. (b/w)

Borsalino X French gangster number with Jean-Paul Belmondo and Alain Delon larking about under Jacques Deray's direction. Old hat, even in 1970. (c)

The Boss √ Corruption in St Louis after First World War exposed by John Payne; rather good of its kind, thanks to Byron Haskin's meticulous direction; 1956. (b/w)

The Boston Strangler √√ Exciting and, on the whole, well-made (by Richard Fleischer) partisan account of the deeds and apprehension of real-life murderer. Tony Curtis, as the strangler, and Henry Fonda, interrogator, are solidly backed by George Kennedy, Jeff Corey, Sally Kellerman; 1969. (c)

Botany Bay √ Formula follow-up to *Mutiny on the Bounty* by same authors, has James Mason as Blighted captain, Alan Ladd as convict hero; would you believe Patricia Medina as a ladylike lady prisoner being transported, too? John Farrow turned in pro job; 1953. (c)

Bottom of the Bottle √ Or of the barrel. Successful lawyer pretends alcoholic brother is just a friend. Van Johnson and Joseph Cotten act like made, but Henry Hathaway hasn't attempted any of the subtlety of the Simenon book it's taken from; 1956. (c)

Bottoms Up XX If, by some personal aberration, you happen to think Jimmy Edwards in his Will Hay-type schoolmaster role is funny, don't let us stop you from chortling over this nonsense about rebellion at his school; others, keep away; 1960. (b/w)

Boxcar Bertha √√ Director Martin Scorsese, who was to make *Mean Streets*, *Alice Doesn't Live Here Anymore* and *Taxi Driver*, shot this unusual thriller in 1972. Centred round Barbara Hershey, a whore who worked the trains in which hobos travelled America in the thirties, it uplifts her to legendary status, along with David Carradine with whom she forms a gang. He gives his share of the loot to the union who are fighting the train bosses. They are the ones who finally catch and crucify him (on a boxcar). Not as trite as it may sound, the film is strong and involving. (c)

The Boy Cried Murder X The boy who cried 'Wolf' sees a murder, nobody believes him; filmed in Yugoslavia by George Breakston with Veronica Hurst; 1966. (c)

Boy, Did I Get a Wrong Number X Well, yes he did, except that it's No 312 on Variety's list of all-time US box-office grossers, which can't be bad. Otherwise, it's strictly for Bob Hope fans, as their lad involves himself with Elke Sommer as disillusioned film star, his wife Marjorie Lord and maid Phyllis Diller misunderstanding him. George Marshall; 1966. (c)

The Boy Friend XX Ken Russell works his familiar magic, which consists of taking an interesting theme and ruining it. In 1971 his heavy hands clawed at Sandy Wilson's charming pastiche of the Twenties, and turned it into his idea of a Thirties musical. Poor little Twiggy out-acts Christopher Gable, and only Tommy Tune's tap-dancing is worth watching TV for. The songs, when they are not camped up, are delightful, but then they always were. (c)

Boy on a Dolphin √ Sophia Loren in and out of the water discovering sunken statue and trying to make a dishonest buck (or, rather, seeing it's Greece, drachma) selling its whereabouts to Clifton Webb. Unfortunately, tepid Alan Ladd plays an archaeologist and foils her; Jean Negulesco made it all very easy to look at, if not to think about; 1957. (c)

The Boys X Nothing looks more outdated than films about Youth, and this 1962 effort with Robert Morley, Felix Aylmer, Wilfred Brambell, Richard Todd suffers more than most. Yet Sidney J. Furie's inventive direction and ensemble playing of (then) teenagers makes this effort at understanding worth trying to watch. (b/w)

The Boys from Syracuse √ Beguiling screen transfer in 1940 of Rodgers and Hart reworking of *The Comedy of Errors*. Includes 'This Can't Be Love', 'Sing For Your Supper'; plus Martha Raye, Alan Mowbray, Eric Blore. Notable direction from Edward Sutherland. (b/w)

Boys' Night Out √ Tony Randall does his usual job of saving wobbly movie, as one of four men who decide to share a girl and an apartment. Snags are that the girl is (a) a sociology student

49

studying them and (b) she's Kim Novak, the worst actress ever to become a household name. Director Michael Gordon makes it all move merrily enough along; 1962. (c)

Boys' Town X This schmaltz won almost every award in sight in 1938, but it comes over as awfully gooey now, despite Spencer Tracy's sincere attempts at being sincere. Mickey Rooney is toughie transformed. Incidentally, as the result of this movie, the Boys' Town charity has become one of the wealthiest in the world, living on its interest. Norman Taurog pulled out all the stops. (b/w)

The Boy With Green Hair √ Early (1948) message pic about discrimination, worth seeing for Dean Stockwell's kid, veterans Pat O'Brien and Robert Ryan and Joseph Losey's first mannered essay in directing. (c)

The Brain X Phoney sci-fi horror flick that has scientist discovering who was the murderer by probing dead man's brain; Anne Heywood, Cecil Parker. Gerard Oury; 1965. (b/w)

Brainstorm X Jeff Hunter, Anne Francis, Dana Andrews are triangle in so-so thriller about attempted suicide and murder. William Conrad directed unimaginatively; 1965. (b/w)

The Bramble Bush X Richard Burton sits uneasily in soap-opera part of doctor returning to Cape Cod to perform op on dying friend and falling for his wife, Barbara Rush. Holds the superficial interest well enough, and Daniel Petrie has strong supports in Jack Carson, Angie Dickinson; 1960. (c)

Branded X Anastasiac western, with diminutive Alan Ladd pretending to be Charles Bickford's long-lost son; snag is he falls in love with Mona Freeman for some reason, like the script – so has to produce the real son before it can all end happily ever after. Rudolph Maté directs ably enough; 1950. (c)

Brannigan √ Mechanical John Wayne vehicle, which casts him in the mould of Clint Eastwood in *Coogan's Bluff* as a visiting detective in a big city (this time London). Richard Attenborough plays a British detective whose exchanges with the big American are supposed to be wryly funny. The story concerns a wanted man (John Vernon) who has apparently been kidnapped. Some neat twists in the plot, albeit absurd, are vitiated by Douglas

Hickox's relentless sightseeing direction; 1975. (c)

The Brass Bottle X The old F. Anstey novel, disastrously updated to contemporary New York with Tony Randall as the man who buys Aladdin-type curio and conjures up a particularly pompous demon in Burl Ives. The smashing Barbara Eden is the lady he nearly gets parted from in ensuing shenanigans. Harry Keller could surely have done better with these ingredients; 1964. (c)

The Brass Legend √ Raymond Burr makes a splendid villain in this western about an 11-year-old boy in jeopardy; Gerd Oswald; 1956. (b/w)

The Bravados √ Superior adult western in which Gregory Peck realises that tracking down killers of his first wife with such single-minded thirst for vengeance has drained him of love and mercy. He tries to make amends with Joan Collins, doing her best (which isn't that good). Henry King makes it exciting, sustained viewing; 1958. (c)

The Brave Bulls √ Despite the double disadvantage of casting Mel Ferrer as matador and Anthony Quinn as his manager, producer-director Robert Rossen manages to translate Tom Leas' novel about the Mexican bullring into a more than competent film; at least Ferrer's doleful countenance makes his wracked indecision believable. Don't worry, soft-hearts, the moments of truth are off screen; 1951. (b/w)

The Brave One √ Sad story of little Mexican boy who loves a bull only to see it matched against matador; Irving Rapper's direction will pull at your heartstrings; 1957. (c)

Breakaway XX 1957 suspenser-that-isn't about racketeers and others' attempts to obtain secret formula for overcoming fatigue in flight. Better to have looked for one to overcome fatigue caused by watching such bosh. Tom Conway, Honor Blackman, Bruce Seton. (b/w)

Breakfast at Tiffany's √√ Whacky New York playgirl Audrey Hepburn shocks, charms small-town George Peppard in cleverly-bowdlerised (by George Axelrod) version of Truman Capote novella. Confidently directed by Blake Edwards; 1961. (c)

The Breaking Point √ Hemingway's *To Have and Have Not* was filmed under its own name (Bogart, 1944), once as *The Gun Runners* (Audie Murphy, 1958) and here, 1950, with

John Garfield as the fishing boat skipper who rents boat to baddies then shoots it out with them. Patricia Neal and Patricia Thaxter have been written in as tramp and wife. Otherwise, Michael Curtiz did competent job, and got the most out of Juano Hernandez's death scene. (b/w)

Break in the Circle XX If you can believe Eva Bartok is a Scotland Yard agent you can take the rest of this routine smuggling-scientist-out-of-Red-infested-Germany 'thriller'; Forrest Tucker is boat-owner; Val Guest knocked it off in 1955. (b/w)

Breakout √ (1) 1959: conventional PoW escape drama, set in Italian camp with Nazi commander; Richard Todd, Richard Attenborough, Michael Wilding. Don Chaffey directed competently enough. (b/w)

Breakout X (2) 1960: Lee Patterson, Hazel Court, Billie Whitelaw in quickie about jailbreak. Peter Graham Scott. (b/w)

Breakout X (3) 1967: James Drury, Red Buttons in mountain escape thwarted by little boy lost situation. Richard Irving. (c)

Breakout √ (4) 1975: the several jailbreaks become repetitive but never completely lose interest, as Charles Bronson, a convincing mercenary, tries to spring Robert Duvall from Mexican prison. Plenty of stunt flying and some broad fun in Randy Quaid's disguise as a tart; Tom Gries directed expertly. (c)

A Breath of Scandal XX The scandal is to have made this awful picture at all, let alone spend goodness knows how much on re-creating Austria of the Habsburgs and their nasty minds. Michael Curtiz hurries it along embarrassedly, Sophia Loren is angry as compromised princess (and doubtless that's not all she's angry about), John Gavin is plain inadequate, Maurice Chevalier forced to parade all his schmaltzy charm; 1960. (c)

Breezy X William Holden as lonely, rich Older Man becomes infatuated with unconvincingly kookie hitch-hiker Kay Lenz. Under Clint Eastwood's 1973 direction and Michael Legrand's sickly score, this becomes a Man Meets Girl, Man Loses Girl, Man Gets Girl sentimentality, a disappointment after the actor's first two films as director, *Play Misty for Me* and *High Plains Drifter*. (c)

Brewster McCloud √ Unusual and rewarding comedy about Bud Cort trying to learn to fly. Sally Kellerman plays a Being who was probably once a bird herself, encouraging him. Cult director Robert Altman (M*A*S*H, Nashville) asks for a suspension of disbelief that is worth making for the surrealistic pleasure to be had from the visuals (mostly in and around Houston airport) and a varied and talented cast of grotesques; 1970. (c)

The Bridal Path XXX Really awful comedy about rough-hewn Scot, Bill Travers, on mainland in search of a wife; Frank Launder should have known better; 1959. (c)

The Bride of Frankenstein √√ Generally agreed to be about the best horror film ever, flowering of James Whale's directorial talents, Boris Karloff's likeable monster and, above all, Elsa Lanchester's incredible bride, with stunning help from make-up. Made in 1935, when they really cared. (b/w)

Brides of Dracula √ 1960 Hammer horror: Martita Hunt keeps her bloodsucking son under lock and key but he cons a girl to let him out; it's lucky Peter Cushing is around to catch him, or he might have sucked director Terence Fisher's blood instead of vice versa; 1960. (c)

The Bride Wore Red XX Only those interested in a fashion show of 1937 styles will warm to this lurid Joan Crawford vehicle about singer-Cinderella who makes it to riches via Franchot Tone. One of the few pre-war movies directed by a woman, Dorothy Arzner. (c)

The Bridge at Remagen X One of those war pix that pretend to philosophise about war while milking it of all the excitement it can provide. This one is particularly nasty because of director John Guillermin's penchant for blood and brutality; George Segal, Ben Gazzara, E. G. Marshall are among the Americans; Robert Vaughn, Peter van Eyck among the Germans who meet on the bridge. It's got an extremely noisy soundtrack; 1969. (c)

The Bridge on the River Kwai √√√ Justly-famous dramatisation of the building of railway under Japanese coercion by British PoWs, commanded by a punctilious CO (Alec Guinness). Ending is obscure, but Alec Guinness recently told us that the fall 'is sort of fifty-fifty accidental, and as the character dies he is meant to be regretting his action'. Jack Hawkins, William Holden manage to avoid too many heroics for a 1957 picture; David Lean directed. (c)

Bridge to the Sun X Carroll Baker as American girl married to Japanese diplomat and her life during the Second World War filmed in situ, Tokyo. It's all a bit naïve and propagandoid for Japanese-US relations, but Etienne Perier makes you almost believe in it; 1961. (b/w)

The Bridges at Toko-Ri √ Personally, we can't see why anyone wants to cheer on war pictures, but obviously plenty of people do – this was the top moneymaker of its year – and you can't do any better than this if you're among them. William Holden, Fredric March, Mickey Rooney, Grace Kelly in detailed account of Navy carrier-based jet pilots and helicopter rescue teams during Korean War. Won Oscar 1955 for its special effects. Mark Robson handled the whole naval structure, cosmic battles and personal dramas within them with a firm, strong hand. (c)

Brief Encounter √ David Lean's direction of Noel Coward's script about Celia Johnson and Trevor Howard's furtive meetings to Rachmaninov's second piano concerto moved the whole forties generation to tears; 1945. (b/w)

Brigadoon X Disappointing version of stage musical about Scottish village coming to life on only one day every 100 years; Gene Kelly, Van Johnson, Cyd Charisse out of their element and director Vincente Minnelli clearly ill at ease; 1955. (c)

The Brigand of Kandahar XXX – Kandahahaha, more like. None of the cast look as if they have been nearer India than the Taj Mahal Tandoori Restaurant; weak Ronald Lewis is the hero, petulant Oliver Reed the villain in this pathetic John Gilling-directed mini-epic a long way after *Gunga Din*; 1965. (c)

Brighton Rock √√ More than adequate 1947 version by the Boulting brothers of Graham Greene novel with Richard Attenborough outstanding as Pinkie, Alan Wheatley as gang boss he murders, Carol Marsh as 16-year-old he marries to keep quiet. (b/w)

Bright Victory √ Arthur Kennedy won New York critics' poll as best actor of 1952 for his part as blinded GI who learns to readjust and find love; Mark Robson directed delicately, avoiding maudlin dangers. (b/w)

Bringing up Baby √√ Delicious Cary Grant-Katharine Hepburn comedy made when they knew how (1938) by a man who knew how (Howard Hawks). Later plagiarised (it's called 'homage') for *What's Up, Doc?* Wild leopard mistaken for pet provides hilarious sequences. (b/w)

Bring Me the Head of Alfred Garcia √√ Violent (but tender in its love scenes) hunt for the gruesome head of a Mexican bandit, to prove his death. Director Sam Peckinpah, famous for his bloody battles, takes his main protagonist, Warren Oates, through several, involving Gig Young, Robert Webber, Kris Kristofferson, among others; 1974. (c)

Brink of Hell X William Holden trying to win back superior's confidence in his flying during Korean War; Mervyn Le Roy does best in the air; 1956. (b/w)

Broadway √ Amusing curiosity from 1942 with Pat O'Brien. George Raft is a Prohibition gangster playing (and dancing) autobiographical part. Broderick Crawford, S. Z. Sakall giving strong support. William A. Seiter directed. (b/w)

Broadway Melody of 1940 √ Cole Porter score includes 'Begin the Beguine' and 'I Concentrate on You'. Backstage yarn features Fred Astaire and Eleanor Powell as struggling dance team. George Murphy, Florence Rice, Frank Morgan support; Norman Taurog directs. (b/w)

Broadway Rhythm √ Minor musical from 1943, based on Kern-Hammerstein's stage show *Very Warm for May*. George Murphy plays Broadway producer, Ginny Sims, Gloria de Haven, Lena Horne are hopeful stars; director, Roy Del Ruth. (c)

The Broken Horseshoe XX Deliberate hit and run involves Elizabeth Sellars and Robert Beatty in drug ring. Martyn C. Webster; 1953. (b/w)

Broken Journey X One of those how-each-reacts-in-air-plane-crash movies; Phyllis Calvert, James Donald, Francis L. Sullivan were in this 1948 version. Ken Annakin. (b/w)

Broken Lance √ This 1954 vehicle for Spencer Tracy provoked bitchy comment from Clark Gable: 'Spence *is* the part. The old rancher is mean, unreasonable and vain. All he has to do is show up and be photographed.' Result was pretty spectacular with Spence as patriarch failing to unify family of Robert Wagner, Richard Widmark, Hugh O'Brien, tautly directed by Edward Dmytryk. (c)

Bronco Bullfrog √√ Remarkable feature made for £17,000 in the East End of London by Barney Platts-Mills, graphically showing how frustrating life is for teenagers there – even if they get lucky and manage to buy a motorbike. Much more than a curiosity, it is a clearer view of life in 1970 than most documentaries. (b/w)

Bronco Buster √ Rodeo star John Lund teaches Scott Brady the ropes, but soon they are rivals for Joyce Holden; made with Budd Boetticher's usual economical directorial skill in 1952. (c)

Brother, Can You Spare a Dime? √ While the newsreel footage and extracts from Thirties films which make up this compilation are interesting, they appear to have been chosen by Philippe Mora almost at random. Also disconcerting is the choice of James Cagney to join F. D. Roosevelt as the archetype of the decade. The songs on the track are fun. (b/w)

The Brotherhood X The movie that proves that it wasn't the subject that made *The Godfather* such a compelling film, and the reason Paramount took so much persuading to give the ultimately No 1 box office grosser the financial backing it needed. This 1968 attempt at the same sort of Mafia plot, even down to the Sicilian scenes, was ruined by Kirk Douglas' insensitive performance and director Martin Ritt's nerveless grasp. Luther Adler makes it live for the moments he is on the screen, but that isn't enough. (c)

The Brotherhood of Satan √ Effective horror movie with Strother Martin and L. Q. Jones, in which children's toys are transformed into murder weapons; director Bernard McEveety; 1970. (c)

Brother John √ Is Sidney Poitier harmless, is he an agitator from the North or an emissary from another planet? However, the film isn't too silly, and Will Geer contributes a useful presence. Director, James Goldstone; 1970. (c)

Brother Orchid √√ Funny 1940 gangster movie with boss Edward G. Robinson hiding in monastery gradually becoming converted to the simple life. Humphrey Bogart is rival gang-leader, Ann Sothern girlfriend, Ralph Bellamy square rancher. Lloyd Bacon provides neat directorial touches. (b/w)

Brothers-in-Law √ Boulting Brothers' pretty successful attempt to do a *Doctor in the House* about the bar; Richard Attenborough, Ian Carmichael, Terry-Thomas, Irene Handl, John Schlesinger (John Schlesinger?), George Rose enjoy themselves; 1956. (b/w)

The Brothers Karamazov X The story's the same – or nearly – but this Pandro S. Berman production has about as much to do with Dostoyevsky as Peyton Place has with real life. Richards Brooks, writer-director, has turned it into a yarn of murder, false trial and escape, period. Casting is awful with Maria Schell, Yul Brynner, Lee J. Cobb, Claire Bloom, Richard Basehart either incompetent or unconvincing; 1958. (c)

The Brothers Rico √ Richard Conte gets involved with gangster threatening his family; briskly and tautly directed by Phil Karlson in 1957. (b/w)

Broth of a Boy X Barry Fitzgerald holding out for more money as TV readies for celebration of his birthday; he's world's oldest man (or is he?) Hugh Leonard's play makes pleasant vehicle for Fitzgerald, and director George Pollock lets him get on with it; 1959. (b/w)

The Browning Version √ Michael Redgrave makes the most of school-teacher-in-crisis part in Anthony Asquith's rather literal translation of Terence Rattigan's play; 1951. (b/w)

Brute Force √√ Perhaps the best-ever prison-break thriller, with Hume Cronyn as beastly warden; Burt Lancaster, Charles Bickford, Jeff Corey, Sam Levene among others inside; Jules Dassin; 1947. (b/w)

The Buccaneer X The blind leading the blind when Anthony Quinn tries his hand at directing Yul Brynner, Claire Bloom, Charlton Heston, Charles Boyer in remake of 1938 success (Fredric March) about pirate Jean Lafitte helping US in war of 1812. Very stiff and spotty; 1958. (c)

Buchanan Rides Alone √ Better-than-average western with Randolph Scott in danger of hanging for befriending Mexican who killed to avenge sister; Budd Boetticher; 1958. (c)

Buck and the Preacher √ Sidney Poitier and Harry Belafonte in a black version of *Butch Cassidy and the Sundance Kid*, helping freed slaves to get way from unscrupulous Cameron Mitchell, hoping to use them for cheap labour. The jokey style Poitier adopts as director is at odds with the film's serious message, and the result is neither light-hearted nor socially redemptive; 1971. (c)

Buck Privates XX Abbott and Costello

in the Army, 1941, Arthur Lubin (b/w). Sequel, *Buck Privates Come Home*, is about smuggling little French boy into America – stupid stuff; Charles T. Barton; 1947. (b/w)

Buffalo Bill √ (1) 1944 William Wellman biog of legendary cowboy with Joel McCrea. (c)

Buffalo Bill X (2) 1965 oater with Gordon Scott taming ambitious young Sioux. (c)

Bugles in the Afternoon X Ray Milland, stripped of rank for assaulting cavalry officer, rejoins as private. You can guess the rest; Roy Rowland churned out usual actioner in 1952. (c)

Bulldog Jack X Creaky museum piece from 1933, saved by Jack Hulbert's insouciant Drummond-substitute chasing jewel thieves in the London underground. Ralph Richardson, Fay Wray grace director Walter Forde's cast. (b/w)

A Bullet for Joey √ George Raft gets a fit of unlikely conscience when kidnapping atomic scientist on behalf of foreign power; Edward G. Robinson hams along under Lewis Allen's direction; 1955. (b/w)

A Bullet is Waiting √ Sheriff Stephen McNally force-lands with prisoner Rory Calhoun on Jean Simmons' ranch on way to murder trial; Jean falls for Rory; John Farrow turned out this competent, incredible melo in 1954. (c)

Bullitt √√√ Stunning duel between detective Steve McQueen and DA Robert Vaughn for possession of key witness; brilliantly shot in San Francisco and the second best car chase ever put on film (first is in same producer's *The French Connection*). Peter Yates; 1968. (c)

Bundle of Joy X Once upon a time, 1939 to be exact, Ginger Rogers made a lovely picture called *Bachelor Mother*. Casting around for a vehicle to show off the minuscule combined talents of the newly-married Eddie Fisher and Debbie Reynolds in 1956, the eyes of some bright Hollywood lads fell upon the old movie and they decided it would be a good idea to remake this story of shopgirl picking up baby from steps of orphanage and thus getting her job back from sympathy. They gave it to Norman Taurog to direct, and they were wrong. It was a rotten idea and this is a rotten film. (c)

Bunny Lake is Missing √ Laurence Olivier makes a believable policeman, Carol Lynley makes an almost believable mother whose child disappears, Keir Dullea makes an unbelievable brother, while Noel Coward doesn't even try to make his sinister neighbour believable. But, then, credibility never was Otto Preminger's strongest point; it's entertaining, all right; 1965. (b/w)

Bunny O'Hare XX Bette Davis sued the production company, AIP, for transforming what she had thought was going to be a social commentary with humorous overtones into tasteless and inartistic slapstick. So it proves, with the ageing star (63 in 1974) having to dress up as a hippie to rob banks. The director, Gerd Oswald, supported her complaint. (c)

Buona Sera, Mrs Campbell √ For the first nine reels this is a smart, amusing comedy about three ex-GIs, returning to Italy with their formidable wives (Shelley Winters outstanding) who all believe they are father to Gina Lollobrigida's child; Phil Silvers, Peter Lawford, Telly Savalas competent 'fathers'. But Melvin Frank's invention (he directs, produces, co-writes with Denis Norden) flags at the end, and it lacks that extra twist that would have made it memorable; 1969. (c)

The Burglars X 1970 remake of *The Burglar* (1957; Dan Duryea), with Omar Sharif (crooked police inspector) and Jean-Paul Belmondo. Climactic caper in grain warehouse is a long time coming. Director Henri Verneuil fails to convince. (c)

Burke and Hare XX Poor effort from director Vernon Sewell, more concerned with Edinburgh brothels than grave-robbings. Harry Andrews and Yootha Joyce do their best, but the main casting, Derren Nesbitt and Glynn Edwards, invited disaster; 1971. (c)

The Burning Hills XX Man-on-the-run drama is sunk by casting of Tab Hunter. Natalie Wood, in her ingenue days (1957), is Mexican maiden who shelters him; Stuart Heisler directed. (c)

Bushfire X Commies holding Americans prisoner in SE Asia, made in 1962 before war became too shameful a subject to make gung-hos about; John Ireland and Everett Sloane; directed and produced by young Jack Warner. (b/w)

Bus Riley's Back in Town √ Ann-Margret wants Michael Parks back when he is demobbed from the Navy; moodily shot by Harvey Hart, it does build a sentimental but convincing picture of small-town life; 1965. (c)

Bus Stop ✓✓ In 1956, back from 18 months at Lee Strasberg's actors' studio, Marilyn Monroe really gave a performance here - even if director Josh Logan had to retake scenes 20 times because she kept forgetting her lines. Her part as night-club floozie picked up by cowboy (Don Murray) fitted her beautifully. George Axelrod adapted from William Inge play. (c)

The Buster Keaton Story X Keaton himself supervised the making of this biopic but, perhaps because of that, it doesn't really work. Donald O'Connor gives a faithful enough imitation and Peter Lorre is at hand as film director but real director and co-writer Sidney Sheldon lets it all get very vacuous; 1957. (b/w)

Busting ✓ Elliott Gould and Robert Blake as unbelievable, naïve cops chasing after drugs supremo Allen Garfield. They are the only uncorrupt policemen around, it seems, and finally learn their lesson. Cynical and depressing, this familiar thriller is convincing enough while it lasts, thanks to first-time director Peter Hyams; 1973. (c)

Butch Cassidy and the Sundance Kid ✓✓✓ Fashion-setter for whimsical male companionships, this 1969 blockbuster gave Robert Redford and Paul Newman roles to relish - even if Katharine Ross was inadequate as the third member of the rumbustious western gang. George Roy Hill directed (1969) with an elegant if ingratiating touch. (c)

But Not For Me ✓✓ Clark Gable acts his age (58 in 1959) as Broadway producer chased by his secretary, Carroll Baker. Lilli Palmer stands there laughing as his ex-wife, while Lee J. Cobb provides an unusually light (for him) rendering of anxious playwright. Altogether fun, and Walter Lang has done a neat job, recalling something of Noel Coward's *The Scoundrel*. (b/w)

The Buttercup Chain XXX Dreadful semi-incestuous (they are cousins) sex fantasy with Hywel Bennett, Jane Asher and others who should have known better. Robert Ellis Miller directed, prettily but uncomfortably, in 1971. (c)

Butterfield 8 ✓ Elizabeth Taylor as the nympho can't help it in a rather milky adaptation of John O'Hara novel; Daniel Mann hasn't got much of a cast apart from her - Laurence Harvey, Eddie Fisher, Jeffrey Lynn, it reads like a list of the weaker available leading men in 1960. (c)

Butterflies Are Free X - but you have to pay for this movie with your time. Do you really want to see Goldie Hawn giggling her way through a love affair with blind neighbour Edward Albert, being thrown out by his disapproving Mom, Eileen Heckart, and ending it all happily? Director, Milton Katselas; 1972. (c)

By Love Possessed X Too many plots spoil the book when it comes to making this movie. James Gould Cozzens's bestseller had some insight - but John Sturges has ironed all that out. Mind you, what could any director do with such poor leads as Lana Turner, George Hamilton, Efrem Zimbalist Jr.? Next layer - Jason Robards, Barbara Bel Geddes, Tom Mitchell, Everett Sloane - can't save the wreck; 1961. (c)

Bye Bye Birdie ✓ Put on a happy face and forgive this 1963 stage adaptation about rock-'n'-roll singer called up into the army for Paul Lynde's splendid father and recently-rediscovered Ann-Margret. George Sidney. (c)

By the Light of the Silvery Moon ✓ Wholesome Doris Day and clean-limbed Gordon MacRae awash in sentiment as he returns from war to 1918 America. Directed 1953 by David Butler. (c)

C

Cabaret ✓ Immensely professional film of the musical of the play of the book *I Am a Camera*, with virtuoso performance from Liza Minelli as Sally Bowles, quasi-innocent as the Nazis are coming to power. Michael York makes a barely adequate bisexual boyfriend, but Joel Grey walks off with the film as the skull-grinning Master of Ceremonies; Bob Fosse does a fine directorial job on the production numbers; 1972. (c)

Cabin in the Sky ✓ All-Negro retelling of Faust legend reflects 1943 attitudes, but Ethel Waters, Lena Horne's singing and Louis Armstrong's playing transcend 'simple souls' attitude of white director Vincente Minnelli. (b/w)

The Cabinet of Dr Caligari XX Disappointing 1962 remake of silent classic horror with Dan O'Herlihy, Glynis Johns, directed and produced by the over-ambitious Roger Kay. (b/w)

Cactus Flower √√ For those with an eye for great comedy acting, nothing Walter Matthau does can be unwatchable. Here he has Goldie Hawn to play against, and Ingrid Bergman as his secretary, impersonating his wife so that he can 'divorce' her to marry Goldie (he has always told her that the barrier to their marriage was that he was married already). Director Gene Saks deftly avoids that you-can-tell-it-was-a-play feeling; 1969. (c)

The Caddy X Jerry Lewis outshines partner Dean Martin to score with several amusing solos, but the whole thing, only nominally directed by Norman Taurog (he seems to have let them get away with whatever came into their heads) is pale stuff vaguely about golf; 1953. (b/w)

Caesar and Cleopatra √ Gabriel Pascal's best attempt at a Shaw play but still pretty grotty; he supplied the lavish dressing, G.B.S. the clever chat, and luckily Vivien Leigh and Claude Rains managed to play it as though they were being well-directed; 1946. (c)

Caged √ Eleanor Parker goes to prison a framed innocent and emerges a hardened criminal, of course. John Cromwell enjoys worrying us with details, and Agnes Moorehead turns in her usual fine performance as the warden; 1950. (b/w)

Cahill X Lacklustre John Wayne 1973 western, with the old (too old) fella having to avoid most of the action. It is left to George Kennedy as a black villain and Wayne's two 'sons' to provide what excitement there is: the boys rebel against his strictness by helping the baddies, but are of course ultimately rescued from them by Wayne. Director, Andrew V. McLaglen. (c)

The Caine Mutiny √√ Taken, unfortunately, more from the novel than from the stage-play, this 'opened out' the court-martial drama which was the whole play, thus rather pre-empting the ultimate trial. Heavy plusses, though, as Humphrey Bogart's sadistic, framed, crumbling Queeg, Fred MacMurray's shifty officer and Van Johnson's simple mutineer. Edward Dmytryk used special effects excel-lently, and worked loyally to Stanley Kramer the producer; 1954. (c)

Cairo X George Sanders leads caper to steal Tutankhamun jewels which comes unstuck partly through his weakness for belly dancers; Richard Johnson; directed by Wolf Rilla; 1962. (b/w)

Calamity Jane √ Doris Get Your Gun would have been better title as Miss Day chases success of Annie Oakley; she's a spirited gal, but Howard Keel's Wild Bill Hickock is a booming bore and the songs are poor; David Butler did his best, but that just weren't good enough, pard, in 1953. (c)

California √ Routine western with Barbara Stanwyck gambling for love and money and Ray Milland as wagon-master with a past. 1946, directed by John Farrow. (c)

California Split √ Elliott Gould and George Segal proved too 'laid back' to make this gambling comedy work properly. However, later acquaintance with director Robert Altman's inconsequential style may make this 1974 effort seem more persuasive when seen again. (c)

Callan √ Superior to the usual run of TV rip-offs, this thriller has Edward Woodward's put-upon agent being framed by Eric Porter, but able to turn the tables; Don Sharp directed, in 1974, with brio. (c)

Calling Bulldog Drummond √ Oh-so-dated, but still fascinating Victor Saville view (1951) of what the pre-war fictional legend was all about. Walter Pidgeon is a pleasant Bulldog, with the teeth of his Sapper-sadism drawn; Margaret Leighton co-starred. (b/w)

Call Me Bwana XX All Bob Hope's frantic wisecracking can't bring to life this silly story of him as phoney author competing with Red agent Anita Ekberg for missile head lost in Africa; all you can do is ignore the mechanics and look for peripheral laughs from Lionel Jeffries. Gordon Douglas directed in what looks more like deepest Pinewood than the Dark Continent; 1963. (c)

Call Me Madam √ If you can stand noisy Ethel Merman bounding about singing some inferior Irving Berlin tunes, you'll quite enjoy this snappy story based on the real hostess-with-the-mostest, Pearl Mesta, in Liechtenstein. But Walter Lang is so indulgent that he doesn't seem to have controlled George Sanders and 'young lovers' cocky Donald O'Connor and Vera-

Ellen, who doesn't even sing her own songs either. Billy de Wolfe is momentarily amusing but the whole thing drowns in its own Broadway Babycham; 1953. (c)

Call Me Mister XX Rather boring back-stage musical about Betty Grable staging a troop show in Japan after that little unpleasantness at Hiroshima and Nagasaki. A thousand laughs – all falling flat; Lloyd Bacon fails to bring it home; 1951. (c)

The Call of the Wild XX Poor 1972 remake (of William Wellman's 1935 version – worth watching if it does pop up) from Jack London's magnificent Alaskan novel, reduced to a-man-and-a-dog sentimentality. Director Ken Annakin and star Charlton Heston turned it into an all-too-obvious *Call of the Tame*. (c)

Camelot √ The music's fine, although there isn't a hit in the whole Lerner-Loewe score. But everything else about this attempt to make a popera out of Mallory and T. H. White is heavy going; Richard Harris outdoes David Hemmings in the winceability ratings; Vanessa Redgrave outdoes them both; no wonder none of them has appeared in a major musical since 1967. Josh Logan directs with too much regard for the stage original; it needed more of a film director to make a film – all it gets is opulent photography. (c)

Camille √ Garbo's finest performance was needed by this kitsch old tear-jerker, and she came up with it. She makes you believe in the dying classy fallen woman, battling against Robert Taylor's wooden acting, Lionel Barrymore's self-indulgence and MGM's vulgarity. Only Henry Daniell as her current Baron helps with a fine performance. George Cukor did all he could but Metro in 1937 was only concerned with a vehicle for Garbo, Cukor was just the chauffeur. (*b/w*)

Campbell's Kingdom √ Rugged attempt to make a British western set in the Rockies, but not filmed there. Dirk Bogarde's long-suffering look fits his part of claimant to mining valley but may also have come from having to act out a limpid script; about the performances of Stanley Baker, Michael Craig and Barbara Murray there is nothing to be said except that they are better than their counterparts in *Hopalong Cassidy*. Ralph Thomas; 1957. (c)

Canadian Pacific X Randolph Scott pushes the railroad through, with help and hindrance from Jane Wyatt, J. Carroll Naish, Victor Jory and director Edward L.Marin; 1950. (c)

The Canadians √ After Custer's Last Stand, the whole Sioux nation crossed into Canada; this western-with-a-difference shows what happened to them. Robert Ryan; director Burt Kennedy; 1960. (c)

Can-Can X Ignore the rest and enjoy Frank Sinatra strolling unconcernedly through the frenzied attempts to make the greatest musical ever and finishing up among the – well, not quite the worst, but the lower end of the league. Juliet Prowse dances better than Shirley MacLaine but can't deliver lines as well. Maurice Chevalier outdoes Louis Jourdan in acting stage Frenchmen. Cole Porter's songs are divine ('It's Alright with Me', 'You Do Something to Me', 'Let's Do It', 'Just One of Those Things', 'I Love Paris', *et al*), but not always well delivered. If this one goes down in history it will be because it upset Mr Khushchev who was visiting Hollywood when it was being made in 1960. It won't do much for you, either. (c)

Cancel My Reservation X Bob Hope slowing down by 1972 and this weary comedy, too respectfully directed by Paul Bogart, shows it. Discovering dead bodies on his ranch, getting arrested for murder by Keenan Wynn, encountering Bing Crosby, John Wayne, Flip Wilson, he is too predictable, too ordinary. (c)

The Candidate √√ Robert Redford, as a Kennedyesque idealist, coached in becoming a senator by Peter Boyle, is charming and convincing. Among the other pleasures of Michael Ritchie's quietly-directed film are Melvyn Douglas as his estranged father and a documentary edge to the campaigning that leaves the former idealist feeling lost; 1972. (c)

Can Hieronymus Merkin Ever Forget Mercy Humppe and Find True Happiness? XX Can Anthony Newley ever remember that he is just a pleasant light comedian and settle down to earn an unpretentious living? Pity Joan Collins, Milton Berle, Stubby Kaye, Patricia Hayes, Judy Cornwell, Joyce Blair for being mixed up in this actor-director-writer-producer's ego trip; 1969. (c)

Cannon for Cordoba √ Action-filled Mexican western with George Peppard and Raf Vallone uninvolvedly fighting over a powerful gun; Paul Wendkos directed expertly in 1970. (c)

Canon City √ On December 30, 1947, twelve desperate men broke out of Colorado State Prison; this film is dramatic documentary of their escape to limited freedom, with some of the people playing real-life parts; actors include Scott Brady, Jeff Corey; director Crane Wilbur; 1949. (b/w)

A Canterbury Tale √ Who is pouring glue over the hair of girls who go out with Americans in 1944? Powell-Pressburger created an atmospheric thriller, with Eric Portman, Sheila Sim, Dennis Price. (b/w)

Canyon Crossroads X Man against helicopter in uranium search; mildly exciting stuff with Phyllis Kirk and Richard Basehart; Alfred L. Werker; 1955. (b/w)

Canyon Pass X Patricia Neal only reason for watching this dim 1951 oater directed by Edwin L. Marin. She's girl on the make, marrying ranch-owner Dennis Morgan. (b/w)

Canyon River X George Montgomery first makes deal with rustlers, then fights them. Harmon Jones; 1956. (c)

Cape Fear √√ Super thriller with Robert Mitchum perfectly cast for once as ex-con out to terrorise the man who sent him down, Gregory Peck, and his family, climaxing in a haunting section on and around a moored houseboat. J. Lee Thompson twists the thumbscrews tighter and tighter. Weak-hearts, don't watch it alone in a lonely spot; strong supporting cast includes Polly Bergen, Martin Balsam, Telly Savalas, Jack Kruschen; 1962. (b/w)

Cape Town Affair X Claire Trevor, James Brolin and a sleepwalking Jacqueline Bisset in South African remake of *Pick-up on South Street*. Funny sort of Cape Town where there aren't any blacks; 1967. (c)

Capone √ Old-fashioned gangster biopic tricked up with permissive values in 1975 by producer Roger Corman and protegé-director Steve Carver. Ben Gazzara as the legendary Al has some strong support in Sylvester Stallone and John Cassavetes; 1975. (c)

Caprice √ Doris Day meets Richard Harris in comic spy plot with help of writer-director Frank Tashlin; glossy rubbish but good fun; 1967. (c)

Captain Boycott √ Robert Donat makes brief appearance as Parnell in Frank Launder's satisfactorily souped-up slice of Oirish history, with Cecil Parker as horrid, eponymous Boycott;

young (it's 1947) Stewart Granger as stubborn hero; Abbey-full of character actors. (b/w)

Captain Eddie X Fred MacMurray as veteran flyer Eddie Rickenbacker looks back over his life from a raft in the wartime Atlantic. Lloyd Bacon shuffles Charles Bickford, Thomas Mitchell, James Gleason, Lloyd Nolan about in various heroics; 1945. (b/w)

Captain from Castille X Tyrone Power displays his startling good looks and lack of personality in this expensive costume drama about Spaniard in the New World. Competently directed by Henry King in 1947. (c)

Captain Horatio Hornblower, RN √ Gregory Peck duelling his way to the greater glory of Nelson's England; the supports are a bit weak (director Raoul Walsh must have asked the casting department for three ha'porth of British he-men and to hell with whether they can act) and Virginia Mayo's wayo out of place. Nevertheless, it moves so fast and furious that a good time is had by all; 1951. (c)

Captain Lightfoot X W. R. Burnett wrote this yarn about nineteenth-century Irish rebellion against the British, Rock Hudson leads the rebels. Douglas Sirk directed; 1955. (c)

Captain Nemo and the Underwater City √ Attempt by James Hill to provide a sequel to Jules Verne story, full of neat effects. Robert Ryan, Chuck Connors, Kenneth Connor; 1969. (c)

Captain Newman M.D. √ Gregory Peck plays officer-psychiatrist at war with Army; strong cast includes Angie Dickinson as admiring nurse, Tony Curtis as unorthodox orderly and Bobby Darin in strong role as guilt-ridden flier. David Miller failed to make this a premature M*A*S*H but directed it all competently enough; 1963. (c)

Captains Courageous √√ 1937 sea epic in which Victor Fleming achieved exciting action on the fishing boats. It is also Kipling's story of Spencer Tracy with a Portuguese accent teaching the spoiled brat Freddie Bartholomew (perfectly suited for the part) what it means to be a Man. Tracy won an Oscar; Lionel Barrymore, Melvyn Douglas, and in a small part, Mickey Rooney, pitched in well (b/w)

The Captain's Paradise √ Neatly-made comedy of bigamist Alec Guinness with wives Yvonne de Carlo and Celia Johnson at either side of the

Straits of Gibraltar that comes unstuck when they both change character; Anthony Kimmins produced-directed; 1952. (b/w)

The Captain's Table XXX Stilted nonsense about John Gregson's vicissitudes as captain of luxury liner: Peggy Cummins, Maurice Denham, Richard Wattis go through the motions. Jack Lee; 1958. (c)

The Captive City √ It's Athens in 1944 (the movie was made in 1963) and there is considerable confusion who's a goodie and who's a baddie because the Reds have risen after fighting with our lads against the nazis. In the midst of this, David Niven has to guard some armaments, and Joseph Anthony's direction ensures a tight hour or so with the help of Ben Gazzara and Michael Craig. (b/w)

The Captive Heart X PoW's, womenfolk at home, readjustment; Michael Redgrave, Mervyn Johns, Basil Radford. Basil Dearden; 1946. (b/w)

Carbine Williams X James Stewart in biopic of the carbine gun's inventor who was jailed for shooting revenue man. The casting and direction (by Richard Thorpe) tends to make him sympathetic, although he behaves most unpleasantly. Wendell Corey backs up doggedly; 1952. (b/w)

The Card √ Alec Guinness delightful in Ronald Neame's careful transition of Arnold Bennett's book about loan shark who becomes mayor. Glynis Johns, Michael Hordern stand out of rather old-fashioned cast; 1951. (b/w)

The Cardinal X Otto Preminger's colourful picturisation of Henry Morton Robertson's novel about priest's rise from Boston to Rome, filled with strong cameos, including John Huston's older cardinal, Burgess Meredith, Dorothy Gish. Unfortunately, main player Tom Tryon was one of Preminger's try-ons that didn't work; 1963. (c)

Career XX Why anyone should be presumed to care about the career of the nasty young actor played here by Tony Franciosa is beyond comprehension; neither his performance, Dean Martin's as a director or Carolyn Jones' as an agent move or intrigue. Shirley MacLaine is given a few moments by director Joseph Anthony, but it's all familiar stuff; 1959. (b/w)

Carefree √ These old Ginger Rogers-Fred Astaire musicals might not quite stand up today (this one was made in 1938) but it's a pleasure to hear the songs ('Change Parners', 'I Used to be Colour Blind') and see them dance. Mark Sandrich. (b/w)

The Caretaker √√ For those who have not yet dreamed of picking up their papers in Sidcup, a magical experience awaits. For the rest of us, a chance to re-enter the closed mocking world of Davies (if that is his name), Aston and Mick – Donald Pleasence, Robert Shaw, Alan Bates – Pinter's archetypes, respectfully filmed by Clive Donner in 1963. (b/w)

The Carey Treatment X James Coburn becomes avenging angel when a doctor colleague is wrongly sacked and arrested after a 15-year-old girl dies from an abortion. Director Blake Edwards; 1972. (c)

Caribbean X Harmless costume yarn (1952) with heroic John Payne and plastic Arlene Dahl tackling pirates and slave traders; might keep the kids quiet. Director, Edward Ludwig. (c)

The Cariboo Trail X Routine settlers v. cattlemen and Randolph Scott v. Victor Jory. Edward L. Marin; 1950. (c)

Carlton-Browne of the F.O. √√ Lovely satire on diplomacy by the Boulting Brothers with Terry-Thomas as forgotten ambassador; plus Peter Sellers, Ian Bannen, Miles Malleson, Irene Handl; 1958. (b/w)

Carmen Jones √√ Otto Preminger's dazzling switch of Bizet's opera to black army camp. Embarrassingly, neither Dorothy Dandridge, Harry Belafonte nor Joe Adams actually sang in the picture; their voices were supplied by Marilyn Horne, Le Vern Hutcherson, Marvin Hayes; Pearl Bailey's for real; 1954. (c)

Carnal Knowledge √√ Remarkable account, written by Jules Feiffer, directed by Mike Nichols, of three episodes, over a period of years, in the lives of friends Jack Nicholson and Arthur Garfunkel. The women in their lives are played by Candice Bergen, Ann-Margret, Rita Moreno, Cynthia O'Neal, Carol Kane; 1971. (c)

Carnival XX (1) 1935 – Lee Tracy must marry or welfare will take his baby away from him and the circus. Herbert Wilcox. (b/w)

Carnival XX (2) 1946 – draggy British ballet film with Sally Gray and Michael Wilding. Stanley Haynes. (b/w)

Carnival XX (3) 1956 – Sydney Chaplin as carnival barker who elopes with mayor's daughter. (b/w)

Carnival of Souls √ Very low-budget but extremely well-made supernatural thriller about a girl who may have been drowned but may equally well be hypnotised; Herk Harvey directs and also plays The Man, the mysterious stranger who seems to control Candace Hiligloss; 1962. (b/w)

Carnival of Thieves X Caper in Pamplona; Russell Rouse has motley, many-accented and largely uninspired lot of actors, including Stephen Boyd, Yvette Mimieux, Giovanna Ralli; 1967. (c)

Carnival Story X Anne Baxter plays a trapeze lady whose partner is killed by a jealous barker. Will her new boyfriend, a photographer, finish up the same way? Kurt Neumann knows that you know the answer and hasn't the heart to direct the picture with any conviction, although he was co-writer, too; 1954. (c)

Carousel √√ 'If I loved you' . . . 'June is busting all over' . . . 'You'll never walk alone' . . . 'Mister Snow' . . . Shirley Jones, Gordon Macrae . . . Rodgers and Hammerstein . . . Henry King. Top money-maker of 1956. (c)

The Carpetbaggers XX Harold Robbins's novel (not about Howard Hughes?) was given the lusty, audience-teasing treatment you'd expect in 1964, just before films got permissive. Edward Dmytryk was lumbered with a mostly inferior lot of actors by producer Joe Levine; George Peppard as the aviation-movie tycoon, Alan Ladd, Robert Cummings, Carroll Baker *et al* come out as petty and unsympathetic characters. (c)

Carrie √ William Wyler's 1952 movie of farm girl who runs off with married man, becomes famous actress, and discards those who helped her. Laurence Olivier does the carrying, Jennifer Jones is carried. (b/w)

Carrington V.C. √ David Niven takes battery office funds in protest at not getting back pay; Margaret Leighton, Clive Morton, Mark Dignam and cast of solid British character-players make this a satisfying exercise; Anthony Asquith from Dorothy and Campbell Christie play; 1955. (b/w)

Carry On Abroad X Package holiday on Spanish island provides writer Talbot Rothwell and director Gerald Thomas with predictable opportunities for ghastly jokes, puns, *doubles entendres* and frilly knickers; 1972. (c)

Carry On Admiral X Not one of the regular *Carry-Ons* but a stage farce *Off the Record*; director Val Guest. David Tomlinson, Peggy Cummins, A. E. Matthews, Joan Sims, Ronald Shiner, Alfie Bass; 1957. (b/w)

Carry On Again, Doctor X Fatigued attempt to do another doctor vulgarity, in 1969. Kenneth Williams, Sid James, Jim Dale and the usual lot in thin plot about fat ladies. (c)

Carry On at Your Convenience XX A lavatory factory provides a suitable setting for the 21st *Carry-On*, but it all should have been flushed down the drain. A poor effort; Gerald Thomas; 1971. (c)

Carry On Cabby √ The 1963 vintage wasn't a bad year, with Sid James and Hattie Jacques as rival husband and wife taxi-owners. plus such joys as Kenneth Connor, Charles Hawtrey, Jim Dale, Liz Fraser. Gerald Thomas directed. (b/w)

Carry On Camping √ Nudist nuttery with Barbara Windsor, Terry Scott, and regulars. Gerald Thomas; 1969. (c)

Carry On Cleo √ Kenneth Williams plays Caesar, Sid James Mark Antony, Amanda Barrie Cleopatra – and if you think that's funny you'll love it. Gerald Thomas; 1965. (c)

Carry On Constable √ Eric Barker welcome guest in this 1960 farce about Sid James, Kenneth Connor, Leslie Phillips sent to a police station where they made Dock Green look like serious drama; Joan Sims winsome WPC. (b/w)

Carry On Cowboy √ Sid James as The Rumpo Kid; plus the usuals and Angela Douglas; Gerald Thomas; 1966. (c)

Carry On Cruising √ Captain finds that on the eve of his departure for the Med he has a Fred Karno crew of Kenneth Connor, Kenneth Williams and the rest of the carriers-on. Wilfred Hyde White a guest in this 1962 lark. Gerald Thomas. (c)

Carry On Dick X 1974 excursion into Dick Turpin-time, with Sid James as the highwayman and the rest of the gang popping out of their clothes and bedrooms. (c)

Carry On – Don't Lose Your Head √ 1967 lark with Sid James Jim Dale, Kenneth Williams, Charles Hawtrey involved in the French Revolution. Gerald Thomas. (c)

Carry On Girls XX Sunk in a morass of bad puns, the series seemed on the edge of expiration with this 1973 stuff about a beauty contest; alas, it wasn't. (c)

Carry On Henry √ The 1971 edition, with Sid James as Henry VIII, was slightly more fun than most of the later Carry Ons. (c)

Carry On Jack √ Juliet Mills and hard-trying Donald Huston guest in Jolly Roger-land on the rolling Spanish Main when Nelson expected every man to pay his duty; Gerald Thomas; 1964. (c)

Carry On Loving XX Terrible 1970 edition was about a marriage bureau run by Sid James and Hattie Jacques. (c)

Carry On Matron √ Moderately amusing 1972 effort from Gerald Thomas with the usual lot doing the hospital jokes all over again. (c)

Carry On Nurse √ One of the best Carry-Ons, with Kenneth Connor as boxer with broken wrist, Kenneth Williams as nuclear student, Wilfrid Hyde White as race-loving patient, Charles Hawtrey, Hattie Jacques, Irene Handl; Gerald Thomas; 1959. (b/w)

Carry On Regardless √ The one about the Labour Exchange and the extremely odd job men; Sid James, Kenneth Connor, Liz Fraser, Joan Sims; directed, as always, by Gerald Thomas, his fifth; 1961. (b/w)

Carry On Screaming X Poor example of the type with Harry H. Corbett and Fenella Fielding looking unhappy; Gerald Thomas; 1966. (c)

Carry On Sergeant √ William Hartnell turning Bob Monkhouse, Kenneth Connor, Charles Hawtrey, Kenneth Williams into soldiers. This 1959 effort was one of the very best Carry Ons, directed of course by Gerald Thomas. (b/w)

Carry On Spying X Owing to a fatal shortage of spies, Kenneth Williams is sent to recover a stolen formula, with the help of Barbara Windsor, Bernard Cribbins, Charles Hawtrey; Gerald Thomas; 1964. (b/w)

Carry On Teacher √ Fair (1963) and funny, with Leslie Phillips and Ted Ray as additions to regulars Kenneth Connor, Kenneth Williams, Joan Sims. Gerald Thomas. (b/w)

Carry On Up the Jungle X By 1970 the series was dragging. Frankie Howerd was in this one instead of Kenneth Williams. Also missing: Kenneth Connor, Barbara Windsor; director, Gerald Thomas; 1970. (c)

Carry On . . . Up the Khyber √ Perhaps the best, certainly the most lavish of the series, sending up the Bengal Lancers – and you know where. Additions to Gerald Thomas's regulars include Roy Castle, Angela Douglas. Great fun; 1969. (c)

Carson City X Dull oater supposedly about the founding of the cattle town, as railroad pushed settlers around; Randolph Scott, Raymond Massey fight it out under André de Toth; 1952. (c)

Carve Her Name with Pride X Virginia McKenna giving a not very convincing portrayal of real-life heroine parachuted into France twice, caught and dying a heroine's death; Lewis Gilbert does what he can with Jack Warner, Sidney Tafler, Bill Owen; gets fine performances from Paul Scofield, Billie Whitelaw, Harold Lang; 1957. (b/w)

Casablanca √√√ Play it again, Sam – and again and again. Somehow the hokum has such durable powers that when Bogie sends Bergman packing (literally) you really believe he would. It won three Oscars in 1943 (Best Picture, director, Michael Curtiz, screenplay), and among the nominees were Humphrey Bogart and Claude Rains; even Ingrid Bergman – an over-rated actress if ever there was one – manages to score, as do Sidney Greenstreet and Peter Lorre. One of the greats. (b/w)

Casanova Brown √ Gary Cooper chose this light comedy about a divorced wife who finds she's pregnant, for his first movie free from Paramount in 1944. Couldn't go wrong with Teresa Wright, Frank Morgan, Anita Louise helping and Sam Wood directing. (b/w)

Casbah XX Peter Lorre is only saving grace of this otherwise execrable musical version of Pepé Le Moko, jewel thief of Algiers. Tony Martin, would you believe, plays the Charles Boyer-Jean Gabin part; John Berry directed nervily; 1948. (b/w)

Cash McCall √ James Garner as unconvincing plastics businessman making deals and Natalie Wood. E. G. Marshall outstanding among colleagues and rivals; Joseph Pevney; 1960. (c)

Casino Royale X Messy mish-mash cashing in on James Bond novel's success; somehow the producers of the Sean Connery opi didn't have the rights to this one, so the lads who did tricked it up with every star who could spend a few days, half a dozen directors and a simply awful script that rattles along on three flat tyres. David Niven, Orson Welles, Ursula Andress manage to get some mileage out of it; Woody Allen, Daliah Lavi, Peter Sellers, Deborah Kerr do not; 1967. (c)

Cass Timberlane √ Spencer Tracy married to Lana Turner; will she have it away with friend Zachary Scott? Actually, George Sidney's transfer of novel is less crude than this, doing its best within the 1947 conventions to be honest. Mary Astor, Albert Dekker strong back-ups. (b/w)

Cast a Dark Shadow √ Strong drama of retribution with Dirk Bogarde as wife-murderer, Margaret Lockwood earmarked as his next victim; Lewis Gilbert; 1955. (b/w)

Cast a Giant Shadow XX Kirk Douglas as Jewish hero, formerly with US forces in second world war, then Palestinian freedom fighter. Melville Shavelson wrote, produced and directed it in 1966 with more stodgy reverence than professional ruthlessness. It also co-starred Yul Brynner, Topol, Frank Sinatra and John Wayne. See it only if you intend to read Shavelson's wise-cracker account of the troubles it took to make in *How To Make A Jewish Movie* (W. H. Allen); *that* he should film. (c)

Cast a Long Shadow X Audie Murphy in western adult enough to cast him as bastard son who returns prodigally to ranch and makes it a going concern instead of cashing it in, thanks to luvverly Terry Moore; Thomas Carr; 1959. (b/w)

Castle Keep √ A superior war picture, with Burt Lancaster as a commander who is deaf to pleas of Jean-Pierre Aumont and Patrick O'Neal to save historic castle filled with art treasures. Peter Falk plays one of his men who moonlights as a baker (with the baker's wife, too). The fantasy element of the original novel (by William Eastlake) hasn't altogether gone, but director Sydney Pollack's vulgar touch effectively flattens it down; 1969. (c)

Castle of Evil XX The most evil thing about this tired old plot (about the mad scientist who invites the five people he hates most to the lair where he has created an electronic robot in his own image) is the *chutzpah* needed to make it all over again. Virginia Mayo reminds us what a pretty girl she used to be (this is 1967 and it may be bounderish to say she was 45 but she was) and Francis D. Lyon directed it without much imagination. (c)

Castle of the Living Dead X Count counted out by own petrifying liquid; Christopher Lee, Donald Sutherland a long way from M*A*S*H; 1964. (b/w)

Cat! XX Wildcat saves boy when rustler attacks him; not as exciting as it sounds. Peggy Ann Garner is only near-name around. Director, Ellis Kadison; 1966. (c)

Catacombs XXX Awful little British pic with Gary Merrill as wife-murderer who's afraid she's still alive; Gordon Hessler seems to be directing from a script he made up from pages found on a tour of Wardour Street dustbins; 1965. (b/w)

Cat and Mouse X Poor thriller with Kirk Douglas unconvincing as inadequate science teacher who, when taunted, takes to murdering his wife (Jean Seberg) and sundry other people; Daniel Petrie's routine direction does not help; 1974. (c)

Cat Ballou √√ Spoof western that made stars out of Lee Marvin (in double role of drunken gunfighter and arch-enemy with silver nose held in place by elastic band) and Jane Fonda, the eponymous school-teacher who is due to be hanged at the start of the movie. The music palls, but otherwise director Elliott Silverstein did a great comedy job; 1965. (c)

Catch Me a Spy X Kirk Douglas walks his way through this muddled light thriller from Dick Clements and Ian La Frenais. Giving up all pretence at reality before the end, it drags in various nationals (Marlene Jobert, Tom Courtenay) as well as the American star in an effort for international appeal; 1971. (c)

Catch-22 √√ This 1970 version of Joseph Heller's modern classic was forced to select from the novel, but did so with some distinction. In Alan Arkin, director Mike Nicholas found an adequate protagonist and some of the supports (Richard Benjamin's slimy Major; Anthony Perkins's inept chaplain) are impressive. Air Force planes provide a chorus, and there is the renowned contradiction of the title ('no sane man would wish to fly, therefore anyone wishing to stop cannot be insane'). (c)

Catch Us If You Can X Humble beginning for director John Boorman, trying to make the Dave Clark Five acceptable cinema fare in 1965. They played film stuntmen and thus didn't have to do very much but stand aside while real stuntmen took over. Barbara Ferris provided minimal romantic interest. (b/w)

Cat on a Hot Tin Roof √√ Tennessee Williams lifts the lid from rich Southern family to reveal impotence, alcoholism and Big-Daddy-domination simmering away. Elizabeth Taylor marvellous as love-yearning girl married into family via tormented Paul Newman; Burl Ives perversely patriarchal. Richard Brooks directed, 1958, with lush atmospherics. (c)

The Cat People √√ Classic horror picture so superior to most of the genre that it mustn't be missed by anyone who likes to be scared; Simone Simon is convinced that when her passions are aroused she turns into a large dangerous cat. When clawings begin is it she – or what? Jacques Tourneur made it in 1942. (b/w)

Cattle Drive √ Kid, Dean Stockwell, learns what life is really all about (perhaps) during big drive from veteran Joel McCrea; Kurt Neumann; 1951. (c)

Cattle Empire √ Joel McCrea on cattle drive again (see previous entry), this time in 1958, with revenge of those who once jailed him, in mind; Charles Marquis Warren. (c)

Caught √ Barbara Bel Geddes discovers she is married to nutter – Robert Ryan – and worse. Max Ophuls gave it some distinction; 1949. (b/w)

Cause for Alarm √ Loretta Young being set up for murder rap by husband Barry Sullivan; Tay Garnett; 1951. (b/w)

Cavalry Command X Richard Arlen helps to restore law and order in Philippine village during Spanish-American war; a bit unconvincing, but then so was the war; 1965. (c)

Cave of Outlaws √ Among those present are Macdonald Carey, Alexis Smith, Edgar Buchanan, Victor Jory – all searching for gold hidden after Wells Fargo hold-up; William Castle; 1952. (c)

Caxambu! X The title refers to a head-hunting Amazon tribe, who are after a crashed plane-load of human meat. The fliers were on their way to cut up 2,000 carats of diamonds. W. Lee Wilder (Billy's brother) directed John Ireland and gang in 1967. (c)

The Ceremony XX Limp crime and sex (don't expect much actual – it was made in 1963) yarn about springing master criminal from Tangier jail; both Laurence Harvey (also directing, a mistake) and Robert Walker fancying Sarah Miles. (b/w)

A Certain Smile XX Practically all of Françoise Sagan's bittersweet charm has been evaporated by clumsy script; instead, the cloying obviousness that is director Jean Negulesco's trademark takes its place, seen at its worst in the indulgence he permits to Rossanno Brazzi's really sickening playing of his 'older man' part. French actress Christine Carère, who went to Hollywood to play heroine, made only one other major picture, and no wonder; 1958. (c)

Chad Hanna √ Henry Fonda is Chad Hanna, who is so impressed with 19th-century bareback rider Dorothy Lamour that he joins the circus. Linda Darnell, Guy Kibbee, Jane Darwell, John Carradine fulfil their type-cast roles under Henry King; 1940. (c)

Chain Lightning X Mainly airborne pic, from war bombers to testing jets, with Humphrey Bogart sacrificing scruples and honour but winning all back in climax; Raymond Massey, Eleanor Parker are around; 1950. (b/w)

The Chalk Garden √ Hayley Mills being set on right path by governess Deborah Kerr under gaze of Edith Evans. Sob-stuff, but it works. Ronald Neame directed, 1964, from Enid Bagnold play. (c)

The Challenge X Pre-war (1937) British epic about mountaineering and rival climbers Luis Trenker, Robert Douglas, as Jean Antoine Carrel and Edward Whymper, on the Matterhorn. Director, Milton Rosmer. (b/w)

A Challenge for Robin Hood XXX Pathetic British picture, 1968 vintage, sketching the familiar Robin Hood stuff but never making it fresh or even interesting; Barrie Ingham an inadequate Robin against Errol Flynn or even Richard Todd; James Hayter and Alfie Bass can't save it; much of the blame must be allocated to director C. M. Pennington Richards. (c)

Challenge to Lassie √ Will the wonder dog be put to death for having no owner in cruel Edinburgh? Edmund Gwenn, Donald Crisp, Reginald Owen say No, under Richard Thorpe's 1949 direction. (c)

Chamber of Horrors XX Afraid it is; this rip-off from House of Wax desperately needs that old camp magic of Vincent Price; all it has is Wilfrid Hyde White ambling through as if he can smell the staleness of the plot; Hy Averback; 1967. (c)

The Champ √ Creaky though this 1931 tear-jerker about boxer (Wallace

Beery) who makes a comeback for his adoring son (Jackie Cooper) may be, there is something compulsive about King Vidor's direction. Remade in 1979. (b/w)

Champagne for Caesar √ Ronald Colman's last starring picture gave an enjoyable opportunity to score as professor who won't stop doubling his money in radio quiz show. Celeste Holm is one hazard planted by the panicky radio company that he overcomes. Vincent Price camps it up as sponsor. Richard Whorf can't really keep it going, but it's fair enough fun; 1950. (b/w)

The Champagne Murders √ Superficially a whodunit, this Chabrol-directed, Derek Prouse-co-written drama is also study of French bourgeoisie under pressure. Anthony Perkins, Yvonne Furneaux; 1968. (c)

Champion √√ Strong prize fight drama based on Ring Lardner's book about a heel who becomes champ. Kirk Douglas was dead right and should have stuck to playing unsympathetic parts after this breakthrough in 1949. It made the reputations of director Mark Robson and producer Stanley Kramer, as well; 1949. (b/w)

Change of Habit XX Mary Tyler Moore makes a miscast nun, but no more than Elvis Presley as a doctor in the slums. Perhaps not surprisingly, this 1969 effort, directed by William Graham, was never commercially distributed in Britain. (c)

The Chapman Report X Inexplicitly sexy (1962 was too early for orgiastic couplings), it's a four-stranded hokum about Kinseyish researchers adding to the statistics. Jane Fonda and Shelley Winters stand out and lie down under George Cukor's direction. (c)

Charade √√ Absolutely delightful Hitchcockian thriller given rather more comedy than the Master would have permitted, by director-producer Stanley Donen. Cary Grant and Audrey Hepburn fit perfectly, Walter Matthau, James Coburn solid support, Henry Mancini's hummable theme tune will stick in your mind; 1963. (c)

Charge at Feather River XX 3D western rather tame in 2D; Guy Madison rescuing Vera Miles from Indians, Gordon Douglas directing; 1953. (c)

Charge of the Lancers XX Paulette Goddard as gypsy is only flicker of interest in this hokum supposedly set in Crimean War; William Castle; 1954. (c)

The Charge of the Light Brigade √ (1) 1936 bit of excitement taking place mainly in India but switching to Crimea for Errol Flynn, Olivia de Havilland to live and love under the shadow of the great self-sacrifice. (b/w)

The Charge of the Light Brigade X (2) 1968 version by Tony Richardson is nearer historical truth but inferior in almost every other way. Trevor Howard, John Gielgud, Vanessa Redgrave are encouraged to go off on their own wavelengths, while David Hemmings is just blush-making. The animated political cartoons by Richard Williams that interrupt the action may have sounded a good idea, but they don't really work, either. (c)

Charley One Eye √ Something of a curiosity: a British-made, Spanish-located, American-set religious allegory that uses western action to spell out its message of tolerance. The Black Man (Richard Roundtree) first enslaves then befriends The Indian (Roy Thinnes), is captured by The Bounty Hunter (Nigel Davenport) but set free by The Indian, who shoots up a church crucifix with dire results; Don Chaffey directed in 1972 as though it were a straightforward western. The executive producer was vicar's son David Frost; the production manager was Jesus Gorgales. (c)

Charley's (Big-Hearted) Aunt XX A reworking of the Brandon Thomas play to accommodate Arthur Askey, Richard Murdoch and various other British comedy stars (using the phrase pejoratively). Walter Forde; 1940. (b/w)

Charley Varrick √√√ Gorgeous comedy-thriller with Walter Matthau being chased by the Mafia as well as the cops after robbing a bank. Don Siegel directed in 1973. (c)

Charlie Bubbles √ This is the 1968 drama, about a successful man revisiting his Northern background, that couldn't get a proper distribution even though it was directed by Albert Finney and starred himself and Liza Minnelli. It's constantly held up by some critics as an example of the wrongheadedness of the commercial cinema system, but the industry chieftains may have shown better critical faculties than the critics in this case. Really, it wasn't much of a film, and Finney is all too obviously worrying about how the shots look to concentrate on his acting; Billie Whitelaw (wife) and Colin Blakely (mate) turn in their usual solid performances but they aren't enough to save a pretentious picture. As Minnelli (mistress), she is desperate. (c)

Charlie Chan √ These movies vary considerably, but the best are the early (1931-37) ones with Warner Oland; the Sydney Toler ones (1938-46) are less good but more polished; the final ones with Roland Winters are worse. They all feature wise Oriental detective biting off wise Oriental sayings while snubbing No 1 and No 2 sons while solving murder mysteries. On the whole, great fun. (b/w)

Charly √ Flashy director Ralph Nelson has come up with a different kind of love story here. He (Cliff Robertson) is feeble-minded, briefly supernormal. She (Claire Bloom) is a therapist who falls in love with him. Sadly, it ends up as sickeningly coy; 1968. (c)

Charro! X The reformed outlaw riding into a trap outside Mexican border town is none other than Elvis Presley. This 1969 oater goes on to show him being framed for theft of cannon cast in precious metals. Director Charles Marquis Warren did his best. (c)

The Chase √√ Enormously interesting failure to say something profound about the nature of evil and the American South. The making (in 1965) was marred by moody fights between star Marlon Brando, writer Lillian Hellman ('decision by democratic vote is a fine form of government, but it's a stinking way to create', she said afterwards), director Arthur Penn and producer Sam Spiegel. Yet the movie itself, with Robert Redford as victim, Brando as *High Noon*-type sheriff, Jane Fonda, Angie Dickinson, is marvellous in places, and if you share any of Brando's masochism, very exciting. (c)

Chase a Crooked Shadow X Is Richard Todd really Anne Baxter's brother or only pretending to be? Various British minor players pretend to care under Michael Anderson's routine direction; 1958. (b/w)

The Chastity Belt XX Also known as *A Funny Thing Happened on the Way to the Crusades*, it's that sort of weak rip-off, with Monica Vitti, Tony Curtis, Hugh Griffith camping it up in the Middle Ages. Director Pasquale Festa Campanile makes it all slightly sordid as well as unfunny; 1967. (c)

Chato's Land √ Straightforward bloody western about tracking down a sheriff's killer (Charles Bronson). Old-timers Richard Basehart and Jack Palance take on new life under Michael Winner's 1971 direction, which contains most of his gory trademarks. (c)

Che! XXX Strong candidate for worst movie of 1969, with Omar Sharif's Guevara only worsened by Jack Palance's Castro. Maybe it's all a deep plot by director Richard Fleischer to goad Cuba into disastrous war with America. (c)

Cheaper by the Dozen √ Charming turn of the century story of the 12 real Gilbreth children, their organising father Clifton Webb and patient mother Myrna Loy. Walter Lang's 1950 box office runaway escaped sentiment by dry, humorous playing of its stars. (c)

Checkpoint X Routine motor racing drama with Stanley Baker as saboteur and wooden Anthony Steel as hero. Ralph Thomas directed in 1956. (c)

Cheyenne Autumn √√ Outstanding John Ford account of the deceit practised on tribe of Cheyenne Indians who were fooled out of their land and pushed on to arid territory 1,500 miles away. In 1878 they really did attempt to march back to their own place, touching the whole American nation. Fine cast carries this epic story along: James Stewart, Edward G. Robinson, Karl Malden, Dolores Del Rio, Richard Widmark, Carroll Baker, Sal Mineo; 1964. (c)

The Cheyenne Social Club √ Likeable though unbelievable comedy set mostly in a brothel that James Stewart inherits and decides, with his equally naïve fellow cowpuncher Henry Fonda, to close down. Directed by Gene Kelly without much sparkle; 1970. (c)

Chicago, Chicago X So recently has the language changed that this was called *Gaily, Gaily* when it came out in 1969. Nothing to do with gays, it shakily chronicles the early days of newspaperman Ben Hecht (Beau Bridges) in old Chicago. However, Norman Jewison mistakenly cast Melina Mercouri, Wilfrid Hyde-White among supports. (c)

Chicago Confidential XX State attorney breaks up crime syndicate; Brian Keith v. Beverly Garland; Sidney Salkow; 1957. (b/w)

Chicago Syndicate √ Rather a nifty little thriller about an accountant being planted on the racketeers by the police. Dennis O'Keefe can't convince in the main part and he's happier being chased with the evidence than adding up the figures; but Paul Stewart's a great heavy and director Fred F. Sears keeps it moving; 1955. (b/w)

Chicken Every Sunday √ Heartwarming, if your heart warms to *schmaltz*, boarding-house owner Celeste Holm and her lovable no-goodnik of a husband Dan Dailey. Set at turn of the century and belonging there, not even to 1948, when it was made. George Seaton. (b/w)

Chief Crazy Horse X Director George Sherman couldn't make up his mind whether this 1955 western was supposed to be a sensitive biography of the greatest of the Sioux (improbably played by Victor Mature, better known as The Hunk) or an excuse for as many screeching Red Indian attacks as he could work in. Final stool-falling denouement simply doesn't work; 1955. (c)

A Child in the House XX Mandy Miller bringing happiness to Eric Portman, Stanley Baker, and Phyllis Calvert in Charles de Latour's sudsy 1956 drama. (b/w)

A Child is Waiting √ Burt Lancaster and Judy Garland fight over retarded children's treatment. John Cassavetes directed with honesty; 1963. (b/w)

Children of the Damned √ Six otherworldly children defy the military; sequel to *Village of the Damned* has Ian Hendry and Barbara Ferris involved; Anton Leader doesn't add much directorwise; 1964. (b/w)

Child's Play XX Super quiz-kids beat security to play with atomic apparatus; most unlikely; Mona Washbourne is biggest star it can boast; 1954. (b/w)

Child's Play X When Marlon Brando departed this film in the making, Robert Preston seemed an unlikely substitute for the role of popular but sinister master in this yarn of malevolence in a boys' school. So it proved when the film was shown in 1973; James Mason and Beau Bridges stood little chance of saving the day. Nor did Sidney Lumet's discouraged direction. (c)

Chimes at Midnight √ Long-in-the-making Orson Welles attempt to put Falstaff in the centre of *Henry IV*, Parts One and Two; John Gielgud, Jeanne Moreau, Keith Baxter seem ill-at-ease, while Welles appears to be wondering where the next injection of finance is coming from. However, the good bits are very good indeed; 1967. (b/w)

China Seas √√ Piracy, romance on the high seas in this great pre-war (1935) actioner with smashing cast of Clark Gable, Jean Harlow, Wallace Beery, Rosalind Russell, Robert Benchley, C. Aubrey Smith; directed by Tay Garnett. (b/w)

Chinatown √√√ Evocative and exciting 1974 thriller in which Roman Polanski made effective use of 1937 Los Angeles – also the range that Jack Nicholson is able to call on in his development of a Philip Marlowe-type character. Faye Dunaway had her best role as the mysterious daughter of John Huston, land-owner; 1974. (c)

China Venture √ Edmond O'Brien capturing Jap general given some distinction by Don Siegel's sharp direction; 1953. (b/w)

Chisum √ Amiable western, with a tired, ageing (63 in 1970) John Wayne doing much more talking than riding. The usual fights between two clans, good and evil, are adequately handled by director Andrew McLaglen. (c)

Chitty Chitty Bang Bang √ Ian Fleming's magic car takes wings under Ken Hughes' cheerful direction and Dick Van Dyke's driving. Jolly cast includes Sally Ann Howes, Lionel Jeffries; 1969. (c)

A Christmas Carol √ 1951 version with Alastair Sim a highly satisfactory Scrooge and the emphasis on ghosts. (b/w)

Christopher Columbus X Yawnful 1949 attempt to make organisation of expedition to discover America into drama. Fredric March and English cast struggle but David MacDonald's direction and talky script bogs them down. (c)

Chubasco X Poor little youth movie, made in 1968, about the regeneration of Christopher Jones as tuna-fisherman, with help from old-timers Ann Sothern, Richard Egan; Susan Strasberg; Allen H. Miner wrote-directed. (c)

Chuka √ Made in 1967 when westerns were at last growing up, this attacked-fort drama was rather more real than others before it, with John Mills commanding a batch of drunks, Rod Taylor speaking up for the starving Injuns, Ernest Borgnine lumbering around. The hard-trying director was Gordon Douglas. (c)

A Chump at Oxford √ Laurel and Hardy sent up Robert Taylor's *A Yank at Oxford* with this funny version of education at the varsity; Alfred Gould-ing directed; 1939. (b/w)

Cimarron X Dreary 1960 remake of 1931 super-western with Richard Dix and Irene Dunne. Glenn Ford and Maria Schell are totally inadequate substitutes, and Anthony Mann can't match the sweep and vigour of the earlier Wesley Ruggles. (c)

The Cincinnati Kid √√ *The Hustler* in spades, poker replacing pool as the showdown game. A hard, brainy Steve McQueen confronts the seasoned and civilised Edward G. Robinson. Nor-man Jewison; 1965. (c)

Cinderella Liberty X James Caan is a sailor on more or less permanent leave who adopts a whore (Marsha Mason) and her family. Mark Rydell's direc-tion tries too hard, and the hero's adventures in Seattle are too diffuse and sentimental; 1973. (c)

Cinderfella XX Jerry Lewis produced this floperoo for the sole benefit of Jerry Lewis, who is in front of the camera and twice as big as anyone else around – which is a shame, when some of the others are Ed Wynn, Judith Anderson and Count Basie. Frank Tashlin served his guv'nor well – much too well, the concept of a male Cinderella, complete with wicked stepbrothers and all, doesn't gel; 1960. (c)

Circle of Danger √ Ray Milland returns to England to find out who killed brother and discovers that two governments are involved; shot by Jacques Tourneur in Britain; 1951. (b/w)

Circle of Deception X Can you believe that Bradford Dillman is set up to be captured by the Nazis, having been filled with false information, in the expectation that he will reveal all he knows and thus trick them? If you can't, forget this rather nasty thriller directed in 1961 by Jack Lee from a Nigel Balchin script. Suzy Parker inadequately fills the American quota, while British backbones Harry Andrews, Paul Rogers, Robert Stephens look as if they are on the side of those who can't believe it. (b/w)

Circus of Fear XX Police seek robbery cash at circus winter quarters, run into several suspicious characters including Christopher Lee; director John Moxey; 1967. (c)

Circus of Horrors √ Compelling little British chiller about plastic surgeon Anton Diffring taking over a circus to escape from vengeance of bungled

patients and staffing it with ladies he has put together again; when he has to get rid of them all the accidents you fear in real circuses actually occur – like the trapezist falling, the knife-thrower not missing; Donald Pleasence; direc-tor Sidney Hayers; 1960. (c)

Cisco Pike √ Kris Kristofferson as a reluctant dope-pusher; Gene Hack-man as the crooked cop who forces him into business; Karen Black as the girlfriend. Bill L. Norton directed moodily; 1972. (c)

The Citadel X Pre-war best-seller made into competent 1938 movie by King Vidor pretends to be realistic but really plays on worst instincts. Of course, nobody can fault the selfless Robert Donat as he spurns Harley Street to practise in Welsh valley but his solution for solving typhoid problem is melodramatic and dangerous; Ralph Richardson abets him; Rex Harrison, Emlyn Williams in their younger days, are around. (b/w)

Citizen Kane √√√ A poll of interna-tional critics voted this the best film of all time in 1972, 21 years after it was made, and their verdict stands unchal-lenged today. The direction and acting of Orson Welles, Herman J. Man-kiewicz's script (modelled on megalo-maniac publisher William Randolph Hearst), Gregg Toland's camera, Ber-nard Herrmann's music are all best of their kind, and the performances of Joseph Cotten (Kane's friend), Everett Sloane (his manager), Agnes Moore-head (his mother), George Coulouris (his guardian), Ray Collins (his politi-cal opponent), Paul Stewart (his butler), Dorothy Comingore (his second wife) launched most on giddy careers. Above all towers Orson Welles, as actor – playing the many ages of the crusading newspaperman who does the dirt on everyone but somehow retains our sympathy to the end – and as producer-director – opening new vistas for the art of film with every dazzling scene, from the pastiche of the March of Time to the endless crane shot of his lifetime's possessions. True film-lovers will be hunched in front of the screen, chanting the lines with the players; and if by any chance you've never seen it, look forward to a stunning experience. It's a bit sad to see Orson Welles and Joseph Cotten made up to be the ages they now are, but fascinating to compare the make-up man's guesses with the reality. (b/w)

City Beneath the Sea X Robert Ryan and Anthony Quinn diving for gold bullion off Jamaica; directed by Budd Boetticher; 1953. (c)

City of Bad Men √ Unusual western caper in that it recreates big prize fight between Bob Fitzsimmons and Jim Corbett; Dale Robertson, Richard Boone are involved in attempt to rob the gate money; Harmon Jones; 1953. (c)

City of Fear X That stolen canister contains dangerous radioactive cobalt, not money, for once; Vince Edwards; directed by Irving Lerner in 1959. (b/w)

City That Never Sleeps X Gig Young in the days before he developed into leading light comedian (1953) as cop who nearly throws away his good name (ha-ha); John H. Auer; 1953. (b/w)

City Under the Sea X Appalling script defeats veteran director Jacques Tourneur's attempt to make British horror movie with Vincent Price as ruler of subterranean world, and Tab Hunter discovering it woodenly. David Tomlinson does what he can with silly-ass; and the underwater fighting goes on and on; 1965. (c)

Clambake XX Elvis Presley as rich boy (at 33 in 1968 he ought to know better – if he didn't, a glance at the size of his waistband might have helped) changing places with water-ski instructor to see if any girl will love him for himself. Oh, dear. Arthur H. Nadel (director) must have been well paid or desperate. (c)

Clash by Night √ Strong stuff with strong cast (Barbara Stanwyck marrying Paul Douglas, liaising with Robert Ryan; Marilyn Monroe, J. Carroll Naish supporting), strongly directed by Fritz Lang from strong script by Alfred Hayes from tough Clifford Odets play. Could even have done with a little weakening; 1952. (b/w)

Class of '44 X Blatant 1973 attempt to dredge up some more nostalgia after the success of *Summer of '42*, this melo of drafts and exam-cheating is overlaid by a surface attention to period detail that does not, alas, extend to subtler and more difficult undercurrents of the time. Gary Grimes couldn't quite carry the main role, nor Paul Bogart the direction. (c)

Claudelle Inglish XX Phoney Erskine Caldwell novel makes phoney Gordon Douglas film about jilted Diane McBain Burning the Candle at Both Ends; 1961. (b/w)

Claudia X Dorothy McGuire growing up; strictly soap-opera. Edmund Goulding; 1943. (b/w)

Claudia and David X Dorothy McGuire's married life; even soapier; Walter Land; 1946. (b/w)

Claudine √ Harmless little ghetto yarn with greater pretensions, about Diahann Carroll and James Earl Jones struggling with large unruly families and the generation gap, to find love at last; director, John Berry; 1974. (c)

Cleopatra √ (1) 1934: considering the date this is a very sexy item, what with its seductions, slave-girls, near-nudity and (in the famous barge set-piece), whipping and suggested animalism. Director Cecil B. de Mille knew what he was doing, but did the Hays Office? Claudette Colbert looks right as Cleo; Warren Williams, Henry Wilcoxon are rather wooden Caesar, Antony. (b/w)

Cleopatra X (2) 'Who do you sleep with to get out of this picture?' was just one of the jokes that went the rounds when the 1962 version was made by writer-director Joseph L. Mankiewicz, the most expensive (over $30,000,000) fiasco in the history of pictures. Liz Taylor and Richard Burton were being extra-marital while filming. The result was awful. It managed to pick up minor Oscars for photography, sets, costume and special effects, but the critics gave it the booby prize otherwise. (c)

The Climbers XX Social, that is, Andrea Parisy brings destruction to marriage in clawing way up ladder; who cares? Edmond O'Brien, Richard Basehart have to make like they do; 1964. (c)

Clive of India √ All-starring (Ronald Colman, Loretta Young, C. Aubrey Smith, Cesar Romero), all-talking, all-action epic of 1935. About empire-building, made when we still were. Director Richard Boleslawski. (b/w)

Cloak and Dagger √ Fritz Lang spy thriller set in Second World War with Gary Cooper probing Nazi atomic progress; 1947. (b/w)

A Clockwork Orange √√ One of those disturbing movies that the better they are the worse they are. While it is hard to fault Stanley Kubrick's meticulous direction of this story of the near future, or Malcolm McDowell's chief hoodlum, one must ask how much nearer a film like this brings the nightmare future about which it is presumably warning us. There is no doubt that gangs of teenage 'droogs' were encouraged in their anti-social behaviour by seeing it in 1972. Doubtless their younger brothers will be when it's on the 'telly'. (c)

The Clouded Yellow √ Jean Simmons trying to prove she didn't do murder in loony haze, with help of ex-MI5's Trevor Howard; Ralph Thomas's direction is notable for some splendid location shots all over England, including Lake District; 1951. (b/w)

The Clown X Those who saw *The Champ* will recognise this as a 1953 updating of the same sob-story by Frances Marion. Only here, the champ is a clown, the come-back is on television, the old wino is Red Skelton and the little chap who takes good care of him is Tim Considine; Robert Z. Leonard does his best to open your tear-ducts. (b/w)

Coast of Skeletons XX A bit of a rip-off from *Sanders of the River* which will probably cause all concerned (director Robert Lynn, actors Richard Todd, Derek Nimmo, Dale Robertson) to cover their faces with shame when it comes on the TV screen; it's that old hokum about how the lust for gold ruins all who are touched by it; 1965. (c)

The Cobweb √ Inside a mental institution played strictly for soap-opera, and it's a bit unnerving the way the picture keeps stopping and starting as though reaching the end of one thrilling, cliff-hanging episode before lurching on to the next. Lauren Bacall and Richard Widmark are young lovers (that shows how long ago it was made – 1955), and supporting inmates include Oscar Levant, Charles Boyer, Gloria Grahame, Susan Strasberg. Vincente Minnelli. (c)

Cockleshell Heroes X Jose Ferrer kindly did us the favour of coming to Britain to direct and star in this 1956 account of a British raid in five small boats on occupied Bordeaux; no wonder Trevor Howard fights with him the whole time. Too much of the picture is taken up with training, and it only flares briefly into life for the actual raid; Anthony Newley among the heroes, which is pretty depressing news. (c)

The Colditz Story √ Straightforward, well-made can-this-prison-hold-our-brave-PoWs story with John Mills, Eric Portman, Lionel Jeffries, Bryan Forbes, Ian Carmichael, Richard Wattis, directed by Guy Hamilton; 1955. (b/w)

Cold Sweat XXX Terrible, creaky French-Italian thriller, dully directed by Terence Young in 1970, with James Mason forcing Charles Bronson to undertake crooked motor-boat trip on the French Riviera, using Liv Ullman as hostage. A bore. (c)

Cold Turkey √√√ Few critics liked this broad-stroke satire on American greed when it appeared in 1970, but we found it amazingly funny and full of unexpected pleasures. Dick Van Dyke is the vain preacher who convinces his small town to go in for a contest to stop smoking. Norman Lear directed with a sharp eye for contemporary greeds and follies. (c)

A Cold Wind in August √√ Example of how a low-budget sexploitation sleeper (*le mot juste*) can outstrip (ditto) fancier films by knowing what it's doing. Lola Albright's seduction of 17-year-old is honest as well as erotic, and no one must have been more surprised than director Alexander Singer when his 1961 effort got taken up as OK intellectuals' movie. (b/w)

The Collector √ William Wyler tried to realise the significance in John Fowles's novel, only to discover that there wasn't any. Result is a rather tame, rather silly thriller about a nutter (competently played by Terence Stamp) who kidnaps a girl (Samantha Eggar); 1965. (c)

Colorado Territory √ Moody, fatalistic western from Raoul Walsh (1949) with Joel McCrea escaping law. (b/w)

The Colossus of New York X Mad scientist puts dead son's brain into robot; Eugene Lourié achieves some great effects; 1958. (b/w)

Colt 45 X Scotts wha' hae: Randolph chases Zachary in this tame 1950 'tribute to the great six-shooting gun'; Edward L. Marin just treats it as one more western. (c)

Column South X Mediocre western with a touch of concern for the Navajo Indians, as Union officer Audie Murphy fights for their protection; credibility bites the dust early in this story directed by Frederick de Cordova; 1953. (b/w)

Comanche X Dana Andrews' job is to try to help the Indians see that it's more sense to make peace not war; director George Sherman's job is to make you stay watching. He tries hard but might not be able to manage it; 1955. (c)

Comanche Station √ One of the best Budd Boetticher-Randolph Scott small-scale westerns, with the tall leathery hero escorting Nancy Gates

The Comancheros ✓ Everyone seems to have enjoyed making this lark of a western, with John Wayne and Stuart Whitman playing hard-drinking goodies, lined up against baddies Lee Marvin, Nehemiah Persoff, Edgar Buchanan. Michael Curtiz strays convincingly into John Ford territory; 1961. (c)

Come Back Charleston Blue ✓ Agreeable comedy-thriller with Godfrey Cambridge and Raymond St. Jacques doing their Harlem detectives bit again, in 1972. This time, all the heroin in the area has been hijacked and the ghost of a razor killer may or may not have returned to 110th street. (c)

Come Back, Little Sheba ✓ 1952 adaptation of William Inge Broadway play, which won Shirley Booth, as sluttish housewife, an Oscar and Burt Lancaster, as alcoholic husband, undeserved upstaging by that award; he was extraordinarily subtle – for him. Daniel Mann directed, but never quite opened up the idea from inhibiting stage structure. (b/w)

Come Blow Your Horn ✓ Sinatra as expert on swinging life finds he doesn't know everything. Bud Yorkin's first film, 1963, takes Neil Simon's Broadway winner and makes it rattle along in a series of frantic jokes. Lee J. Cobb is father. (c)

The Comedians ✓ Graham Greene's novel of Papa Doc's Haiti transferred moodily to the screen by Peter Glenville, with a rather theatrical cast of Burton-Taylor, Peter Ustinov, Paul Ford, Lillian Gish; but Alec Guinness walks away with it – possibly he is well suited and sympathetic to Greene's tortured Catholic world; 1967. (c)

The Comedy Man X Unusual showbiz backstage story with Kenneth More as actor who finally makes it in commercials; Billie Whitelaw, Dennis Price do their very best but are let down by Alvin Rakoff's spotty direction; 1964. (b/w)

The Comedy of Terrors ✓ Macabre slapstick about two undertakers who improve business by creating a few corpses, it has a gorgeous cast –Vincent Price, Peter Lorre, Boris Karloff, Basil Rathbone – and Jacques Tourneur making his first (1963) comedy. Great fun and quite thrilly at times. (c)

Come Fill the Cup ✓ James Cagney is ex-drunk who now guides newspaper proprietor's son on to the straight and narrow. It's all a bit simple and silly, but Cagney's charisma counts for a lot, and the supports are strong: Raymond Massey, Gig Young, Jimmy Gleason. Gordon Douglas; 1951. (b/w)

Come Fly With Me X Three airline hostesses get involved with romance on a trip to Paris and Vienna; strictly for the wide blue yonder, though Karl Malden almost saves the picture with his skilful warmth; Henry Levin keeps it flying; 1963. (c)

Come Next Spring ✓ Rather a touching little picture with Ann Sheridan and Steve Cochran, usually in flashier, worse pictures than this 1956 idyll by R. G. Springsteen, determined to make their Arkansas farm work . . . come next spring. (c)

The Come-On X Anne Baxter is crook's partner involved with honest boatowner; Russell Birdwell spins murder story with help of Sterling Hayden; 1956. (b/w)

Come September ✓ Early (1961) Robert Mulligan-directed comedy about the annual holiday Rock Hudson and Gina Lollobrigida take in his villa overlooking Positano, only to find, arriving early, that Walter Slezak uses it as an hotel; mildly funny and glossy but beware, Bobby Darin sings 'Multiplication'. A big box-office hit. (c)

The Command ✓ Unpretentious little western directed by David Butler that falls down only in its principal players – Guy Madison, James Whitmore, Joan Weldon; civil war soldier v. the Indians; 1954. (c)

Command Decision X Clark Gable wants to send bombing planes deeper into Germany in this 1948 actioner, made when bombing was not a dirty word; John Hodiak, Walter Pidgeon, Edward Arnold involved in heartsearching under veteran director Sam Wood. (b/w)

The Committee X So breathtakingly pretentious is this parable that it almost gets away with breaking all the rules. Paul Jones kills the driver of a car he has hitched a lift in by cutting off his head, then he sews it back on and the chap drives on. And that's only the start. The rest is Kafkaesque stuff about being summoned before an all-powerful, all-mysterious Body. You've got to hand it to Peter Sykes and Max Steuer for actually making it and not just talking about it; 1968. (b/w)

Companions in Nightmare X Which nutter is killing the others at therapy institute? Melvyn Douglas, Anne Baxter, Dana Wynter, Gig Young, all getting on a bit in 1967. (c)

Company of Killers √ Made in 1968 for American TV, this exciting if predictable will-they-catch-him was shown in the cinemas here. Old-timers Ray Milland, Van Johnson, Fritz Weaver go through the motions under Jerry Thorpe's reasonably taut direction. (c)

Compulsion √√ Richard Fleischer's strong adaptation of Meyer Levin's book about Leopold and Loeb 'thrill-killers', earlier inspirers of Hitchcock's *Rope*. A bit too much courtroom, with Orson Welles delivering Clarence Darrow speeches. Set 1920s, shot 1959. (b/w)

Comrade X XX Soviet bus conductress Hedy Lamarr is romanced by Clark Gable and the American way of love; despite presence of Sig Rumann and Oscar Homolka raises few laughs or even hackles; King Vidor; 1941. (b/w)

The Condemned of Altona √ The Hamburg ship barons, as seen by Jean-Paul Sartre, made over by Abby Mann in 1963; with Fredric March as chief capitalist, Maximilian Schell as lingering Nazi officer son, Sophia Loren. (b/w)

Confessions of an Opium Eater XX Not your de Quincey, but your Vincent Price hamming it up among San Francisco slave-girls; Albert Zugsmith didn't believe it, either; 1962. (b/w)

Confidential Agent X Disappointing attempt by stage director Herman Shumlin (never to make another picture, understandably) to bring the Graham Greene novel about fascist business dealings to life. Despite super cast (Charles Boyer, Peter Lorre, Katina Paxinou, Miles Mander, Lauren Bacall) he never convinces for a moment. Read the book instead; 1945. (b/w)

Confidential Report √ The butchered remains of an Orson Welles masterpiece, this tells of the shady past of an eccentric and mysterious financier. Unfortunately, control passed out of Welles' hands, and what should have been a meaningful and exciting thriller with deeper undertones became a confusing release in 1955, with Welles, Michael Redgrave, Akim Tamiroff, Mischa Auer involved in impenetrable goings-on. Still, enough remained of Welles the director-writer to make it

fascinating for those who worship at his shrine. (b/w)

Conflict √ Humphrey Bogart as wife-killer versus Sidney Greenstreet, psychiatrist; Curtis Bernhardt directed with high competence; 1945. (b/w)

Conflict of Wings √ Gentle British (very) battle between RAF and villagers over a bird sanctuary. John Gregson, Kieron Moore are leaders, so you can guess it's all a bit stilted and low-key. Director, John Eldridge; 1953. (c)

Connecting Rooms X Two fine artistes, Bette Davis and Michael Redgrave, are unfortunately trapped in an old-fashioned romantic drama. They are both pretending to be what they are not, and in the end all comes out nicely. Poor stuff, unimaginatively treated by writer-director Franklin Gollings in 1969. (c)

The Connection √√ Remarkable mock *ciné-vérité* of junkies waiting for a fix; Shirley Clarke magically managed to involve the audience, which was much easier in the theatre; 1961. (b/w)

Conquest of Cochise X Routine William Castle movie with Robert Stack trying to subdue blacked-up John Hodiak's braves; 1953. (c)

Conquest of Space XX 1955 guesses at the future animated by George Pal are not very impressive now we have lived through the reality. Walter Brooke, Eric Fleming search for raw materials on Mars; director Byron Haskin. (c)

Conquest of the Planet of the Apes X Rotten 1972 using-up of the costumes and discarded ideas from previous *Ape Planet* movies; J. Lee Thompson. (c)

Conrack √√ Sentimental, old-fashioned (in 1974) heart-warming drama about a teacher who brings joy and understanding to his young charges on an island off South Carolina, and gets fired for his trouble. Jon Voight responded well to Martin Ritt's direction which was particularly effective in its use of the channel between island and mainland as metaphor (Voight teaches them to swim it). (c)

Conspiracy of Hearts √ Nuns shelter Jewish children in wartime Italy and get away with it because Ronald Lewis as Italian commander turns a blind eye. But then German officer Albert Lieven takes charge and it's all very tricky, exciting and sentimental for Lilli Palmer, Sylvia Syms, Yvonne Mitchell; set in 1943, made 1959, directed by Ralph Thomas. (b/w)

Conspirator X Taylors, Elizabeth and Robert, in a silly little Gaslit story about a husband ordered by the Reds to whom he is in thrall (for some unexplained reason) to kill his wife; Victor Saville did uninspired directorial stint in 1949. (*b/w*)

The Conspirators √ Smudged carbon of *Casablanca*, with Paul Henreid doing his freedom fighter bit, Peter Lorre and Sidney Greenstreet as lovable villains, but it's Hedy Lamarr who is the fatal femme this time. Jean Negulesco directed in Lisbon (or Warner's back-lot) in 1944. (*b/w*)

The Constant Husband √ Rex Harrison's stylish performance almost saves silly comedy of multi-married amnesiac, with Kay Kendall, Margaret Leighton. Launder-Gilliatt; 1955. (*c*)

The Conversation √√√ –Riveting thriller about the 'best bugger on the West Coast', as Gene Hackman's electronic surveillance expert is called. A bit of a mystery himself, he guards his own secrets as ruthlessly as he pries into other people's. The viewer becomes as obsessed as he does with a tape-recording he makes in a park, and with the subsequent tracking-down of a murder. Allen Garfield is equally convincing as a friendly rival, and the whole film is a monument to Francis Ford Coppola's skill as writer-producer-director; 1974. (*c*)

Convict 99 √ Lovely old (1938) Will Hay-Graham Moffat-Moore Marriott comedy of mistaken identities, with Googie Withers, Basil Radford, Kathleen Harrison in and out of jail. (*b/w*)

Convicts Four X True story of John Resko (Ben Gazzara), who was freed after serving large part of 17-year stretch because of understanding warden's (Stuart Whitman) interest in his paintings. Great back-up cast include Ray Walston, Vincent Price, Rod Steiger, Brod Crawford, Jack Kruschen. Alas, director Millard Kaufman couldn't put any zip into dull script he wrote himself; 1962. (*b/w*)

Convoy XX Stiff-upper-lip time for Clive Brook, John Clements, Michael Wilding over U-boats and Judy Campbell; director, Pen Tennyson; 1940. (*b/w*)

Coogan's Bluff √√ Sleeper of its year, 1968 – that is to say, the suprise success – thanks mainly to veteran director Don Siegel's way with a thriller. Given an A-picture budget for a change, Siegel made this yarn of a small-town cop (the wooden Clint Eastwood, his

unacting ability well-used in this steely part) tracking down his man in wild New York, exciting and involving. Lee J. Cobb turned in one of his usually impressive performances as the Manhattan tough-cop driven wild by the hick. (*c*)

Cool Hand Luke √√ Haunting drama of chain-gang prisoner Paul Newman with strong undercurrent of comedy as he sasses his bosses; stunning camerawork by Conrad Hall makes Stuart Rosenberg's direction look even better than it is. Jo Van Fleet contributes marvellous cameo as his mother, while George Kennedy and Dennis Hopper stand out in brilliantly marshalled cast; 1967. (*c*)

Cops and Robbers √√ Beguiling and thoroughly amusing if it wasn't so evidently based on fact. The point is that the cops *are* the robbers in this neat comedy thriller – and in factual reports from New York City police department – in 1973. Director Aram Avakian handles his unknown cast beautifully and makes the central caper really exciting. (*c*)

Cornered √ Good, tough little thriller with Dick Powell searching Europe and Argentina for Nazi killers of his wife; before its time in 1946; Edward Dmytryk. (*b/w*)

The Corn is Green √ Bette Davis woefully miscast but battling on like a good trouper in Emlyn Williams' famous autobiography of teacher who puts star pupil through university. Disguised propaganda for private (school) enterprise, this version, directed by Irving Rapper, manages to catch the Welsh ambience; 1946. (*b/w*)

Corridors of Blood √ Although Boris Karloff is in it and despite title, this is reasonably sincere account of introduction of anaesthetics to relieve suffering. Slips over the top when he goes mad because of overdose turning him addict; Robert Day; 1958. (*b/w*)

Corruption XXX Crazy Peter Cushing mutilating ladies so that girlfriend's vanished beauty can be restored. Horribly done, in every sense of the word. Robert Hartford-Davis has some pretty sick ideas, and obviously hopes that you share them; 1968. (*c*)

Cosa Nostra — Arch Enemy of the FBI X This clumsy title comes from the fact that this was originally two episodes of *The FBI* TV series put together; it's a pre-*Godfather* (1967) view of the Mafia as simple gangsters, beefed up with a few over-the-hill stars

- Walter Pidgeon, Celeste Holm, Telly Savalas, Susan Strasberg. Don Medford directed. (c)

Cotton Comes to Harlem √ Comedy thriller using a raft of leading black actors (Godfrey Cambridge, Raymond St. Jacques, Calvin Lockhart, Red Foxx) to make an enjoyable romp through familiar double-crossing territory. Unfortunately it leads to a weak climax. Director Ossie Davis clearly knew his milieu; 1970. (c)

Countdown √√ Sci-fi thriller with outstanding credentials. Made in 1967 by Robert Altman, who went on to *Nashville*, *M*A*S*H*, etc., it starred James Caan and Robert Duvall, both in *The Godfather*. This one is about a panic flight by a US aeronaut in a clapped-out rocket, just to beat the Russians to the moon. (c)

The Counterfeit Traitor √ Spy thriller with William Holden as Swedish businessman forced by Allies to snoop on Nazis; Lilli Palmer, Hugh Griffith. Supposedly it all really happened. George Seaton; 1962. (c)

Counterpoint X Rather awful adaptation of Alan Sillitoe's novel *The General* further vitiated by Ralph Nelson's insensitive direction. Maximilian Schell is Nazi officer who captures symphony orchestra led by Charlton Heston, whose spirited performance is the only bright spot in a dull landscape; 1968. (c)

A Countess from Hong Kong X Charles (to give him the pompous Christian name he insisted on when directing) Chaplin's howling failure to make a thirties-type comedy out of State Department official Marlon Brando finding stowaway Russian countess Sophia Loren in his cross-Pacific cabin. Should have been thrown overboard but will doubtless hang around as monument to an old man's hubris; 1967. (c)

The Count of Monte Cristo √ First glimpsed on television in 1938 (at Radiolympia), this swashbuckler was directed four years earlier by Rowland Lee. Robert Donat was the wrongly imprisoned Count, Louis Calhern chief heavy. Elissa Landi was heroine. (b/w)

Country Dance XX Understandably suppressed by film distributors, this 1969 farrago directed by J. Lee Thompson has Peter O'Toole as a loony landowner, Susannah York the sister he covets. (c)

The Country Girl √ Oscar-winning performance from Grace Kelly, holding up drunken Bing Crosby with encouragement from William Holden. Strong stuff and competently directed by George Seaton; 1954. (b/w)

Count the Hours √ Macdonald Carey takes blame for pregnant wife Teresa Wright when employers are murdered; Don Siegel made it tight and trim in 1953. (b/w)

Count Three and Pray X Raymond Burr, one of the great Hollywood heavies in both senses of the word, tangling with Van Heflin, rogue turned pastor. Joanne Woodward is romantic interest in this 1955 western. George Sherman. (c)

Count Yorga, Vampire √ 1970 version of the Dracula theme, rather neatly translated to present-day Los Angeles. Bob Kelljan's cast were unknowns. (c)

Count Your Blessings XX Deadly comedy with some of the deadliest stars in the business: Deborah Kerr, Maurice Chevalier, Rossano Brazzi, directed by the deadly Jean Negulesco. How a che-ild brings parents together again; 1959. (c)

Courage of Lassie X Elizabeth Taylor reforms Lassie, used in war as killer. Directed by Fred Wilcox; 1946. (c)

The Court Jester √ Made by Panama-and-Frank while Danny Kaye was still as funny (in 1956) as he later thought he was, this is a romp through the Middle Ages with Basil Rathbone and Cecil Parker backing up nicely (and rather nastily, but that's only the plot). (c)

The Courtneys of Curzon Street XX While this tosh about three generations of a Mayfair family was just about acceptable in 1947 as an antidote to austerity, Michael Wilding, Anna Neagle, Gladys Young and Michael Medwin merely look quaint today; Herbert Wilcox. (b/w)

The Courtship of Eddie's Father XX Quite horrible comedy with Glenn Ford as widower giving up the girl he wants to marry (fashion consultant Stella Stevens) for the nurse who lives next door (Shirley Jones), at the grinding insistence of his ghastly 6-year-old son (the precocious Ronny Howard). Vincente Minnelli, who should have known better, perpetrated this cute concoction in 1963. (c)

A Covenant with Death √ Death and deceit in the Twenties. Gene Hackman in early (1967) role as police chief arresting Earl Holliman for murdering wife. George Maharis is nominal lead. Director, Lamont Johnson. (c)

Cowboy √ The imaginative idea of filming Frank (*Life and Loves*) Harris's adventures as a 19th-century cow-poke (and that's nearly the right word) grinds to a disappointing movie as Delmer Daves makes compromise after compromise with convention, ending up as just another western with Glenn Ford and Jack Lemmon trading chitchat, and Brian Donlevy doing his usual bit. 1957. (c)

The Cowboy and the Lady XX Gary Cooper and Merle Oberon meet in the West of 1939. One of those tiresome plots where a rich girl pretends to be her own maid. Director is Henry C. Potter. (b/w)

The Cowboys √ *Emil and the Detectives* transposed to the Wild West, with gruff, kindly, hard taskmaster John Wayne depending on a gang of eleven kids to help him drive his cattle. When vicious Bruce Dern and desperadoes do him in, the cow-*boys* regain the cattle and finish the drive; Mark Rydell makes it all a bit cute; 1972. (c)

Crack in the Mirror √ Laudable attempt to try something different; Orson Welles, Juliette Greco, Bradford Dillman each play two parts in parallel love stories set in Paris. Richard Fleischer; 1960. (b/w)

Crack in the World √ Superior 1965 sci-fi about Dana Andrews trying to harness earth's energy but only succeeding in causing vast earthquakes. Janette Scott screams convincingly but real star is director Andrew Marton's special effects. (c)

Crack-Up √ One of those whatever-happened - while - I - lost - my - memory thrillers with Pat O'Brien, spotter of master forgers, being manipulated. Claire Trevor, Herbert Marshall, Ray Collins, Wallace Ford give good value under director Irving Reis; 1946. (b/w)

Crazy Joe √ Mafia movie that is at least aware of its mythical status, with a strong cast - Peter Boyle, Paula Prentiss, Charles Cioffi, Rip Torn, Luther Adler, Eli Wallach - and lively direction from Carlo Lizzani; 1973. (c)

Creature from the Black Lagoon √ Allegorical and beautifully filmed sci-fi, directed by Jack Arnold, 1954. A Gill-Man lives in the depths of the Amazon, menacing our moral world in general and Julie Adams in particular. If you don't like the genre, it's easy to laugh at this low-budget example; but

if you will allow yourself to enter into its premises you may find it haunting and unsettling. Achieved added fame when Marilyn Monroe went to see it in *The Seven Year Itch* and sympathised with the Creature. (b/w)

Creature from the Haunted Sea X Villain plans to blame mythical monster for crime; then - how did you guess? - real one appears; 1961. Roger Corman. (b/w)

Crime and Punishment, USA √ Dostoievsky's much-filmed drama of death and retribution transferred to Santa Monica and the 1959 beat set; George Hamilton is adequate as the law-student, but the attempt of brothers Terry and Denis Sanders founders on trying to do too many things (tell the story, bring out the meanings, transfer the locale) all at once. (b/w)

Crime in the Streets √ Don Siegel's rather sentimental yarn about juvenile delinquents on the East Side: John Cassavetes, Sal Mineo, Mark Rydell; 1957. (b/w)

Crime of Passion √ Sad little story of love and the police; Barbara Stanwyck's ambition for her husband leads her to commit adultery and murder; Sterling Hayden, Fay Wray, Raymond Burr; Gerd Oswald kept his ambition low and achieved it; 1957. (b/w)

The Criminal √√ Exciting if overly symbolic (is freedom outside jail or inside yourself?) yarn with sharp Alun Owen script and closely-observed performances from Stanley Baker, Sam Wanamaker, Patrick Magee. Despite later acclaim, Joseph Losey has never done better than this 1960 thriller. (b/w)

The Crimson Kimono √ San Francisco detectives fall out over art student Victoria Shaw while investigating murder of a stripper; Samuel Fuller gave this B-pic his special touch in 1959. (b/w)

The Crimson Pirate √ Burt Lancaster playing the buccaneer in what might have been intended as a spoof but ends up another swashbuckler under Robert Siodmak's direction; 1952. (c)

Cripple Creek X George Montgomery on the trail of gold bandits poses as member of the gang; this 1952, Ray Nazarro-directed western must not be confused with *Cripple Creek Bar-Room*, made in 1898 and the first western ever made, although you might have preferred seeing the latter. (c)

Crisis √ Cary Grant as American doctor forced to treat South American dictator; Richard Brooks did it competently in 1950. (b/w)

Criss Cross √ Burt Lancaster in tough gangster yarn directed by Robert Siodmak that grips the interest, partly because it isn't too obvious; only snags are Yvonne de Carlo as his wife and rest of weak cast except for Dan Duryea; 1949. (b/w)

Critic's Choice X Presenting the flimsiest ethical problem of 1963: should Bob Hope review wife Lucille Ball's play? Don Weis contrives to make it as appealing as possible, which isn't very. (c)

Cromwell X Spectacular but ultimately boring historical essay on Cavaliers v. Roundheads. Alec Guinness makes a sombre Charles, Richard Harris a pretentious Cromwell. His brutalities in Ireland are conveniently ignored, so that writer-directory Ken Hughes can present him sympathetically. This does no service to the man, to history, or to us; 1970. (c)

The Crooked Road X Robert Ryan in British-made, Don Chaffey-directed Balkan thriller about a dictator and a newspaperman; not very convincing; 1965. (b/w)

Crooks and Coronets XXX Dreadful failure involving Dame Edith Evans as unendearingly eccentric old lady that the self-consciously funny-peculiar Telly Savalas hopes to rob; Cesar Romero and Harry H. Corbett try throwing in echoes of some of their other, more successful roles, but it doesn't help. Jim O'Connolly wrote and directed, so he must take the main share of the blame; 1969. (c)

Crooks Anonymous √ Harmless little British comedy about villains trying not to be. Ken Annakin had a better cast than the thin script deserved: Leslie Phillips, Stanley Baxter, Wilfrid Hyde White, Julie Christie, Robertson Hare, Harry Fowler, John Bennett, Dick Emery, Dandy Nichols, Alfred Burke, Norman Rossington; 1962. (b/w)

Crooks in Cloisters XX Barbara Windsor, Bernard Cribbins, Ronald Fraser, and confederates hide out in monastery; Joseph O'Conor and Francesca Annis are among the inmates. Jeremy Summer's leaden direction numbs; 1963. (c)

Crossfire √√ Strong thriller about anti-semitic killer (Robert Ryan) who tries to pin the rap on soldier-buddy. Robert Young makes a fine detective who states the theme – that persecution is sickness and Jew-hating is evil. Edward Dmytryk made this 1947 Doré Schary production taut and exciting all the way. (b/w)

Crossplot XX Indistinguishable from a routine *Saint* churn-out, this 1969 effort has Roger Moore preventing the assassination of a visiting statesman; Alvin Rakoff skims through it with the help of a batch of familiar TV faces. (c)

Crosswinds X Dashing John Payne, after cargo of gold from a plane that crashed in New Guinea, inevitably meets headhunters and Rhonda Fleming. Directed 1951 by Lewis R. Foster. (c)

The Crowd √ Lovely 1928 silent film about the ups and downs of Eleanor Boardman and James Murray, directed by King Vidor. Some fascinating documentary records of the New York of the time. (b/w)

Crowded Paradise √ Tight little drama about how badly Puerto Rican immigrants are treated in New York, with Hume Cronyn; 1956. (b/w)

The Crowded Sky X One of those who-will-be-saved air disaster yarns with Anne Francis, Efrem Zimbalist Jr, Dana Andrews, Keenan Wynn among possibly-doomed; Joseph Pevney; 1960. (b/w)

The Cruel Sea √ Rugged account of corvette in battle of the Atlantic convinces and sobers; in a huge distinguished cast Jack Hawkins, Donald Sinden, Denholm Elliott, Alec McCowen stand out. Charles Frend directed, from Eric Ambler's script from Nicholas Monsarrat's novel; 1953. (b/w)

Cry Blood, Apache √ Despite the title, this is claimed to be more of a psychologically violent thriller than the routine bang-bang. Revenge for massacred Indians is theme; Joel McCrea's son Jody doubles for his father as a young man. Director Jack Starrett plays a small role himself; 1968. (c)

Cry Danger √ Creditable product of tough Hollywood school with Dick Powell as convict paroled under say-so of ambiguous pillar of the community. William Conrad among those threateningly present. Nice tight job from Robert Parrish; 1951. (b/w)

Cry for Happy XX Dull little comedy about expectations of American sailors Donald O'Connor, Glenn Ford over services performed by geisha girls in

Japan; George Marshall makes the best (which isn't very good) of it; 1961. (c)

A Cry from the Streets X Max Bygraves, Barbara Murray, Kathleen Harrison, sundry children in modest 1958 yarn about homeless kids and social workers; Lewis Gilbert's sympathetic direction helps. (b/w)

Cry Havoc X Nurses on wartime Philippines include Margaret Sullavan, Ann Sothern, Fay Bainter, Ella Raines; director Richard Thorpe; 1943. (b/w)

A Cry in the Night √ Peeping Tom kidnaps girl, and the chase that follows. Plenty of incident and tension served up by Frank Tuttle with the help of Natalie Wood, Raymond Burr, Edmond O'Brien, Brian Donlevy; 1956. (b/w)

Cry of Battle X Contrasting Americans Van Heflin and James MacArthur (later to settle down in his rightful place as minor support in *Hawaii Five-O*) caught in the Philippines at outbreak of war; tame direction from Irving Lerner doesn't help; 1963. (c)

Cry of the City X Childhood mates grow up to opposite sides of the law; kid brother could go either way; Richard Conte, Victor Mature, Shelley Winters. Robert Siodmak made it all so predictable; 1948. (b/w)

Cry of the Hunted X Louisiana marsh locations give this routine chase a touch of distinction; otherwise, some tiresome philosophising interrupts the action. Polly Bergen, Barry Sullivan; director Joseph H. Lewis; 1953. (b/w)

Cry Terror! √ One of those family-held-hostage movies, this time with Rod Steiger as chief heavy and James Mason as father of beleaguered family; Andrew Stone plays it for thrills and should succeed in holding your attention, at least; 1958. (b/w)

Cry, the Beloved Country √ This 1952 version of Alan Paton's novel about apartheid undoubtedly has its heart in the right place but so much has changed in twenty years. It couldn't be shot in South Africa now; and the moral that men of goodwill of all colours must work together seems pathetic. Sidney Poitier and Canada Lee acted with dignity; Zoltan Korda directed. (b/w)

Cul-de-Sac √√ Gorgeously conceived and carried out black comedy-thriller with the superb Lionel Stander forcing himself on Donald Pleasence and Françoise Dorléac on Holy Island

Roman Polanski made this one unforgettable; 1966. (b/w)

The Culpepper Cattle Company √ Western made 1972, that is after the bloody influence of *The Wild Bunch* had changed the look of oaters, probably for ever. Hero of this violent rustler drama is Gary Grimes as 16-year-old who earns his manhood during the cattle drive. Dick Richards directed without discernible purpose except to give the audience a thrill excused by some moral posturing. (c)

The Cure for Love X Robert Donat having to get rid of fiancée Dora Bryan (27 when this was made in 1949) to marry Cockney Renée Asherson; he also directed and produced it, nine years before his death. (b/w)

The Curse of Frankenstein √ Hammer horror with Peter Cushing, Christopher Lee, going through the usual antics; it's a flashback of how the Baron comes to be awaiting death sentence. Terence Fisher directed competently; 1956. (c)

The Curse of the Cat People √√ Although she's in it, this isn't really a sequel to Simone Simon's earlier *Cat People* (q.v.). This title was forced on director Robert Wise and producer Lew Lewton by the studio. Instead, it's a sensitive and haunting story of the impression a visit to a cranky old lady has on the mind of a 7-year-old, caught in a world of terror while the grown-ups squabble and disregard her; beautifully done; 1944. (b/w)

Curse of the Mummy's Tomb X Uninspired remake of the old mummy plot by Hammer's Michael Carreras in 1964; stiff Terence Morgan stars in this one which does at least have a surprise twist of sorts in that the heavy isn't the one you first think. (c)

Curse of the Undead X The only horror western? Gunman who turns out to be a vampire; E. Dein crashing between stools in 1959. (b/w)

Curse of the Voodoo XX Native chief curses safari hunter; could have been exciting, but like so many British horror-attempts it tails off to boredom. Dennis Price gamely soldiers on, Lisa Daniely screams; director Lindsay Shonteff; 1965. (b/w)

Curse of the Werewolf X Oliver Reed was bewitched in this rather ordinary horror pic directed by Terence Fisher; 1960. (c)

Custer of the West √ Robert Shaw, Mary Ure, Robert Ryan in attempt to marry epic western (originaly made in

Cinerama) and political tract with dubious origins; Robert Siodmak; 1967. (c)

Cyrano de Bergerac X Disappointing version of Rostand's play, founders less on the size of Jose Ferrer's nose than the inadequacy of his performance; Michael Gordon directs faithfully from a rather desperate Carl Foreman script; 1950. (b/w)

D

Daddy Long Legs √ 1955 musical remake of 1919 Mary Pickford and 1930 Janet Gaynor vehicles, with Leslie Caron as the orphan who loves her benefactor, this time Fred Astaire. Johnny Mercer supplied some pretty tunes (including 'Something's Gotta Give') and Jean Negulesco's schmaltzy directorial style is well-suited to this load of sentiment. (c)

Daddy's Gone A-Hunting √ Carol White being chased round San Francisco by a photographer all set on killing her little baby; all very far-fetched and only moderately chilling; Mark Robson; 1969. (c)

Dad's Army √ Bigger, costlier, coarser than the TV original, this 1971 screen version was a disappointment. Director Norman Cohen had the money to introduce a detachment of the German army, never seen in the TV show, and Mainwearing is allowed to become an unlikely and daring hero – but the essence is missing. (c)

Daisy Kenyon X Joan Crawford in 1947 Otto Preminger epic he'd rather forget; should she marry Dana Andrews now he's divorced or stay with nice Henry Fonda? You guessed. (b/w)

Daisy Miller √ Worth watching for Peter Bogdanovich's loving, if blurred, reconstruction of fashionable Switzerland and Rome in the days of Henry James, and for his blind devotion in casting hopeless Cybill Shepherd as the convention-defying heroine. For the rest, despite the presence of the formidable Mildred Natwick and Cloris Leachman, he failed to evoke any true Jamesian feeling; 1974. (c)

Dakota Incident √ Linda Darnell's in the stagecoach, the Indians are outside attacking; Lewis R. Foster; 1956. (c)

Daleks' Invasion Earth 2150 A.D. √ It may be 2150 in the title but it looks strictly 1966 from here. Quite an amusing comic strip, with Bernard Cribbins scoring as special constable from the sixties caught up in the future. Peter Cushing plays Dr Who; unfortunately he was ill during the filming which is the real reason he is absent through so many of the adventures; director Gordon Flemyng. (c)

Dallas √ Gary Cooper's the goody, Raymond Massey and Steve Cochran the baddies in standard western, nothing to do with the recent soap-opera, directed by Stuart Heisler in 1950. (c)

The Dam Busters √ Michael Redgrave as Dr Barnes Wallis, the man who made the bouncing bomb to destroy Möhne and Eder dams. Michael Anderson directed this one with a straight bat in 1954 and got absolutely decent performances from Richard Todd as Wing-Commander Gibson, Basil Sydney, Nigel Stock, Robert Shaw; but it's Redgrave's film. (b/w)

The Damned √ On the level of sci-fi thriller this 1962 Joseph Losey parable works fine; only when it starts taking itself seriously does it stumble. A bunch of cold-blooded (literally) kids are kept in a cave to repopulate the world after the holocaust – and at anything but the lowest level it gets pretentious and confusing. Poorly cast with Macdonald Carey, Shirley Ann Field, Alexander Knox, Oliver Reed each adding their contribution to the general unbelievability. (b/w)

The Damned √√ Impressive saga of a German family up to the time when the SS took over completely. Visconti's strong direction creates a sombre, baroque mood, and Dirk Bogarde is almost matched in intensity by Ingrid Thulin; 1969. (b/w)

Damn Yankees √√ Irresistible-sounding idea of an ageing baseball fan being Fausted into great player, becomes slightly more resistible amid all that alien home-running; somehow the opening-out of the stage play hasn't helped. But Ray Walston's Devil and Gwen Verdon as his tempting helper are fine. Her 'Whatever Lola Wants' stops the show. Stanley Donen gave it polish; 1958. (c)

Dan Candy's Law √ Donald Sutherland as Mountie, declaring vengeance against Red Indian Gordon Tootoosis for attacking Kevin McCarthy; Canadian-shot oater; 1973. (c)

The Dance of Death √√ National

Theatre's production of Strindberg drama about a chained marriage photographed by director David Giles with only a desultory minute's opening-out for filming. Olivier incredibly powerful, Geraldine McEwan adequate, Robert Lang plodding; 1969. (c)

Dance of the Vampires √ This heavy-handed satire on horror movies has taken on a totally different and macabre aspect since its star Sharon Tate, wife of its director Roman Polanski, was so tragically involved in manifestations of occult madness. Polanski appears himself with Jack MacGowran as vampire hunters. Sad that it wasn't a better memorial; 1968. (c)

A Dandy in Aspic X Russian-British double-agent Laurence Harvey is told to kill the spy we know to be himself; he manages to make it all languorous and tiresome, abetted in his general stupefaction by Mia Farrow, Tom Courtenay, Peter Cook, all of whom shuffle around as if waiting for the funny lines director Anthony Mann promised them. Only Lionel Stander ignored the general apathy and hams it up as Russian spymaster; 1968. (c)

Danger By My Side XX Maureen Connell, a little star who flickered briefly in 1959, working undercover to avenge her brother's murder; director, Charles Saunders. (b/w)

Dangerous √ Bette Davis won an Oscar for this bravura performance as actress saved from drink and herself by Franchot Tone. Alfred E. Green directed in 1935. (b/w)

The Dangerous Days of Kiowa Jones √ Robert Horton is the awkwardly-named hero in this superior western, taking two captured murderers to jail, meeting up with Diane Baker, surprisingly driving a covered wagon around at the time. As the baddies, Nehemiah Persoff and Sal Mineo turn in strong performances, and the whole effort was a restrained and distinguished first film for director Alex March; 1966. (c)

Dangerous Mission √ The Glacier National Park is the real star of this otherwise heavy-going drama with Victor Mature and William Bendix on the side of Good; Vincent Price representing Evil; Louis King seems happier with the scenery than the automatons he is directing. Piper Laurie saw a murder and fled there; 1954. (b/w)

Dangerous Moonlight X Brian Desmond Hurst's 1941 romantic tear-jerker that launched the Warsaw Concerto upon us. Famous Polish pianist Anton Walbrook meets American journalist Sally Gray in shattered Warsaw, escapes to join a bomber squadron to avenge his country. (b/w)

Dangerous When Wet X Routine Esther Williams swimerama in which she is member of family swimming the Channel under sponsorship of a drink called Liquapep. She falls for French prince Fernando Lamas. Small compensation from Charlotte Greenwood as her Ma and Jack Carson as Liquapep's promoter. Charles Walters directed; 1953. (c)

Danger Route XX Hard to care about this cold-spy melo. Richard Johnson fails to inject spy with any charm and director Seth Holt to discipline a wayward and gnomic story; 1967. (c)

Danger Within √ PoW-camp drama – which soldier is the informer: Richard Todd, Bernard Lee, Michael Wilding, Richard Attenborough, Dennis Price, Donald Houston, William Franklyn, Vincent Ball? Don Chaffey keeps you idly guessing; 1958. (b/w)

Darby's Rangers X William Wellman directed this yarn about assault troops in Second World War led by James Garner, and it was not one of his better efforts. Jack Warden, Stuart Whitman are among supports; 1958. (b/w)

The Daring Game X Lloyd Bridges in his *Sea Hunt* kit doing his underwater bit, combined this time with parachuting, to save American scientist and daughter trapped in South America; unconvincing story is just about saved by the special effects; veteran director Laslo Benedek has tried hard; 1968. (c)

The Dark at the Top of the Stairs √√ If William Inge play was more profound in the theatre, this version of family - and - neighbours small - town drama, with Eve Arden, Angela Lansbury, Dorothy McGuire, Robert Preston, escapes banality. Delbert Mann; 1960. (c)

Dark City √ Charlton Heston made his modern-dress debut in this 1950 thriller as a shady bookmaker who becomes target of a hit-man. Ed Begley and Jack Webb are his confederates; Lizabeth Scott, Viveca Lindfors, Dean Jagger complete an impressive cast for director William Dieterle. (b/w)

The Dark Man XXX Double murder in seaside town brings out the worst in British B-pictures, including Maxwell

Reed, William Hartnell, Sam Kydd; director, Jeffrey Dell; 1950. (b/w)

The Dark Mirror √ Trick photography is better than the plot as Olivia de Havilland plays twin sisters – one goodie, one baddie. Lew Ayres makes an unconvincing analyst; Robert Siodmak directed; 1946. (b/w)

Dark of the Sun √ Thriller set in troubled Congo well-directed by ex-cameraman Jack Cardiff in 1968. Rod Taylor and Jim Brown are mercenaries, hardly heroic figures, one would have thought. (c)

Dark Passage √√ Humphrey Bogart escapes from prison to prove he isn't wife-killer; helper is Lauren Bacall; Agnes Moorehead among splendid cast; tautly and excitingly directed by Delmer Daves; 1947. (b/w)

The Dark Past √ How a psychiatrist tries to talk his way out of being held hostage by potty killer; William Holden, Lee J. Cobb; director Rudolph Maté; 1948. (b/w)

Dark Places √ Enjoyable if grisly horror pic with some sturdy players – Christopher Lee, Robert Hardy, Joan Collins, Jane Birkin – mostly loony in some form or other. Will they find the £200,000 in the old dark house? What else will they find? Don Sharp; 1973. (c)

Dark Purpose XX Hammy old Rossano Brazzi is the heavy, conning lightweight Shirley Jones to come to Amalfi to catalogue his paintings; but who has he hidden upstairs, Rochester-style? It's terribly hard to care and veteran director George Marshall can't make you; 1964. (c)

Dark Star √√ Cult success which matched *Star Wars*'s lavishness with intelligence. Blowing up unstable stars is crew's job, but they don't notice their own troubles until too late. Director was John Carpenter, who went on to make such hits as *Halloween*; 1974. (c)

Darling √√ Overrated triple Oscar-winning (the 1965 doorstops for female actress, Julie Christie; story, Frederic Raphael; costumes, Julie Harris) purports to show that upward drift of mod model – including abortions, orgies, conversion, a prince for a husband-only brings unhappiness. John Schlesinger's skill only partly conceals emptiness of the film, Dirk Bogarde among saving graces. (b/w)

Darling Lilli XX Overblown First World War spy comedy in which Julie Andrews, directed by ever-loving husband Blake Edwards, fell flat on her face in 1969. Rock Hudson plays gamely opposite her, but the whole shebang is likely to make you wince. (c)

The Darwin Adventure X 1971 movie that has been displaced by the longer, more complete and more authentic BBC series made in 1978. This one had Nicholas Clay as the explorer-naturalist-theoretician and a cast of hardworking, undistinguished minor British players; Jack Couffer directed with some pains. (c)

A Date with a Lonely Girl √ Any female character named T. R. Baskin and always called 'T. R.' is obviously in danger of plunging a movie into sentimentality. When Candice Bergen, the most overrated actress in American serious cinema, plays her, you can be sure that cuteness will outweigh truth. However, Peter Boyle's presence as a nice guy prepared to exploit her sexually, is some compensation. James Caan, as his straight friend, is less welcome; Herbert Ross, 1971. (c)

David and Bathsheba √ Slightly better than the usual Hollywood Biblical epic in that it has Gregory Peck giving the appearance of integrity as only he knows how. For the rest, it's stilted dialogue, a doll-like Susan Hayward as Bathie, and competent direction by Henry King, particularly of the battle scenes. The supporting cast doesn't much; 1951. (c)

David and Lisa √√ Outstanding Frank and Eleanor Perry movie underrated by the industry in 1962 (never properly released) but hailed by critics and gaining Academy Award nomination. Keir Dullea, Janet Margolin as inmates of school for disturbed adolescents who reach out for mutual help. (b/w)

David Copperfield √√ (1) 1934: David Selznick proved two important lessons: don't tamper with a classic; don't worry about a picture's length, as long as it is good. Reminded that Dickens made no mention of Micawber's juggling, W. C. Fields (who played him) replied: 'He probably forgot it.' Freddie Bartholomew, Basil Rathbone, Roland Young; George Cukor directed. (b/w)

David Copperfield √ (2) 1969: inferior in every way except casting (Micawber: Ralph Richardson rather more faithful to the original; Mr Creakle: marvellous horrid Olivier; Ron Moody's slimy Uriah Heep; Wendy Hiller, Michael Redgrave, Susan Hampshire, Edith Evans), this slow and oddly time-structured version, directed by Delbert Mann, doesn't satisfy either Dickensians or non-Dickensians. (c)

Davy Crockett √ Fess Parker in the Disney live-actioner that did so well in 1955. The King of the Wild Front Ear has Buddy Ebsen to help him keep law'n'order's racoon hat on. (c)

Dawn at Socorro √ Standard western about gambler who intends to reform (Rory Calhoun) and Piper Laurie as the girl who prays for him in the shoot-out; George Sherman; 1954. (c)

The Dawn Patrol √ 1938 remake of 1930 flying adventure, *The Dawn Patrol*, using original footage. Errol Flynn was in the Richard Bathelmess part of roustabout who sobers up when he takes command. Basil Rathbone, David Niven, Donald Crisp, Barry Fitzgerald, Peter Willes among familiar names directed by Edmund Goulding. (b/w)

A Day at the Races √√ 'Marry me and I'll never look at another horse,' says Groucho to Margaret Dumont; and Marxists won't need reminding of Chico's ice-cream vendor-cum-racing-tipster. Sam Wood; 1937. (b/w)

A Day in the Death of Joe Egg √√ Example of the inferiority of the cinema to the stage in some crucial respects. In the theatre, Peter Nichols's depiction of life with a seriously spastic child (he is the father of one) could be seen without having to study the child. On the screen this wasn't possible, and the whole balance is altered. Alan Bates lacks the comic seriousness that Joe Melia brought to the role of the father in the theatre; Janet Suzman projects the mother well enough, and one is carried along with her attempt at euthanasia. Peter Medak directed sympathetically, in 1971. (c)

Day of the Badman √ Fred Mac-Murray in standard western (1958) about judge determined to hang despite condemned man's brothers trying to free him; Harry Keller. (c)

The Day of the Dolphin √ Bizarre and uncomfortably sensational account of how two dolphins are kidnapped and trained to destroy the President's yacht. George C. Scott makes a puzzled scientist; director Mike Nichols did his best with material that could have been purely sentimental; 1973. (c)

The Day of the Jackal √ Straightforward account of an event that did not happen, the near-assassination of President de Gaulle in 1963. Since you know he is not going to die, all the elaborate preparations made by Edward Fox fail to thrill. Fred Zinnemann was much-praised for this effort at direction in 1973, but it's really a ramshackle job, as when the otherwise precise killer forgets to arrange an escape route. The backgrounds are authentic but the English cast is oh, so English. (c)

The Day of the Locust √√ Despite some splendid set-pieces, notably the riot at the end outside Grauman's Chinese Theatre, John Schlesinger's 1974 version of Nathaniel West's novel misses in evoking either the forked vision of the original or Hollywood as it was in 1938. Caricatures abound: Donald Sutherland is the passive set designer; Karen Black the whore he worships; Burgess Meredith her ex-vaudevillian father; Geraldine Page, the faith healer who doesn't. (c)

Day of the Outlaw √ Two days of terror in a cattle town changes a lot of lives, including those of Robert Ryan (as herd-owner), Tina Louise (another man's wife he fancies), Burl Ives (leader of the hell-raisers); strong direction by André de Toth makes this 1959 western a cut above most. (b/w)

The Day of the Triffids X Disappointing version of John Wyndham's novel about scary veg. and blinding of Earth's inhabitants, preparatory to taking over, has as least one superior sequence – just before the blind turn on the the blind in frustrated anger. And Janette Scott gives a better performance as scientist fighting the menace than director Steve Sekeley has managed to get from the rest of his somewhat inadequate cast, led by Howard Keel(!); 1963. (c)

The Day the Earth Caught Fire √√ One of the best sci-fi movies ever made in Britain, this is the one about the earth's axis having been tilted by atomic explosion so that we get too dangerously near the sun. Set mostly in the *Daily Express* offices, it starred a brisk and likeable Edward Judd and Janet Munro, both excellent, and a whole gallery of believable performers. Val Guest co-wrote with Wolf Mankowitz, produced, directed and never did better; 1962. (b/w)

The Day the Fish Came Out XX Pretentious Michael Cacoyannis rubbish about seeking planeload of atomic material on Greek isle; the second-eleven cast (Tom Courtenay, Sam Wanamaker, Colin Blakeley, Candice Bergen) don't help; 1969. (*c*)

The Day the Earth Stood Still √ Superior sci-fi about convincingly wooden Michael Rennie visiting from another planet. Pat Neal, Sam Jaffe play supports to flying saucer; Robert Wise made it most watchable; 1951. (*b/w*)

The Day the World Ended √ Roger Corman sci-fi about small group that survived atomic radiation; Richard Denning, Lori Nelson, Adele Jergens; 1956. (*b/w*)

The Day They Robbed the Bank of England X Only Peter O'Toole (restrained and wry in 1960, before he started believing his own publicity) makes this standard caper movie worth looking at. Nominal star Aldo Ray is a bit of a pill; supports Elizabeth Sellars, Hugh Griffith, Kieron Moore likewise. John Guillermin. (*c*)

Days of Wine and Roses √√ Jack Lemmon's an alcoholic, marries Lee Remick and gets her on the bottle, too. Daddy Charles Bickford's appalled; AA member Jack Klugman tries to help them kick it. It's all a bit pat, but Blake Edwards does tight (sorry) directorial job that falls just short of slickness; 1962. (*b/w*)

Dayton's Devils XX Rather wearisome caper about stealing 1½ million from US Army base; Jack Shea hasn't got the tautness in his direction that's needed for a good robbery movie, and cast of Leslie Nielsen, Rory Calhoun and unknowns haven't the charisma; 1968. (*c*)

D-Day The Sixth of June XX Weak effort with Robert Taylor unconvincing as American soldier about to invade Germany, which he eventually does most unconvincingly. Only Edmond O'Brien turns in anything like a performance as a blustering GI under Henry Koster's flaccid direction; 1956. (*c*)

Dead Cert XX That's what director and co-writer Tony Richardson must have thought he was on to in 1974 with one of Dick Francis's yarns of doped horses and the Grand National. Alas, he comes off at the first fence, with all sorts of racing howlers, lack of genuine atmosphere; wooden acting by horses and humans alike. (*c*)

Dead End √ Famous 1937 blockbuster shot in one huge set, with gang of delinquents torn between baddie Humphrey Bogart and goodie Joel McCrea. So is Sylvia Sidney. William Wyler directed and Claire Trevor, Marjorie Main, Allen Jenkins provided stronger support than the unconvincing Dead End Kids. The whole thing is intolerably twee under the tough-guy wrappings, but so was almost everything Sam Goldwyn touched. (*b/w*)

Deadfall √ Bryan Forbes out of his depth trying to make a plushy Riviera caper into a signficant character study. He's not helped by the performances of Michael Caine, Giovanna Ralli, Eric Portman and Mrs Bryan Forbes; 1968. (*c*)

Dead Heat on a Merry-go-Round √√ Cheerful caper about robbing an airport when it's all taken up with the arrival of VIP; James Coburn carries it disarmingly, and writer-director Bernard Girard provides some nifty touches; 1965. (*c*)

Deadlier Than the Male XX Exceptionally boring and tedious Miss J. Bond thriller with the gimmick that it's the ladies (Elke Sommer, Sylvia Koscina – groan!) who do the killing. Nigel Green employs them, Richard Johnson as Bulldog Drummond exposes them. A waste of all their time – don't add yours; Ralph Thomas; 1967. (*c*)

Deadline √√ Strong newspaper stuff from Richard Brooks, directing a particularly well-cast Humphrey Bogart as Front Page-type managing editor fighting to save a dying daily with crime scoop in last issue. Solid support from Ethel Barrymore, Ed Begley, Kim Hunter, Paul Stewart, Martin Gabel; 1952. (*b/w*)

The Deadly Affair √ Sidney Lumet must have hoped that this would get under the tape before sordid-spy cycle ended, but 1967 was too late for this *In From the Cold*-type thriller, even though it was from John le Carré's *Call for the Dead*. James Mason and Simone Signoret do their best, but it has got the chilly breath of failure about it all – of course, it's meant to have, but not this deep. (*c*)

The Deadly Bees XX – but not so deadly as this slow-moving, creaky old movie, which has Frank Finlay as an obvious nut and Suzanne Leigh as an obviously dim girl who takes refuge (hah!) in his house; Freddie Francis; 1967. (*c*)

The Deadly Companions √√ A remarkable first film by Sam Peckinpah in 1962, foreshadowing many of the themes and excitements that later established him (*The Wild Bunch, Straw Dogs*) as an original if abrasive talent. The escorting of a coffin over Indian territory becomes a violent and riveting parable; Maureen O'Hara, Brian Keith, Steve Cochran. (*c*)

The Deadly Mantis √ New York is threatened by giant insect from the Arctic; can Craig Stevens save the city? Director Nathan Juran; 1957. (*b/w*)

Deadly Strangers XX Hayley Mills in lame thriller that depends on withholding information from the audience to build tension and is totally unconvincing when the denouement comes. Sidney Hayers directed, in 1974, with dogged determination, but you can only feel sorry for actors like Peter Jeffrey and Sterling Hayden for having to act in such tosh for their daily bread. (*c*)

The Deadly Trackers XX If Sam Fuller had directed this western, as originally intended, it might have worked. But he and star Richard Harris got across each other and Barry Shear took over. Unfortunately, the new director seems to have allowed Harris's ego to override the revenge story, and the result is an over-exposed hunk of manhood under the impression that he is Marlon Brando; 1973. (*c*)

Dead Image √ Bette Davis playing murderous twins, planning to do herself in and then pretend to be herself; of course it's all absurd hokum, but as *Time* said in 1964: 'Two Bette Davises are better than one . . . exuberantly uncorseted, her torso looks like a gunnysack full of galoshes . . . .her face like a U2 photograph of Utah. And her acting, as always, isn't really acting; it's shameless showing-off. But just try to look away'. Paul Henried. (*b/w*)

Dead of Night √√ Classic 1945 chiller in which Cavalcanti, Basil Dearden, Robert Hamer each directed episodes, dreams within a dream, most haunting of which is Michael Redgrave's ventriloquist controlled by his doll. (*b/w*)

Dead or Alive √ Early (1968) spaghetti western: Alex Cord is an epileptic bounty-hunter, Robert Ryan a pardoning governor, Arthur Kennedy a US Marshal. Director, Franco Giraldi. (*c*)

Dead Reckoning √√ Humphrey Bogart, unofficially investigating death of paratrooper pal, finds that Lizabeth Scott (the poor man's Lauren Bacall) is at the centre of the web; John Cromwell; 1946. (*b/w*)

Dear Brigitte XX Why a star of the stature of James Stewart permits himself to be embroiled in this kind of farrago is beyond comprehension. He's the father of an 8-year-old boy who's a whizz at picking winners but won't do so until he has met Brigitte Bardot. So – would you credit it? – Jimmy schlepps him all the way to France and BB does us all a favour with a guest appearance. Positively embarrassing all round, and Henry Koster (producer as well as director) should blush; 1965. (*c*)

Dear Heart X Glycerine magazine story about spinster Geraldine Page meeting lonely Glenn Ford and getting together; Delbert Mann's poor taste runs right down to the weak casting which includes Angela Lansbury and Michael Anderson Jr.; 1965. (*b/w*)

Death Curse of Tartu XXX Dreadful nonsense about reincarnations of a witch doctor protecting graves from desecration – and the plot's the best thing about it; William Grefe is the name of the director; 1968. (*c*)

Death in Venice √√ Thanks to Dirk Bogarde's beautifully-judged performance, and Visconti's evocation of the turn-of-the-century Venice Lido, Thomas Mann's paean to paedophilia almost works. As it is, there is enough sumptuousness and sensuality to satisfy; 1971. (*c*)

Death is a Woman XXX A really awful attempt to show that Patsy Ann Noble is an actress – and one capable of playing a triple murderess. And the worst thing about it is that she's the best thing in the picture. Desperately padded and badly made in all departments, this stands as a monument of inefficient moviemaking. Director Frederic Goode must take most of the blame, although anyone who accepted any assignment having read Wally Bosco's script obviously needed the money; 1967. (*c*)

Death of a Gunfighter √ Old-style Marshal Widmark won't resign, so he has to be bumped off out of office is theme of this unconvincing western. But Richard Widmark, Lena Horne, John Saxon, Carroll O'Connor get some mileage out of the improbabilities, thanks to direction by 'Allan Smithee', a pseudonym for Don Siegel and Robert Totten; 1969. (*c*)

Death of a Salesman √√ More important for its influence than its profundity, this filming of Arthur Miller's stage success about failure hopped effortlessly about in time and space, as it traced Fredric March's reasons for not wanting his son to follow his saga in search of the fast buck. Competently directed by Laslo Benedek, 1951, it did rather romanticise the stage-play's meaner salesman. (b/w)

Death Wish √ Nasty but effective thriller in which urban liberal Charles Bronson is transformed into the Nemesis of muggers by an attack on his wife and daughter. Everyone loved him in 1974 – the picture's police (who let him go) and the cinema audiences who cheered him on. Singlehanded he brings down New York's mugging rate, thus 'proving' that the birch, capital punishment and summary execution should be introduced immediately for all crimes of violence. The gospel according to Michael Winner. (c)

Deception √ Hysterical hokum played to the hilt by pianist Claude Rains and benefactress Bette Davis; directed by Irving Rapper in 1946. (b/w)

Decision at Sundown √ Superior Budd Boetticher western has Randolph Scott arriving to kill John Carroll thinking he was responsible for his wife's death during the Civil War; 1957. (c)

The Decks Ran Red √ Broderick Crawford's murderous plan is to kill off the crew of a rusty old tub for the salvage money; James Mason, the cap'n, is out to thwart him; made by the Andrew and Virginia Stone reliable team of thrill-raisers in 1958. (c)

Decline and Fall X By avoiding doing Waugh's novel in its only possible setting, the twenties, John Krish has thrown away most of the chance to make this progress towards enlightenment work. What's left is a rather ordinary tale, not more than competently acted by Robin Phillips and Genevieve Page, and allowing too much indulgence to Donald Wolfit and Leo McKern; 1968. (c)

The Deep Blue Sea √ Vivien Leigh as tragic heroine, with Kenneth More as her RAF lover. Eric Portman and Emlyn Williams are fine in slow, stagey version (1955) of Terence Rattigan's play. (c)

Deep End √√ Remarkable attempt by Polish director Jerzy Skolimowski to show the initiation of a 15-year-old into the mysteries of sex, set mostly in a London municipal swimming pool. John Moulder-Brown is convincing as the lad; Jane Asher makes an impres-

sive temptress; Diana Dors has a powerful little cameo as she hugs him to her ample bosom in orgiastic chattering; 1970. (c)

Deep In My Heart XX Pretty awful musical biography of one of the weaker popular composers – Sigmund Romberg – soggily cast (Jose Ferrer, Merle Oberon, Helen Traubel, Walter Pidgeon, Paul Henreid) and directed by Stanley Donen; 1954. (c)

The Deep Six XX Rather nasty and embarrassing Second World War actioner that features Alan Ladd, ashamed of his previous pacifism, leading a dangerous naval attack; Rudolph Maté; 1958. (c)

The Deerslayer XX Lex Barker, Forrest Tucker, Rita Moreno in disappointing adaptation of James Fenimore Cooper's novel about white boy brought up by Indians; Kurt Neumann; 1957. (c)

The Defector √ Unusual espionage thriller in that it is 1966 Franco-German co-production, with Montgomery Clift in last role, Hardy Kruger as communist agent and Jean-Luc Godard *acting*. Raoul Lévy directing. (b/w)

The Defiant Ones √√ Stanley Kramer's still powerful 1958 racial drama of two Southern chain-gang convicts on the run. Superb performances from Sidney Poitier and Tony Curtis. (b/w)

The Delicate Delinquent √ In this 1957 comedy Jerry Lewis went it alone for the first time as a petty crook open to reform. Don McGuire directed and wrote the script, which is more helpful to Lewis than some of his later mush. (b/w)

Deliverance √√√ Brilliant and involving film about city-dwellers Jon Voight, Burt Reynolds, Ned Beatty, Ronny Cox vaingloriously braving the rapids to prove how rugged they are. Terrible things happen to them on the way. Exciting, involving and meticulously directed by John Boorman, in 1972, it works on several levels. (c)

Demetrius and the Gladiators √ The 1954 follow-up to the previous year's epic, *The Robe*, stars Victor Mature, not the most sensitive of actors, and features Anne Bancroft before Hollywood realised she was Academy Award potential. (c)

Dentist in the Chair XX Usual sort of deadly British comedy, circa 1960. This one has Bob Monkhouse as dental student, grimacing with Peggy Cummins. Director, Don Chaffey. (*c*)

Dentist on the Job XX Painful Bob Monkhouse 1961 comedy about endorsing toothpaste. Kenneth Conner, Shirley Eaton; directed by C. M. Pennington-Richards; 1961. (*b/w*)

Derby Day XX Boring collection of British character actors (Anna Neagle, Michael Wilding, Googie Withers, Gordon Harker among them) converge on Epsom for four linked yarns all solved by the big race; Herbert Wilcox; 1952. (*b/w*)

The Desert Fox √√ Exciting and cool account of Field-Marshal Rommel, the North African war and his part in anti-Hitler plot. James Mason, Luther Adler, Everett Sloane; directed by Henry Hathaway; 1951. (*b/w*)

Desert Legion X With Alan Ladd in the Foreign Legion; utterly predictable; director Joseph Peveney; 1953. (*c*)

The Desert Rats √√ Second World War suspenser about the siege of Tobruk saved by Richard Burton's tough officer slowly winning respect of troops. James Mason does his splendid Rommel (as in *The Desert Fox*) and there's an outstanding performance from Robert Newton as professor turned soldier. Robert Wise's 1953 direction is action-packed. (*b/w*)

The Desert Song XX Extremely boring version of the old Sigmund Romberg operetta; Gordon Macrae, Kathryn Grayson. Only Raymond Massey gives it flicker of life; H. Bruce Humberstone; 1953. (*c*)

Designing Woman √ Stylish 1957 comedy directed by Vincente Minnelli with Gregory Peck as sports-writer who marries Lauren Bacall after whirlwind courtship and finds that she's top fashion designer. Nub is conflict between their worlds. Dolores Gray, Sam Levene give strong support. (*c*)

Desirée XX A quite awful rendering of the Napoleon story with Marlon Brando ludicrous as Bonaparte and Jean Simmons not much better as the lady of the title. Daniel Taradash's script is balderdash, and the luckless Henry Koster stumbles directorially about letting the chat go on and on, and vainly trying to marshal the rest of his weak cast to little effect; 1954. (*c*)

Desire in the Dust X Ex-con Ken Scott gets mixed up with Raymond Burr's family, and the bloodhounds come out in an overcooked ending; William F. Claxton; 1960. (*b/w*)

Desire Under the Elms √ This is the poorly-cast (Sophia Loren, Burl Ives, Anthony Perkins), poorly-set (you can smell the studio arc lamps burning, not the farmyard dung), poorly directed (Delbert Mann) 1958 version of Eugene O'Neill's long, passionate drama. A pity because basically it's splendid. (*b/w*)

The Desk Set √√ Katharine Hepburn heads a research team threatened by new office broom Spencer Tracy; also in the cast are Gig Young and Joan Blondell. Do you need to know any more except that Walter Lang let them enjoy themselves hugely in 1957? (*c*)

The Desperados X Parson Jack Palance rides into town with his sons ready to avenge his dead wife; son Vince Edwards rebels, but Pop goes after him, too. It all ends badly. As a matter of fact, it starts and goes on badly, too. Unfortunately, director Henry Levin makes it all seem loose and lacking in tension; Palance does well enough but everyone else in sight seems uncertain. 1969. (*c*)

The Desperate Hours √√ High tension nail-biter as three escaped convicts hide out in a suburban home, terrorising a family. With Humphrey Bogart at his meanest. Directed 1955 by William Wyler. (*b/w*)

Destination Gobi √ Workaday war pic, sharply directed in 1952 by Robert Wise, with Richard Widmark, Don Taylor trekking through the desert. (*c*)

Destination Inner Space X Undersea sci-fi drama about monster terrorising marine research station; looks like director Francis D. Lyon was told to economise on the special effects and the result isn't as scary as it should be; Sheree North loons around; 1966. (*c*)

Destination Moon X This was huge success in 1950, thanks to George Pal's meticulously-assembled special effects team, but underneath the scientific blah it's a hollow vessel with poor story and acting, largely overlooked by director Irving Pichel as he struggled with his other priorities. Today, it looks pretty ludicrous all round. However, any serious student of sci-fi must have it logged. (*c*)

The Destructors XX Despite some lively moments and the occasional imaginative touch from director Francis D. Lyon, this is essentially just another Chinese communist-spy-foiled - by - American - counter - intelligence plot that rarely wholly grips. Richard Egan's physical flabbiness (it was made in 1967 when he was 46) is excused by some lines of dialogue suggesting that he's afraid of middle age, but he has got a flabby film to go with him. (c)

Destry √ This is *Destry Rides Again*, remade in 1954 without the satire. Now it's just Audie Murphy as sheriff who keeps law'n' order without using the guns he's shy of; George Marshall, same director as classic version, seems only too aware of the stars he lacks. (c)

Destry Rides Again √√ A landmark both as a western and in Hollywood comedy was this 1939 slam-banger with James Stewart as pacifist marshal, Marlene Dietrich singing ' See What the Boys in the Back Room Will Have', Una Merkel fighting with her in classic unladylike brawl, and Brian Donlevy as the heavy. George Marshall put it all together with wit while retaining respect for the conventions of the oater. (b/w)

The Detective √√ If only this had been directed by someone with flair instead of Gordon Douglas it might have reached real heights; as it is, it's still an exciting, unusual murder thriller with a domestically-troubled cop, believably played by Frank Sinatra, arresting a man he suspects isn't guilty of the murder. Original references to homosexuality and other real-life events may result in a few cuts; hopefully it won't be butchered too much; 1968. (c)

Detective Story √√ One day in New York precinct station, with burglars, shoplifters and sundry crooks dealt with by contrasting detectives, concentrating on bent Kirk Douglas. Made in 1951 by William Wyler. (b/w)

The Devil at Four O'Clock √ Frank Sinatra and Spencer Tracy are two of a quartet who volunteer to bring out patients and staff of volcanic island's leper colony when the eruption occurs. Mervyn Le Roy could be trusted to wring every ounce of action and sentiment out of this basically phoney yarn; 1961. (c)

The Devil Doll √√ Legendary Tod Browning directed this fascinating version of Devil's Island escapee (Lionel Barrymore) shrinking humans to doll-size, in 1936. Maureen O'Sullivan, Frank Lawton shone. (b/w)

Devil Doll √ Modest but genuinely creepy little thriller using the ventriloquist idea from *Dead of Night* to transfer 'soul' into dummy; William Sylvester fine; director Lindsay Shonteff; 1964. (b/w)

The Devil Is a Woman √ Classic Dietrich-von Sternberg drama slowly builds up as Cesar Romero disregards fate of his best friend at the hands of temptress Marlene. Much enthused about by buffs, but rather creaky to modern eyes; 1935. (b/w)

The Devil Rides Out X Surely a better version of Dennis Wheatley's yarn about black magic could have been contrived than this stilted, silly effort? Director Terence Fisher must take a large part of the blame, though script and production values are equally null. Christopher Lee and Charles Gray just flounder; 1968. (c)

The Devils X Unpleasant piling-on of agonies by Ken Russell, using John Whiting's serious play from Aldous Huxley's factual book as starting-point for hysterical piece of exhibitionism. Vanessa Redgrave is to be pitied; 1970. (c)

The Devil's Agent XXX Scandalously bad and mutilated in the cutting room. It's supposed to be one of those double-agent dreams, but if you or anyone else (including Peter van Eyck, Macdonald Carey, Christopher Lee or Marius Goring) can work out what's happening or, at the end, what happened, you are gifted with second sight. Director John Paddy Carstairs obviously gave up early; 1964. (b/w)

The Devil's Brigade X Another attempt at *The Dirty Dozen*'s box-office bonanza doesn't come off under Andrew McLaglen's so-so direction. The battle scenes aren't as good as they should be, and William Holden can't hold it together. He looks awfully tired, poor chap, and no wonder; 1968. (c)

Devil's Canyon √ Marshal, jailed for self-defence shoot-out, becomes involved in prison riot; Dale Robertson, Virginia Mayo; director Alfred L. Werker was a worker; 1953. (c)

The Devil's Disciple √ Olivier is best thing about rather uninspired adaptation of Shaw's War of Independence drama directed by Guy Hamilton in 1959, in a different class from Burt Lancaster, Kirk Douglas; but Harry Andrews supports strongly. (b/w)

The Devil's 8 XX Federal agent breaks up 'moonshine' liquor gang, using it to gain power in the South; Christopher George just isn't up to this sort of part and such weak casting as Fabian doesn't help Burt Topper's efforts at authenticity; 1969. (c)

The Devil-Ship Pirates √ Rather a good Hammer movie, which says something about the nature of collaborators as a Spanish privateer puts into a Cornish port in 1588 and cons the local squire and villagers into thinking that Spain has won the war and they are part of occupying force. Christopher Lee is unbending as the captain of the ship although Natasha Pyne makes a weak heroine; conscientiously and occasionally imaginatively directed by Don Sharp; 1964. (c)

Devils of Darkness √ Some efforts have been made to produce as authentic a picture about vampires as possible and the care pays off; set in the West Country and Chelsea, it has Hubert Noel as a 400-year-old Frenchman who needs the blood of an occasional virgin to keep going; directed by Lance Comfort; 1965. (c)

The Devil's Own (more likely to turn up as **The Witches**, so see under this title).

Diagnosis: Murder XX Christopher Lee as baddie doctor chased by Inspector Jon Finch in 1975 actioner that hardly sustains the interest, although there is a certain amount of tricksy plotting; Sidney Hayers churned it out. (c)

Dial M for Murder √√ It took Hitchcock only thirty-six days to direct this theatre classic in 1954. Tennis player Ray Milland is worried about rich wife Grace Kelly's friendship with novelist Robert Cummings. Princess Grace loses her cool but will she lose her life? Tension runs high. (c)

Diamond Head X Charlton Heston playing the heavy brother in Hawaii when sister Yvette Mimieux, not one of the greatest actresses of our time, wants to marry 'beneath her'. As cobbled by Guy Green in 1963, it's strictly for the pineapples. (c)

Diamond Horseshoe X Poorly-cast musical with Betty Grable renouncing all for medical student Dick Haymes; set in gaudy real-life nightclub. Only real moment of pleasure – song 'The More I See You' muted by singing; George Seaton; 1945. (c)

Diamonds Are Forever √ More Bond set-pieces, linked by a nothing plot. The last 007 epic for Sean Connery, it had Jill St. John and Bruce Cabot among those elaborately threatening and threatened; Guy Hamilton; 1971. (c)

Diamonds for Breakfast XX Weak comedy about diamond caper (the Soviet government handily keeping the Russian Crown Jewels in English country house!) with Marcello Mastroianni utterly unbelievable as thief so irresistible to the ladies that seven of them act as his accomplices. Directed by Christopher Morahan; 1968. (c)

Diane X The only interesting fact about this costumer is that it was written by Christopher Isherwood, though you wouldn't notice by the time David Miller has finished directing the inadequate cast of Lana Turner, Pedro Amendariz, Roger Moore. It's supposed to be about the relationship of France's Francis I and Diane de Poitiers, but isn't; 1956. (c)

Diary of a Bachelor XX Mild little comedy of engaged fella who reforms only to find that his wife isn't as pure as he'd thought; director Sandy Howard's cast were unknowns and have stayed that way; 1964. (b/w)

The Diary of a Chambermaid √√ (1) Paulette Goddard in the 1946 Jean Renoir American production managed remarkably well with the nuances of Mirabeau's novel of sexual deviation, mad neighbours and villainous valets. (b/w)

The Diary of a Chambermaid √ (2) Jeanne Moreau was, by comparison, disappointing – especially as one hoped much more from her – in Bunuel's 1964 French version. (both b/w)

Diary of a Mad Housewife √√√ Brilliantly-funny adaptation of Sue Kaufman's observant novel of a middle-class marriage, with Richard Benjamin superb as pretentious husband, driving wife Carrie Snodgress to extreme action. Frank Perry did a scintillating directing job in 1970. (c)

Diary of a Madman X De Maupassant story of magistrate who thinks evil spirit in man whom he condemned has entered into him, hokumised by Vincent Price and director Reginald Le Borg; 1963. (c)

The Diary of Anne Frank √√ True story of Nazi occupation of Amsterdam seen through eyes of 13-year-old couldn't fail; although George Stevens's 1959 casting of Millie Perkins in main part nearly makes it founder. It's saved by supporting performances from Shelley Winters (it won her an Oscar), Ed Wynn, Joseph Schildkraut. (b/w)

Did You Hear the One About the Travelling Saleslady? XX If you happen to be a fan of Phyllis Diller you'll enjoy this mishmash about a crazy inventor in the American backwoods. Otherwise, not. Director Don Weis clearly didn't know how to handle her talents; 1967. (c)

Dilemma XX Peter Halliday finds a body in his bathroom. For some reason he assumes that his wife, Ingrid Hafner, is the murderer. He disposes of the remains under the floorboards but when wife arrives, she says she didn't do it. Director Peter Maxwell has a team of cut-price British players to fill in the next hour or so; 1962. (b/w)

Dillinger √√ (1) Exciting account of Public Enemy No. 1, tautly played by Lawrence Tierney, with Elisha Cook Jr. and Edmund Lowe shooting along; Max Nosseck; 1945. (b/w)

Dillinger √√ (2) Exciting gangster biopic set in 1933, made in 1973 by John Milius, breaking out from scriptwriting (*Magnum Force*). Told sparsely and unpretentiously, it coaxed convincing performances from Warren Oates, Richard Dreyfuss and Baby Face Nelson. (c)

Dimension Four XXX Phoney little Red Menace (they're going to blow up Los Angeles with an atom bomb for some reason) yarn made even less interesting by a sci-fi gimmick in which the hero can go forward or backward in time by pressing a button; hardly surprising that the Reds are foiled, is it? Jeffrey Hunter and France Nuyen are trapped in this nonsense; directed by Franklin Adreon; 1967. (c)

Dingaka XXX South African drama, in line with racist government's policy to show how primitive and backward native tribesmen are; Stanley Baker is tough lawyer, Juliet Prowse his wife; Jamie Uys directed; 1964. (c)

Dinner at Eight √ Classic but, one must admit, rather over-rated MGM 1933 drama in which Jean Harlow argues with Marie Dressler; Wallace Beery is boorish; John Barrymore articulates; plus brother Lionel, Lee Tracy, Edmund Lowe, Billie Burke. Directed by George Cukor from the George S. Kaufman and Edna Ferber play. (b/w)

Dirty Dingus Magee X Sad to see the mature (in 1970) Frank Sinatra capering about in poor comic western, with captures, escapes, hiding treasure and getting into scrapes with ladies (Anne Jackson, Lois Nettleton, Michele Carey). Main opponent is George Kennedy, and director Burt Kennedy (no kin) fails to provide much in the way of laughs. (c)

The Dirty Dozen √√ Lee Marvin, Ernest Borgnine, Charles Bronson, John Cassavetes, Jim Brown, George Kennedy, Trini Lopez and half a dozen other dirties are released from jail to form suicide squad against the Nazis. Brilliantly made by Robert Aldrich. See it when it appears, and whatever you may think of its morals, violence or subject, you'll be gripped; 1967. (c)

Dirty Harry √√ Unpleasant as Clint Eastwood's cop is, there is so much excitement in this 'loner' plot about his rule-breaking obsession to nail killer Andy Robinson that it carries the audience along, unprotesting. Don Siegel is past master at thrillers, and this one is probably his best; 1971. (c)

Dirty Little Billy √ Dirty little movie with Michael J. Pollard as 17-year-old in the West learning about life and sex from gunmen and whores; there's a certain amount of keen observation from director Stan Dragoti; 1972. (c)

Dirty Mary, Crazy Larry X . . . and Silly Movie. Peter Fonda is a wild driver who commits a robbery (solely for cash for his souped-up cars, so we are supposed to like him), and dashes across California with Susan George, miscast as a Goldie Hawn figure, and Adam Roarke. They are chased by Vic Morrow. The gratuitous ending recalls the days of the Hays Code; after all it was made in 1974 and we had grown up a little by then. Director, John Hough. (c)

The Disorderly Orderly √ If you happen to like both Jerry Lewis and movies set in hospitals you'll adore this 1964 Frank Tashlin writer-director effort. Otherwise, you'll be turned off by the usual mugging and posturing and a total effect of sentimental grossness. (c)

Distant Drums √ Straightforward western about hero falling in love with Indian maid after attacking fort held by gun-runners, given distinction by the fact that it's Gary Cooper in the main part. Raoul Walsh did routine job of direction; 1951. (c)

A Distant Trumpet XX Not so much distant, as out of sight. If westerns can ever be boring, this is the one. And if Troy Donahue, Suzanne Pleshette are capable of being anything other than wooden, Raoul Walsh isn't the man to enliven them, not with John Twist's script about the army fighting Indians, anyway; 1964. (c)

Dive Bomber √ 1941 aviation story about overcoming pilot blackout made for an exciting movie, with Michael Curtiz getting the best out of Fred MacMurray, Ralph Bellamy, Errol Flynn and some good effects. (c)

The Divided Heart √ Based on true-life story about boy torn between two mothers in wartime. Charles Crichton coaxes best perfomances Yvonne Mitchell, Theodore Bikel, Alexander Knox are capable of; 1954. (b/w)

Divorce American Style X From the man who later adapted *Steptoe and Son* and *Till Death Us Do Part* for American television, Norman Lear, comes title rip-off of *Divorce – Italian Style*, a funnier, earlier, foreign language pic. This one, directed for producer Lear by Bud Yorkin, has Dick Van Dyke and Debbie Reynolds at its soft centre; Jason Robards and Jean Simmons as veterans of the divorce hassle, put them to shame; 1967. (c)

Doberman Patrol √ James Brolin is mugged in department store loo and staggers out after the place has closed. Six huge dogs are loose, to attack intruders, and they try to kill him. Susan Clark is meanwhile trying to locate him. Will she be in time? Taut low-budget suspenser, adequately directed by Frank de Felitta in 1973. (c)

Doc √√ Director Frank Perry (*David and Lisa*, *Diary of a Mad Housewife*) takes a trip out West to make yet another oater about Wyatt Earp (Harris Yulin), Doc Holliday (Stacy Keach), Katie Elder (Faye Dunaway) and other mythical heroes. Although he insists on surface realism, he is more interested in personal conflict than in exploring myths or making just another exciting cowboy picture; 1971. (c)

The Dock Brief √ Opening-out of John Mortimer's television play about a lawyer and his client by James Hill stretches it a bit too far, and Peter Sellers and Richard Attenborough know it and try to over-compensate; 1962. (b/w)

Doctor Faustus X The late Sixties were disaster-time for Richard Burton and Elizabeth Taylor, and this 1967 version of Marlowe by the Oxford University Players, with a few minutes of La Taylor, was part of the awful era; Burton produced and directed, too. (c)

Doctor . . . In the House √ Dirk Bogarde, 1954, very funny; . . . **At Sea**, Dirk Bogarde, 1956, quite funny but spoiled by extravagancies of the pompous James Robertson Justice, who has continued to dominate the series with his smugness ever since; . . . **At Large**, Dirk Bogarde, 1957, still amusing but beginning to run out of steam; . . . **In Love**, Michael Craig, 1960, without Bogarde it flags; . . . **In Distress**, Dirk Bogarde, 1963, it is rather – in distress; . . . **In Clover**, 1966 Leslie Phillips; reduced to *Carry On* proportions without that marvellous Crazy Gang; . . . **In Trouble**, Leslie Phillips, 1970; at 46, Phillips is getting just a bit old for being the bright young doctor. All Ralph Thomas. (all c).

Doctor Blood's Coffin XX Notable only for Sidney J. Furie, later to become successful Hollywood director, cutting his teeth in this gruesome 1960 yarn about mad son of a Cornish doctor. Unfortunately, the casting of Kieron Moore in the main part ensured that Furie had no real chance. (c)

Doctor Jekyll and Sister Hyde √ Better-than-average Hammer horror, with some impresive metamorphoses between Ralph Bates and Martine Beswick. If Brian Clemens's script stuffed in too many Victorian stock horrors (Jack the Ripper; Burke and Hare), Roy Ward Baker's direction at least kept the plot moving; 1971. (c)

The Doctor's Dilemma √ Over-talky Shaw play treated reverently by Anthony Asquith in 1958. Dirk Bogarde tries to humanise the young patient, but Robert Morley, Alastair Sim, John Robinson and Felix Aylmer walk off with the honours as the Harley Street harlots. Leslie Caron is miscast and inadequate; 1958. (c)

Doctor's Wives X Cast – Dyan Cannon, Gene Hackman, Rachel Roberts, Richard Crenna – is too good for this yarn about Dyan's revelation that she has slept with three local husbands. George Schaffer directed, sloppily, in 1971. (c)

Doctor, You've Got to be Kidding √ Sandra Dee is rushed to hospital, giving birth, with three blokes all begging to marry her. George Hamilton must be favourite – he gets first billing. Others in this 1967 romp, directed by Peter Tawksbury, are Mort Sahl, Celeste Holm, Bill Bixby. (c)

Dodge City √ Errol Flynn puts down Bruce Cabot and the other baddies to make the town a place for decent folks (until the next western). Olivia de Havilland is nice girl, Ann Sheridan bad (but golden-hearted). Michael Curtiz directed this archetypal western in 1939. (c)

Dodsworth √√ Despite Walter Huston's memorable portrayal in 1936 of Sinclair Lewis's retiring hero, and Mary Astor's performance, the sentiment and the sets let down William Wyler's direction. Ruth Chatterton played his thrill-seeking wife; Paul Lukas and David Niven the thrills. (b/w)

Dog Day Afternoon √√ Fascinating and successful caper with couple of twists. First is that Al Pacino could profit so little out of his bank robbery; the second is that he is staging it so that his second 'wife' can have a sex-change operation. Sidney Lumet based his film on a real-life gay bank robbery on a Chase Manhattan Bank in Flatbush, Brooklyn; 1975. (c)

A Dog of Flanders √ What chance have even Donald Crisp and Theodore Bikel against appealing dog and kid in this happy tear-jerker for children? James B. Clark laid it on thick; 1959. (c)

A Doll's House √ (1) Director: Patrick Garland. First of 1973's two adaptations of Ibsen's play was based on an uninspired modernised text by Christopher Hampton, prompting conventional performances from Claire Bloom as Nora, the wife who forged her father's name and is about to be betrayed to her husband (Anthony Hopkins) by Denholm Elliott. (c)

A Doll's House √√ (2) Director: Joseph Losey. Rather better was Jane Fonda's awakening to her doll-like marriage in a version shot in Norway and tingling with icy behaviour. David Warner and Trevor Howard improve on Hopkins and Ralph Richardson, although Edward Fox and Delphine Seyrig must yield to Denholm Elliott and Anna Massey. Above all, this is a film; unlike Garland's stagebound version, the play photographed. (c)

The Don Is Dead √ Post-*Godfather* confection reminiscent of the old gangster movies of the Thirties, with current (1973) philosophy about the mob being run on sound business lines adding a contemporary ingredient. Anthony Quinn is the Don who only puts out the rumour he is dead as a ploy; Richard Fleischer. (c)

Do Not Disturb X After this disastrous effort in 1965, Doris Day (then pushing 42) decided to give up being a giggly kid and has since made some grown-up movies. But this nadir, an embarrassing echo of her prev. delightful frothy comedies, still has he_ as a young married (to Rod Taylor) who loses her husband, then gets him back in a giddy whirl. Part of the blame is director Ralph Levy's, who seems to have gone along blindly with the whole thing. (c)

Donovan's Brain √ Rather better than routine sci-fi with Lew Ayres as scientist who seeks to control kept-alive brain but is himself taken over by it; writer-director Felix Feist; 1953. (b/w)

Donovan's Reef √ John Ford enjoying himself in Hawaii in 1963 with John Wayne and Lee Marvin as ex-navy men scrapping and drinking and wenching (with Elizabeth Allen, Dorothy Lamour). All good tough fun. (c)

Don't Bother to Knock √ Devotees of Marilyn Monroe will squirm with delight at the sight of her first dramatic part – a loony babysitter – in 1952. The rest of you can enjoy Richard Widmark, the debut of Anne Bancroft, Roy Baker's not too certain direction. (b/w)

Don't Bother to Knock XX Unremarkable farce with Edinburgh travel agent Richard Todd, in love with good girl June Thorburn, handing out his flat keys to Elke Sommer and others. Directed (1960) by Cyril Frankel. (b/w)

Don't Give Up the Ship √ – Just the movie, unless you enjoy the antics of Jerry Lewis, circa 1959. Here he is looking for a boat he lost in the war. (b/w)

Don't Go Near the Water X Dull little comedy with Glenn Ford romancing Gia Scala on Pacific isle during naval occupation. Only Fred Clark scrapes by, doing his usual bluff bit; Charles Walters; 1957. (c)

Don't Just Stand There XXX Remarkably unfunny comedy about Mary Tyler Moore and Robert Wagner trying to smuggle girl out of Paris brothel; Glynis Johns lurks around as man-hungry novelist. Clearly director Ron Winston is not much of a dab at judging how to make people laugh; 1969. (c)

Don't Look Now √√√ Nicholas Roeg's absorbing supernatural thriller set in wintertime Venice chills and thrills as well as exciting the imagination. Julie Christie and Donald Sutherland carry the main parts more than adequately, but it is death in the compellingly convincing prologue and frightening

...ce later that haunts anyone ...s the movie; 1973. (c)

...ake Waves X Tony Curtis as ...ing pool salesman with the arch ...lia Cardinale lurking around; ...a falling-in – including a house ...the sea; Robert Webber, Mort ...il look dismayed, as well they might. Sad that Alexander Mackendrick, who made *The Ladykillers* and *Sweet Smell of Success,* should come to this in 1967. (c)

Don't Raise the Bridge, Lower the River XX Jerry Lewis' British picture couldn't be called a success by any standards. Despite efforts from all concerned, the mixture – like the bridge – failed to rise; Jerry Paris from a Max Wilk script about turning an estranged wife's home into a Chinese restaurant; 1968. (c)

Doppelgänger X Gerry and Sylvia Anderson show that although you can treat puppets as people (they made *Thunderbirds,* etc.), it doesn't work the other way round; Ian Hendry, Patrick Wymark, Herbert Lom and others discover new planet which is mirror-image of ours. Strictly for the puppets. Director Robert Parrish; 1969. (c)

Double Bunk X Could have been called 'Carry On Down the River' as Ian Carmichael and Janette Scott sail the Thames in an old houseboat, helped and hindered by Sid James, Liz Fraser, Dennis Price, Irene Handl, Terry Scott, Gerald Campion, Graham Stark; directed by C. M. Pennington-Richards; 1960. (b/w)

Double Crossbones X Pirate jollifaction, helping to amortise Universal's investment in water tanks and galleons on their backlot and swashbuckling clothes in their wardrobe department. 1950 yarn has Donald O'Connor taking to sea after being accused of dishonesty. He makes a rotten pirate; director, Charles T. Barton. (c)

Double Indemnity √√√ Sharp, sour, stunning *tour de force* about wife (Barbara Stanwyck) who seduces insurance salesman (Fred MacMurray) to kill husband and collect huge insurance. Billy Wilder, who directed, co-wrote the script with Raymond Chandler from a James M. Cain novel, and it's a masterpiece of driving economy; Edward G. Robinson, Porter Hall perfect too; 1944. (b/w)

A Double Life √√ Ronald Coleman won 1947 Oscar for performance as actor whose work so affects his life that he becomes schizophrenic and mur-

derous; George Cukor made what is basically hokum into convincing melodrama; Edmond O'Brien, Shelley Winters, Ray Collins helped considerably. (c)

The Double Man XX Yul Brynner in two-part spy bore along with Britt Ekland and the CIA in the Austrian Alps. Franklin Schaffner; 1967. (c)

Double Trouble XX Elvis Presley as bodyguard for Annette Day, chosen for the part after worldwide publicity stunt. She never made another film. Norman Taurog directed; 1967. (c)

The Dove XX Monumentally boring round-the-world voyage, with Joseph Bottoms playing the part of Robin Lee Graham. There are the occasional moments of excitement, but mostly it's travelogue stuff, unimaginatively directed by Charles Jarrott in 1974, with an occasional visit ashore for a quick nibble at a love story with Deborah Raffin. (c)

Down Argentine Way X Tuneful, empty, garish musical with Betty Grable chasing Don Ameche round the pampas. Carmen Miranda does her thing better than her billions of imitators. Charlotte Greenwood and J. Carroll Naish support; director Irving Cummings keeps them at it; 1940. (c)

Downhill Racer √ Ski movie, with Robert Redford and Gene Hackman, that has become a cult film. However, those uninvolved in skiing may find it a bit dull. Michael Ritchie directed with style in 1969. (c)

Do You Know This Voice? X Dan Duryea in British kidnapping drama, with Gwen Watford, Isa Miranda; director Frank Nesbitt, 1964. (b/w)

Dracula √√ (1) Bela Lugosi was original in 1931 Tod Browning classic. (b/w)

Dracula √ (2) 1957: Peter Cushing and Christopher Lee were in Terence Fisher's excellent version which used the trappings of heart-stakes and neck-fangs with good effect. (c)

Dracula XX (3) 1973: Jack Palance is quite wrong in the Lugosi role. Despite claims that this version, directed by Dan Curtis, is the first accurate adaptation, there are several changes, all for the worse. (c)

Dracula Has Risen From the Grave √ Best of the three sequels Hammer produced from its own *Dracula;* Freddie Francis took over as director of this 1968 effort and improved it colourwise, sexwise and subtlewise. However, a certain gusto is missing, although Christopher Lee is his usual menacing self. Rupert Davies weighs in with a priest-cum-avenger. (c)

Dracula – Prince of Darkness X Fisher's own 1966 rip-off, like most of the later attempts to cash in on the brand-name, didn't equal the original. (c)

Dracula's Daughter √√ 1936 sequel to first *Dracula*, this was scrupulous and convincing, achieving a near-Lesbian quality between biter (Gloria Holden) and bitten; Lambert Hillyer. (b/w)

Dragnet X Spin-off from the once-successful Jack Webb TV series has the solemn-faced actor-director going through the routine of bringing in suspect and pinning gang-murder on him; 1954. (c)

Dragonwyck √ High drama, romance, terror, murder in a big mysterious old mansion; Gene Tierney is the girl, Walter Huston, Vincent Price are part of the creaking furniture; Ernst Lubitsch produced, Joseph L. Mankiewicz directed; 1945. (c)

Dr Crippen X Who didn't murder his wife, according to this unconvincing version by Leigh Vance, directed with even less *élan* by Robert Lynn – it was all an accident, like the movie. Only Donald Pleasence as the archetypal worm-that-turned is worth switching on for; but neither Coral Browne as Belle, nor Samantha Eggar as Ethel, convinces; 1964. (b/w)

Dreamboat √√ Great fun: Ginger Rogers and Clifton Webb in 1952 spoof about his old movies being shown on television. Lovely old 'clips' from silents; Anne Francis and Elsa Lanchester add to the enjoyment under Claude Binyon's direction. (b/w)

Dream of Kings X Anthony Quinn overacting all over the screen as Chicago Greek trying to raise the money to send ill son to Greece; unfortunately, he's so unsympathetic that none of director Daniel Mann's schmaltzy tricks can make us care; Irene Papas enjoys herself as long-suffering wife; Sam Levene is almost only non-Greek in rest of large cast; 1969. (c)

Dream Wife X Weak little snippet about man who believes men are superior and wives should be subservient. When Eastern princess turns up as his bride for State Dept. reasons he demonstrates his theories to fiancée. Most amazing fact is that Cary Grant plays the chap; Deborah Kerr's his girl – they must have been mad to take the parts; Sidney Sheldon; 1953. (b/w)

Dressed to Kill √ Odd name for a Sherlock Holmes adventure: Basil Rathbone and Nigel Bruce on the trail of three identical music boxes, one of which holds the key to forgery; Roy William Neill directed in 1946. (b/w)

Drive, He Said √√ Jack Nicholson's first picture as a director (he isn't in it) may be a bit confusing, but is saved by a sharp eye for detail. Bruce Dern dominates as a hysterical athletics coach, trying to keep his star, William Tepler, along the rah-rah-rah straight and narrow. But the influence of radical Michael Margotta and adulteree Karen Black frustrate him; 1970. (c)

Dr Jekyll and Mr Hyde √√ (1) 1932: Splendid version directed by Rouben Mamoulian transformed Fredric March by making different parts of his make-up sensitive to different light filters; Miriam Hopkins is distressed lady. (b/w)

Dr Jekyll and Mr Hyde √ (2) 1941: Disappointing Victor Fleming version with Spencer Tracy trying too hard, what with Freudian dream sequences and all. Neither Ingrid Bergman nor Lana Turner were at home in foggy London. (b/w)

Dr No √√ This is the best of the cycle it spawned. Sean Connery *v.* Joseph Wiseman in Jamaica, with Ursula Andress in bathing suit, are slick and exciting; Terence Young directed; 1963. (c)

Drop Dead Darling X Solid cast (Tony Curtis, Lionel Jeffries, Nancy Kwan, Fenella Fielding) wasted in rubbishy stuff about con-man marrying and murdering for money. Ken Hughes; 1967. (c)

The Drowning Pool √ Director Stuart Rosenberg muffed this 1975 follow-up to *The Moving Target* (1966), in which Paul Newman's private eye, Harper, is called by Joanne Woodward to her Louisiana hothouse to solve the usual Marlowe-type melange of blackmail and murder. Instead of going either for steamy atmosphere or straightforward detection, the film teeters on the edge of parody and settles for being smart. (c)

Dr Strangelove or How I Learned to Stop Worrying and Love the Bomb √√√ Stanley Kubrick's brilliant, if chilling, 1964 comedy which won pre-release Presidential approval. Peter Sellers is at his best in a triple performance. What happens when the

Button is pressed and Doomsday arrives . . . (b/w)

Dr Terror's House of Horror √ Peter Cushing reads grim tarot cards for five future victims of supernatural death and we dutifully follow their dead-of-night fates; unfortunately, this is one of Milton Subotsky's quick-buck British churn-outs and Freddie Francis's best efforts can't overcome a painfully derivative script and low budget; a good cast (Christopher Lee, Donald Sutherland, Harold Lang included) try hard; music by Elisabeth Lutyens and Tubby Hayes; 1965. (c)

The Drum √ Polished 1938 adventure about rebel tribesmen in British India attempting to usurp Prince Sabu's throne. Raymond Massey makes a powerful heavy; Roger Livesey, Valerie Hobson suitably weak sahib, memsahib, and Zoltan Korda directed for brother Alex. (c)

Drum Beat √ Alan Ladd warring, peace-parleying with Indians; tautly directed by Delmer Daves in 1954. (c)

Drummer of Vengeance XX British-made western featuring the inadequate Ty Hardin in various disguises as he takes his revenge on the men who killed his wife and son. Robert Paget directed, listlessly. (c)

Drums Across the River √ Considering it's only an Audie Murphy vehicle, this 1954 western is really rather good. Gold-seekers push Indians off their lands, with Hugh O'Brien and Walter Brennan in the serviceable cast; Nathan Juran. (c)

Drums Along the Mohawk √√ Classic 1939 actioner with Claudette Colbert, Henry Fonda, Edna May (scene-stealing) Oliver, John (varmint) Carradine fighting against and with the Indians isn't a western, more an Eastern. The drums are those of Iroquois paid by the British to fight Fonda, Colbert and fellow Americans during the revolution; John Ford's first colour film used the new medium superbly, particularly in silhouette sequence of hero's flight. (c)

Dr Who and the Daleks XX Vulgarised version of an already vulgar TV series, far removed from the wit and nuances of good science fiction. This is comic-book stuff, and a bad comic at that. Peter Cushing takes the main part but without even the depth of character the TV Doctors Who have had; the story is about his meeting with the Da-a-a-aleks for the first time; 1965. (c)

Dry Rot X Long-running stage farce about switching horses makes rather too broad a film without audience laughter; Ronald Shiner, Brian Rix, Sid James, Joan Sims; directed by an indulgent Maurice Elvey; 1956. (b/w)

Duck Soup √√ The (four) Marx brothers, Margaret Dumont, Louis Calhern, Edgar Kennedy in classic 1933 spoof of banana republics. Groucho says it's their craziest. Banned by Mussolini. Director, poor chap: Leo McCarey. (b/w)

Duel √√√ Have you ever overtaken a lorry that turns out to have a malevolent driver, determined to 'do' you for having the temerity to cut in on him? That is what happens to Dennis Weaver in this terrifyingly recognisable movie that was modestly made for American TV by Steven Spielberg (later to direct *Sugarland Express, Jaws* and *Close Encounters of the Third Kind*) but which became a cult cinema hit in Britain. There develops a chase to make you cover your eyes in terror; 1972. (c)

Duel at Diablo √√ More than a western, a bloodbath. Ralph Nelson, who was later to direct the infamous *Soldier Blue*, warmed up for it with this Indian ambush with the blood spilling like a hot-dog bathed in tomato ketchup – which is probably what it is, too. But he does get the best out of James Garner, Sidney Poitier, Bibi Andersson; 1966. (c)

Duel in the Jungle XX Is between sterling insurance detective Dana Andrews and horrible David Farrar, swindler and jungle-dweller; set in pre-UDI Rhodesia, in 1954. George Marshall fails to excite. (c)

Duel in the Sun √√ *Gone With the High Noon*? – five directors (mainly King Vidor, but William Dieterle shot Tilly Losch dance opening), eight stars (Jennifer Jones, Joseph Cotten, Gregory Peck, Lionel Barrymore, Lillian Gish, Herbert Marshall, Walter Huston, Charles Bickford), orchestrated by David Selznick in the big-spending days of 1946. (c)

Duffy X One of those near-spoof capers with the increasingly tiresome James Coburn putting himself about in a pretentious, over-dressed, over-produced thriller about stealing a million from a liner. Some good English players – James Mason, James Fox, Susannah York, John Alderton – are pushed around by him and director Robert Parrish; 1968. (c)

Dulcima X Carol White finds out that

'orrible old John Mills has a secret fortune so she becomes his house-keeper, then his mistress. He is supposed to be overtaken by an obsessive lust for her, but Frank Nesbitt's direction never has the courage of H. E. Bates's convictions, from whose story the script was taken; 1971. (c)

Dunkirk √√ Leslie Norman's ambitious 1958 account of historic event succeeds partly because he avoids unnecessary false heroism, partly because of graphic, almost documentary, approach. Top performances from stalwarts John Mills, Richard Attenborough, Bernard Lee, Robert Urquhart. (b/w)

Dutchman √√ Gripping little film of the LeRoi Jones one-acter tightly directed by Anthony Harvey with Al Freeman Jnr. as black passenger and Shirley Knight (Hopkins) as flaunting white passenger in New York subway, recreated in London studio; 1967. (b/w)

Dynamite Man from Glory Jail √ Three outlaws (James Stewart, Strother Martin, Kurt Russell) go through various excitements in their efforts to cash a cheque which is rightly theirs; Andrew McLaglen directed, in 1971, in his usual competent, uninspired way. (c)

E

The Eagle and the Hawk X Dennis O'Keefe and John Payne thwarting plots in Texas when it was still part of Mexico; Lewis R. Foster never manages to hold the interest; 1950. (c)

The Early Bird XXX Dreadful British comedy with Norman Wisdom as milkman who loves his horse and somehow saves his boss from a takeover bid. Hard to care about milkman, boss, or horse. Director Robert Asher; 1965. (c)

The Earth Dies Screaming X The one about Beings from Another Planet turning us all into zombies. Enough of this kind of movie wll do the trick, too. A 1963 effort, when little-known Americans (Willard Parker in this case) were given leads in inferior British pix, with inferior British supports. Director, Terence Fisher. (b/w)

Earthquake √ Two tremors, two shocks and the bursting of a dam provide this disaster movie with plenty of action. Ava Gardner, Charlton Heston, George Kennedy, Lorne Green, Richard Roundtree are soon submerged, literally as well as metaphorically. Neither their dilemmas not their acting are up to much. Director Mark Robson understandably paid more attention to his special effects in 1974. (c)

Earth II √ Orbiting space station is menaced by Red China. Gary Lockwood to the rescue. Director Tom Gries does as well as he can on a *Star Trek*-sized budget; 1971. (c)

Easter Parade √√ Judy Garland, Fred Astaire, a couple of swells; Fred's trying to forget ex-partner Ann Miller; plus sixteen other Irving Berlins. Charles Walters; 1948. (c)

East of Eden √√ Elia Kazan's successful interpretation of (part of) Steinbeck's novel about Cal (James Dean's great performance) rebelling against father (Raymond Massey). Julie Harris his equal as strange local girl; and Jo Van Fleet won Oscar for her Kate. Set in 1917, made in 1955. (c)

East of Sumatra √ Budd Boetticher gives some distinction to this routine adventure about mining engineer in Far East, with Jeff Chandler and Anthony Quinn; 1952. (c)

Easy Come, Easy Go X Elvis Presley was so taken up with a (sadly false) vision of himself as an actor that he sang only three songs in this 1967 stuff about a frogman. Maybe the frog was in his throat? John Rich indulged him. (c)

Easy Rider √√ The movie that caused a revolution in picture-making in 1969. Until then, nobody had quite realised that the young provided such a huge untapped market, but for this low-budget odyssey of producer-directors Peter Fonda and Dennis Hopper travelling across the southern states by motorbike chopper, they turned out in their millions all over the world. Jack Nicholson, as a drunken lawyer who joins them for a while, walks away with the acting honours. While much of the action and dialogue is banal, the film does have guts, and the end is genuinely horrific. (c)

Easy to Love X Esther Williams in water-spectacle, falling for boorish boss Van Johnson; Charles Walters managed to make water-skiing quite lavish; 1953. (c)

The Eddie Cantor Story XX The

comedian's own voice emerges, spirit-wise, out of the mouth of the just-competent Keefe Brasselle (actor who later unhappily turned TV executive). If you happen to adore Mr Cantor you might find this not too distasteful; otherwise, it's just creepy; Alfred E. Green; 1952. (c)

The Eddy Duchin Story X George Sidney directed this 1956 biopic about Thirties pianist. Tyrone Power gave it more than it deserved, Kim Novak about as good as she got. (c)

Edge of Eternity √ Don Siegel actioner in, around and over the Grand Canyon; unfortunately, actors Cornel Wilde, Mickey Shaughnessy can't match it in any particular; 1960. (c)

Edward My Son √ Compelling performance from Spencer Tracy as the father who not quite honestly builds a fortune for his son, and discovers that he and his wife, Deborah Kerr, and their precarious marriage drove the boy to suicide. George Cukor's 1949 direction is a touch gimmicky, but Ian Hunter, Mervyn Johns and Felix Aylmer lend strong support. (b/w)

The Effect of Gamma Rays on Man-in-the-Moon Marigolds √ The awful title has a literal meaning in the science experiments that slatternly Joanne Woodward's daughter (Nell Potts) does at school. There is doubtless also a metaphysical interpretation. Paul Newman's directorial debut (from a play by Paul Zindel) is the kind of movie that, when you see a girl's pet rabbit, you know it will be killed by the end. The drama is primarily a dissection of the Woodward character's disintegration, climaxing in her getting drunk in public; 1972. (c)

The Egg and I √ Chicken farmer Fred MacMurray marries city slicker Claudette Colbert, who learns how to survive on a farm. Supposedly true story introduces Ma and Pa Kettle who were spun off to make long successful series of their own. Chester Erskine; 1947. (b/w)

The Egyptian X Darryl F. Zanuck's 1954 biblical epic owes most to set and costume designers. Edmund Purdom, Jean Simmons, Peter Ustinov, Victor Mature, Michael Wilding and 5,000 extras are lavished on indifferent story. But director Michael Curtiz loads on the spectacle. (c)

The Eiger Sanction X Dull actioner with preposterous premises sends Clint Eastwood and George Kennedy climbing a mountain in a Bondish plot.

Eastwood is required to kill a couple of heavies up there. He directed himself so there were no excuses in 1975. (c)

Eight on the Run XX Dire attempt at humour about bank clerk on the run as suspected embezzler. Bob Hope is cute enough, but here is out-joked by a veritable galaxy of unfunnies including Phyllis Diller, Jonathan Winters, seven children and a big dog. Shirley Eaton must have thought she was going to make it big after being cast in this 1968 'comedy' but it turned out to be a killer for her career; George Marshall. (c)

80,000 Suspects √ Disease is the villain of this 1963 suspenser set in Bath in the middle of smallpox and flu epidemics; Val Guest does usual uninspired professional job with the help of Claire Bloom, Cyril Cusack. (b/w)

El Cid √ It's a long time between high-lights (a single-handed combat near the beginning and the final battle) during which Charlton Heston slowly unites the Moors and Christians of Spain under one king. You'll have plenty of time to study director Anthony Mann's deliberate composi-tions; 1962. (c)

El Dorado √ In 1959 Howard Hawks made Rio Bravo; in 1967 he made this, and it's pretty hard to tell them apart, particularly as John Wayne's in both of them. Robert Mitchum's along for the ride this time, and the old master knows how to rope your attention. (c)

An Elephant Called Slowly XX Viginia McKenna and Bill Travers return to the land of *Born Free*, where they look up old friends. A herd of elephants provide some pretty if familiar pictures, but director James Hill can't cope with a boring script cobbled out by Travers and himself; 1969. (c)

Elephant Walk √ Elizabeth Taylor, Peter Finch, Dana Andrews, and herd of rampaging elephants in *Rebecca*-type story in Ceylon; William Dieterle; 1953. (c)

11 Harrowhouse XX Unconvincing comedy-thriller in which Charles Grodin makes a half-hearted jewel thief: the title is an address where diamonds worth billions are kept. The film includes a double-cross by Trevor Howard; treachery by James Mason; with some relief from John Gielgud and Peter Vaughan. Aram Avakian directs erratically, apparently as baffled by British methods as his hero; 1974. (c)

El Greco X Worthy, well-photographed but boring account of the painter from Crete who lived in Toledo. Mel Ferrer produced it as a vehicle for himself. Maybe director Luciano Salce would have preferred a better actor but didn't quite like to say so? 1967. *(c)*

Elizabeth of Ladymead XX Weak four-generation yarn presents Anna Neagle as a quartet of ladies (one at a time, from different generations) in a Georgian mansion, awaiting husbands away in the army; Herbert Wilcox directed lovingly and routinely; 1949. *(b/w)*

Elmer Gantry √√ Well-cast Burt Lancaster as charlatan evangelist exploiting Jean Simmons' touring pulpit in 1920s Midwest. Arthur Kennedy is journalist out to expose him, Shirley Jones discarded girlfriend-turned-prostitute. Neatly directed (1960) by Richard Brooks from Sinclair Lewis's novel. *(c)*

The Elusive Pimpernel √ David Niven is the Scarlet Runner in this 1950 version, directed by Powell and Pressburger. *(c)*

Embassy √ Richard Roundtree and ageing Broderick Crawford have to smuggle defector Max von Sydow out of the American embassy in Beirut on to a plane. But KGB assassin Chuck Connors almost rubs him out. Director Gordon Hessler does a competent job with familiar situations. *(c)*

Emergency √ Neat little British thriller about finding rare blood donor to save dying girl. Glyn Houston makes a dour detective; Zena Walker, Dermot Walsh play the parents. Francis Searle directed; 1963. *(b/w)*

Emperor of the North √√ Lee Marvin is the king of the hobos in Robert Aldrich's powerful, violent allegory set in 1933. He has a running battle with Ernest Borgnine and a complicated relationship with fellow-hero Keith Carradine; 1973. *(c)*

The Emperor Waltz √ Quite what Billy Wilder was doing in a studio like this except earning his living in 1948 isn't altogether clear, but he manages to put a few nice touches into Viennese yarn about travelling salesman Bing Crosby meeting Austrian princess Joan Fontaine circa 1901. Should have been called 'The Emperor Schmaltz'. *(c)*

The Enchanted Cottage √ Pirandello play desperately whimsied up by director John Cromwell but still retaining enough of its depends-who-you-are origins to take story of ugly girl (Dorothy McGuire) and broken flyer (Robert Young) interestingly out of the rut; Herbert Marshall, Spring Byington giving their stock performances don't help; 1945. *(b/w)*

Enchanted Island X If you can guess the origin of this tritely produced 1963 tale of two sailors jumping ship and living idyllic South Sea island life, you must be psychic; particularly with casting of Dana Andrews and Jane Powell, and Allan Dwan's lighthearted direction. It's a Herman Melville novel. *(c)*

Endless Night XX Alas, it's the film that seems endless as Hayley Mills takes a long time a-dying. Hard to believe that it comes from an Agatha Christie novel when Sidney Gilliat makes the plot, involving Hywel Bennett, Britt Ekland and George Sanders, both so obvious and unbelievable; 1971. *(c)*

The Endless Summer √ Paean of praise for the joys of surfing, directed, produced, edited and narrated by Bruce Brown. Sometimes very beautiful, interesting for a time, absorbing only if you are an addict; 1966. *(c)*

The End of the Affair X Adaptation of the Grahame Greene novel about finding God after infidelity. It's too American in influence, with Van Johnson as the lover and Edward Dmytryk the director. Deborah Kerr and Peter Cushing as the other sides of the triangle are adequate, and the rest of the cast is old-school English; 1955. *(b/w)*

The Enemy Below √ Duel between Robert Mitchum's destroyer and Curt Jurgens's U-boat is unlikely but moderately successful pacifist plea; Dick Powell turned out to be more than competent director in 1957. *(c)*

The Enforcer √ Assistant DA Humphrey Bogart *v.* crime boss Everett Sloane in no-nonsense toughie, with Zero Mostel; director Bretaigne Windust; 1951. *(b/w)*

The Engagement XXX If ever Tom Stoppard is rich enough he will doubtless buy up all the copies of this disastrous incursion into film-writing and burn them. David Warner, the main character, spends an afternoon in a taxi trying to raise some money. Director Paul Joyce leaves his players floundering; 1970. *(c)*

England Made Me √ Graham Greene has not fared well with his screen adaptors, and this 1972 transposition of his first major novel (1935) from

Sweden to Nazi Germany is just the first vulgarisation from director Peter Duffell (others include an incestuous kiss for twin Michael York from Hildegard Neil – both miscast). Peter Finch did his best with the character of ruthless financier, but the smaller parts (Joss Ackland as his executioner, Michael Hordern as a timid little journalist with dramatic scoop leaked to him) come off best. (c)

Ensign Pulver √ Drama? Comedy? Comedy-drama? It isn't clear with this story of a very junior member of the Navy taking on the hated captain of his boat, and that's typical of the way the whole film falls (or rather, plunges, mostly at sea) between stools. But Burl Ives pulls off the feat of making the martinet sympathetic, and Walter Matthau is the ship's doctor. Unfortunately, Robert Walker can't reach the demands of the main part, though the blame (and the praise – it's not that bad) must go to Joshua Logan, who produced and directed from a play by Josh Logan that he wrote with someone else, having rewritten it for the screen with another partner; 1965. (c)

Enter Laughing √ Carl Reiner, comedy writer turned director, obviously thought he was going to deliver a mighty laugh in this thin but basically autobiographical tale of a boy's first Broadway chance, but he mucked it up by casting Reni Santoni as the lad and Jose Ferrer as an ageing actor. Only Elaine May, as his daughter, really works well. Pity. 1967. (c)

The Entertainer √√√ Stunning performance by Laurence Olivier as music hall comedian who tries heartbreakingly hard to kid himself that he's going to make it. John Osborne's play translates smoothly to the screen, and Brenda de Banzie, Joan Plowright, Roger Livesey, Albert Finney, Thora Hird provide matching contributions. Tony Richardson's direction doesn't intrude on star or script; 1960. (b/w)

Entertaining Mr Sloane √ Unimaginative working-out of Joe Orton's outrageous play about murder, seduction and homosexuality, with Beryl Reid, Harry Andrews, Peter McEnery. Directed by Douglas Hickox; 1969. (c)

Escapade √ Neat and thoughtful play about the sons of world peace campaigner John Mills embarrassing him with school larks. Alastair Sim does his headmaster bit; Andrew Ray and Peter Asher are two of the schoolboy sons (it was 1955). Roger McDougall's play is not particularly well served by director Philip Leacock. (b/w)

Escape from East Berlin XX Factual-based account of how 28 East Germans tunnelled through to the West under the Wall. Don Murray and Christine Kaufmann starred in this 1962 casualty of cold war hysteria. Director Robert Siodmak held the patient's hand to no avail; it expired from over-earnestness. (b/w)

Escape from Fort Bravo √ Cavalry western with William Holden chasing four Southern prisoners, while Eleanor Parker holds her throat in suspense. Director, John Sturges; 1953. (c)

Escape from the Planet of the Apes √ Second (1970) sequel to original conveniently brings Roddy McDowell and Kim Hunter to present-day Los Angeles. Their adventures are not completely banal; director, Don Taylor. (c)

Escort West X Victor Mature beating the Red Indians and winning his daughter's affection, at the end of Civil War; Faith Domergue; director F. D. Lyon; 1958. (c)

Esther and the King X Failed attempt at epic by Raoul Walsh, with dull battles and even duller performances by Joan Collins and Richard Egan; 1960. (c)

Eve X Forty minutes shorter than Joseph Losey originally intended, this impenetrable fable of loquacious Welsh writer being destroyed by a *femme fatale* never takes a grip, and the Venice-in-winter backgrounds acquire the importance that scenery only does when the foreground action is boring or inconsequential. Jeanne Moreau does what she can with the inexplicable and unexplained Woman of the World; Stanley Baker can't do anything with the writer who fancies himself too much. As empty and pretentious as an issue of 1963 *Vogue,* and just as dated. (b/w)

Evel Knievel √ Biography of the daring young man which is more than a cheap exploitation of the morbid interest his near-suicide attempts provoke, to the credit of director Marvin Chomsky and producer-star George Hamilton. They have somehow got the Knievel's permission to show him and wife (Sue Lyon) as less than ideal characters. He is depicted as a bundle of nerves, who fears irrational dangers like earthquakes, real ones like diarrhoea and is upset at having fewer men to guard him than Elvis Presley had; 1971. (c)

Evergreen √ Jessie Matthews became a film star in 1934 when her stage musical *Ever Green* was adapted for the screen and she danced on the ceiling. Rodgers and Hart wrote the songs for her, but she remembers the filming with horror – 'my crucifixion' she calls Victor Saville's direction. Her estranged husband, Sonnie Hale, played opposite her. (b/w)

Everybody Does It √ 'It' being singing, not what you were thinking. Celeste Holm thinks she has a voice, but hasn't; Paul Douglas, husband, doesn't think he has, but has; Nunnally Johnson's story is neat as usual, Edmund Goulding's direction unassuming; 1950. (b/w)

Every Home Should Have One XX Marty Feldman, leering and grimacing all over the place, is enough to put anyone off this melange of hopeful jokes about advertising and television, but director Jim Clark has gone for a *Carry On* approach, as well. The result is that such excellent people as Shelley Berman, Penelope Keith, Dinsdale Landen and Frances de la Tour are swept away in a flood of *double* and single *entendres*; 1970. (c)

Every Little Crook and Nanny √ Mild farce with Lynn Redgrave posing as a nanny and kidnapping 12-year-old son of Mafia boss Victor Mature (he was, rather, by 1972 – aged 57). Cy Howard directed competently. (c)

Everything I Have is Yours √ Dancers Marge and Gower Champion in routine backstager about couple coming together, splitting, reuniting. Director Robert Z. Leonard has brought out some nice sly observations on marriage, however; 1953. (c)

Everything You Always Wanted to Know About Sex but were Afraid to Ask √ Seven uneven but, at their best, genuinely funny sketches with Woody Allen in his timid sex-obsessed persona. He directed himself, in 1972. Others to be glimpsed include Tony Randall, Burt Reynolds, Gene Wilder, John Carradine. (c)

The Evil of Frankenstein X Peter Cushing busily reviving the monster he thought dead but was, luckily for Hammer, only ice-bound; Freddie Francis is the director in this 1963 extension of a profitable but clapped-out series. (c)

Excuse My Dust √ Worth staying during the faintly tedious, good-old-summertime stuff for climax of early buggy race; lead Red Skelton's a bit wearing, though; director Roy Rowland; 1951. (c)

The Executioner √ Conventional but efficient spy thriller hinging on George Peppard's need to expose the traitor in the midst of MI5. Sam Wanamaker directed smartly enough in 1970 to get the best (in some cases that's not much) out of Joan Collins, Judy Geeson, Oscar Homolka, Nigel Patrick. (c)

Executive Action √√ Mark Lane's theory that John F. Kennedy's assassination was the work of a right-wing group who used Lee Harvey Oswald as a fall guy, scripted by Dalton Trumbo and director David Miller. Burt Lancaster and Robert Ryan play the leaders of the conspiracy. However, time has given other theories greater credence: the FBI, Mafia, CIA, Castro, Cuba, KGB as villains are all more convincing. Still, that gunman on the grassy knoll, as shown here, has now been confirmed as more than likely. (c)

Executive Suite √ Power game in the American furniture-making world, circa 1954, with William Holden, Fredric March, Paul Douglas, Walter Pidgeon among the strugglers; Barbara Stanwyck, Shelley Winters, Nina Foch soften it, and Robert Wise directed with jumpy cutting. (b/w)

Exodus X Mort Sahl is said to have stood up at the preview of this long, apparently endless chronicle of the birth of Israel after three hours and shouted to producer-director Otto Preminger 'Let my people go!' Luckily you can always turn off, although Paul Newman, Ralph Richardson, Lee J. Cobb should delay bottom-ache; 1960. (c)

The Exorcist √√ Efficient horror movie with 12-year-old Linda Blair inhabited by demons. Too solemn (maybe mock-solemn) in its approach to its subject, it is full of clever tricks, like her head turning full circle. Ellen Burstyn, Max von Sydow and Lee J. Cobb are among fine players slickly directed by William Friedkin in 1973. (c)

The Extraordinary Seaman √ David Niven as more than a mere mortal in a confusing spoof of wartime movies. Surprising effort from John Frankenheimer (*The Manchurian Candidate*, *Seven Days in May*), who usually takes war more seriously; Faye Dunaway, Alan Alda, Mickey Rooney as humans; 1968. (c)

Eye of the Cat √√ Highly satisfactory

and well-made low-budgeter about the way cats take over as murder agents when the family of Eleanor Parker, Gayle Hunnicutt and Michael Sarrazin get to murdering each other. You'll find yourself glancing at your own mog in quite a new way as the pic unfolds; David Lowell Rich milks it well; 1969. (c)

Eye of the Devil XX Dreadful attempt at suggesting how supernatural forces threaten a family, that succeeds only in documenting a fight between the risible and the incredible, rather than the intended one between good and evil. David Niven looks thoroughly embarrassed, as well he might, as chatelaine, although David Hemmings and Deborah Kerr seem under the mad impression that they are taking part in a serious film. J. Lee Thompson is director of the farrago and seems to have settled for restlessness in the camerawork in an attempt to disguise the poor material he is stuck with; 1968. (c)

Eye Witness √ The one about the witness who sees a murder but no-one will believe him/her. In this case, Mark Lester is an 11-year-old (it's 1970) who sees an assassination on Malta. Susan George is his sister; Lionel Jeffries, Peter Vaughan, Jeremy Kemp, Peter Bowles flesh out from John Gough's routine direction. (c)

F

The Face at the Window XX Creaky old Tod Slaughter melodrama about murders in 19th-century Paris. The direction (George King) is as old-fashioned (1939) as the setting. (b/w)

A Face in the Crowd √√ Superficially a protest movie about the manipulation of the public by a cynical entertainer, this is in fact a brilliant example of Elia Kazan's contempt for the public who'll believe anything as long as it looks as if it is on their side. Andy Griffith and Patricia Neal are startlingly good; 1957. (b/w)

Face of a Fugitive √ Fred MacMurray, on the run in a western town, makes good and proves his innocence; Paul Wendkos; 1959. (c)

The Face of Fu Manchu √√ Rather fun – a carefully preserved relic from an earlier world where oriental super-villains lurk and the assistant commissioner of Scotland Yard takes on the Man Who Wants to Rule the World Single-handed. Full marks ʻo director Don Sharp for not allowing it all to become campy spoof; instead, he has given us a delicious re-creation of what people used to pass the time agreeably with before television arrived. Christopher Lee makes a splendid Fu Manchu; 1965. (c)

Faces √ Pretentious, long-winded, action-starved account of middle-class American marriage whose ambience conned critics into thinking they were seeing something profound. John Cassavetes' direction is significant for its indulgence and he was lucky to have cameraman Al Ruban to save his excesses – he could have done with an equally tough editor. Cassavetes used friends and spouses who improvise adequately; 1968. (b/w)

The Facts of Life √ Considering that Bob Hope and Lucille Ball play the main parts, this is a remarkably quiet and understated comedy of thwarted adultery; credit must go to director Melvin Frank. Still, it was a strange and rather weak choice for the Royal Film Performance of 1961. (b/w)

Fahrenheit 451 √ Portentous Truffaut version of Ray Bradbury sci-fi. Julie Christie makes a mess of heroine's role, and Oskar Werner is almost as dull as member of the firing (setting fire to books) squad. Cyril Cusack, Anton Diffring came off a bit better; 1966. (c)

Fail Safe √√ Relatively unnoticed in the fall-out from *Dr Strangelove*, this 1964 Sidney Lumet suspenser postulates B52 bombers being sent to Moscow by mistake, and not even President Henry Fonda can stop them. Walter Matthau, Fritz Weaver add to masterly, all-too-convincing warning. (b/w)

Fair Wind to Java XX Pirate yarn with skipper Fred MacMurray and slave girl Vera Ralston searching for buried treasure; Joe Kane produced and directed; 1953. (c)

The Fake XX Dull British B-picture about theft of Leonardo with Denis O'Keefe guarding one at the Tate (an unlikely gallery to show it, to start with). Godfrey Grayson directed; 1953. (b/w)

Fallen Angel √√ Good strong early (1945) Otto Preminger about Dana Andrews marrying nice girl Alice Faye only so that he can get her money to run off with bad girl Linda Darnell. But then there's a murder and the plan gets all fouled up; earthily done with strong supports Charles Bickford, Bruce Cabot, John Carradine. (*b/w*)

The Fallen Idol √√ Absorbing tragedy of embassy butler and secretary as observed by protective but blundering small boy (Bobby Henrey); Ralph Richardson and Michèle Morgan marvellous in these parts, but the picture belongs to Carol Reed for bringing Graham Greene's screenplay from his short story so convincingly to life; 1948. (*b/w*)

The Falling Man X Looks as though director Billy Michaels shot a straightforward thriller about a framed cop and then someone decided it was too ordinary. So he recut it, renamed it and did the whole thing as a flashback as the man (Henry Silva) falls slowly forward. By the time he crashes down we know who has framed him – and don't care; 1972. (*c*)

The Fall of the House of Usher √ Roger Corman's first big success – in 1960 – is ponderous and poorly acted (Vincent Price *et al*), but is reasonably true to Poe's story. (*c*)

Fall of the Roman Empire XX Illustrates better the reasons for the Fall of the Hollywood Empire. Vast sets, chariot races and duels are no substitute for a strong script, and you can't get good acting just by hiring good actors. James Mason, Alec Guinness look embarrassed; Sophia Loren and Stephen Boyd let it all wash over them; Christopher Plummer apparently takes it seriously; Anthony Mann must be kidding; 1964. (*c*)

False Witness √ George Kennedy, discovering he has a terminal disease, works out an ingenious if over-complicated way to make a pot of gold to leave to his widow, Anne Jackson. Eli Wallach plays his lawyer. Richard A. Colla fails to make the most of his distinguished actors, however, and the film finally fails to thrill as much as it should; 1970. (*c*)

Fame Is the Spur √ Solid adaptation of Howard Spring's book by the Boultings is a chronicle of the long rise from poverty of politician Michael Redgrave. Rosamund John, Sir Seymour Hicks supported in 1946. (*b/w*)

The Family Jewels XX Unbelievably unfunny Jerry Lewis script-direction-acting shows no signs of awareness of the dire results; it's supposed to be about a 9-year-old orphan heiress choosing one of her uncles as a new father. The most awful thing is that Jerry Lewis plays them all; 1965. (*c*)

Family Life √ Cunningly made but ultimately unconvincing case-history of girl (Sandy Ratcliff) driven into deeper madness by ghastly family and drug-oriented psychiatry. Director Ken Loach brings considerable skill to his espousal of R. D. Laing's views as dramatised by David Mercer. It was called *In Two Minds* on television; 1971. (*c*)

The Family Way √ Adaptation of Bill Naughton's play *All in Good Time*, exploring two sets of working-class relationships. Parents are John Mills (never quite getting the earthiness of the character but making a splendid try) and Marjorie Rhodes (excellent). Son (Hwyel Bennett) and Hayley Mills (right in her bright little way) agonise through the reasons for the non-consummation of their marriage. As good as anything John and Roy Boulting ever did; 1967. (*c*)

Fanatic √ For the first part a fine menace movie about crazy old lady – Tallulah Bankhead, dahlings –imprisoning son's fiancée. Silvio Narizzano lets it get out of hand towards the end, but it was a lovely shiver in 1965 and still is. Strong TV names support: Peter Vaughan, Yootha Joyce, Maurice Kaufman. (*b/w*)

Fancy Pants √ Can you believe Bob Hope in Charles Laughton role? This is *Ruggles of Red Gap* musicalised by George Marshall in 1950, with Lucille Ball helping to make it amusing if not rollicking. (*c*)

Fanny X Sloppy sentimental broadening of the Marcel Pagnol trilogy brought to the American screen via the stage by Joshua Logan. Leslie Caron coos her way through the little waif bit, lumbered by clumsy Horst Buchholz, but comforted by kindly, wrinkly-eyed old Maurice Chevalier in a Marseilles that never existed. Charles Boyer, Lionel Jeffries gamely play along; 1961. (*c*)

Fantastic Voyage √√ Exciting idea of miniaturised sub with scientists in, speeding through bloodstream of body to wipe out brain lesion, is somewhat let down by obviousness of story about rugged hero (Stephen Boyd), shapely cutie (Raquel Welch), naughty villain (Donald Pleasence) inside; but effects are marvellous. Richard Fleischer; 1966. (*c*)

The Far Country √ James Stewart

bringing law'n'order to the Wild West, pursued by Steve Brodie and other villains, Bad Girl Ruth Roman and Good Girl Corinne Calvert. Anthony Mann; 1953. (c)

Farewell My Lovely √√√ (1) 1945: Dick Powell as Raymond Chandler's beaten-about private eye in classic thriller directed by Edward Dmytryk; Claire Trevor, Otto Kruger stand out among supports. (b/w)

Farewell My Lovely √√ (2) 1975: far from disastrous remake with Robert Mitchum in the Philip Marlowe part, and Charlotte Rampling doing her best to impersonate Lauren Bacall. The private eye emerges as rather more liberal than the original; director, Dick Richards. (c)

A Farewell To Arms XX David O. Selznick's great floperoo. The remake of the famous Helen Hayes-Gary Cooper 1933 version in 1957 was meant to be a crowning achievement for him and his wife Jennifer Jones. But he wouldn't listen to advice, forced first director John Huston to resign, tried to cower replacement Charles Vidor and spent money in grand, hopeless gestures. Although Ernest Hemingway had long before signed away his rights on his First World War novel about a nurse and a soldier, Selznick cabled him that he was allocating £50,000 of the profits as ex gratia payment. Hemingway cabled back that the chances of a profit on any film by Selznick with the 38-year-old Mrs S playing his 24-year-old heroine were nil, but if a miracle did occur Selznick could go change the money into nickels and shove them up himself until they came out of his ears. (c)

Far From The Madding Crowd √ Rare evocation of the English country-side rather let down by bare attempt to convey the strength of Hardy's plot; John Schlesinger never really convinces with absurdly modern miss Julie Christie, Alan Bates looking wan in a part that one reviewer commented 'might have been written for a well-mannered Airedale'; Terence Stamp making his usual unsuccessful attempt to get by on his looks. Only Peter Finch manages to seem at all convincing, and even he is too samey; 1967. (c)

The Far Horizons XX Unbelievable to the point of subversiveness, this prettied-up account of Lewis and Clark's epic journey through the wilderness of early America is plain awful; Fred MacMurray and Charlton Heston are supposed to be feuding but really they are engaged in a sorry battle over which is the worse actor. Astonishing that such an old reliable as Rudolph Maté let himself be roped in to direct such a dreadful script; 1955. (c)

The Fastest Gun Alive √ Moral-studded western about a store-keeper who had gun-slinging reputation foisted on to him, is then challenged by a real gunman. Russell Rouse directed, 1956, and Glenn Ford, Broderick Crawford, Jeanne Crain kept the idea and pace moving towards inevitable stand-up-and-fight climax. (b/w)

The Fast Lady XX 1962 British comedy with Stanley Baxter, Leslie Phillips and James Robertson Justice which could be called Carry On Vintage Driving and is notable only for Julie Christie's debut; Ken Annakin. (c)

Fat City √√ Although two boxers (Stacy Keach, Jeff Bridges) occupy centre-screen, John Huston's 1972 tragedy is not a boxing film. It is a sad story of failure, hype, and aimless illiteracy which could have been about any of a score of jobs, and there is not much boxing on the screen. Successful in what it sets out to do, it gives the audience a real insight into the characters' lives; 1972. (c)

Fate is the Hunter √ Glenn Ford investigating why a plane crashed. Was it Rod Taylor's fault? Ralph (Soldier Blue) Nelson directed, 1964; supports include Dorothy Malone, Jane Russell, Nehemiah Persoff, Wally Cox. (b/w)

Father Brown √ Alec Guinness in the 1954 – and only – English film of G. K. Chesterton's detective. Robert Hamer had dream cast to direct: Guinness plus Joan Greenwood, Peter Finch, Cecil Parker, Bernard Lee, Sid James. (b/w)

Father Came Too XX Stanley Baxter, Ronnie Barker dragged down by James Robertson Justice, Leslie Phillips and poor script in 1963 rubbish about newly-weds; director, Peter Graham Scott. (c)

Father Goose √ Featherweight comedy with Cary Grant as undercover agent disguised as shiftless South Seas beachcomber. Along trips schoolmarm Leslie Caron and miniature St Trinian's. With Trevor Howard, Jack Good, directed by Ralph Nelson. It won the 1964 Oscar for writers, but looks a bit coy now. (c)

Father of the Bride √√ Spencer Tracy as harassed dad carries this 1950 comedy of the problems of Elizabeth Taylor marrying namesake Don Taylor. Joan Bennett, Billie Burke add to the fun, directed by Vincente Minnelli. (b/w)

Father's Little Dividend √ Same cast and director as *Father of the Bride*, takes story on a stage when Spencer Tracy is going to be a Grandpa; 1951. (b/w)

Fathom √ Entertaining spoof of spy thriller with the minus of Raquel Welch as skydiver who plummets into middle of villainous Tony Franciosca, Ronald Fraser, Clive Revill, Tom Adams. Director Leslie Martinson makes it all good fun; 1967. (c)

The FBI Story √ Without James Stewart this would have been one more feds-and-hoods picaresque drama, but his patina and Mervyn Le Roy's 1959 direction lift it up by its shoulder-holster. (c)

Fear in the Night √ One of those plots where they don't believe the lady because she has a history of mental instability. This time it's Judy Geeson who swears she was attacked by a one-armed bandit. Joan Collins, Ralph Bates, Peter Cushing, Gillian Lind record various expressions of disbelief and guilt under Jimmy Sangster's routine 1972 hammer. (c)

Fear Is the Key √√ Barry Newman and Suzy Kendall are swept through the excitements of Alistair MacLean's thriller by director Michael Tuchner, showing pace and flair with a double-crossing, revenge-tinted plot. (c)

Fear Strikes Out √√ Don't be put off by subject, which superficially is baseball. In fact, it's a gripping and sympathetic true story of father's obsessive driving of son to glory, and the boy's crack-up and treatment. Karl Malden, Anthony Perkins marvellous. Robert Mulligan-Alan Pakula's director-producer debut; 1957. (b/w)

Female on the Beach √ Joan Crawford thinks Jeff Chandler is trying to murder her in this 1955 toughie. Is he? Joe Pevney directed with gusto. (b/w)

The Feminine Touch √ (1) Author of treatise on jealousy (Don Ameche, miscast) succumbs to it when he thinks wife (Rosalind Russell) is carrying on with Van Heflin, while she thinks he fancies Kay Francis; old-fashioned but has that 1941 Woody Van Dyke style. (b/w)

The Feminine Touch XX (2) Five girls train to be nurses; unfortunately, this was dated when it was first shown in 1956, and is desperately antique now. Pat Jackson assembled cast of nice competent second-raters but couldn't make it catch fire. (c)

Ferry to Hong Kong √ Curt Jurgens and Orson Welles ham it up as perpetual inadequate, unable to land either in Hong Kong or Macao, and boat's skipper; director Lewis Gilbert didn't seem to know whether it was meant to be comedy or melodrama; 1959. (c)

Fever Heat XXX Boring little film about dirty work in stock car racing, with Nick Adams and Jeannine Riley hopelessly inadequate; same goes for director Russell S. Doughton; 1968. (c)

A Fever in the Blood √ Three men all try to use a murder trial to further their political ambitions; an unusual and quite gripping melo with Efrem Zimbalist Jr., Don Ameche, Herbert Marshall and Angie Dickinson as the girl in the middle; but director Vincent Sherman ran out of conviction in 1960. (b/w)

Fiddler on the Roof √ Hugely successful, desperately vulgar haze of nostalgia about the old country (this time the Ukraine), with Topol sobbing and stomping away with a chorus of Jewish types. Easy laughs, easy sentimentality, uneasy history; Norman Jewison; 1971. (c)

Fiddlers Three X Tacky British copy of *Roman Scandals*, with Tommy Trinder attempting the Eddie Cantor bit in 1944. Francis L. Sullivan camps around and there's a glimpse of Frances Day, top musical comedienne of the time; Harry Watt directed. (b/w)

The Fiend Who Walked the West √ Western for grown-ups is about psychopathic killer in cowboy gear; Gordon Douglas made this one genuinely exciting in 1958; Hugh O'Brien. (b/w)

The Fiercest Heart XX White men pushing Red Indians out of their territory and made heroes for it in western movies are bad enough, but Boers shoving Zulus out of their land in South Africa and having heroic films made about them seem much worse somehow. Are Stuart Whitman, Juliet Prowse, Geraldine Fitzgerald, Raymond Massey happy about this 1961 adventure, looking back? George Sherman. (c)

55 Days At Peking √ The Boxer Rebellion and siege of the legations retold with some idea of its being allegorical plea for Uniting Nations; Charlton

Heston and Ava Gardner strike attitudes among the fireworks; Nicholas Ray directs manfully; 1963. (c)

The Fighting Prince of Donegal X A chunk of Irish history that's a bit too heavily served to swallow easily; Peter McEnery attempts an Errol Flynn role with moderate success; Susan Hampshire, Gordon Jackson among other Elizabethan period furniture; Michael O'Herlihy; 1966. (c)

Figures in a Landscape √ Ambitious Joe Losey attempt in 1970 to translate a closed Kafkaesque world to the wide open spaces, as Robert Shaw and Malcolm McDowell are pursued by a helicopter. Whence and whither are not explained, and all the tension comes from the personalities of the hunted pair, inter-acting on each other as well as against the terrain and the pursuers. (c)

The File of the Golden Goose XX Only the smaller parts played by such dependables as Edward Woodward, Graham Crowden, Charles Gray, manage to make this picture worth a desultory look. Yul Brynner's arrogant walk-through as American undercover agent breaking up counterfeiting gang is his usual terse, boring performance; Sam Wanamaker's idea of direction is to whizz through as many London locations as possible; 1969. (c)

The Final Hour √ Western with the difference that the antagonism is between ranchers and Polish workers imported for the coal-mines. Robert Douglas directs imaginatively and Lee J. Cobb lends distinction; 1963. (c)

The Final Programme √ Sci-flick about a self-reproducing human being, born of Jenny Runacre. Jon Finch plays a Nobel prizewinner intent on averting the end of the world as we know it. Robert Fuest wrote and directed in 1973. (c)

The Final Test √ Terence Rattigan enjoying himself writing about cricket and the last game that a father is playing. He wants his son to watch him but the lad isn't interested. Anthony Asquith squeezes the last drop of Englishness out of a very posh script, and Robert Morley stands out; 1954. (b/w)

Finders Keepers XX One of a string of weak comedies made by Cliff Richard in his hey-hey-heyday, 1966 in this case. Peggy Mount and Robert Morley mug ferociously but can't breathe much life into this yarn about 'Mighty Mini' bombs dropped in Spain by an American aircraft. Director, Sidney Hayers; 1966. (c)

A Fine Madness √ Berserk poet Sean Connery soon becomes tedious, despite Joanne Woodward's hard work as his wife; Jean Seberg and Patrick O'Neal don't help. Director Irvin Kershner has done better with New York locations than the people in this attempt at crazy comedy; 1966. (c)

Finian's Rainbow √ Made in 1968 before 'Godfather' Francis Ford Coppola became the golden boy of Hollywood, this rather pleasant and expensive version of the stage musical (*How Are Things In Glocca Morra?*) never made it with the public, but pleased discerning critics. An ageing Fred Astaire (69) still managed to appear sprightly, and it is perhaps unfair that Tommy Steele hasn't been asked to make a major movie since. (c)

Fireball 500 XX The stock cars in this racing low-budgeter are fine; Frankie Avalon and Fabian not so fine; William Asher; 1966. (c)

The Firechasers X Routine who-started-it hunt for arsonist, with American investigator Chad Everett drafted in to help London cop James Hayter and the U.S. box-office. Anjanette Comer plays one of those unlikely girl newshounds. Keith Barron, Rupert Davies, Robert Flemyng muddle along under Sidney Hayers's direction; 1970. (c)

Firecreek XX Both Henry Fonda and James Stewart have proved in their choices of television series to be utterly incapable of selecting material worthy of their talents and charisma, and this 1968 western seems to suggest that the rot set in at around their sixtieth birthdays (Fonda was born 1905, Stewart 1908). It's dull, slow-moving, poorly-scripted, inadequately-directed (by Vincent McEveety). Fonda's a villain, leader of a bunch of hired hands terrorising the community where Stewart is part-time sheriff. Not until the final shoot-out, when a crippled Stewart takes on the whole gang, does it rise even to the lowest heights. (c)

Fire Down Below X Robert Mitchum and Jack Lemmon fighting in a tramp steamer for tramp Rita Hayworth. Made in England for some reason (like blocked currency), it used a lugubrious lot of British actors as weak supports. Director Robert Parrish; 1957. (c)

The First Men in the Moon √ Amiably-eccentric version of the H. G.

Wells story, made in 1964, with gorgeous special effects by Ray Harryhausen and equally gorgeous performance by Lionel Jeffries as the first lunar-tic, claiming the moon for Queen Victoria. Director Nathan Juran. (c)

The First of the Few √ In 1942 Leslie Howard produced, directed and starred in real-life story of R. J. Mitchell, designer of the Spitfire, who died early, in 1937. It was Howard's last film: in 1943 he died in a shot-down aircraft. David Niven, Rosamund John, Roland Culver; Sir William Walton's famous score. (b/w)

The First Texan √ Joel McCrea as Sam Houston who led the fight for the state's freedom and became President; Byron Haskin; 1956. (c)

The First Travelling Saleslady X She's Ginger Rogers desperately trying to sell barbed wire to Texans, James Arness, Clint Eastwood among them; Arthur Lubin; 1956. (c)

Fitzwilly Strikes Back XXX Acute embarrassment is the only possible reaction to this outsized booboo with Dick Van Dyke as butler organising crime syndicate to keep distressed gentlewoman in the style to which she is accustomed. Dame Edith Evans must have been mad to accept the part of the eccentric dowager, and Delbert Mann's direction is so sentimental that it defies belief; 1968. (c)

Five √ The last quintet on Earth after an atomic explosion are all unknowns, but Arch Oboler, who directed and produced in 1951, is dab hand at the scientifically-fictitious. (b/w)

Five Against the House √ Reno casino caper – Guy Madison and Brian Keith stand out as college buddies in the gang; Kim Novak is their inside girl. Director Phil Karlson; 1955. (b/w)

Five Branded Women √ Jeanne Moreau with a shaven head is the most distinguished of the unlikely band of guerrillas formed in Yugoslavia after being thus marked for associating with the Nazis. Others: Silvana Mangano, Vera Miles, Barbara Bel Geddes. With direction by Martin Ritt, there is a much-needed undercurrent of reality. Among the males: Van Heflin, Richard Basehart, Steve Forrest; 1960. (b/w)

Five Card Stud √ Late (1968) attempt by veteran Henry Hathaway to come up with something new in westerns (*Ten Little Indians* in a game of poker, with each of the players getting shot in turn). However, he hasn't been able to make it sufficiently different from his routine work to distinguish it and the whodunit element is never exploited. Dean Martin, Robert Mitchum and Roddy McDowell turn in fairly obvious performances. (c)

Five Easy Pieces √√ Jack Nicholson, a middle-class slummer in the bars and oil-rigs of the blue-collars, visits his impeccable and artistic home, with a pregnant waitress (Karen Black) in tow. After some argumentative and sexual skirmishes, he leaves again. Although director Bob Rafelson extracts some power from this fable, the character ultimately fails to convince. Along the way, however, there are more than enough resonances and bits of sheer fun to repay watching; 1970. (c)

Five Finger Exercise X Disappointing version of Peter Schaffer play that was gripping in the theatre but has been coarsened in its screen translation directed by Daniel Mann. Nor are Rosalind Russell, Jack Hawkins convincing as parents of family disrupted by German student Maximilian Schell; 1962. (c)

Five Fingers √√ Splendid performance from James Mason as the Operation Cicero spy rifling the safe of the British ambassador to Turkey. Joseph L. Mankiewicz; 1952. (b/w)

Five Golden Dragons XX Robert Cummins is an innocent entangled in a Chinese smuggling ring. Dan Duryea, George Raft, Christopher Lee are directed, if that's the word, by Jeremy Summers; 1967. (c)

Five Man Army X Peter Graves leads train robbers for $500,000 gold hoard. The scene is Mexico, 1914; the location was Italy, 1970. Director, Don Taylor. (c)

Five Miles to Midnight √ Sophia Loren well-cast for once as Italian wife of American living in France who plots to swindle insurance company after he survives air-crash; Gig Young, Jean-Pierre Aumont support. Anatole Litvak made it moderately gripping; 1962. (b/w)

The Five Pennies X Supposed biopic of jazz musician Red Nichols in the twenties, all so familiar you want to chant the next lines even if you haven't seen it before. To make things worse, Danny Kaye does usual hammy over-acting; Barbara Bel Geddes is given an awful hair-do and told not to steal the picture – that's left to Louis Armstrong; Mel Shavelson; 1959. (c)

Five Weeks in a Balloon √ Splendid

spoof of Victorian exploration, with race across Africa to claim territory; Red Buttons, Barbara Eden, Cedric Hardwicke, Peter Lorre, Billy Gilbert, Herbert Marshall, Reginald Owen make up strong cast for Irwin Allen in 1962. (c)

The 5,000 Fingers of Dr T √ Imaginative nightmare of little boy who dreams of a 500-seater piano, lush apartments, dreary dungeons in Dr Terwilliker's Musical Academy, with Peter Lind Hayes. Director Roy Rowland; 1953. (c)

The Fixer √ A clash of opposites that never gel is the fault of this well-meaning, often moving, but rarely satisfactory account of one Jew's persecution in Czarist Russia. Dalton Trumbo's talky script fights with John Frankenheimer's natural flashy but suppressed style of direction. Symbolic importance of the theme fights with cliché lines ('Where there is no fight for it, there is no freedom'; 'I'm not a hero, I'm an accident'). And the casting – with the exception of Alan Bates as the hero/accident, who surprisingly overcomes his physical wrongness for the part – is awry: a whole string of British bit players doing their nuts (Georgia Brown, Ian Holm, David Warner, Carol White among the most out of place) and Dirk Bogarde indulges himself as a lawyer; 1969. (c)

The Flame and the Arrow √ Burt Lancaster as Italian Robin-Hood-type hero in the 12th century, Virginia Mayo the gal he wins; Jacques Tourneur lets everyone enjoy themselves, including you, if sufficiently uncritical; 1950. (c)

The Flame and the Flesh XX This dreary soaper with Lana Turner as bad woman and Pier Angeli as good is fortunately dominated by some scenes of Naples; Richard Brooks understandably preferred it to the plot and the principals; 1954. (c)

Flame in the Streets X Dated yarn about racial prejudices in 1961 Britain with Sylvia Syms falling for black teacher and causing her parents' marriage (John Mills, Brenda de Banzie) to blow up; Earl Cameron, Johnny Sekka, Ann Lynn, Wilfrid Brambell, do their best with a Ted Willis script; director Roy Baker. (c)

Flamingo Road X Joan Crawford, stranded carnival queen in small town, gets involved with politician Sidney Greenstreet, while losing heart to Zachary Scott. Michael Curtiz desperately tries to make sense out of twisting and often motiveless plot; 1949. (b/w)

Flaming Star √ What? a good movie with Elvis Presley in it? Well, not quite, but nearly. Possibly because as half-breed Indian, he has to share the lead with Steve Forrest and Dolores Del Rio, and Nunnally Johnson had a hand in the script. But most likely it's because the director was Don Siegel, since recognised (this was made in 1960) as one of Hollywood's major talents. (c)

Flareup √ Considering the original Barbie Doll, Raquel Welch, is one of two girls in mortal danger from potty Luke Askew, this James Neilson-directed thriller is not too bad; 1970. (c)

A Flea in Her Ear XXX There have been few more disastrous attempts to cash in on the success of a stage play than this profoundly unamusing version of Feydeau's farce which was helplessly funny on the stage. Perhaps it was that the mechanics of opening the wrong doors at the right time and dressing up to get out of naughty situations needs the magic box of the theatre. Or it may be that Rex Harrison, Rosemary Harris, Louis Jourdan and Rachel Roberts are simply unsuited to high farce. Or that Jacques Charon is a rotten director; 1968. (c)

Flesh and Blood XX One of Alexander Korda's self-important but bruisingly dull British spectaculars, circa 1951. Based on Bridie's *A Sleeping Clergyman*, director Anthony Kimmins puts wooden Richard Todd through a double role (mainly as doctor), attended by a whole gallery of earnest players, including Glynis Johns, Joan Greenwood, George Cole, Michael Hordern. (b/w)

Flesh and Fury X The presence of Tony Curtis as a boxer might tempt you into watching this, but be warned, he's deaf and dumb, and is given his hearing back by magazine writer Mona Freeman; Joseph Pevney must have known it was hokum, but he bravely puts a good face on it; 1951. (b/w)

The Flesh and the Fiends X Filmmakers are endlessly fascinated by the Burke and Hare grave-robbing mythology, and this is a 1960 version of the Edinburgh anatomist story with Peter Cushing, Donald Pleasence, Billie Whitelaw, directed by John Gilling. (b/w)

The Flesh is Weak XX Trite little melo

about tarts and bully-boys in London; nifty direction by Don Chaffey is about all it's got; 1957. (b/w)

Flight From Ashiya X One of those back-flashing melos about characters caught in air-sea rescue, sunk before it starts by a banal script well matched by the luckless direction of Michael Anderson, never the man to add inspiration. Richard Widmark and Shirley Knight manage to rise a little above the general boredom; Yul Brynner and George Chakiris don't; 1964. (c)

Flight of the Phoenix √ Superior survivors-in-the-desert drama with stand-out performances from James Stewart as crashed plane's pilot, Richard Attenborough as his navigator. Beautifully understated direction from Robert Aldrich overcomes tendency to stereotyping among the others. They gradually fight to rebuild the plane, and the climax is guaranteed to keep you on the edge of your seat; 1966. (c)

Flight to Tangier X Jack Palance, soldier of fortune, and Joan Fontaine, pilot's girlfriend, seek survivors in North African plane crash; Charles Marquis Warren wrote and directed in 1953, without much flair. (c)

Flipper √ Pleasant little Florida adventure with, one suspects, a whole school of dolphins acting the part of Flipper. After all, we wouldn't know them apart, would we? Strictly boy-meets-dolphin, boy-loses-dolphin, boy-gets-dolphin despite hurricane. Director, James B. Clark; 1963. (c)

Flipper and the Pirates X Luke Halpin, Pamela Franklin and precocious dolphin in run-in (and swim-in) with ex-convicts. But there aren't any pirates. Leon Benson; 1964. (c)

Flower Drum Song X Endless musical about Chinese girl from Hong Kong who loves Chinese boy in San Francisco but he loves Chinese stripper; no great songs from Rodgers and Hammerstein and no great shakes from director Henry Koster; Nancy Kwan, James Shigeta, Juanita Hall; 1961. (c)

Fluffy XXX Boring and predictable yarn about a pet lion on the loose that wastes the talents of owner Tony Randall, Shirley Jones, Celia Kaye, Jim Backus; director is Earl Bellamy, who does his best with over-stretched material; 1964. (c)

The Fly √ A huge success in 1958, surprising its makers, who thought they had an average-to-good low budgeter

(it cost £350,000; made £3 million in its first few weeks' release) but had reckoned without the morbid attraction of a man's head and arm being fixed by scientific mischance on to a fly – and vice versa. Vincent Price admits he couldn't keep a staight face during filming, but although producer-director Kurt Neumann didn't exploit the possibilities, it remains genuinely chilling. (c)

Flying Leathernecks √ The standard army drama transferred to the flying corps with John Wayne as the tough commander and Robert Ryan, resenting him, finds he has to act the same way when he takes over. Nicholas Ray gives it great zing; 1951. (c)

Folies Bergère √ Maurice Chevalier plays a double role in musical museum piece with vast chorine members, Ann Sothern, Merle Oberon; director Roy del Ruth; 1935. (b/w)

Follow Me X Poor remake of Peter Schaffer's one-act *The Public Eye*, with Topol disastrous as the detective who establishes a relationship with the wife (a trite Mia Farrow) he is following. As the husband, Michael Jayston is unable to generate much sympathy, while director Carol Reed has failed to imprint his usual touch; 1971. (c)

Follow That Dream √ The best Elvis Presley vehicle - though that's not saying much. He's a country hick moving to Florida in order to homestead and he beats the slickers at their own game; Director Gordon Douglas; 1962. (c)

Follow That Horse XX British comedy directed by Alan Bromly wastes a marvellous cast of good character actors in rubbish about horse swallowing microfilm; David Tomlinson, Cecil Parker, Richard Wattis, Dora Bryan, George A. Cooper, Arthur Lowe; 1959. (b/w)

Follow That Man XX Sydney Chaplin, Dawn Addams in Jerry Epstein-directed tripe about a con man and a journalist; 1960. (b/w)

Follow the Boys X Low-spirited comedy of American gals who (nicely) traipse after the American fleet in the Med. Picture postcards of Cannes and Santa Margherita; pleasant legs in front of them belong to Paula Prentiss, Janis Paige. The rest is noise; Richard Thorpe; 1963. (c)

Follow the Fleet √√ 'Let's Face the Music', 'Eggs in One Basket', 'We Joined the Navy' are among the numbers in this 1936 Astaire-Rogers joyousness. Actually, he joins the navy because Ginger turns him down. Then they meet again in San Francisco; Mark Sandrich directed. (b/w)

Follow the Sun X Over-dramatised biopic of golfer Ben Hogan's fight against accident damage; Glenn Ford, Anne Baxter, Sam Snead. Sidney Lanfield; 1951. (b/w)

Folly to be Wise √ One of the funnier British comedies of the early fifties (1952 to be precise) has Alastair Sim organising and embarrassing 'brains trust'; Roland Culver, Martita Hunt, Miles Malleson helped Frank Launder come up with a smiler. (b/w)

Fools Rush In XX Weak British comedy of 1949 about on-off-on wedding directed by John Paddy Carstairs in rather limp style and with thoroughly undistinguished cast. (b/w)

Footsteps in the Fog √ Gas-lit melo with Stewart Granger as wife-murderer – is Jean Simmons next on the list? Arthur Lubin does his best to milk the suspense; 1955. (c)

For a Few Dollars More √ Sequel to A Fistful of Dollars, this spaghetti western has Clint Eastwood and Lee Van Cleef searching for an outlaw. These once-despised European-shot oaters under Sergio Leone have gone up in critical opinion since their influence became so pervasive and their moody violence became the norm for Hollywood; 1967. (c)

For Better For Worse X Dirk Bogarde gives this thin little domestic comedy about young couple facing early years of marriage what distinction it has with Cecil Parker backing him up solidly. Distaff side weaker, with Susan Stephen and Eileen Herlie less convincing; J. Lee Thompson; 1954. (c)

Forbidden XX Twisty-ended thriller about Douglass Montgomery planning death of his wife, scheming Hazel Court. Motley crew of British players attempt to support: Ronald Shiner, Kenneth Griffith, Andrew Cruickshank, Patricia Burke. George King directed; 1947. (b/w)

Forbidden Planet √√ Raves John Baxter in Science Fiction in the Cinema: 'Was and still is the most remarkable of sf films, the ultimate recreation of the future'. Loosely based on The Tempest, it has Walter Pidgeon as survivor of AD 2000 expedition to Altair, with Anne Francis as his Miranda of a daughter; a robot is their Caliban. Done with more verve and imagination than scientific accuracy or plausibility,

it is nevertheless a major achievement for director Fred. M. Wilcox and special effects expert Joshua Meador; 1956. (c)

The Forbin Project √ One of those computer-takes-over sci-flicks, with Eric Braeden and Susan Clark wrestling with the implications of US's electronic brain teaming up with Russians. Director, Joseph Sargent, 1969. (c)

Force of Arms √ Updating of Hemingway's A Farewell to Arms to Second World War but based on a short story by Richard William Tegaskis. William Holden is battle-weary soldier, Nancy Olson a WAC officer frightened to fall in love again; Michael Curtiz treats it as superior soap-opera, which is what it always was; 1951. (b/w)

Foreign Correspondent √√ Classic 1940 Hitchcock with Joel McCrea caught up in web of international espionage, and Herbert Marshall, George Sanders, Laraine Day, Robert Benchley turning in their best work under his direction. Gary Cooper turned it down because it was a thriller, and Hitchcock has since criticised McCrea as being too easy-going. (b/w)

Foreign Intrigue √ Robert Mitchum uncovering Neo-Nazis, with Genevieve Page; Sheldon Reynolds directs-produces this competent, if ultimately disappointing thriller; 1956. (c)

The Foreman Went to France √ Tommy Trinder as humble factory-worker thrust into France with Clifford Evans to wrest vital parts from advancing Nazis. The refugee reconstruction by director Charles Frend has popped up in genuine retrospectives, a tribute to its apparent authenticity; 1941. (b/w)

Forever Amber X Otto Preminger took over after John Stahl had already shot two million dollars' worth of unusable film. He told Darryl Zanuck then he couldn't even finish reading the book, but he was under contract. Then they rowed about the star – he wanted Lana Turner but Zanuck insisted on Linda Darnell. 'The picture, in spite of all the whittling that was done, the censorship difficulties, the cuts that were made for the Catholic League of Decency, brought back its money and eventually made a profit.' (Otto Preminger in Gerald Pratley's book.) It shouldn't have – it just shows the power of the dirty word; 1947. (c)

Forever Darling XX James Mason sorts out Lucille Ball and Desi Arnaz's marital problems. He plays the part of an angel, as he did again in Warren Beatty's *Heaven Can Wait* in 1978. Directed by Alexander Hall; 1956. (c)

Forever Female √ Satisfyingly bitchy glimpse into world of the theatre with Ginger Rogers as ageing actress, husband-producer Paul Douglas, ambitious playwright William Holden; Irving Rapper; 1953. (b/w)

For Love of Ivy XX Appalling longueur on the part of Sidney Poitier (who devised and starred in it), Daniel Mann (who directed) and all aboard this so-called comedy about a racketeer who woos a housemaid for the despicable purpose of keeping her employed by white household. Offensive to anyone, black or white, who sees the need for radical change. Poitier, doing very nicely thank you out of the present situation, obviously isn't among them; 1967. (c)

For Love or Money X Widow Thelma Ritter hires lawyer Kirk Douglas to be matchmaker for her three daughters; the only question which might idly occupy your attention is which one he'll end up marrying himself. Bright little, dull little Mitzi Gaynor is closest to a star so she's the favourite; William Bendix and Gig Young can't save it from Michael Gordon's nerveless grasp; 1963. (c)

For Pete's Sake √√ Agreeable crazy comedy in which Barbra Streisand has to work for a number of shady employers in settlement of a debt to loan sharks. Michael Sarrazin, Estelle Parsons support, gamely. Peter Yates, hitherto known as a thriller man, directed; 1974. (c)

The Forsyte Saga X A bit of a laugh, when Errol Flynn is Soames, Robert Young the architect Bossiney, Greer Garson moderately well cast as Irene; pity poor Compton Bennett having to squash it all into a couple of hours. Can't be done; 1950. (c)

Fort Apache √ Classic John Ford 1948 super-western, with Henry Fonda as embittered officer in charge of outpost, John Wayne as his disgusted aide. Shirley Temple makes an unexpected entry as Fonda's daughter – she was 20 at the time. (b/w)

Fort Defiance √ Coward deserts during Civil War, causing all but one man in his company to be killed; the survivor pledges revenge. Dan Clark and Ben Johnson do well in main parts; John Rawlins directs competently; 1951. (c)

For the First Time XX Mario Lanza

fans can tune in for a weep-in as our stodgy star, playing of course a temperamental opera king, falls for a beautiful girl who is deaf – fortunately? With Johanna von Koczian, Zsa Zsa Gabor, directed (1958) by Rudy Maté. (c)

For the Love of Ada XXX Weak opening-out of weak series with Wilfred Pickles and Irene Handl. Virtually plotless as well as witless; director Ronnie Baxter; 1972. (c)

For Them That Trespass X One of those earnest British movies about plucky girl (Patricia Plunkett) fighting to clear unjustly accused (Richard Todd). Patronising about the working class, as many films were in 1949, despite being directed by Alberto Cavalcanti. (b/w)

For Those Who Think Young XX Cheap little picture about the extra-curricular activities of girl at college, with James Darren and Nancy Sinatra; only occasionally amusing; Leslie H. Martinson; 1964. (c)

Fort Massacre X Joel McCrea takes over command of survivors of Indian massacre, determined on vengeance; Forrest Tucker; director Joseph Newman; 1958. (c)

Fort Osage X The fort was the last safe stop for pioneers heading into the West; Rod Cameron fronts routine western using it as background; Leslie Selander; 1952. (c)

Fort Ti X On TV, 3D effects are unfortunately missing from this otherwise standard western. All that's left is George Montgomery riding to the rescue in French-Indian war of late 18th century; William Castle; 1953. (c)

The Fortune X Director Mike Nichols doesn't seem sure whether to make this a black comedy, a farce or a satire, but the threesome of Jack Nicholson, Warren Beatty and Stockard Channing is irresistible. She's an heiress in 1920, when the Mann Act forbade transportation for immoral purposes across a state line, so she must marry Jack although Warren's her lover. Murder follows. Billy Wilder would have given it a mordant edge: Nichols settled for urbane fun, in 1974. (c)

The Fortune Cookie √√√ Divine Billy Wilder satire about insurance frauds with shady lawyer Walter Matthau (Whiplash Willie) advising Jack Lemmon on how to milk the insurance company; 1966. (b/w)

Fort Worth X Randolph Scott has to pick up his guns again when his newspaper can't rid the town of scoundrels – a dubious message. Edwin L. Martin; 1951. (c)

Forty Carats XX Liv Ullmann had a disastrous career in Hollywood during the seventies. After *Lost Horizon*, she tried romantic comedy with this 1973 tale of middle-age-loves-youngster (the 22-year-old son of comedian Eddie Albert, Edward Albert). Sadly, Liv couldn't do the light-hearted bit and the result is deplorable. Gene Kelly and Binnie Barnes add to the feeling of geriatric benefit week; director, Milton Katselas. (c)

Forty Guns √ A Samuel Fuller script-production-direction of Barry Sullivan coming up against the forty-strong gang headed by Barbara Stanwyck, Gene Barry, Dean Jagger; 1957. (c)

Forty Guns to Apache Pass X Routine 1966 Cavalry adventure, with Audie Murphy fighting the Indians and his treacherous sergeant, Robert Brubaker. William Witney directed without much flair. (c)

Forty Pounds of Trouble √ A bit cute but often amusing comedy about gambling casino owner Tony Curtis having to cope with 5-year-old girl left on his hands; Phil Silvers, Stubby Kaye score, and there's a lot of Disneyland. Norman Jewison brought some nice touches to what could have been insufferably whimsical; 1962. (c)

Forty-Second Street √√√ Archetypal 1933 Busby Berkeley-choreographed musical in which Bebe Daniels breaks a leg and so can't star in Warner Baxter-directed show. Ruby Keeler, this is your big chance - get out there and slay them! Among others present: Ginger Rogers, Rudy Vallee, George Brent, Guy Kibbee, Una Merkel, Ned Sparks. Among the songs: 'You're Getting to be a Habit with Me', 'I'm Young and Healthy', 'Shuffle Off to Buffalo'; director, Lloyd Bacon. (b/w)

For Whom the Bell Tolls √ Sam Wood's war film, with a convincing Gary Cooper and a less-so Ingrid Bergman, carefully played down Hemingway's essential placing of it in the Spanish Civil War. Despite this, it probably educated a large number of hitherto isolated Americans about which side was which in the world conflict they had somehow become embroiled in (it was made in 1943). The tendency was towards cartoon in Katina Paxinou's and Akim Tamiroff's performances, but the whole effect was exciting and involving. (c)

The Fountainhead X Gary Cooper gravely miscast as hero of Ayn Rand's philosophical novel about modern architect battling with Establishment. 'I thought it should have been someone like Bogart, a more arrogant type of man,' said King Vidor, looking back. 'But Pat Neal I thought marvellous, splendid.' 1949. (b/w)

Four For Texas √ Clanny romp through the Wild West with Frank Sinatra, Dean Martin, Anita Ekberg, Ursula Andress. Robert Aldrich gave it expert touch; 1963. (c)

Four Guns to the Border XX Rory Calhoun as bank-robber laid low by pretty Colleen Miller; director Richard Carlson makes it last from fight to clinch to fight somehow; 1954. (c)

The Four Horsemen of the Apocalypse XX Not, alas, the 1921 Valentino version but Vincente Minnelli's 1962 updating to Second World War which only revealed story's novelettishness and Glenn Ford's inadequacies. Divided loyalties in Argentinian family in Paris. Those old horsemen come thundering through in visions. (c)

Four In the Morning √√ Three sets of London stories intertwine to make an unusual and memorable film which gives the impression that director Anthony Simmons allowed his talented cast (Judi Dench, Norman Rodway, Joe Melia in outstanding episode; Ann Lynn, Brian Phelan in another) to improvise. Some nice moody shots of London, too; 1966. (b/w)

The Four Musketeers — the Revenge of Milady X Inferior sequel to 1973's *The Three Musketeers*, brought out in '74. Directed by Richard Lester at the same time as the original, this should have been as funny and inventive, but somehow wasn't. The jokes don't seem so amusing, and the high camp of Faye Dunaway, Charlton Heston, Geraldine Chaplin and the little band of adventurers themselves falls flat. (c)

The Fourposter X Made in 1952, when Rex Harrison and Lilli Palmer were married, they are the only players in filming of dreary Jan de Hartog play about various stages of a married life with the title-bed as part of each scene's action. Sadly, it's neither very sexy nor edifying; Irving Reis; 1952. (b/w)

Four Rode Out XX Nasty western full of rape (mostly Sue Lyon's) and revenge (ditto). Director John Peyser just keeps it moving, but it's a long trek for all concerned, not least the audience. 1969. (c)

Fourteen Hours √ Will Richard Basehart throw himself off skyscraper edge? Can Paul Douglas or Barbara Bel Geddes save him? Can you spot Grace Kelly in a sub-plot? Henry Hathaway; 1951. (b/w)

The Fox √ In the dear dead pre-permissive days of 1968 this was a great sensation with implied lesbianism and a glimpse or two of bared breasts, but now it's just an unsatisfactory attempt to translate the D. H. Lawrence story to the screen, with awful overplaying by Keir Dullea, Anne Heywood and Sandy Dennis. Director Mark Rydell must take part of the blame. (c)

The Foxes of Harrow X Lush mush with Rex Harrison, Maureen O'Hara, Victor McLaglen put through tiresome hoops by John M. Stahl in 1947 failure to recapture copied grandeur of *Gone With The Wind*. (b/w)

Foxfire XX A very ill-assorted pair (Jeff Chandler as Apache miner, Jane Russell as posh girl from the East) somehow meet and get married. Their problems and their search for a gold-mine take up this drama routinely directed by Joseph Pevney; 1955. (c)

Framed XX Joe Don Baker revenging his imprisonment, which he and we are supposed to think is false, although we see him beat a deputy to death in the first few minutes of the film. Director Phil Karlson; 1975. (c)

The Franchise Affair √ Michael Denison and Dulcie Gray in neat thriller about what may or may not be a kidnapping; Lawrence Huntington directed in 1952. (b/w)

Francis X First of seven pretty grim comedies about a talking mule, with Donald O'Connor as his mate (1950); spawned **Francis Goes to the Races** (1951); **Francis Goes to West Point** (1952); **Francis Covers the Big Town** (1953); **Francis Joins the WACS** (1954); **Francis in the Navy** (1955), all munch of a munchness (and that's about the level of the jokes); when director Arthur Lubin went on to create Mr Ed, a talking horse (wonder where he got the idea?) on TV, Charles Lamont made a final film with Mickey Rooney replacing Donald O'Connor, **Francis in the Haunted House** (1956). (all b/w)

Francis of Assisi X No, not a follow-up to the above. This sixth film on the animal-loving saint is pictorially beautiful, being made on the actual locations in Italy, but a bit dull. Still, that's better than being sensational. Bradford Dillman plays St. Francis carefully, and Dolores Hart, Finlay Currie, Athene Seyler don't give offence; Michael Curtiz probably achieves the effect he was seeking if not the success; 1961. (c)

Frankenstein √√√ A great, great movie, much more than just a horror picture, unlike so many of its imitators. Director James Whale wrung masterly performances from Boris Karloff in 1931; you feel sympathy and understanding for this almost-human and, through him, for all life's abnormals. (b/w)

Frankenstein Created Woman X And Terence Fisher created disappointment in this creaky 1967 attempt to project the myth further than it will stretch; Peter Cushing does his best. (c)

Frankenstein Meets the Wolf Man X Scientist tampering with the unknown in 1943 was Patric Knowles. Instead of finding Dr Frankenstein's diary he unearths Bela Lugosi and Lon Chaney. Director Roy William Neill was forced by Lugosi's age to cheat his more active scenes. (b/w)

Frankenstein Must Be Destroyed X But you can bet he won't as long as he goes on making money with such farragos as this 1969 one about the Doc transplanting brains; Peter Cushing and Freddie Jones, directed perfunctorily and bloodily by Terence Fisher (lots of c)

Frankenstein 1970 X Time has overtaken this lame attempt to squeeze one more chiller out of the old story; it wasn't made in 1970 but twelve years earlier and is about Boris Karloff being made in the basement while a TV crew films a programme about him upstairs. Strictly for collectors; Howard W. Koch. (c)

Frankenstein — The True Story √ Who did Christopher Isherwood and Don Bachardy think they were kidding in 1973 when they claimed that? This is just one more run around the monster, cut to two hours from the original US-TV length of four hours, with Michael Sarrazin as Boris Karloff, James Mason as the Doctor, and Leonard Whiting as F. The presence of Gielgud and Richardson in Jack Smight's cast adds interest. The most novel suggestion is a sort of gay relationship between monster and creator. (c)

Frankie and Johnny X As Elvis Presley vehicles go, this one from 1966 isn't too awful. Frederick de Cordova keeps it lively and Harry Morgan has some quite jolly comedy lines to say. Nancy Kovack makes a sweet Nellie Bly. (c)

Fraternally Yours √√ Laurel and Hardy live it up while their wives think they are on holiday for their health; director, William A. Seiter; 1933. (b/w)

Fraulein X Prettied-up version of novel which dwelt lovingly on all the degradations a German had to go through as the war collapsed. Here, Dana Wynter finds love with an American officer after a certain amount of tough times but nothing to the book; Henry Koster; 1958. (c)

Fraulein Doktor XX Hard going for Suzy Kendall as real-life spy, Anna Maria Lesser, in the First World War. Director Alberto Lattuada can't get the best out of Kenneth More, James Booth, Alexander Knox. Nobody can out of Capucine; 1968. (c)

Freebie and the Bean √ Usual 1974 mixture of buddy-buddy cops (Alan Arkin, James Caan) in the midst of the department's corruption, violence, car chases, gays, blacks, cynical comedy. The result is familiar but quite engaging. Director Richard Rush. (c)

Freedom to Die X Paul Maxwell escapes jail, intent on revenge. He should have turned on writer Arthur La Bern and director Francis Searle. Bruce Seton, T. P. McKenna can't save it; 1961. (b/w)

The French Connection √√√ Marvellously observed and realised chase thriller with outstanding direction by William Freidkin and convincing performances from Gene Hackman (a little too lovable for his repulsive detective), Fernando Rey (smooth villain), Roy Scheider (tough cop). The thrills are a bit mechanical and the sadism too obvious; but it keeps you watching; 1971. (c)

French Connection II √√ As in so many seventies' movies, the most important credit here is Stunt Co-ordinator (Hal Needham), as detective Gene Hackman chases Fernando Rey round Marseilles. John Frankenheimer kept it all moving, in 1975, and there is sufficient characterisation to keep you alert between stunts. (c)

French Dressing XX Awful Ken Russell debut which at least doesn't have the pretentiousness of his later epics. Imagine casting a dull little Austrian actress, Marisa Mell, as a French starlet when there were so many French possibilities. From this beginning the half-hearted attempt to satirise the English seaside is just gloom-plunging, despite James Booth and Roy Kinnear doing their best; 1964. (b/w)

The French Line XXX Jane Russell has quite big breasts. When you've said that, you have exhausted all possible points of interest about that over-publicised lady. Certainly this dull comedy about heiress looking for man not after her money and going to Europe to find him has none. Lloyd Bacon slices it thin; 1954. (c)

Frenchie √ Stongly-cast – Joel McCrea, Shelley Winters, Elsa Lanchester – western about a gambling lady; Louis King; 1950. (c)

Frenchman's Creek X Daphne du Maurier novel not all that well translated to the screen but making an undemanding swashbuckler with Arturo de Cordova as the pirate who's a perfect gent and Joan Fontaine as grand lady with romantic ideas; Basil Rathbone, Nigel Bruce were their 1945 best; Mitchell Leisen. (c)

Frenzy √√ Splendid old-fashioned Hitchcock thriller, set in Covent Garden and district, in 1972. A 'necktie murderer' terrorises London, and disposes of Barbara Leigh-Hunt and Anna Massey before our eyes: rape shows a new side of Hitchcock. While Barry Foster blossoms under the direction of the Master, Jon Finch fumbles along in a thankless part. (c)

Freud –The Secret Passion √ While avoiding the usual biopic pitfall of glamorising his subject, John Huston hasn't made Freud at all believable. He isn't helped by a monotonous, pop-eyed performance from Montgomery Clift; nor is the rest of this poorly chosen cast very convincing; it's sensational enough, in parts, and the Viennese locations are authentic. But there's a block somewhere. When did you first start having these dreams of being a significant film director, Mr Huston? 1962. (b/w)

Friendly Persuasion √√ Delightful morality tale of Quaker family (Gary Cooper, Dorothy McGuire, Tony Perkins) whose pacifism is put to the test in the Civil War. William Wyler; 1956. (c)

The Friends of Eddie Coyle √√ Strong drama from director Peter Yates: Robert Mitchum is neatly turned into an informer by treasury agent Richard Jordan and his life threatened by Peter Boyle. Set in Boston, a change from San Francisco, Paul Monash's script provides a solid basis; 1973. (c)

The Frightened City XX Tedious British thriller about wicked Herbert Lom's intention to amalgamate the six gangs that run London's protection racket. John Gregson, Sean Connery are on hand; director, John Lemont; 1961. (c)

Frogs √√ One of the most frightening horror movies ever made, with swamp creatures – frogs, turtles, snakes, toads, lizards and leeches too – turning on the humans that have relegated them to inferior status. Ray Milland is the only name among the humans; somehow it's comforting to remember that director George McCowan was right there behind the camera all the time; 1972. (c)

From Hell to Texas √√ Superior western with Don Murray on the run from a crime he hasn't committed. Dennis Hopper is among well-etched band of characters he runs into. Henry Hathaway can usually be relied on to bring the best out of an oater script and certainly did so here in 1958. (c)

From Here to Eternity √√ Conflict between director Fred Zinneman and producer Harry Cohn over length (Cohn insisted on two big scenes being cut so as to bring it under two hours) and casting of this drama of army life in Hawaii at start of Second World War; Joan Crawford was Cohn's choice for the part Deborah Kerr turned sexy in, and it was only when she walked out over a fight about the wardrobe that he gave in. And he accepted Frank Sinatra cheap (£1,000 a week) after the then-failed singer offered to pay to get into the picture; Sinatra was right – it marked the turning point in his career and won him one of its seven Academy Awards. See *The Godfather* for fictionalised version of how Sinatra got the role; Donna Reed also won Oscar for it; 1953. (b/w)

From Russia With Love √√ The second James Bond film – the one about his being snaffled in Istanbul as he goes after Russian cipher machine; usual slick *mélange* of guns, athleticism and sex, presided over by Terence Young. Sean Connery does his famous bit, aided by Robert Shaw, Lotte Lenya, Pedro Armendariz; 1963. (c)

From the Earth to the Moon X Pretty ludicrous adaptation of Jules Verne sf about a millionaire who chooses to stay

on the moon for love of a lady; somehow Joseph Cotten, George Sanders, Debra Paget got involved in 1964 version of 1868 yarn. Byron Haskin directed. (c)

From the Terrace √ Paul Newman as another of his early ruthless, ambitious working boys marrying (Joanne Woodward) social status, from John O'Hara chronicle. Myrna Loy is splendid as drunken mother; directed, 1960, by Mark Robson. (c)

The Front Page √√ Enjoyable remake of 1930 (Pat O'Brien-Lewis Milestone) newspaper play (which became *His Girl Friday* with a sex-change in 1940) by Billy Wilder in 1974. Walter Matthau plays the hard-hearted editor, Jack Lemmon the star reporter who hides the escaped prisoner for a scoop. Enormous fun. (c)

Front Page Story X One of those incredible newspaper yarns. Editor Jack Hawkins has to cope with divorce, lost children, murder and mutiny, besides getting the paper out. Weak supports include Eva Bartok, Derek Farr, Elizabeth Allan; director, Gordon Parry; 1953. (b/w)

The Fugitive √ Critics were upset in 1947 because John Ford softened Graham Greene's *The Power and the Glory* by not making Henry Fonda's priest alcoholic. But this produced a greater challenge in that he never has this excuse. It is now recognised as Ford's most personal work, celebrating the solace of religion, and Fonda's sincerity is matched by Dolores del Rio as his Mary Magdalene, J. Carrol Naish his Iscariot, Pedro Armendariz his Pilate. (b/w)

The Fugitive Kind √√ Marlon Brando as drifting Romeo ready to settle. As try-outs he gets involved with passionate Anna Magnani and powerful Joanne Woodward – who gives a great performance. Sidney Lumet's uneven 1959 direction don't quite do justice to Tennessee Williams's original *Orpheus Descending*, but it smoulders along satisfactorily. (b/w)

Full of Life √ The superb Judy Holliday as pregnant wife dependent on excitable father-in-law Salvatore Baccaloni; a good laugh. Highly efficient direction by Richard Quine; 1956. (b/w)

Funeral in Berlin √ This is the Len Deighton about Colonel Stok (Oscar Homolka) purportedly defecting, with Michael Caine as bespectacled hero from *The Ipcress File*. Guy Hamilton didn't manage the coherence of the book; 1966. (c)

Fun in Acapulco XX Elvis Presley might have had some fun counting the money he was going to make from this rotten movie, but it doesn't extend to us. He's supposed to be a trapeze artist who regains lost nerve when high-diving in this fancy Mexican resort; Paul Lukas scores as temperamental chef; Ursula Andress wears bathing suits. Richard Thorpe; 1963. (c)

Funny Face √ Photographer Fred Astaire lures bookshop assistant (Audrey Hepburn) into becoming model girl; lots of pleasant dancing, singing and clothes; Stanley Donen; 1956. (c)

Funny Girl √√ Sometimes a performance is so legendary that audiences don't see the person – only the myth. This was the case with Barbra Streisand's film debut in the performance that had already conquered Broadway and the West End, in a show allegedly based on the life-story of Follies star Fanny Brice. The first half transferred well to the screen under veteran William Wyler's respectful direction, but after the interval it goes to pieces when her drama with her unsatisfactory husband (played with inappropriate self-satisfaction by Omar Sharif) has been opened out. The end is pure Streisand, singing a song that wasn't in the original show, 'My Man', in a manner quite unlike Miss Brice's. The rest of the cast are only back-drops to La Streisand; 1968. (c)

Funny Lady XX Unfortunate sequel to *Funny Girl*, with Omar Sharif again popping in and out of Barbra Streisand (as Fanny Brice)'s life. James Caan makes an absurd Billy Rose, whose show numbers, which were vulgar but worked, are replaced by director Herbert Ross with antiseptic glamour; 1975. (c)

Funnyman √ Low-budgeter which shows with some success, some over - pretentiousness, how young San Francisco revue actor searches for something to make his life meaningful. Altogether too pleased with itself; John Korty; 1968. (part c part b/w)

A Funny Thing Happened on the Way to the Forum √ But not nearly as funny as everyone involved seems to think. The original stage musical was a bit yawny, but the frantic opening-out by fey Dick Lester is even more so; ancient Rome must have been wittier than this lumbering attempt to weld Buster Keaton, Zero Mostel, Phil Silvers and Swinging Rome into any kind of satisfactory whole; 1966. (c)

The Furies √ Routine epic western about cattle-baron feud, with Barbara Stanwyck as defiant Juliet (it was made in 1950 when she was 43!) and Walter Huston her crusty old pop; Anthony Mann directed. (b/w)

Further up the Creek X Frankie Howerd turns last voyage of naval frigate into paying holiday cruise with David Tomlinson, Shirley Eaton, Thora Hird among passengers and crew. Provides a laugh or two. Director: Val Guest; 1958. (b/w)

Fury √ 'MGM's picture *Fury* is a powerful and documented piece of fiction about a lynching for half its length, and for the remaining half a desperate attempt to make love, lynching and the Hays Office come out even' (*The Film Criticism of Otis Ferguson*). Spencer Tracy (36 in 1936) was chosen by Fritz Lang, making his American picture debut, as innocent victim who turns the tables; Alistair Cooke called it 'best film of this or maybe of any coming year' – but it's a bit disappointing now. (b/w)

Fuzz √ Moderately successful comedy-drama set in Ed McBain's 87th Precinct, with Burt Reynolds and Jack Weston the two detectives. The main weakness is the casting of the mytho-logical, incompetent Raquel Welch as a third detective. The sight of highly paid Yul Brynner in the cast list may spoil guesswork as to who the heavy will turn out to be; 1972. (c)

G

Gaby XX *Waterloo Bridge* updated to Second World War, with Leslie Caron not a patch on Vivien Leigh and John Kerr a poor substitute for Robert Taylor; Curtis Bernhardt; 1956. (c)

Gallant Bess XX Boy loves horse, boy loses horse, boy gets horse. Confusing and dull, but the horse is good. George Tobias and Chill Wills do their best. Director, Andrew Marton; 1947. (c)

The Gallant Hours √ Admiral Halsey biopic served better than might have been expected by fine performance from James Cagney and a low-key script. Robert Montgomery directed reverently (in 1960) and the movie is stopped from degenerating into usual string of naval battles by the fact that Halsey was mostly stuck at HQ. (b/w)

Gambit √√ Michael Caine recruits Shirley MacLaine for a caper; Ronald Neame directed in 1966 with unsure hand, but the best bits are excellent. (c)

The Gambler √ Karel Reisz directed James Toback's script with economy and persuasion in 1974, but why should one want to watch a masochist enjoy losing – and having his face slashed? James Caan does not provide an adequate reason. (c)

The Gambler From Natchez XX It's Dale Robertson in the usual mythical riverboat rubbish, directed this time by old reliable Henry Levin. Debra Paget is belle; only Kevin McCarthy's superior performance reminds one what a load of cold tea the rest is; 1954. (c)

Games √ If rich and beautiful young couple James Caan and Katharine Ross invited moneyless salesgirl Simone Signoret to stay with them because they fancied her, we might have had a superior sexpic. As it is, we've got an inferior whodunit. Pity. Curtis Harrington; 1967. (c)

The Games X Attempt to make fiction more interesting than fact (Zatopek, Jim Peters) fails in the hands of Michael Winner. Charles Aznavour (an athlete? huh!) and Michael Crawford in a straight part are equally unconvincing. What should have been exciting fails to stay the course; 1969. (c)

The Gang's All Here √ 1944 boy-meets-loses-gets-girl musical with Alice Faye, Carmen Miranda; rapidly becoming collector's item since director Busby Berkeley was canonised. (c)

Gangster Story XX Walter Matthau wasn't being funny when he directed and starred in this straightforward cops-and-robber about nice girl mixed up with a guy like that. Pity he wasn't; 1960. (b/w)

The Gang That Couldn't Shoot Straight √ Based on a novel by humorous columnist Jimmy Breslin, this frantic black comedy about incompetent gangsters has some funny moments, two considerable personalities (Lionel Stander, Robert De Niro) and rather desperate directions from James Goldstone; 1971. (c)

Garden of Evil √ Fine old-fashioned big-league western with Gary Cooper, Cameron Mitchell, Richard Widmark, hired by Susan Hayward to extricate her husband from goldmine; Apaches and greed thicken stew and Henry Hathaway keeps it boiling; 1954. (c)

The Garment Jungle √ Lee J. Cobb shines as dress manufacturer in this gangster-union drama set unusually in the Seventh Avenue enclave. Vincent Sherman got the credit but it was Robert Aldrich who directed most of it and kept it exciting; 1957. (b/w)

Gaslight √√ Even if Ingrid Bergman didn't really deserve the 1944 Best Actress Oscar as Victorian wife being driven mad (preferred over Barbara Stanwyck's *Double Indemnity*), it's a powerful piece. Charles Boyer is sinister husband, Dame May Whitty, Angela Lansbury, Joseph Cotten support strongly. Décor won award, too, but not George Cukor's direction. (b/w)

A Gathering of Eagles X Rock Hudson neglects his wife for his Strategic Air Command planes, so enter Rod Taylor eyeing Mary Peach; director Delbert Mann takes wings in the air, crashes on the ground; 1963. (c)

The Gatling Gun X Straightforward western, tricked up with crocodile tears about the noble Indians who get slaughtered and some fancy camera-work from director Robert Gordon; 1972. (c)

Gay Purr-ee X Warner Brothers tried to do a Disney in 1963 with this full-length cartoon about cats, but hadn't got the touch; despite Garland and Gingold on the sound-track and pastiches of Lautrec and van Gogh, it just didn't come off; Abe Levitow. (c)

The Gazebo XX Silly little attempt at a funny whodunit from a play by the artifice-prone Alec Coppel, which gets the poor performances it deserves from Glenn Ford, Debbie Reynolds. Director George Marshall does his best which isn't much help; 1960. (b/w)

The Geisha Boy X Jerry Lewis in Japan. That's really all that needs to be said. Frank Tashlin; 1959. (c)

The General √ Luckily this silent classic is beyond criticism, or one would be tempted to say it is not quite as funny as everyone agrees. Buster Keaton's 1926 single-handed fighting of the Civil War is hallowed. He was helped in his direction by Clyde Bruckman. (b/w)

Genevieve √ One of the few authentic British movie classics. This race, between John Gregson's old crock, a 1904 Darracq (passenger Dinah Sheridan), and Kenneth More's 1904 Spyker (passenger Kay Kendall), has weathered the years since it was made by Henry Cornelius in 1953 to become a vintage film itself. (c)

Genghis Khan X James Mason, Eli Wallach and Robert Morley cheerfully send up this pretentious costumer shot in Yugoslavia for some reason (like cheap extras) in 1964, but Omar Sharif, Stephen Boyd and Françoise Dorleac take it all more seriously with disastrous results. Old-timer Henry Levin must have known it was hokum, but maybe he thought it wiser not to tell them. (c)

Gentle Giant X Cuddly child actor Clint Howard meets cuddly animal actor bear cub in story about stolen bears. Dennis Weaver, Vera Miles, Ralph Meeker soon find out the truth of the adage about never acting with children and animals. Director, James Neilson; 1967. (c)

Gentleman Jim X Biopic of boxing champ James J. Corbett, not very convincingly impersonated by Errol Flynn in 1942; director, Raoul Walsh. (b/w)

Gentleman's Agreement √ Don't be fooled by the 1947 Oscars (best picture; best support, Celeste Holm; director, Elia Kazan), it was slick then, and it's out-of-date now. Gregory Peck's goody-goody journalist posing as Jew to experience anti-semitism seems stiff; only John Garfield's cameo as genuine Jew stands up. Still it's a fascinating period piece, especially for outraging Un-American Activities Committee. (b/w)

Gentlemen Marry Brunettes X Hopeless attempt to repeat flavour and success of *Gentlemen Prefer Blondes* without the main ingredient, M. Monroe. Jane Russell couldn't sustain a suntan, let alone a major movie, and Jeanne Crain, as her friend, isn't much help. The Paris locations are pretty but Richard Sale seems to know he is fighting a losing battle; 1955. (c)

Gentlemen Prefer Blondes √ Howard Hawks cast Marilyn Monroe as the classic dumb blonde bombshell, an image she was never able to lose. But without her and Jane Russell, as two big little girls from Little Rock on the make in Paris, Hawks's 1953 film would have served Anita Loos's novel poorly. Great comedy support from Charles Coburn, but film – especially

'Diamonds are a Girl's Best Friend – is all Monroe's. (c)

The Gentle Rain XXX Christopher George is Brazilian mute in this terrible little movie about the frigidity of Lynda Day; Burt Balaban is the director and the bossa-nova isn't all bad; 1965. (c)

Geordie XXX Frank Launder's awful 1955 yarn about puny youth who takes a bodybuilding course to stop the world kicking porridge in his face and heads for Olympics via Highland Games. Dull, depressing stuff. With Bill Travers, Alastair Sim. (b/w)

The George Raft Story X It's supposed to be a true biopic, but don't you believe it. Ray Danton isn't bad at impersonating Raft, the gang groupie turned film star, but it might have made a more amusing pic if Joseph Newman had let Frank Gorshin – seen here in a smaller role – do his famous take-off of the coin-spinning star. Jayne Mansfield, Julie London provide less than competent distaff interest; 1961. (b/w)

Georgy Girl √ Lynn Redgrave only too well cast as plain girl who gets involved with Older Man James Mason and zany Alan Bates; London had stopped swinging by 1966, but Silvio Narizzano hadn't noticed. Now all those tricksy shots and cuts look fit for a museum. (b/w)

Geronimo √ Chuck Connors does well as legendary Indian chieftain of the Apaches and his struggles against injustice; Arnold Laven is producer-director; 1962. (c)

The Getaway √√ Steve McQueen in partnership with the supremely accomplished Sam Peckinpah is dragged down by Ali MacGraw as his less than honest wife. Having been set up to do a theft for Ben Johnson, he has to shoot his way out of a series of obstacles on the way to Mexico. The final result is often impressive and gripping; 1972. (c)

Get Carter √√ The successful British gangster movie is a rare bird indeed, but Mike Hodges managed it impressively in 1971 with this vehicle for Michael Caine. John Osborne makes a smiling villain, along with Ian Hendry. Britt Ekland is fleetingly but revealingly seen. (c)

Get Off My Back X Inept attempt to show how ex-junkies are readied for normal life in Californian home, Synanon. Quite unbelievable, despite attempts by Edmond O'Brien as unit head, Chuck Connors and Alex Cord as inmates. Richard Quine produced-directed and had the ludicrous idea that Eartha Kitt could act; 1966. (b/w)

Getting Straight √ Very much of its time (1970), this comedy attempts to expose the weaknesses of the educational establishment, but in doing so is forced to take sides with equally unimpressive student protesters. Elliott Gould manages to catch the humorous strengths of the main protagonist; Candice Bergen is less successful as his girlfriend. Director, Richard Rush. (c)

The Ghost Catchers √ Great fun in a haunted house with Olsen and Johnson. The ghost concerned is a soft-shoe dancing gentleman from the nineties and his manifestation is a treat; Leo Carrillo, Andy Devine add to fun; Edward Cline; 1944. (b/w)

The Ghost Goes West √√ Delightful pre-war (1936) comedy of Eugene Pallette unknowingly purchasing Robert Donat's ancestor when he buys Highland castle to rebuild in America. Robert Sherwood co-wrote, René Clair lightly directed. (b/w)

Ghost in the Invisible Bikini XXX What on earth are Francis X. Bushman, Boris Karloff, Basil Rathbone doing in a mess like this? Even Nancy Sinatra is too good for this dreary mishmash of a teenage beach romp and the haunted house cliché – and that's really saying something; Don Weis is director; 1966. (c)

Ghost of Frankenstein √√ If the Frankenstein saga was tiring in 1942, when Erle C. Kenton took over direction, Lon Chaney Jr. gave a creditable impersonation of Boris Karloff and Bela Lugosi was still around to do his Ygor bit. (b/w)

Giant √√ Cattle barons, oil tycoons and a tremendous cast make this one of the big ones. Of course, it's all bombast but is great stuff and George Stevens milks Edna Ferber's novel for all it can give. Among those present: Elizabeth Taylor (at her 1956 peak), Rock Hudson, James Dean, Carroll Baker, Jane Withers, Mercedes McCambridge. (c)

GI Blues X Cash-in on Elvis Presley's return from the army in 1960 has him as private who dates a night-club singer for a bet, in Germany. Good location shots let down by studio-bound rest and Norman Taurog's idea of how Germans look and sound. (c)

Gideon of Scotland Yard √ Surprisingly directed in England in 1959 by John Ford. Jack Hawkins as the detective taken over on TV by John Gregson. Shows one day in Gideon's life, Anna Massey supporting. (c)

Gidget X 1959 forerunner of endless series (e.g. **G. Goes Hawaiian,** 1961; **G. Goes to Rome,** 1963), in which Sandra Dee as Girl-Midget was involved with beachboy Cliff Robertson; Paul Wenklos rendered it all harmless, and pretty funless. (c)

Gift Horse √ One of those Second World War muted heroics British studios were so fond of around 1952, when Compton Bennett directed this one. Trevor Howard as captain of lease-lend destroyer ultimately winning his men's respect; with Richard Attenborough, and Sonny Tufts for US sales. (b/w)

The Gift of Love √ Tear-jerker with Lauren Bacall about how important little adopted girl becomes to Robert Stack after wife's death; suits Jean Negulesco's schmaltzy style; 1957. (c)

Gigi √√ Eight 1958 Oscars were won by this musical version of Colette story (best picture, screenplay, photography, art direction, costumes, editing, scoring, direction – Vincente Minnelli), although Leslie Caron won no honours for her wide-eyed rebel who prefers marriage to concubinage. Lerner-Loewe wrote the music, Beaton designed, as in My Fair Lady. Maurice Chevalier remembered it well, thanked heaven for little girls – the dirty old man. (c)

Gigot XX Should be watched on an empty stomach, otherwise you might make a nasty mess when you throw up over the excessive sickly saccharine that director Gene Kelly smears over this already sticky yarn about a deaf-mute (Jackie Gleason) who befriends animals and children. Yuch! 1962. (c)

Gilda √ Rita Hayworth in archetypal forties film (actually 1946) about South American café owner hiring American Glenn Ford, with complicated Gilda as wife; Charles Vidor. (b/w)

The Girl and the General XX Dull little squib about Rod Steiger as Austrian general captured by two Italian peasants who decide they love each other. So what? Virna Lisi can't convince as a peasant, and director Pasquale Festa Campanile doesn't seem to know what he's all about; 1969. (c)

The Girl Can't Help It √ Edmond O'Brien wants to buy his girlfriend Jayne Mansfield into movie stardom; Tom Ewell is broke so he helps. But then the complications set in. Occasionally funny moments from director Frank Tashlin; 1956. (c)

The Girl from Petrovka XX Goldie Hawn miscast as Soviet ballet dancer who falls for American correspondent Hal Holbrook. Robert Ellis Miller directed poorly and the film was shelved in 1974 but has emerged on TV. (c)

Girl in the Headlines XX Soppy little murder hunt whose cast (Ian Hendry, Ronald Fraser, Margaret Johnston, Jeremy Brett, Jane Asher, Zena Walker, James Villiers) might attract you into wasting your time watching it. Director Michael Truman really should have done us better; surely the obvious inconsistencies and thin-ice skating could have been avoided? 1963. (b/w)

The Girl in the Red Velvet Swing √ The real-life scandal of Stanford White-Evelyn Nesbit Thaw, architect-showgirl-millionaire triangle provided basis for adequate movie about life in New York, 1906. Joan Collins, trying hard; Ray Milland, Farley Granger, too; directed by Richard Fleischer; 1955. (c)

A Girl Named Tamiko X Laurence Harvey well-cast for once as unpleasant half-Russian, half-Chinese photographer in Tokyo, choosing between the American passport marriage with Martha Hyer would bring and True Happiness with France Nuyen; Michael Wilding lurks charmingly; John Sturges; 1963. (c)

Girl of the Golden West XX Jeanette MacDonald and Nelson Eddy thrilled their queasy way through this Sigmund Romberg operetta in 1938. Eddy doubles as sheriff and bandit; Walter Pidgeon, Leo Carillo, Buddy Ebsen join in under Robert Z. Leonard's direction. (b/w)

Girl of the Night XX Proves that a call girl can go straight if she wants to, though it takes psychiatry and goodness knows what else. It's all rubbish, and director Joe Cates' cursory way with the plot shows that he thought so, too. Anne Francis is the girl, Lloyd Nolan her therapist, John Kerr her leering pimp whom she loves for some deep reason not vouchsafed to the audience; 1961. (b/w)

The Girl on a Motorcycle X A rather unpleasant adaptation of André de Mandiargue's novel about the fantasies of a schoolmaster's wife (the inadequate Marianne Faithfull), most of which involve riding a bike without anything under her fur-lined catsuit to see her love (the even more inadequate Alain Delon). Jack Cardiff's romantic style with a camera and director's chair seems both too explicit and yet to miss the point; 1968. (c)

Girl on Approval X Modest little 1963 effort all shot on location in a children's home about a teenage girl 'on approval' to foster parents, Rachel Roberts and James Maxwell. Annette Whiteley, as the girl, can't quite meet the demands of the script, but director Charles Frend did a competent, likeable job. (b/w)

Girls at Sea XX Awful little 1958 remake of Ian Hay's *The Middle Watch*, with Ronald Shiner doing his best to put some fun in the proceedings. His best isn't good enough. Director Gilbert Gunn. (c)

Girls, Girls, Girls! X Elvis Presley sings a dozen songs, romances Stella Stevens and Laurel Goodwin in featherweight item about fishing boats; Norman Taurog slogs along, as usual; 1962. (c)

Girl Stroke Boy XX Amazing how filmmakers actually make films like these, especially when the producer and co-scriptwriter of this one was the professionally tasteful Ned Sherrin. There are two jokes: one is that the central heating gets hotter and hotter throughout a weekend (so why not open a window and let in the snowy atmosphere outside?). The other is that the son of Michael Hordern and Joan Greenwood has a girlfriend whom they suspect to be a boyfriend. End of jokes. End of interest. Bob Kellett directed; 1971. (c)

The Girl Who Knew Too Much XX But not enough to stay out of this farrago about Red Chinese plot to take over the American rackets and thus weaken the great old USA. Nancy Kwan's the girl, Adam (Batman) West's the hero, Nehemiah Persoff the chief heavy. Francis D. Lyon; 1969. (c)

Girl With Green Eyes √√ Rita Tushingham had the critics cheering in 1964 with her young Edna O'Brien provincial let loose in Dublin, falling for Older Man Peter Finch. 'Embodies all that is naïve and silly and noble and wonderful and heart-breaking and funny about being young,' wrote Judith Crist in *New York Herald Tribune*. Desmond Davis directs. (b/w)

The Glass Bottom Boat √ Nice 1966 Doris Day diversion mixing spies and tourist high-jinks. Writer-director Frank Tashlin makes time pass pleasantly. (c)

The Glass Key √√ 1942 version of Dashiell Hammett thriller about political boss Brian Donlevy accused of murder. In *Magic and Myth of the Movies*, Parker Tyler comments: 'If ever there was a mannequin gangster, he was Alan Ladd in *The Glass Key*, and if he ever reached for the upper crust and took down a mannequin moll to load his mannequin gat for him, she was Veronica Lake.' (b/w)

The Glass Menagerie √ Inside the dream worlds of Tennessee Williams; a slow, fey but entrancing weepie with Gertrude Lawrence and Arthur Kennedy (right); Jane Wyman and Kirk Douglas (wrong). Irving Rapper; 1950. (b/w)

The Glass Slipper XX Tepid 1954 version of *Cinderella*, with Leslie Caron as poor Cinders, Michael Wilding an ineffectual Prince Charming. Roland Petit did the ballets; Charles Walters directed. (c)

The Glass Web √ *Crime of the Week* is a TV show. One week it features a murder, just too similar to real-life one of girl blackmailer. Could murderer be show's authority, Edward G. Robinson? Jack Arnold; 1953. (b/w)

The Glenn Miller Story √ James Stewart plays the bandleader in 1954 biopic which includes all his biggest hits meticulously played; strong support from June Allyson, Frances Langford, Louis Armstrong, Gene Krupa; director Anthony Mann manages it all excellently; 1954. (c)

A Global Affair X One of those effortful Bob Hope comedies, this time involving children. 1964 attempt had him a bachelor UN official having to look after baby, with Russians (in the person of an unlikely gynaecologist Lilo Pulver) stirring up international trouble; Jack Arnold does his best. (b/w)

The Glory Guys √ They're Andrew Duggan, who disobeys general's order to attack the Sioux on a certain date and brings his men into battle a day early to claim the victory for himself, and his men. Sam Peckinpah wrote the script but the direction is by Arnold Laven, who does well, considering the shadow he is working in; 1966. (c)

The Go-Between √√√ Pinter's script and Losey's direction complement L. P. Hartley's delicate novel of divided loyalties. In the hothouse atmosphere of a turn-of-the-century house party, Dominic Guard runs errands between Julie Christie and Alan Bates. Margaret Leighton, Edward Fox stand out in a faultless cast; 1970. (c)

The Goddess √ Kim Stanley as Hollywood star who could never find lasting love gives fine methodical performance in script by Paddy Chayevsky, humbly directed by John Cromwell; 1958. (b/w)

The Godfather √√√ Marlon Brando's remarkable study of the patriachal mobster, and his fighting family – notably Al Pacino and James Caan. Only Diane Keaton looks miscast and out of place as Pacino's WASP wife. The rest is simply the gangster movie you can't refuse. Francis Ford Coppola; 1972. (c)

The Godfather, Part Two √√ Although extravagantly praised, this companion piece to Francis Ford Coppola's Mafia blockbuster comes off as muted and sprawling. Made in 1974, it is both a sequel (Al Pacino's wife Diane Keaton leaves him) and a prologue (Robert De Niro makes a surprisingly convincing young Brando) to the 1972 epic. John Cazale does particularly well as the passed-over brother, weakly trying to get his revenge; so does Lee Strasberg as a rival Jewish mobster. (c)

God's Little Acre √ For once, a movie that is better than the original novel. Erskine Caldwell's novel was a steamy sexy yarn of lusts down on the farm; this 1958 version directed by Anthony Mann, prevented by censorship from being too randy, has developed a sense of humour instead. So Robert Ryan's pitting of holes thoughout his farm looking for gold (and continually moving the tract of the title) becomes amusing, and his crucial decision to stop looking for gold and get on with being a farmer the force of reality. (b/w)

Going My Way √ Famous sentimental throat-lumper (or sick-maker) about young, new-broom priest, Bing Crosby, winning over old tetchy but lovable priest Barry Fitzgerald and gang of poor New York kids with a smile and a song. Director Leo McCarey carried off seven 1944 Academy Awards to the tune of 'Too-ra-Loo-ra-Loo-ra'. (b/w)

Gold XX Unpleasant adventure yarn shot in South Africa and tacitly endorsing the social order there. The guilty players include Roger Moore, a simple hero; Susannah York, his adulterous girlfriend; Ray Milland, a mine-owner, Bradford Dillman, the villain. Peter Hunt directs with the aim of telling a simple story. Alas, it is the people who shore up the South African self-image who are simple; 1974. (c)

The Gold Hawk X Frank Yerby swashbuckler with Rhonda Fleming sailing the troubled Caribbean; Sidney Salkow made it all very actionful in 1952. (c)

The Golden Rabbit XX Silly little bit of rubbish about man who can make gold – it's *The Man in the White Suit* without any clothes on. Timothy Bateson, Maureen Beck; director David MacDonald; 1962. (b/w)

Golden Salamander √ Gentlemanly archaeologist Trevor Howard gets involved with delicious Tunisian beauty Anouk Aimée and gang of gun smugglers. Directed 1949 by Ronald Neame, with Herbert Lom, Wilfrid Hyde White, Miles Malleson. (b/w)

Goldfinger √√ Bond-lovers cheer when this appears on the little screen, but those who never worshipped at the shrine of vulgar art direction, nifty sadism and unsexy sex may wonder what all the fuss was about; Sean Connery judges with Honor Blackman, saves Fort Knox, shows off the special Aston Martin. Shirley Eaton in gold make-up all-over is worth a glimpse – which is about all we get. Guy Hamilton; 1964. (c)

Go Naked in the World √ An appealing idea – son Anthony Franciosa dates the town whore Gina Lollobrigida, not realising who she is, but Papa Ernest Borgnine knows only too well – thrown away in histrionics. Needs remaking in today's more honest atmosphere; 1961. was too early for implications to be explored properly, and director-writer Ranald MacDougall had to make too many compromises. (c)

Goodbye Again X Anatole Litvak's rotten title for *Aimez-Vous Brahms*, Françoise Sagan's novel. Anthony Perkins, coming between Ingrid Bergman and Yves Montand, manages to suggest that he feels more attraction for Montand than Bergman. It's all a bit world-weary and dull, however, despite the French locations; 1961. (b/w)

Goodbye Charlie X All the skills of author George Axelrod and comedian Walter Matthau can't make this one stand up. Plot is a murdered man returning to Earth (with vengeance in mind) in the shape of Debbie Reynolds. Tony Curtis looks as baffled as us; Vincente Minnelli; 1964. (c)

Goodbye Columbus √ Hello, *The Graduate*; but Richard Benjamin, lacking the charm of Dustin Hoffman, is matched only too well by the arch self-satisfaction of Ali MacGraw. A disappointing translation of Philip Roth's novella about sex and money in the American Jewish country club set. Larry Peerce; 1969. (c)

Goodbye Mr Chips √√ (1) Vintage 1939 Sam Wood version of schoolteacher weepie with Robert Donat winning Academy Award and Greer Garson winning hearts. Look out for the young John Mills. (b/w)

Goodbye Mr Chips XX (2) Unfortunate 1969 musical remake with Peter O'Toole manages to screw most of the charm out of the story, with awful Leslie Bricusse music and Michael Redgrave, Pet Clark looking lost. Partly blame director Herbert Ross. (c)

The Good Die Young √√ Strong caper, with Lewis Gilbert's firm 1955 touch bringing out the best in Richard Basehart, Gloria Grahame, Stanley Baker, Margaret Leighton and even Laurence Harvey. (b/w)

The Good Earth √√ Simple-minded but magnificent reconstruction of Chinese farm-life up to the revolution, made on a spectacular scale and winning Oscars for Luise Rainer's wife and Karl Freund's camera. Special effects like the locust plague are stunning, and Paul Muni's phlegmatic playing suits part of peasant visited by it as punishment for taking dancer Tilly Losch as second wife. Director Sidney Franklin deserves credit for keeping theme of the land, which ran through Pearl Buck's bestseller, always in forefront; 1937. (b/w)

The Good Fairy √ Margaret Sullavan in schmaltzy old (1935) William Wyler-directed romance in which Budapest usherette insists on doing good. Herbert Marshall, Frank Morgan, Alan Hale, Cesar Romero submit to having good done to them. (b/w)

The Good Guys and the Bad Guys √ Attempt to make a funny western by Burt Kennedy is let down by selfconscious direction and performances by Robert Mitchum, George Kennedy, as good, bad, respectively, joining forces to fight progress. Morally, politically, artistically shaky; 1969. (c)

Good Morning, Boys! √ Will Hay-

Graham Moffatt-Charles Hawtrey classic, supposedly about prison-break but really an excuse for incomparable music-hall act. Marcel Varnel; 1937. (*b/w*)

Good Morning, Miss Dove X Gooey yarn of schoolteacher Jennifer Jones solving everyone's problems except yours; should you turn off or will it get any better? Henry Koster; 1955. (*c*)

Good Neighbour Sam √ Jack Lemmon in tailor-made 1964 role as frustrated ad-man. David Swift (who co-wrote, too) spins it along from chuckle to snort, although Dorothy Provine and Romy Schneider drag it all up a bit. (*c*)

Good Sam X Disappointing 1948 Gary Cooper 'comedy' in which the lanky veteran is put through sentimental jogtrot about a fumbling good Samaritan; Leo McCarey just didn't have astringent enough touch. (*b/w*)

The Good, the Bad and the Ugly √ Spaghetti westerns, attacked for their violence when made (in the sixties – this one is 1967) are now enshrined in movie mythology as forerunners of the moody oater. Clint Eastwood is his usual mysterious stranger, Eli Wallach a Mexican gunman and Lee Van Cleef a sadistic killer. They are all searching for a cashbox containing $200,000; Sergio Leone directed. (*c*)

Good Times X Sonny and Cher fans may enjoy this exposure of the singers in various roles as Cher has some on-screen nightmares, with George Sanders always the villain. Director, William Friedkin; 1967. (*c*)

The Goose Steps Out X Will Hay in double part as German spy and harmless schoolteacher asked to parachute into Germany for King and Country. Among those present in the far-off days of 1942 were Peter Ustinov, Julien Mitchell, Peter Croft; Basil Dearden helped Will Hay to direct himself. (*b/w*)

Gorgo √ She's a prehistoric monster whose offspring is captured by sailors William Sylvester and Bill Travers (whose acting is pretty monsterlike at the best of times). When the human race puts the babe on exhibition Gorgo rises from the sea and, Kong-like, devastates London to rescue it. Director Eugene Lourié is great special effects whizz and pulls off a stunner here; 1960. (*c*)

The Gorgon √ Plenty of Hammer horrors here; though they didn't persist with the idea of a Medusa snake-haired lady after this promising

1964 start. Terence Fisher brought out the best in his talented cast (Peter Cushing, Richard Pasco, Barbara Shelley) although Christopher Lee's a bit unhappy as a goodie. (*c*)

Gorilla at Large √ Strong cast – Anne Bancroft, Lee J. Cobb, Raymond Burr, Lee Marvin, Cameron Mitchell – in circus whodunit. Gorilla is chief suspect. Harmon Jones; 1954. (*c*)

The Graduate √√√ Hilarious, wry, influential comedy of young Dustin Hoffman's affairs with married Anne Bancroft and her daughter, Katharine Ross. Mike Nichols rightly won 1967 Oscar as director; wonder is that *In the Heat of the Night* beat it for best picture and actor. (*c*)

Grand Hotel √√ Don't expect to see very much of Garbo in this, her 19th film. She had to share equally with John and Lionel Barrymore, Wallace Beery, Joan Crawford in creaky, multi-storied extravaganza based on Vicki Baum's bestseller. But as a tired ballet star who falls in love with a crook she completely dominated the others. See what the word 'glamour' really means. Director, Edmund Goulding; 1932. (*b/w*)

Grand Prix √√ Lively blockbuster about Formula One motor racing that's marvellous on the track, but tends to break down off it. See it on as large a screen as possible because John Frankenheimer indulges himself in countless splitting into two, three and lots more simultaneous images. Yves Montand, James Garner drive; Eva Marie Saint waits; 1967. (*c*)

Grand Slam √√ Bank caper with Edward G. Robinson and Janet Leigh, and Rio de Janeiro at carnival time; Giuliano Montaldo orchestrates international cast neatly and the plot is taut; 1968. (*c*)

The Grapes of Wrath √√√ This account of the Okies fleeing the Oklahoma dustbowl in piled-high jalopy and finding little to cheer them in the golden hope of California, touched the conscience of the nation, as director John Ford intended. Although set in the Depression years, it seemed only too relevant to a nation that contained so many poor in 1940. All the performances were great, but Jane Darwell won an Oscar for her Mother, and Henry Fonda is unforgettable as the young Joad. (*b/w*)

The Grass is Greener X Too-too-old-fashioned stage drama that went down awfully well in Shaftesbury Avenue but bores in a sub-sub-*Private Lives* sort of way. Stanley Donen failed to make it catch fire in 1960 despite presence of Cary Grant. Rest of cast – Deborah Kerr, Jean Simmons, Robert Mitchum – just not up to it. (*c*)

The Gravy Train √ Reasonably exciting thriller about a heist that goes right but causes betrayals afterwards. Notable for some closer observation (director: Jack Starrett) than is usual in such yarns. Stacy Keach plays the much put-upon hero; 1974. (*c*)

The Great Bank Robbery X Zero Mostel and Kim Novak make an engaging pair of robbers; Clint Walker a watchable lawman, keen to break into the bank for upright reasons. Starts well, under Hy Averback's direction, but goes gradually downhill to a ludicrous climax; 1969. (*c*)

The Great Caruso X The music, if you like the more obvious operatic arias and such corn as *The Last Rose of Summer*, is all right, but the plot (boy meets girl, boy pursues girl, boy gets girl, boy dies) is only matched in awfulness by the acting of Mario Lanza and Ann Blyth; Richard Thorpe does his best to make him seem like an actor, but can't win; 1951. (*c*)

Great Catherine XX It must have sounded a good idea – Jeanne Moreau and Peter O'Toole in Shaw's playlet extended with some fooling from Zero Mostel. Under Gordon Flemyng's direction it was a disaster; Akim Tamiroff, Jack Hawkins swept along on a current of awfulness; 1968. (*c*)

The Great Dictator √√ Chaplin's burlesque of Hitler, like a brilliant marionette show. Unfortunately, final pompous speech lets it down; 1940. (*b/w*)

The Great Escape √√ Three hours of escaping prisoners-of-war with Americans Steve McQueen, Charles Bronson scoring over typecast James Donald, Richard Attenborough; John Sturges laid on the excitement; 1963. (*c*)

The Greatest Show on Earth √√ If you like circuses you'll like this celebration of the love affair that Cecil B. de Mille naturally had with them. However, you may be frustrated when the documentary opening gives way to a rather ordinary series of lovely plots involving Betty Hutton, Cornel Wilde, James Stewart, Dorothy Lamour, Charlton Heston. If you hate 'em, forget it; 1952. (*c*)

The Greatest Story Ever Told X Jesus Christ! the book was better. All very tasteful, but Bergman rep. player Max von Sydow as New Testament lead only proves what a good director Ingmar is – unfortunately, it's George Stevens in charge here. The result, partly shot in Monument Valley, is a Monumental bore. Charlton Heston, Dorothy McGuire, David McCallum are among unlikely cast; 1965. (*c*)

Great Expectations √√ (1) Best Dickens film ever, gripping from marvellous Finlay Currie in graveyard, through the young (it's 1947) Alec Guinness and John Mills, to Martita Hunt's Miss Havisham and Jean Simmons as young, Valerie Hobson as older Estella. Nice that Dickens altered the end to make it happy. David Lean's direction faultless. (*b/w*)

Great Expectations XX (2) 1975: Pretty awful adaptation with several characters missing, unevocative sets, unsympathetic direction (Joseph Hardy) and some serious miscasting including Sarah Miles as a too-sophisticated Estella; beefy Michael York as Pip, James Mason a suave Magwich. (*c*)

The Great Gatsby √√√ Enchanting version of F. Scott Fitzgerald's novel, savaged by the critics in 1974, but full of loving direction from Jack Clayton, a sufficiently faithful script by Francis Ford Coppola and some memorable performances. Robert Redford is the legendary millionaire; Mia Farrow his lost love; Bruce Dern her horrid husband; Karen Black the husband's mistress. Sam Waterston makes a modest narrator. The period (1922) re-creation is delightful, the clothes and music making up for a slight feeling of artificiality. (*c*)

The Great Impostor √√ In real life, Ferdinand Demara really did get away with passing himself off as, variously, a Canadian naval surgeon, prison warden and Trappist monk, among other hoaxes, and Tony Curtis enjoys passing himself off as Ferdinand Demara. Robert Mulligan's direction helps us to enjoy it almost as much, too; 1961. (*c*)

The Great Jesse James Raid √ Rather superior western about the old outlaw's last caper; Willard Parker, Tom Neal respond to Reginald Le Borg's 1953 direction. (*c*)

The Great Lie √ Definitive soaper with Bette Davis battling Mary Astor in 1941 after George Brent is in air crash; Astor won one fight – for the Oscar as best support of the year; Edmund Goulding served them faithfully. (*b/w*)

The Great Lover √ Bob Hope on a ship with a bunch of boy scouts and Roland Young, murderer; Rhonda Fleming's the girl, Alexander Hall's the director; 1949. (b/w)

The Great Man √ Jose Ferrer does an Orson Welles on this one, but only proves that it takes more than sheer nerve to direct, co-write and play the main part. Indeed, with other people doing these various jobs Al Morgan's novel of the truth about a popular radio idol might have become a masterpiece of clay-feet exposure. As it is, the movie is just a minor piece of hokum, with Ed Wynn walking away with the honours under Ferrer's nose with a cameo about the man who started the idol off; 1957. (b/w)

The Great McGinty √√ This 1940 Preston Sturges has become political comedy classic; chronicling Brian Donlevy's rise to fame and fortune. (b/w)

The Great McGonagall XXX Spike Milligan and director Joe McGrath collaborated on the script of this truly apalling example of how far wrong a comedian can go in convincing himself he is funny. Milligan as the worst poet in Scotland (and most other places) fails to allow the ghastliness of McGonagall's verse to make its own point. Instead, we are nudged, poked and pushed into trying to find him, Peter Sellers as Queen Victoria and McGrath's usual rep company hilarious. They aren't. (c)

The Great Missouri Raid X Wendell Corey, Macdonald Carey in routine western about Jesse James and brothers; Gordon Douglas couldn't make it live; 1950. (c)

The Great Northfield Minnesota Raid √ Interesting, old-fashioned Jesse James (Robert Duvall) western, with fellow-folk hero Cole Younger (Cliff Robertson) being canonised. Director Philip Kaufman pretends documentary realism, but his daguerreotype-type camerawork hardly conceals the old-style plot about goodie-baddies; 1971. (c)

The Great Race √√ Genevieve with lots of knobs on, including Tony Curtis in the nice John Gregson part, Jack Lemmon as demonised, moustachioed Kenneth More. This time it's New York to Paris and three long hours of it. Blake Edwards almost manages to keep it going, but you may finally conk out before it does; 1965. (c)

The Great St Trinian's Train Rob- bery XX Pathetic attempt to wring something out of more train robberies or St Trinian's – Launder and Gilliat didn't seem to care which in 1966 – but only, alas, to fail miserably on both counts. Neither Dora Bryan nor Frankie Howerd can do anything right and those girls seemed impossibly out of date even then. (c)

The Great Sioux Raid √ Joseph Cotten in superior account of Custer's Last Stand; Sidney Salkow; 1965. (c)

The Great Waldo Pepper √√ Robert Redford is a stunt flyer in 1926 who finds himself matched with his First World War enemy, Bo Brundin, as they have to dogfight as movie stunt men; George Roy Hill directed with flair in 1975. (c)

The Great Waltz XX Dull, interminable epic about the Strauss family that hopes to substitute vast dance formations for true spectacle, and histrionics (with some mediocre players) for drama. Any director who casts the posturing Rossano Brazzi, Horst Buchholz, Nigel Patrick and Yvonne Mitchell as Strausses and friends deserves disaster; Andrew Stone gets it; 1972. (c)

The Great White Hope √ James Earl Jones's magnificent performance as Jack 'Jefferson' (in real life Jack Johnson), who becomes the first black heavyweight champion of the world, lifts this 1970 tract out of the rut of didacticism into which it has been steered by director Martin Ritt, and makes you feel for the man, if not the race. No doubt Johnson's flaunting of his white mistress (Jane Alexander) did upset the white establishment and lead to his hounding to prison. But director Ritt allows melodrama to overtake reality. Unfortunately, the final fight, which the champ has agreed to lose, does not grip as it should. (c)

The Great Ziegfeld √ Lush 1936 biopic of the Broadway producer, Flo Ziegfeld, who was later to turn up as a character in Funny Girl and Funny Lady. William Powell is miscast as the impresario, and Myrna Loy as Billie Burke is the wrong shape, as keen moviegoers know. Luise Rainer somehow won an Oscar for performance as Anna Held. Director, Robert Z. Leonard. (b/w)

The Green Berets XX Whatever you may think about John Wayne as an actor there's no doubt that morally and politically his heart was in the wrong place. By this 1968 effort, glorifying

American troops in Vietnam, he may well have put more full-blooded patriots off the war there than all the platitudes of the peace lobby, so inept, so callous and so meretricious did it show itself through the Goodies-and-Baddies veneer. He directed it himself, with Ray Kellogg, and it is not without significance that 1968 was the year the opinion polls first showed that the majority of Americans were ashamed of what they were doing in south-east Asia, and wanted Out. (c)

Green Fire XX Rather more green than fire about this rather tame South American adventure yarn with Stewart Granger and Paul Douglas as mining engineers, Grace Kelly as coffee plantation owner. Andrew Marton settles for the easy thrills; 1954. (c)

The Greengage Summer √√ Susannah York incredibly good as the schoolgirl on holiday in France who grows up as the result of a fascination with a rotter – Kenneth More, too nice to be able to convey the necessary rottenness. Danielle Darrieux a bit tight as proprietress of chateau hotel where they are staying. But director Lewis Gilbert never falls into the trap of sentimentality; 1961. (c)

Green Grow the Rushes √ Richard Burton in 1951 union-financed attempt to break out of film industry grip which produced interesting if tame comedy about illegal whisky-brewing; Derek Twist. (b/w)

The Green Helmet XXX Wretched little British effort using some exciting newsreels of motor racing to save shooting their own. Bill Travers his usual wooden self as driver, Ed Begley's only role is to give it some US appeal. Sid James gets no chance to show any subtlety. The director was Michael Forlong; 1961. (b/w)

The Green Man √ Pleasant, accomplished comedy with Alastair Sim attempting to do in erring politician Raymond Huntley. Sim's assassinating past is told in delightful flashbacks. Terry-Thomas, George Cole tend to broaden Sim's subtlety under direction of Roday Day; 1957. (b/w)

Green Mansions XX Pretty disastrous attempt by actor-turned-director Mel Ferrer to steer his then (1959) wife Audrey Hepburn through a version of W. H. Hudson's novel. She plays Rima, 'spirit of the forest', a sort of refined lady Tarzan, with Anthony Perkins as gold-seeker whose life she saves. It's all very coy and embarrass-

ing and not helped either by Villa-Lobos's music, Katherine Dunham's dancers or the location pix of Venezuela, Colombia and British Guiana. (c)

The Grip of Fear √√ Lee Remick has to steal $100,000 or she and her young sister will be done in; San Francisco has served as backdrop for many an excitement, and this is one of the most exciting, thanks to director-producer Blake Edwards; 1962. (b/w)

The Grissom Gang X Another version of *No Orchids for Miss Blandish*, with Kim Darby as the kidnapped heiress this time, 1971. Robert Aldrich meretriciously followed *Bonnie and Clyde* and *Bloody Mama* in the hopes of the same box office success, but it's an unpleasant thriller, with slobbering rape and the insulting misconception that that's what women really want. (c)

The Groundstar Conspiracy √ Moderately exciting and well-plotted identity thriller with a whodunit element centring on a secret space project. Michael Sarrazin is meant to be zomboid; George Peppard just is. Director, Lamont Johnson; 1972. (c)

The Group √ Disappointing attempt to translate Mary McCarthy's evocative, astringent novel of whatever-happened - to - the - girl - you - were - at - college-with by Sidney Lumet. For the reasons for failure see Pauline Kael's long, bitchy but engrossing account of how the film was made, in *Kiss Kiss Bang Bang*; Shirley Knight and Candice Bergen shine out best; 1966. (c)

Guadalcanal Diary √ If you like war films, this is for you. Made in 1943, only a year after real-life first victory against Japan, Lewis Seiler was more concerned with glories of war than the horrors. Hard-sweating cast includes Preston Foster, Lloyd Nolan, William Bendix, Anthony Quinn, Lionel Stander. (b/w)

Guess Who's Coming to Dinner √ Hailed at the time as 'a human document of great importance for the future of all free-thinking peoples' (one Roy Moseley, critic, in *Films & Filming*), this can now be seen as a cash-in on liberal sensibilities towards black people. Indeed, by 1968 anyone thinking free could see that this rich, charming, intelligent, healthy, handsome, successful young doctor would have been welcomed as a son-in-law by crusty old heart-in-the-right-place Spencer Tracy with wide-open arms even if he had been green, let alone black like Sidney Poitier. So what were he and Katharine Hepburn agonising about? Someone should remake it with the prospective addition to the family as a dope-pushing, homosexual flashy pimp that the girl loves – then we'd see where liberal sensibilities really belonged. Stanley Kramer directed this slick slice of meretriciousness. (c)

A Guide for the Married Man X Even Walter Matthau's desperate and skilful attempts can't salvage this series of black-out sketches in which cocky Bobby Morse teaches him how to cheat on his wife. Frank Tarloff writes, Gene Kelly directed and they are obviously going for the cheap laugh at every point. Only the episode with the man convincing his wife that she didn't see what she saw is genuinely comic – the rest just trip up. Basically, a nasty, dishonest film; 1967. (c)

Gulliver's Travels √ Well, not all of them – just the first voyage, to Lilliput. Max Fleischer challenged the Disney monopoly with this full-length cartoon in 1939, and if it's got the crudity of his *Popeye* against the comparative subtlety of *Snow White*, it should keep the smaller children happy. (c)

Gumshoe √√ Splendid combination of writer Neville Smith, director Stephen Frears and star Albert Finney makes a beguiling yarn about a smalltime comedian who wants to write *The Maltese Falcon*, record 'Blue Suede Shoes' and play Las Vegas. The reincarnation of the Bogart persona in Lancashire surprisingly comes off a treat; 1971. (c)

A Gunfight √√ Unusual and watchable western, financed by a rich Red Indian tribe, in which part-Indian singer Johnny Cash plays a down-at-heel gunfighter; Kirk Douglas a fighter who agrees to shoot it out with him for money; Karen Black a saloon girl. Lamont Johnson directed in 1970. (c)

Gunfight at Comanche Creek X Audie Murphy as undercover detective who thwarts particularly unpleasant gang of bankrobbers, forcing escaped prisoners to commit crimes so that the price on their heads will go higher and they can make a good profit handing them back. But it stays filmbound; you can never really believe in it, thank goodness. Frank McDonald; 1963. (c)

The Gunfight at Dodge City √ Welcome change from standard western is Joseph M. Newman's rather ironic yarn of Joel McCrea's clean-up of outlaw-plagued town; 1959. (c)

Gunfight at the OK Corral √ John Sturges tries this time, but John Ford did it better in the classic *My Darling Clementine*. Burt Lancaster and Kirk Douglas are the legendary ex-friends who shoot it out. Leon (*Exodus*) Uris wrote the script but he doesn't make you really care; 1957. (c)

The Gunfighter √ Superior western with Gregory Peck as the man who has learned to dislike his own title as top gun of the West but who has to go on fighting against those who would take it off him or avenge the past. Director Henry King; 1950. (b/w)

Gunfight in Abilene X Will Bobby Darin recover his nerve in time to shoot it out with the outlaws? Well, if he doesn't, the title's a cheat. Director William Hale; 1967. (c)

Gun for a Coward √√ Fred Mac-Murray tries to keep the peace between his two younger brothers in a western that for once puts a believable human conflict before cattle drives and suchlike. Abner Biberman does superior directing job; 1957. (c)

Gung Ho! √√ While on the surface this is just another Second World War actioner of marines taking a Jap-held island, there is a far greater subtlety in Ray Enright's direction than one sees with half an eye. The way he holds Randolph Scott and crew captive in a submarine while they sweat out their days of waiting gives a dimension of understanding and horror that is notably lacking in many war pix; 1943. (b/w)

Gun Glory X Stewart Granger proving that he has reformed and is no longer a baddie; routine western by Roy Rowland; 1957. (c)

The Gun Hawk √ A western weepie? Well, maybe that's unfair, but this 1963 departure of actually giving an oater a theme as well as a plot is an innovation to be cheered. Paternalism is the theme and is explored in real situations such as Rory Calhoun's relationship with his father, the town drunk; in the way he runs hotel for wanted men; and his particular attitude towards one young man he has befriended but cannot guide away from Evil. If all this sounds suspiciously like a Bette Davis tearjerker in drag, there are similarities. But at least it's interesting, for a change. Director Edward Ludwig manages to ride both horses – conventional western and emotional heart-stringer – at the same time, and do it well. (c)

Gunman's Walk √ Tab Hunter and James Darren as fightin' sons of rancher Van Heflin. Rather better than most westerns in having characters instead of ciphers; Phil Karlson did intelligent director's job; 1958. (c)

Gunn X Just a bigger-budget long episode from the TV series with Craig Stevens, directed by Blake Edwards. There's a neat surprise ending but nothing much else to recommend it over any halfway-watchable American cops-and-robbers series chunk; 1968. (c)

Gunpoint X An Audie Murphy western with the doughty lad as sheriff hunting kidnapped Joan Stanley; a 1966 effort from Earl Bellamy. (c)

The Gun Runners X Disappointing 1958 version of Hemingway's *To Have and Have Not* with Audie Murphy far inferior to Bogart and Garfield, who preceded him. Director Don Siegel must have had an off-month – it's below his best by a long chalk; Eddie Albert and Everett Sloane look ready to respond, but can't find what to. (b/w)

Guns at Batasi X African-set skirmishes with frightfully British performances from Jack Hawkins, Richard Attenborough, Flora Robson; climax is Red Indian-style attack on the whites. Mia Farrow is love interest; John Guillermin; 1964. (b/w)

Guns for San Sebastian X Cross between *The Power and the Glory* and *Seven Samurai* doesn't come off, partly because Anthony Quinn hams it up as adventurer mistaken for priest, but mostly because of Henri Verneuil's uninspired direction; 1968. (c)

Guns in the Afternoon √√√ A really great western – strictly for adults – by Sam Peckinpah, which since its unheralded debut in 1961 has taken its place as one of the cult movies of recent times. It tells of an ageing Joel McCrea's attempt to transport some gold in his care, but it's the astonishingly lifelike set pieces that stay in the memory – the saloon with its flabby Madame and raddled girls; the wedding celebration where all four of the bridegroom's brothers intend to have the bride; and the final insane shoot-out with Randolph Scott. (c)

The Gunslinger √ Roger Corman can be relied on to come up with something different and this yarn of Beverly Garland taking over as town marshal

after her husband's ambush has a nicely equivocal undertone; 1956. (c)

Gunsmoke X Nothing to do with the TV series but a 1953 Audie Murphy with him turning over a new leaf and marrying the ranch boss's daughter, Susan Cabot. Pleasantly directed by Nathan Juran. (c)

Guns of Darkness √ Literate – perhaps over-literate – script by John Mortimer gives this South American actioner, about David Niven and Leslie Caron helping wounded ex-president of banana republic to escape, a dimension usually missing in this kind of movie. Anthony Asquith directs unobtrusively; 1962. (b/w)

The Guns of Fort Petticoat X Audie Murphy teaches Texas ladies how to ward off Indian attack; George Marshall makes it all fair fun; 1957. (c)

The Guns of Navarone √√ Massive Second World War actioner about Gregory Peck and explosives expert David Niven destroying two big guns on island. At climax of shooting, Niven became seriously ill, which was inconvenient for writer-producer Carl Foreman. So, Niven recalls, he was 'pumped full of drugs, went back to work against doctor's orders . . . and suffered a relapse that lasted seven weeks. The Big Brass never even sent me a grape.' Never mind, the movie made a lot of money. Director, J. Lee Thompson; 1961. (c)

Guns of the Magnificent Seven X Same old Seven stuff, this time in a 1969 version directed by Paul Wendkos who vainly hoped that his fine compositions and well-shot fights would make us forget the original; George Kennedy and James Whitmore come off best among the Seven Deadly Dwarfs but nobody manages very well. (c)

Guns of the Timberland X When it's Alan Ladd as leader of the loggers versus Jeanne Crain, leader of the ranchers whose land they invade, guess how it all ends. Frankie Avalon embarrasses everyone in sight by singing a couple of songs, but this was 1960, when the great rock boom was under way and producers desperately tried to get into the act. As Ladd had some money in it – director is Robert Webb – he can't complain if the action is slowed while the lad warbles. (c)

Guns of Wyoming √ This western has Robert Taylor as successful rancher defending his land against hired gunmen and Robert Middleton.

Towering old Tay Garnett gives this one guts; 1962. (c)

The Gun That Won the West X It's the Springfield rifle that's celebrated in William Castle's efficient oater; Dennis Morgan is chief shooter; 1955. (c)

The Guru X Director James Ivory, who has made some charming vignettes of the Indian scene, comes to grief when presented with the resources of 20th Century Fox to make a wide-screen, star-filled (Michael York, Rita Tushingham) study of the effect on Beatlesy musician who seeks enlightenment on the sub-continent; 1969. (c)

Guys and Dolls √ Fun musical of Damon Runyon stories that has become almost vintage since it was made in 1955. Marlon Brando works pretty well as lead; Frank Sinatra was at his peak; but dolls Jean Simmons and Vivian Blaine manage to wrest the honours from under their famous noses. Writer Joseph L. Mankiewicz does adequate directorial job, and if the whole show's a bit stagebound, that suits its theatrical essence. After all, it could hardly have been done realistically. (c)

Gypsy √ Although this 1962 biopic of Gypsy Rose Lee suffers from unpleasant story of mother-driving domination, miscasting of Rosalind Russell as Ma and Natalie Wood as daughter, Mervyn Le Roy does manage to catch tawdry fascination of dying vaudeville. Stephen Sondheim's lyrics flow happily out of the action – 'Let Me Entertain You','Everything's Coming Up Roses', included. (c)

The Gypsy and the Gentleman X Joseph Losey's second credited picture in 1957, after Hollywood blacklisting, seems to have depressed him. Not that swashbuckling plot about Regency rake and girlfriend cheating sister out of inheritance gives much scope, but Melina Mercouri, Keith Michell and Patrick McGoohan might have responded to enthusiasm. (c)

The Gypsy Moths √ Disappointing John Frankenheimer epic about early air circus in a Kansas town, wonderful in the air, rather less so on the ground. Burt Lancaster, Deborah Kerr are supposed to be leads, but Gene Hackman and Sheree North take it away from them; 1969. (c)

H

Hail the Conquering Hero √√ Great piece of satire from Preston Sturges; Eddie Bracken is returning soldier, mistakenly thought to be medalwinner. Ella Raines, Raymond Walburn, William Demarest, Franklin Pangborn outstanding; 1944. (b/w)

Half Angel XX Feel sorry for Joseph Cotten and Loretta Young in this embarrassing comedy about a sleepwalking nurse; Richard Sale; 1951. (c)

Half a Sixpence X Director George Sidney lets over-lavish production swamp charm that H. G. Wells's original story and stars Tommy Steele, Julia Foster have in this musical version of Kipps; 1968. (c)

The Half-Breed √ One of the earliest westerns (1952) that sided with the Red Indians against the white man. Robert Young is gambler who takes on white supremacists Barton MacLane, Porter Hall, Reed Hadley. Stuart Gilmore's heart was in the right place, even if his camera wasn't always. (c)

The Halfway House √ Mervyn Johns, Françoise Rosay, Glynis Johns, Tom Walls in a sort of Outward Bound drama as they discover they are on the way to heaven – or hell; Basil Dearden directed at Ealing in 1944. (b/w)

The Hallelujah Trail √√ A fun sendup of the western in which five groups of different predators all want to get their hands on forty wagon-loads of whisky; Burt Lancaster's fine (the title was changed from The Hallelujah Train, to avoid confusion with The Train), and Lee Remick, Donald Pleasence, Martin Landau all enjoy themselves. With John Sturges fully in command (if a bit over-indulgent), so should you; 1965. (c)

The Halliday Brand √ Joseph Cotten plays dominating rancher whose despotism leads to bloody revolt among his workers and family. Betsy Blair, Viveca Lindfors; directed by Joseph Lewis; 1957. (b/w)

The Halls of Montezuma √√ Strong and mostly successful Second World War drama, with Richard Widmark, Jack Palance, Robert Wagner, Richard Boone fightin' and dyin' for the flag on island like Okinawa; makes an honourable companion to director Lewis Milestone's All Quiet on the Western Front and A Walk in the Sun; 1950. (c)

Hamlet √√√ (1) Olivier's five-Oscar-winning version in 1948 was a clear reading of the text, presented as a Portrait of a Man Who Could Not Make Up His Mind; his Oedipal attitude towards his mother was emphasised with the kiss smack on her lips; Jean Simmons and Eileen Herlie did best after his own towering performance. (b/w)

Hamlet XX (2) 1964: Richard Burton in a 15-simultaneous camera job that fails technically, and doesn't do justice to Gielgud's straightforward production. Burton's awful. (b/w)

Hamlet √ (3) 1969: Nicol Williamson, in Tony Richardson's close-up version shot at the Round House in darkness, is scornful and cynical. Marianne Faithfull makes an inadequate Ophelia; Judy Parfitt and Anthony Hopkins well-cast as Gertrude and Claudius. (c)

Hammerhead XX Depressing little thriller set mostly in Portugal with Peter Vaughan as erotically trendy spy foiled by American agent Vince Edwards. Judy Geeson, Diana Dors, Michael Bates, Beverly Adams swan around. Director David Miller tries desperately hard, but just can't make it; 1969. (c)

Hammersmith Is Out X One of the mistakes made by Elizabeth Taylor and Richard Burton in the early seventies (specifically 1972), this is a pretentious thriller co-starring and directed by Peter Ustinov. Mental patient Burton bribes Beau Bridges to let him out, and they form a partnership that leads to an Ambassadorship for Burton and a wheelchair for Bridges. The longer it goes on, the more you wonder at the existence of a script credit. (c)

Hand in Hand XX Soppy little comedy-drama about two children who overcome religious differences between their Jewish and Catholic backgrounds; Philip Leacock manages OK with the kids, but the adult scenes are more embarrassing; 1960. (b/w)

The Hand of Night XXX A right mess of Egyptological pretensions with William Sylvester as guilt-ridden archaeologist; Frederic Goode; 1968. (c)

The Hands of Orlac XXX Poor little effort that couldn't even get distribution when it was made in 1958, about concert pianist, played by a pallid Mel Ferrer, who believes that a murderer's hands were grafted on to him after accident; Edmond T. Greville. But if 1934 version (Karl Freund) with Peter Lorre surfaces, don't miss. There's a 1924 Conrad Veidt silent one, too. (all b/w)

Hands of the Ripper X Delectable Angharad Rees, from Poldark, here plays Jack the Ripper's daughter who has inherited his penchant for mass disembowelment. Eric Porter tries to help her over this little quirk; Peter Sasdy directed in 1971. (c)

The Hanged Man √ Remake in 1965 by Don Siegel of the 1947 Robert Montgomery thriller, Ride the Pink Horse. Nice touches like the climax at the New Orleans Mardi Gras, but Robert Culp can't carry the main part of small-time crook blackmailing the union boss Edmond O'Brien. (b/w)

Hang 'Em High X Clint Eastwood survives a lynching and tracks down the nine men who strung him up; ritualised killing follows, but Ted Post has no redeeming point of view. It's brutality for its own sake – and that of the box office; 1968. (c)

The Hanging Tree √ Gold fever in the Old West mixes uncomfortably with justification for medicine as practised by Dr Gary Cooper in this 1959 drama. Karl Malden is lecherous half-wit. Delmer Daves falls between stools, but does have George C. Scott and Maria Schell in the cast to help out. (c)

The Hangman √ An adult western for childlike minds. Robert Taylor can't just rescue Tina Louise – he has to talk about it and his inner problems, too; Michael Curtiz directed the action bits splendidly in this 1959 fashionable oater, but nobody could have made that script stand up. (b/w)

Hangmen Also Die X Incredibly, this uneven 1943 Second World War drama about assassinating Nazi leader was written by Bertolt Brecht and directed by Fritz Lang; Gene Lockhart shines as framed man. (b/w)

Hangover Square √ The superb and lamented Laird Cregar in horror-emphasised 1945 version of Patrick Hamilton's novel; Edwardian composer becomes unconscious homicidal maniac. John Brahm lets it all go over the top in the climax. (b/w)

Hannibal Brooks X An elephant crossing the Alps with a British PoW (Oliver Reed) meeting up with American guerrilla (Michael Pollard) must have sounded irresistible as an idea. Unfortunately, under Michael Winner's direction (1968) it proves only too resistible. (c)

Hannie Caulder XX Raquel Welch, clad only in a blanket, escapes after being widowed (and raped) by Ernest Borgnine, Strother Martin and Jack Elam. She picks up Robert Culp to help her wreak vengeance on the baddies. Pretty ludicrous stuff, with director Burt Kennedy unable to disguise his stars' inabilities; 1971. (c)

Hans Christian Andersen X Sickly script purporting to tell life of great storyteller is made worse by Danny Kaye's nauseous performance in the title role; however, the dancing's fine and the music – 'Inchworm', 'Ugly Duckling' – pleasant; Charles Vidor; 1952. (c)

The Happening √ Shame about that desperately 1967 title, which dates much more than the movie, a wry parable of kidnapped big-shot who can't find anyone — associates, wife, mother – who likes him enough to put up the ransom money. Then he – Anthony Quinn – and captors – Faye Dunaway, Michael Parks outstanding – join forces against those whom he feels have betrayed him; Eliot Silverstein makes all this almost credible. (c)

The Happiest Days of Your Life √ Margaret Rutherford in 1950 role of girls' headmistress billeted on boys in charge of Alastair Sim. Superior to subsequent St Trinian's saga. Frank Launder directed. (b/w)

Happy Anniversary X Mild domestic spatting provides what comedy there is in this David Niven-Mitzi Gaynor effort which dates from the period (1959) when Hollywood regarded television as its arch enemy.Villain is the TV set they buy and which causes domestic divisions; David Miller does his best to make it work, but it's awfully uphill work. (b/w)

The Happy Ending XX Phoney look at American Marriage, 1969 style, with Jean Simmons in a sub-Doris Day part as disillusioned wife who flees her wedding anniversary to live it up in the Bahamas. There she meets Bobby Darin, but returns to set up on her own, only to start new romance with – yes, you guessed, her stuffy husband (John Forsythe). If this is the best Jean Simmons's husband, writer-producer-director Richard Brooks, could do for her, it's a wonder she didn't get restless herself. (c)

Happy Go Lovely X Edinburgh Festival provides unlikely background for musical about producer and chorus girl Vera-Ellen; David Niven, Cesar Romero. Bruce Humberstone directed; 1950. (c)

Happy is the Bride XX – if not the audience. This remake of *Quiet Wedding* in 1959 creaks with gentility. Ian Carmichael, Janette Scott, Cecil Parker, and a clutch of comics thrown in with the vain hope of raising a laugh of two – Terry-Thomas, Joyce Grenfell, Eric Barker among them. Director, Roy Boulting. (b/w)

The Happy Thieves √ Farce about three unlucky posh crooks in Madrid, marred by taking itself a bit too seriously; Rita Hayworth, Rex Harrison, directed by George Marshall; 1962. (b/w)

The Happy Years √ A boys' school in the 1890s. Dean Stockwell is naughty but nice pupil, becoming even more aggressive at establishment meant to tame the unruly. William Wellman directed; 1950. (b/w)

A Hard Day's Night √√ The first Beatles film, 1964, and it tells of a mythical day in their lives; stands up well as a museum piece, and Dick Lester's direction is always neat and apposite. (b/w)

The Harder They Come √√ Tough, lively, musical biography of someone like Jimmy Cliff, who plays the hero. Filmed in Jamaica by Jamaican Perry Henzel it won a cult following in 1972, and also had a wider appeal for reggae fans. (c)

The Harder They Fall √ Humphrey Bogart's final film – 1956 – was as nasty a boxing story as ever made the screen. From Budd Schulberg's novel about the exploitation of a South American giant; Rod Steiger, Jan Sterling, Mike Lane, Nehemiah Persoff come off well, and there are appearances by real-life fighters Max Baer and Jersey Joe Walcott; Mark Robson directs. (b/w)

Harem Holiday XX Ten songs in a plodding 1966 Elvis Presley vehicle, about the lad as a sheiky film-star, kidnapped when visiting the Middle East for a première; cursory direction from Gene Nelson. (c)

Harlow √ (1) Not quite as ghastly as it might have been, this pseudo-biography of early thirties sex symbol leaves out a couple of marriages and the all-important Christian Science of her mother. The rise to stardom is competently told, however, and the marriage to an impotent executive tactfully – too tactfully? – alluded to. What redeems it are the performances by Carroll Baker in the main part and

Martin Balsam as a slimy studio boss; for the rest, director Gordon Douglas can't wring convincing performances from Red Buttons, Peter Lawford or Angela Lansbury, but that might not be his fault; others have tried and failed, too; 1965. (c)

Harlow X (2) At the same time, Alex Segal was shooting another version with Carol Lynley miscast as the sex symbol, which had the advantage of Ginger Rogers as her mother but little else; 1965. (b/w)

Harold and Maude √ Black comedy that works most of the time, although leaves one with an unsatisfied feeling. Bud Cort is obsessed with death; at one of the funerals he attends for fun, he meets Ruth Gordon, a 79-year-old who gets her kicks in the same way. Eventually he proposes marriage; but death is aptly waiting. Hal Ashby directed in 1971. (c)

Harriet Craig √ Joan Crawford as ruthless wife in 1950 remake of *Craig's Wife*; Rosalind Russell played the part in 1936. Crawford gave it more histrionic value but the script has withered with the years. Or maybe it was Vincent Sherman's direction. (b/w)

Harry and Tonto √ Sentimentality from director-writer-producer Paul Mazursky in 1974. Art Carney plays his usual lovable old man, this time on a long and boring trip across America with some hippies, calling in on daughter (Ellen Burstyn), old love (Geraldine Fitzgerald) and son (Larry Hagman) on the way. Tonto is a cat he insists on taking with him. Carney won a surprise Oscar for his performance. (c)

Harry Black and the Tiger X Fearless tiger killer Stewart Granger is visited by old friends Barbara Rush and Anthony Steel in steaming Indian jungle. Disloyal love makes it even steamier, which must be how the plot got lost. Directed, if that's not too strong a word, by Hugo Fregonese in 1958. (c)

Harry in Your Pocket √ Pickpocketing team is made up of James Coburn, Michael Sarrazin, Trish Van Devere, and Walter Pidgeon, the fence. Director Bruce Geller has made a rather laboured romantic thriller out of a fascinating subject, and it's a cop-out because he never shows exactly how the dexterous hands achieve their alleged amazing successes; 1973. (c)

Harvey √√ James Stewart scores in famous role as drunk who is accompanied by six-foot rabbit; Josephine Hull won 1950 Oscar as his upset relation. Henry Koster faithfully translated stage play. (b/w)

The Harvey Girls √ One of Judy Garland's best (made in 1946 before limelight burned her up). She's one of an invasion of classy waitresses trying to alter ways of Western town. Songs won an Oscar (e.g. 'Atcheson, Topeka and The Santa Fé') and deserved to. Director, George Sidney. (c)

Hatari! X Howard Hawks clearly fell in love with the hunting of wild beasts and wouldn't sacrifice any of the endlessly repetitive chases in this long, long film; as they are the best thing about this jungle pic (apart, perhaps, from Henry Mancini's score), it's a hard slog to sit through – particularly as you have to put up with the incompetent Hardy Kruger, Elsa Martinelli, Red Buttons and a Fordless John Wayne; 1962. (c)

The Hatchet Man √ Tong wars in San Francisco, with Edward G. Robinson as a mandarin; Loretta Young falls for him. William Wellman failed to make it credible in 1932. (b/w)

A Hatful of Rain √ Powerful, if specious, drug-addiction movie, 1957; Eva Marie Saint and Don Murray shone under Fred Zinnemann's direction. (b/w)

The Haunted and the Hunted √ This was knocked off by Roger Corman's callow young assistant, Francis Coppola (in the days – 1963 – before he put the Ford in the middle of his name and made *The Godfather*). Corman had a crew in Europe, and Coppola pointed out that for another $20,000 they could make a quickie in Ireland. 'I described a scene of some lady who goes into a pond and sees the corpse of a little child and gets axed to death – everything I knew Roger would like.' The censor did some hacking of his own, but the result is still exciting stuff, if hokum. The cast were all unknowns and most have stayed that way. (b/w)

The Haunted Palace √√ A really enveloping horror movie that chills you deep into your spine; Roger Corman disciplines Vincent Price, for once, into ironing out his weakness for sending himself up, and manages to extract a double performance of virtuosity as both victim and evil-doer. Do those deformed children come from his experiments or from puritans' own repressed imaginations? Lon

Chaney gives a superior performance, too, as a sinister butler; 1963. (c)

The Haunting √√ Creepy respectfully directed by Robert Wise in 1963 from Shirley Jackson story. Elegant and literate, it has Claire Bloom as lesbian assistant to scientist Richard Johnson, menacing Julie Harris. (b/w)

Hawaii XX The story of missionary Max von Sydow and his wife Julie Andrews (enamoured of sea captain Richard Harris), who go and destroy the happy sinful lives of the South Sea Islanders, bringing in return a grubby Christianity that corrupts them. Long (over three hours), frequently boring, plagued by inadequate casting, and without a truly sympathetic character, it still manages to impress with sheer weight of sincerity. And with George Roy Hill's painstaking direction; 1967. (c)

The Heartbreak Kid √√ Elaine May's second film (1972), another extension of her famous duologues with Mike Nichols. First there is Charles Grodin's discovery of the enormity of the mistake he has made in marrying Jeannie Berlin; then his hilarious courtship of Cybill Shepherd; finally his exchanges with her irate father, Eddie Albert. The boy meets girl, boy loses girl, boy gets girl plot is a framework on which to hang some very funny dialogue and several wry characterisations. (c)

The Heart is a Lonely Hunter √ Weepie about deaf-mute who is shown to be so superior to the other characters as to be almost unbelievable, if it wasn't for Alan Arkin's fine interpretation; directed by Robert Ellis Miller from the Carson McCullers novel. Stacy Keach in a minor role; 1969. (c)

Heart of a Child X About little boy, his dog and nasty Daddy (Donald Pleasence), all predictable and stoically directed by Clive Donner in 1958. (b/w)

The Heart of the Matter √ Fair 1953 try by George More O'Ferrall at the Graham Greene novel about a police commissioner in Sierra Leone tortured over his sinful love – Trevor Howard for Maria Schell – But Greene's plots are less important than his words and ideas, and these lost out, as usual in the films from his books. (b/w)

Heaven Can Wait √√ Ernst Lubitsch told Don Ameche's story, as head of posh family, from tenderest age until he is turned away from the gates of hell by perfectly-cast Laird Cregar; Gene Tierney made an appealing wife; 1943. (c)

Heaven Knows, Mr Allison √ Got the critical thumbs-down when shown in 1957, as being too obvious a reworking of *The African Queen*, also by John Huston, with Robert Mitchum and Deborah Kerr alone on an island instead of a boat and the Japs replacing the Germans. She was a nun this time. (c)

Heavens Above! √ The Boultings take on Christianity, and it's no surprise that they should come out the losers. However, there are compensations in Peter Sellers's beautifully judged performance as the well-meaning vicar that even the dogs pee on. There are also some rather nasty cracks at 'skyvers' on the social services, some gipsies who cheerfully bite the hands that feed them, a long way after Bunuel's *Viridiana*. A gallery of splendid British comic actors keep it going happily – Cecil Parker, Eric Sykes, Ian Carmichael, Irene Handl, Miriam Karlin, Eric Barker, Roy Kinnear, Kenneth Griffith – but the total effect isn't all that pleasant; 1963. (b/w)

Heaven With a Gun √ Pastor Glenn Ford forces peace between the cowboys and the sheep-herders with frequent use of firearms; sadly, the implications of this on the Christian religion are not even considered and Lee H. Katzin directs as though it had no possibility of being more than a conventional western; 1969. (c)

The Heiress √√ Shows the winsome way Olivia de Havilland won the Oscar in 1949 as daddy-dominated plain girl falling victim to fortune hunter Montgomery Clift. As a father even more horrid than Mr Barrett, Ralph Richardson acted everyone else into mere appendices to his case-history. Adapted from Henry James's *Washington Square*. William Wyler directed with prosy elegance. And there's that lovely moment at the end that will greatly appeal to all scorned women. (b/w)

The Heist √ Ambitious attempt to use very short takes and quick cutting to build into a complete long film. Although film buffs will be fascinated by Richard Brooks's technique, others will be exasperated by the absurd plot and inconsequential way it is resolved. Warren Beatty plays a bank employee who robs safe deposit boxes while incarcerated in the safe by a bomb scare. Goldie Hawn is his accomplice; 1971. (c)

Helen of Troy XX Although Brigitte Bardot is in the cast, she doesn't play the title role; this belonged to plump, pouting Rossana Podesta in 1955, and director Robert Wise must still be kicking himself round the cutting room for acquiescing in this monumental mistake. It wasn't the only one in this huge, expensive epic: the script was another howler. Stanley Baker, Cedric Hardwicke, Harry Andrews battle gamely on, but it's disaster all the way. (c)

The Helicopter Spies XX Tired and boring Man from UNCLE with Robert Vaughn and David McCallum saving the world yet again; sad to see such excellent supports as Lola Albright, John Carradine, Julie London reduced to capering about for cliché-director Boris Sagal in 1968. (c)

Hell and High Water XX This routine submarine rubbish may awake critical interest because it is the 1954 work of Samuel Fuller, one of the most respected American *auteurs*. But beware – even Fuller's hagiographer, Nichola Garnham, in his book on his idol admits 'I find *Hell and High Water* almost unwatchable.' So what about the rest of us? Condolences to Richard Widmark, Cameron Mitchell, Bella Darvi. (c)

Hell Below Zero XX Whoever dreamed up the idea of a girl commanding a whaler while she hunted for her Daddy's killer must have been bemused; then whoever cast Joan Tetzel in the role must have been even pottier. Plucky Alan Ladd does his best as her number two, but he's right out at sea, as are Stanley Baker and Basil Sydney. Director Mark Robson appears to have gone along with the whole thing; 1954. (c)

Heller in Pink Tights √√ Unusual western with Sophia Loren in a blonde wig as star of travelling theatrical company saved by killer Steve Forrest; she's the 'heller' or hell-raiser concerned. George Cukor brings off some nice touches – Loren tied to a galloping horse; Indians dressing up in troupe's costumes after they raid them – and there's strong support from old-timers Margaret O'Brien, Ramon Navarro, Anthony Quinn, Edmund Lowe; 1960. (c)

Hellfighters X The one about putting out oil fires that has been coming round ever since movies were made,

this time with John Wayne and Jim Hutton among the fire-dampers; if the story is formula, so is Andrew McLaglen's direction; 1969. (c)

The Hellfire Club XXX Really dreadful little costumer about aristocrat who becomes circus performer; Robert S. Baker and Monty Berman share the credits and the discredit of having produced one of the worst films ever to come out of a British studio – and that's saying something. Condolences to Keith Michell, Adrienne Corri, Peter Cushing, Andrew Faulds, Miles Malleson – all of whom have appeared in better movies; 1961. (c)

Hell in the Pacific √√√ A remarkable film in many ways, not least in taking a situation that lesser writers (Alex Jacobs and Eric Bercovici here) and directors (John Boorman) would have allowed to degenerate into the sort of boring war-pic that the poor title suggests, and creating a parable of great power. American Lee Marvin and Japanese Toshiro Mifune find themselves in a Robinson Crusoe situation during the war. How they make their personal peace, only to find it shattered on return to 'civilisation' is brilliantly conveyed, particularly in the use of our expectations aroused by lesser, earlier films of the same genre. 'Personal contact', typified in the Christmas meeting across the trenches in the first war and so many sentimental movies since, is not, alas, the answer to international conflict and that's brought out here. The roots of that lie deep, deeper than the cinema usually permits itself to peer; 1969. (c)

The Hellions XX A rotten 'western' set in the Transvaal, with Richard Todd as the sheriff or whatever he's called there, and such great classical actors as Marty Wilde to marvel at; director was Ken Annakin; 1962. (c)

Hell is a City X Location crime thriller on the American model provides Stanley Baker, Donald Pleasence, Billie Whitelaw with some exciting moments in Manchester and Oldham, culminating in the inevitable roof-top fight; Val Guest copies faithfully, but his studio sequences between Inspector Baker and wife Maxine Audley come over as very artificial; 1960. (b/w)

Hell is for Heroes √ Technically brilliant war drama from Don Siegel, with Steve McQueen, Bobby Darin, Fess Parker attacking German pillbox in 1944 Belgium. But all it says is War is Hell all over again; 1962. (b/w)

Hello Dolly! √ Bits are wonderful – the Barbra Streisand-Louis Armstrong routine with the title number, Walter Matthau's misogynist, the huge scale of the sets – but too much else is strained. Tommy Tune leaves Michael Crawford standing. Surely director Gene Kelly and choreographer Michael Kidd could have made more of the dancing; 1969. (c)

Hello, Frisco, Hello XX Dreary 1943 musical comedy with Alice Faye trying to make a break, plus John Payne, Jack Oakie and Oscar-winning song 'You'll Never Know'. H. Bruce Humberstone directs. Goodbye, movie, goodbye. (c)

Hell on Frisco Bay √ The ex-con who's out to uncover how he got framed is a standard plot and Frank Tuttle's direction doesn't attempt to lift it above the hackney carriage. But the cast is so strong they have their own momentum: Edward G. Robinson, Alan Ladd, Paul Stewart, William Demarest, Joanne Dru, Fay Wray; 1955. (c)

Hell's Island XX John Payne in weak little murder mystery in the Caribbean, momentarily enlivened by Francis L. Sullivan; Phil Karlson; 1955. (c)

Hell to Eternity X 1960 look back to trueish story of Japanese-American marine behind the enemy's lines – the Japanese, that is; he isn't too sure at first, either. Jeffrey Hunter acts to the limits of his ability, which aren't much; David Janssen, Vic Damone are buddies. Director Phil Karlson seems to have had a big budget. (b/w)

The Hell With Heroes √ Improbable, familiar smuggler-in-Algeria plot is redeemed by fast cutting and Joseph Sargent's slick direction; although neither Rod Taylor nor Claudia Cardinale are capable of more than perfunctory characterisation; 1969. (c)

Hellzapoppin √√ If it isn't quite as funny and novel now as it was in 1941, that's because it has been copied a hundred times since. But this zany farce deserves a place in any celebration of the history of the movies for the way it liberated the screen. Olsen and Johnson, Mischa Auer, Martha Raye, Hugh Herbert all gorgeous, and director H. C. Potter did more than just translate the Broadway hit to film. (b/w)

Help! √ From the standpoint of history, which the Beatles now are, this second movie they made – in 1965 – isn't a patch on their first, documentaryish effort, *A Hard Day's Night*, also directed by Dick Lester. The elaborate, nonsensical plot involving magic rings never fulfils its eastern promise, and there is far too much indulgent scampering around; Roy Kinnear and Victor Spinetti slow things up further in superfluous subplot. (c)

Hennessy √ Rod Steiger attempting a Guy Fawkes job on the Houses of Parliament because his wife and daughter are killed in Ulster. There is the usual last-minute will-they-stop-him stuff as Richard Johnson co-operates with IRA chief Eric Porter (fearing public reaction). Don Chaffey brought his long B-picture experience to doing a workmanlike direction chore in 1975. (c)

Henry V √√√ Hailed as 'one of the movies' rare great works of art' (*Time* magazine), the thirty-odd years since its first showing (1944) have unfairly eroded its reputation. Yet Olivier's production, direction and playing are consummate, the well-assimilated borrowings from the earlier films are triumphantly justified, the bold but honourable re-arrangements of Shakespeare's text never jar, the performances of Robert Newton (Pistol), Renée Asherson (the French princess), Leo Genn (Constable of France), rich and human. And Olivier's 'Gentlemen of England now abed' at Agincourt is still among the most rousing minutes of speech on film. (c)

Henry VIII and His Six Wives √ A sort of remake of the BBC series in 1972, with Keith Michell playing the part again and most of the familiar made-up faces from the serial. Unfortunately the ladies flash in and out, and the film cannot stand the comparison with Charles Laughton's lovingly remembered hamming. (c)

He Ran All The Way √√ John Garfield's last movie (1951) was this suspenser about criminal-on-the-run holding up Shelley Winters's nice American family. John Berry did more than adequate directing job. (b/w)

Here Comes Mr Jordan √√ Much-copied 1941 comedy about Robert Montgomery popping off before he was supposed to and given a new body by Heaven; Alexander Hall got the best from a cast that included Claude Rains, Edward Everett Horton. (b/w)

Here Comes the Groom X Frank Capra steers Bing Crosby, Jane Wyman,

Franchot Tone, Anna Maria Alberghetti through sticky newspaper comedy with Bing needing a Mum for the two orphans he impulsively adopts; 1951. (b/w)

Here Come the Co-Eds XX Abbott and Costello lunacy, without much magic, places them as caretakers at girls' college, where Peggy Ryan is cavorting; director, Jean Yarbrough; 1945. (b/w)

Here Come the Girls X Dull little musical with Bob Hope in his younger (well, a bit younger – he was 49 when this was made in 1953) days as chorus boy involved with star Arlene Dahl, threatening boyfriend, and his True Love Rosemary Clooney; Claude Binyon directed cheerfully. (c)

Here We Go Round the Mulberry Bush X This was dated when it appeared in 1968 and is even more of a museum piece of the early sixties now. The out-of-dateness is further emphasised by the swinging way in which Clive Donner has shot and edited it all, looking like the television commercials he himself made at the time. Barry Evans is adequate as the virgin-obsessed main boy; Judy Geeson, Angela Scoular, Adrienne Posta are sufficiently different to provide acceptable contrasts; Denholm Elliott and Michael Bates as usual walk off with the honours. (c)

He Rides Tall XX Routine western. Dan Duryea being villainous is the only bright bit in prairie landscape; director R. G. Springsteen; 1964. (b/w)

Her Jungle Love X Dorothy Lamour vehicle from 1938, in which she plays a jungle girl whom the natives believe is a goddess. Crashed flyer Ray Milland is most impressed. Director George Archainbaud throws in a typhoon, an earthquake and a tidal wave. (c)

The Heroes of Telemark X Three attempts to destroy Nazi heavy water plant have to be made so that they won't get the atomic bomb first. Kirk Douglas and Richard Harris are chief destroyers and neither is particularly convincing. The script has more holes in it than the bombed factory, and such incidentals as Malcolm Arnold's music are pretty awful. Anthony Mann is trapped into conventional war-stuff by inauthentic introduction of girl at saboteurs' camp; 1966. (c)

The Heroin Gang XX David McCallum as a really nasty hero, Sol Madrid. Utterly ruthless, he even kills his best friend on the vague suspicion that he

may be mixed up in the Mafia-drug biz being investigated in Mexico; the appearances of Telly Savalas, Ricardo Montalban, Rip Torn, Pat Hingle, Paul Lukas are welcome but not enough to save this Brian G. Hutton-directed damp squib; 1968. (c)

Hero's Island √√ Not quite a pirate pic, although James Mason does play the bearded captain of a pirate ship. Put ashore on a raft, he comes to the aid of the widowed Kate Manx and helps her claim the island that's rightfully hers. Leslie Stevens directs resourcefully and the whole unusual drama really comes off; 1961. (c)

Her Twelve Men XX Repulsively coy comedy with Greer Garson smilin' her way thru' troubles at a boys' school where she teaches. A measure of the general ghastliness is that the men of the title are boys. Robert Ryan and Barry Sullivan shuffle noiselessly around; Robert Z. Leonard directed; 1954. (c)

Hester Street √√ Charming but hard-centred fable of immigrant life in the New York ghetto at the turn of the century. A wife, fresh off the boat, turns the tables on her philandering husband. Beautifully directed, without fuss, by Joan Micklin Silver, 1974. (b/w)

He Who Rides a Tiger X 1966 drama from veteran director Charles Crichton is about recidivist who gets involved with orphanage girl thinking she's rich; Tom Bell, Judi Dench. (b/w)

Hickey and Boggs √ Robert Culp (directing as well as starring) and Bill Cosby, who made a break-through white-and-black partnership in the TV series I Spy, team up again as down-at-heel private eyes in a thriller that seems at first as if it is going to have some originality, but soon settles for ordinariness; 1972. (c)

Hide and Seek XX Comedy-thriller that is neither, alas; Ian Carmichael, Janet Munro, Curt Jurgens, lost in a rambling script, which director Cy Endfield does nothing to clear up; 1964. (b/w)

The Hideaways √ Considering the incipient cuteness of the subject – kids running away to hide in the Metropolitan Museum of Art – Fielder Cook kept this yarn under fairly strict control in 1973. Ingrid Bergman clearly enjoyed herself as stern but relenting old lady they go and see; camp George Rose even more as her butler. (c)

The High and the Mighty X One of those multi-storey dramas, 1954, of passengers on disabled aircraft each flashbacking to their reasons for living; Robert Stack, Laraine Day, John Wayne, Claire Trevor come off best under William Wellman's direction. (c)

The High Bright Sun XX Embarrassing naive drama about the British in Cyprus that must surely make everybody concerned blush to the roots of their hair today. Made in 1965, when almost everyone except this film's makers, director Ralph Thomas and producer Betty Box, realised that British days in Cyprus were numbered – and rightly so – they chose to make a Union Jack-waving piece of propaganda. Dirk Bogarde plays the major who persuades American neutral Susan Strasberg to come out against the 'terrorists' (mainly sneaky George Chakiris). (c)

The High Command X Lionel Atwill being blackmailed in 1937 melodrama about guilty secrets in a West African garrison, directed by Thorold Dickinson. James Mason, then a stripling of 28, was the lead. (b/w)

The High Cost of Loving XX Jose Ferrer directing himself in tepid little tragedy of an over-the-hill employee who loses his job when his firm is taken over. The screenplay is by Rip van Ronkel – obvious jokes are hereby avoided; 1958. (b/w)

High Noon √√√ Oscar-laden classic about Marshal Gary Cooper searching for support against outlaws against the clock (time-span of film is from 10.40 a.m. to noon). Fred Zinnemann directed, Carl Foreman wrote, Grace Kelly, Thomas Mitchell, Otto Kruger, Lon Chaney acted. And do not forsake Dimitri Tiomkin's haunting music; 1952. (b/w)

High Plains Drifter √√ Powerful if confusing use of the western as symbolism by Clint Eastwood in his second director-star effort, 1972. Up to the last moment, we are unsure of the moral commitment of the stranger who rides into town, teaches the citizens how to defend themselves and finally takes his revenge. Surrealistic devices like painting the whole place red and changing its name to Hell come off remarkably well in an unusual, almost operatic style. (c)

High Sierra √ Convict Humphrey Bogart is sprung to stage hold-up. On the way he falls for Good Girl Joan Leslie and then gets mixed up with Bad Girl Ida Lupino; you can't believe a frame, but Raoul Walsh manages to make you suspend disbelief; 1941. (b/w)

High Society √√ Cole Porter's music ('Who Wants To Be A Millionaire', 'Well Did You Evah?'); Sinatra and Crosby's singing and fooling; Grace Kelly's poise, Celeste Holm's bite, sadly can't combine to make you forget original *Philadelphia Story*. Charles Walters, 1956. (c)

High Time √ Pleasant trifle about middle-aged Bing Crosby enrolling in college and giving the young (Fabian, Tuesday Weld, Richard Beymer) a lesson in how to enjoy themselves. Blake Edwards skilfully avoids its being patronising. The songs aren't much cop, however; 1960. (c)

High, Wide and Handsome √ Lumbering musical with over-rated talents – Irene Dunne ('Can I Forget You?', 'The Folks That Live on the Hill'), Dorothy Lamour ('The Things I Want') and Randolph Scott. Charles Bickford, William Frawley, Akim Tamiroff, Raymond Walburn among others directed by Rouben Mamoulian in yarn about early days of oil boom; 1937. (b/w)

A High Wind in Jamaica √√ A beautiful film of great integrity from Richard Hughes' novel. Director Sandy Mackendrick has brought off the feat of sailing between an ordinary (if exciting) pirate adventure and an earlier-set *Lord of the Flies*, in telling this tale of children captured by pirates and the way they are made to turn against them. If you're left with too much sympathy for the pirates, this is probably due to Anthony Quinn's ingratiating performance as their chief. But James Coburn and all the children are marvellous; 1965. (c)

Hilda Crane XX Embarrassing detergent opera about Finding Happiness, with Jean Simmons doing her plucky best. Philip Dunne; 1956. (c)

The Hill √√ Brutality in a North African prison camp during the last war, imposed by Ian Hendry on Sean Connery, Jack Watson, Roy Kinnear and Ossie Davis. Main punishment is running up the hill of the title. It's hard to see why such a stark, horrid drama was made; unlike *The Brig*, which it resembles, the punishment no longer applied in 1965. Perhaps director Sidney Lumet felt that he was exposing military sadism of all kinds. Others present are Ian Bannen, Michael

Redgrave, Harry Andrews, Alfred Lynch, Norman Bird. (b/w)

A Hill in Korea √ Korean war film in which the supports outshine the star, George Baker. Among those in the National Service patrol: Michael Caine, Robert Shaw, Stanley Baker, Stephen Boyd. They all achieved greater eminence after this 1956 effort, directed by Julian Aymes. (b/w)

Hills of Home √ 1948 follow-up to *Lassie Come Home* with Edmund Gwenn, Donald Crisp and the wonder dog stealing scenes from each other in story of doctors in the Highlands; Fred M. Wilcox. (c)

The Hired Hand √ High-aiming western which fails to hit most of its targets, partly due to Peter Fonda's ineptness as director and self-indulgence as main character. Warren Oates turns in a fine job as his buddy; Verna Bloom makes the most of the unusually detailed characterisation of an abandoned wife provided for her by writer Alan Sharp; 1971. (c)

The Hireling √ Robert Shaw as ex-Sgt. Major with pretensions to posh Sarah Miles's hand. Losing her to Peter Egan, he is driven to extremes; Alan Bridges directed as well as he could from Wolf Mankowitz's too-obvious script, in 1973. (c)

His Butler's Sister X Title may sound like naughty-naughty Charing-X Roader, but it's ever-so-pure Deanna Durbin falling in love with employer – Franchot Tone, Pat O'Brien. Director Frank Borzage; 1943. (b/w)

His Girl Friday √√√ Sparkling remake of *The Front Page* with sex of quitting reporter switched so that Rosalind Russell can score in part and Ralph Bellamy as her drippy fiancé. Cary Grant's the managing editor who connives to keep her working, and Gene Lockhart, Porter Hall, Frank Jenks, Billy Gilbert all shine under Howard Hawks' creative 1940 direction. (b/w)

The History of Mr Polly √ John Mills in tame version of H. G. Wells novel of lower middle-class shopkeeper's revolt. Directed by Anthony Pelissier; 1949. (b/w)

The Hitchhiker √ Edmond O'Brien picks up nutter; premature woman's-libber Ida Lupino directed and co-wrote this one in 1953 and kept it pretty exciting. (b/w)

Hitler XX Inept, incompetent, inefficient, unconvincing attempt to whizz through the dictator's life. Richard Basehart was a ludicrous choice as Hitler and he's the best actor in it. Director Stuart Heisler couldn't really have tried; 1962. (b/w)

Hitler: The Last Ten Days X Unconvincing sojourn in the Berlin bunker, with Alec Guinness doing more of an impersonation than a portrayal under Ennio de Concini's compromised direction. Despite Prof. Trevor-Roper's endorsement, this was surely not what it was like down there – for one thing, Hitler himself was a broken, physical wreck by then. Nor can they have moralised incessantly; 1973. (c)

Hit the Ice X Abbott and Costello in Sun Valley. They play would-be press photographers who get sucked into bank raid by Sheldon Leonard. Director, Charles Lamont; 1943. (b/w)

H. M. Pulham Esq √ Robert Young lets his stuffing out as he goes into middle-aged fling; from John P. Marquand novel; Hedy Lamarr was flingee in 1941. King Vidor the director. (b/w)

HMS Defiant √√ Super-patriotism on Nelson's high seas, from the novel *Mutiny* by Frank Tilsley; Alec Guinness, Dirk Bogarde, Anthony Quayle all more than adequate under Lewis Gilbert's direction; 1962. (c)

Hobson's Choice √√ Charles Laughton could have over-weighted this custom-made comedy from Harold Brighouse's play, but he settles down comfortably to some fine ensemble playing with Brenda de Banzie and Daphne Anderson. John Mills is built up by one of his rebellious daughters as his rival in the Lancashire of the eighties. David Lean; 1954. (b/w)

Hoffman X Peter Sellers, desperately trying to win the love of Sinead Cusack, resorts to blackmailing her to spend a week with him. The soft ending, telegraphed way ahead, pre-empts suspense, and one is left with a series of comic episodes that owe more to Sellers's own routines than Alvin Rakoff's direction; 1969. (c)

Hold Back the Dawn √ Charles Boyer conning Olivia de Havilland into marriage so that he can get into the USA. Mitchell Leisen directed. The script may have had some heartfelt feeling as it was written by Billy Wilder and Charles Brackett in 1941, only a few years after Wilder, a refugee from Germany, married the daughter of a Californian attorney. (b/w)

Hold That Ghost √ Best Abbott and Costello farce has Joan Davis as girl whose job in life is to scream on the radio; Arthur Lubin's frantic direction makes it great fun; 1941. (b/w)

A Hole in the Head √√ Delightful 1959 Frank Capra sentimental comedy about Frank Sinatra's money troubles, beset by an irascible brother (Edward G. Robinson), sister-in-law (Thelma Ritter), nasty old buddy-buddy (Keenan Wynn), and warring ladies (Eleanor Parker, Carolyn Jones). All are at their best under Capra's relaxed and masterly direction. (c)

Holiday √√ Katharine Hepburn and Cary Grant in Philip (*Philadelphia Story*) Barry's play neatly adapted for the screen about rebel Grant clashing with society gal Hepburn. George Cukor got the best out of them in 1938 with Binnie Barnes, Edward Everett Horton, Henry Daniell fine supports. (b/w)

Holiday Camp XXX The *Huggett* comedy series grew out of this 1947 romantic comedy – and there couldn't be greater condemnation than that. Jack Warner and Kathleen Harrison are two of the gallery of British characters holidaying in a bizarre manner all those years ago. Dennis Price, Flora Robson among the wasted; Hazel Court, Jimmy Hanley, Susan Shaw in their element. Ken Annakin directed. (b/w)

Holiday for Lovers XX Doubtful if the intention of this 1959 tour round South America was to show up how embarrassing and awful some American tourists are, but that's the result that Henry Levin achieves. Papa is Clifton Webb, Mom Jane Wyman, nubile daughters Jill St John and Carol Lynley. (c)

Holiday in Mexico XX Walter Pidgeon, Jane Powell are OK if undistinguished in this yarn about ambassador's daughter in love with a musician, but Jose Iturbi and Xavier Cugat should have stuck to their instruments. George Sidney directed; 1946. (c)

Holiday on the Buses XXX An insult to all concerned: those who took part and those who are expected to give up their time (and in 1973 their money) to watch. All the usual terrible jokes about holiday camps with the TV team, who were never very funny in the first place. The director was Brian Izzard. (c)

Hollywood or Bust X Dean Martin and Jerry Lewis in broad (the 'bust' in the title is, nudge-nudge, a *double entendre*) comedy about sweepstake-winners

crossing USA to see Anita Ekberg; Frank Tashlin directed, vulgarly, in 1956. (c)

Hombre √√ Although Martin Ritt was obviously trying to move the western on a pace or two by making his hero as much an anti-hero as the film is an anti-western, the genre is so strongly fixed in our experience and imagination that it works only intermittently. Yet if the script is too talky, the performances – particularly Paul Newman in the main part – are outstanding; 1967. (c)

Home at Seven √ Cosy whodunit with plenty of twists, directed by and starring Ralph Richardson. One of those amnesia stories in which there has been a murder and a theft during the time he can't remember; Margaret Leighton, Jack Hawkins support loyally; 1952. (b/w)

Home Before Dark √ Typical 1958 Warner Bros drama about a distraught Jean Simmons returning from a mental hospital. Veteran Mervyn Le Roy directed slickly. Dan O'Herlihy is heavy husband, Efrem Zimbalist reliable friend. (b/w)

Home from the Hill √ Solid two-and-a-half hours-worth of Southern drama with Robert Mitchum unhappily married to Eleanor Parker, and strong performance from Everett Sloane; George Peppard and George Hamilton are around; Vincente Minnelli directed in his florid 1960 style. (c)

Home is the Hero X Sentimental drama about readjustment after five-year prison term. Directed by J. Fielder Cook with cast of Abbey Theatre players; 1959. (b/w)

Home of the Brave √ Black soldier finds wartime discrimination worse than the enemy; strong stuff for 1949; Douglas Dick, James Edwards; director Mark Robson makes it feel real. (b/w)

Hondo √√ Signs are that this 1953 western with John Wayne working for John Farrow instead of John Ford, for once, set out to push the frontier of the genre on a bit but took fright before the final film was issued. Certainly the script is far more ambiguous and literate than usual, and the relationship between the scout and widder Geraldine Page more interesting. (c)

Hondo and the Apaches X Poor relation to John Wayne's *Hondo* is this spin-off with Ralph Taeger as Hondo Lane, former Cavalry scout waging peace between warlike Indians and the white men – specifically Michael Rennie, Robert Taylor, Noah Beery Jr. Director Lee H. Katzin; 1966. (c)

Honeymoon XXX Boring trip round Spain with Anthony Steel, Ludmilla Tcherina, with ballet interludes; Michael Powell; 1958. (c)

Honeymoon Hotel √ An oh-so-familiar mix-up in a hotel reserved for honeymoon couples, with Robert Goulet, Robert Morse, Nancy Kwan, Jill St John – and Elsa Lanchester stealing it from under their noses as a comic chambermaid. The wonder is the lateness of the date – 1964. You might have reasonably expected this sort of inconsequence to have passed away long before then. Henry Levin. (c)

The Honeymoon Killers √√ Powerful horror stuff, all the more horrible for being based on true story of couple who posed as brother and sister, advertised for lonely hearts, and killed them for their money. Leonard Kastle's initial strength was not to cast the main parts from the cosmeticised stars that a big budget movie would have made them, but to use Shirley Stoler and Tony Lo Bianco, who look pretty off-putting here; 1969. (b/w)

The Honeymoon Machine √ Unremarkable comedy about two sailors with a scheme to beat the roulette wheel in Monte Carlo saved by Steve McQueen, Jim Hutton, Paula Prentiss. Richard Thorpe directed; 1961. (c)

The Honey Pot √ Rex Harrison invites three old girlfriends back to his palazzo in Venice but Maggie Smith is there already; Susan Hayward and Cliff Robertson were strange choices of writer-director Joseph L. Mankiewicz, but it all keeps going cheerfully – and there's a murder; 1967. (c)

Hong Kong X Tedious tale of Ronald Reagan as GI tangling with improbable mission teacher Rhonda Fleming in bid to rob Chinese waif. Directed 1951 by Lewis R. Foster against plywood Hong Kong. (c)

The Honkers √ One of a rash of movies about ageing rodeo performers around 1972. James Coburn stars this time; director Steve Ihnat died soon after making this, his only feature. (c)

Honky Tonk X Dull romantic western in which Clark Gable takes over a town and Lana Turner, Frank Morgan, Claire Trevor, Marjorie Main, Albert Decker, Chill Wills don't get enough to do; 1941. (b/w)

Honor Thy Father X The Godfather without flair or excitement. Based on

real happenings among the Mafia in 1967, it has the right names (the Bonnanos, played by Joseph Bologna, Raf Vallone, Brenda Vaccaro) but the wrong feelings for either reality or imaginative fantasy; Paul Wendkos does a surprisingly poor directorial job. (c)

The Hoodlum Priest X First hour is muddled record of priest's attempts to set up reform home for criminals. Last section shows young crook Keir Dullea judicially murdered in the gas chamber; Don Murray wrote (under a pseudonym), co-produced and played the priest; Irvin Kershner directed, in 1961. (b/w)

The Hook X Routine will-the-escaped-prisoner - blow - up - the - ship drama given a Korean War setting; Kirk Douglas, Nehemiah Persoff, Robert Walker give competent but uninspired performances under George Seaton's direction; 1962. (b/w)

Horizons West √ Budd Boetticher western (which guarantees its superiority) with Rock Hudson, Robert Ryan as brothers on rival sides of the law; Julie Adams, Raymond Burr stirring it; 1952. (c)

The Horizontal Lieutenant X Awful example of the way a director can ruin a film: played fast fast fast, this comedy of accident-prone Jim Hutton capturing pilfering Japanese guerrilla could have been quite funny; as it is, it's so slow that it droops away under Richard Thorpe's uninspired touch; Paula Prentiss, Jack Carter look as wearied as we do; 1962. (c)

Hornet's Nest X Lacklustre war thriller about blowing up a dam, made rather late in the day (1970) and consequently over-concerned to impart a compensatory message. Rock Hudson goes through the motions under Phil Karlson's slick direction, but the whole enterprise seems pretty pointless. (c)

The Horrors of the Black Museum XX Michael Gough and less than stunning cast nervelessly handled by Arthur Crabtree in incredible hypno-tised-murderer yarn; 1959. (c)

Horse Feathers √√ The one about Groucho as college president fixing the football game in which Harpo zanily shines; Norman McLeod; 1932. (b/w)

The Horsemen XX Ludicrous attempt to turn a Hollywood backlot into Old Afghanistan, and Omar Sharif and Jack Palance into proud Tartars. This is compounded by a silly plot and unconvincing supporting players;

John Frankenheimer must have fallen off his horse in 1970. (c)

The Horse's Mouth √ As well as acting the main part of Gully Jimson, the artist who can't stop painting murals on every empty wall he sees, Alec Guinness wrote the screenplay for this mild comedy from Joyce Cary's novel. Director Ronald Neame seemed over-awed by the combination in 1959 and came up with a slightly disappointing movie. Great Artists are notoriously difficult to convey, particularly when their genius is the excuse for spoiled brat behaviour. Still, John Bratby painted some convincing pictures, and Guinness won the acting award at the Venice Film Festival for his performance. (c)

The Horse Soldiers √√ Big-budget Civil Warrer by John Ford with contemptuous John Wayne and William Holden; based on a true incident when the north raided deep into the south, defended only by its women and the children of a military academy; the emphasis is even more action than usual in Ford movies, with the character clash between Colonel Wayne and Doctor Holden providing most of the character tension. Two notable bit players are both called Gibson – tennis star Althea and veteran cowboy actor Hoot; 1959. (c)

The Hospital √√ Harshly comic exposé of the ghastliness of American hospitals, with a hard central performance from George C. Scott as a doctor. Diana Rigg is less impressive as the daughter of a homicidal patient who tries to get the doctor to flee the city and responsibilities with them. Arthur Hiller directed more than adequately in 1971. (c)

Hostile Witness XX Poor rendering of a threadbare courtroom drama. Sad that Roy Milland should have bothered to star in and direct such rubbish in 1968. Sylvia Syms is his junior (he's a barrister accused of murder) who secretly loves him. Whodunit? Who cares? (c)

Hotel XX The star is the set, a remarkable mock-up of a grand hotel in New Orleans, the centre of a takeover bid; there are a number of sub-plots involving various guests, but it's never very gripping – due to feckless direction by Richard Quine and his weak ideas on casting (Rod Taylor, Catherine Spaak, Michael Rennie, Merle Oberon, Richard Conte). Melvyn Douglas has some moments as the

place's proud owner and Karl Malden manages to lift the action slightly whenever he does his hotel thief bit. But you may want to check out early; 1967. (c)

Hotel Paradiso X Alec Guinness, Gina Lollobrigida, Robert Morley, Peggy Mount, Akim Tamiroff, Douglas Byng, Robertson Hare may seem a disparate lot to bring life to a Feydeau farce – and so it proved. Though made in 1966, it had to wait until 1971 for release, and then understandably flopped. Peter Glenville who produced-directed and helped to script must take most of the blame for allowing a wild farce to turn into a mild comedy. (c)

Hot Enough for June X Unfortunate attempt by Ralph Thomas to make spy spoof involves Robert Morley as M-type and Dirk Bogarde as 007-type; the city of Prague comes off best, as do the Czechs altogether; 1964. (c)

Hot Millions √ Ustinov versus the computer, with the human embezzler winning; pleasant and unassuming with the humour coming from character – Ustinov's own warmth supplemented by a peach of a performance from Maggie Smith as his helpmate; Karl Malden, Robert Morley contribute their strengths, too. If Eric Till didn't turn out to be the greatest new director of 1968, he at least didn't detract from the proceedings. Ustinov wrote himself in a scene where he conducts a symphony orchestra because he had never done it before. (c)

Hot Rods to Hell XX Nasty little drama of Dana Andrews and Jeanne Crain tormented by car freaks; unsympathetic to the young but hardly showing the middle-aged in a very kindly light; John Brahm directed; 1967. (c)

Hot Spell √ Anthony Quinn is sleeping around while Shirley Booth tries to hang on to drifting children; Daniel Mann directed tautly; 1958. (b/w)

Houdini XX Conventional show-biz biography of great escapologist, made 1953, illustrated with tricks. Tony Curtis (born Bernie Schwartz) plays Harry Houdini (born Henry Weiss). Janet Leigh, then married to Tony/Bernie, plays his wife, very unlike the real Mrs H.; George Marshall. (c)

Hound Dog Man XX The only surprise about this routine 1960 teenage mush is the director – Don Siegel, king of the crime thrillers. Otherwise it's just Fabian and Stuart Whitman chatting up Carol Lynley and Dodie Stevens. (c)

The Hound of the Baskervilles √ (1) 1939 Sidney Lanfield version with Basil Rathbone as Sherlock Holmes, Nigel Bruce as Dr Watson, doesn't convince in its Englishness, but is full of excitement otherwise. (b/w)

The Hound of the Baskervilles X (2) 1959 version is oddly dull, plodding down the beaten track without benefit of surprise, inspired direction (though Terence Fisher's is workmanlike enough) or distinguished acting (Peter Cushing and André Morell as Holmes and Watson; Christopher Lee as Sir Henry B.). Perfectly competent, nothing more. (c)

Hour of the Gun √ Ten years before this 1967 western, director John Sturges ended *Gunfight at the OK Corral* with the famous shoot out between the Earps and the Clantons. This is what happened next; if it isn't quite so exciting, it is at least authentic, with James Garner and Jason Robards looking, moustachewise, rather more like Earp and Doc Holliday than is usually shown in movies and TV. (c)

The Hour of 13 XX Peter Lawford in this London-shot thriller is a gentleman crook at the turn of the century, helping to trace a Ripper-type killer. Director Harold French had a rather obvious list of character supports, none doing very well here; 1952. (b/w)

Houseboat √ Sophia Loren has said she learnt more from this, playing with Cary Grant as *au pair* hired by widower for his three kids, than from any other actor (guess what happens – and you're right!) Mel Shavelson directed; 1958. (c)

A House is Not a Home X No, and despite the title-song in this case it's a brothel. Doubtful if Miss Polly Adler (played by Shelley Winters) who wrote a book about her famous real-life cathouse, was anything like the bewildered innocent shown here. And despite 1964 freedoms, it's still an awfully respectable place. Robert Taylor plays her gangster-protector with an air of familiarity – he has seen the character in as many movies as we have; Russell Rouse. (b/w)

House of Bamboo √√ Tough little thriller about American gang in Tokyo led by Robert Ryan was filmed there in 1955. Director was Samuel Fuller, now a cult figure. (c)

House of Dark Shadows √ *Dark Shadows* was an American horror soap opera that was never seen in Britain. This 1970 version, with Joan Bennett the only name in the cast familiar to British audiences, is freed from the constraints of American TV rules, so is pretty gory. Director, Dan Curtis. (c)

House of Dracula X Frankenstein's monster and the Wolf Man (Lon Chaney) are thrown in for good measure in this skimped variation on the tale of scientist (Onslow Stevens) turning into vampire; Erle C. Kenton directed in a hurry; 1945. (b/w)

The House of Fear √ Holmes/Watson (Rathbone/Bruce) investigate murder club. Based vaguely on Conan Doyle's *Adventure of the Five Orange Pips*. Director, Roy William Neill; 1945. (b/w)

House of Frankenstein √ Mad scientist this time is travelling freak-showman Boris Karloff. That's all this rip-off has to do with *Frankenstein*. However, Lon Chaney, John Carradine, J. Carroll Naish, Lionel Atwill are thrown in for good measure in 1944; Erle C. Kenton. (b/w)

House of 1000 Dolls XX Dreadful plot and dialogue about white slave traffic in Tangiers is partly compensated for by Vincent Price's enjoyment as magician who literally makes girls disappear; but Jeremy Summers can't make it exciting or even interesting; 1968. (c)

House of Strangers √ Strong stuff from Joseph L. Mankiewicz with Edward G. Robinson as paterfamilias who uses his sons ruthlessly; Richard Conte is the eldest; Luther Adler, Susan Hayward support; 1949. (b/w)

House of the Damned √ Freaky, in more ways than two, is this thriller about a mysterious house with strange goings-on; it's all quite creepy in a mechanical sort of way, and at least the explanation is logical if far-fetched; Maury Dexter directs an unknown cast with competence; 1963. (b/w)

The House of the Seven Hawks X Robert Taylor seeking Nazi gold with aid of map he finds on murdered man on his charter ship. Richard Thorpe directed in 1959, using Dutch locations. Adapted from novel by Victor Canning called *The House of the Seven Flies* – but hawks do better at the box office. (b/w)

House of Wax √ This version of *The Mystery of the Wax Museum* was made for viewing through 3D glasses in 1953. André de Toth directed, Vincent

Price starred. The old story still packs a thrill or two. (c)

House on Haunted Hill √ Veteran horror director William Castle had Vincent Price as his sinister host in this 1958 creepie. Mind you, a spot of oil on the hinges and half the excitement would be gone. Stay with it for Elisha Cook Jr.'s famous last line. (b/w)

The House on 92nd Street √ *The March of Time* was never as strictly accurate as some cinemagoers imagined, using recreations quite calculatingly. Similarly, this FBI *v.* the Nazis semi-documentary by the same producer, Louis de Rochemont, may have aped authenticity but wasn't quite as scrupulous as it pretended. Lloyd Nolan, Gene Lockhart stood out in what was to start a cycle of true-to-life location-shot dramas; Henry Hathaway; 1945. (b/w)

House on Telegraph Hill √ Thrills despite unconvincing plot about assumed identities. Creaking doors and lines, but Robert Wise got better than expected performances from Richard Basehart, Valentina Cortesa in 1951. (b/w)

How Green Was My Valley √√ Winning 1941 Oscars as best picture, best support (Donald Crisp), best direction (John Ford), best photography (Arthur Miller) was a bit excessive in the year that also produced *Citizen Kane* and *The Maltese Falcon*; but the Welsh mining village story can still warm hearts and catch throats. (b/w)

How I Won the War X Richard Lester's frantic, frenetic, flash-backing comedy-to-make-you-weep, sending up war movies more than war. John Lennon remarkably accomplished as bespectacled private, Michael Crawford a bit one-note as officer; Roy Kinnear, Michael Hordern doing their familiar acts. It's really *Carry on Sergeant* treated surrealistically, and Charles Wood's script soon folds under the attempt; 1967. (c)

How Sweet It Is XX Pretty dreadful updating of traditional Hollywood comedy, comes into line with 1968 teenage morals by showing how broadminded Pop James Garner and Mom Debbie Reynolds react to their son's holidaying in Europe with his girlfriend; Jerry Paris lets it all slip through his nerveless fingers. (c)

How the West Was Won √ Cinerama pageant that looks very dwarfed on the little screen. Three major directors – John Ford, George Marshall, Henry Hathaway – directed a raft of stars (Carroll Baker, Lee J. Cobb, Henry Fonda, Karl Malden, Gregory Peck, Robert Preston, Debbie Reynolds, James Stewart, Eli Wallach, John Wayne, Richard Widmark) but as it's just a comic-strip of clichés, they don't accomplish much; 1961. (c)

How to be Very, Very Popular X Features the Betty Grable of 1955, with that hair and those legs, as a chorus kid on the run with girl friend Sheree North. They hide out in a college fraternity house – but where else? – and meet Robert Cummings wearing his vacant face (the other one is earnest). The comedy is a bit frantic, but see North do a wild shake, rattle and roll number that steals Grable's thunder. Nunnally Johnson. (c)

How to Commit Marriage XX Desperate Bob Hope comedy, in which he plays a divorcing parent (from Jane Wyman) whose daughter's impending marriage is threatened by the revelation of their split. Jackie Gleason is the groom's heavy father, and the feeble plot involves Hope in various tedious impersonations; 1969. (c)

How to Marry a Millionaire √√ Marilyn Monroe, Betty Grable, Lauren Bacall, generously helped by William Powell, Fred Clark, witty Nunnally Johnson script, Jean Negulesco direction, in gold-digger of 1953. Marilyn is funny as well as gorgeous as near-sighted dope who won't wear glasses. (c)

How to Murder a Rich Uncle XX Dull 1957 Nigel Patrick-directed, Nigel Patrick-starring 'comedy thriller' (i.e. a film that is neither) in which he tries to do Charles Coburn in but knocks off others by mistake. Spot Michael Caine, Anthony Newley. (b/w)

How to Murder Your Wife X What could have been another tart comment on contemporary life, written by George Axelrod and starring Jack Lemmon, becomes, in the hands of director Richard Quine, more than a bit gooey. It needed a Billy Wilder to bring out the ironies of explaining to the world in a comic-strip just how he was going about doing in Virna Lisi; but it all ends 'happily', with American Woman very much American Mom, however shapely she looks in this version; 1964. (c)

How to Save a Marriage — and Ruin Your Life √ Fairly sophisticated comedy with Dean Martin, Eli Wallach, Anne Jackson, Stella Stevens,

139

about stealing mistresses to save marriages. Fielder Cook directed, 1967. (c)

How to Steal a Diamond in Four Uneasy Lessons √ Agreeable caper comedy with a splendid quartet – Robert Redford, George Segal, Zero Mostel, Ron Leibman – stealing and double-crossing each other. Peter Yates directed in fine style in 1972, even if it does get a bit silly towards the end. (c)

How to Steal a Million √√ Peter O'Toole and Audrey Hepburn in slick, enjoyable 1966 caper about Paris museum theft. William Wyler expertly juggles stars plus Charles Boyer, Eli Wallach, Hugh Griffith. (c)

How to Steal the World XX The Men from UNCLE saving the world yet again; ho-hum. David McCallum and Robert Vaughn walk through their parts as if zombied by the nerve gas which is this particular villain's secret weapon. Barry Sullivan and Eleanor Parker sort of pretend they aren't there; and director Sutton Roley doesn't seem to mind; 1968. (c)

How to Succeed in Business Without Really Trying √√ One of the better and relevant musicals of the sixties (1967 to be precise), well-translated from the stage with Robert Morse, who played the part of the thrusting junior on Broadway, repeating his success without trying too hard. Rudy Vallee also repeats his stage bumbler. David Swift produced, wrote, directed this version, and does well, while not realising all the possibilities. (c)

Huckleberry Finn XXX Dreadful 1974 attempt by J. Lee Thompson to turn Mark Twain's story into a musical, with terrible songs, boring pictures and lifeless acting. The jokes are particularly awful, and blacks horribly patronised. (c)

The Hucksters √ Sending up advertising doesn't seem so daring now as it was in 1947, when Jack Conway directed a fine bunch of players – Gable, Gardner, Greenstreet, Deborah Kerr – and some nice satires on commercials. (b/w)

Hud √√√ Portrait of a heel who, unlike so many horrid heroes on TV, is properly seen to be nasty, alienating everyone including the audience. Paul Newman superb; director Martin Ritt master of western setting and complex characterisations; Oscars won by stunning Pat Neal, Melvyn Douglas; 1963. (b/w)

Hue and Cry √√ Alastair Sim and Jack Warner plus bunch of kids in splendid chase after gang of thieves. Fine location direction by Charles Crichton in 1946, trendsetter of British comedy-realism. (b/w)

Humoresque √ They don't make movies like this any more – solid vehicles for confident stars, here Joan Crawford striding through her tears as the wealthy lover and patron of violinist John Garfield, fated to part despite their love. Jean Negulesco; 1946. (b/w)

The Hunchback of Notre Dame √√ Grotesque masterpiece of German director William Dieterle, made in Hollywood, 1939, with Charles Laughton at his imitable best as lonely dwarf, Maureen O'Hara his love-object, Edmond O'Brien explorer of Breughelish medieval underworld, Thomas Mitchell king of the beggars. Avoid 1956 remake with Anthony Quinn (director: Jean Delannoy). (b/w)

Hungry Hill XX Daphne du Maurier has expressed herself as disappointed with most of the adaptations of her stories for the screen (one exception: Don't Look Now) including this one. She has cause for complaint as director Brian Desmond Hurst shoves competent cast (Jean Simmons, Dennis Price, Margaret Lockwood) through their paces in lacklustre way; 1947. (b/w)

The Hunters X Drama among the Korea War air force, with Robert Mitchum romancing May Britt, wife of alcoholic Lee Phillips; it isn't much more gripping in the air, either; produced-directed by Dick Powell in 1958. (c)

The Hunting Party XX Slice of sadism in which Gene Hackman spends the whole film torturing Oliver Reed for succeeding with Candice Bergen where he failed. Nasty stuff in the West; Don Medford; 1971. (c)

The Hurricane √√ Jon Hall and Dorothy Lamour make it heavy going for John Ford until he can unleash his massed wind machines on the biggest blow in motion pictures; Raymond Massey is nasty governor of island which numbers Mary Astor, Jerome Cowan, Tom Mitchell, John Carradine among its inhabitants; 1937. (b/w)

Hurry Sundown √√ With its heart not only in the right place but on its sleeve, too, this Otto Preminger indictment of Southern whites is marred by being, if you will excuse the expression, too black and white. The whites are all nasty in various ways; the blacks are all virtuous. The whites hate; the blacks suffer. It isn't that way in real life, but then real life has never been Preminger's main aim. As a cinematic exercise it's superior stuff, however, and Jane Fonda is given the opportunity to act; Faye Dunaway, George Kennedy, Michael Caine do more than adequately, too. Set in 1946, it was shot in 1966. (c)

Husbands √√ An adult version of *On the Town*, with three American middle class husbands on the loose in London. Director John Cassavetes, Peter Falk and Ben Gazzara play the parts, improvising as they carouse. The most serious implications include their reaction against materialism in the USA; 1970. (c)

Hush, Hush, Sweet Charlotte √√ Gorgeous performances from Bette Davis, Olivia de Havilland, Agnes Moorehead, Mary Astor in this scary in the *Baby Jane* tradition; Robert Aldrich directed again with such a lack of subtlety that it's like watching a send-up of horror movies at times; at others, though, it's genuinely frightening; 1965. (b/w)

The Hustler √√√ Charismatic Paul Newman a cocky young billiard player out to beat Jackie Gleason as ageing legendary king Minnesota Fats in Robert Rossen's memorable 1961 film of dingy pool hall circuit – and youth *v.* age universally. George C. Scott as gambling manager is just right. (b/w)

I

I Accuse X Jose Ferrer unexcitingly directs Jose Ferrer in disappointing 1958 retelling of Dreyfus case; plus Viveca Lindfors, Anton Walbrook. (b/w)

I Aim at the Stars XX Glorification of the German scientist Werner von Braun, whose V2 rocket-bombs caused so much damage in Britain, and who later led the dizzily costly American prestige effort into space. Curt Jurgens plays the man sympathetically, and J. Lee Thompson seems prepared to forgive and forget, even if many of his British audience won't; 1960. (b/w)

I am a Camera XX It started with Isherwood in Berlin; became a John van Druten play; turned into this weak little film with Julie Harris and Laurence Harvey both miscast and showing it; then it became a Broadway show with music, *Cabaret*; and finished up as the Liza Minnelli movie. This 1955 stop along the way, directed by Henry Cornelius, was not exactly a highspot. (b/w)

I am a Fugitive from a Chain Gang √√ Harrowing tale of an innocent (which is a cop-out) prisoner subjected to barbaric punishment. *Films in America, 1929-1969* recalls: 'Director Mervyn Le Roy has contended that the picture was responsible for chain gangs being taken off the road in Georgia . . . Many feel this is Muni's top screen performance, far superior to Pasteur and Zola'; 1932. (b/w)

I Believe in You X – but it's hard to believe that Cecil Parker (kindly probation officer), Celia Johnson, Harry Fowler, Joan Collins, Laurence Harvey or Sid James ever looked so young. Shot in 1951 under Basil Dearden, it's well-meaning but hardly convincing. (b/w)

I Can Get It For You Wholesale √ Not much left of Jerome Weidman's novel about New York rag trade except the title. But director Michael Gordon got good performances from Susan Hayward, as ruthless designer who wants to get ahead and doesn't mind how, Dan Dailey, George Sanders in 1951. (b/w)

Ice Cold in Alex √ A *Wages of Fear* translated to the Libyan desert during the last war with nitro-glycerine as cargo, and nurses plus a spy to complicate the lives of drivers John Mills and Harry Andrews. You may not be too aware of the soggy script in J. Lee Thompson's taut direction; 1958. (b/w)

Ice Palace √ Old-fashioned melodrama about ruthless Richard Burton sacrificing Robert Ryan and Carolyn Jones, among others, on his way to the top. Set in Alaska, with a bit of history of the place thrown in. Vincent Sherman made it the equivalent of a good old-fashioned read in 1960. (c)

Ice Station Zebra √ Unpretentious adventure yarn has Rock Hudson, Ernest Borgnine, Jim Brown, Patrick McGoohan aboard submarine on a secret mission to the North Pole. John Sturges did an honest job of work in

1968, and it's great stuff for little boys of all ages. (c)

I Confess √ Hitchcock disappointed in 1953 with this slow-moving story of priest (Montgomery Clift) who refuses to reveal murderer's confession to police even when he finds his own freedom at stake; strong support from Anne Baxter, Karl Malden. Hitchcock confessed failure. (b/w)

I Could Go On Singing √ What was at the time (1962) dismissed as mawkish, now posthumously comes over as Judy Garland's own heartbreak: it's all there – public Palladiumising, private despairs. Director Ronald Neame and co-star Dirk Bogarde hold Judy up magnificently. (c)

An Ideal Husband XX Stiff and ultimately boring transfer of elegant theatre piece to the screen; failure's not Oscar Wilde's so it must be director Alexander Korda's. Certainly his casting of Paulette Goddard was off-key, and the rest of the cast is terribly British but terribly second-rate; 1948. (c)

I Died a Thousand Times √ 1955 remake of Bogart's *High Sierra* with Jack Palance as gangster who loves dog and club-foot girl. Stuart Heisler hams up direction, but Shelley Winters and Lee Marvin make it viewable. (c)

Idiot's Delight √ Clark Gable as song-and-dance man stranded at hotel near Italian border, encountering Norma Shearer and assorted luminaries such as Edward Arnold, Joseph Schildkraut. Clarence Brown directed, 1939, but never quite achieved the passion of the Pulitzer Prize pacifist play by Robert E. Sherwood upon which it's based. (b/w)

The Idol XX Pedestrian little number with Jennifer Jones uncomfortable in role of remarrying but seduceable divorcée, which she took over in 1966 at the last minute from the more suitable Kim Stanley. American director Daniel Petrie is equally far from home in that boring old Swinging London, and has cast the supports from type. They might accept this England in the Middle West – but you know better. (b/w)

I'd Rather be Rich X 1964 remake of Deanna Durban's *It Started With Eve*, with Sandra Dee in role originally played by Robert Cummings – they switched sexes. Updated fairy story with Andy Williams, Maurice Chevalier, Charlie Ruggles. Jack Smight directed from earlier script. (c)

If . . . √√ Lindsay Anderson's masterly parable. Fantasies in public school – expressed and merely imagined – of masters and boys. Malcolm McDowell gives outstanding performance as intelligent rebel; 1969. (c)

If a Man Answers XX Newlyweds Sandra Dee and Bobby Darin think they have problems. With such weak starts and a silly plot director Henry Levin certainly did in 1962. Don't waste your time. (c)

If He Hollers, Let Him Go X Absurd plot involving negro on the run being forced to murder Kevin McCarthy's wife but twists and double-twists screw everything up. Charles Martin, who wrote, directed, produced in 1969, can't escape the blame. Raymond St. Jacques does well in the main part. (c)

If I Had a Million √√ Series of episodes about reactions of people handed a million dollars: classic 1932 omnibus had bevy of directors (among them Ernst Lubitsch, James Cruze), and Gary Cooper, George Raft, Mary Boland, Charles Laughton, W. C. Fields, Charlie Ruggles, Jack Oakie *et al.* (b/w)

If It's Tuesday, This Must Be Belgium X Even in 1969, this send-up of American tourists 'doing' Europe looked dated. With a bundle of sub-plots, no discernible main plot, and a bus-load of types whizzing round the continent under the lugubrious, self-regarding charge of Ian McShane, the film is uniformly unmemorable; director, Mel Stuart. (c)

I Know Where I'm Going √ Wendy Hiller outstanding as heiress who flees the rich life for true love in Scotland; Powell-Pressburger coaxed lovely performances, too, from Roger Livesey, Finlay Currie, and a 14-year-old Petula Clark; 1945. (b/w)

I'll Be Your Sweetheart XX Not with creaky old British musicals like this one, you won't. Margaret Lockwood trills her way through 'The Honeysuckle and the Bee'; Vic Oliver and Moore Marriott try to put their songs on the map. Director Val Guest introduced some quasi-serious stuff about the fight to establish copyright claims, but it's all about as wet as leading men Michael Rennie and Peter Graves; 1945. (b/w)

I'll Cry Tomorrow √√ Triumph for Susan Hayward as the real-life alcoholic star Lillian Roth, her mother (Jo Van Fleet), and husbands (Richard Conte, Eddie Albert, Don Taylor).

Daniel Mann's relatively restrained direction made this stand out in 1955. (b/w)

Illegal √ Modest but exciting Edward G. Robinson thriller. He plays former DA who gets involved with baddies; Lewis Allen even got effective brief performance out of Jayne Mansfield, though Nina Foch was star; 1955. (b/w)

Ill Met by Moonlight √ Famous war movie made in 1957 about dashing Dirk Bogarde kidnapping German General Marius Goring in Crete. Powell and Pressburger keep it rattling along. (b/w)

I'll Never Forget You XX Poor 1951 remake of *Berkeley Square*. Tyrone Power time-slips back into 18th-century London and love with Ann Blyth. Roy Baker directed only too forgettably in 1951. (c)

I'll See You In My Dreams √ Formula musical biography treatment of songwriter Gus Kahn's life with 1951 vintage bubbly Doris Day, Danny Thomas; director Michael Curtiz. (b/w)

I'll Take Sweden XX If we tell you it's about father Bob Hope protecting daughter Tuesday Weld's virtue in 'sexy' Sweden, you could guess the rest. One would have thought they were more grown up in 1965. Frederick de Cordova directed. (c)

The Illustrated Man √ Ray Bradbury's knock-out book of sixteen short stories taking off from the tattoos on one man's (Rod Steiger's here) body has been reduced to three. While the prologue and epilogue, involving the tattooed gentleman, a wayfarer and an enigmatic spirit (Claire Bloom — Mrs Steiger at the time) are fine, none of the stories really work. Director Jack Smight uses his camera effectively enough, but the special effects are mouldy; 1969. (c)

I Love Melvin √ Pleasant enough time-passer if you happen to love Debbie Reynolds and Donald O'Connor. She's a chorus girl, he's a magazine photographer, but director Don Weis knew that was just an excuse for some lively but undistinguished song-and-dance routines; 1953. (c)

I Love My Wife X Elliott Gould walks through this 1970 sex comedy that, like his earlier *Bob and Carol . . .*, never really faces up to the problems it is so cynically flip about. Brenda Vaccaro plays the neglected wife sent to health farm to become attractive again – and when she does, she becomes someone else's girlfriend. Mel Stuart directed, fitfully. (c)

I Love You, Alice B. Toklas X There is – anyway, there was in 1969 – a marvellous film to be made about the comic clash of the two cultures of middle-class Jewish America and the world of the hippie, but this isn't it. Occasional flashes such as the conversations between straight Peter Sellers and sex-manual-obsessed Joyce Van Patten have a momentary brilliance; but the descent into slapstick when he embraces the creed of the flower-children just embarrasses. And why do directors like Hy Averback put up with unconvincing performances from non-Jewish actors pretending to be Jewish when there are so many good real ones around? Ditto Hughes. The end is a cop-out. (c)

Images √√ Clever and unnerving thriller in which Susannah York is tormented by her inner demons which take the shape of dead lovers before her eyes (and ours). Gradually she is sucked into a completely paranormal world in which she kills hallucinatorily. Director Robert Altman adds an extra tricksy layer of unreality by giving his characters the first names of other players in the cast: Susannah York is Cathryn, Cathryn Harrison is Susannah, René Auberjonois her husband Hugh, Marcel Bozzuffi is René, and Hugh Millias is Marcel; 1972. (c)

I'm All Right, Jack √ Cynical, malicious comedy from the Boulting Brothers, attempting to satirise both sides in industrial relations but finishing up as a union-bashing exercise, partly due to Peter Sellers's brilliance in portraying archetypal (falsely archetypal, but enduringly so) shop steward and Irene Handl's knowing-her-place wife. Plenty of beautifully-composed cameo performances, but the whole film leaves a nasty taste in the mouth; 1959. (b/w)

I Married a Monster from Outer Space √ Off-putting title hides well-made thriller about alien planet taking over human beings; ex-film editor Gene Fowler Jr. made it good and taut in 1958. (b/w)

I Married a Witch √√ Beguiling René Clair-directed original of *Bewitched* has Veronica Lake peek-a-booing deliciously at Fredric March, descendant of Salem-burners and bumblingly endearing Robert Benchley; 1942. (b/w)

143

I Married a Woman XX Overworked George Gobel married to oversexy Diana Dors; Hal Kanter didn't give it any sparkle in 1958. (b/w)

Imitation General X That's Glenn Ford taking officer's place in George Marshall-directed second world war comedy with Red Buttons, Taina Elg; 1958. (b/w)

Imitation of Life √ (1) Soppy but just credible version of Fannie Hurst book with Claudette Colbert making a million out of pancake recipe of ole black lady whose daughter passes for white; John M. Stahl; 1934. (b/w)

Imitation of Life X (2) Over the top in 1959 remake with Lana Turner, and Susan Kohner as the white-passer; the death of the black mommy is sobbiest sickiest scene of its kind ever filmed; Douglas Sirk. (c)

I'm No Angel √ Cary Grant is memorably invited to come up and see Mae West and peel her a grape in this 1933 classic comedy; Wesley Ruggles directed from Mae's own script. (b/w)

I, Monster √ Superior rendering of *Dr Jekyll and Mr Hyde*, with Christopher Lee as the goodie/baddie and Peter Cushing as his solicitor; a promising 1970 debut for 23-year-old director Stephen Weeks. (c)

Impasse √ Burt Reynolds looking for the loot he and three pals buried during the war in the Pacific. He allegedly did his own stunts, despite director Richard Benedict's objections; 1972. (c)

The Importance of Being Earnest √√ Oscar Wilde's impeccably-mannered comedy splendidly cast with grave Michael Redgrave, Michael Dennison, Dorothy Tutin, Joan Greenwood, and Edith Evans the definitive Lady Bracknell. Plus bonus of Margaret Rutherford, Miles Malleson and Richard Wattis and elegant direction by Anthony Asquith; 1952. (c)

The Impossible Years XX David Niven, Lola Albright wasted as thoroughly modern parents worried about daughter Christina Ferrare's virtue. Hard to believe director Michael Gordon raised even a snigger in 1968. (c)

Inadmissible Evidence √ Disappointing adaptation of John Osborne's riveting play about a totally unsatisfactory man, brilliantly realised by Nicol Williamson, here as on the stage; though Anthony Page and Osborne have fallen into the trap of 'opening it out' and inserted a comic-strip running gag about a court case. On film, it's more difficult to believe that he is tolerated in running the office and home where he somehow stays as boss. But film is always involving and unlike most surface-skimming movies; 1969. (b/w)

In a Lonely Place √√ Humphrey Bogart at top of his form in 1950 as Hollywood scriptwriter suspected of hat-check girl murder, shielded by neighbour Gloria Graham. Nicholas Ray directed, with eye for detail and the sickly smell of corrupt Hollywood hangs over the whole film. (b/w)

Incendiary Blonde XX Tiring Betty Hutton as equally fatiguing Texas Guinan, queen of the night-clubs in the twenties. True story has been laundered by writers and director George Marshall, who also has unfortunate penchant for character-caricaturers like Charlie Ruggles, Barry Fitzgerald, Albert Dekker; 1945. (c)

The Incident √ Passengers on New York subway are held prisoner by vicious hoodlums; director Larry Peerce rather overdid it in 1967, with Tony Musante, Beau Bridges. (b/w)

Incident at Owl Creek √√√ Classic half-hour of the thoughts and memories of a hanging man (Roger Jacquet), superbly realised by Robert Enrico, from Ambrose Bierce's *An Occurrence at Owl Creek Bridge*; 1962. (b/w)

Incident at Phantom Hill √ Straightforward western about an ambushed Union army convoy in Texas; Dan Duryea, Robert Fuller scrap under Earl Bellamy's 1965 direction. (c)

In Cold Blood √√ Richard Brooks's narrative pseudo-documentary, based on Truman Capote best-seller about two hold-up men who rob a farmer and make sure there are no witnesses left alive, and the judicial murder of them after a lengthy trial. Undeniably gripping, it is flawed by the device of jumping over the killing in the first part of the film so it can be shown near the end. There are no surprises and, since one knows the end, the only *raison d'être* is to condemn the death penalty. Or, of course, ghoulishness on the part of the makers and audience. Robert Blake and Scott Wilson, unknowns, play the killed killers; Jeff Corey, Paul Stewart, with their well-known faces, seem rather out of place; 1968. (b/w)

The Incredible Mr Limpet X Incredible plot, too, about a timid Don

Knotts turning into a dolphin and helping US Navy during Second World War. Kids may like it. Arthur Lubin; 1964. (c)

The Incredible Shrinking Man √√ 'Arguably the peak of sf film,' writes John Baxter in Science Fiction in the Cinema. A man gets smaller and smaller until spider is monster menace; but it has a message, too: there's a place for everybody and everything in the universe, no matter what their size. Jack Arnold directed; 1957. (b/w)

The Indian Fighter √ Routine but lively western with Kirk Douglas, Elsa Martinelli, Walter Matthau; director André de Toth keeps it moving; 1955. (c)

Indiscreet √√ Stylish comedy had Cary Grant and Ingrid Bergman in and out of love (though not in and out of bed — after all it was only 1958); a sumptuous Mayfair background and some solid British support (Cecil Parker, Phyllis Calvert, Megs Jenkins, David Kossoff). Stanley Donen gave it plenty of gloss. (c)

Indiscretion of an American Wife X Will Jennifer Jones go back to her husband or stay with lover Montgomery Clift? She obviously cares, but will you? Director Vittorio de Sica tried to make you in 1954. (b/w)

In Enemy Country √ Neat and exciting double-espionage thriller, with Tony Franciosa framing his girlfriend so that she can marry German officer and betray his secrets. Reflects 1968 ethos in suggesting there was not much to choose between the two sides in the last war. Harry Keller. (c)

I Never Sang for My Father √√ Strong family drama, with Melvyn Douglas and Gene Hackman doing some of their best-ever work as father and son who can neither come to terms nor break the bond between them. The son is determined to leave his father in New York while he goes away to marry a Californian. Estelle Parsons is the daughter of the family. Gilbert Cates achieved, in 1969, a notable piece of direction, easily surpassing the rather clumsy stage productions in London and New York. (c)

Inferno √ Lovers Rhonda Fleming, William Lundigan leave husband, Robert Ryan, to die in desert – they think. Director Roy Baker keeps us in suspense; 1953. (c)

The Informer √√ Victor McLaglen as shambling Gypo who plays Judas during the Irish Troubles, winning director John Ford his first Oscar in 1935; successful on a variety of levels, this version of the Liam Ó'Flaherty novel has never been bettered in its theatrical statements on men under pressure. (b/w)

The Informers √ Rather well-made (by Ken Annakin) police yarn about Nigel Patrick (beautifully polished and always better when not directing himself) as inspector getting framed for the killing when one of his snouts is killed; realistic support from Colin Blakely, Frank Finlay, Michael Coles, George Sewell; 1963. (b/w)

In Harm's Way X Otto Preminger had big-star cast of John Wayne, Kirk Douglas, Henry Fonda, Dana Andrews, Franchot Tone, Patricia Neal, Brandon de Wilde, Paula Prentiss, Burgess Meredith, making love and war after Japanese attack on Pearl Harbour. It was poorly received in 1965, but isn't quite that bad. (b/w)

Inherit the Wind √ Flawed retelling of real-life Dayton Monkey Trial, when schoolteacher was arrested for teaching evolution. Stanley Kramer directed Spencer Tracy as Clarence Darrow, Fredric March as Bryan in 1960, but departed from truth in having heart attack kill one of them, when it was really overeating, and tacking on false final twist. (b/w)

In Like Flint X James Coburn as carbon-copy James Bond manages to be both smug and boring in tedious comic strip about stealing the President and replacing him with living, breathing doll. As if there'd be any difference! Gordon Douglas probably thought he was directing slickly and amusingly, in 1967; he wasn't. (c)

In Love and War X Sentimental Second World War melodrama about effects of war on lives and loves of three young marines – Robert Wagner, Bradford Dillman, Jeffrey Hunter. Philip Dunne directed; 1958. (c)

Inn for Trouble XXX Desperately unfunny translation of the never-very-funny TV Larkins family to the big screen in early (1960) attempt to cash in on what was later in the decade to become an industry in itself – the switching of British TV comedy to the cinema. All sorts of well-known faces (Peggy Mount, David Kossoff, Leslie Phillips among them) stumble about from one silly situation to the next; Pennington Richards. (b/w)

Innocent Bystanders X Poor example of secret agent-type flick, directed in

1972 by Peter Collinson. Donald Pleasence is head of British Intelligence; Dana Andrews, his American opposite number; Stanley Baker, Sue Lloyd, Derren Nesbitt his competing agents. Geraldine Chaplin adds to the complications of freeing a Russian agent. (c)

The Innocents √√ Atmospheric rendering of Henry James's *The Turn of the Screw* with emphasis on governess Deborah Kerr's fight against 'forces of evil' in children, which with our post-Freudian hindsight we might interpret less supernaturally. A good chill, though. Jack Clayton; 1961. (b/w)

Innocent Sinners X 1958 adaptation of sickly Rumer Godden novel about two cockney kids, *An Episode of Sparrows*. Philip Leacock directs June Archer, Christopher Hey, Brian Hammond, Flora Robson, David Kossoff, Andrew Cruickshank with restraint. (b/w)

The Inn of the Sixth Happiness √ Successful tearjerker despite all its faults (Ingrid Bergman's ludicrous accent in a part that is supposed to be utterly English; the obviousness of the set pieces, the over-simplification of character), from Mark Robson. The story holds up even if it isn't very convincing; both Robert Donat and Athene Seyler stand out; Curt Jurgens gets by; 1959. (c)

In Old Chicago √ Early (1938) disaster movie which has a twenty-minute climax of the 1871 great fire of Chicago. It was all Alice Brady's fault, for leaving an oil lamp near a kicking cow. Tyrone Power, Alice Faye, Don Ameche, Brian Donlevy, Andy Devine make a barren raft of principals under Henry King's lifeless direction. (b/w)

Inserts √√ Wry joke about Hollywood in 1930 (shot 1975) with Richard Dreyfuss as director fallen on hard times and blue films. His star is dependent on heroin; his backer (Bob Hoskins, later of *Pennies from Heaven* fame) confiscates the footage; Clark Gable wants him to direct his next film. Writer-director John Byrum keeps one amused. (c)

Inside Daisy Clover √ Robert Mulligan's working-over of Gavin Lambert's screenplay from his cliché-ridden novel about the rise of a teenage film star was given some sharp teeth in 1966, but somehow fails to bite. Natalie Wood is never less than adequate as the girl concerned, but neither Robert Redford, Christopher Plummer, nor Roddy McDowall can

quite bring off important contributory roles. Nor is the ending convincing. But, having knocked, one has to say that there are compensations like the vivid picture of thirties Hollywood and Ruth Gordon's mother; let's hope that one day TV restores the 20 minutes cut out by the British distributor. (c)

Inside Job √ Mild little caper with retiring parole officer leading ill-assorted gang (Larry Hagman, Leonard Nimoy, James McEachin) in gold bullion heist. Robert Michael Lewis directed – quickly – in 1973. (c)

The Inspector X Neither a thriller nor a melodrama nor a character-study, this is a nothing of a film about a girl saved from white slavery in 1946 (it was made 16 years later); routine acting from Stephen Boyd, Leo McKern, Donald Pleasence, Robert Stephens, mostly the fault of director Philip Dunne. (c)

An Inspector Calls √√ Alastair Sim at his enigmatic best in J. B. Priestley flash-backer on family responsibility; Guy Hamilton directed stolidly; 1954. (b/w)

Inspector Clouseau X Heavy-handed third in series has Alan Arkin replacing Peter Sellers, and yawns replacing jokes. Arkin, who arbitrarily dispenses with Sellers' irritating mannerisms in the part, doesn't replace them with anything worth watching, and director Bud Yorkin lacks both wit and style. The supports – Frank Finlay, Beryl Reid, Richard Pearson and a string of other familiar players – do not seem to be able to respond to anything comic in either the script or the direction; 1969. (c)

The Intelligence Men X Despite an appalling script, an attempt to turn them into characters different from their established personas, awful support acting and pathetic direction from Robert Asher, Eric Morecambe and Ernie Wise rise above it all to do their sublime act, only occasionally being dragged down by aforementioned disadvantages; 1965. (c)

Intent to Kill X Jack Cardiff's directional debut in 1958 had unoriginal script idea about the South American dictator (here in a Montreal hospital) whom Richard Todd and Alexander Knox are trying to save, while Warren Stevens tries to do him in. Herbert Lom plays the dictator in his usual beetle-browed style. Quite exciting in a less than nailbiting way; (b/w)

Interlude √ That weepy old one about falling in love with a married man who can't get a divorce. In 1957 *she* was nice young American girl, June Allyson, *he* was European conductor Rossano Brazzi; director was Douglas Sirk. In 1968 *she* was nice young English girl Barbara Ferris, *he* was Oskar Werner and still a conductor; director was Kevin Billington. (both *c*)

Intermezzo √ Called *Escape to Happiness* when shown in Britain in 1939, this sweeping romantic drama was a remake of a movie Ingrid Bergman had made in Sweden three years before, and was her English-speaking debut. One of those lush yarns in which the girl runs away from the man she loves (Leslie Howard, holding a violin). Gregory Ratoff, better known for acting comic Russians, directed; the cast includes such female stiff-upper-lippers as Ann Todd and Edna Best. (*b/w*)

The Internecine Project √ Neat if silly thriller in which four members of an industrial espionage gang are set up to kill each other by James Coburn. They are Harry Andrews, Ian Hendry, Michael Jayston and Christine Kruger. Director Ken Hughes manipulates the complicated action with competence but without inspiration; 1974. (*c*)

The Interns X Soap opera about hospital life with Cliff Robertson, James MacArthur, Michael Callan, Suzy Parker. You've seen it all before in countless TV series and so had director David Swift in 1962. (*b/w*)

Interrupted Journey XX Richard Todd, the cad, leaves gracious Valerie Hobson and runs off with Christine Norden. But he gets his comeuppance when suspected of murder on a train; Daniel Birt was the director; 1949. (*b/w*)

Interrupted Melody √ Moving story of Majorie Lawrence, the real-life opera singer who survived polio. Director Curtis Bernhardt got fine performances from Eleanor Parker and Glenn Ford in 1955. (*c*)

In the Cool of the Day XX Jane Fonda, Peter Finch, Arthur Hill in Greece should have been glossy, fascinating. In fact, only Angela Lansbury pleases, under Robert Stevens's 1963 direction. (*c*)

In the Doghouse XX Leslie Phillips as a vet, with James Booth as wicked partner, Peggy Cummins (37 in 1962) still playing the ingenue, Hattie Jacques, Joan Heal. Director, Darcy Conyers. (*b/w*)

In the French Style X Jean Seberg learning the hard way that sex and sophistication in Paris isn't as satisfying as life with a solid doctor in America. This message is so obviously packaged for Stateside consumption and the whirl of Paris reduced to a gentle wind so as not to offend (the date is 1963, too early for the sexual explicitness demanded by the theme) that Irwin Shaw's treatment of his stories becomes anodynical; Miss Seberg turns in a good performance; directed by Robert Parrish. (*b/w*)

In the Good Old Summertime √ Made in the good old days of 1949 when Judy Garland and Van Johnson could fall in love by mail, and Cuddles Sakall and Spring Byington could cluck schmaltzily on the porch. Only Buster Keaton gives much life; Robert Z. Leonard. (*c*)

In the Heat of the Night √√√ 1967 Oscars rightly went to Rod Steiger for his racist policeman who learns live-let-live, Stirling Silliphant for script. Norman Jewison's best film falls into usual trap of making Sidney Poitier too goodie, but it's exciting and must have been educative in its setting, the Deep South. (*c*)

In the Nick √ 1960 British comedy about prison psychologist, Anthony Newley, trying to reform racketeer James Booth; with Harry Andrews, Bernie Winters, Anne Aubrey, Ian Hendry. Ken Hughes gave it some laughs. (*b/w*)

In This Our Life √√ Bette Davis as prize bitch in director John Huston's second movie (a year after his smashing *Maltese Falcon*), ruining everybody's life including sister Olivia de Havilland's; 1942. (*b/w*)

Intruder in the Dust √ Faulkner's lynch-mob novel transfers well under Clarence Brown's direction, 1949; Claude Jarman Jr., Porter Hall do best. (*b/w*)

Invaders From Mars √ Flying saucer brings nasties from outer space who insert crystals into brains of Jimmy Hunt's parents; when he runs to police, chief has scar too. William Cameron Menzies makes it all belief-suspensible; shot in 1953. (*c*)

Invasion XX One of those slices of hokum about another world invading ours. Some respected TV names (director Alan Bridges, writer Roger Marshall, actors Edward Judd, Valerie Gearon, Tsai Chin, Barrie Ingham, Glyn Houston) fail to make it credible or even technically competent; 1966. (b/w)

Invasion of the Body Snatchers √√√ Silly title for powerful picture that Don Siegel thinks is his best. Framework is alien world taking over human beings, but Siegel uses this to criticise contemporary zombiedom. Dana Wynter, Carolyn Jones; 1956, remade in 1978. (b/w)

Invasion Quartet XX Spike Milligan, John le Mesurier and Eric Sykes are almost the only excuses for looking at this pathetic 1961 effort at a wartime comedy, crassly directed by Jay Lewis, who clearly had no idea how to get the best from his cast or just how rotten a script he was trying to film; it's supposedly about a private invasion to spike (or milligan) a German gun. (b/w)

An Investigation of Murder √ Disappointing detective story in pictorial San Francisco, with Walter Matthau miscast as obsessed cop and Bruce Dern as his thick new partner. Director Stuart Rosenberg fails to illuminate motives, and the result is an old-fashioned B-pic in 1973 stars' clothing. (c)

Invitation XX Glossy 1952 tearjerker has rich girl (Dorothy McGuire) worrying that father (Louis Calhern) 'bought' husband (Van Johnson) to brighten up her last days. Gottfried Reinhardt didn't seem to worry too much, and nor should you. (b/w)

Invitation to a Gunfighter X Director Richard Wilson didn't deserve the good performances he got from Yul Brynner as hired gunman and George Segal as victim. Apart from Janice Rule, nothing else convinces; 1964. (c)

Invitation to the Dance √ Most of this Gene Kelly attempt to make an all-ballet film in 1957 has passed into the great museum of moviedom, although 'Sinbad the Sailor' is still fun in its own right. (c)

In Which We Serve √ Noel Coward's tribute to the Navy, 1942. No fool he, Coward got Anthony Havelock-Allan as his co-producer, David Lean as his co-director and Noel Coward as his scenarist. He also played Captain D. of HMS Torrin (based on Lord Louis Mountbatten's HMS Kelly). As her crew cling to a float, upper-lips stiff as ramrods, they remember their loved ones. Impossible to fault without appearing unpatriotic. (b/w)

I Only Arsked XXX Poor 1959 filming of soppy TV series The Army Game, with

Bernard Bresslaw's catchphrase making the title. Alfie Bass, Norman Rossington, Charles Hawtrey, Michael Medwin carry on under frantic director Montgomery Tully. (b/w)

I Passed for White XXX Sick little story of black girl who wishes she wasn't; they *couldn't* make films like that any more, thank goodness and Black Power. Fred M. Wilcox directed James Franciscus and Sonya Wilde; 1960. (b/w)

The Ipcress File √√ Spy stuff adapted from Len Deighton book with Michael Caine as bespectacled special agent. Nigel Green makes perfect dept. boss; Sidney J. Furie; 1965. (c)

I Remember Mama √ Extremely sentimental, about plucky Irene Dunne raisin' her brood in San Francisco; George Stevens piled on the goo but those who like a good cry will love it. Barbara Bel Geddes does well among daughters; 1948. (b/w)

Irish Eyes Are Smiling X 1944 Irish-American blarney about songwriter's troubles with inevitably fiery-tempered colleen, has little plot, familiar tunes, Dick Haymes, June Haver, Anthony Quinn, director Gregory Ratoff. (c)

Irma la Douce XX One of Billy Wilder's few failures was this attempt to stretch already thin musical play without its sixteen numbers. It makes a silly comedy about a ponce who's so jealous that he disguises himself to be his girl's only client; Jack Lemmon flounders in the part Keith Michell was able to gloss over by song in the stage version, Shirley MacLaine just doesn't have the presence to make the golden-hearted tart anything but fitfully interesting; 1963. (c)

The Iron Maiden XX Made by Carry On producer Peter Rogers and director Gerald Thomas, this appallingly dreary comedy is only significant in showing how important those comedians are in the Carry Ons. Without them (and with Michael Craig, Noel Purcell and Cecil Parker) the script and direction reveal a terrible sense of flop, and the story of traction engines and British aircraft is equally dull; 1963. (c)

The Iron Mistress X Alan Ladd inventing the Bowie knife while standing on a box. Virginia Mayo is his inadequate girlfriend; directed by old reliable if uninspired Gordon Douglas in 1952. (c)

The Iron Petticoat XX Katharine

Hepburn and even Bob Hope wasted in embarrassing 1957 Ralph Thomas-directed comedy about cold Russian Air Force captain (Hepburn) melting under charm of American pilot (Hope). (c)

Isadora √√ Intermittently brilliant, this biopic of the modern dancer and free soul is marred by remembrances of movies past, as though Karel Reisz couldn't or didn't want to get away from the MGM screen biographies of the thirties. However, Vanessa Redgrave makes a persuasive Isadora and her expressionistic love-scenes are as good as anything filmed of this kind. James Fox as Gordon Craig does better than Jason Robards as her husband. And that end, which we all know is waiting for us, when the scarf catches in the wheel of the car, does work; 1969. (c)

I Saw What You Did √ They didn't really; it was just two silly girls (Andi Garrett, Sarah Lane) playing a practical joke over the telephone. But how was their 'victim' (John Ireland) to know? And how were they to know they'd picked on a dangerous psychopath? Thrills begin as they start to find out, but director William Castle could have done a more chilling job. Joan Crawford disappears early on; 1965. (b/w)

I See a Dark Stranger √ Superficial melo about Trevor Howard trying to stop Deborah Kerr from innocently helping nasty spies. All very Irish under Launder and Gilliat's supervision in 1947. (b/w)

I Shot Jesse James √ Actually, Samuel Fuller did, in 1948, the first that the writer also directed, and the forerunner of a distinguished series of westerns; John Ireland begins a dishonourable tradition for Fuller by shooting his best friend in the back. Preston Foster is lead. (b/w)

Island Escape XX Tawdry, unconvincing reconstruction of the one American left alive on the island of Guam after over two years of Japanese occupation; Jeffrey (*I Was a Teenage Jesus*) Hunter weak; only the newsreels convince. John Monks, who wrote, produced and directed all the bits between the authentic clips, doesn't either; 1962. (c)

Island in the Sky X Best thing about this William Wellman air rescue drama is the marvellous photography; John Wayne, Lloyd Nolan, James Arness aren't nearly as impressive; 1953. (b/w)

Island in the Sun X Old-fashioned (1957) view of black *v.* white struggle in Jamaica, poorly adapted from Alec Waugh novel. Robert Rossen directs garish cast of James Mason, Joan Fontaine, Dorothy Dandridge, Joan Collins, Stephen Boyd, Harry Belafonte, who must at least have got a nice holiday out of it all. (c)

Island of Love √ Robert Preston as conman, Walter Matthau as gangster he conned, Tony Randall and beautiful Greek locations should have added up to something more; maybe it was director Morton Da Costa's fault; 1963. (c)

Island of Terror X Poor example of the *Creature from the Sea* genre directed by Terence Fisher in 1966; Peter Cushing manages his usual competent job. It's kinder to their hard-working agents who miraculously got them parts in this one, not to name the rest of the cast. (c)

The Island of the Blue Dolphins √ Taken from an account of a female Robinson Crusoe who lived off California from 1835 to 1853, this modest children-oriented adventure, directed by James B. Clark, is beguiling enough; Celia Kaye plays the main, monologuey part; 1965. (c)

Island of the Lost X Richard Greene in 1967 mix-up of head-hunters, giant reptiles, dangerous ostriches and so on; directors John Floria, Ricou Browning. (c)

Is Paris Burning? X Only from embarrassment at such a poor film being made of its liberation and confused Nazi orders as to its fate; René Clément just couldn't control his cast from going off in all directions – Charles Boyer, Leslie Caron, Alain Delon, Kirk Douglas, Glenn Ford, Gert Fröbe, Simone Signoret, Claude Dauphin – the list reads like a party-game of overrated actors; what was Orson Welles doing mixed up with this lot? 1966. (b/w)

Istanbul XX Tired Joseph Pevney-directed hokum, about stolen jewels and lost love Cornell Borchers suffering from amnesia, is strictly for Errol Flynn fans; 1957. (c)

Istanbul Express X A made-in-Hollywood 1969 mock-up of the Orient Express provides the luxurious setting for a predictable but pleasant spy adventure, whose premise is no sillier than most Saintly TV episodes. Strictly second-eleven 'stars' fill the main stereotyes – Gene Barry, Senta Berger, John Saxon – but Richard

Irving knows he's only providing entertainment and more or less manages to. (c)

I Start Counting √ Jenny Agutter finds blood-stained sweater thrown away by foster brother. Could he have committed sex murders? Bryan Marshall, Simon Ward, Madge Ryan, Fay Compton; directed by David Greene; 1969. (c)

It Ain't Hay X – and it ain't much of a movie either, unless you are a confirmed Abbott and Costello fan; based on a Damon Runyan yarn about the wrong horse being given away, Eugene Pallette is in a supportive part; director, Erle C. Kenton; 1943. (b/w)

The Italian Job √ Notable only for the appearance of Noel Coward as imprisoned mastermind and the antics of stunt drivers with their Minis, this thriller suffers from the combined weight of Michael Caine, Benny Hill, Rossano Brazzi, Irene Handl, Fred Emney, Robert Powell; and the direction of Peter Collinson; 1969. (c)

It Always Rains on Sunday √ One day in the East End from Arthur La Bern's novel, directed by Robert Hamer in 1947 with the minimum of genteel falsification and a melancholic charm. Googie Withers, Jack Warner, Alfie Bass responded. Perhaps someone will remake it as it was originally written – sexy and gritty. (b/w)

It Came From Outer Space √ Clever trick photography is best thing about this routine sci-fi with Richard Carlson, Barbara Rush, Charles Drake. Jack Arnold directed; 1953. (b/w)

I Thank a Fool X Mercy-killing mélange, with Peter Finch and Susan Hayward harrowed among crowd of British types (including Diane Cilento, Cyril Cusack, Richard Wattis, Athene Seyler, Miriam Karlin). Director, Robert Stevens; 1962. (c)

It Happened at the World's Fair X If it didn't have Elvis Presley in it, this could be dismissed as a lousy film that desperately uses the 1962 World's Fairground in Seattle in an effort to inject some novelty. With Elvis, it's a lousy film with ten musical numbers that desperately uses the 1962 World's Fairground in Seattle in an effort to inject some novelty; Norman Taurog must be the most faithful, if not the most inspired director ever in Hollywood. (c)

It Happened Here √√ Remarkable reconstruction of what would have happened if the Nazis had occupied Britain; ten years in the financing and making by Kevin Brownlow and Andrew Mollo, it was publicly shown in 1966; Sebastian Shaw is only well-known full-time actor in the cast. (b/w)

It Happened in Athens XXX Really awful 'comedy' about the earliest Olympic games, with Jayne Mansfield kindly offering herself (in marriage) to winner of the marathon; Andrew Marton, director, must be kidding – but if so, why aren't we laughing? 1962. (c)

It Happened One Night √√ Frank Capra's classic holds up well despite its age – it was made in 1934 – and its famous set-pieces – hitching a lift with a glimpse of stocking, hanging the blanket between their sleeping arrangements – still work; Clark Gable, Claudette Colbert enchant as reporter and heiress. (b/w)

It Happened to Jane √ Comedy has Doris Day and Jack Lemmon selling lobsters, and a villainous Ernie Kovaks; Richard Quine made it quite a lot of fun in 1959. (c)

It Happened Tomorrow √ René Clair 1944 fantasy (set at turn of century) about newspaper reporter getting tomorrow's news today; Dick Powell, Jack Oakie, Edgar Kennedy, Sig Ruman play their familiar parts energetically; a young (21-year-old) Linda Darnell enchants. (b/w)

It's a Great Feeling √ Musical excuse (by I. A. L. Diamond, director David Butler, 1949) for cameo performances by Gary Cooper, Joan Crawford, Errol Flynn, Sidney Greenstreet; Edward G. Robinson et al, in story of Jack Carson trying to direct a movie with himself and Doris Day. (c)

It's Always Fair Weather √ Reunion of three ex-army pals (Gene Kelly, Michael Kidd, Dan Dailey) is excuse for a musical send-up of TV; co-directors Kelly and Stanley Donen gave it zing in 1955. (c)

It's a Mad Mad Mad Mad World √√ Over, over, over, overlong comedy chase after money, money, money, money, which wearies at least an hour before the end of its 192 (cinema) minutes, involving six greedy people chasing after loot that Jimmy Durante, before pegging out, confides he has buried. Stanley Kramer has endless cast of comedians (among them: Phil Silvers, Terry-Thomas, Milton Berle, Jonathan Winters, Jim Backus, Edward Everett Horton, Buster Keaton, the Three Stooges, Andy Devine,

Zasu Pitts, Buddy Hackett, Sid Caesar, plus Spencer Tracy) pulling every gag in the Joe Miller gag book. Best bits are the car crashes, but you hate yourself for enjoying their wanton destructiveness – but, then, all the film is rather unpleasant, if you think about it; 1963. (c)

It's a 2' 6" Above the Ground World XXX Tasteless stuff about a bra manufacturer and his wife (Hywel Bennett, Nanette Newman) going in for contraceptives after six children, and a sub-plot about a pregnant Angharad Rees. Directed lugubriously by Ralph Thomas from Kevin Laffan's play; 1972. (c)

It's a Wonderful Life X Dated bit of whimsy lifted by James Stewart as dejected, hard-working citizen suddenly shown good things of life by obliging angel. Donna Reed, Lionel Barrymore. Directed (1946) by Frank Capra. (b/w)

It Should Happen To You √√ Treat from George Cukor in 1954 has out-of-work model (delicious Judy Holliday) renting advertising space for herself on New York billboard; Jack Lemmon, Peter Lawford help keep up the fun. (b/w)

It's Only Money X Down the drain, as far as we're concerned. Jerry Lewis fans will probably love him, though, as TV repair man in Frank Tashlin-directed slapstick with Zachary Scott, Joan O' Brien; 1962. (b/w)

It Started in Naples XX And finishes in a yawn. Clark Gable, Sophia Loren, Vittorio de Sica go through some cumbersome motions in what is supposed to be a Mel Shavelson comedy about custody of a rather repulsive little waif; the scenery comes off best, though there's rather too much even of that; Gable is an American lawyer, Loren a hard-up Italian auntie, battling for the kid, so if you have ever seen a film before you'll be able to guess the ending; 1960. (c)

It Started in Tokyo XX Butchered to get down to length in England, this moderate thriller directed by Joseph M. Newman played as a second feature in 1962. Agnes Moorehead and William Demarest were cut completely out, and the plot, about a murderer and missing heiress, has been rendered meaningless. David Janssen and Jeanne Crain are still there, but it's all a muddle, so don't watch unless it's at least 85 minutes long when it reaches your screen. (b/w)

It Started with a Kiss X Painless comedy about Debbie Reynolds newly-married to GI Glenn Ford had some striking Spanish backgrounds; also Eva Gabor, Fred Clark and easy direction from George Marshall in 1959. (c)

It's That Man Again XX Made in 1943 to cash in on Tommy Handley & Co's immense popularity; nostalgic wallow for the over-40s, and an explanation to those younger why Dad and Mum think such phrases as 'TTFN' and 'This is Funf speaking' are funny. Director, Walter Forde. (b/w)

Ivanhoe √ If you can overlook the American accents you'll enjoy star-studded (Elizabeth Taylor, Robert Taylor, Joan Fontaine) 1952 Richard Thorpe version done with just the right panache. (c)

I've Gotta Horse XXX Billy Fury, the Bachelors, Michael Medwin, Jon Pertwee, Fred Emney, Bill Fraser sink this leaky vehicle about dogs and racehorses, weakly directed by Kenneth Hume in 1965. (c)

I Walked with a Zombie √√ And very terrifying it is, as Frances Dee takes catatonic Christine Gordon through the dark cane fields to meet voodoo priest in Haiti; Jacques Tourneur and producer Val Lewton turned this into one of the most frightening films on the screen; 1943. (b/w)

I Walk the Line √ Gregory Peck betrays his wife and his sheriff's badge for love of Tuesday Weld. John Frankenheimer does well by the Deep South: you can feel the steamy sweat; 1970. (c)

I Want To Live! √√ Susan Hayward won Oscar for her histrionics in this Robert Wise-directed 1958 attack on capital punishment. She plays real-life drug-addicted whore, unfairly (it says) convicted for part in brutal attack on old woman. (b/w)

I Want You XX Effect of Korean War on typical American family - or rather how director Mark Robson imagined it in 1951. Phoney and embarrassing, and poor cast of Dana Andrews, Farley Granger, Dorothy McGuire doesn't help. (b/w)

I Was a Fireman √√ Better known as *Fires Were Started* which is how it was billed on ITV in 1976 and presumably will be again. Dramatised documentary about firemen in the blitz; writer-director Humphrey Jennings; 1943. (b/w)

I Was Happy Here √ Desmond Davis' rather muted version of an Edna

151

O'Brien short story, with Sarah Miles. Moving and sensitive, if never completely absorbing; 1966. (b/w)

I Was Monty's Double X To fool the Germans, British Intelligence sent M. E. Clifton-James off to North Africa dressed as General Montgomery; he did it all over again in 1958 for this mild but amusing actioner, with John Mills and Cecil Parker; John Guillermin directed competently enough. (b/w)

I Wonder Who's Kissing Her Now X June Haver, Reginald Gardiner in very ordinary eighties musical, pleasantly directed by Lloyd Bacon; 1947. (c)

J

Jack of Diamonds √ Routine caper with the weak George Hamilton playing jewel thief in league with Maurice Evans, Joseph Cotten planning to lift diamond and ruby necklace from Munich bank. Momentarily enlivened by two 'famous film stars' playing themselves as his victims – it's a measure of Don Taylor's minuscule budget that the best they could afford were Carroll Baker and Zsa Zsa Gabor; 1967. (c)

The Jackpot √ James Stewart wins it and how it changes his life. Unfortunately, it's all terribly dated, being made in 1950 – even the quiz game he wins is on radio and not TV; Walter Lang directs adequately. (b/w)

Jacqueline XX Terrible old (1956) weepie about drunken Oirish father (John Gregson) whose son runs away from home in shame. The little boy is Richard O'Sullivan, much later to become star of *Robin's Nest* and *Dick Turpin*. Director, Roy Baker. (b/w)

Jailhouse Rock √ Despite the lamentable title, this isn't a bad Elvis Presley vehicle, with the lad as convict who can play the guitar and sing; having Richard Thorpe direct, in 1957, helped; they don't go in for class directors much in Presley movies. (b/w)

Jamaica Inn √ Charles Laughton and director Alfred Hitchcock didn't get on too well, a battle that showed itself on the screen in this less than compelling 1939 version of Daphne du Maurier's smuggling yarn. Maureen O'Hara,

Robert Newton provided the romance. (b/w)

Jane Eyre √√ (1) The most pornographic novel in the English language, D. H. Lawrence called it, and Robert Stevenson, the director, conveyed its heavy eroticism splendidly in this 1944 version. But it more strongly bears the imprint of Orson Welles, playing Rochester and casting long shadows (actual as well as metaphorical) with his Mercury mates, actress Agnes Moorehead, co-writer (with Aldous Huxley) John Houseman, composer Bernard Herrmann, designer William Pereira. If Joan Fontaine is just too one-note as Jane, the rest of the cast (including the young Elizabeth Taylor and a malicious Henry Daniell) make up for her. (b/w)

Jane Eyre X (2) 1970. George C. Scott's dry, sharp Rochester dominates this version if only because he is so much on the screen. Poor Susannah York pales into insignificance, while all the other characters (Jack Hawkins, Ian Bannen, Nyree Dawn Porter etc.) are allowed to go for almost nothing, as are the set pieces. Jean Marsh, later to shine in *Upstairs, Downstairs*, makes an unusually young first Mrs R. Director, Delbert Mann. (c)

Jason and the Argonauts √√ Special effects help this little attempt to inject some grandeur into the Argos's voyage to find the Golden Fleece; the cast comes from the less expensive pages of *Spotlight*. Don Chaffey directs, hopefully; 1963. (c)

Jaws √√ One of those blockbusters that are above criticism. Director Steven Spielberg handled the yarn of the killer shark deftly, although the fish itself is a bit mechanical. Robert Shaw grimly played a reach-me-down Cap'n Ahab; Roy Scheider, Richard Dreyfuss contribute manfully to this child of disaster married to horror; 1975. (c)

The Jayhawkers XX Talky 'psychological' western about unbelievable character played by Jeff Chandler who intends to take over Kansas with his outlaws. The fact that he lives in a book-lined cave, drinking wine and entertaining ladies, doesn't add to the rapidly-evaporating feeling of authenticity; Melvin Frank, better known as a comedy writer and producer, unintentionally added another farce to his long list in 1959. (c)

Jazz on a Summer's Day √√ Best jazz film ever made, with Anita O'Day, Chico Hamilton, Gerry Mulligan,

Louis Armstrong, Mahalia Jackson beautifully shot and recorded against the background of the Newport Jazz Festival, 1958; a bit long, but nearly always a joy. Bert Stern. (c)

The Jazz Singer √ (1) The first talkie – or rather, 300 words on a silent movie that changed the world. Al Jolson turned on the syrup, upsetting his cantor father's sensibilities with his songs. Most people of discrimination's, too. Director, Alan Crosland; 1927. (b/w)

The Jazz Singer X (2) Danny Thomas takes over the Al Jolson role in a 1953 remake of the early talkie, as a cantor's son who makes it big in show biz; as corny as ever and drippy entertainment. Director Michael Curtiz. (c)

jeanne Eagels √ The speed is too fast for Kim Novak in this story of real-life twenties star who drove herself to an early grave. Luckily Agnes Moorehead and Gene Lockhart are there to give it some distinction. George Sidney; 1957. (b/w)

Jennifer on My Mind X Inconsequential black comedy-drama, with Tippy Walker as a heroin addict entangled with Michael Brandon, who spends the flashbacking film trying to get rid of her body and confiding his story to a tape-recorder; Noel Black; 1971. (c)

Jeopardy √ Barbara Stanwyck runs for help when husband Barry Sullivan falls off a jetty. But she meets 'orrible Ralph Meeker instead. John Sturges keeps the excitement going; 1953. (b/w)

Jeremiah Johnson √ Robert Redford, in private a keen conservationist, shows how man can live idyllicly in the wild. He marries an Indian but offends the tribe, and they kill her. He spends the next years exacting a terrible revenge. Narratively the film is flat; Sydney Pollack's direction is irritatingly tricksy. (c)

Jesse James √ Ambitious western that made a hero out of title villain in keeping with Tyrone Power's 1939 box-office standing. Henry Fonda plays brother and director Henry King's supports include reliable Randolph Scott and Brian Donlevy. (c)

Jessica XX Angie Dickinson as American nurse in Italian village; unconvincing direction by Jean Negulesco leaves Agnes Moorehead and Maurice Chevalier high and dry along with the ill-served Angie; 1962. (c)

Jesus Christ, Superstar X The commercial success of the musical on which this even more vulgar (black Judas, gay Pilate) version by Norman Jewison is based suggests there is an extraordinarily large market for religion without faith. 1973. (c)

Jet Over the Atlantic X Neither director – Byron Haskin – nor cast – George Raft, Guy Madison, Virginia Mayo – can inject much excitement into this corny old one about will the, won't the, plane crash; 1960. (b/w)

Jet Pilot X $5,000,000 budget, and all they could come up with was John Wayne as airman falling for Russian spy Janet Leigh. Howard Hughes kindly let Josef von Sternberg direct in 1958. (c)

Jet Storm √ Richard Attenborough gives fine performance as father of murdered child who plans to blow up plane in revenge. On board: Stanley Baker, Diane Cilento, Virginia Maskell, Harry Secombe, Mai Zetterling and other dependables. Cy Endfield keeps the tension driving, even if the sub-plots do get lost in the end; 1959. (b/w)

Jezebel √ 1938 winner of Oscars for Southern Belle Bette Davis and aunt Fay Bainter. Henry Fonda and George Brent are duelling suitors. William Wyler's set pieces are so successful that you can almost forgive the famous red dress, that scandalises polite society, for not being in colour. (b/w)

Jigsaw XX Dull little British detective plodder with Jack Warner as a promoted PC 49 in plain clothes and Ronald Lewis as Sgt. to his Insp. It's mostly just a series of long and boring interrogations and there are no characters, only cliché-cartoons; Val Guest's to blame – he wrote, produced and directed, as well as being married to one of the more decorative members of the cast; 1962. (b/w)

Jimmy the Gent √ Lovely to see the 1934 incarnations of Bette Davis and Jimmy Cagney in this Michael Curtiz-directed comedy about searching for heirs to claim fortunes. (b/w)

Jivaro X Unconvincing jungle journey with Indian siege and triangle plot with Fernando Lamas, Rhonda Fleming, Brian Keith. Ho-hum direction by Edward Ludwig; 1954. (c)

Joanna XX Indulgent – to writer-director Michael Sarne's psyche and his vapid heroine's aimless life – and overlong. Tour round the never-never land of swinging London does have some nice performances, notably from Calvin Lockhart and Donald Sutherland. Eponymous Genevieve Waite is a dead loss. On the strength of this dubious exercise, Sarne was invited to Hollywood to make the disaster of all time, *Myra Breckinridge*. They should have got themselves a good director and asked *Joanna*'s cameraman Walter Lassally instead; perhaps they didn't realise where the credit for this well-photographed exercise should have gone; 1969. (c)

Joan of Arc XX Pretty dull adaptation of Maxwell Anderson's turgid play about the Maid, not helped by wooden casting of Ingrid Bergman in the part, supported by such so-so performers as Jose Ferrer, J. Carroll Naish, Ward Bond; director Victor Fleming went with the wind; 1948. (c)

Joe Dakota X Mystery western with Jock Mahoney as a man called the Stranger, always an ominous sign. Turns out he used to own the land now discovered to be rich with oil, and he wants his cut. Richard Bartlett directed; 1957. (c)

Joe Kidd √ Clint Eastwood, in his usual role as the embodiment of law'n'order, tracks down Mexican bandit John Saxon, disposing of land baron Robert Duvall on the way. Director John Sturges holds our interest; 1972. (c)

Joe Macbeth X Interesting idea of adapting Shakespeare's *Macbeth* to New York quickly runs out of steam, partly due to poor casting (Paul Douglas, Ruth Roman, Sid James, Bonar Colleano) but mostly to direction of Ken Hughes; 1956. (b/w)

Joey Boy XXX Hopelessly unfunny comedy of skyving soldiers, involving raft of good TV comics – Harry H. Corbett, Stanley Baxter, Bill Fraser, Reg Varney – that director Frank Launder simply doesn't know how to get going; 1965. (b/w)

John and Mary √ Slick sentimentality disguised as cynicism provides a cold undertone for Peter Yates's reworking of Mervyn Jones's British novel in a chic New York setting. Dated in its end-of-the-sixties mood, it ends up as a slight vehicle for two fashionable stars, Mia Farrow, Dustin Hoffman. (c)

John Goldfarb Please Come Home XX and stop this tiresome movie. Shirley MacLaine as forerunner to that ghastly *Shirley's World* reporter and Richard Crenna as football coach assigned to improve Middle East king Peter Ustinov's football team. This is a J. Lee Thompson comedy, made in 1965, and he hasn't made one since –

understandably. Notre Dame football team, parodied here, sued; 1964. (c)

Johnny Belinda √√ Sentimental, slushy and successful. Jane Wyman won 1948 Oscar for her deaf-mute in Nova Scotia who, raped, has to fight to keep bastard with help of Dr Lew Ayres. Director Jean Negulesco had wax poured into her ears so that she really couldn't hear. Charles Bickford and Agnes Moorehead won supporting nominations. (b/w)

Johnny Concho X Frank Sinatra is the coward who has to find courage; he set it up in 1956 and gave old pal Don McGuire first chance to direct. He also put his current flame Gloria Vanderbilt in star role, but as she was no actress they had a row and she left, to be replaced by Phyllis Kirk. Don't be fooled by his speed on the draw at the end – it's a trick spring holster. (b/w)

Johnny Cool X Sixties (1964 to be precise) gangster melo with the characteristic amorality of this period; a Sicilian bandit takes on gangster's identity at his request to become instrument of his revenge. Far-fetched and calculatingly horrid it may be; it still has some nicely-judged moments from director William Asher and a host of old-time names (Elisha Cook, Jim Backus, Mort Sahl, Sammy Davis Jr.) backing up Telly Savalas and Henry Silva. (b/w)

Johnny Got His Gun √ Anti-war movie that seemed out-of-date in 1971, but Hollywood Ten victim Dalton Trumbo wrote and directed with such sincerity that it's hard to cavil. Timothy Bottoms plays a soldier so badly wounded that he wakes up to find he no longer has arms, legs, eyes, ears, nose or mouth. Communicating by morse code he asks to be either exhibited as an Awful Warning or decently killed; grim stuff. (c)

Johnny Guitar √√ Outstanding western for the conflict between Joan Crawford as saloon owner and Mercedes McCambridge as gangleader. Nicholas Ray picked sides among Hollywood's toughest hombres to make their teams, and the plots ride forcefully over the prairie alongside Dr Freud. McCambridge records that Crawford's hatred for her wasn't reserved for the screen – a group of technicians applauded after McCambridge finished a scene and that maddened Crawford –'quite understandably' says the lesser star, magnanimously; 1954. (c)

Johnny Nobody XX One of that 1960

crop of movies shot over here for cheapness with American stars to sell it back home, and as botched as most of them. Nigel Patrick directed himself, Yvonne Mitchell and Abbey-full of Irish, in Dublin-based murder. Aldo Ray and William Bendix statutory Yanks. (b/w)

Johnny Reno X Low-budget western shows its penny-pinching when R. G. Springsteen uses fights scene and tracking shot of hero Dana Andrews on horesback twice over. He is lawman who alienates community as he tries to prove that murder rap is frame up. Jane Russell, alas, shows her years – she was 45 when this was made in 1966 – and other old-timers like Lon Chaney, Tom Drake, Richard Arlen, John Agar don't all wear too well, either. (c)

Johnny Tiger X When Robert Taylor arrives to Americanise the Seminole Indians in Florida there's bound to be trouble. Paul Wendkos makes the most of it, with Chad Everett well-cast as younger tribesman who wants to reject parents' values; Geraldine Brooks is doctor attracted to the teacher. All a bit pat, but quite pleasant; 1966. (c)

John Paul Jones X Sprawling historical biopic of the founder of the American Navy, back in the War of Independence. Doubtless the fervent patriotism went down well in the Middle West in 1959, but it's a bit cold-leaving now. John Farrow can't really control his vast cast, and Robert Stack is inade-. quate as John Paul (he added Jones later). If you're still watching after nearly two hours, you will be rewarded with a three-minute glimpse of Bette Davis. (c)

The Joker is Wild √ Frank Sinatra film fictionalising own myth: the cynical swinger. Charles Vidor directed this true story of Joe E. Lewis, singer forced to turn comedian when Al Capone's sidekick slashed his vocal cords. Good 1957 recreation of roaring twenties. Includes 'All The Way', Mitzi Gaynor. (b/w)

The Jokers √ Time-passing Michael Winner 1967 caper about Oliver Reed and Michael Crawford pinching the Crown Jewels; all a bit obvious, like the supporting cast (Harry Andrews, Michael Hordern, Frank Finlay, et al), but amusing enough. (c)

A Jolly Bad Fellow √ Leo McKern given his gargoyle's head in *Cruel Hearts and Coronets*-type of black comedy partly written by Robert Hamer just before his death in 1963 and directed by Don Chaffey. Oxford professor finds poison-without-trace and proceeds to dispose of rivals and others he dislikes; Dennis Price, Leonard Rossiter, Janet Munro help to make it wicked fun; 1964. (b/w)

The Journey XX Deborah Kerr, Robert Morley, E. G. Marshall, Jason Robards as travellers held up by Hungarian uprising with Yul Brynner hammering it as nasty Red. Anatole Litvak; 1959. (c)

Journey Back to Oz X Seems that never-never lands have their Good Old Days, too. Certainly, Oz has seen better times than in this 1971 attempt to rekindle the old magic, with Liza Minelli (Judy Garland's daughter, of course) providing the voice for a doll-like Dorothy cartoon. Other voices: Ethel Merman as the Bad Witch, Mickey Rooney as the Scarecrow; director, Hal Sutherland. (c)

Journey Into Fear √√ Spy melo that was started by Orson Welles in 1942, taken over by Norman Foster, but is still gripping for Welles' performance and that of Joseph Cotten. (b/w)

Journey to Shiloh √ Seven young men set out to fight in the Civil War. Only one remains alive. William Hale makes this more than a western, if less than a major film; Michael Sarrazin, James Caan are among the seven; 1969. (c)

Journey to the Centre of the Earth √√ Boisterous adaptation of Jules Verne novel, directed by Henry Levin with at least one eye on the children, who should enjoy the ludicrous but delightful adventures as James Mason, Pat Boone, Arlene Dahl descend via Iceland and emerge in the Mediterranean; 1959. (c)

Joy in the Morning X Richard Chamberlain and Yvette Mimieux unbelievable as young marrieds at college; luckily, Arthur Kennedy's Pop learns to understand them. Alex Segal; 1965. (c)

Juarez √√ Paul Muni as Mexican leader almost having the screen stolen from under his make-up by Brian Aherne as his opponent, the gentle, baffled Maximilian. Other inspired bits of William Dieterle's casting were John Garfield as Mexican gunman and Claude Raines as Napoleon III; 1939. (b/w)

Jubal √√ Tough stuff on the ranch in this adult, gory western, with Glenn Ford, Ernest Borgnine, Rod Steiger, Noah Beery Jr. at each other's throats and women, Valerie French and Felicia Farr; directed moodily by Delmer Davis; 1956. (c)

Judgement at Nuremberg √ TV original has been expanded here to 190 minutes (cinema running time). This isn't the Nuremberg Trials of Goering and Co, but a dramatic affair of four judges pleading that all they were doing was obeying the law of their land. Unfortunately, what could have been a sharp political examination has been debased by Stanley Kramer into an entertaining series of histrionics, with Marlene Dietrich, Judy Garland, Montgomery Clift, Maximilian Schell (he won 1961 Oscar for it), Burt Lancaster all doing their nuts, while Spencer Tracy presides. The critics divided sharply; Gavin Lambert called it an All-Star Concentration Camp Drama, with Special Guest Victim Appearances. Others responded to its pretensions to greatness with homilies as to the vital importance of going to see it 'if you have the slightest concern for the future of civilisation'. Bitingly, Pauline Kael called its dramatisation of large issues 'ludicrous'. Writer Abby Mann, she says, 'accepted his Academy Award, with excruciating humility, not only for himself, but for all intellectuals'. (b/w)

Judith XX Banal melodrama set in Israel in first days of independence, with ex-Nazi planning Syrian attack. Oddly enough his ex-wife is Jewess Sophia Loren and she obligingly shoots him. Peter Finch unconvincing as Jewish leader; and Daniel Mann directs with verve (and should it be nerve?) in the hope that somehow the literate paucities of the uncinematic Lawrence Durrell script will be concealed; 1966. (c)

Juggernaut √ Efficient disaster movie about hijacked ocean liner. Among those involved: Richard Harris, Omar Sharif, David Hemmings, Anthony Hopkins, Ian Holm, Cyril Cusack, Freddie Jones, Michael Hordern, Tom Chadbon – mostly tiresome and mannered players that perhaps one wouldn't mind seeing disappear beneath the waves; Richard Lester directed without his usual jokiness – and all the better for that - in 1974. (c)

The Juggler X Kirk Douglas doing his Israeli bit again, this time in a chase after he has clonked a cop; lucky for him, Milly Vitale is waiting on a kibbutz. Edward Dmytryk; 1953. (b/w)

Julie XX Doris Day being terrorised in 1956 by crazy husband Louis Jourdan. Would you believe that Doris the stewardess could fly the plane herself? Director Andrew Stone seems to expect you to swallow it. (b/w)

Julius Caesar XX (2) 1970. Apallingly Joseph Mankiewicz in 1953 with Marlon Brando memorably spouting the 'Friends, Romans, Countrymen' speech and Gielgud's serpentine plotting against (an ill-cast) Louis Calhern's Caesar. The ladies – Greer Garson, Deborah Kerr – are pretty awful, and James Mason has a tough slog as Brutus. (b/w)

Julius Ceasar XX (2) 1970. Apallingly cast: Charlton Heston as Mark Antony, Richard Johnson as Cassius, Robert Vaughn as Casca, Richard Chamberlain as Octavius Caesar: even the redoubtable Jason Robards is way off beam as Brutus, leaving Gielgud to struggle on alone as Caesar. Stuart Burge's direction is ill conceived, with unfortunate pictorial inserts attempting to 'open out' the action but merely taking the attention away from the central human conflicts.(c)

Jumbo √ Called *Billy Rose's Jumbo* in America. Safe, dull, pretty two-circus picture (son of one spies on another, falls for daughter); Doris Day, frankly too old – 38 in 1962 – for this kind of ingénue role; Martha Raye, Jimmy Durante along for the laughs. Charles Walters tries to recapture the innocence of the thirties, inevitably fails. (c)

June Bride √ Bette Davis and Robert Montgomery slide easily over the surface of slight story about magazine writers and weddings; Bretaigne Windust directed in 1948, but not to Miss Davis's satisfaction. (b/w)

Jungle Street XX Dreary little thriller made in 1961, before David McCallum went to Hollywood and became an UNCLE. He is a cosh boy in this one, boringly directed by Charles Saunders. (b/w)

Junior Bonner √√ Strong Western-set family drama, with Steve McQueen as broke rodeo star; Robert Preston as his father who wants to emigrate to the still wide-open spaces of Australia; Ida Lupino his mother; and Joe Don Baker as younger brother who is solely concerned with turning a fast buck. Sam Peckinpah brings skill and understanding to one of the last remaining heroes of the West; 1972. (c)

Just For You √ Bing Crosby 1952

musical about his relations with his kids – Natalie Wood, Robert Arthur – and how Jane Wyman, without a touch of jealousy, shows him how to cope; Elliott Nugent directed this fairystory. (c)

Justine √ Shaky adaptation of Durrell's *Alexandria Quartet* serving as melodramatic plot for Dirk Bogarde, Anouk Aimée, Anna Karina, Michael York; director, George Cukor; 1969. (c)

Just Like a Woman X Little programmer episodically showing what happens to Wendy Craig and Francis Matthews when they split up. She's always reliable, in any part, and makes the best of this rewarding one. Matthews fumbles most of his chances. Director Robert Fuest has managed lots of splendid little touches, but they don't add up to anything like a compulsive film; 1967. (c)

J. W. Coop √√ Likeable personal film from Cliff Robertston, who wrote, produced, directed as well as starred in it in 1971. An ageing rodeo star returns after ten years in prison, determined to win the national title in one season. Rather meandering and a shade too obvious, it nevertheless has plenty of nice touches. (c)

K

Kaleidoscope √√ 1966 thriller about successful caper into factory to mark playing cards for Warren Beatty and Susannah York; credibility becomes strained when Clive Revill, as her father, turns out to be Scotland Yard detective who offers a deal. Jack Smight cast small parts splendidly: John Junkin, Yootha Joyce, Eric Porter, Jane Birkin, Murray Melvin. (c)

Kansas City Bomber X Raquel Welch, in conspiracy with director Jerrold Freedman, drags down what might have been an interesting exposure of the seamy world of roller-skate racing to a career v. motherhood and femalecats - scratching - each - others' - eyes - out type comedy; 1972. (c)

Kansas Raiders √ How Audie Murphy got leads like this when there were such fine actors as Brian Donlevy, Tony Curtis, Richard Arlen in it is one of the

minor Hollywood mysteries, but here he is as Jesse James, joining up with well-known fellow-dodgers to wreak revenge on the Yankees after the Civil War; 1951 Ray Enright direction. (c)

Keeper of the Flame √√ Katharine Hepburn-Spencer Tracy team job, 1942, has her as widow of distinguished hero, him as much-raking reporter. Donald Odgen Stewart wrote, George Cukor directed. (b/w)

Kelly's Heroes √ Routine big-budget Second World War actioner, with Clint Eastwood, Telly Savalas, Don Rickles, Donald Sutherland, Caroll O'Connor providing the good guys comedy-thrill team. Director, Brian Hutton (*Where Eagles Dare*); 1970. (c)

The Kentuckian √ In his ill-starred effort as a director (1955) Burt Lancaster couldn't decide whether he was making a farce, a drama or a movie of significance. Actually, it was just a western with his own face in front of the camera most of the time. Walter Matthau, Una Merkel, John Carradine didn't get much of a look in. (b/w)

Kes √√ Moving, touching, convincing tale of a boy with a falcon and the awfulness of contemporary (1969 – and it hasn't improved) secondary education. Ken Loach's direction is affectionate and understated; producer Tony Garnett's choice of then unknown actors to support the remarkable boy, David Bradley, was triumphantly justified – Colin Welland, Brian Glover, Lynne Perrie among them. (c)

The Key X Blown-up, over-long (134 minutes when in the cinema) wartime triangle drama in which Trevor Howard, inopportunely killed off halfway through, comes back as a ghost to haunt William Holden and Sophia Loren. Oddly enough, Carol Reed directed; 1958. (b/w)

Key Largo √√ Humphrey Bogart dominates this transposed (by Richard Brooks with director John Huston) Maxwell Anderson play, about gangster taking over Florida hotel in storm; others in closed set included Edward G. Robinson, Lauren Bacall, Claire Trevor, Lionel Barrymore. It's all a bit predictable but never loses its grip; 1948. (b/w)

The Keys of the Kingdom √ Epic is the none-too-complimentary word for this big-deal adaptation of A. J. Cronin novel of missionaries in 19th-century China. Young (1944) Gregory Peck and Vincent Price are priests, Thomas

Mitchell is crusty old unbeliever; and plot is mostly about bandits. John M. Stahl directed from Mankiewicz-Nunnally Johnson script. (b/w)

Khartoum √√ A good, solid reconstruction of the relationship and ultimate battle between General Gordon (Charlton Heston, not at all bad, considering he has evidently been cast more for his American box office appeal than proven acting ability) versus the Mahdi (a blacked-up Olivier, superb, as always). Meanwhile, back in London, Ralph Richardson's brilliant Gladstone plays devious political games. If the other parts are disappointingly cast and Basil Dearden's direction borders on the mundane, at least Robert Ardrey's script is literate and the camels look lovely; 1966. (c)

Kid Blue √ Comedy western, with Dennis Hopper an easy-riding ex-outlaw who finds that his efforts at working hard like other folks are constantly frustrated. So he goes back to robbing, and despite a few deaths, it's all one big laugh. Peter Boyle, Warren Oates, Ben Johnson join in the fun under James Frawley's amiable direction; 1973. (c)

A Kid for Two Farthings XX Phoney, phoney, phoney East End types in phoney, phoney, phoney yarn about boy who thinks goat is unicorn; even Carol Reed can't do much with schmaltzy Wolf Mankowitz script and some indulgent performances from Celia Johnson, Diana Dors, David Kossoff, and sundry boxers; 1956. (c)

The Kid From Brooklyn √ Danny Kaye is no Harold Lloyd and it shows when he tries remaking *Milky Way*, the story of milkman who accidentally becomes boxer; best in Norman Z. Macleod's cast are Lionel Stander, Fay Bainter, Steve Cochrane; 1946. (c)

Kid Galahad √√ (1) 1937 Bette Davis-Edward G. Robinson boxing story, with Robinson as promoter building up Wayne Morris but losing his gal to him; Humphrey Bogart is rival manager, who also carries a gun. Michael Curtiz. (b/w)

Kid Galahad √ (2) 1963 remake had Elvis Presley in the boxer role, Gig Young and Lola Albright excellent pinch-hitters for Edward G. and Bette D., but somewhat soft-centred direction from Phil Karlson loses much of the punch of the original; mind you, what could the poor guy do when Elvis

insisted on keeping his singing voice in training? (c)

Kidnapped X (1) 1938 version of R. L. Stevenson's Scottish adventure of the mid-18th century had the sickening little Freddie Bartholomew as the lad, plus Warner Baxter, C. Aubrey Smith, John Carradine, Nigel Bruce, all playing their usual type-cast roles. Alfred L. Werker directed. (b/w)

Kidnapped X (2) 1948 attempt had the interesting Dan O'Herlihy, Jeff Corey but too low a budget to do it justice. William Beaudine. (b/w)

Kidnapped √ (3) Michael Caine made a bit of a fool of himself by doing a version for Delbert Mann; with an accent that came and went as the wind changed o'er the heather; 1971. (c)

The Kidnappers √ Get your furtive handkerchief ready for this 1953 sobstory about flint-hearted Nova Scotian Duncan Macrae who drives his grandchildren into stealing a baby because he won't let them have a pet. Philip Leacock's direction makes it almost believable. (b/w)

The Killers √√ (1) Robert Siodmak shot this 1946 version of Hemingway's story with tense authority, with Burt Lancaster making his first big success as the ex-boxer who won't run away; Edmond O'Brien, Albert Dekker, Sam Levene all outstanding, and Ava Gardner at her most effective. (b/w)

The Killers √√ (2) Don Siegel, commissioned to remake it for television in 1964, produced such 'a flippant view of violent death and nihilistic philosophy' that he horrified the sponsors, according to John Baxter's *Hollywood in the Sixties*. So he obtained a cinema release. 'Siegel and actor Lee Marvin crystallised the sixties gangster movie – flip, artificial, hinged on a poetic use of violence... To him, corruption and sudden death are so common and essential to modern life they cannot be wrong.' John Cassavetes plays the victim who won't run away – but not from courage. If you can bear the amorality, you will be gripped finding out why. Angie Dickinson excellent, as was Ronald Reagan in his last movie before becoming Governor of California. (c)

Killer's Kiss X Frank Silvera sees red when boxer Jamie Smith comes courting Irene Kane. Only the fact that this was director Stanley Kubrick's second movie (1955) makes it of any interest. (b/w)

The Killing √√ Tough, tight, tantalising

thriller about racetrack robbery that made 27-year-old Stanley Kubrick's reputation in 1956. Elisha Cook Jr. and Sterling Hayden are convincing crooks. (b/w)

The Killing of Sister George √ Robert Aldrich, who has commercialised and coarsened Frank Marcus' funny and fairly tender stage play (with the help of professional scriptwriter Lukas Heller) must be charged with exploiting lesbianism as a box office attraction. Where the original was frank but subtle, this 'opening out' is crude. Only the performances lift the film above the level of vulgarity: Beryl Reid is splendid as the actress whose imminent demise in her daily serial makes life such hell for her and results in the slipping away of her girlfriend, marvellously played by Susannah York; 1969. (c)

Kill or Cure XX Jokey whodunit with Terry-Thomas as part-time detective, aided by a youthful Eric Sykes (1962). Dennis Price, Lionel Jeffries, Ronnie Barker, Moira Redmond, Derren Nesbitt among victims and suspects. Director, George Pollock. (b/w)

Kim √ Kipling's Indian adventure made satisfactorily rousing 1950 actioner for Errol Flynn, subduing the restless natives and fighting the conniving Russians on behalf of the Queen; Dean Stockwell as the young courier; Paul Lukas, Thomas Gomez weigh in with strong portrayals; Victor Saville shot on the actual locations, and it paid off. (c)

Kimberley Jim XX Jim Reeves in weak little South African actioner about gamblers who win diamond mine. Director Emil Nofal; 1965. (c)

Kind Hearts and Coronets √√√ Alec Guinness plays the eight victims of Dennis Price's insouciant murderer in Robert Hamer's 1948 stylish comedy. Beautifully achieved in all departments. (b/w)

A Kind of Loving √√ Tail-end of Angry Young Man movement now notable for John Schlesinger feature debut in 1962. When Alan Bates 'has to' marry June Ritchie, can their marriage succeed? Waterhouse and Hall script still works and Thora Hird's mother-in-law is archetypal. (b/w)

King and Country √√ Joseph Losey's powerful 1965 piece about the private who walked away from the First World War (Tom Courtenay doing his hurt innocence bit) and the rather more interesting complexities of his defending officer (Dirk Bogarde grasping the opportunity brilliantly). It's all a bit simplistic and overloaded but none the less moving for this. Losey insists that it isn't a war picture ('there are no scenes of battle, and the only scenes of death and desolation are stills or static'). For him, it's a restatement of his continuous theme, hypocrisy – about people who 'have to face the fact that they have to be rebels in society . . .with all the penalties this entails, or else they have to accept hypocrisy' (*Losey on Losey*, Secker & Warburg, 1967). (b/w)

The King and Four Queens √ Ironic title, as by the time Clark Gable came to churn this one out in 1956 he was no longer King – and this was the sort of squandering of his talent that brought him down. It's supposed to be how he rides into town and charms four bandits' widows into telling him where their late husbands hid the swag. Utterly unbelievable, except for Jo Van Fleet's tough mother. Raoul Walsh. (c)

The King and I √√ Yul Brynner and Deborah Kerr are outstandingly good in Rodgers-and-Hammerstein's musical version of *Anna and the King of Siam*, and it transplants beautifully to the screen; Deborah Kerr provides the face for Marni Nixon's top notes. The songs endure: 'Getting to Know You', 'Shall We Dance?', 'Hello Young Lovers'; and the movie stands up. Walter Lang; 1956. (c)

King Creole √√ Elvis Presley's third film (1958) was his best; he had a strong director, Michael Curtiz; a solid plot from a Harold Robbins novel about musician caught up among New Orlean gangsters; and outstanding actors like Walter Matthau, Paul Stewart, Carolyn Jones, Dolores Hart, to back him up. If he had taken this as the starting-point for a serious career he might really have achieved something besides adoration and money, but presumably he didn't like having to be just one of a team. (b/w)

King Kong √√√ The unsurpassed classic of 1933, with the lovable, pitiable, oversized gorilla, sexily (but not as much as intended – the censor's scissors were busy) grabbing Fay Wray, buzzed by biplanes on top of the Empire State building. Great stuff, and we're forever in the debt of directors Merian C. Cooper and Ernest B. Schoedsack. (b/w)

King Lear √ Peter Brook's adaptation,

set in Jutland, is cold, dusty and depressing. There is little magnificence in Paul Scofield's craggy old monarch; Jack MacGowran's Fool is what he should never be – foolish; Irene Worth, Susan Engel and Annelise Gabold are not perfectly cast as the daughters; 1970. (c)

King of Hearts √ Alan Bates is met by inhabitants of local asylum and zoo as he enters French town to defuse time bomb at end of First World War. He also meets Genevieve Bujold. Director, Philippe de Broca; 1966. (c)

King of Kings XX Or *I Was a Teenage Jesus*. Directors can be miscast just as easily as actors and Nicholas Ray was simply the wrong man to attempt a meaningful, emotion-involving life of Christ. And his casting is ludicrous – Jeffrey Hunter as Jesus, Ron Randell as Lucius the Centurion, Robert Ryan as John the Baptist, Rip Torn as Judas...it's like a sick game to choose the least apt Hollywood hams for the divine parts. This 1961 effort had the same title as de Mille's 1927 epic, which was pretty grotesque but preferable to this mess. (c)

The King of Marvin Gardens √√√ Jack Nicholson and Bruce Dern as brothers involved in the rackets of an out-of-season Atlantic City: an elegaic, moving study of brotherly love and hate in an almost mythical landscape, with performances of hallucinatory power from Ellen Burstyn and Julia Anne Robinson as mother and stepdaughter the brothers mixed up with. Bob Rafelson, as director and co-author, made a major contribution with this 1972 masterpiece. (c)

King of the Khyber Rifles X Not a very entertaining *Northwest Frontier* effort with Tyrone Power unconvincing as half-caste British officer who leads the Queen's troops to victory over the troublesome natives; veteran director Henry King had a weak cast to back up his star in 1953 – Terry Moore, Michael Rennie, John Justin, Guy Rolfe. (c)

King Rat √√ This sets out to be realistic account of life in Japanese PoW camp, but has three disadvantages. First is the melodrama that has to be introduced if it has any hope of a mass-market success; second is that emaciated actors are hard to come by (maybe they should have paid them to starve for a couple of months before shooting?); and third is Bryan Forbes' fatal fascination with heroics. In its

favour, however, are remarkable performances from John Mills, Tom Courtenay, Leonard Rossiter; and George Segal acquits himself well in the inevitable bit of casting for that hopeful American appeal; 1965. (b/w)

King Richard and the Crusaders XXX Settle down for a good laugh at this one – in all the wrong places. David Butler has managed to reduce Sir Walter Scott's *The Talisman* to a bad comicbook, and actors Rex Harrison and George Sanders to the level of travesty. Laurence Harvey and Virginia Mayo were there already. It isn't even strong on the fighting; 1954. (c)

Kings Go Forth √ Glib, incredible war drama about Frank Sinatra falling in love with white-passing daughter of black millionaire (what?), who switches to psychotic Tony Curtis. Naturally, they are sent out on mission together, and it all ends happily. The tragedy is that Sinatra was never easier to believe in, and Delmer Daves is such a dab hand that he almost makes it credible for as long as it's on the screen; 1958. (b/w)

Kings of the Sun XX Depressing trivialisation of noble theme – the Mayan civilisation's collapse – minimised by J. Lee Thompson's direction and Yul Brynner's performance into a rather poor western in slightly changed costumes. A mess; 1964. (c)

King Solomon's Mines √√ This 1950 version didn't trust Rider Haggard's plot or its uninspired cast (Stewart Granger, Deborah Kerr, Richard Carlson) and went all out for African spectacle; the result is an eye-catching entertainment, directed jointly by Compton Bennett and Andrew Marton in a manner old-fashioned even in 1950, but perfectly acceptable. (c)

The King's Pirate √ The one about the naval officer (Doug McClure, very UnBritish) who joins the pirates to expose them; a fun-film, with nothing intended to be taken seriously – certainly hope not, anyway - considering what a confused lot of historical hokum it is. Jill St. John (oddly clothed), Torin Thatcher, Guy Stockwell enthusiastically respond to Don Weis's cheerful direction; 1967. (c)

King's Row √√ One of the big ones of 1941. Sam Wood's wide-sweep of small town at turn-of-the-century, with eager Ann Sheridan, Claude Rains as local doctor, Betty Field his loony daughter, young physician Robert Cummings, the future

Governor of California Ronald Reagan in his best-ever part, superbly shot by James Wong Howe. (b/w)

The King's Thief X David Niven, George Sanders, Alan Mowbray enjoy themselves in 17th-century hokum about the Cavaliers at the court of Charles II, and carry us and director Robert Z. Leonard along with them. The more wooden Roger Moore, Edmund Purdom, and Ann Blyth don't seem too sure of what's happening, but plunge gamely on; 1955. (c)

Kismet √ (1) Lush version of *Arabian Nights* romp (1944) directed by William Dieterle. Ronald Colman and Marlene Dietrich - she dances with that fabulous body painted gold. (c)

Kismet X (2) Remade from the Broadway musical taken from first film, in 1955, it had two smashing songs – 'Baubles, Bangles and Beads', 'Stranger in Paradise' – ripped off from Borodin - but despite presence of Monty Woolley and Dolores Gray, precious little else. Vincente Minnelli simply couldn't make Howard Keel or Ann Blyth believable. (c)

A Kiss Before Dying XX Robert Wagner, Mary Astor, Joanne Woodward in dreadful will-he-get-caught directed by Gerd Oswald, from Ira Levin's slightly better book; 1956. (c)

Kisses For My President XXX Only as recently as 1964 the idea of a woman president was so comic that Curtis Bernhardt could attract quite reasonable players like Polly Bergen (as Madame President), Fred MacMurray as her frustrated husband, and Eli Wallach to act in this comedy laughing at it. (b/w)

Kiss Her Goodbye √ Elaine Stritch used to act in American B-pictures before she became a comedienne in British TV. This is about goings-on at a *Psycho*-type motel; director Albert Lipton; 1958. (b/w)

Kissin' Cousins X If one Elvis Presley turns you off (or on) prepare to be doubly repulsed (or excited) when he plays both a clever Air Force officer and a hillbilly determined not to let the Army use his land as testing site; the wrong Presley wins. Gene Nelson directs, sporadically; 1964. (c)

The Kissing Bandit XX 1948 was a down year for Frank Sinatra and Laslo Benedek's directorial debut did nothing to halt the rot. He plays a tenderfoot son of western bandit. Not even a decent song to relieve tedium. (c)

Kiss Me Deadly √ Mickey Spillane thriller suited Robert Aldrich's sadistic style and this broody gangster-private eye melo works with strong performances from Ralph Meeker, Albert Dekker, Paul Stewart, Cloris Leachman; 1955. (b/w)

Kiss Me Kate √√ The bouncy stage musical of *The Taming of the Shrew* translated happily to the screen in 1953. None of the leads (Howard Keel, Ann Miller, Kathryn Grayson, Keenan Wynn) has much charisma, although George Sidney manages to project a reasonable facsimile. The music is what counts, however, and all hail to Cole Porter's 'So in Love', 'I Hate Men', 'We Open in Venice', 'From This Moment On', 'Always True to You in My Fashion'. (c)

Kiss Me, Stupid √√ 'Tasteless' was the word that greeted this wild Wilder-Diamond collaboration in 1964, though 'gamey' would have been a better gastronomic metaphor. Dean Martin sends himself up rotten; Kim Novak ('Why does your husband call you lamb chop?' – 'Maybe because I wear paper panties'), Felicia Farr, Ray Walston splendid in satire on small-town America. (b/w)

Kiss of Death √ Hard, tight, exciting 1947 thriller about stool-pigeon (Victor Mature, convincing for once) pursued by killer he fingered (Richard Widmark). Solid script by Ben Hecht and Charles Lederer brought to real life by New York locations and Henry Hathaway's taut direction. (b/w)

Kiss of Fire XX So what did you expect with a title like that, art? What you get is Jack Palance and Barbara Rush on the way up from Mexico in the 17th century; she renounced the Spanish throne to remain in the New World. Joseph M. Newman; 1955. (c)

Kiss of the Vampire √ Rather sprightly and entertaining Draculoid thriller, neatly directed by Don Sharp in 1962, with bats playing *The Birds* and a solid battle between Good and Evil. Clifford Evans is the mysterious Professor Zimmer. (c)

Kiss The Blood Off My Hands X Despite the come-on in the title, this mish-mash of two accidental murders is never gripping, partly due to Robert Newton's eye-rolling performance, but mostly to Norman Foster's inadequate direction; Burt Lancaster, Joan Fontaine can't rise above it; 1948. (b/w)

Kiss Them For Me X What was Cary

Grant doing backing and appearing in this soapsy 1957 wartime comedy about three naval officers on leave? Maybe Suzy Parker is the answer. Sadly, neither they nor Jayne Mansfield, Ray Walston nor director Stanley Donen could make it come alive. (c)

Kiss Tomorrow Goodbye X And tonight, too, if you waste your time watching this sub-standard gangster melo with James Cagney parodying himself in 1950 under Gordon Douglas's lacklustre direction; he's supposed to be escaped con who gets married but can't escape from himself; only Luther Adler as lawyer pleases. (b/w)

Kit Carson X Jon Hall plays title-role, Dana Andrews is cavalry officer, Lynn Bari femme. Made in 1940 by George Seitz when westerns didn't have to be adult. (b/w)

The Kitchen XX Cut-price attempt to translate Wesker's play to screen in 1961 failed lamentably. In the theatre, it had a vitality partly due to the conjuring-trick of miming all the actions in the restaurant kitchen. Made concrete here, it sinks like a stone with Carl Mohner, Mary Yeoman. James Hill directed. (b/w)

Kitty Foyle √ Ginger Rogers as working-class girl loving rich boy won her 1940 Oscar but looks awfully faded today; from Christopher Morley's novel, directed by Sam Wood. Eduardo Ciannelli does well as waiter. (b/w)

The Klansman √ Vulgarisation of William Bradford Huie's thoughtful novel examining white motives in a Southern town, beleaguered by civil righters. The novel's deft characterisations have been sacrificed to give big, obvious starring roles to Lee Marvin (knife-edged sheriff), Richard Burton (alcoholic recluse), Cameron Mitchell (racist lyncher), and O. J. Simpson (black avenger); director, Terence Young; 1974. (c)

Klute √√√ Immensely exciting murder story, with Jane Fonda as a high-class call-girl and Donald Sutherland as the eponymous investigator. Roy Scheider, Morris Strassberg, Charles Cioffi among those turning in convincing performance under Alan J. Pakula's intense direction in 1971. (c)

The Knack √ Ray Brooks, with it; Michael Crawford, without it; Rita Tushingham, object of it in Dick Lester's much too jazzed-up 1965 version of Ann Jellicoe's play. (b/w)

Knights of the Round Table X Only in the fights does Richard Thorpe manage to make this King Arthur stuff even begin to be acceptable; performances are awful, so raspberries for Robert Taylor, Ava Gardner, Mel Ferrer, Anne Crawford, Stanley Baker; 1954. (c)

Knight Without Armour √ Naive but charming account of Robert Donat playing Scarlet Pimpernel during Russian Revolution. Getting Countess Marlene Dietrich out is his main preoccupation. Others around: Irene Vanbrugh, John Clements, Miles Malleson, Raymond Huntley; French director was Jacques Feyder; 1937. (b/w)

Knock On Any Door √ Humphrey Bogart as defending attorney picks a loser in slum boy; a bit heavy with social significance. Nicholas Ray handles the court scenes well; 1949. (b/w)

Knock on Wood X Those who happen to like Danny Kaye will find this 1954 indulgence by Panama and Frank hugely enjoyable; the rest of us will wonder where on earth he ever got his reputation. (c)

Konga XX Dreadful little rip-off from *King Kong*, with Michael Gough as a Dr Frankenstein who injects an ape with serum to make him bigger and bigger. Ends with the usual smashing of London by the monster; you've seen it all before, more convincing. Best moment is when the enlarged ape kills off Jess Conrad, who richly deserves it for the performance he has been giving. John Lemont; 1961. (b/w)

Kotch √ Walter Matthau as a garrulous old codger whose son and wife want put in a home, but who opts for independence and a sort of Santa Claus life. The parts are sharper than the whole, and Jack Lemmon, directing his first movie in 1971, escapes banality if not sentimentality. (c)

Krakatoa, East of Java X 1968 forerunner of disaster movies, involving volcanic eruption and motley passengers on Java-bound ship. Maximilian Schell is the captain; among his largely unconvincing charges are Brian Keith, Rossano Brazzi, Sal Mineo, John Leyton, Jacqui Chan. Director, Bernard L. Kowalski. (c)

The Kremlin Letter XX Waste of some giant talents (Orson Welles, Bibi Andersson, Lila Kedrova and director John Huston's own) in yet another tortuous Cold War spy farrago. Some rather nasty set-pieces are introduced to stop you falling asleep. Doubtful if they will; 1970. (c)

L

Lad: A Dog XX Soppy sub-*Lassie* tale, about a collie and a crippled child. Aram Avakian directed; 1961. (c)

The Ladies' Man XX Jerry Lewis-directed comedy about Jerry Lewis working in girls' hostel soon fizzles out; 1961. (c)

Ladies Who Do √ Charladies that is. Peggy Mount, Dandy Nichols, Miriam Karlin pick up stock market tips from the wastepaper bins in the offices where they work. Robert Morley, Harry H. Corbett; C. M. Pennington-Richards directed in 1963. (b/w)

Lady Be Good √ Busby Berkeley-choreographed epic, with Eleanor Powell surrounded by countless chorus boys and pianos while dancing 'Fascinatin' Rhythm'. Story of boy and girl songwriting team. Robert Young and Ann Sothern helped by Lionel Barrymore, Red Skelton, Virginia O'Brien, Tom Conway, Reginald Owen, Phil Silvers. Gershwin score; director was Norman Z. McLeod; 1941. (b/w)

Lady Caroline Lamb XX Awful sentimentalisation and distortion of the affair between potty Caroline (Sarah Miles, unable to give her the mad charm she must have had) and posing Byron (Richard Chamberlain desperately miscast), and the disastrous consequences. Neither historically true nor romantically convincing, writer-director Robert Bolt has made it all seem tedious, dragging down Olivier, John Mills, Margaret Leighton, Pamela Brown and other luminaries in the process; 1972. (c)

The Lady Eve √√ Preston Sturges' memorable 1941 comedy of millionaire son falling for Barbara Stanwyck, daughter of a card-shark. Henry Fonda, Charles Coburn, Eugene Pallette. Poorly remade in 1956 as *The Birds and the Bees*. (b/w)

The Lady from Shanghai √√ Few films have had such sharply divided critical comment as this one: ever since Orson Welles directed it in 1948 (way over budget and in total confusion), some have hailed it as a thriller masterpiece, others have dismissed it as incomprehensible, murkily photographed, badly sound-recorded. All agree, however, that the final scene in the mirror maze is fantastic. Welles cast himself as young, devil-may-care Irishman involved with wicked Rita Hayworth (they were about to divorce in real life) and old pal Everett Sloane. Do not adjust your set, only your ears. (b/w)

Lady Godiva of Coventry XX Considerably less than the bare truth about that famous ride through Coventry. Arthur Lubin's direction doesn't encourage anyone to be a Peeping Tom. Maureen O'Hara, Victor McLaglen; 1955. (c)

Lady Godiva Rides Again XX Pauline Stroud wins beauty contest, is smooth-talked by film star Dennis Price and is eventually disillusioned. On the way she meets Stanley Holloway, Kay Kendall, George Cole, Diana Dors, Dora Bryan. Produced-directed by Launder and Gilliat; 1951. (b/w)

Lady Ice X Run of the mill diamond robbery by Donald Sutherland; whimsical romance with Jennifer O'Neill; Robert Duvall, Patrick Magee also appear. Tom Gries directed routinely in 1973. (c)

Lady in a Cage √√ Genuinely frightening 1964 thriller about Olivia de Havilland caught in private lift and menaced by intruders. Director Walter Grauman's use of oppressive heat and the world outside's apathy is particularly effective; as is his working on audience's ambivalence towards helpless but nasty victim. (b/w)

Lady in Cement √ Frank Sinatra in the follow-up to *Tony Rome* looked a bit tired of it all in 1969, which goes well enough with the world-weary private detective but gives a slightly so-so look to the film. Gordon Douglas has managed to get some cheerful balancing performances from most of the cast (not from Raquel Welch – nobody could desynthesise her); Martin Gabel, Dan Blocker, Richard Conte particularly. (c)

The Lady in the Car with the Glasses and the Gun XX As silly as its title, this lukewarm thriller is one of those amnesiac plots in which Samantha Eggar is in trouble for doing nasty things she can't remember. Oliver Reed, her boss, and John McEnery might be implicated in a terrible conspiracy. Directed by Anatole Litvak; 1970. (c)

Lady in the Dark √ If you're going to make a movie out of a Moss Hart theatre piece, why leave out most of the songs? Particularly when they are by Kurt Weill. Maybe Ginger Rogers objected to their doubtless hidden communist undertones in 1944. The result is that Mitchell Leisen turned out respectable (i.e. dull) film about dreams, with Ray Milland, Warner Baxter supporting Ginger. (*c*)

Lady in the Lake X Robert Montgomery is too posh director-star in this 1946 version of Raymond Chandler thriller. What makes it mildly interesting is use of camera as hero's eyes. Audrey Totter's awful. (*b/w*)

The Lady is a Square XXX Utterly appalling Herbert Wilcox-Anna Neagle farrago, with Frankie Vaughan as dude 'butler' with the mission to make her groovy. A 1958 disaster, directed by Herbert Wilcox. (*b/w*)

The Lady Killers √√ Funny 1955 charmer from Sandy Mackendrick about inept gang of bank robbers. Alec Guinness masterminds Peter Sellers, Cecil Parker, Herbert Lom, Danny Green. Plus Katie Johnson as dear old lady who thwarts them all. (*c*)

Lady L XX $2,000,000 had already been spent when Peter Ustinov arrived to take over script and direction. Sophia Loren married to both aristocrat David Niven and chauffeur Paul Newman simultaneously and happily is an engaging enough idea. But Ustinov admits 'there was no real story there. [It was] too ambitious [and] on the wrong scale'; 1965. (*c*)

The Lady Says No XX So will you to silly story of Joan Caulfield as writer of best-selling anti-man book finding herself not quite so anti dishy magazine photographer David Niven. Frank Ross; 1952. (*b/w*)

Lady Sings the Blues √ Vulgarisation of the life of Billie Holiday, as impersonated by Diana Ross, directed by Sidney J. Furie. The songs are right; the voice is subtly wrong; the facts are travestied; 1972. (*c*)

The Lady Vanishes √√√ The last great thriller Hitchcock directed in England before first going to Hollywood – made in 1938. Scripted by Launder and Gilliat (who were so furious the reviews didn't mention them that they immediately set up as director-producers on their own) from Ethel Lina White's novel *The Wheel Spins*. It's a version of the famous old fable about a young woman being convinced by a conspiracy that an older one didn't exist (a later version of the original was Terence Fisher's 1950 *So Long at the Fair*). It all takes place on a train with Margaret Lockwood as the girl, Dame May Whitty as the older woman, Michael Redgrave helping the lady in distress, Naunton Wayne and Basil Radford exchanging endearing banalities, Paul Lukas and Cecil Parker. Poorly remade in 1979. (*b/w*)

The Lady with a Lamp XX Anna Neagle painfully trying to recreate Florence Nightingale with the assistance of director-husband Herbert Wilcox; 1951. (*b/w*)

The Lamp in Assassin Mews XX Mild little English comedy about a couple who are so against progress that they murder a trio of vacuum salesmen and almost do in a 'progressive' councillor, Francis (Paul Temple) Matthews. As the gentle assassins, Amy Dalby and Ian Fleming have a certain charm, even if Godfrey Gayson's direction doesn't; 1962. (*b/w*)

Lancelot and Guinevere X Lots of swash and buckle in 1962 film directed by and starring Cornel Wilde, with Brian Aherne as an unlikely King Arthur. Wilde was also executive producer: he cast Jean Wallace as Guinevere. (*c*)

The Landlord √ Intriguing black comedy with Beau Bridges, naive heir to a fortune, buying a house to turn into a private discotheque, but becoming involved with the people he has to turn out. 1970 directorial debut of Hal Ashby, later to make the amusing *Harold and Maude* and impressive *The Last Detail*. (*c*)

Land of the Pharaohs X Jack Hawkins, Joan Collins in spectacular-looking Ancient Egypt epic about, among other things, the building of a pyramid – no wonder Howard Hawks needed all those extras. William Faulkner had an unexpected hand in the script; 1955. (*c*)

Land Raiders X Violent western, made in Spain by Hollywood director Nathan H. Juran, in which horrible Telly Savalas gets his comeuppance from younger brother George Maharis under the disillusioned eye of wife Arlene Dahl; 1969. (*c*)

Lassie Come Home √ One of the best naive films: story of collie, parted from owners, who makes own way back to them. Fred M. Wilcox directed super 1943 cast: Elizabeth Taylor, Roddy McDowell, Donald Crisp, Edmund

Gwenn and male dog Pal playing part of bitch Lassie. (c)

Lassie's Great Adventure XX Tepid dog-and-boy story that even the smallest children will realise is pretty grim – absurd, unbelievable adventures about being carried off by balloon into the Canadian wilderness. You so often catch the dog and the kid waiting for instructions on how to do what they are supposed to be doing and what to do next that it's positively embarrassing. Director William Beaudine has a lot to answer for; 1964. (c)

The Last American Hero X Hard to care about Jeff Bridges buzzing round the stock car racing circuits to make money for his jail-widowed old mum. Mild peripheral pleasures are Valerie Perrine's golden-hearted groupie and Ned Beatty's near-crooked promoter, but the central theme is dissipated by director Lamont Johnson, who understandably appears to have little faith in William Robert's script, claimed to have been 'based on articles by Tom Wolfe'. 1973. (c)

The Last Angry Man √ Paul Muni, Luther Adler, Godfrey Cambridge in 1959 portrait of slum doctor; director Daniel Mann. (b/w)

The Last Blitzkrieg X Van Johnson just doesn't convince as German spy in routine Arthur Dreifuss-directed Second World War drama; 1959. (b/w)

The Last Command X The Battle of the Alamo all over again, this time (1955) with Sterling Hayden, Ernest Borgnine, J. Carrol Naish, directed as a spectacle by Frank Lloyd. It does go on; 1955. (c)

The Last Day of the War √ Moderately exciting thriller about George Maharis searching out an SS-man who is trying to kill a scientist; director Juan Antonio Bardem (it was a 1969 Spanish co-production) had made better films, including *Death of a Cyclist*. (c)

The Last Detail √√√ Wonderfully observed journey of two petty officers (Jack Nicholson, Otis Young) escorting a harshly-sentenced but apathetic 18-year-old sailor (Randy Quaid) to jail, and giving him a taste of life on the way. Director Hal Ashby does marvels with Robert Towne's tight script; 1973. (c)

The Last Escape XX Stuart Whitman liberating rocket scientist Pinkas Braun from the Nazis and Russians; Walter Grauman directed for America; 1970. (c)

The Last Frontier X Cavalry v. Indians, with Our Hero Victor Mature (well, Anne Bancroft and director Anthony Mann's, anyway) v. Bancroft's horrible cavalry commander husband, Robert Preston. You can guess who wins in both cases; 1955. (c)

The Last Grenade X Jungle mercenaries in revenge story: Stanley Baker, Richard Attenborough, John Thaw among those betrayed by Alex Cord. Gordon Flemyng directed in 1969. (c)

Last Holiday √√ Alec Guinness, doomed to die (he thinks), goes on a last fling. J. B. Priestley wrote and Henry Cass directed an absorbing story. Kay Walsh, Bernard Lee, Sid James, Wilfrid Hyde White among supports; 1949. (b/w)

The Last Hunt X Stewart Granger and Robert Taylor, as nice and nasty buffalo hunters, just aren't competition for the buffaloes which are director Richard Brooks's real stars; 1956. (c)

The Last Hurrah √ John Ford enjoying himself directing gift-wrapped fable from Edwin O'Connor novel about political chicanery, with Spencer Tracy marvellous as Boston's mayor fighting his final campaign. Backing him up are the peerless Pat O'Brien, James Gleason, Ed Brophy and Donald Crisp; against him are Basil Rathbone and John Carradine. If all this sounds earlier than 1958 (and the presence of Jane Darwell, Frank McHugh, Wallace Ford certainly adds to the impression), it can all be forgiven for the sheer fun of the thing. Incidentally, Mayor Curley was the real-life original of the Tracy part. (b/w)

The Last Mile √ Strong stuff in 1959, this Howard W. Koch drama about Death Row prisoners – including an excellent Mickey Rooney – still grips today. (b/w)

The Last of Sheila √√ Elegant, insubstantial, satirical whodunit by musical composer and puzzle-setter Stephen Sondheim and actor Anthony Perkins (who is not in it). Director Herbert Ross happily shuffles his stars round a yacht, rather like a 1973 precursor of *Death on the Nile*. Among them: Richard Benjamin, Dyan Cannon, James Coburn, James Mason, Raquel Welch. (c)

The Last of the Badmen X Chicago detective agency sends two operatives West to find out who killed one of their men. Director Paul Landres tries hard to make you care, but George

Montgomery and so-so cast militate against him; 1957. (*c*)

The Last of the Fast Guns X Search for long-lost missing brother by hired gunslinger runs into various predictable obstacles. Gilbert Roland is only semi-name in uninspiring cast. Director, George Sherman; 1958. (*c*)

The Last of the Mohicans √ Exciting stuff, showing that even in 1936 not all Red Indians were baddies. Director, George B. Seitz; Randolph Scott as Hawkeye. (*b/w*) Remade as *Last of the Redskins* in 1947 by George Sherman, with Jon Hall blacking up. (*c*)

Last of the Red Hot Lovers √ Neil Simon stage play that remains sofabound as Alan Arkin struggles through three attempts at seduction – Act 1, Sally Kellerman; Act 2, Paula Prentiss; Act 3, Renée Taylor. Director Gene Saks; 1972. (*c*)

The Last of the Secret Agents? XX Comics Marty Allen and Steve Rossi in a pale imitation of Laurel and Hardy. They become involved with spy group called THEM. Presence of Nancy Sinatra doesn't help much; director, Norman Abbott; 1966. (*c*)

The Last Picture Show √√√ Beautifully realised evocation of 1951 America (in 1971) by director Peter Bogdanovich. He has wrought wonderful performances from Timothy Bottoms, Cybill Shepherd among the younger generation, and Cloris Leachman, Ellen Burstyn, Ben Johnson among the older inhabitants of a small town, incidentally at the point of transition from cinema to TV-watching. As a dumb boy, Sam Bottoms is particularly moving. (*b/w*)

The Last Run √ One of those this-is-the-last-job-for-me thrillers, which signals that the lovable old bloke (George C. Scott in this case) is going to finish up in trouble. Scott helps gunman Tony Musante and girlfriend Trish Van Devere escape from double jeopardy. John Huston is said to have walked out after he tried to change the script; Richard Fleischer took over; 1971. (*c*)

The Last Safari X African thriller with dubious morals, glorifying hunters (in the person of Stewart Granger) who make a living out of slaughtering disappearing species. Human conflict is between Granger, on his way to kill an elephant called Big Red, and Kaz Garas, playing a bumptious playboy. Henry Hathaway directed; 1967. (*c*)

Last Summer √√ A beach party romp

done for real. Kids (Barbara Hershey, Richard Thomas) pal up with others, have various adventures, some of which ring true. The excellent Frank Perry makes best use of wife Eleanor's script; 1969. (*c*)

The Last Sunset X Kirk Douglas, Rock Hudson, Dorothy Malone, Carol Lynley, Joseph Cotten all look as fed up with this predictable Robert Aldrich-directed western about a round-up as you'll probably feel. Let's hope the cattle enjoyed themselves in 1961. (*c*)

The Last Time I Saw Archie XX *Dragnet*'s Jack Webb produces, directs and co-stars, as sidekick to con-man Robert Mitchum, in unfunny Army comedy; 1961. (*b/w*)

The Last Time I Saw Paris XX Genuinely touching Scott Fitzgerald short story, *Babylon Revisited*, blown up into vulgar flash-backing melodrama about Van Johnson and Elizabeth Taylor destroying each other. Director and co-writer Richard Brooks must shoulder a lot of the blame; 1954. (*c*)

Last Train from Gun Hill √ In spite of local opposition, marshal Kirk Douglas is determined to get on it – with the prisoner he's taken. If he seems particularly anxious to see justice done, that's because his wife was their victim. Anthony Quinn, Carolyn Jones, Brad Dexter and lots of tense moments in exciting 1959 John Sturges western. (*c*)

The Last Valley √ Michael Caine, ruthless soldier, *v.* Omar Sharif, tender humanist, in an Alpine village during the 17th century's Thirty Years' War. Director James Clavell has managed his Shangri-La convincingly, and you may be caught up in both the inner and outer struggles despite initial lack of sympathy for the participants; 1970. (*c*)

The Last Voyage √ Ageing liner sinks – will George Sanders, Dorothy Malone, Robert Stack, Edmond O'Brien go down too? Writer-director Andrew Stone usually makes exciting movies and this is one of them; 1960. (*c*)

The Last Wagon √ Superior western with good baddie Richard Widmark, who's on a murder charge, reluctantly relied upon by pioneers and Felicia Farr to lead them through hostile injun territory. Delmer Daves directed; 1956. (*c*)

The Last Warrior XX Misbegotten mix-up which attempts to make a wild comedy out of Red Indians' contemporary (1970) fight for better conditions, and ends up being insulting to them. Carol Reed is way out of his depth on the reservation, and Anthony Quinn makes a Greek-looking redskin. Called *Flap* in America, it would have been better titled *Flop*. (c)

The Last Woman on Earth XX The only remote interest this tiresome piece of 1961 sci-fi has is that it was directed by Roger Corman. Otherwise, its slender little plot – about a threesome who go skin-diving in Puerto Rico and find that the world has been depopulated while they were swimming – is below naive as well as sea-level. (c)

The Las Vegas Story X Jane Russell, Victor Mature, Hoagy Carmichael, Vincent Price in routine murder melo. Robert Stevenson; 1952. (b/w)

The Late George Apley √ Hard to know if this lush portrait of Boston posh families squabbling over Romeo and Juliet story is meant to be satire or not. John P. Marquand's novel made splendid vehicle for Ronald Colman in 1946, aided by Joseph L. Mankiewicz's sympathetic direction. (b/w)

Latin Lovers X Is dashing Brazilian Ricardo Montalban after heiress Lana Turner's money? Wealthy John Lund certainly isn't, but then he's not as good-looking. Director Mervyn Le Roy didn't make us care too much either way in 1953. (c)

Laughter in Paradise √ A good laugh, too, not so much for Audrey Hepburn's first noticeable screen appearance as for Alastair Sim, Fay Compton, George Cole, Bea Campbell going through some wild hoops to earn inheritance. Mario Zampi directed; 1951. (b/w)

Laughter in the Dark √√ Nabokov's 1933 novel trendily made over in 1969 by Tony Richardson with an Edward Bond script. In the book Nabokov describes the plot as a rich, respectable, happy man (Nicol Williamson) who one day 'abandoned his wife for the sake of a youthful mistress; he loved; was not loved; and his life ended in disaster'. It has a bitter, haunting last half-hour when Williamson, blind now, imagines himself alone with mistress Anna Karina but her lover, Jean-Claude Drouot, is there. (c)

Laura √√ Tyro Otto Preminger was allowed to direct this highly successful thriller after Darryl F. Zanuck took big-shot director Rouben Mamoulian off it. Gene Tierney plays title role and Dana Andrews the detective who's in love with her before they even meet; 1944. (b/w)

The Lavender Hill Mob √√ Tibby Clarke won Oscar for story and screenplay, quite a feat for an English movie in 1952. But it's so rich and comic that it couldn't be denied. Enjoy Alec Guinness as gold thief aided by Stanley Holloway, Sid James, Alfie Bass. Can you spot Audrey Hepburn? Director, Charles Crichton. (b/w)

Law and Disorder √ (1) 1958. Pleasant Ealing-type comedy, with Michael Redgrave, a confidence trickster, pretending to his son (Jeremy Burnham) that he has been on missionary work when he has really been in jail. Back-up cast includes Robert Morley, Joan Hickson, Lionel Jeffries, Brenda Bruce, John Le Mesurier; director, Charles Crichton. (b/w)

Law and Disorder √ (2) 1974. Wry comedy about what happens when Ernest Borgnine and Carroll O'Connor (in similar role to his Archie Bunker of *All in the Family*) form themselves into vigilante group in New York. Quickly defeated by the urban jungle, they retire in a bathetic scene. Karen Black is unfortunately used as a sexy stereotype. Emigré director Ivan Passer seemed unsure of his material. (c)

The Law and Jake Wade √ Not one of John Sturges' best, but it has Robert Taylor as outlaw-turned-lawman and Richard Widmark as old friend-turned-foe on buried treasure hunt; and some exciting action should hold your interest; 1958. (c)

Law and Order √ This title became slogan for its star, Ronald Reagan, when he ran for Governor of California years after it was made in 1953. He plays retiring marshal urged to pin badge back on to run Preston Foster out of town. Nathan Juran directed. (c)

The Law and the Lady X Poor remake of *The Last of Mrs Cheyney*, with an unconvincing Greer Garson, too posh for her part as ladies' maid, and Michael Wilding in a double role(those old twin brothers again) fleecing the rich; director, Edwin H. Knopf. (b/w)

The Lawless Breed √ Straightforward 1953 western, directed by Raoul Walsh, with Rock Hudson making sure his son doesn't follow in his naughty footsteps; Hugh O'Brien, Dennis Weaver. (c)

A Lawless Street X Routine Randolph Scott cleaning-up-the-town western directed in 1955 by Joseph H. Lewis. Angela Lansbury plays euphemistic dance-hall hostess. (c)

167

Lawman √ Unusual western with old-timers Burt Lancaster, Robert Ryan, Lee J. Cobb shooting it out as Lancaster crosses the seven wanted men off his list one by one. Nattily tricked out by Michael Winner, in 1970, there is weak ending and gallons of blood. (c)

Law of the Lawless X Strongly-cast, poorly-scripted western that disappointingly stays indoors almost the whole time. Judge Dale Robertson tries old pal John Agar for murder, under pressure from Agar's pa, Barton MacLane; also threatens gun-duel with Bruce Cabot. Sheriff, William Bendix, and Yvonne de Carlo recreate their familiar roles. Director William F. Claxton might have made something of the ingredients, but didn't, in 1964. (c)

Lawrence of Arabia √√√ Superbly photographed (Freddie Young) pageant of the life of that most enigmatic of Englishmen. Robert Bolt's literate screenplay simplifies him and perhaps takes too straightforward a line. But giving the best performances of their careers, Peter O'Toole and Omar Sharif make Lawrence and Sherif Ali convincing dramatic, if not always human, personalities. Three-and-a-half hours is a long time to sit through a movie, but this one justifies its length. Won Best Picture, Best Director (David Lean), and five other Oscars; 1962. (c)

The Lawyer √ Original of the series *Petrocelli*, this mild thriller has Barry Newman defending doctor accused of murdering his wife. Sidney J. Furie gets the best out of a very straightforward court case by pointing up small town cynical values. There are elements of the real-life Dr Sam Sheppard case; 1968. (c)

Laxdale Hall X *Passport to Pimlico* meets *Whisky Galore:* Hebridean islanders refuse to pay their car licences until they get a road. General Ronald Squire and spirited daughter Kathleen Ryan give Raymond Huntley MP what-ho in 1953 comedy. Now familiar faces include Fulton Mackay, Prunella Scales, Roddy McMillan. Director, John Eldridge. (b/w)

The League of Gentlemen √ Snob caper that comes off. And then? Then they have to be caught, and that's a bore. Jack Hawkins, Nigel Patrick, Richard Attenborough make gentlemanly gentlemen; Bryan Forbes who wrote it plays one of the ex-officers;

Mrs Bryan Forbes appears. Basil Dearden directed competently enough; 1960. (b/w)

The Learning Tree √ Black director Gordon Parks went on to worse things (*Shaft*-type thrillers) after this sensitive autobiographical dramatisation. Kyle Johnson plays Parks growing up in Kansas in the twenties; made 1969. (c)

Lease of Life √ Robert Donat's penultimate film (1954) was painful drama of a vicar with only a short time to live. Charles Frend directed conscientiously, bringing out the conflicts of integrity. (c)

The Leather Boys √ Drama about a marriage (Rita Tushingham and Colin Campbell) that doesn't work and the boy's gradual realisation that he has drifted into a homosexual affair (with Dudley Sutton). It would be fascinating to know what happened after the ending – which is better than a pat tying-up of all the ends, but is still frustrating. Sidney J. Furie directed this in 1963 with just a bit too much flashiness, but altogether it's a creditable job and never lets up. (b/w)

The Leather Saint XXX Awful little programmer about priest (John Derek) turned boxer to raise money for a polio hospital. Paul Douglas and Cesar Romero are embarrassed participants in this inept yarn, weakly directed by Alvin Ganzer; 1956. (b/w)

Leave Her to Heaven √ Highly-coloured drama of wife so possessive that she commits murder to hold on to her husband. Based on Ben Ames Williams's best-seller and well-enough thought of to win Leon Shamroy the 1945 Oscar for photography. John M. Stahl adrenalised cast of good second-raters – Gene Tierney as the wife, Cornel Wilde, Jeanne Crain, Vincent Price, Ray Collins, Gene Lockhart. (c)

The Left-Handed Gun √√ This 1958 literate Western contains much of director Arthur Penn's own childhood, respect for violence and a super performance by Paul Newman as the sinistral Billy the Kid. (b/w)

The Left Hand of God X Humphrey Bogart as a priest? Not quite; only a flyer pretending to be one after having been stranded in China and serving as adviser to a bizarrely-made-up Lee J. Cobb. He fools Gene Tierney though, who gets sexy, guilty feelings about fancying a man of God, and E. G. Marshall (tricked up not as Chinaman, but as missionary) and wife Agnes

Moorehead (also made up, just too much so). Edward Dmytryk was responsible for all this make-up and the rather stilted progress of the melodrama in 1955. (c)

Left, Right and Centre XX Political comedy so good-natured as to be positively non-existent. Launder and Gilliat obviously hoped to have it both ways and eat it, too, in 1959, and go off on an irrelevant joke about stately homes that's boring in its obviousness and embarrassing in its playing. Alastair Sim, Ian Carmichael, even Richard Wattis seem ill-at-ease. (b/w)

The Legend of Hell House √ Eerie stuff about four psychic investigators agreeing to spend a week in house known to be haunted by murderous spirit. Gayle Hunnicut, Pamela Franklin, Roddy McDowell, Roland Culver and you are among those to be terrified. Director John Hough keeps it scary; 1973. (c)

The Legend of Lylah Clare XX Would you believe that Kim Novak looks just like the tragically dead wife of Peter Finch? And that she was a film star whose story would make a Great Movie? And that Finch decides to remake her story with Novak in the part and that he falls in love with her all over again and it all happens tragically all over again and so on and so on? Robert Aldrich hoped you would in 1968. Maybe you will again, just like before. . . . (c)

The Legend of Machine Gun Kelly √ Low-key and fairly effective gangster biopic, with Dale Robertson chasing Harry Yulin, and Dick Sargent as a kidnapped millionaire. Dan Curtis directed from a story by John Milius in 1974. (c)

The Legend of Nigger Charley X Heavily censored for its violence, this yarn of freed slave Fred Williamson reluctantly helping a white man defend his homestead was crudely directed by Martin Goldman in 1972. It neither edifies nor thrills. (c)

Legend of the Lost XX Right old load of rubbish with John Wayne, Rossano Brazzi in desert duel over the love of Sophia Loren, on the way to rediscover an archaeological treasure. Henry Hathaway fools nobody with this one; 1957. (c)

The Lemon Drop Kid √ Lots of laughs with Bob Hope as racetrack tout in gangster's debt. Sidney Lanfield; 1951. (c)

Lenny X Lenny Bruce was too big and original an artist to be confined by this Hollywood biopic, made in 1972, eight years after his death. Dustin Hoffman tries hard enough, but neither he nor director Bob Fosse begin to convey the comedian's outrage at conventionality or the reasons why he rejected marriage and respectability to die from the drugs he chose to take. Valerie Perrine is equally unhappy in an unrewarding role – the stripper he married and who hounded him for money. (b/w)

The Leopard √ Burt Lancaster at his most enunciatingly earnest is the unlikely star of Visconti's study of replaced aristocracy. Alain Delon, Claudia Cardinale revolve round him. The star supervised the English dubbing which the director disowned in 1963. (c)

The Leopard Man √ Dressed as a leopard, somebody is terrorising Mexican village, killing off the inhabitants. Then a real leopard escapes from a circus. Director Jacques Tourneur, good with horror, made this one pretty scary in 1943. Among the frightened: Margo, Dennis O'Keefe. (b/w)

Leo the Last √ Messy attempt to marry surrealism to political realism that earns John Boorman some marks for trying. But Marcello Mastroianni, as an exiled prince living in a poor London street and gradually becoming involved with its black and white (in more ways than one) denizens, appears so bored and superficial that all involvement dies. We are left with an unconvincing story artily told; 1969. (c)

Les Girls X Kay Kendall as one of three flash-backing show girls is by far the best thing about this 1957 George Cukor-directed musical. Otherwise Cole Porter tunes mostly disappoint, as do Gene Kelly, Mitzi Gaynor and dance numbers. (c)

Les Misérables √ Ninth film version of Victor Hugo's classic with, this time, Michael Rennie as the escaping prisoner, Valjean, and Robert Newton as his dogged pursuer. Lewis Milestone did a competent enough job in 1952, but it couldn't compare with Richard Boleslawski's 1935 version with Fredric March and Charles Laughton. (b/w)

Let No Man Write My Epitaph X Bobby Darin makes a poor job of fighting for existence in urban jungle with the help and hindrance of drunk Burl Ives, addict mum Shelley

169

Winters, pusher Ricardo Montalban, Jean Seberg, Ella Fitzgerald. Britain's Philip Leacock was out of his milieu and his element in 1960. (b/w)

Let's Dance X Fred Astaire's dancing doesn't make up for boring plot about ex-partner Betty Hutton's tug-of-war with society-in-laws over her son. Norman Z. McLeod; 1950. (c)

Let's Do It Again X Blurtingly honest title for 1953 remake of 1937's *The Awful Truth*, with Ray Milland in Cary Grant's part as adultering husband, Jane Wyman in Irene Dunne's as wife who invents an affair that lands them in the divorce court. Alexander Hall added some songs to make it a musical, but nothing else – like wit, lightness or charm. (c)

Let's Get Married XX Is a pregnant and abandoned woman marrying her doctor funny? Ken Taylor's script assumes it is, and director Peter Graham Scott throws in as much slapstick as he can devise to confirm this dubious assumption. As Anthony Newley and Anne Aubrey play the main parts, it becomes even less funny, and the result is a centrepiece of unsurpassing non-jokery, flecked with comic bits from Bernie Winters, James Booth, Lionel Jeffries and John Le Mesurier; 1960. (b/w)

Let's Make It Legal X Mild comedy about middle-aged couple (Claudette Colbert, Macdonald Carey) planning 'friendly' divorce after twenty years of marriage. Zachary Scott awful; Marilyn Monroe lovely; Robert Wagner supports nicely; Richard Sale directs; 1951. (b/w)

Let's Make Love X Marilyn Monroe's penultimate film before final *The Misfits* was a pretty sad affair about a millionaire posing as just another hoofer to make Marilyn fall in love with him. Yves Montand looks pretty embarrassed about his part; not so Frankie Vaughan as his singing rival, who should have been. Only George Cukor's expert and tactful direction kept it going, although Marilyn's challenge to Mary Martin in singing 'My Heart Belongs to Daddy' is spirited and delightful; 1960. (c)

The Letter √ Maugham's murderess provided Bette Davis with splendid opportunity for histrionics in 1940, though William Wyler kept her in check. (b/w)

Letter from an Unknown Woman √ Joan Fontaine continues to love Louis Jourdan, the pianist she is infatuated with, tho' the years roll on, like this nostalgic sentimental movie softly, sweetly directed by Max Ophuls in 1948. (b/w)

A Letter To Three Wives √√ 'You see, girls, I've run off with one of your husbands' – but which? Ann Sothern, Linda Darnell, Jeanne Crain flashback worriedly; is it Kirk Douglas? Paul Douglas? Jeffery Lynn? Joseph L. Mankiewicz won both script and director Oscars in 1949; a little bit excessive in the year of *Bicycle Thieves?* (b/w)

Libel X Stuffy courtroom drama, with upper class Dirk Bogarde – accused of murder and impersonation – suing for libel. Wife Olivia de Havilland has doubts about his identity – which isn't really surprising, as director Anthony Asquith has Bogarde playing three roles. Old-fashioned, even for 1959. (b/w)

The Liberation of L. B. Jones √√ Powerful thriller of racism in the Deep South. William Wyler's 1969 indictment is both sophisticated and understanding, and does not rely on nice blacks and nasty whites. Lee J. Cobb is the only familiar face in the cast, and he is not central to the murderous action. (c)

Licensed to Kill XX Called *The Second Best Secret Agent in the Whole Wide World*, in America, this weak rip-off of James Bond on the cheap, made in Britain, has Tom Adams protecting a scientist who can alter gravity. Veronica Hurst, Peter Bull are some compensation. Director, Lindsay Shonteff; 1966. (c)

The Life and Death of Colonel Blimp √ 'By Gad, sir, Goebbels was right! If you want to turn a villain into a hero, show him in love.' That's what's happened to Low's selfish, stupid, pompous old fool with the droopy white moustache. In Powell-and-Pressburger's 1943 whitewash job he became loving (Deborah Kerr in three disguises) and lovable (Roger Livesey, all soft-centred and funny foibles). But Anton Walbrook's sympathetic German friend was a welcome surprise during the war. (c)

The Life and Times of Judge Roy Bean X Desperately described by director-actor John Huston as 'a romp', this is a tedious chronicle of a real outlaw who proclaimed himself judge in a Western town and brought it prosperity. Despite the presence of Paul Newman, Ava Gardner (as Lillie

Langtry), Stacy Keach, Anthony Perkins and Ned Beatty the story of gangs, oil and cantankerousness seems interminable; 1972. (c)

Life at the Top √ Lacks the bite of *Room at the Top*, of which it's the ten-years-after sequel in 1965. Clinches are franker, however. Laurence Harvey is Man; Jean Simmons Mrs; Honor Blackman is bit on the side. Ted Kotcheff directed Mordecai Richler's script. (b/w)

Lifeboat √√ Hitchcock's wartime (1943) drama entirely taking place in a lifeboat should be particularly good on TV, as he shot it mostly in close-and semi-close-up. Tallulah Bankhead, John Hodiak, William Bendix and five other torpedoed passengers are joined by Nazi sailor Walter Slezak. As thriller progresses the characters of each emerge. Hitch intended it to be allegory of disparate Allies having to pull together to defeat singleminded Germans, but John Steinbeck's script wasn't good enough for him. He brought in another couple of writers, ended up rewriting it himself. His own statutory appearance was hard to arrange: he had intended to be dead body floating by but was afraid he'd sink; finally he ingeniously put himself as the before-and-after figure in a newspaper ad for Reduco. (b/w)

Life for Ruth √ Strong, didactic, over-simplified 1962 drama about a husband (Michael Craig) with fundamentalist religious beliefs, who won't let his wife (Janet Monro) give permission for a blood transfusion for their little daughter. She dies and Dr Patrick McGoohan makes a national scandal of it. Basil Dearden directs it all. (b/w)

Life in Emergency Ward 10 XXX Dreadful little rip-off from *Emergency Ward 10* deserves a special place in Wardour Street's Chamber of Horrors as one of the first films to be made from an ITV television series – in 1959. Otherwise, the worst of the British film industry has been grafted on to the worst of television. Michael Craig and Wilfrid Hyde White were added to the regular cast but do not improve it. The script was even more exposed at full length; Robert Day directs. (b/w)

A Life in the Balance √ Boy stalks murderous Lee Marvin across Mexico City in weak adaptation of Georges Simenon yarn. Anne Bancroft and colourful locations are the best director Harry Horner could come up with in 1954. (b/w)

Life is a Circus XX Unfortunately it isn't despite the Crazy Gang's attempts to prove otherwise. They find Aladdin's lamp and summon the genie to keep their circus going. (Why? Why not just ask for a million each and to hell with it?) Val Guest wrote and directed, but he has doubtless forgotten it by now. Before it all gets junked (the sooner the better) someone should transfer the scene where Flanagan and Allen sing 'Underneath the Arches' to the National Film Archives; 1960. (b/w)

The Life of Emile Zola √ Slow, dated, cliché-ridden, but still powerful story of the Dreyfus Affair, but miscalled because Paul Muni, Warner Brothers' contract star, insisted on his role always being the title. Despite Muni's screen-hogging, Joseph Schildkraut manages to edge him off when it comes to real acting, as the persecuted Jewish officer. William Dieterle's flat 1937 direction serves. (b/w)

A Life Of Her Own X A rare miss for George Cukor. Will fashion model Lana Turner return her rich boyfriend to his crippled wife? This was 1950, remember. Not even Ray Milland, Tom Ewell, Louis Calhern can save this slush. (b/w)

Life With Father √ William Powell is tyrannical father, Irene Dunne mother, in Michael Curtiz lavish period comedy, based on Clarence Day best-seller. Particularly good music score by Max Steiner; 1947. (c)

The Light at the Edge of the World XX Unsuccessful attempt by Kevin Billington to film Jules Verne's novel about commandeered lighthouse. Yul Brynner (baddie) and Kirk Douglas (goodie) chase each round the ragged rocks, with Samantha Eggar alternating between them; 1971. (c)

Light in the Piazza XX What Mama (Olivia de Havilland – not really up to the role) does when daughter (Yvette Mimieux, pleasant) attracts eligible bachelor (Italianate George Hamilton) in Florence is complicated by the fact that the girl is mentally retarded – should Mama point it out? Guy Green confuses the whole issue by letting the whole cast behave as if it's mentally retarded, though what does it matter as long as they're happy? 1962. (c)

Lightning Strikes Twice X Richard Todd drags down this King Vidor thriller as a released convict who goes home to the ranch to find his wife's killer. Mercedes McCambridge almost

171

makes up for him and Zachary Scott; 1951. (b/w)

The Light Touch √ An innocent Pier Angeli exerting good influence over art thief Stewart Granger isn't as sickly as it sounds under director Richard Brooks' light touch; Italian locations, and George Sanders' sophisticated villain, are lovely; 1951. (b/w)

Li'l Abner √ Energetic visualisation of Al Capp's comic-strip land of Dogpatch hillbillies had 1959 political overtones. Mel Frank directed from Broadway musical. Earlier, in 1940, Granville Owen had made an experimental movie with masked characters attempting to match the strip. But the Frank attempt was only a near-miss, with Stubby Kaye and Julie Newmar remarkably close to the best-ever strip. (c)

Lilacs in the Spring XX Anna Neagle plays four roles in this preposterous tale – Queen Victoria, Nell Gwyn, an ENSA performer and her own mother – and Errol Flynn's her father who marries her – get it? It's a right old mish-mash with amnesia and sentimentality jostling for first place in Herbert Wilcox's old-fashioned (it was, alarmingly, made as recently as 1954) direction. (c)

Lili √ Sentimental tale of Leslie Caron being wooed by Mel Ferrer through his puppets. Includes song 'Hi-Lili, Hi-Lo' and should keep little girls of all ages glued to the set. Charles Walters; 1953. (c)

Lilies of the Field X Sickly, sentimental tale of handyman Sidney Poitier building nuns a chapel; made in 1963. Ralph Nelson directed; Poitier won an Oscar. (b/w)

Lilith √ The last film Robert Rossen made before his death, and 'his noblest and most lyrical failure' says Andrew Sarris. Warren Beatty is therapist in love with mental patient Jean Seberg. Peter Fonda, Gene Hackman support ably; 1964. (b/w)

The Limbo Line XX Craig Stevens solves the mystery of who is kidnapping defecting Russians; watch for Jean Marsh (*Upstairs Downstairs*) in minor role. Sam Gallu directed from Victor Canning novel; 1967. (c)

Limelight √ Appallingly sentimental yarn of ageing comedian who makes a comeback thanks to the devotion of the ballet-dancing protegée he once saved from suicide. However, as Charlie Chaplin plays the main part and made it himself in 1952 it has an interest far beyond its dreadfully banal story. Claire Bloom is the dancer and there are appearances for various members of the Chaplin family, including son Sydney as Bloom's *inamorate*. The tune has outlived the film. (b/w)

The Limping Man XX – in a limping thriller, made in 1954. One of those British efforts starring an American second-division star – Lloyd Bridges this time – with such genteel players as Moira Lister, Helene Cordet, Leslie Phillips articulating their way through an unbelievable plot. Director, Charles de la Tour. (b/w)

The Line-Up √ Tough, tight little thriller directed by cult-figure Don Siegel in 1958 about drug-pusher (Eli Wallach) holding two women hostages. (b/w)

The Lion X Is Pamela Franklin taming her pet lion? Or is it turning her savage? Do we care? William Holden has to. Jack Cardiff directed; 1962. (c)

The Lion Has Wings √ A real museum piece: a 1939 Ministry of Information-sponsored propaganda effort, rolling the drum for Great Britain, with a thin fictional story about Squadron Leader Ralph Richardson and his wife, Merle Oberon. The film links chunks of newsreels and the 1936 film *Fire Over England*, starring Flora Robson as Queen Elizabeth. A joint directional effort, it may have inspired some soldiers to fight harder for King and Country. (b/w)

The Lion in Winter √√ Winning 1968 Oscars for Katharine Hepburn, composer John Barry and writer James Goldman, this cross between a costume *Peyton Place* and *Who's Afraid of Virginia Woolf?*, set in the combined English and French courts of the 12th century, is adequately guided by Anthony Harvey. He welds the team of Hepburn, Peter O'Toole, Jane Merrow, John Castle, Timothy Dalton, Anthony Hopkins, Nigel Stock and Nigel Terry into a single ensemble of great power. The immediate question is who shall succeed Henry II (O'Toole). When he vomits at a revelation in the plot, Hepburn turns to the audience and asks: 'What family doesn't have its ups and downs?' It takes a self-confident film to say that – and to talk as much as this one does – and a very good one to get away with it. (c)

The Liquidator X This came at tail-end of James Bond boom (1966) and attempts twist with hero (Rod Taylor) as inefficient bumbler. Trevor Howard and Wilfrid Hyde White do their best but director Jack Cardiff can't thrill as much. No wonder projected sequels never happened. (c)

Lisbon √ Ray Milland, Claude Rains, Maureen O'Hara and complicated kidnap plot are all upstaged by the scenery. Ray Milland directs as well; 1956. (c)

The List of Adrian Messenger X Self-indulgent 1963 Irish extravaganza by John Huston, supposedly a murder mystery, most notable for appearances by heavily disguised Tony Curtis, Kirk Douglas, Burt Lancaster, Frank Sinatra, Robert Mitchum (disguised?), with George C. Scott in mainline part. (b/w)

Lisztomania XXX Ken Russell's 1975 contribution to the cinema was this embarrassing marriage of rock stars (Roger Daltry, Ringo Starr, Rick Wakeman) and their music with 19th-century romantic composers Wagner, Chopin and so on. The ridiculous story, supposedly about Franz Liszt, is acted so feebly and edited so frantically that it is impossible to guess even at his intentions. (c)

Little Big Man √√ Dustin Hoffman looking back over his 121 (yes, 121) years in the Wild West could have been an excuse for a brainless epic. As it is, Arthur Penn's thoughtful film remains an episodic collection of morality plays, never less than interesting – often absorbing. Faye Dunaway, Martin Balsam lead a long, strong list of supports; 1970. (c)

Little Boy Lost X Bing Crosby in France trying to find the son he last saw as baby isn't quite as sloppy a it sounds. George Seaton; 1953. (b/w)

Little Fauss and Big Halsy X Robert Redford in an unsympathetic role as the braggart of the motorcycle racing circuit. Sidney J. Furie passively allows the film to lose the excitement of the racetrack that a lesser – or less pretentious – director would have welcomed, and Michael Pollard's exploited sidekick who grows tall – metaphorically – is taken from *Bonnie and Clyde*, not life; 1970. (c)

The Little Foxes √√ Bette Davis at her best in 1941, despite constant rows with director William Wyler, taking merciless revenge on husband Herbert Marshall for refusing to invest in her brother's business. Teresa Wright, Dan Duryea. (b/w)

The Little Hut X Ava Gardner, Stewart Granger and David Niven enjoy themselves in adaptation of boulevard play about castaway triangle on a desert island, more daring than most movies in 1957, if less than most today. Director, Mark Robson. (c)

Little Malcolm and His Struggle Against the Eunuchs √ By the time it was made (1974), the period of revolutionary youth was over, but David Halliwell's stage play transferred nicely to the screen. John Hurt's weakly fascist leader of a local coup that will clearly never happen works well. David Warner makes his hopeless conspirator sympathetic, while Rosalind Ayres does her usual excellent job as the girl Führer Hurt fancies but can't pursue. (c)

Little Murders √ Alan Arkin directed and starred in this adaptation of Jules Feiffer's play about sniper terrorising New York, rather further down the road to anarchy than it actually was in 1971. Elliott Gould has main role. (c)

Little Nellie Kelly √ Little Judy Garland (18 in 1940) reconciling stubborn Irish policeman father George Murphy and grandfather Charles Winniger in St. Patrick's Day parade. It's a great film for the Irish. The song 'Singin' in the Rain' features again (it was first heard in Hollywood revue of 1929). Director, Norman Taurog. (b/w)

Little Old New York X With the help of Alice Faye (get that Scottish accent), Richard Greene invents the steamboat. Fred MacMurray builds it for him. Henry King directed in 1940 with a fine disregard for historical fact. (b/w)

The Little Ones √ Films about sweet little children usually tend to get very mawkish. This one, written and directed by Jim O'Connolly, is an exception. A low-budget effort, it's about a search for a father; 1965. (b/w)

The Little Prince XX Disastrous musical by Stanley Donen, despite music from Lerner and Loewe and the presence of Gene Wilder in the cast. Saint-Exupery's fragile, sad little book, with its simple illustrations, is clearly not the stuff from which rumbustious musicals are made. Richard Kiley and Steven Warner do adequately as the Pilot-Narrator and the Prince, but it's a forlorn enterprise; 1974. (c)

Little Women √√ (1) 1933 version by George Cukor of Louisa May Alcott favourite had Katharine Hepburn,

Joan Bennett, Paul Lukas, Frances Dee, Edna May Oliver. (b/w)

Little Women √ (2) 1949 remake by Mervyn Le Roy starred Elizabeth Taylor, June Allyson, Margaret O'Brien, Janet Leigh, Mary Astor. (c)

Live and Let Die √ Expensive in 1973 (costs at £3,000,000) but cheap in its thrills, this seventh Bond adventure was the first starring Roger Moore. The heavy is Yaphet Kotto, who was to make a more dignified use of his black power five years later in *Blue Collar.* (c)

Live It Up XX In his humble days of 1963, David Hemmings starred in this 18-day pop quickie that was better than it deserved to be, thanks mainly to Lyn Fairhurst's observant script and Lance Comfort's experienced direction. He plays one of four messenger boys who form a pop-group and finally Make It. All very naive and silly now, but it retains a certain museum interest. (b/w)

The Lively Set XX Motor racing-cum-teenager-fun pic that isn't much fun. Jack Arnold puts some cars, James Darren and Pamela Tiffin through their paces. Mostly, the cars work; 1965. (c)

Live Now, Pay Later √√ The world of hire-purchase, celebrated in a Jack Trevor Story script that lets the nasties win. Nice Liz Fraser can't stand the repayment grind and ends up under a car. But Ian Hendry is mesmerically good as the villain-hero, conning the housewives, and takes Jay Lewis's otherwise clumsily-directed drama up to quite dizzy heights; 1962. (b/w)

The Lives of a Bengal Lancer √ Made in 1935 by Henry Hathaway during a period when Hollywood tried, with awed respect, to reflect a sun already setting on the British Empire. 19th-century India has Gary Cooper, Franchot Tone and C. Aubrey Smith, some ludicrous dialogue, terrific narrative-tug and a marvellous snake-charming sequence. (b/w)

Living Free XX Tepid 1972 sequel to 1965 *Born Free* is particularly infuriating because it pretends to have documentary realism but is all too obviously phoney – from wishy-washy story to unskilfully faked photography. Nor does its cuddly attitude towards wild animals genuinely help the cause of conservationism; pity Susan Hampshire and Nigel Davenport for finding themselves in this. Director, Jack Couffer. (c)

Living It Up X Jerry Lewis as suspected

174

radiation victim, Dean Martin as doctor, Janet Leigh as journalist covering the story in so-so Norman Taurog 1954 remake of *Nothing Sacred.* (c)

Lizzie X A sort of *Three Faces of Eve*, with Eleanor Parker as triple schizo, Richard Boone as her psychologist. Joan Blondell and actor-director Hugo Hass support weakly; 1957. (b/w)

Lock Up Your Daughters XX And don't bother to put the set on, it isn't worth the effort. This mish-mash of *Rape Upon Rape* and *The Relapse* relies on Restoration naughtiness which quickly palls. The combination of heavy-handed director and heavy-footed lead Christopher Plummer produces a deadening effect. Fenella Fielding, Susannah York, Georgia Brown, Peter Bayliss and Peter Bull lighten the gloom for a moment or two, but it sorely misses the music that it had in the Mermaid's theatrical revival; 1969. (c)

The Lodger X Only version likely to find its way to your home screen is John Brahm's 1944 effort with the dreadful Merle Oberon not quite balanced by the gorgeous Laird Cregar, George Sanders and Cedric Hardwicke. Hitchcock's 1926 simpler effort about the lodger who is suspected of being Jack the Ripper (the first real Hitchcock film) and Maurice Elvey's 1932 version might seem just too remote now. (b/w)

Lolita √ Despite Vladimir Nabokov's credit as adaptor of his own novel, this is only remotely the book of the film. By making the nymphet appear between 15 and 17, it destroyed the essence of the affair between a 12-year-old and the near-psychopathic obsessional. Despite this and some heavy overacting by Shelley Winters as Humbert Humbert's wife and a performance by Peter Sellers as Quilty which shows him to be more mimic than actor, the film remains fascinating. James Mason's Humbert is remarkably effective despite his physical unsuitablility for the part, and Sue Lyon does all that is required of her except look right. Above all, Stanley Kubrick's direction keeps a firm grip and makes for an entertaining if not exciting view; 1962. (b/w)

The Loneliness of the Long Distance Runner √ Faultless performance from hungry-looking Borstal boy Tom Courtenay out to humble superior upper-class Governor Michael Redgrave. Over-directed in 1962 by Tony

Richardson but good tight script from Alan Sillitoe. Strong support from James Bolam, James Fox. (b/w)

Lonely Are The Brave √ Interesting contemporary (1962) David Miller-directed western with Kirk Douglas excellent (for once) as old-time cowboy on the run from sheriff Walter Matthau, great as always. (b/w)

Lonelyhearts X Couldn't help but fail to have the bite and surrealism of Nathanael West's novel about a newspaper advice columnist (Montgomery Clift). It would need a director of genius; this version – with Robert Ryan, Myrna Loy, Dolores Hart – got Vincent J. Donehue instead; 1959. (b/w)

The Lonely Man √ Jack Palance plays an ageing gunfighter in this 1957 western, trying to redeem himself in the eyes of society and his son, Anthony Perkins. But Neville Brand rides in, out of his past. Henry Levin directed. (b/w)

The Lone Ranger X Full-length version of radio and TV series that was big in 1956. Clayton Moore is the wooden hero, Jay Silverheels is Tonto the wooden Indian. Lyle Bettger is the villain who plans to destroy an Indian reservation, ex-child actress Bonita Granville, 33, plays the heroine; Stuart Heisler directed. (c)

Lone Star √ While Texas fights for independence, there's a routine good guy v. bad guy western scene going on. But routine doesn't matter quite so much when they're Clark Gable and Broderick Crawford; Ava Gardner, who they're feudin' about, and Lionel Barrymore, Beulah Bondi, Ed Begley are around. Don't trust the history – they got it all wrong. Vincent Sherman; 1952. (b/w)

The Long and the Short and the Tall √ Broke new ground in 1961 by treating Second World War as hell. Leslie Norman's slightly stagey version misses presence of Peter O'Toole from original play; he's replaced by bigger box office name (then!) of Laurence Harvey. (b/w)

The Long Arm X How the police painstakingly trace the thief who robbed a Covent Garden safe is shown in meticulous detail, but since 1956 we have seen too many *Softly-Softlys* and similar reconstructions for us to feel much interest in this bloodless caper. Jack Hawkins plays his Detective-Supt. with his usual competence and Charles Frend's direction cannot be faulted, but there's a mechanical air about this end-of-Ealing drama. (b/w)

The Long Day's Dying X Charles Wood's intelligent, probing script from the novel by Alan White, about war in the persons of three soldiers who don't know quite what to do with a prisoner they have captured, gets a let-down from Peter Collinson's insensitive, modish direction. David Hemmings, Tom Bell and Tony Beckley do their best but seem to be fighting the director; 1968. (c)

Long Day's Journey Into Night √ Eugene O'Neill's brooding play about his own family, revealing, in a setting of claustrophobic pre-First World War anti-macassars, the reasons why Mum was a morphine addict, Dad compulsively mean, the elder son a drunk and the younger one a morbid poet. Katharine Hepburn, Ralph Richardson, Jason Robards and Dean Stockwell, respectively, do these characters magnificently, and Sidney Lumet's direction doesn't feel trapped in close-up or within the play's one-room set; 1964. (b/w)

The Longest Day √ D-Day, mostly from the American point of view (but not forgetting that the Germans were there, too) made as super-budget, super-roadshow drama which is fairly exciting, accurate and heartless, not to say pointless. Among those present: John Wayne, Robert Mitchum, Henry Fonda, Robert Ryan, Robert Wagner, Edmond O'Brien, Rod Steiger, Mel Ferrer (Americans); Curt Jurgens, Peter van Eyck, Gerd Froebe (Germans); Richard Burton, Richard Todd, Kenneth More, Sean Connery (British); Bourvil, Jean-Louis Barrault, Christian Marquand, Arletty (French). Directors: Bernhard Wicki, Ken Annakin, Andrew Marton, and Darryl F. Zanuck; 1962. (b/w)

The Longest Yard √√ Tough prison thriller with a difference - football. Burt Reynolds is jailed sports star who is ordered, under pain of extra punishments, to get together a team of convicts and then to lose to the guards. Will he revolt? Robert Aldrich directs with gusto; 1974. (c)

The Long Goodbye √√ Despite a changed ending and different villains from Raymond Chandler's original, Robert Altman made this 1973 version of the Philip Marlowe thriller into an agreeable two hours. Elliot Gould is surprisingly effective and idiosyncratic private eye; among strong supports are Nina van Pallandt, Sterling Hayden, Mark Rydell, Henry Gibson. (c)

The Long Gray Line √ Sentimental but affectionate 1955 John Ford tribute to real-life West Point coach, played by Tyrone Power; Maureen O'Hara is his wife. (c)

The Long Haul XX A long drag with truck-driver Victor Mature, a Yank in Liverpool, falling for glamorous (1957) Diana Dors, moll of crook Patrick Allen, and being forced to work for them. Directed by Ken Hughes. (b/w)

The Long Hot Summer √ Brooding drama about outsider's effect on neurotic Southern family, based on William Faulkner stories. Director Martin Ritt's splendid cast – Paul Newman, Orson Welles, Joanne Woodward, Lee Remick, Angela Lansbury, Anthony Franciosa – gave it conviction in 1958. (c)

Long John Silver √ Broad, humorous performance from piratical Robert Newton still buccaneering his way after Flint's gold. He meets up again with Jim 'Awkins from *Treasure Island* days, and with lots of swash and buckle they're off again. Byron Haskin; 1954. (c)

The Long, Long Trailer √ Slick (under Vincente Minnelli's direction) vehicle for Lucille Ball and Desi Arnaz as couple honeymooning in caravan; 1954. (c)

The Long Night XX Weak remake of *Le Jour se Lève* reset from Paris to Pittsburgh had particularly poor performances from Vincent Price and Barbara Bel Geddes, as seducer and seduced. Henry Fonda looked charmingly tortured as the hunted murderer holed up in a tenement, but Anatole Litvak's moody direction simply looked cheap against Marcel Carné's original; 1947. (b/w)

The Long Ride Home √ Roger Corman's name was dropped from the credits and Phil Karlson got his name on as director in 1968, but it was Corman who set up and shot most of this end-of-the-Civil-War tragedy as Glenn Ford is forced to pursue George Hamilton and some escaping Confed soldiers who have kidnapped his girl, Inger Stevens. Exciting, wide-ranging stuff. (c)

The Long Ships X Vikings (Richard Widmark, etc.) v. Moors (Sidney Poitier et al.) in Jack Cardiff-directed costume epic. Well, it makes a change from cowboys v. injuns, but that's not

enough to recommend it; 1964. (c)

The Long Voyage Home √ Visually ravishing (thanks to Gregg Toland's stunning photography) this knitting-together of four Eugene O'Neill playlets about life at sea isn't altogether happy in its cast (Ian Hunter stiff; London characters absurd) but contains so many memorable moments that you forgive John Ford's lapses of taste and mood. John Wayne, Thomas Mitchell come off best among the leaky tramp steamer's crew; 1940. (b/w)

The Long Wait XX And nothing to show at the end of it, so don't waste your time with this slow Micky Spillane yarn about amnesiac Anthony Quinn falsely accused of murder. Who cares? Director Victor Saville certainly didn't seem to in 1954. (b/w)

Look Back in Anger √√ Richard Burton made it possible for Tony Richardson and John Osborne to transfer their Royal Court success to the screen in 1959 by agreeing to play Jimmy Porter. He was OK and the film is more than an accurate record of the play. Yet, as almost everything Richardson does, there was an unsatisfactory edge to it that comes from the inability to project technically the height of his pretentious ambitions. (b/w)

Look for the Silver Lining XX Conventional showbiz biomusical (1949) about Marilyn Miller, Broadway star, hazily interpreted by June Haver and directed by David Butler. (c)

Looking for Love XXX Stupid little sub-musical with Connie Francis thinking she's in love with Jim Hutton when really she's in love with Joby Baker. You know the sort of thing. Don Weis churned it out for teenage morons in 1964. (c)

The Looking Glass War √ John Le Carré doesn't write spy thrillers, he draws character studies of people caught up in the bureaucracy of espionage. Unfortunately director Frank R. Pierson has set out to make a spy thriller from this Le Carré novel and the result is predictably unsatisfactory. The main casting (Christopher Jones, Pia Degermark) is equally inept, although supports Ralph Richardson, Anna Massey, Timothy West, Paul Rogers almost save the day; 1969. (c)

Loot X Near-miss by Silvio Narizzano in opening up Joe Orton's outrageously funny play. He is not helped by Galton and Simpson's broader script, Richard Attenborough's central performance as Truscott of the Yard (very different from Michael Bates's *tour de force* in the theatre), Hywel Bennett's villain and idiosyncrasies from Milo O'Shea and Dick Emery. Lee Remick is never at home as the murderous nurse; 1970. (*c*)

Lord Jim X Disastrous big-scale attempt to give Conrad's novel wide-screen life. Between them, director Richard Brooks and self-conscious star Peter O'Toole have destroyed the strength and poetry and mystery of the sailor ashamed of his cowardice who finds regeneration in the jungle. Instead, we are offered a sprawling spectacle, with Big Names doing their cameo bits (James Mason, Curt Jurgens, Eli Wallach, Jack Hawkins, Paul Lukas, Akim Tamiroff) and a glib dissipation among battles and explosions; 1965. (*c*)

Lord Love a Duck X Some funny moments, but George Axelrod's 1965 comedy about American teenagers looks out-of-date now – as do Tuesday Weld and Roddy McDowall. (*b/w*)

Lord of the Flies √√ The fable of small boys reverting to savagery when marooned on a desert island may not be as powerful on the screen as in William Golding's book; but in Peter Brook's adaptation, which he directed himself in 1961/3, it retains enough primitive power to hold, move and disturb. For an advocate of the Theatre of Cruelty he is strangely hesitant about picturing the worst excesses of the boys, but enough is shown to make you weep with Piggy, hate Jack and sympathise with Ralph. (*b/w*)

The Lords of Flatbush √√ While lacking the intensity and understanding of *Mean Streets*, this evocation of a 1957 Brooklyn youth gang has some strong scenes and a sense of humour. The presence of both Sylvester Stallone and Henry Winkler should ensure a bigger TV audience than writers-producers-directors Stephen V. Verona and Martin Davidson could have guessed in 1974. (*c*)

Loser Takes All XX Desperately disappointing tale of winning system at roulette and the difference it makes to newlyweds Rossano Brazzi (terrible) and Glynis Johns. Weak in almost every department, the blame is only partly director Ken Annakin's. Everyone expected better from the script-writer, who took it from his own short story – Graham Greene; 1956. (*c*)

Lost XX Sincere attempt to tell the story of child stolen from pram may be a bit too pedestrian for modern tastes, but Guy Green made it acceptable in 1956. Second-eleven cast, headed by David Farrar. (*c*)

Lost Battalion XX 1962 B-picture allegedly set behind the Japanese lines in the Philippines but all too obviously shown up by the newsreels which keep it interesting. The action sequences are OK but the talk (should a white girl – Diane Jergens – fall in love with a local guerrilla – Leopold Salcedo?) is embarrassing. And the final twist of the plot is a *deus ex machina*. Eddie Romero directed. (*b/w*)

Lost Command √ Anthony Quinn, George Segal, Alain Delon, Claudia Cardinale, Michèle Morgan all doing their bit for one or other side in French-Algerian war. Director Mark Robson makes it all a bit specious, but there's a nice irony in the final shots; 1966. (*c*)

The Lost Continent X Better than usual Hammer horror about how boatload of quite interesting characters (Eric Porter, Hildegard Knef, Suzanna Leigh, Nigel Stock) survive a hair-raising voyage on a ship filled with explosives. Among other excitements they are in a hurricane and get trapped in some man-eating seaweed. Director Michael Carreras took this from a Dennis Wheatley novel in 1968. (*c*)

Lost Horizon √√ (1) 1937 Adult fairy story about Ronald Colman finding a valley in Tibet where nobody grows old; Margo's sudden withering in his arms as they leave the place is one of the great moments of cinema; Frank Capra. (*b/w*)

Lost Horizon XX (2) 1972 Risible remake directed by Charles Jarrot, with Peter Finch encountering John Gielgud in his worst-ever part as Chang the High Priest; Liv Ullman and Sally Kellerman singing and dancing (it's a musical, wouldn't you know?); Bobby Van tap-dancing with what seems to be Hare Krishna beggars from Oxford Street. (*c*)

The Lost Man √ Mainly interesting for those who have warm memories of the original *Odd Man Out*, this 1969 reworking of F. L. Green's novel fails to develop either the revolutionary aspect or the human inter-relationships of Carol Reed's 1946 insight into Irish rebels. Joanna Shimkus is an inadequate Cathy, and Poitier himself long ago lost credence. (*c*)

The Lost Weekend √√ First attempt to treat alcoholism as a movie subject was

177

immense success, winning 1945 Oscars for best film, best actor Ray Milland, best director Billy Wilder, best script Wilder and Charles Brackett. Deliberately slow-paced, it builds up into horrendous climax in Bellevue's alcoholic ward after Milland succumbs to his need for a drink, tottering up Third Avenue with his typewriter to pawn, finally selling his girl's coat to buy a gun to shoot himself. Jane Wyman's regeneration of him was not in the book and should be ignored as window-dressing. (b/w)

The Lost World XX Prehistoric monsters don't like the arrival of explorers Michael Rennie, Claude Rains, Jill St. John one bit and you can't blame them. Irwin Allen remade silent 1924 classic in ludicrous fashion in 1960. (c)

The Loudest Whisper X This 1962 effort to present Lillian Hellman's stage play (from the author's own adaptation) runs into trouble when it tries to make social ostracism believable. People just don't behave that way any more, and neither Audrey Hepburn, Shirley MacLaine nor director-producer William Wyler can remotely suggest any reason why a hint of homosexuality might send them into such a tizzy. (b/w)

Louisiana Story √√ Robert Flaherty's 1948 lyrical paean to nature is as slow as the waters of the bayous, but story of boy in a boat watching big oil prospectors (it was sponsored by Standard Oil) is wonderfully evocative of the struggle for existence and a child's awakening. (b/w)

Love Among the Ruins √ Shown at the London Film Festival, but originally made in 1974 for American TV, Katharine Hepburn consults old flame Laurence Olivier, without realising who he is. Some nice twists in static situation aren't enough to dissipate the ennui. George Cukor directed; 1974. (c)

Love and Death √√ Woody Allen rewrites, directs and acts in this squint-eyed version of *War and Peace*. Oddly enough, the idea comes off fairly well, and we follow him through the duels, battlefields, and drawing-rooms, laughing. As always, Diane Keaton works beautifully with him; 1975. (c)

Love and Pain and the Whole Damn Thing √ Maggie Smith, dying of an incurable disease, meets Timothy Bottoms, asthma-sufferer, on a bus in Spain. He says 'Let's go sightseeing.' She says 'I'm strangely attracted.' And the consequence is they go their separate ways in New York. Sob. Alan J. Pakula, producer-director, sadly doesn't lift his material much higher than that; 1972. (c)

The Loved One X Tony Richardson was so obviously the wrong chap as director of Evelyn Waugh's flaying satire on California burial rites that it's amazing how producers John Calley and Haskell Wexler (who also did the photography) chose him. Predictably, he took all the caricature elements in Terry Southern and Christopher Isherwood's adaptation of the novel and compounded them with a cast he seems to have encouraged to over-act. Thus despite the presence of Rod Steiger, Anjanette Comer, Robert Morse, Jonathan Winters, Milton Berle, John Gielgud, Margaret Leighton, Liberace, Robert Morley, Lionel Stander, all we got in 1965 was a series of jokes to replace Waugh's scalpel strokes. The plot, such as it is, is cluttered with all sorts of irrelevant jibes at other Los Angeles follies. (c)

The Love Goddesses √√ Fascinating 1965 compilation, mostly from Paramount, of clips linked by refreshingly literate narration. The obvious ones – Harlow, Monroe, Bardot, etc. – are included, but far juicier are the barge scene from De Mille's *Cleopatra*; choice Busby Berkeley number; the gorilla who turns out to be Dietrich; and some scenes to remind us that there was an era before censorship. (b/w)

Love Happy XX Weak 1950 Marx Brothers comedy notable for a walk-on by Marilyn Monroe. David Miller; 1950. (b/w)

Love Has Many Faces XXX Simply awful soaper with Lana Turner as ageing playgirl (this was 1964), Cliff Robertson and Hugh O'Brien as gigolos in Acapulco. Alexander Singer directed tastelessly. (c)

Love in a Goldfish Bowl XXX Daft little teenagerer with Tommy Sands and Toby Michaels slipping off together for a platonic holiday (oh, Toby's a girl) which sends their college authorities into a frenzy of moralising. This must have been old-fashioned in 1961 – it's positively antediluvian now. Written and directed by Jack Sher. (c)

Love in Las Vegas X And boredom for you unless you happen to be an Elvis Presley fan. His 1964 vehicle was this nonsense about being a waiter-cum-mechanic-cum-racer wooing swimming instructress Ann-Margret. George Sidney staged the musical numbers efficiently but he could hardly believe in the plot either. (c)

The Love-Ins XX Nasty Hollywood cash-in on the 1960s hippy scene, made 1967, with Richard Todd, James MacArthur; Arthur Dreifuss directed. (c)

Love in the Afternoon √√ Gary Cooper - a bit old for the part (56 in 1957) but who's counting? - wooing Audrey Hepburn in gentle Billy Wilder - I. A. L. Diamond comedy filmed in Paris; Maurice Chevalier as Audrey's papa provides local colour along with the locations. (b/w)

Love is a Ball XX Pretty Riviera setting for silly yarn about heiress Hope Lange and fortune hunters Glenn Ford, Charles Boyer. David Swift; 1963. (c)

Love is a Many-Splendored Thing X You've heard the song, now see the film - but only if you'd love a good cry at *Madame Butterfly*-type romance between war correspondent William Holden and unbelievable Eurasian girl Jennifer Jones. Henry King; 1955. (c)

Love is Better Than Ever X The way she looked in 1952, it's a mystery why it takes Elizabeth Taylor so long to hook Larry Parks (why she should want to is even more mysterious). Stanley Donen spun it out. (b/w)

The Love Lottery XX Soft little British comedy with David Niven as the prize in a sweepstake. But he really loves Anne Vernon, for some reason. Charles Crichton wasn't able to give it much zing, things being what they were in 1953. (c)

Lovely To Look At X Howard Keel, Kathryn Grayson, Red Skelton in 1952 Mervyn LeRoy remake of Astaire-Rogers musical, *Roberta*, set in high-fashion Paris. Jerome Kern songs like 'Smoke Gets In Your Eyes', 'I Won't Dance' still lovely to listen to. (c)

A Lovely Way To Go X Ex-cop Kirk Douglas trying to prove Sylvia Koscina didn't murder her husband. David Lowell Rich didn't make us care one way or the other in 1968. (c)

Love Me or Leave Me √ Doris Day as Ruth Etting, the twenties singer, famous for 'Smoke Gets In Your Eyes' and highly dramatic personal story, turned to good account by Charles Vidor in 1955. James Cagney memorable as Marty the Gimp. (c)

Love Me Tonight √√ Made in 1932 with bravura by Rouben Mamoulian, it has a Rodgers and Hart score

(including 'Isn't It Romantic?', first sung by Maurice Chevalier in Paris, picked up by all sorts of characters as it carries us into the country), Myrna Loy as a nymphy countess ('Don't - you think of anything but men?' - 'Yes, schoolboys'), Charlie Ruggles, Charles Butterworth, C. Aubrey Smith, and a tailor-meets-princess story. It also has Jeanette MacDonald, but survives magnificently. (b/w)

Love Nest X Silly story about a con man getting his friend jailed so that he can dictate his memoirs in prison, isn't improved by leaden performances from June Haver, William Lundigan and Frank Fay. But Marilyn Monroe in a small part is some compensation. Director, Joseph Newman; 1951. (b/w)

Love on the Dole √ Classic early British working class realism film of Walter Greenwood's novel about a Lancashire family in the Depression. Young Deborah Kerr's mill girl made her a star, well supported by Clifford Evans, Mary Merrall, George Carney. Directed, 1941, by John Baxter. (b/w)

Lover Come Back √ Delicious Doris Day-Rock Hudson comedy with sophisticated Madison Avenue setting; director Delbert Mann gives it plenty of sparkle and Tony Randall adds to the fun; 1962. (c)

Lovers and Other Strangers √√ When Gig Young died so tragically, the screen lost an apparently light comedian who was a better actor than we realised. He uses his insouciant strength in this 1969 comedy of love, seduction and separation, and is partnered by Anne Jackson, another intelligent player, who can suggest depth behind frivolity. Cy Howard directed this concoction of five couples of various ages. (c)

Love Story √ A phenomenon such as this transcends criticism. An ordinary little magazine yarn of boy meets girl, boy loses girl (by death, with violins playing) became an industry in 1970. The film broke all records; the novel was hastily written by scripter Erich Segal to zoom into a blockbusting bestseller; a sequel fixed; and the trite phrase, 'Love means never having to say you're sorry' entered books of quotations. Ryan O'Neal and Ali MacGraw (soon to sink from stardom) were just the right light-weight; Ray Milland as his stern father gruffly staggers through. Director, Arthur Hiller. (c)

Love with the Proper Stranger √

Feckless jazz musician Steve McQueen gets casual lay Natalie Wood pregnant. Realistic New York locations, fine performances and Robert Mulligan's sensitive direction make it all believable, even though things have changed a lot since 1963. (b/w)

Loving √√ Effective little 1970 comedy about George Segal's disillusionment with his marriage to Eva Marie Saint and his job in advertising. Some nice moments and generally deft direction from Irvin Kershner. (c)

Loving You XX Elvis Presley's second film (1957) was predictable yarn of small-town boy facing up to overnight fame and fortune; with Lizabeth Scott, Wendell Corey; director, Hal Kanter. (c)

Lovin' Molly √ Interestingly structured country tale of girl (Blythe Danner) and two men in her life (Beau Bridges, Anthony Perkins), told by each of them in turn, and with incidents strung out between 1925 and 1964. Sidney Lumet coaxed his players through a difficult task, but failed on the rural ambience; 1973. (c)

The L-Shaped Room √ Despite critical raves, Leslie Caron seems miscast as unwed pregnant girl in love with fellow-lodger Tom Bell. It's not director Bryan Forbes's fault that what seemed real in 1963 looks dated now. (b/w)

The Luck of Ginger Coffey √√ Absorbing drama about an Irish family of immigrants to Canada and the way they get split up. Robert Shaw and Mary Ure are painfully true-to-life. Director Irvin Kershner did well by Brian Moore's script from his own novel; 1965. (b/w)

Lucky Jim √ Ian Carmichael was monumentally miscast as hero of Kingsley Amis's novel shoved on to the screen by the Boultings in 1957 with no regard for subtleties. The belly-laughs are still there for the farcical bits (Terry-Thomas, Hugh Griffith upped the milieu while broadening the incidents) but there is no sign of why novel should have become symbol of redbrick revolution against Establishment. (b/w)

Lucky Me X Lucky Jack Donohue had Doris Day, Phil Silvers, Robert Cummings to give this dreary musical about out-of-work showgirls a bit of life; 1954. (c)

Lucky Nick Cain X Gambler George Raft framed for murder on Italian Riviera in otherwise conventional gangster yarn. Joseph M. Newman; 1951. (b/w)

Lucy Gallant √ Ambitious career girl Jane Wyman makes a huge success of everything except – you've guessed it – her personal life, oilman Charlton Heston in this case. Robert Parrish; 1955. (c)

Lullaby of Broadway √ You could do worse than let this Doris Day musical with songs by Cole Porter and Gershwin wash over you. Gladys George is fine as Doris's Broadway-singer Mom. David Butler directed; 1951. (c)

Lust for Life √ Not as ghastly as the usual 'great artist' biopic, but let down by inadequacies of Kirk Douglas as Van Gogh and Anthony Quinn as Gauguin. The paintings are great, however, and Vincente Minnelli's attempt to recreate them in moving pictures not at all bad. Pamela Brown, Everett Sloane, Jill Bennett, Lionel Jeffries support; 1956. (c)

The Lusty Men √ Nicholas Ray's vivid and authentic picture of rodeo life more than makes up for rather conventional storyline; Robert Mitchum, Susan Hayward, Arthur Kennedy convince too; 1952. (b/w)

Luv XX The blame for the failure of this one must lie with director Clive Donner. He had three splendid stars in Jack Lemmon, Elaine May and Peter Falk and the original Murray Schisgal play about middle-class New Yorkers was very funny Broadway hit. So what went wrong, Mr Donner? 1967. (c)

Lydia Bailey X Kenneth Roberts, who wrote *North West Passage*, concocted this Haiti-based extravaganza which director Jean Negulesco glossed into some sort of a shine in 1952. Dale Robertson was the American lawyer trying to get signature on legal document from Anne Francis, then becoming entangled in Napoleonic subversion. (c)

M

M √ Quickie (20 day) 1951 remake by Joseph Losey of child murderer hunt which doesn't begin to match Fritz Lang's German classic with Peter Lorre in 1931, despite presence of

Luther Adler and Martin Gabel and a very close sticking to the original script. (b/w)

Ma and Pa Kettle XX, Hillbillies from *The Egg and I* make their own debut in this mild 1949 comedy. Marjorie Main and Percy Kilbride win an electronic house – not like a real home, of course. Director, Charles Lamont. (b/w)

Ma Barker's Killer Brood X Lurene Tuttle does fine in Bill Karn's rather crude version of true-ish life-story of Bloody Mama, remade with Shelley Winters ten years after this 1960 version. (b/w)

Macao √ For most, this will be a moody sub-*Casablanca*, with Robert Mitchum and Jane Russell fighting an equivocal sexual duel. But for the cinéaste it provides a chewy puzzle: who directed what? When Howard Hughes asked the legendary Joseph von Sternberg to direct it, he expected trouble; what he got was chaos, with rows on the set and tantrums all round. He so hated the rushes that he brought in Nicholas Ray to reshoot some scenes. But how much of the finished film was Ray's? (b/w)

Macbeth √ (1) 1948. Orson Welles whizzed through this in three weeks, but managed some imaginative filming. (b/w)

Macbeth X (2) 1960. Maurice Evans is the ambitious Thane, in an unimaginatively photographed version of the play, directed by George Schaefer. (c)

Macbeth √√ (3) 1971. Roman Polanski, with the help of Kenneth Tynan and *Playboy,* had a weak Thane in Jon Finch but a strong Lady M. in Francesca Annis. (c)

Machine Gun Kelly √ Charles Bronson plays mad-dog gangster under Roger Corman's tough 1958 direction. (b/w)

Mackenna's Gold √ Great long super-western sprawls unconvincingly over a huge canvas, shooting off in all directions about some gold that by the end you simply don't care about. J. Lee Thompson has been provided with a stellar cast by co-producer Carl Foreman (Gregory Peck, Omar Sharif, Telly Savalas, Keenan Wynn, Raymond Massey, Lee J. Cobb, Anthony Quayle, Edward G. Robinson, Eli Wallach, Eduardo Cianelli) and a narrator, Victor Jory, thrown in to stitch the uncomfortably-fitting pieces together. Unfortunately, he can find little for them to do, and this series of disappointments plus inferior special effects, add up to one huge disappointment; 1969. (c)

Mackintosh and T.J. √ Return of Roy Rogers in 1975, after twenty years off the Hollywood range, with a broken down pick-up truck on a real ranch in West Texas. He's a drifter who teams up with rebellious young Clay O'Brien; director, Marvin J. Chomsky; 1975. (c)

The Mackintosh Man X Predictable and somnolent 'thriller' from John Huston, remarkable only in the type-casting of everyone in sight (Paul Newman in his *Torn Curtain* role; James Mason in his *North by Northwest* one; the usual parts for Harry Andrews, Ian Bannen, Michael Hordern, Peter Vaughan, Noel Purcell, Niall MacGinnis etc.). Only Dominique Sanda is a newcomer to this tired old double-crossing spy stuff, and she was a mistake; John Huston should (and almost certainly did) know better; 1973. (c)

The Macomber Affair √ Hemingway African short story made clumsily over to give Gregory Peck, Joan Bennett, Robert Preston starring roles. Zoltan Korda exaggerated the dramatics in his direction; 1947. (b/w)

Mad About Men X Tame sequel to *Miranda,* in which girl and look-alike mermaid change places. Glynis Johns plays them; Margaret Rutherford, Donald Sinden back up. Ralph Thomas; 1954. (c)

Madame Bovary X Just one of the many movies ruined by Jennifer Jones grabbing the main part when quite unsuited to it. Here she mucks up Flaubert's novel of a calculating woman, dragging down James Mason, Van Heflin with her. Vincente Minnelli obliged directorially; 1949. (b/w)

Madame X X Real old thirties-type weepie given 1965 production values but little else by David Lowell Rich's unashamed twanging on the heart-strings. Ex-shopgirl Lana Turner is forced by horrid mother-in-law Constance Bennett to leave her husband and pretend she's dead. All she did was have a fling with Ricardo Montalban. She hides away but kills blackmailing Burgess Meredith, to be defended by Her Own Son, Keir Dullea. Previous Madame Xs: Gladys George, 1937; Ruth Chatterton, 1929; Pauline Frederick, 1920; original was play by Alexandre Bisson. (c)

The Mad Bomber √ Vince Edwards traps Chuck Connors after a career disposing of people and institutions which he doesn't like. If the police

181

methods reveal an unnerving reliance on hunches and coincidences, this is mostly glossed over by Bert I. Gordon's lively direction; 1972. (c)

Made X Contemporary (well, 1972) morality story about what happens when nice girl Carol White moves in with transient pop star Roy Harper. Despite the presence of Margery Mason as her mother, director John Mackenzie does little to lift the material above trendy soap operatics. (c)

Made in Paris X But confected in Hollywood; this is the one about the American girl (Ann-Margret) who, on a tour of the sights of the naughty French capital, can't make up her mind which of three men she should marry. Louis Jourdan, the only 'name' around, must start favourite. Boris Sagal directed it all very smoothly in 1966 but it needed more than slick production to get by. (c)

The Mad Genius √ 1931 Svengali rip-off as vehicle for John Barrymore to do his ham act in a top hat and beard. This time it was about ballet. Names who were to blossom later included Boris Karloff, Donald Cook, Charles Butterworth, and director Michael Curtiz. (b/w)

Madigan √ √ Emergence of Don Siegel into the big-time after years and years of making the best B pix was this 1968 super-thriller which presents a couple of New York detectives (Richard Widmark and Harry Guardino), almost indistinguishable from the scum they hunt, given 72 hours to pull in a sadistic killer. Henry Fonda, who prides himself on being a clean detective, is their chief but he turns out to be as corrupt in his fashion as the rest of the characters in this violent, exciting, nasty, compelling parable of the urban jungle. (c)

Madison Avenue XX Dreary tale about the advertising industry, without bite or bile, or even any pretensions to either. Eleanor Parker and Jeanne Crain expose themselves (alas, not literally) and the man they have built up, Dana Andrews, when they realise he could become a danger to dear ol' America – Bruce Humberstone directs with a straight face; 1961. (b/w)

Madonna of the Seven Moons XX Belongs to the bad old days of British films, 1944, when Phyllis Calvert, Stewart Granger, Patricia Roc, Jean Kent – all of whom can be seen posturing about in this soppy yarn about a gypsy curse – ruled the roost. Director, Arthur Crabtree. (b/w)

The Mad Room √ Horror thriller in which Stella Stevens, companion to Shelley Winters, plans to marry into the family. The snags are her homicidal teenage brothers and sisters. They are given refuge in . . . the mad room. Director, Bernard Girard; 1969. (c)

The Madwoman of Chaillot √ Dreadfully theatrical piece of theatre by Jean Giraudoux never sits easily on the screen despite star-cramming (Katharine Hepburn, Margaret Leighton, Giulietta Masina, Edith Evans as madwomen; Donald Pleasence, Charles Boyer, Yul Brynner, Paul Henreid, as heavies; Danny Kaye, Richard Chamberlain, and sundry others playing parable parts like The Folk Singer, The Flower Seller, The Juggler, the Deaf Mute, the goodies). It's all too schmaltzy and zany in its self-consciously fantasy manner. Bryan Forbes directed with a heavy hand, in 1969. (c)

The Maggie √ Paul Douglas was imported to play financier who loses out to canny Scots over cargo of tramp steamer; well directed by Alexander 'Sandy' Mackendrick in 1954. (b/w)

The Magic Box √ A cast of British stars as long as your nose graces this Festival of Britain (1951) celebration of William Friese-Greene, inventor of the cinema camera. John Boulting assembled Robert Donat, Laurence Olivier, Eric Portman, Glynis Johns, Emlyn Williams, Richard Attenborough, Margaret Rutherford, Peter Ustinov, among others. Considering it's a (misplaced) Tribute movie, it isn't too bad. (c)

Magic Fire X One of those Great Composer biopics, this time about the unpleasant Richard Wagner, who comes out as a nicer chap than he was in real life, thanks to Alan Badel's sympathetic performance and director William Dieterle's need for a hero. Yvonne de Carlo, Rita Gam and Peter Cushing mope about in unreasonable facsimile of moviedom's idea of how a composer's satellites behave, and only Valentina Cortese makes a real stab at catching the period and emotions as the woman who inspired Tristan und Isolde. Actual locations are used wherever possible and the matching sets are scrupulously correct; but the opera excerpts evidently embarrassed the film-makers as much as they will bore the uninitiated (by being too long) and annoy the addict (by being too short); 1956. (c)

The Magnet √ Cosy, charming Ealing comedy about childhood directed by Charles Frend. The leading child William Fox grew up to become actor James Fox; 1951. (b/w)

The Magnificent Ambersons √√√ Made twenty years before its time, in 1942, when movie families had to be Andy Hardy's parents, not disquieting real-life aliens. Superb performances from Tim Holt, arrogant scion of best family in town, who gets his come-uppance; Dolores Costello as his doting mother; Agnes Moorehead as his screaming bitter old maid of an aunt; Richard Bennett as patriarch; Joseph Cotten, Anne Baxter, Ray Collins. The great director (who also wrote the screenplay from Booth Tarkington's novel) wasn't allowed by the money boys to finish and it ends abruptly three reels before he meant it to with a tacked-on sequence in a hospital by another hand. He was permitted to speak the final credits, however. His name is Orson Welles. (b/w)

Magnificent Obsession √ Successful soaper about Jane Wyman going blind and Rock Hudson curing, loving her. Douglas Sirk directed this 1954 remake of 1935 Robert Taylor - Irene Dunne - John M. Stahl tearjerker. (c)

The Magnificent Seven √√√ A great western, taken from Kurosawa's *Seven Samurai* and surviving the transposition – well, magnificently. Director John Sturges has managed to get real characterisation and tension out of the septet of gunmen – Yul Brynner, Horst Buchholz, Steve McQueen, Charles Bronson, Robert Vaughn, Brad Dexter, James Coburn – and Eli Wallach's bandit chief they protect the village from is equally memorable, not least for its unexpected casting; 1961. (c)

The Magnificent Seven Deadly Sins X A series of sketches, not all of them new, skated through by a battery of TV comics (Bruce Forsyth, Roy Hudd, Harry Secombe, Leslie Phillips, Harry H. Corbett, Ian Carmichael, Spike Milligan, Ronald Fraser). Director Graham Stark doesn't manage to impose a uniformity of style, and the hit-and-miss atmosphere only emphasises the misses; 1971. (c)

The Magnificent Seven Ride √ 1972 version of the 1960 yarn, with Lee Van Cleef as chief rider. George McCowan makes a fine job of storytelling, and the climatic gunfight is particularly well-prepared and mounted. (c)

The Magnificent Showman √√ Strictly for lovers of big westerns and circuses, this is a huge drama, filled with all sorts of catastrophes and John Wayne lording over all. Director Henry Hathaway serves it up expertly; 1964. (c)

The Magnificent Two X Another of Morecambe and Wise's unhappy forays into the cinema; this 1967 effort, under Cliff Owen's direction, has Eric as a South American rebel leader. The comedy is interrupted by rather nastily literal action sequences. (c)

Magnum Force √ With the philosophy that nothing is wrong with shooting as long as the right people get shot, Clint Eastwood's Dirty Harry takes on crooks and crooked cops alike with a great show of blood and guts. Unpleasant as all this is (and the critics panned it), the movie was a huge box office hit. Director Ted Post served up almost as expert a dish as Don Siegel did with the original Dirty Harry, two years before; 1973. (c)

The Magus XXX Pretentious treatment under weak director Guy Green of John Fowles novel. If the labyrinthine script hadn't sunk it, casting (Anthony Quinn, Michael Caine, Candice Bergen, Anna Karina) would have anyway; 1968. (c)

Mahler X Usual Ken Russell vulgarisation, with Nazi parodies and absurd domestic scenes. Robert Powell looks and sounds wrong as the composer; spotty casting leaves a few fine players (Ronald Pickup, Georgina Hale) lost in a sea of caricatures. Only the music survives – just; 1974. (c)

The Main Attraction XX Dull little circus story climaxing in night in mountain hut where Pat Boone and Nancy Kwan are unaware they are in the path of an avalanche. Weak supports Mai Zetterling, Yvonne Mitchell, Kieron Moore, Warren Mitchell don't get the direction they badly need from Daniel Petrie; 1962. (c)

The Major and the Minor √√ Billy Wilder's first shot at direction (1942) was this fast-paced comedy about Ginger Rogers dressing up as a child to save the train fare and falling for Ray Milland. Great fun. (b/w)

Major Barbara √√ Best of Gabriel Pascal's adaptations of Bernard Shaw's plays (what charm the little chap must

183

have had to con Shaw into letting him ruin play after play) was this one with Wendy Hiller as the Salvation Army girl, Rex Harrison, Robert Morley, Robert Newton, Emlyn Williams, Deborah Kerr, Sybil Thorndike; 1941. (b/w)

Major Dundee √√ One of the most important American movies of the last decade, if you can believe the enthusiasts for director Sam Peckinpah, whose third picture (1964) this was. But most audiences will see only a moderately exciting, rather scruffy western, with Federal officer Charlton Heston leading a band of ex-Confederate prisoners, under a resentful Richard Harris, against the Apaches. Look for deeper meanings, despite drastic re-editing over Peckinpah's head. (c)

A Majority of One √ Schmaltzy 1961 story of Jewish widow Rosalind Russell, whose son was killed in the war, meeting and resenting Japanese industrialist Alec Guinness. Sympathy triumphs but it takes too long. Unimaginative direction from Mervyn Le Roy leaves it stage-bound. (c)

Make Me an Offer √ Tepid antique (in many senses) comedy from Wolf Mankowitz novel; Peter Finch as dealer involved with Wedgwood vase. Directed patiently by Cyril Frankel; 1955. (c)

Make Mine Mink XX Pathetic little British comedy made in 1960 at the end of the 'zany period', about retired officer (Terry-Thomas) who joins up with three posh old ladies (Athene Seyler among them) to steal for charity. Some good players (Hattie Jacques, Irene Handl, Billie Whitelaw) shamefully wasted on a weak Michael Pertwee script and Robert Asher's lack-lustre direction. (b/w)

The Male Animal √√ Elliott Nugent directs from his and Thurber's play about triangle with professor Henry Fonda, Olivia de Havilland, Jack Carson. Light, sophisticated 1942 comedy. (b/w)

The Maltese Falcon √√√ This was John Huston's first (1941) direction and he never bettered it. In fact, nobody has ever bettered it in its own field – the shady, seamy, semi-underworld of the private eye, played ever-memorably by Humphrey Bogart, never fooled for a moment (well, not many moments) by Mary Astor's calculating schemer, Peter Lorre's frightened operative, Sydney Green-

street's bland flatterer, partner Jerome Cowan's weak womaniser, Gladys George's clinging adulterer, and the whole shenanigans about the little black bird whose worth is greater than you will ever know. Aficionados will also treasure continual needling of Elisha Cook Jr. and Daddy Walter Huston's literally staggering aid to his son as he wanders in with the treasure. (b/w)

Mame √√ At 64 in 1974, Lucille Ball was frankly too old for the nifty trouper Aunt Mame should have been. And too ingratiating where Patrick Dennis's novel portrayed as imperious. Rosalind Russell's 50-year-old Auntie Mame in 1958 was altogether more impressive. Director Gene Saks doesn't manage to suggest that life with Aunt Lucille was much fun. (c)

A Man Alone √ Ray Milland directing himself in superior western about a fugitive from lynching taking refuge with sheriff's daughter Mary Murphy. Ward Bond, Raymond Burr, Lee Van Cleef among the heavy mob; 1955. (c)

Man at the Top X Tiresome, amoral 1973 spin-off from a spin-off – the TV series that followed John Braine's dilution of his original *Room at the Top*. Joe Lampton, as portrayed by Kenneth Haigh, is a monotonous chip-on-shoulder toughie; a weak supporting cast fails to convince under Mike Vardy's direction. (c)

Man Behind the Gun √ Dull oater about Randolph Scott building Los Angeles, with help of Alan Hale, Patrice Wymore; Felix E. Feist directed; 1952. (c)

The Man Between X James Mason earnestly supported by Claire Bloom and Hildegarde Neff in 1953 Carol Reed-directed drama of cold war in Berlin. (b/w)

A Man Called Horse X Lord Richard Harris becomes an honorary Indian chief after being suspended by his nipples in a scene to thrill all masochists. This 1970 adult western was successful enough to warrant a sequel, despite most of the dialogue being in Sioux and the rest in absurd English. (c)

A Man Called Peter XX Richard Todd as real-life Senate chaplain in dull account of his life. Director Henry Koster; 1955. (c)

The Manchurian Candidate √√√ Tremendously exciting hokum about Laurence Harvey being turned into walking zombie ready to do the Red

Chinese's wicked deeds (like sniping at presidents) without realising it, given immense zip by John Frankenheimer in 1962. Frank Sinatra is the officer who gets through the turn-on code, but the acting honours belong to James Gregory and Angela Lansbury as a nasty couple of political crooks. (b/w)

A Man Could Get Killed X One of those heavily mixed-up melos in which James Garner is taken for a spy, Melina Mercouri for a thief, Roland Culver pretends to be a doctor and Tony Franciosa passes himself off as someone else. Directors Ronald Neame and Cliff Owen appear not to have taken each other completely into their confidence; 1966. (c)

Mandingo XX Insult to both audiences and blacks alike, this farrago from a flopped play adaptation of a novel about slavery is an excuse for prolonged sadism. James Mason over-acts as villainous plantation owner; Susan George along; the slaves slave and lust. Director Richard Fleischer lingers lovingly over every flayed back and death by boiling water; 1975. (c)

Mandy √√ Tearjerker directed by Sandy Mackendrick in 1953, about little Mandy Miller who turns out to be deaf and dumb. Jack Hawkins, Phyllis Calvert face bravely up to the problem of how to raise her. (b/w)

A Man For All Seasons √√√ Superb transfer to the screen of Robert Bolt's play, produced and directed by Fred Zinnemann with tact and depth, in 1967. Paul Scofield repeats his towering performance as Sir Thomas More who goes through so much, remains so steadfast, and has magnificent support from Wendy Hiller as his wife; Susannah York as his strong-willed daughter; Leo McKern the squitty Cromwell; Vanessa Redgrave (unbilled) as Anne Boleyn; Orson Welles as a grand Wolsey; Robert Shaw as the young Henry VIII; and John Hurt is a marvellously evil Rich. A treat in all departments, which was rewarded by a raft of Oscars and both critical and box-office success. (c)

A Man for Hanging X Peter Breck plays a mad bandit, raping and murdering his way across the Wild West wearing a leather mask to hide his hideously scarred face. Director Joseph A. Mazzuca; 1970. (c)

The Man from Colorado √ Glenn Ford takes over western territory as judge and reveals himself to be corrupt and power-mad. It takes William Holden to break him up; Henry Levin; 1948. (c)

The Man from Laramie √ James Stewart rides into town looking for the gun-runner who caused his brother's death; how he is avenged keeps this oater taut. Director Anthony Mann has it on his conscience, however, that this movie introduced sadism into the western in 1955, when Alex Nichol deliberately shoots Stewart through the hand. (c)

The Man from the Alamo √ Glenn Ford in strong Budd Boetticher-directed US v. Mexico war drama; 1953. (c)

The Man from the Diners' Club √ Quite a fun picture from Danny Kaye – one of a minority – in which he has all sorts of adventures in chasing a lost credit card that Telly Savalas has pinched. Frank Tashlin directs slickly from a script he co-wrote; 1963. (b/w)

Man Hunt √ Walter Pidgeon stalking Hitler, disappointingly directed by Fritz Lang in 1941. (b/w)

Maniac XX Sloppy Hammer thriller about American artist in France having affair with café-owner, arousing daughter's anger. Meanwhile her husband escapes from an asylum. Unknown actors stayed that way. Michael Carreras churned it out; 1963. (b/w)

The Man in Grey X The only reason this thin historical nonsense ever became popular was because in 1943 it provided a chance to see something elaborate as a relief from austerity Britain – cleavage for one thing (or two). So Leslie Arliss found himself directing a boom picture, and Margaret Lockwood, James Mason, Phyllis Calvert, Stewart Granger became major stars. (b/w)

The Man in the Gray Flannel Suit √ Gregory Peck doing his usual sincere bit in long and not altogether tedious story of life in an American corporation; Fredric March is president of the company whose marriage provides a poor example to Peck. Nunnally Johnson wrote and directed from Sloan Wilson's best-seller in 1956. (c)

The Man in the Iron Mask √ Louis Hayward is incarcerated twin brother of Louis XIV in this 1939 remake of Douglas Fairbanks 1929 classic. James Whale keeps action spinning; with Joseph Schildkraut, Alan Hale and Joan Bennett. Based on supposedly true story (though the mask was velvet) fictionalised by Alexandre Dumas. (b/w)

Man in the Middle √ Keenan Wynn murders a British sergeant in wartime India; Robert Mitchum has the job of defending him, knowing that Anglo-American relations demand he should be found guilty. Guy Hamilton's direction somehow fails to involve the audience, despite strong performances from Trevor Howard and Barry Sullivan and a Waterhouse-and-Hall script; 1964. (b/w)

Man in the Moon X Mildly entertaining satire-that-misses about Kenneth More being sent up to the moon as a kind of working-class guinea pig. Basil Dearden's direction and the Michael Relph-Bryan Forbes screenplay are redolent in gags and attitudes that must have been outdated when it was made in 1961, let alone now. Michael Hordern, Shirley Ann Field, Norman Bird go through familiar motions competently enough and, as usual, Kenneth More delivers beyond the call of duty. (b/w)

The Man in the Net X Alan Ladd looking pretty silly as an artist suspected, for no apparent reason, of killing his wife, hiding out in the woods and exposing the real killer with the help of the local kids; directed by Michael Curtiz without any sign that he believed it either; 1959. (b/w)

The Man in the Sky √ Test pilot Jack Hawkins refusing to leave failing airline company's promising prototype when it catches fire in flight. Elizabeth Sellars is wife who waits, plus Lionel Jeffries, Donald Pleasence. Charles Crichton directs; 1956. (b/w)

The Man in the White Suit √√ Sandy Mackendrick's 1951 comedy wears well, mainly because of Alec Guinness as an inventor who discovers a fabric that doesn't get dirty or wear out. Brilliantly co-written by Roger MacDougall; and supports Joan Greenwood, Ernest Thesiger, Cecil Parker all turn in lovely performances. (b/w)

Man in the Wilderness XX Richard Harris spends most of this dreary adventure limping along in order to revenge himself on John Huston for leaving him for dead; then when he catches up with him, he doesn't. Director Richard C. Sarafian seems to have meant some metaphysical truth to shine out of all this, but that doesn't, either; 1971. (c)

A Man is Ten Feet Tall √ Martin Ritt's first film has strong echoes of *On the Waterfront*, with John Cassavetes as the docker who learns to stand up to bullying boss. Also stars Sidney Poitier; 1957. (b/w)

Man of Aran √√ Robert Flaherty's famous romantic (some say romanticised) look at the people (or rather, the folk) of the Aran Islands, off Ireland, and their age-old fight against the elements. But you can't knock the photography and the trail-blazing; it was made in 1934. (b/w)

The Man of a Thousand Faces X It's Lon Chaney; but don't expect a fascinating montage of his own silent pix. Instead, Joseph Pevney painstakingly re-directed James Cagney in a 1957 mock-up of some of the most famous horror roles. It's all joined together by a routine, unconvincing biography in which Dorothy Malone, Jane Greer and Marjorie Rambeau pluckily string along; the make-up by Bud Westmore's great, though. (b/w)

Man of La Mancha XX Don Quixote as a musical may sound a bizarre undertaking, but it worked well enough on Broadway. Translated for the screen, under Arthur Hiller's direction and miscast with Peter O'Toole, James Coco and Sophia Loren, it proved disastrous in 1972. Most of the action takes place in a prison cell where Cervantes and friends act out the story, instead of on the plains of Spain; 1972. (c)

Man of the West X Sadistic western that wastes Gary Cooper as outlaw trying to go straight but forced to participate in some nasty business. A disappointment from writer Reginald Rose and director Anthony Mann in 1958. (c)

Man on a Swing X Joel Grey stands out in whodunit about a psychic's involvement with murder investigation; Cliff Robertson was the star of this 1975 Frank Perry-directed thriller. (c)

Man on a Tightrope √ Fredric March liberating his circus across the Iron Curtain, including Terry Moore, Gloria Grahame. Adolphe Menjou, a leader of the McCarthy pack in Hollywood, must have been gratified to appear in Elia Kazan's 1953 anti-Red picture. (b/w)

Man on Fire X This 1957 attempt to establish Bing Crosby as non-singing dramatic actor sent him back to singing roles. The sincerity of the main plot (child caught up in divorce tug-of-war) was undermined by such ludicrous sub-stories as lawyer's assistant falling for Bing (relax, she's a girl) and the tritest of dialogue. Ronald Mac-Dougall was responsible for that, as well as the direction. (b/w)

The Man on the Eiffel Tower √ Actor Burgess Meredith turned director in 1949 to guide this exciting story of murder investigation; Charles Laughton, Franchot Tone and Meredith himself stand out. (c)

Man on the Flying Trapeze √√ Classic W. C. Fields comedy from 1935, with his much put-upon persona coping with wife, mother-in-law, policemen, judges, singing burglars. Clyde Bruckman directed. (b/w)

Manpower √ One of those movies they don't make any more about two tough buddies both lusting after the same woman, with action (power lines here) alternating with wisecracks alternating with love-scenes. Raoul Walsh was an expert at them and this 1941 concoction had Edward G. Robinson and George Raft as the dudes, Marlene Dietrich as the dame. (b/w)

Man's Favourite Sport √ Fishing, as if you hadn't guessed. It's all on this level of nudge-nudge vacuity, but Rock Hudson, Paula Prentiss turn in competent comedy jobs under Howard Hawks; 1963. (c)

Man-Trap XX Inept in every department, this is a thriller that just doesn't. The only (not surprising) solo directing attempt by actor Edmond O'Brien also suffers from a ridiculous script, as inexplicable as it is incredible, about a robbery that goes wrong. There isn't much that Jeffrey Hunter, David Janssen and Stella Stevens can do but hang on. Miss Stevens does so with great bravado; 1962. (b/w)

Manuela XX If the crew can accept Elsa Martinelli as a boy when she dresses up to be with Pedro Armendariz, they must all be more short-sighted than you. She falls for Captain Trevor Howard (smashing performance as drink-sodden skipper), but Donald Pleasence, Jack MacGowran, Warren Mitchell still don't catch on. Director Guy Hamilton won't fool you, however, despite documentaryish authenticity of the tramp steamer; 1956. (b/w)

The Man Upstairs √ Successful attempt in 1958 by ACTT, the trade union, to inject some exciting realism into British films. Taut economical script by Alun Falconer, sparely realised by Don Chaffey, who gets fine performances from Richard Atten-borough (as shrinking psychopath), Bernard Lee (as a policeman who thinks), Kenneth Griffith, Alfred Burke. (b/w)

The Man Who Came to Dinner √√ Bravura performance by Monty Woolley as the world's rudest man, forced to stay in small-town household because he breaks his hip. Bette Davis, Reginald Gardner, Billie Burke, Ann Sheridan are further spurs to watching. William Keighley directed this photographed stage play in 1941; thirty years later Orson Welles essayed the role in taped version for American TV (but made in Southampton, England) and came as big a cropper as larger-than-life Sheridan Whiteside. (b/w)

The Man Who Could Cheat Death √ Sci-flick about Dr Anton Diffring, who is 100 years old but doesn't look it – thanks to magical injections and operations. Suddenly, he can't get his fix and comes out of his personal Shangri-La to age fearfully. Old horror alumni Christopher Lee, Hazel Court and director Terence Fisher join in; 1959. (c)

The Man Who Finally Died X Stanley Baker is English innocent jazzman in Germany seeking his dad who was supposed to have been killed during the war. Peter Cushing, Mai Zetterling, Eric Portman, Nigel Green adopt various brands of accents and heaviness as Nazis, neo-Nazis and neo-neo-Nazis, and you won't believe a word of it. Quentin Lawrence directed Lewis Greifer's adaptation of his own TV serial; 1963. (b/w)

The Man Who Knew Too Much √√ Gorgeous 1956 remake by Hitchcock of his own 1934 British masterpiece; the story is altered but the suspense is as taut as ever. James Stewart and Doris Day are dandy as the couple in the middle. Surely that shot at the Albert Hall – to be fired at the clash of a cymbal – can't kill; yet will it, after all? Everything else is so right that you can forgive the sloppy post-synchronisation of Daniel Gelin's lip-movements.(c)

The Man Who Loved Cat Dancing X Maybe the lurid death of Sarah Miles's manager that took place during the filming of this western cast an unshakable pall over it. Whatever the reason, she and Burt Reynolds make a lacklustre kidnapped and kidnapper who, of course, fall for each other. Lee J. Cobb, George Hamilton track along behind. The obscure title refers to an

Indian maid named Cat Dancing who is dead before the picture starts; director, Richard C. Sarafian; 1973. (c)

The Man Who Never Was √ Fooling the Germans as to where the invasion is going to take place by planting phoney papers on a drowned man as Clifton Webb and Stephen Boyd, with Gloria Grahame as an unbelievable tart for relief. Ronald Neame directs with painstaking care from Nigel Balchin script; 1956. (c)

The Man Who Shot Liberty Valance √√ Strong John Ford western with Lee Marvin as the heavy gunman hired by wealthy cattlemen to terrify ranchers. When John Wayne is one of the latter and James Stewart an unintended hero, you know how it will all turn out; 1962. (b/w)

The Man Who Understood Women XX Except that he doesn't. Nor, on this evidence, do scriptwriter-director Nunnally Johnson or Romain Gary, from whose novel *Colours of the Day* it was adapted. How could any man who understood women fail to consummate his marriage to Leslie Caron, unless he was gay? And there's no sign that Henry Fonda is supposed to be. He's a Great Film Director (no proof of actual films here) who hires an assassin to kill his wife's lover on the Riviera and then tries to stop him. Hokum, hokum, hokum; 1959. (c)

The Man Who Wouldn't Talk XXX A really terrible script by Edgar Lustgarten is matched by appalling performances by Anna Neagle (as a clever-clever QC), Zsa-Zsa Gabor (a Russian secret agent) and Anthony Quayle (a scientist who knows how to give humans myxomatosis). Neagle gets Quayle acquitted for not shooting Gabor. Director Herbert Wilcox wouldn't get off so easily; 1958. (b/w)

Man Without a Star √ Kirk Douglas showing off in run-of-the-prairie western, 1955, all nice and easy-going until Jeanne Crain's bullyboys set on him. Claire Trevor is on hand with repeat of her *Stagecoach* golden-hearted whore. King Vidor keeps the action going. (c)

The Man With the Golden Arm √ Slick Otto Preminger drama about drug addiction, with Frank Sinatra OK as the weak monkey who tries to break the habit with the help of Kim Novak; as if this wasn't enough, there's a second plot about a perfect murder which Eleanor Parker couldn't have committed because she's a cripple – or is she? All a bit too much; 1956. (b/w)

The Man With The Golden Gun X 1975 James Bond nonsense, with Roger Moore established in the role of post-Connery agent. The set pieces no longer dazzle, such novelties as a flying car seem tame, the glamorous ladies who want nothing more than a roll in the hay with Our Hero seem out of date. Perhaps director Guy Hamilton was just tired. (c)

The Man With the X-Ray Eyes √√ Roger Corman horror-sci-fictioner about Ray Milland who, in an effort to improve the human eye, injects himself so much with his secret serum that he literally sees through everything, until his inner knowledge drives him mad. There could be a 'profound philosophical commentary' on Life here, but fortunately Corman has chosen to go for the more exciting aspects of the story; 1964. (c)

Many Rivers to Cross X Poor comedy western with Eleanor Parker shrewishly chasing thick Robert Taylor; Victor McLaglen is her Pop. Roy Rowland directed, adequately, in 1954. (c)

Mara Maru XX Errol Flynn as a deepsea diver searching for a rich prize – a cross of diamonds – at the behest of heavy Raymond Burr. He fancies his partner's wife, Ruth Roman. Gordon Douglas did what he could with a weak script in 1952, but the ending is pure bathos. (b/w)

The Marat-Sade √√ Or *The Persecution and Assassination of Jean-Paul Marat as performed by the Inmates of the Asylum of Charenton under the direction of the Marquis de Sade.* The performers have to be separated from the curious visitors by bars. But not from you. They tell their story of the French Revolution. And much about themselves. And the end is chaos. Glenda Jackson, Patrick Magee and the rest of the Royal Shakespeare Company make it come to life. Peter Brook directs. You might need a strong drink in your hand as you watch; 1967. (c)

The Marauders X Little rancher *v.* the big ranchers. Dan Duryea, Jeff Richards, Keenan Wynn. Gerald Mayer directed routinely; 1955. (c)

The March Hare XXX Irish whimsy about a racehorse, directed with utter disbelief by George More O'Ferrall, 1956. It has Terence Morgan as the Irish milord whose fortunes the animal could save by winning the Derby. Among other little people: Cyril Cusack, Martita Hunt, Wilfrid Hyde White. (c)

Marco the Magnificent XXX Hopeless attempt by Denys de la Patellière to retell Marco Polo story comes to grief despite presence of Orson Welles, Anthony Quinn, Horst Buchholtz, Omar Sharif, Elsa Martinelli (actually, looking down that list of hams, maybe it was because of, not despite); 1966. (c)

Mardi Gras XX Routine little behind-the-showbizscenes comedy about starlet involved with military cadets Pat Boone, Tommy Sands, Gary Crosby. Dull stuff, with lifeless direction by Grand Old Man Edmund Goulding, who was obviously taking it easy by 1958, a year before his death – he had been churning 'em out since 1920, with *Grand Hotel* and *The Old Maid* along the way. (c)

Margie √ Premature *Thoroughly Modern Millie* has something of the same period and musical charm. Jeanne Crain is such a nice girl; Henry King; 1946. (c)

Margin for Error X Only in the rarest cases can directors direct themselves convincingly; Otto Preminger proved the disaster rule again in 1943. Milton Berle as Jewish policeman whose job it is to guard the German ambassador before America went into the war just isn't funny now. (b/w)

Marie Antoinette √ Heavyweight historical romantic biopic from MGM, starring studio head Irving Thalberg's wife Norma Shearer. Others in this 1938 powdered-wig epic include Robert Morley (aged 29) playing Louis XVI, Tyrone Power, John Barrymore, Gladys George, Joseph Schildkraut. (b/w)

Marie Walewska X Greta Garbo encouraging Charles Boyer, as Napoleon, for the sake of Poland and the box office in 1937. Usual thirties MGM rep. co. supports: Reginald Owen, Henry Stephenson, Dame May Whitty, under direction of Clarence Brown. (b/w)

Marjorie Morningstar √ Herman Wouk's novel about a stage-struck Jewish girl becomes a weak vehicle for an unbelievable Natalie Wooden with a crush on swinging Gene Kelly; Claire Trevor and Everett Sloane as Yiddisher parents. Astonishing how Jewish film-makers manage to miss the ambience of their own culture so completely – Irving Rapper, you should have known better! 1958. (c)

The Mark √ Simple, intelligent, decent attempt (1961) to show what happens to a man who has served his time for

attack on 10-year-old girl, let down by its own dodgy attitude towards its-persecuted hero. While you're mentally applauding Stuart Whitman, psychiatrist Rod Steiger, director Guy Green, ask yourself what you would feel if he *had* been raving dangerous attacker; would you and the film have as much sympathy then? Yet you should have – making hero not guilty is familiar cop-out in such 'crusading' movies. (b/w)

Mark of the Hawk X Should the blacks resort to force to get their just demands? That's the vital theme of this actioner set in Africa and made in far-off 1958 by Michael Audley, when the answers that were acceptable to white audiences were different from what we have come to recognise as historical inevitability today. Diminished by poor casting of Eartha Kitt, Sidney Poitier. (c)

The Mark of Zorro √ Effective 1940 remake of the 1920 Douglas Fairbanks actioner can't be criticised on anything but its own, highly enjoyable terms, which are strictly comic strip. It's Tyrone Power *v.* Basil Rathbone, folks, and you may find yourself on the side of evil, so compelling is Rathbone and so weak Power. Rouben Mamoulian made sure everybody enjoyed themselves, including you. (b/w)

Marlowe √ At last, in 1969, the movie of Raymond Chandler's *The Little Sister*, given a more contemporary brutal name and brought up to date with some more recent slang. Fortunately, the story is the same, and James Garner doesn't make a bad private eye (or private fuzz, as he's called here). The deceitful ladies are all OK, too; particularly Rita Moreno and Gayle Hunnicutt. Carroll O'Connor is the real law. Paul Bogart directed. (c)

Marnie √√ One of those Hitchcock movies that have gained in reputation since it was first shown (in 1964), this is the one where Sean Connery is attracted to Tippi Hedren in a fetishist sort of way just because she is a thief. He uncovers the secret of why she compulsively steals. Over-simplified, poorly cast (bluntly, Sean Connery comes from the wrong – too low – class as Hitchcock now admits; and Tippi Hedren isn't much of an actress), too glib, it nevertheless grips as only Hitchcock can. (c)

Maroc 7 XX Dull little jewel caper movie with staff of fashion mag. highly unlikely set of thieves. Takes place mostly in Morocco, but Gerry O'Hara doesn't get much mileage out of the location. Gene Barry, Elsa Martinelli, Cyd Charisse have been packaged for the international market, but it still shows at the seams as a very British picture, with Leslie Phillips (also the film's producer), Denholm Elliott, Eric Barker, Angela Douglas moving about rather aimlessly; 1967. (c)

Marooned X Gene Hackman stuck in space, while Gregory Peck masterminds an attempt by David Janssen to save him. As bare of character as the moon's face, this would-be suspenser runs out of rocket fuel around the same time as the astronauts. John Sturges's direction does little to save the situation; 1969. (c)

The Marriage-Go-Round XX Soppy comedy about Julie Newmar proposing to James Mason that he fathers her child, with the consent of wife Susan Hayward. It could have been witty, sly, honest, even devastatingly frank. All it is, is coy. Pity the stars caught up in Walter Lang's hangdog direction and Leslie Stevens's smutty script; 1961. (c)

The Marriage of a Young Stockbroker √ Richard Benjamin in his *Diary of a Mad Housewife* persona, with the added characterisation of being a compulsive voyeur. Unfortunately the women in the cast (Joanna Shimkus, Elizabeth Ashley) are not in the Carrie Snodgress class, and director Lawrence Turman has to settle for threadbare plot-exposition; 1971. (c)

Marriage on the Rocks X Frank Sinatra's daughter Nancy plays his daughter in 1965 marriage-and-divorce mix-up with Deborah Kerr getting split from him, spliced with Dean Martin, but all ending happily. Cesar Romero's caricature of Mexican judge so angered locals that Sinatra was barred from the country. Director Jack Donohue allowed himself to be rather swamped by stars' slap-happy attitude. (c)

The Marrying Kind √ Nice blend of comedy and marital drama directed with panache by George Cukor (particularly in opening Central Park sequence). Judy Holliday gave studio bosses heart failure by appearing before Un-American Activities Committee just before it was released in 1952, but they got her testimony suppressed until the film had made its money, later in the year. (b/w)

The Marseilles Contract XX Curiously lifeless thriller limping after *The French Connection* and countless assassination thrillers, with few of the usual thrills. Michael Caine, Anthony Quinn and James Mason sleepwalk through, under Robert Parrish's 1974 direction. (c)

Marty √√√ Ernest Borgnine rightly won Academy Award for this shy, shambling butcher who finds love with Betsy Blair. Notable for Paddy Chayefsky script written originally for television when American TV still put on single plays. Since 1955, every real-life film has been influenced by it and Delbert Mann's documentary-type direction. Film, script, direction and Borgnine all won Oscars. (b/w)

The Marx Brothers at the Circus √√ The floating bandstand . . . the case at the circus . . . J. Cheever Loophole . . . 'The night I drank champagne from your slipper – two quarts' . . . Edward Buzzell; 1939. (b/w)

The Marx Brothers Go West √√ 'Any of you boys got change of ten cents? Well, keep the baggage' . . . Groucho setting out to swindle the others out of $10 and losing $60 himself . . . the chase for the missing deeds . . . the train chopped up for firewood as it goes along . . . Edward Buzzell; 1940. (b/w)

Maryland √ Fay Bainter closes her stables when her husband is killed by a horse, but lovable old Walter Brennan and keen young John Payne make her change her mind. Charlie Ruggles, Hattie McDaniel, Brenda Joyce play their obvious roles; Henry King directed, spaciously, in 1940. (c)

Mary, Mary √√ Smooth translation of the Jean Kerr stage play to the screen preserves most of the laughs, and veteran Mervyn Le Roy has added some subtle openings-out of the story of the splitting married couple (Debbie Reynolds, Barry Nelson) who come together again over a tax form; 1964. (c)

Mary, Queen of Scots X 1971 retelling by the uninspired director Charles Jarrott of the conflicts between Elizabeth of England (Glenda Jackson) and Mary (Vanessa Redgrave). Lacks visual sense. (c)

M*A*S*H √√ A sort of inspired 'Carry On in Korea', this 1970 original is often brutally and rudely funny. Donald Sutherland and Elliott Gould are memorable as the maverick medics (so much so that one remembers them vividly despite having seen a hundred episodes of the TV copy). Sally

Kellerman and Robert Duvall are equally superior as the baited lovers. Put together by Robert Altman. (c)

The Mask of Dimitrios X Peter Lorre-Sydney Greenstreet vehicle with the little man flash-backing over life of villain Zachary Scott; moodily, mysteriously directed by Jean Negulesco from Eric Ambler novel that now seems creaky and dated; 1944. (b/w)

The Masque of the Red Death √√ Imaginative horror pic by fast-worker Roger Corman, made in England in 1964, has Vincent Price as 12th-century Italian nobleman renouncing God for the Devil, from an Edgar Allan Poe story. Jane Asher, Patrick Magee come off well, and his use of colour is gorgeous and exciting. (c)

Masquerade √√ Spiffing tongue-in-cheek comedy-thriller with Cliff Robertson nicely restrained as he gets involved with secret agent Jack Hawkins, sending himself up delightfully. Spoofs a dozen or more straight thrillers yet emerges as professional and exciting in its own right; as good as anything Basil Dearden and Michael Relph ever produced-directed; 1965. (c)

Massacre XXX Unpleasant little western directed by Louis King, 1956, about illegal supply of guns to Red Indians. Unknown cast deserves to stay that way. (c)

Mastermind √ Not another TV-into-movie, but Zero Mostel in a frantic Japanese-set thriller as Inspector Hoku Ichihara. Director Alex Marsh let it all get out of hand, but it's still enjoyable; 1969. (c)

The Master of Ballantrae √ Errol Flynn in whitewashed version of the Robert Louis Stevenson novel, made in England in 1953 to utilise frozen Warner Brothers' dollars. In the book, he's a scoundrel who fights for the Stuarts and in the end both he and his brother (Anthony Steel, loyal to King George II) die. But not here. This is all happiness after some wild adventures. Director William Keighley was much helped by Jack Cardiff's fine photography. (c)

Master of the Islands X If you relished James A. Michener's novel, *Hawaii*, or the movie of the same name, you might actually look forward to this. The rest of us are in for a slog through more of the saga taken from the same novel. Charlton Heston is the hero; the island takes second place. Director, Tom Gries, 1970. (c)

Master of the World √ Interesting little 1961 sci-fictioner about Vincent Price taking it on himself to destroy the world's armies, adapted from two Jules Verne stories. Unfortunately, director William Witney doesn't realise the possibilities. (c)

Masterson of Kansas X Just one more western involving Doc Holliday, Wyatt Earp and Bat Masterson, churned out by William Castle in 1954. George Montgomery, Nancy Bates go through the standard motions. (c)

Matchless XX Patrick O'Neal has discovered the secret of invisibility and puts it to the service of his country, in this witless spy spoof. Donald Pleasence is around, but so is Ira Furstenberg. Alberto Lattuada directed in Italy (note the atrocious post-synching); 1966. (c)

The Matchmaker √ Why, hello Dolly, fancy seeing you back where you belong – in original 1958 version by Joseph Anthony of Thornton Wilder's play. Just the story without the tiresome songs and dances. Shirley Booth in Barbra Streisand's part. Tony Perkins, Shirley MacLaine. (b/w)

The Mating Game √ How lovable farmer Paul Douglas works exclusively on the barter principle thus screwing up city slicker tax man Tony Randall. Directed by George Marshall in 1959 from H. E. Bates's *The Darling Buds of May*, with nice little parts for Debbie Reynolds, Fred Clark, Una Merkell. But it's all strangely lifeless, probably due to transatlantic transplant. (c)

The Mating of Millie X Evelyn Keyes wants to adopt this child and so Glenn Ford magnanimously says he'll marry her although he's not in love with her. Well, after a while, he realises that . . . but why spoil the obvious plot? Henry Levin expertly works on the tear-ducts; 1948. (b/w)

A Matter of Life and Death X Extravagantly awful 1946 charade about RAF flyer going to heaven, told not as a comedy but as a serious, ludicrous drama; David Niven, Roger Livesey, Raymond Massey ploughed their way through turgid plot under Powell-Pressburger team, who showed occasional moments of insight and imagination. Achieves spurious fame as first film to be selected for Royal Film Performance, an accolade that was soon to become very tarnished as industry jockeyed for this commercial fillip for bad movies. (c & b/w)

A Matter of WHO XX Odd little

comedy-thriller about Terry-Thomas (in a part written for Noel Coward) tracking down where an epidemic started from. Richard Briers is assistant; Honor Blackman, Carol White, and sundry stalwarts of the British supporting actors' guild make brief appearances. But the whole thing smells of a 1961 commercial for the World Health Organisation, and director Don Chaffey never seems happy with his material. (b/w)

The Maverick Queen X Barbara Stanwyck is bandit lady tempted to reform for the sake of undercover detective Barry Sullivan. Joseph Kane lacked the touch to get the most out of script potential; 1956. (c)

Mayerling √ (1) The 1936 French version directed by Anatole Litvak made stars of Danielle Darrieux and Charles Boyer in the rather apocryphal roles of the Austrian Archduke Rudolph and his sweetheart. (b/w)

Mayerling XX (2) The 1968 version had Omar Sharif and Catherine Deneuve monumentally miscast and floppily directed by Terence Young. Ava Gardner and James Mason were equally unhappy. (c)

Maytime in Mayfair XX One of those pathetic Herbert Wilcox-Anna Neagle extravaganzas. She's a Hartnellish dress designer, Michael Wilding the owner of her salon, busy outwitting Peter Graves. Ho-hum-yawn-yawn; 1949. (c)

McCabe and Mrs Miller √√ Although you may find the words difficult to comprehend, this cult success has the strength of Robert Altman's personal film-making, with cross-cut incidents and large numbers of players impressively orchestrated. The central plot – Warren Beatty sets up Julie Christie in a successful brothel but dies as the result of *folie de grandeur* – should be unusual enough to hold you; 1971. (c)

The McConnell Story X Alan Ladd plays jet pilot, June Allyson long-suffering wife; Gordon Douglas did usual plodding directional job; 1955. (c)

The McKenzie Break √ Superior prisoner of war escape yarn, set in Britain for a change, with German troops (split between U-boat and Luftwaffe factions) outwitting Brian Keith, Ian Hendry, Jack Watson; director Lamont Johnson; 1970. (c)

McLintock √ Clan pictures tend to be great fun for the participants but not quite as much for the suckers who sit and watch a gang of old mates fool around for an expensive home movie. This falls into an even clannier type, the family film. John Wayne is the star; Patrick Wayne, his son, has a major part; Alissa Wayne, his daughter, appears; Michael Wayne, another son, produces; Victor McLaglen's son, Andrew, directs; and fellow-actors Maureen O'Hara, Bruce Cabot, Chill Wills, Hank Worden all appear; and the technical credits are nearly all by folk who have worked on many a Wayne pic. So it's not surprising that the end result is plotless, self-indulgent, and quite good fun if you're in the mood. It's one long fight between the hard-drinking Wayne and the divorcing O'Hara in a Western setting; 1963. (c)

The McMasters . . . Tougher than the West Itself! √ Despite the trebly misleading title (there's only one McMasters – Burl Ives; he's not all that tough, getting killed before the end; and it's not in the West), this is an unusual racial drama in which a black Unionist soldier goes back home to farm. The white townsfolk won't work for him, but some Indians do until they see he's no different from a white taskmaster and reject him. Alf Kjellin directed; 1969. (c)

McQ √ No, not Steve McQ but John Wayne, the oldest cowboy hero in the West, come to town as a detective in the modern (1974) *Dirty Harry* tradition. Thrown out of the force for going his own way, Wayne becomes a private eye, and despite being refused his licence by grudge-nursing Eddie Albert, shoots the baddies in the end; John Sturges did his usual lively job of direction. (c)

Me and the Colonel √ Episodic fable of ill-assorted couple's escape from the Nazis – Akim Tamiroff, who learns humility, and Danny Kaye's modest little Jew. Alas, Peter Glenville's static and unimaginative direction crippled what might have been a great film, although he does at least draw a memorable and self-effacing performance from Kaye. From Franz Werfel's *Jacobowsky and the Colonel*; 1958. (b/w)

Mean Streets √√√ Stunning thriller which goes beyond surface excitement to explore character and motives of the young villains in a totally convincing Little Italy, New York. Author-director Martin Scorsese makes you believe in his sub-Mafia hoodlums and girlfriends, and a cast headed by Harvey Keitel and Robert De Niro seem impressively real. Not least of its achievements is to give their religious backgrounds unsentimental importance; 1973. (c)

The Mechanic X Amoral account of various assassinations planned and executed by hired killer Charles Bronson and his pupil Jan Michael Vincent. Michael Winner directs in his usual flashy style, and satisfies the blood lust while pretending to pontificate; 1972. (c)

A Medal for Benny √ Hypocrisy in a small town makes a stronger vehicle than lightweight cast of Dorothy Lamour, Arturo de Corduvo can drive. Director Irving Pichel seems to know it. John Steinbeck scripted; 1945. (b/w)

Medium Cool √√ Interesting, if uneven and self-defeating, excursion into the gap between fiction and fact. Starting from the point that cameramen are insensitive about what they photograph, cameraman-director Haskell Wexler shows his main character (Robert Forster) becoming increasingly involved and ultimately the object of an indifferent cameraman himself. The use of real events (assassinations, the Democratic convention of 1968) mingled with fictitious ones (love affairs, runaways), can cause schizophrenia in the viewer. (c)

Meet Danny Wilson √ Interesting singer-meets-racketeer drama in that many critics in 1951 saw it as thinly-disguised biography of Frank Sinatra who himself played crooner Danny Wilson. Raymond Burr is night-club owner who hounds him and partner Alex Nichol for promised 50 per cent of his earnings, while Shelley Winters is in love with Nichol. Sinatra had some smashing songs – 'You're a Sweetheart', 'She's Funny That Way', 'That Old Black Magic', 'All of Me', 'How Deep is the Ocean' among them – but this was his last singing role before his breakthrough the following year with *From Here to Eternity*, so if this was biopic it only told the first half of the story. Joseph Pevney, alas, kept it strictly in the rut, although Sinatra is always in the groove. (b/w)

Meet Me at Dawn XXX Dreadful rubbish about duelling in turn-of-the-century Paris, made in 1947 in England, 'starring' William Eythe and Hazel Court. Reissued in 1958 under the title *The Gay Duellist*, which they couldn't use today. Thornton Freeland directed. (b/w)

Meet Me in Las Vegas √ Sprightly plug for the gambling centre of America, with Dan Dailey as the luckiest guy around – he's got Cyd Charisse. Roy Rowland made it quite entertaining and there are a lot of walk-ons by famous names, including Frank Sinatra, Lena Horne, Debbie Reynolds, Peter Lorre; 1956. (c)

Meet Me in St Louis √√ Judy Garland was delightful, under the spell of Vincente Minnelli in 1944 (two years before they had Lisa), as one of a well-to-do St. Louis family at the time of the World's Fair there. Pa was Leon Ames, Ma Mary Astor, Tom Drake 'the boy next door'. Other songs include 'The Trolley Song', 'Have Yourself a Merry Little Christmas'. (c)

Meet Me Tonight √ Omnibus of three Noel Coward plays – originally called *Tonight at 8.30* – directed by Anthony Pelissier in 1952. Elegantly acted by Valerie Hobson, Nigel Patrick, with robust performance from Stanley Holloway. (c)

Melody √ Jack Wild, Mark Lester, Tracy Hyde in 1971 comedy of childhood, directed by Waris Hussein. Succumbs to the fatal flaw of feyness halfway through, but isn't too stomach-churning. (c)

The Member of the Wedding √ Julie Harris growing up in the Deep South, from Carson McCullers' book; Fred Zinnemann; 1952. (b/w)

The Men √ Marlon Brando's first picture, 1950, while he was waiting for his stage success, *Streetcar*, to be set up as a movie. He plays ex-soldier adjusting to civilian life after paraplegia, with Teresa Wright encouraging him. Fred Zinnemann built it round him. While the film and his performance got raves, it flopped at the box-office. Teresa Wright, Jack Webb, Everett Sloane. (b/w)

Men Against the Sun XX Creaky drama about building the Mombasa-Uganda railway, with animals as the heavies. John Bentley, Zena Marshall lead a tepid 1953 cast. Director, Brendan J. Stafford. (b/w)

Me, Natalie √ She, Natalie (Patty Duke), is the plainest, orneriest gal who ever did go to high school. All kinds of humiliating things happen to her because she's so ugly. Then she goes off to Greenwich Village and gets laid by handsome hippies who realise that it's what a girl's like inside (or, at least, in bed) that counts. Oh, Hans Christian Andersen, what crimes are committed in the name of your Ugly Duckling! Fred Coe directs without too much false pathos. Martin Balsam, Elsa Lanchester strengthen supporting cast; 1969. (c)

Men in War X Realistic action only distinguishing feature in Anthony Mann's 1957 war toughie about personal conflicts in Korean retreat. Predictably manly performances from Robert Ryan, Aldo Ray. (b/w)

Men of Sherwood Forest XX Poor version of Robin Hood (1954), directed by Val Guest. Don Taylor was Robin, Reginald Beckwith Friar Tuck. It was that kind of film. (c)

Men of the Fighting Lady X Korean War 1954 actioner about an aircraft carrier. Van Johnson, Keenan Wynn, Louis Calhern, Walter Pidgeon. Andrew Marton competently. (c)

The Mercenaries X Jack Cardiff enlists sympathy for men who kill for money. Rod Taylor, Jim Brown lead a mission to 'save' inhabitants of town under rebel attack in the Congo. Drunken doctor Kenneth More and Yvette Mimieux are along on the trip; 1968. (c)

Merrill's Marauders √ Jeff Chandler as real-life general in Burma, drives his men (Ty Hardin, Claude Akins *et al*) for more effort in strong, machismoid Samuel Fuller-directed blood and guts; 1962. (c)

Merry Andrew XX Pretty dire 1958 vehicle for Danny Kaye, running away to join a circus and falling in love with Pier Angeli there. He tries so hard to be charming that it's distinctly embarrassing to see him fall flat on his oily grin. Michael Kidd, his director, appears to have let Kaye get away with anything - unfunny jokes, sickly sentiment, flabby acting. (c)

The Merry Widow √√ (1) 1934: sparkling Ernst Lubitsch version of Lehar's familiar operetta, with Maurice Chevalier and Jeanette MacDonald. Edward Everett Horton and Una Merkel also star. (b/w)

The Merry Widow XX (2) 1952: charmless version by Curtis Bernhardt, with Lana Turner and Fernando Lamas. Even Una Merkel, repeating her earlier role, cannot help this one. (c)

Merton of the Movies X Innocent becomes a Hollywood star; Red Skelton, Virginia O'Brien, Alan Mowbray made it mildly amusing, under

the direction of Robert Alton in 1947. (b/w)

Micky One √√ Fascinating (and unfairly dismissed at the time - 1965) experiment in using the familiar props of the American cinema to tell the story of a man weighed down by contemporary anxieties. Arthur Penn is a commercial director who is never afraid to try something new. He has got a moving and haunting performance from Warren Beatty (and veterans Jeff Corey and Franchot Tone) in the picaresque, anguished adventures of a nightclub comedian who no longer believes in his patter. Instead, he seeks some kind of personal freedom to find that it is no longer possible in the land of the free. The final sequence as he auditions in an enormous dark night club is resonant with loneliness and impotence. One tragedy was that this flawed attempt was made two years before Penn and Beatty made *Bonnie and Clyde* - released afterwards, it would have had ten times the audience and critical attention. (b/w)

Midas Run XX Called *A Run on Gold* when seen (briefly) in British cinemas around 1970, this unbelievable yarn about gold robbery is weighted with watchable players (Fred Astaire, Ralph Richardson, Cesar Romero) going through unwatchable motions and spouting unintelligible dialogue. A clanger from director Alf Kjellin. (c)

Middle of the Night √ Kim Novak as divorced receptionist, still sexually hankering after her ex, and Fredric March as widower, seeking happiness together, but being frustrated by all the possessive people around them. The two leads emphatically aren't Jewish, so despite attempts at authenticity, this remains a phoney - and once you start realising that, the overloaded black-and-white characterisations of Martin Balsam, Albert Dekker, Glenda Farrell start to show, too; 1959. (b/w)

Midnight √√ Delicious thirties comedy (1939 actually) in which Claudette Colbert coquettes her way through Brackett-Wilder script, directed by the under-rated Mitchell Leisen with a touch of genius. She pretends to be countess, John Barrymore abets her, Don Ameche threatens to expose her, Mary Astor, Monty Woolley, Hedda Hopper chip in. (b/w)

Midnight Cowboy √√√ A major film and a major achievement of director John Schlesinger. His portrayal and understanding of the two men in uncaring New York – would-be easy-liver Joe Buck and crippled Ratso – created an urban idyll that was both funny and sad, near-realistic and penetrating. Respectively, Jon Voight and Dustin Hoffman filled the enemies-turned-friends roles perfectly and the final scene in the bus to Florida is genuinely pathetic. 1969 Oscar winner for best picture, best direction, best screenplay (Waldo Salt). (c)

Midnight Lace √ A gaslit melodrama of Doris Day being threatened by a mysterious voice; Rex Harrison as her smooth hubby; Myrna Loy and Herbert Marshall bringing some veteran gloss. Yet director David Miller rarely thrills all the way, and to a British audience the London scene is ludicrous; 1961. (c)

The Midnight Man √ With Roland Kibbee, Burt Lancaster produced, wrote and directed this whodunit in 1974 for himself to star in. He plays the only blameless person around the college where he is a security guard. Double-crossings are routine, and he is continually being surprised by twists you will probably have already figured. (c)

A Midsummer Night's Dream √ (1) In 1935 Warner Brothers threw together Shakespeare, famed stage producer Max Reinhardt (plus William Dieterle to show him how to film), choreographer Nijinska (Nijinsky's sister) and a million dollars of scenery, music and general artiness. Then they chucked it all away with a ha'p'orth of tarred casting – Dick Powell (Lysander), Victor Jory (Oberon), Anita Louise (Titania), Olivia de Havilland (Hermia), Mickey Rooney (Puck), James Cagney (Bottom). Only Joe E. Brown and Hugh Herbert (Flute, Snout) worked. (b/w)

A Midsummer Night's Dream √ (2) In 1969 Peter Hall tried to do the film on a shoestring. Practically no attempt was made at actually creating a film: instead the moderately distinguished actors and actresses (David Warner, Diana Rigg, Helen Mirren, Judi Dench) were pushed along at GCE level with frequent use of close-up to disguise the paltry scenery and effects. (c)

Mighty Joe Young √ The poor gorilla's *King Kong*, Ernest B. Schoedsack; 1949. (b/w)

The Mikado X The only version likely to reach TV is Stuart Burge's 1967 record of the D'Oyly Carte company's 1964 production, filmed on the stage of the Golders Green Hippodrome. OK for fans, but otherwise dull. Earlier, more adventurous versions – Kenny Baker as Nanki-Poo in 1939; *The Cool Mikado* (which Harold Baim made in 1962) – seem to have got lost. (c)

Mildred Pierce √ Joan Crawford won the 1945 Oscar for her heartrending performance as doting mother; Ann Blyth is the bitch of a daughter. Zachary Scott as lover of both. Michael Curtiz directed devotedly. (b/w)

Military Policemen X Only confirmed lovers of either Bob Hope or boxing movies will anticipate this 1953 comedy with pleasure. Mickey Rooney, Marilyn Maxwell scamper around. Original title: *Off Limits*; George Marshall directed. (b/w)

The Millionairess √ Unsatisfactory adaptation of Shaw's play allows Peter Sellers to dominate with his classic Indian doctor. Sophia Loren can't manage the strength and personality of the richest woman in the world who feels miffed by his failure to respond to her. Alastair Sim is content to play Alastair Sim playing her twisted lawyer. Dennis Price is lover soon discarded, and the whole thing is petrified in Shaw's ideas, Wolf Mankowitz's hesitant making-over and Anthony Asquith's theatrical direction; 1960. (b/w)

The Million Pound Note XX Gregory Peck made this attempt to capture the flavour of Mark Twain's fable about man given million pound note in England in 1954. But Ronald Neame couldn't make it more interesting. (c)

The Mind Benders √ Dirk Bogarde sets out to prove that his former colleague wasn't a traitor by undergoing rigorous isolation tests like prolonged floating under water which show that after them a man has no will of his own. The actual tests have a documentary interest, but the story is infuriatingly flabby, and Basil Dearden's direction safe-playing; 1963. (b/w)

The Mind of Mr Soames X Terence Stamp well cast as a mindless vegetable, gradually given back the use of his brain by surgeon Robert Vaughn. Before the doctors can agree how he should be prepared for the world, he escapes. Nothing much happens then, this being a serious work, directed by Alan Cooke, not the Hallowe'en-type shocker it might more entertainingly have been; 1969. (c)

Ministry of Fear √ Combination of Graham Greene novel and director Fritz Lang should have produced more compelling thriller than this rather routine spy plot in London during the war. Ray Milland; 1944. (b/w)

The Miniver Story XX Mrs Miniver dying of cancer, upper-lip fluttering. Sequel to the deadly *Mrs Miniver*, this 1950 effort by H. C. Potter about post-war England was even more embarrassing than the original. Greer Garson, Walter Pidgeon again. (b/w)

Minnesota Clay √ Spaghetti western made (in 1964) before Clint Eastwood turned up. Cameron Mitchell from *High Chaparral* is the gunfighter escaping from prison, determined to clear his name. Director, Sergio Corbucci. (c)

Minnie and Moskowitz √√ John Cassavetes (*Shadows, Faces, Husbands*) made this wry comedy in 1971, and it is very much of its time. A rocky romance between two misfits, it ends in the compromise of him cutting his hair if she'll marry him. On the way, there are some delicious moments, with Gena Rowlands and Seymour Cassel playing the main roles. (c)

The Miracle XX if you can believe that while Carroll Baker has run away from her convent, the statue of the Virgin Mary has stepped down to take her place, you will be able to swallow the rest of this rubbish about the Napoleonic Wars. Roger Moore is the lover she runs away to marry. When she thinks he's dead all kinds of naughty (but sadly unexciting) things happen to her. She is saved by gipsies Walter Slezak and Katina Paxinou, both hamming it up outrageously. Irving Rapper; 1959. (c)

Miracle in Soho XXX One of those really awful British comedy-dramas they still made in 1957 with John Gregson as a road-mender who breaks all the hearts in this never-never land which the film-makers must have known wasn't anything like Soho (they only had to look out of their windows) but which director Julian Aymes has the cheek to try and pass off to us as the real thing. Bet Cyril Cusack, Billie Whitelaw, Ian Bannen don't watch this on the box — they'd be too ashamed. (c)

Miracle in the Rain X It never rains but it bores, wrote one reviewer when this came out in 1956. Jane Wyman, Van Johnson are two lonely people who fall in love in New York. Rudolph Maté sloshes his way through in galoshes; 1956. (b/w)

Miracle of Morgan's Creek √√ *James Agee on Film* contains two long raves for this black farce which the former doyen of criticism saw as 'funnier, more adventurous, more abundant, more intelligent, more encouraging than anything made in Hollywood for years . . . as nihilistic as Céline, as deeply humane as Dickens'. Others may regard it as just an overplayed comedy with Betty Hutton conning Eddie Bracken into marriage after she finds she is pregnant by soldier whose name she can't quite remember. Sure it's tasteless, but what's so great about 'good taste'? Preston Sturges asked in 1943. (b/w)

The Miracle of the Bells XX Frank Sinatra more than faintly ludicrous as priest in this more than loudly ludicrous story of a press agent trying to pressure a film producer to release a movie held up for the unlikely reason that the star has died. Then there's a miracle – or is it? – and Frank Sinatra has the dilemma of whether to let it pass as one or not. Ho hum. Director, Irving Pichel; 1948. (b/w)

Miracle on 34th Street √√ Heart-warming fable about big store Father Christmas (Edmund Gwenn) proving to little girl that he really is Santa Claus. Fascinatingly, that little girl is Natalie Wood, who was to be wife-swapped in *Bob and Carol and Ted and Alice* 22 years later – she was 8 in 1947. Maureen O'Hara played Mum; George Seaton was calculatedly sentimental director. Lovely courtroom climax. (b/w)

The Miracle Worker √√ Oscar-winning performance from Anne Bancroft as teacher to deaf, dumb and blind Helen Keller (Patty Duke). Arthur Penn more than faithfully translated moving, sometimes stunning Broadway play; 1962. (b/w)

Mirage √√ Exciting 1965 thriller with Gregory Peck suffering from amnesia, being chased through New York after the leader of the World Peace Movement is murdered; with George Kennedy and scene-stealer Walter Matthau; fast, action-filled direction by Edward Dmytryk. (b/w)

Miranda √ Glynis Johns as mermaid in successful unsophisticated British comedy directed cheerfully by Ken Annakin; 1948. (b/w)

The Misfits √√ Last film (1961) of both Clark Gable and Marilyn Monroe about rounding up wild horses for pet food. Arthur Miller wrote, John Huston directed, and Montgomery Clift (also since died), Thelma Ritter and Eli Wallach were in it too. Yet it wasn't quite the great film it should have been, due perhaps to some stumbling editing and writing as well as Huston's increasing impatience with his actors. It's hard to watch without melancholy overtaking one; 1961. (b/w)

The Missing Juror √ Budd Boetticher thriller about revenge on jury that found innocent prisoner guilty; Jim Bannon, Janis Carter, George Macready; 1945. (b/w)

Mission Mars XXX Dreadful little bit of cheap nonsense about landing on Mars, with Darren McGavin, Nick Adams; director Nick Webster; 1969. (c)

The Missouri Traveller X Undemanding whimsy about orphan boy and his horse determined to make their way in the world. With Brandon de Wilde, Gary Merrill and Lee Marvin – as the villain, of course, as it's 1958; Jerry Hopper. (c)

Miss Robin Hood XX Well, a near-miss, anyway. Margaret Rutherford saves this flabby yarn about rescuing a secret whisky formula, as she did so many mediocre movies. Her task was even tougher in 1952, as she had to atone for the accumulation of Michael Medwin, Eunice Gayson, Reg Varney, Dora Bryan and Richard Hearne. Director was John Guillermin, before he graduated to Hollywood epics. (b/w)

Miss Sadie Thompson XX Pretty terrible 1954 remake of Maugham's *Rain*, in which Rita Hayworth slinks plumply through the role (played in the past by Gloria Swanson and Joan Crawford) as sinner (here called an 'entertainer'). Jose Ferrer furrows his brow as the fanatical preacher; Aldo Ray is the leader of the pack. Director, Curtis Bernhardt. (c)

Mister Jericho X Con trickery between Patrick MacNee and Herbert Lom in harmless, ungripping thriller, involving the usual fake diamonds. Director, Sidney Hayers; 1969. (c)

Mister Moses X One of those unconsciously insulting adventure stories Hollywood used to turn out about retarded African natives, impressed by white men like Robert Mitchum. Although a diamond smuggler, he proves his heart is in the right place by paternalistically leading villagers to safety from a flood; Carroll Baker and Ian Bannen tag along. Ronald Neame directed; 1965. (c)

Mister Quilp XX Despite a battery of superior British supporting players (David Hemmings, David Warner, Jill Bennett, Ronald Lacey, Bryan Pringle, Brian Glover), this musical adaptation of *The Old Curiosity Shop* is a disaster. Anthony Newley mugs his sticky way through the songs and villainy; Sarah-Jane Varley is unbearably cloying as Nell; Michael Hordern mumbling as her grandfather. Michael Tuchner proves that directors, as well as stars, should stick to what they do well; 1974. (c)

Mister Roberts √√ John Ford and Mervyn Le Roy both had a hand in directing this wildly successful wartime comedy-drama of merchant ship that Henry Fonda longs to take into battle. Fonda had created the title role in the smash-hit Broadway play but producer Leland Hayward decided he had been too long away from the screen (seven years) to do the film version. Despite the traumas, the tight Frank Nugent-Josh Logan script stood up under the strain, and with the help of stalwarts James Cagney (slightly potty captain), William Powell (Doc) and Jack Lemmon (lazy Ensign Pulver – won Oscar for support), the movie steamed home as a wild success; 1955. (c)

Mister Ten Per Cent XXX Poor Charlie Drake vehicle stretched to a long, long film and the little man surrounded by vapid support actors, becomes a great big bore. Peter Graham Scott does his best; 1967. (c)

Mixed Company X Well-meaning but dull comedy about the adoption of three children of various nationalities by basketball coach Joseph Bologna and wife Barbara Harris. Melville Shavelson directed - produced - co-wrote, so the blame is his; 1974. (c)

Mix Me a Person √ A bit of a thriller, with Adam Faith as condemned teenager being proven innocent by his defence counsel – Anne Baxter, imported from America in 1962 to improve the box-office prospects there. Husband Donald Sinden thinks Adam must be guilty because, just like Lee J. Cobb in *Twelve Angry Men*, he hates all teenage toughies. Some good British character actors bravely support Leslie Norman's painstaking attempts, which ultimately make a watchable drama. (b/w)

Moby Dick √ His name is Ahab and he sails again in the mad chase to kill the giant whale. Director John Huston provides some visual excitement but Gregory Peck is sadly miscast. Confused backing from Orson Welles, Leo Genn in 1956. Earlier versions were with John Barrymore (1926 – called *The Sea Beast*) and 1930. *(c)*

Model Shop X French director Jacques Demy and his star Anouk Aimée made a disappointing voyage to Los Angeles for this sequel to *Lola*. While the story of a drafted soldier and a woman of the world just about holds the interest, the details of America never convince, and the people seem all wrong. *(c)*

Modern Times √√ Last sight of the silent Chaplin tramp, in 1936, as he and Paulette Goddard walk off hand in hand into the sunset. Up to then, they have had all sorts of adventures singly and together, including the famous opening sequence in the factory when Charlie gets into the cogs. Goddard is an orphan who gets a job as a cabaret dancer. And there's the scene in the store when he joins his fellow-workers in a party at the expense of the management. Beyond (some would say above, some below) criticism. *(b/w)*

Modesty Blaise √ Joseph Losey directed, in 1966, this violent spoof on violence but ended up by tripping over his own intentions. Worth seeing for fluency of action and creepy performance by Dirk Bogarde, although Monica Vitti looked lost, as though mislaid by Antonioni. Clive Revill comes off best. *(c)*

Mogambo √ Clark Gable re-creates role he pioneered in *Red Dust* with Jean Harlow – this time with Ava Gardner (girlfriend) and Grace Kelly (another man's – Donald Sinden – wife) – as great white hunter at home with wild animals but at a loss with wilder women. John Ford directed; 1953. *(c)*

The Molly Maguires √ Martin Ritt's interesting account of a tough secret society that really did flourish in the coalmines of Pennsylvania during the 1870s. However, the film degenerates into a battle between two dull players, Richard Harris and Sean Connery, with the end rarely in doubt. Nor does the casting of very British supports – Frank Finlay, Samantha Eggar – add verisimilitude; 1969. *(c)*

Moment of Danger X Dull little thriller about Trevor Howard and Dorothy Dandridge chasing Edmund Purdom round Spain to get their share of the proceeds of a robbery. Only the caper at the start carries any of the tautness one expects from Laslo *(The Wild One)* Benedek; 1960. *(b/w)*

Moment to Moment XX Sadly silly yarn about Jean Seberg shooting lover in the South of France – which merely gives him amnesia. When he remembers, will he tell? This 1966 drama from old-timer Mervyn Le Roy takes one look at the New Permissiveness and runs back to the old hokum. *(c)*

Money from Home Strictly for Jerry Lewis-Dean Martin fans is this hotch-potch of horse-racing, gangsters and Arab harems; George Marshall; 1953. *(c)*

The Money Trap X A couple of crooked American cops (aren't they all, one wonders sometimes) get hold of the combination of a doctor's safe and decide to take the vast amount of cash he keeps there. Glenn Ford is out-acted by partner Ricardo Montalban in this duo. Joseph Cotten is the doc. What could have been a taut thriller is allowed to go very slack indeed by director Burt Kennedy; 1966. *(b/w)*

Monkey Business √√ (1) The Marx Brothers's third film, made in 1931. They are stowaways involved with gangsters; Norman Z. McLeod directed the traffic. *(b/w)*

Monkey Business √√ (2) Howard Hawks's 1952 farce about over-rejuvenation has stunning cast of Cary Grant, Marilyn Monroe ('half child, but not the visible half'), Ginger Rogers, Charles Coburn. A chimp steals it, though. *(b/w)*

Monkey on My Back √ Dated (1957) warning about dangers of dope addiction, as evinced by boxer Barney Ross. Cameron Mitchell heads undistinguished cast directed by André de Toth. *(b/w)*

Monsieur Beaucaire √ Bob Hope fans will doubtless find his barber sent on suicide mission in historical France, funny enough. But Valentino was funnier in 1924. George Marshall directed this one in 1946. *(b/w)*

Monsieur Verdoux √ Chaplin's fascinating if muddled attempt in 1947 to warn the world against future wars by portraying a criminal who has the same philosophy as governments, conscienceless because the world has lost its conscience. So he murders wives for profit. Of course, being Chaplin, he has to have a soft, squashy interior and is forever making sentimental gestures.

The martinet quality of the main character perfectly suits his own dapper personality. (b/w)

Montana X Errol Flynn played his true nationality, Australian, in this poor little story of sheep-herder invading American West. Alexis Smith is first attracted to him, then against him when she learns he opposes her cattle-ranching, then they all get together; directed by Ray Enright in 1949. (c)

Monte Carlo or Bust √√ Villainous Terry-Thomas (it suits him better than his usual vapid silly ass part), helped by blackmailed assistant Eric Sykes, challenges Tony Curtis to a side-bet in a twenties Monte Carlo Rally race. Other contestants include Peter Cook and Dudley Moore, also better cast than usual as another master-servant team. There's a host of international stars whizzing to Monte Carlo from all over Europe (Bourvil, Walter Chiari, Susan Hampshire, Jack Hawkins, Hattie Jacques, Richard Wattis) and the whole 1969 comedy really is great fun. Ken Annakin. (c)

The Monte Carlo Story XXX A real stinker, with Marlene Dietrich and Vittorio de Sica as two poor noble persons who are gambling mad. It's hard to feel much sympathy for their supposed poverty on their yachts or for the American father and daughter they consider marrying for money. Samuel A. Taylor couldn't even arrange to photograph Miss Dietrich without revealing her true age – 55 in 1957. (c)

Monte Walsh √ A sad western about ageing cowboys (Lee Marvin, Jack Palance) playing with domesticity (Jeanne Moreau) but ultimately caught up in a vendetta. Some attempt is made by director William A. Fraker to defuse the mythology and present a realistic picture of the dying West, but he is defeated by the genre; 1970. (c)

Monty Python and the Holy Grail √√ Too many jokes may seem an unfair complaint, but when one is bombarded with frantic fun before the credits, during the credits, after the credits and on and on, the smile on one's face tends to become a bit fixed. Nevertheless, those who miss *Monty Python's Flying Circus* will enjoy King Arthur's knights undergoing trials and seeking the inaccessible. Terry Gilliam and Terry Jones took turns at directing in 1974. (c)

The Moon and Sixpence √√ George Sanders as Gauguinesque painter in adaptation of Maugham novel, with Herbert Marshall rather unnervingly popping in as the author. Albert Lewin wrote and directed in 1942 debut. (b/w)

Moonfleet √ Stewart Granger swashing many a buckle (or should it be buckling a swash?) on his pirate's progress, George Sanders and Viveca Lindfors co-starring. Worth a look for the fact that it was made in 1955 by Fritz Lang. (c)

The Moon is Blue √ There was a great censorship kerfuffle over Otto Preminger's transfer of F. Hugh Herbert's stage comedy, in 1953. He insisted on keeping hitherto taboo words like 'virgin' and 'seduction' in the script about misunderstanding over Maggie McNamara between David Niven and William Holden. All very naughty-sounding but actually pathetically mild. (b/w)

The Moonraker XX It's George Baker, who helps King Charles escape the Roundheads in this old-fashioned, creaky yarn about Cavaliers in the right and Marius Goring in the wrong; pretty tiresome stuff, unimaginatively directed by David Macdonald in 1958. (c)

Moonrise XX Dane Clark accidently kills a man, runs; Ethel Barrymore, Lloyd Bridges do a little to help a dull one from director Frank Borzage; 1948. (b/w)

Moonrunners XX Poor little backwoods drama about illicit liquor stills. The genre had become boring and debased by 1974; James Mitchum glumly walks through the part of stud blowing up rivals' stills under Guy Waldron's uninspired and (judging by sound quality and some nasty continuity) incompetent direction. (c)

The Moonshine War X Hillbillies in the aftermath of Prohibition fight it out for possession of illicit stills and 150 gallons of whisky. Patrick McGoohan, Richard Widmark and gang try to terrorise Alan Alda. Director Richard Quine ruins some prospectively fine sequences with sub-*Bonnie and Clyde* music and cutting; 1970. (c)

Moon Zero Two XX Hammer and Roy Ward Baker went into orbit in 1969 with this space cowboy-type thriller, but didn't manage much of a job. The moon has been colonised in 2021, but humans still have human greeds. Warren Mitchell is chief heavy, stealing a sapphire asteroid; Catherina von Schell is looking for her brother;

James Olson promises to help her. Come in *Moon Zero Two*, your time is up. (c)

More Dead Than Alive X Pretentious western, with Clint Walker as a sideshow gunfighter, recently released from jail, hunted for revenge by two separate killers. Vincent Price contributes a welcome study of a showman; director, Robert Sparr; 1968. (c)

The More the Merrier √ Jovial comedy of Jean Arthur platonically sharing apartment with Joel McCrea and Charles Coburn, which was awfully ooh-la-la in 1943 (and even in 1966 when it was remade as *Walk Don't Run*) but is accepted as part of life among today's young people. Still, George Stevens squeezed some fun out of it then. (b/w)

Morgan — A Suitable Case for Treatment √ One of the more bitter disappointments of the sixties (1966 to be precise). With the starting-point of a David Mercer television play, Karel Reisz cooked up an extravagant, would-be meaningful soufflé that failed to rise. David Warner plays an artist-in-revolt, whose ideas and antics still attract his ex-wife, although she is remarrying. Most famous moment is when David Warner, dressed in a gorilla suit, breaks up Vanessa Redgrave's wedding to Robert Stephens. Looking back, it's depressing to see how all that really works is the farce (with Irene Handl and Bernard Bresslaw carrying on the best of that). Its political ideas seem as dated as the Aldermaston Marches – which doesn't make them any less valid, only lessens their impact, never very great in the context of such a jazzily shot-and-cut crazy comedy. (b/w)

Morgan the Pirate XX Steve Reeves the pirate is bought by Valerie Lagrange as a slave in Panama. Does he escape and win her love? Need you ask? André de Toth directed in 1960. (c)

Mosquito Squadron X RAF bomber squadron on dangerous mission over France. Can they discover V3 installation without killing PoWs? David McCallum's leader, under Boris Sagal's 1970 direction. (c)

The Most Dangerous Man in the World √√ . . . is Gregory Peck, an American scientist allowed to work with the Red Chinese because they have discovered new formula that the State Department wants. The CIA fits his brain up with a transmitter (via satellite) and, without his knowing, a little bomb to blow him up if they want to. This makes for an exciting picture, which J. Lee Thompson saves from falling into a waiting standard sci-fi rut. As a military bigwig, Arthur Hill has the best lines and takes advantage of it. Chairman Mao is played convincingly by Conrad Yama; 1969. (c)

Moulin Rouge √ Jose Ferrer kneeling and hobbling about as Toulouse-Lautrec in John Huston's 1952 drama-with-music that worked better than most Great Artist biopics partly because he wasn't such a serious painter that he demanded a po-faced treatment. Unsympathetic cast (Zsa Zsa Gabor, Christopher Lee, Ferrer) weakens the effect. (c)

The Mountain √ Spencer Tracy and Robert Wagner talk too much as they climb to a crashed airliner, but there are plenty of thrills. Claire Trevor, William Demarest, E. G. Marshall are strong supports. Edward Dmytryk directed in 1956. (c)

The Mountain Road √ War film (set in 1944, made 1960) about James Stewart blowing up bridges and sundry other bits of road to stop Japanese advance and failing to understand or tolerate Chinese refugees who get in his way. Script by Alfred Hayes from Theodore White novel tries hard to make it into portrait of a man whose power goes to his head, but is defeated by director Daniel Mann's apparent desire to turn in conventional war-pic. (b/w)

Mourning Becomes Electra √ Rosalind Russell, Michael Redgrave, Raymond Massey, Katina Paxinou fit uneasily as co-stars in inevitably talky version of Eugene O'Neill's making over of the Agamemnon myth, avenging death of father. Dudley Nichols; 1947. (b/w)

The Mouse on the Moon √ Follow-up to *The Mouse That Roared* was also the last in the series – understandably. Dick Lester used the idea of a satire on the space race to indulge his penchant for tricks, and fine actors like Margaret Rutherford, Terry-Thomas, June Ritchie, John Le Mesurier got smothered in slick whimsy. Some nice moments between the longueurs, however; 1963. (c)

The Mouse That Roared √ The film that put Peter Sellers on the international map in 1958. Jack Arnold economically directed Roger Mac-Dougall's script of a tiny kingdom that declared war on the US and won by mistake. He saved money by casting Sellers in three roles, including one that Margaret Rutherford adopted in the sequel – see previous entry. (c)

Move Over Darling √ There's something about Doris Day that makes her ideal TV (particularly in colour). Maybe it's the frothiness evident here, as wife returned from dead, confronting newly remarried husband James Garner. Michael Gordon directed this jolly 1963 remake of 1940s *My Favourite Wife*. (c)

The Moving Target √√ Paul Newman convincingly inhabits role of hip Harper, private eye low on funds but high on principle in this William Goldman-scripted version of Ross Macdonald novel that Jack Smight excitingly directed in 1966. Co-stars Lauren Bacall, Bogart's widow. Millionaire-hunt illuminates a world as cold and flashy as neon. This thriller had a huge success and turned Newman into a blockbusting superstar, after 22 films. Others in this 'constant-jeopardy' plot about a kidnap were Robert Wagner, Julie Harris, Janet Leigh (as the wife), Shelley Winters, Robert Webber. (c)

Mr Blandings Builds His Dream House √√ Cary Grant, Myrna Loy and Melvyn Douglas as townies who get taken for a ride when they decide to build a house in the country; H. C. Potter directed stylishly; 1948. (b/w)

Mr Denning Drives North X Tepid British thriller: John Mills mistakenly attempts to buy off the crook who is having affair with his daughter. Phyllis Calvert, Sam Wanamaker, Herbert Lom go through the motions under Anthony Kimmins's stiff direction; 1951. (b/w)

Mr Forbush and the Penguins XX Al Viola made a film from Graham Billing's novel about the terrors of Antarctica, but the producers evidently didn't think it worked. So they got Roy Boulting to shoot another film, with his wife Hayley Mills, featuring Forbush (John Hurt) in London. The result is a right mess; 1971. (c)

Mr Majestyk X The limitations of director Richard Fleischer and dour star Charles Bronson ensure that this hunter-hunted thriller fails to realise its potential. Nominally about a fruit-grower caught in the crossfire of union politics, it avoids social comment and settles for chasing around after – and from – Bronson; 1974. (c)

Mr Ricco √ Praiseworthy attempt to make a thriller that puts black criminals in perspective, foiled by Dean Martin's nonchalance. Director Paul Bogart works hard to give some depth to his characters, and succeeds with harrassed police chief Eugene Roche; 1975. (c)

Mr Sardonicus XX Disappointing horror movie from William Castle about an 18th-century count whose face is set in a horrible grin so he has to wear a mask and have Awful Goings-On in the cellar. Oscar Homolka can't save it; 1962. (b/w)

Mr Skeffington √ And the moral of this soap opera, says Agee, is 'hang on to your husband . . . and count yourself blessed if like Claude Rains in his old age, he is blinded'. Up till then, Bette Davis has been playing one of the biggest bitches in her gallery of bitches, and if you'd enjoy seeing about two hours of her bitchery – and you will, you will – settle down to a good sob (or laugh). Vincent Sherman loyally directed; 1944. (b/w)

Mr Topaze XX Peter Sellers made the mistake of directing himself as simple schoolteacher turned swindler in this unfunny 1961 version of Marcel Pagnol's *Topaze*. (c)

Mrs Brown, You've Got a Lovely Daughter XXX Dreadful little pop film with Peter Noone and Herman's Hermits and Stanley Holloway and some greyhounds and Mona Washbourne and Avis Bunnage and Lance Percival and some dreary music and just about every predictable situation that will flash through your mind as the opening titles drown you. 1968 seems awfully late for this sort of nothing, and the fact that it's produced by Allen Klein should give somebody some uneasy nights. The director is called Saul Swimmer. (c)

Mrs Gibbons' Boys XX Knockabout comedy wrong-headedly adapted for British cast from an American play. Max Varnel misses most of his opportunities, both as director and writer, and Kathleen Harrison is too one-note as Mrs G. Compensations are Lionel Jeffries, Diana Dors, John Le Mesurier, Dick Emery; 1962. (b/w)

Mrs Miniver √ Greer Garson smilin' thru the blitz, Dunkirk and various other wartime traumas, keeping her and her family's upper lips stiff. The fact that they were in Hollywood at the time may have had something to do with the film's glassy unreality. This

1942 weepie, which many Englishmen found nauseating and patronising, won six Oscars (film, actress, female support – Teresa Wright, director – William Wyler, script, photography) and when Greer Garson made her acceptance speech she meandered on for half an hour, much to the embarrassment of the Motion Picture Academy, and thus forcing a subsequent change of routine. (b/w)

Mrs Parkington X Greer Garson and Walter Pidgeon together again two years after *Mrs Miniver*, with her as thrusting society lady when Edward Arnold, Agnes Moorehead, Gladys Cooper outshining the principals. Tay Garnett was tough director; 1944. (b/w)

Mrs Pollifax – Spy X Weary farrago of espionage, with Rosalind Russell showing just how spunky a middle-aged American lady can be. Just one more variation on a theme already overtired by 1970; director, Leslie Martinson. (c)

The Mudlark √ How Queen Victoria emerged from mourning after an urchin wangled his way into the Palace. Oh yeah? Irene Dunne plays the grand dame, Andrew Ray the tiddler. Director Jean Negulesco guaranteed that it was more Hollywood than Osborne. Alec Guinness makes Disraeli dominate; 1950. (b/w)

The Mummy √ (1) The daddy of the Egyptology scaries, with Boris Karloff as the buried-alive priest Im-ho-tep who, aeons later, seeks a princess's reincarnation. Karl Freund, who photographed *Dracula*, directed this one in 1932 and achieved shock-eschewing mood piece. (The early forties saw three sequels with Lon Chaney Jr – *The Mummy's Tomb, Ghost* and *Curse*.) (b/w)

The Mummy √ (2) 1959 Hammer remake with Christopher Lee in Victorian setting. Peter Cushing was the Egyptologist in this rather Freudian version by Terence Fisher, with tongue-pulling for castration and gun-blasts for breasts in the shrouded ghost. (c)

The Mummy's Shroud X Hammer sequel in 1966 by John Gilling, to their remake of *The Mummy*. This time André Morell is nosey scientist who gets murdered for his inquisitiveness. (c)

Murder Ahoy X Fourth Miss Marple comedy-thriller with Margaret Rutherford enjoying herself hugely as Agatha Christie's detective, this time in an original story but still directed, rather haphazardly, by George Pollock. Lionel Jeffries plays the skipper of a training ship where most of the murders and action take place; 1965. (b/w)

Murder at the Gallop X Margaret Rutherford as Miss Marple blithely ignores the awfulness of all around her as she rides through this cursory whodunit, cheerfully directed in 1963 by George Pollock, from an Agatha Christie yarn, *After the Funeral*. Robert Morley's presence ensures a few extra laughs. (b/w)

Murder by Contract √ Interesting low-budgeter about professional killer Vince Edwards who meets woman assigned as his next victim and is suddenly faced with the question of morality. It doesn't shirk from pointing out that what is appalling in our society is perfectly acceptable for soldiers, and Irving Lerner steers a tight directorial course between plain thrills and philosophical reasoning; 1960. (b/w)

Murderers' Row X As Matt Helm, special agent, matched against I-shall-destroy-the-world Karl Malden, insouciant Dean Martin glides his way inconsequently through a series of Saintly predicaments, tricked out with gimmicks like a delayed-action gun. Unfortunately, Henry Levin's direction is similarly slow-moving. Strictly for addicts of mid-Atlantic shooting-wall-paper; 1966. (c)

Murder Incorporated √ 1960 saw an interesting attempt to make a more-or-less truthful account of the gang that could be hired to kill anyone for money. But directors Burt Balaban and Stuart Rosenberg didn't make it taut enough and let Peter Falk go over the top in his portrayal of a sadistic killer; Stuart Whitman and May Britt were the couple scared out of their wits, rather more than you are likely to be; 1960. (b/w)

The Murder Men X Confused jazz movie about dope fiends. Poor Dorothy Dandridge may get hooked again because club owner James Coburn is pushing the stuff. Director John Peyser unclear if he's for the police or against bad laws or both or neither; 1963. (b/w)

Murder Most Foul X Cosy Miss Marple mystery (third with Margaret Rutherford, made in 1964) about crime in a rep. From Agatha Christie's whodunit,

Mrs McGinty's Dead. Andrew Cruickshank, James Bolam, Terry Scott among TV names present. Directed again by George Pollock. (*b/w*)

Murder on the Orient Express √√√ Hugely enjoyable Agatha Christie whodunit, directed by Sidney Lumet in 1974 with a dazzling cast: Albert Finney (as Poirot), Lauren Bacall, Martin Balsam, Ingrid Bergman, Jacqueline Bisset, Sean Connery, John Gielgud, Wendy Hiller, Anthony Perkins, Vanessa Redgrave, Rachel Roberts, Richard Widmark, Michael York, Colin Blakely, George Coulouris, Denis Quilley. (*c*)

Murder She Said √ Nice little adaptation of Agatha Christie whodunit, *4.50 to Paddington*, in which Miss Marple spots a murder in a passing train. Margaret Rutherford is splendid, of course, though nobody else is allowed to come near her by the simple and economical expedient of casting most of the rest of the parts with third-rate actors and actresses. Or perhaps director George Pollock thought they were OK – it would fit in with his idea of how to direct a thriller; 1961. (*b/w*)

Murders in the Rue Morgue √ (1) 1932. Bela Lugosi mixes the blood of his tame King Kong with that of a young girl. But the ape, Eric, falls in love with Sidney Fox. Hey, relax, Sidney's a girl's name in this case. Director, Robert Florey. (*b/w*)

Murders in the Rue Morgue √ (2) 1971. Reworking of Poe's story to give Jason Robards the part of an actor-manager, in conflict with Herbert Lom, who has the power to return from the dead. Christine Kaufman is the girl everything happens to; Lilli Palmer is a vitriol-thrower, Michael Dunn successfully exploits his small size again; director, Gordon Hessler. (*c*)

Murphy's War √ Peter O'Toole obsessed with single-handedly pursuing a U-boat along the coast and up the rivers of Venezuela in an old seaplane, even past the armistice. Peter Yates makes it all quite exciting, but one never cares nearly as much as the character; 1971. (*c*)

The Music Lovers XX . . . among whom director Ken Russell is not counted, judging by the travesty he has perpetrated on the character of Tchaikovsky, and, even more reprehensible, on his music. Although there is no proof that the composer was ever a practising homosexual, Richard Chamberlain has been provided with a partner in the shape of Christopher Gable; the literacy of his wife (Glenda Jackson) has been improved on; the nuances of his extraordinary relationship with his sponsor, Madame von Meck, have not been exploited. As for the symbolism, it is just vulgar; 1970. (*c*)

The Music Man √√ Rousing 1962 transfer by Morton da Costa from stage-hit, keeping Robert Preston's cocksure performance as boys' band organiser intact. Straightforward, jolly tunes, undemanding Shirley Jones, Buddy Hackett. (*c*)

Mutiny on the Bounty √√ (1) Heroic Fletcher Christian (Clark Gable) *v.* arch-villain Captain Bligh (Charles Laughton) in classic sea-story filmed in 1935 and unsurpassed since; Frank Lloyd directed; won Oscar as best film. (*b/w*)

Mutiny on the Bounty X (2) 1962 version failed to establish anything like the same relationship between Christian (Marlon Brando with a ludicrous accent) and Bligh (Trevor Howard). Director Lewis Milestone makes the voyage out more exciting, but comes to grief with Tahiti and the subsequent mutiny. Pity. (*c*)

Mutiny on the Buses XXX Another terrible inflation of a TV episode to cinema size, which gains nothing at being deflated again to the small screen. Director Harry Booth hopes for some laughs from vulgarity and stupidity. That laughter-track from the studio claque is badly missed; 1972. (*c*)

My Blood Runs Cold √ Jolly piece of teenage hokum about a nutty boy (Troy Donahue) who pretends – or is it so? – that he and Joey Heatherton (sorry, she's a girl – it's not that kind of liberated movie) had been lovers in a previous incarnation. There's a murder and a storm at sea and it's all directed neatly enough by William Conrad, the fat detective in TV's *Cannon*; 1965. (*b/w*)

My Cousin Rachel √ A did-she-do-it? mystery plot from Daphne du Maurier novel, directed by Henry Koster. Olivia de Havilland is question-mark; 1953. (*b/w*)

My Darling Clementine √ Climaxing in the great gunfight at the OK corral, this John Ford western is considered by many critics as the greatest ever made. Ford actually knew Wyatt Earp, and it's his story (he's Henry Fonda) and the complex relationship with Doc Holliday (Victor Mature) that got lost in the TV series; 1946. (*b/w*)

My Fair Lady √ √ Elegant, charming, beautiful (Cecil Beaton), firmly-acted (Rex Harrison, Audrey Hepburn) musical version of *Pygmalion*, with impeccable Lerner-Loewe music. A good quiz question would be whose voice is on the soundtrack when Audrey Hepburn sings? The answer: her own for the lower notes, with veteran dubber Marni Nixon for the high ones, thanks to the miracles of the sound engineers; director, George Cukor; 1964. (*c*)

My Geisha XX If, by any remote chance, you can't have too much of Shirley MacLaine, this is the movie for you. She plays an American film star, a geisha girl, Madame Butterfly, and is up there all the time yak-yakking away, supposedly proving to her husband, the film director, she's the girl to play the part. Edward G. Robinson, Yves Montand, Robert Cummings only get a look in, which may be less than you want. Jack Cardiff; 1962. (*c*)

My Lover, My Son XXX Steamy sex-exploitation movie made in swinging '69 which embarrassingly popped up on TV in 1978 and doubtless will again. Romy Schneider fantasises about bed with teenage (actually 21) son Dennis Waterman; husband Donald Houston doesn't like it; a murder ensues. Director, John Newlands. (*c*)

My Man Godfrey √ Competent 1957 remake of the 1936 wacky comedy about butler-and-rich-mistress comes off extremely well, thanks to David Niven's cool and dry performance in the shoes of William Powell. June Allyson is OK as the girl, Jessie Royce Landis brightly *grande dame* as a society hostess. Henry Koster has wisely not tried to improve on the original, and provides a comfortable entertainment. (*c*)

My Old Man's Place √ Three soldiers return from Vietnam to hole up in a broken-down farm. There they reveal how the war has brutalised them. Some strong scenes that may have to be snipped for TV are unnecessary, and director Edwin Sherin seems happier with gore than enlightenment. Arthur Kennedy as the old farmer is the only known face; 1971. (*c*)

Myra Breckinridge XXX From Gore Vidal's witty and evocative Hollywood sex-change novel, director Michael Sarne fashioned a pathetically amateur and hopeless melange in 1970. The casting of Raquel Welch in a role that was widely sought after by some excellent actors and actresses is just the first disaster. Only Mae West provides a reason for watching. Everything else is dross. (*c*)

My Sister Eileen √ (1) Fun in wacky Greenwich Village comedy. Rosalind Russell, Janet Blair are country mice who conquer New York, under Alexander Hall's fatherly direction; 1942. (*b/w*)

My Sister Eileen √ (2) Janet Leigh, Betty Garrett are rather put in the shade by exuberant Jack Lemmon in Richard Quine's musical adaptation; 1955. (*c*)

My Six Loves XX If Debbie Reynolds adopting six children and a dog is your idea of yummy entertainment, you'll have a lovely sentimental time over this one, directed by dancer Gower Champion; Cliff Robertson is oddly-cast Rev. It was cut by twenty minutes when shown here in the cinema – putting it back might make some of the plot references understandable, but would increase the tedium; 1963. (*c*)

Mysterious Island X Rather pointless sci-fi with giant crabs and erupting volcano on Pacific isle from a Jules Verne fantasy. Cy Endfield does his best with what is really only a vehicle for some special effects. A largely inferior cast of British stock actors stumble through it; 1962. (*c*)

Mystery Submarine XX Old-fashioned war film about sending back captured German U-boat with British crew to decoy the rest of the Nazi fleet never really surfaces. Edward Judd is fine as the jut-jawed captain; James Robertson Justice behaves as if he has wandered in from playing his usual straight role in a *Carry On* movie. Director, C. M. Pennington-Richards; 1963. (*b/w*)

My Teenage Daughter XXX Prudish prune of a film made in 1956 by Herbert Wilcox to give wifey Anna Neagle a chance to show off some nice clothes and her pained expressions as teenager Sylvia Syms slips out to the jazz club. (*b/w*)

My Wife's Family XXX A mother-in-law comedy with Ted Ray. If that doesn't put you off try the rest of the cast: Ronald Shiner, Robertson Hare, Greta Gynt. Gilbert Gunn wrote-directed; 1956. (*c*)

N

The Naked and the Dead √ Norman Mailer's war novel could have made a great film, with its raw language, clearly-defined character and action scenes; alas, old-timer Raoul Walsh couldn't quite rise to the occasion as director in 1958, but worth looking at for Raymond Massey; Aldo Ray, Cliff Robertson are other leading soldiers. (c)

The Naked City √√ Jules Dassin's location-shot thriller with police searching real New York for girl's killer. Gave birth to superior TV film series. This original had Barry Fitzgerald, Howard Duff; 1948. (b/w)

Naked Earth XX Turgid turn-of-the-century tale of Irish farmer Richard Todd and French wife Juliette Greco trying to make a go of things in Africa. Mis-directed by Vincent Sherman; 1958. (b/w)

The Naked Edge XX Gary Cooper's 92nd and last picture, made in Britain in 1961, and it looks as though nobody knew whether or not he was a murderer – neither screen wife Deborah Kerr, him, nor director Michael Anderson. Eric Portman is loony ex-barrister, Hermione Gingold and Peter Cushing add characterisations, but the plot is so full of hitches and cock-ups that it's one big yawn. (b/w)

The Naked Jungle √ The humans (Eleanor Parker, Charlton Heston) fortunately matter less than the red ants that surround them, threatening horrible death in the Brazilian jungle, and have been treated somewhat cursorily by Byron Haskin. You'll never look at an anthill in the same way again; 1954. (c)

The Naked Maja XX Trivialisation of the life of Goya (Anthony Franciosa), concentrating on his relationship with the Duchess of Alba (Ava Gardner), cheaply directed (not necessarily inexpensively) by Henry Koster; 1959. (c)

The Naked Prey √√ Interesting attempt to make a chase film with significance directed, produced and starring Cornel Wilde, still trying in 1966 to live down the memory of his Chopin in *A Song to Remember* (who could forget it?). Here, he puts himself in the place of a white hunter captured in 1840 by hostile African tribesmen who give him the 'chance' of being hunted like the 'animals' he was butchering. How he runs from the ten tribesmen after him – across jungle and scrubland – is given Significance by intercuts with the animals. In addition, the 'savages' are not shown as such automatons as the movies usually make them, which alone gives one reason to cheer. And there are others. (c)

The Naked Runner √ Not the most exciting spy story ever made, but British-shot thriller does have Frank Sinatra, Peter Vaughan, Edward Fox; Sidney Furie directs flashily enough to cover the many holes, like how Sinatra happens to have his gun with him on this trip to eastern Europe and how the Secret Service managed to get the patsy to fall in with its plans. As one critic said at the time, if Frank Sinatra took as much care over his movie material as he did over his music we'd have some better pictures; 1967. (c)

The Naked Spur √ James Stewart, Janet Leigh, Robert Ryan in location-shot thriller of group tracking down price-on-head outlaw. Superior direction by Anthony Mann makes them all come alive as characters; 1953. (c)

The Naked Truth √ Dennis Price takes honours as blackmailing publisher in Mario Zampi's 1956 broad comedy, despite Peter Sellers' superbly creepy TV personality and Peggy Mount's bluff novelist. (b/w)

The Nanny √ Is the trusted old nanny a murderess or is it all the malicious imagination of the little boy? As you wait to find out, you have plenty of time to admire Bette Davis, senior citizen among superstars, losing none of her power in 1965. Unfortunately, Seth Holt couldn't do much with Jimmy Sangster's Hammer script which has Jill Bennett screaming on the floor, children dying in the bath and sundry other horrors. (b/w)

The Narrow Margin √ Marie Windsor as widow of murdered gangster menaced on a train as she goes from Chicago to Los Angeles to testify; Richard Fleischer made it all quite exciting in 1952. (b/w)

Nashville √√√ Absorbing panorama of the Country'n'Western town and its interesting inhabitants, wonderfully orchestrated by producer-director Robert Altman. If Lily Tomlin steals the acting honours as a gospel-singing adultress, almost all the huge cast (outstandingly Ned Beatty, Karen Black, Shelley Duvall, Allen Garfield, Henry Gibson, Keenan Wynn) perform convincingly and memorably. Only Geraldine Chaplin as an unbelievable English radio reporter and Keith Carradine as a self-regarding singer jar. But everyone will have his own favourites and aversions; 1975. (c)

The National Health √√ Imagine *Carry On* done with sensibility, compassion and intelligence, and you will get some idea of this funny and clever satire on the usual hospital soap opera, beautifully realised by director Jack Gold in 1973, from Peter Nichols's play. Lynn Redgrave, Sheila Scott-Wilkinson, Donald Sinden and Jim Dale stand out. (c)

National Velvet √√ One of Elizabeth Taylor's best performances was in this 1944 yarn about 12-year-old girl training for Grand National. Despite flaws (e.g. training routine, the race itself), it grips, and Mickey Rooney's surprising performance complements hers. It was Anne Revere's mother that won an Academy Award, though, and Donald Crisp, Angela Lansbury respond almost as well as the horse to Clarence Brown's direction. (c)

Navajo Run √√ Remarkable sleeper produced, directed and starred in by one Johnny Seven, who plays a half-breed Navajo who is bitten by a snake and forces his way into a hostile home of three internecine fighters who help him only grudgingly. The interplay is tautly brought out, and holds you tight; 1966. (b/w)

The Navy Lark √ Pleasant 1959 comedy from the radio series, better than most *Carry Ons*, about Cecil Parker, Ronald Shiner, Leslie Phillips & Co. trying to keep the cushy number they have on an island near Portsmouth; Sid Colin and Laurie Wyman's script involves them in all sorts of risible subterfuges, and Gordon Parry directs good-heartedly. (b/w)

Nearly a Nasty Accident XX Routine British comedy with Jimmy Edwards, Kenneth Connor, Shirley Eaton, Richard Wattis, Eric Barker about mechanic who messes up everything and everybody in the aircraft industry. Patronising. Don Chaffey; 1961. (b/w)

Ned Kelly X Muddled, poorly directed (Tony Richardson), poorly acted (Mick Jagger) tale of the legendary Australian outlaw. Bits are OK, but the whole is a mess that lacks the pace and excitement a less pretentious treatment would surely have evoked; 1970. (c)

Neither the Sea nor the Sand X Nor a very good picture, either. Susan Hampshire's lover, Michael Petrovitch, dies but his slowly decaying body lives on to love her and do nasty things like killing his brother (Frank Finlay). Adaptation of newsreader Gordon Honeycombe's novel directed by Fred Burnley; 1972. (c)

The Neptune Factor √ Ben Gazzara, attempting to free a bunch of scientists trapped beneath the waves. Eels are his main antagonists. Walter Pidgeon, Ernest Borgnine add some Hollywood gloss to director Daniel Petrie's Canadian production; 1973. (c)

Nevada Smith √ This started as a spin-off from *The Carpetbaggers*, in which Alan Ladd played a character with a Past. This is the Past (hunting down the three murderers of his parents and dispatching them each in turn), but before he could make it Ladd died. So, in 1966, Steve McQueen took over. Henry Hathaway produced (and directed) a slick job that should keep you watching to the end. (c)

Never Give an Inch √ A statement from Paul Newman, star and director, about the strength of a family that works together, defying the striking lumberjacks who try to sabotage them. Within the family, headed by Henry Fonda, there are tensions, some of them triggered off by the return of a younger member, Michael Sarrazin; 1971. (c)

Never Let Go √ Richard Todd takes on gangster Peter Sellers (refreshing in uncomic part) as he tries to retrieve stolen car. It's all so unlike real life while pretending to be authentic that it finally sickens (particularly at dirty-fighting climax), but John Guillermin kept the Alun Falconer script rolling, and Adam Faith and Carol White are a couple of youngsters who, as we now know, were to go on to fulfil the promise they showed in this 1960 thriller. (b/w)

Never Love a Stranger X Steve McQueen's first speaking film, 1958 (he was an extra in *Somebody Up There Likes Me*, in 1956), playing hoodlum John Drew Barrymore's boyhood friend. It was a bit of a mess in all departments, thanks partly to director, Robert Stevens, but remains an interesting museum piece for McQueen's debut. (b/w)

Never on Sunday √ Without that twangy theme-tune this 1960 shot-in-

Greece American effort, directed by Jules Dassin, might have lapsed into decent obscurity. As it is, the Melina Mercouri portrayal of a conventional whore's making-over by a guilty American has attained a stature that it never deserved. Amusing but flawed, it provides a pleasant enough vehicle to show off Mercouri showing off. (b/w)

Never Put It In Writing √ Or, at least tear it up before you mail it. That's the lesson of this refreshingly funny film from thriller-merchants Andrew and Virginia Stone in 1964. Pat Boone (groan) writes a very rude letter to his boss complaining of nepotism when he hears he was passed over for promotion, posts it, and then hears he has been made a junior partner in the firm. So he has to retrieve the letter. But the Irish post office won't allow it (he's in Ireland, you see). So he hires a plane and races it to London. Of course, the pilot's potty, and so on and on . . . Nice performances from Milo O'Shea, Reginald Beckwith, Colin Blakely. (b/w)

Never Say Goodbye XX (1) Drippy comedy-drama about how Errol Flynn and Eleanor Parker split up but get back together again for the sake of the child, repulsive Patti Brady. Notable for brilliant impersonation by Flynn of Humphrey Bogart, facilitated by dubbing Bogart's own voice on to the soundtrack. Director James V. Kern; 1946. (b/w)

Never Say Goodbye XX (2) 1956 remake wasn't of above but of William Dieterle's *This Love of Ours*, an even soapier confection, with Rock Hudson meeting Cornell Borchers many years after their separation, and coming together – for the sake of the child. Jerry Hopper directed this, with feeling. (c)

Never So Few X Burma guerrilla actioner not nearly good enough for stars Frank Sinatra, Steve McQueen; also Gina Lollobrigida, Brian Donlevy, Charles Bronson. One point in its favour is that it came bravely out and charged that Chiang Kai-Shek's Nationalist Chinese government sold US arms for profit to Japanese invaders and local bandits. But Sinatra's on-off romance with Lollo, playing Paul Henreid's mistress, is a bit of a pill. John Sturges; 1959. (c)

Never Steal Anything Small √√ . . . when you have the chance of stealing something big, is a-moral of this wicked story of how crooked union boss James Cagney cons his way into a small fortune, the hearts of his union voters, but not into that of married woman (Shirley Jones). Director Charles Lederer put an almost Billy Wilder gloss on to an unproduced stage musical by Maxwell Anderson, called *Devil's Hornpipe*, and came up with a nice black comedy in 1958. (c)

Never Take Sweets from a Stranger XXX Titillatory exercise in child molesting, naturally pretending to be a Solemn Warning and Plea for Medical Treatment of criminally insane. Gwen Watford, Patrick Allen, Felix Aylmer hammered it home in 1960, under Cyril Frankel's opportunistic direction. (b/w)

Never Too Late XX Nasty little comedy about a middle-aged pregnancy and how it annoys her grown-up daughter who decides to have a baby herself. So that's funny? Director Bud Yorkin thought so, but evidently failed to get his conviction over to Paul Ford, Connie Stevens, Maureen O'Sullivan; 1966. (c)

New Face in Hell X Carnography is to blood and violence what pornography is to sex and eroticism, and around 1967 there were a lot of carnographic movies starting to be made. This is one of them, using the hiring of private eye George Peppard by villain Raymond Burr as an excuse for an endless stream of blood. Briton John Guillermin directed in America. (c)

New Faces √ Little more than film of Broadway revue, but has charm, some wit, pretty music. This was start of Eartha Kitt's slinky act, aptly summed up in song 'Monotonous'. But Robert Clary compensates. Harry Horner directed cameras on to Leonard Sillman's stage; 1954. (c)

The New Interns X They can call it New, but it isn't; it's that old hospital multi-drama. In this one there's a doctor who finds he's sterile (he's an obstetrician – get the irony) and various other sub-plots, which are confusing because there isn't any main plot – just like *Emergency Ward 10* and *General Hospital*. Only George Segal rises slightly above the general mush, as a tough new intern. John Rich directed; 1965. (b/w)

A New Kind of Love XX That awful title is derived from an old Chevalier song, and here he momentarily sings it, just to prove we really are in Paris, not some Hollywood back-lot. But are we? Despite Paul Newman and Joanne

Woodward (neither of whose forte is comedy) this remains one of those ooh-la-la Middle Western misconceptions about the naughty French and the terrible things that can happen to nice Americans there. Blame goes to producer-director-writer Mel Shavelson and his weak plot about the love-hate relationship between a career girl and a journalist. Naturally, it contains that scene where she sheds her masculine mien and goes into a beauty shop, to emerge desirable, and un-recognisable to Newman who promptly romances her. As critic Judith Crist wrote: 'Doris Day and Rock Hudson they're not – and shouldn't aspire to be'; 1963. (c)

A New Leaf √√√ Gorgeously funny yarn of Elaine May (directing herself) falling for Walter Matthau's fortune-hunting, but then finding happiness. Apart from their consummate playing, there are lovely cameos from Jack Weston, George Rose and James Coco; 1970. (c)

Newman's Law XX Routine example of genre, very tired by 1974 – the detective who doesn't mind being vicious as long as he gets his man. The wooden George Peppard is the cop; director, Richard Heffron. (c)

New York Confidential √ Richard Conte in gangster thriller made in 1955 by Russell Rouse. Broderick Crawford was Mr Big; Anne Bancroft his daughter. (b/w)

Next to No Time XX Henry Cornelius, who made Genevieve, deserved a better memorial than this posthumous creaky comedy, released in 1958. Kenneth More, blundering about an ocean liner, insulting Roland Culver, is dreadfully miscast, as is Betsy Drake as a film star. (c)

Niagara √ Marilyn Monroe in dresses 'cut so low you can see her knees', as the script says, fights the Falls for attention, and wins. She also fights the story about her murdering her husband, and with director Henry Hathaway's help, holds it to a draw. Made in 1953, it was her 18th film, and gave her Joseph Cotten, Jean Peters as co-stars. (c)

A Nice Girl Like Me X Barbara Ferris, an excellent actress, is pertly miscast as the dreamy innocent of Desmond Davis's 1969 film about two unwanted pregnancies and a third baby shoved into her arms through a train window. Harry Andrews, in a grey beard, plays a different kind of role from the police superintendent or general he usually has – here, for the first time in his life, he has a romantic lead. It's all very sweet on a grown-up story-book level, but it's also rather safe and silly. (c)

Nicholas and Alexandra X Claims that the Russian Revolution was not the result of inevitable conflicts in feudalism and capitalism, but was caused by the Czar and Czarina's over-devotion to their son, the haemophiliac. Franklin J. Schaffner's muddleheaded and simplistic view of history contributes nothing towards an understanding of Russia's turmoil before and during the Revolution. Nor has he cast players who could stride over the minutiae of facts to command an impression by their personalities. Michael Jayston and Janet Suzman appear very second league here; Tom Baker's Rasputin is larger than life, which the old monk was, but not as large as this; 1971. (c)

Nicholas Nickleby √ Dickens adaptation is second-rate due more to undistinguished cast (Derek Bond, Cedric Hardwicke, Mary Merrall, Sally Ann Howes, Bernard Miles) than to Alberto Cavalcanti's game direction; 1947. (b/w)

Night and Day X Unconvincing biography of Cole Porter (not surprising as it had to leave out a central personal fact about him in 1946, when he was still alive and the subject was taboo, anyway). Cary Grant as Cole, under Michael Curtiz's predictable direction, looks as though he knows it's all a fraud. But the music is stunning, of course: 'Begin The Beguine', 'What is This Thing Called Love', 'Miss Otis Regrets', 'Just One of Those Things', 'Do I Love You?', 'My Heart Belongs to Daddy', 'I Get a Kick Out of You', 'You're the Top', 'I've Got You Under My Skin', 'In the Still of the Night', 'Let's Do It', 'Easy to Love', and the title song. (c)

Night and the City √ Jules Dassin directed this thriller set in London: Richard Widmark is wrestling promotor; Herbert Lom his rival; Googie Withers, Gene Tierney romantic interest. All a bit lurid; 1950. (b/w)

A Night at the Opera √√√ Superb example of the Marx Brothers at their best, 1935. Contains the incomparable cabin scene. Sam Wood. (b/w)

The Nightcomers X Marlon Brando and Stephanie Beacham as the governess and gardener who appear as ghosts in The Turn of the Screw. The kids killed them, it seems, because they enjoyed peeping at the couple's sado-masochistic games. This leaden concept (Michael Hastings wrote the script) is made even more deadweight by Michael Winner's direction; 1971. (c)

Night Hair Child XX Britt Ekland is understandably startled when her 12-year-old stepson (Mark Lester) suggests they go to bed together. He also suggests that Daddy (Hardy Kruger) did his real mother in. A tasteless shocker, which also involves Lilli Palmer and Harry Andrews as doctors. Trevor Preston wrote the script; James Kelly directed; 1971. (c)

The Night Has a Thousand Eyes X Edward G. Robinson is stage magician who finds he has genuine gift of precognition. Script lets him and director John Farrow down; 1948. (b/w)

The Night Holds Terror √ One of those never-fail thrillers about a family being held prisoner, tightly directed by expert Andrew L. Stone. Jack Kelly, Hildy Parks, Vince Edwards, John Cassavetes; 1955. (b/w)

A Night in Casablanca X By 1946, the Marx Brothers were running out of steam, and this shows it. Only the opening gag with the wall has the old touch. The rest is strained. Archie Mayo. (b/w)

Nightmare XX (1) Unbelievable thriller about jazz musician Kevin McCarthy killing under hypnosis; don't worry, detective Edward G. Robinson solves it all and the goodies end happily, so you can turn the thing off. Maxwell Shane; 1956. (b/w)

Nightmare X (2) Hammer used the same title for one of its fiendish plots in 1964 with a double-twisting soporific yarn about driving Jennie Linden mad, directed by Freddie Francis. (b/w)

Nightmare Alley √ Tyrone Power as a carnival hanger-on who learns how to 'read minds' and parleys his way to fortune as a society clairvoyant; Helen Walker powerfully chilling as accomplice, Joan Blondell equally convincing as another. Edmund Goulding; 1947. (b/w)

Nightmare in the Sun √ Well-observed chase yarn in which John Derek pays the price for dallying with Ursula Andress by having her husband pinned on him. All the people he trusts while on the run (Lurene Tuttle, George Tobias, Keenan Wynn, Allyn Joslyn stand out) find some reason for betraying him. Shot in 16 days, it was an impressive producer-director movie debut for former small part player Marc Lawrence in 1965. (c)

Night Moves √√ Powerful thriller which keeps moving despite complex parallel plots. Gene Hackman plays a detective with marital problems who has to finish one more case before giving his home necessary attention. But that case, with its stunt-men and daughters of heiresses, proves difficult. One of the more successful attempts to make a detective come real, directed by Arthur Penn; 1975. (c)

Night Must Fall √ Karel Reisz's 1964 re-make of Emlyn Williams's suspense drama lacks the chilling quality of Richard Thorpe's 1937 version. But Albert Finney is convincing and effective, and Susan Hampshire's fear as she slowly realises identity of local homicidal maniac is definitely catching. (b/w)

Night of the Demon √ Jacques Tourneur made a more than efficient spine-tingler from M. R. James' *Casting the Runes* in which Dana Andrews is at first sceptical about the power of an old parchment to conjure up a devil but gradually gives way to terror; 1957. (b/w)

Night of the Eagle √ Occult thriller with Peter Wyngarde aghast to discover how deeply wife Janet Blair is into black magic. Cemeteries with chasing stone eagles and Margaret Johnston as equivocal cripple; Sidney Hayers; 1962. (b/w)

The Night of the Following Day √ Muddled thriller about kidnapping a rich man's daughter, excellently played by Pamela Franklin. As Marlon Brando is the tough man of the plot and the kidnappers fall out among themselves there is bound to be a pretty gratuitous amount of violence, but director-producer-co-writer Hubert Cornfield manages to keep this at a decent minimum and concentrate instead upon the moody shots of the Normandy beach-house where she is held prisoner. Surprise of the film is Rita Moreno, startlingly good as the tripping female member of the gang. And then it's all ruined by a tacked-on it-was-all-a-dream ending – what an unnecessary shame; 1969. (c)

The Night of the Generals X One of the Nazi generals is a murderer (only one? as one character asks). Anyway, that's the main plot – is it Peter O'Toole, Donald Pleasence or Charles Gray?

There's an awful lot more, like the attempt on Hitler's life, Rommel being shot up in a plane, love-stuff between Tom Courtenay and Joanna Pettet, detective Omar Sharif on the trail. Director Anatole Litvak lets it sag and there's a lot left unsaid; 1967. (c)

The Night of the Grizzly √ Clint Walker, broke and desperate, tracks a killer bear that has helped to ruin him, with the dedication of a Captain Ahab; Martha Hyer is his wife, Keenan Wynn the man he's mortgaged to. Joseph Pevney directed, 1966, and the bear doesn't get a credit. (c)

The Night of the Hunter √√ Important curiosity: Robert Mitchum as religious fanatic who is prepared to kill for loot to build church; James Agee wrote script from David Grubb's novel; Charles Laughton directed (his only picture); Lillian Gish returned to play lonely fairy godmother; 1955. (b/w)

The Night of the Iguana √√ Pretentious but always fascinating try at Tennessee Williams symbolism by John Huston, 1964; defrocked priest (Richard Burton) is chased by rapacious teenager (Sue Lloyd) into the arms of bawdy innkeeper (Ava Gardner) watched by suffering spinster (Deborah Kerr) in Mexico. Sundry other colourful characters abound, including iguana. (b/w)

Night of the Living Dead √ Strong, low-budget horror flick, about Duane Jones, Judith O'Dea beset by zombies. Some genuine shivers are activated by director George A. Romero; 1969. (c)

Night of the Quarter Moon XXX Nasty little exploitation movie about racial intolerance, which uses this crucial test of our civilisation for the purpose of titillation (as when octoroon Julie London does a striptease in the annulment courtroom to snap her husband back into sexual life, physically abetted by her black lawyer). Hugo Haas was the director and Albert (*High School Confidential*) Zugsmith the producer; 1959. (b/w)

Night Passage √ James Stewart in 1957 western caper about robbing train payroll. James Neilson keeps it going. (c)

Night People √ Above-average Cold War drama filmed in 1954 Berlin about getting kidnapped American soldier out of Russian zone. Nunnally Johnson wrote and directed Gregory Peck, Broderick Crawford, Rita Gam. (c)

The Night They Raided Minsky's √ An amusing comedy about the accidental tearing of a dress that is supposed to have started striptease. The dress belongs to Britt Ekland, who isn't at all bad in this, her first big chance (in 1969). It was also billed as Norman Wisdom's big international breakthrough, but somehow - not altogether surprisingly - this is the only film he has made in America to date. Jason Robards and Denholm Elliot are fine; also present are Joseph Wiseman as Minsky and Elliot Gould as his son. Director, William Friedkin; 1969. (c)

Night Tide √ Unusual thriller with poetic undertones written and directed by Curtis Harrington in 1967 and giving Dennis Hopper an interesting part as a sailor who falls in love with a mermaid - or, at least a girl posing as one in a sideshow. She's a bit confused about just what and who she is herself, and gets a bit murderous. (b/w)

A Night to Remember √ (1) Brian Aherne, Loretta Young in *Thin-Man*-style whodunit, 1943; director Richard Wallace. (b/w)

A Night to Remember √√ (2) Rather a gripping 1958 account of tragedy of magnificient Titanic on her maiden voyage. Authentic Eric Ambler script, documentary style direction from Roy Baker, strong performances from Kenneth More, Honor Blackman, David McCallum. (b/w)

The Night Walker √ Why does Barbara Stanwyck keep dreaming of lost husband, Hayden Rorke? Horror-director William Castle provides the answer, 1964. One reason might be that Stanwyck was once married to Robert Taylor, who's also around, in real life. (c)

Night Watch X One more disaster for Elizabeth Taylor who made seven bad films in the seventies. In this 1973 thriller, director Brian Hutton humoured her, as all her directors appear to have done, with the usual result. This time, Laurence Harvey, Billie Whitelaw, Robert Lang were involved. (c)

Nine Hours to Rama XX Slow-moving (it almost seems the nine hours of the title), fictitious account of Gandhi's assassination and killer, unconvincingly played by blacked-up Horst Buchholz, with the equally miscast Valerie Gearon as the girl he loves. Jose Ferrer looks cross as the police chief but conveys little else. Only Indian actor J. S. Casshyap emerges with any credit from director Mark Robson's failure – his portrayal of the Mahatma is compelling. The continuation of the film after the climactic shooting is woeful; 1963. (c)

1984 XX It's nearly the year of Orwell's nightmare vision and we seem to be doing OK so far. Tamely directed by Michael Anderson, this has further drawback of Edmond O'Brien in lead (but all British films had to have American stars then). Michael Redgrave, Donald Pleasence, Mervyn Johns are around but they can't salvage weak adaptation and direction; 1955. (b/w)

90 Degrees in the Shade √ Anne Heywood, James Booth, Ann Todd, Donald Wolfit went to Czechoslovakia to appear in this joint production about corruption in a grocery store; Jiri Weiss directed from a David Mercer screenplay; 1964. (b/w)

99 44/100 Dead XX From its meaningless and unpronounceable title to its flip ending, there is nothing in this lifeless melo to suggest that John Frankenheimer ever directed anything of quality – let alone *The Manchurian Candidate*, *Seven Days in May* or *Seconds*. Lumbered with Richard Harris (in specs, for some reason) as hero, he goes through the motions of making an exciting thriller, but all he managed, in 1974, was a tedious series of incidents. (c)

Ninotchka √ As a comedienne, Garbo revealed wit and timing previously swamped in increasing tendency to overact. A stony Red Russian agent on a mission in Paris, slowly melting to the charms of Count Melvyn Douglas. Dated, 1939 sociological chat, smooth Ernst Lubitsch direction. (b/w)

No Blade of Grass √ Nigel Davenport attempts to take his family through an English countryside devastated by deadly virus. Cornel Wilde, tireless campaigner for the environment, directed in 1970. (c)

Nobody Lives Forever √ John Garfield is con-man. Geraldine Fitzgerald is prey. Yet could love be real? Dry those tears, Jean Negulesco will make sure it all comes out right; 1946. (b/w)

Nobody Runs Forever XX Cloak-and-dagger mystery which starts off quite promisingly with the Premier of New South Wales, Leo McKern, instructing Rod Taylor to arrest the High Commissioner of Australia, Christopher Plummer, for an ancient murder. This soon gets buried under routine melodramatics, as Taylor saves Plummer from the lethal wiles of Daliah Lavi. The inept screenplay carefully filters out the social consciousness of the original novel, leaving Ralph Thomas with nothing to direct except familiar old rubbish. Franchot Tone, Clive Revill, Calvin Lockhart are wasted; 1968. (c)

No Down Payment √ Slick, efficient, strangely gripping drama of life in a blue-collar suburb, with Patricia Owens as wife who gets raped, Joanne Woodward as wife of the rapist, Cameron Mitchell. Tony Randall, as the salesman who doesn't realise he's over the hill, and his wife, well-played by Sheree North, add to the authenticity of this Jerry Wald-Martin Ritt 1957 superior soap-opera. (b/w)

No Drums, No Bugles √√ Martin Sheen as conscientious objector who spends three years in cave rather than fight in Civil War; Clyde Ware wrote, produced, directed in 1971. (c)

No Hard Feelings √√ Director Alan Parker won the 1978 British Academy award for his *Midnight Express* but this 1974 effort couldn't get a showing in the cinemas. An evocation of the Blitz, filmed entirely in East London, it features Anthony Allen, Mary Larkin, Joe Gladwin, Kate Williams. (c)

No Highway X James Stewart gives passable unconscious imitation of Groucho Marx walk in a serious role as absent-minded professor who knows he's right – shucks – that the plane's tail is going to fall off, and – see here – he's darn well going to pull this here lever and make sure the plane doesn't go up in the sky until he's proved it. Marlene Dietrich floats in and out as unlikely fairy godmother in the form of Famous Film Star, as widower Stewart romances pretty air hostess Glynis Johns on the side. Unconvincing but harmless enough. From Nevil Shute novel, lifelessly directed by Henry Koster; 1951. (b/w)

No Kidding XXX – and precious few smiles, either, despite frantic efforts by Leslie Phillips and Geraldine McEwan, turning their country house into children's holiday home; *Carry On* director Gerald Thomas fitted it in during 1960. (b/w)

No Love for Johnnie XX Peter Finch is politician with vaulting ambition in 1961 drama directed by Ralph Thomas, supported by Stanley Holloway, Donald Pleasence, Billie Whitelaw, Dennis Price, Paul Rogers, Peter Barkworth, Fenella Fielding, Rosalie

Crutchley, Mary Peach. Posing as neutral politically, it is in fact subtle anti-Labour propaganda, as shown by the final scene where our hero, now sold out, is seen listening cynically to Tory speech caring about the workers he has betrayed. All the left-wing and working class characters are represented unsympathetically, while his true love is a nice upper-middle-class gal. (b/w)

No, My Darling Daughter XX Weak, dated little comedy about Juliet Mills wooed by Michael Craig; Betty Box; 1961. (b/w)

None But the Brave √ Rare Frank Sinatra effort at directing as well as starring (second to Clint Walker); US marines stranded on island with Japanese troops during last war make a unilateral truce, which has to be broken when they get in touch with outside world again. Unfairly attacked as naive at the time (1965) it has something to say about war even if it betrays its own premises by making the fighting too glossy. (c)

None But the Lonely Heart X Cary Grant was anxious to prove in 1944 that he could play the dramatic role of a Cockney drifter in Clifford Odets' version (which he also directed) of Richard Llewellyn's novel. He got an Academy Award nomination, but the film wasn't a success, possibly because the phoniness of the book was intensified by the mainly American cast (Ethel Barrymore, Jane Wyatt, Dan Duryea). (b/w)

No Place for Jennifer XX Supposed to make you cry about a little girl (Janette Scott – Janette Scott? Well, it was made in 1949) with divorcing parents, but you may find yourself sorrier for Leo Genn, Rosamund John and all involved. Henry Cass directed. (b/w)

Nora Prentiss XX Dr Kent Smith risks his career for love of Ann Sheridan. Vincent Sherman directed this mundane semi-thriller in 1947. (b/w)

No Room at the Inn √ Dylan Thomas wrote the script for this melodramatic yarn about evacuees, under the charge of horrid Freda Jackson; director Daniel Birt; 1948. (b/w)

North By Northwest √√√ An Americanised *Thirty-Nine Steps*, with Hitchcock convincing us that he can follow the plot even if we can't ('I am but mad north-northwest: when the wind is southerly I know a hawk from a handsaw' – *Hamlet*). Contains two of his best-known breathcatchers, the crop-dusting plane shooting at Cary Grant in the stubble, and the final chase over the massive stone heads carved out of Mount Rushmore. Luckily Hitch had complete artistic control – otherwise MGM would have cut key scene after the Rushmore chase; 1959. (c)

Nor the Moon by Night XXX Ken Annakin's 1958 film of love on African game reserve offers no surprises but has tragic Belinda Lee, one-time British Bardot, plus Michael Craig and Patrick McGoohan as game warden and brother. Dreadful script, gratuitous sadism. (c)

Northern Pursuit XX Errol Flynn plays a Mountie of German extraction; is he for or against Nazi saboteur Helmut Dantine? Director, Raoul Walsh; 1943. (b/w)

North to Alaska XX Brawling John Wayne steals much of Stewart Granger's thunder in this gold-rush melodrama, with posturing Capucine adding woman trouble. Direction by Henry Hathaway can't hide silliness of the plot and childishness of the characters. Ernie Kovacs has some nice moments as a con-man, but there are more yawns than thrills in the rest; 1960. (c)

Northwest Frontier √ Exciting dash through hostile India with threatened prince; Kenneth More, Lauren Bacall head a large cast, held together by taut direction by J. Lee Thompson who gets some good performances, including one from Herbert Lom as journalist-villain; 1959. (c)

North-West Passage √ Half-made by MGM in 1939; the second half, about the actual passage, was never even started. So this is the settlers-and-Indians saga that was to be the prologue. Director King Vidor wouldn't allow doubles and Spencer Tracy wore out a pair of leather trousers. Robert Young, Walter Brennan supported adequately. (c)

Not as a Stranger √ Frank Sinatra plus Robert Mitchum, Olivia de Havilland, Broderick Crawford, Lee Marvin, epidemics, adultery, surgery, fornication, redemption; Stanley Kramer certainly delivered in 1955. (b/w)

Nothing But a Man √ One of the few treatments of the black man's personal struggle for his rights and dignity that doesn't come over as specious and/or patronising. Made on a shoestring by

Michael Roemer and Robert Young, it was historically true for 1964, when the hero, believably played by Ivan Dixon, found his militancy up against both Alabama whites and his wife's Uncle Tom training. (b/w)

Nothing But the Best √√ Stylish 1963 comedy directed by Clive Donner giving Alan Bates wonderful opportunity as smart lad clawing his way up the business and social ladder, which he takes with both hands, giving us perhaps the finest British comedy performance of the decade. Millicent Martin awfully good as posh little girl he woos. Neat ending. (c)

No Time for Sergeants √ 1958 Mervyn Le Roy comedy about country boy who messes up the army. Spawned TV series of same name. Andy Griffith plays the troublesome hayseed. (b/w)

No Time for Tears XXX Anna Neagle in 1956 tear-jerker that may cause you to weep more for the British film industry than its junior *Ward 10* histrionics. Cyril Frankel directed. (c)

No Time to Die XXX Dull, obvious piece of British war-film flim-flammery surprisingly made in 1958, not ten or fifteen years earlier. Victor Mature, Leo Genn, Anthony Newley, Bonar Colleano, Sean Kelly – all pretty awful – escape from an Italian PoW camp to Fight for Freedom and director Terence Young. (c)

Notorious √√ Ingrid Bergman is planted by FBI man Cary Grant as wife to spy on Claude Rains in South America. A huge hit in 1946, particularly because the 'McGuffin', as Hitchcock calls his major plot devices, was about uranium in wine-bottles. As the movie was planned months before it was revealed that there was such a thing as an atom bomb, the FBI had him under surveillance because they suspected he had been leaked the secrets of Los Alamos. (b/w)

The Notorious Landlady X Disappointing comedy-thriller which places too much weight on the hefty shoulders of Kim Novak as girl who might be planning to do in Jack Lemmon. Unfortunately, Richard Quine fails to spoof the Hitchcockian tradition sharply enough. We're left without laughs or thrills, despite the presence of Fred Astaire, Lionel Jeffries and Estelle Winwood (who has the one exciting scene in a wheelchair running down a slope); 1962. (b/w)

No Trees in the Street XX Sylvia Syms, writer Ted Willis, director J. Lee

Thompson try to impose a nostalgic copper's-eye view of the world on a youth problem that was to make this look as dated as the foxtrot within a few years, and a museum piece now; 1958. (b/w)

Not With My Wife You Don't √ George C. Scott and Tony Curtis as buddy-buddies in the Korean War, both zeroing in on the same Italian nurse, Virna Lisi. One of them marries her, but only by a trick pretending the other's dead. Then he turns up. All good, dirty fun, directed and produced by Norman Panama in 1966. (c)

Now and Forever XX Trite magazine story of chase to Gretna Green in the cause of young love, superficially told and directed by Mario Zampi. Janette Scott does her best, against the grain; 1956. (c)

No Way Out √ Early (1950) violent race-drama has goody black doctor Sidney Poitier accused of murder by bigot Richard Widmark. Its heart is in the right place. Director, Joseph L. Mankiewicz. (b/w)

Nowhere to Go √ Low-budget British thriller about escaped convict looking for fortune with notable debuts by director Seth Holt and co-scriptwriter Kenneth Tynan, in 1958; if the end lets it down, we have had some 80 minutes of excitement before then, and Bernard Lee, Andrée Melly and Bessie Love are fine. (b/w)

Now Voyager √ Famous weepie with Bette Davis brought out of shell by psychiatrist Claude Rains. Transformed from ugly spinster into ravishing beauty she dates Paul Henreid, but gives him up when she realises they can never marry because of his ailing wife. So she settles for looking after his daughter instead. Director Irving Rapper chose to exaggerate the soapier elements – after all he couldn't go for authenticity with that plot; 1942. (b/w)

The Nun's Story √ Long, overblown saga of Audrey Hepburn taking vows and finally renouncing them, without any clear motivation at either end. Full of interesting rituals and painstakingly directed by Fred Zinnemann, but ultimately defeating his evident purpose of making us admire the self-sacrificing life of devotion in showing just how mindless the obedience of the postulants has to be. Peter Finch does the little he has to do rather well, and Dames Ashcroft and Evans turn in their usual flawless performances; 1959. (c)

O

Objective Burma XX When this war actioner was shown in 1945 in London, it had to be withdrawn after a week because of protests that it suggested that America had a major part in the Burma campaign. Not until seven years later was it publicly shown again here, this time with a tactful prologue. The script does give a false impression that an American paratroop attack was decisive and Errol Flynn's popularity was permanently affected in Britain. The movie itself is the usual collection of heroics, reinforced by a particularly loud and inapposite music track. Raoul Walsh did his usual lush but competent directing chore. (*b/w*)

The Oblong Box √ Exciting horror thriller about long-delayed retribution, neatly directed by Gordon Hessler in 1968. Alastair Williamson seeks revenge on Vincent Price for keeping him chained up; Christopher Lee is doctor about to cut him up, thinking he is dead. (*c*)

Ocean's Eleven √ Frank Sinatra, Dean Martin, Sammy Davis Jr. and other members of that old ratpack enjoying themselves rather more than the audience in this 1960 caper about robbing Las Vegas. Director Lewis Milestone deserved danger money for keeping this lot in line. (*c*)

The October Man XX John Mills loses his memory: did he commit that murder? Lose yours and forget to switch on. Roy Baker; 1947. (*b/w*)

The Odd Couple √√ Walter Matthau and Jack Lemmon set up house when divorce looms. Neil Simon's very funny dialogue gets a great work-out. Gene Saks directed expertly, in 1968. (*c*)

Odd Man Out √√√ Tremendously exciting Carol Reed masterpiece of suspense about the last hours of Irish rebel James Mason's life as he is hunted by police. Robert Newton, Kathleen Ryan, Dan O'Herlihy, Robert Beatty, Fay Compton, Cyril Cusack all did their finest screen work in this 1947 thriller. (*b/w*)

Odds Against Tomorrow X White and black bank robbers forced by circumstances into crime has strong cast of Harry Belafonte (whose company also produced), Robert Ryan and Shelley Winters as his nagging wife. Robert Wise somehow failed to make it as exciting as it should have been – perhaps he was too concerned to get over message of racial tolerance? 1959. (*b/w*)

The Odessa File √ Routine chase-the-neo-Nazis thriller, tricked out with big production values and dull direction by Ronald Neame. Jon Voight is the chaser, Maximilian Schell his main quarry; 1974. (*c*)

Odette X Anna Neagle as resistance heroine, with Trevor Howard, Marius Goring, Peter Ustinov in Occupied France. Herbert Wilcox hammed up the direction which made it unreal in 1951, and subsequent revelations have suggested that even the story he based film on wasn't quite as it seemed. (*b/w*)

The Offence √ John Hopkins's play *This Story of Yours*, about a copper who kills a suspected child molester during interrogation, fails to catch fire on the screen. Sean Connery is inadequate in the central introspective role, while Vivien Merchant and Trevor Howard are clearly unhappy under Sidney Lumet's direction; Ian Bannen does better as the suspect; 1972. (*c*)

Of Human Bondage Maugham's vaguely autobiographical yarn about club-footed medical student and a whore has been filmed three times, each one getting worse.

√√ (1) Leslie Howard and Bette Davis in 1934, directed by John Cromwell. 'Probably the best performance ever recorded on the screen by a US actress', *Life* raved about Bette Davis. (*b/w*)

X (2) Paul Henreid and Eleanor Parker in 1946, directed by Edmund Goulding. A routine, sub-standard version. (*b/w*)

XX (3) Laurence Harvey and Kim Novak in 1964, directed by Ken Hughes and Henry Hathaway. A glorious mess, with the two leads outacting each other in a poor screenplay by Bryan Forbes and providing embarrassment all round, particularly for Siobhan McKenna and Mrs Bryan Forbes. (*b/w*)

Of Love and Desire XXX This 1964 extravaganza is one of the very worst films ever made. Merle Oberon plays the part of a nymphomaniac who got that way because of her incestuous desires for her brother, Curt Jurgens. It takes the love of a good Steve Cochran to set her right in a fade-out.

Everything about this monumental piece of nonsense is to be treasured as the apotheosis of bad cinema, the music (Sammy Davis Jr. singing 'Katherine's Tune'), the photography, above all the truly appalling direction of Richard Rush achieve a composite that connoisseurs of the awful still chuckle over together during the long winter evenings. A strong contender for the booby prize of all time. (c)

Oh Dad, Poor Dad, Mama's Hung You in the Closet and I'm Feeling So Sad XX Best thing about this transfer of Arthur Kopit's play (once avant garde, now old stuff) is the title. Rosalind Russell, Robert Morse, Jonathan Winters fail to make zany tale of widow who keeps her husband's embalmed body in the wardrobe light enough, while 25-year-old son has affair with his baby-sitter (yes, he's supposed to be retarded or something). Richard Quine; 1967. (c)

O. Henry's Full House √ Five stories by O. Henry transferred to the screen in 1952 from a not very sparkling Lamar Trotti script by a clutch of top directors. Worth seeing the first one, though, for richly comic performances from Charles Laughton and Marilyn Monroe. He's a tramp who finds it hard to get arrested and thus spend a nice warm winter in jail; he accosts a lady in the street – but she turns out to be every man's dream tart. Henry Koster directed this bit. (b/w)

Oh Men! Oh Women! √ Stylish high-comedy acting from David Niven, Tony Randall, Dan Dailey and Ginger Rogers in frothy tale of marital mix-ups. Nunnally Johnson adapted and directed it in 1957. (c)

Oh Mr Porter √ Famous Will Hay comedy, directed in 1938 by Marcel Varnel, about incompetent station master clearing up Irish branch line of gun-runners; Hay inimitable as bungling centre of gravity to Graham Moffat and Moore Marriott. (b/w)

Oh Rosalinda XXX Oh Michael Redgrave! What were you doing in this stiff musical comedy concoction in 1955, when you were old enough to know better? Others attracted by Powell and Pressburger to exhibit themselves in yarn about practical jokes in Old Vienna were Mel Ferrer, Anthony Quayle, Anton Walbrook, Dennis Price. (c)

Oh What a Lovely War √ Although rapturously received and much-honoured, this adaptation by Richard Attenborough of Joan Littlewood's didactic stage knock-out about the First World War is a prettied-up, fashionable cartoon in which various Grand Actors (Ralph Richardson, John Gielgud, Kenneth More, Jack Hawkins, John Mills, Maggie Smith, Michael Redgrave, Laurence Olivier, Susannah York, Dirk Bogarde, Phyllis Calvert, Vanessa Redgrave) are allowed the illusion that they are contributing to a devastating exposure of the horrors of war while really indulging themselves in Attenborough's harmless shadow-boxing. Tarting up Brighton Pier as a set sounded a nice idea, but it limits the action. The linking family is palely drawn – although the final shot is effective. A modish, filleted effort which only retains a fraction of the original's power – yet that is still potent enough to move; 1969. (c)

Oklahoma! √ Disappointing literal version of the stage smash hit musical relies too much on photographing the show and doesn't create a real film. The Rodgers - and - Hammerstein music's fine, of course, ('Oh, What a Beautiful Morning'; 'The Surrey with the Fringe on Top'; 'People Will Say We're in Love'; 'Many a New Day'), and Rod Steiger is outstanding as the heavy. But Shirley Jones and Gordon MacRae are no more than pleasant, and Fred Zinnemann seems to have been under orders to keep it theatrical; 1955. (c)

Oklahoma Crude √√ Singleminded Faye Dunaway and shifty George C. Scott drilling for oil in 1913. John Mills plays her father, Jack Palance also stars. Stanley Kramer directed with expertise and without too much moralising about greed; 1975. (c)

Old Acquaintance X A gilded sinkful of soapy suds is this yarn about competing novelists, Bette Davis the noble, Miriam Hopkins the ignoble. James Agee wrote at the time (1943), 'The odd thing is that the two ladies and Vincent Sherman, directing, make the whole business look fairly intelligent, detailed and plausible; and that on the screen such trash can seem even mature and adventurous'. He was too kind. (b/w)

The Old Dark House √ Comedy-thriller that's actually both quite funny and frightening about night in 'haunted' mansion where Robert Morley, Janette Scott, Peter Bull, Fenella Fielding are among those threatened by murderer. This is 1962 remake by William Castle of 1932 Karloff-Laughton movie which came from the unlikely source of a J. B. Priestley novel, *Benighted,* adapted by Benn Levy. (*c*)

The Old Maid √ Fascinating glimpse of young Bette Davis as unmarried mother battling bitchy cousin Miriam Hopkins for love of her unknowing daughter. Hate sizzles in Civil War setting as director Edmund Goulding pulls out all emotional stops. (*b/w*)

The Old Man and the Sea √ Hemingway's mock-simple tale of a fisherman, his tremendous, self-imposed task of catching a marlin and then having it eaten under his eyes by the sharks, was faithfully transferred to the screen in 1958 by John Sturges (replacing Fred Zinnemann after early dramas). While it makes a strong, clear narrative, the deeper philosophical 'meanings' are intrusive and given too much weight, which extends even to James Wong Howe's fine photography (supplemented by second and third units who roamed the Atlantic and Pacific looking for fish and sunsets plus an underwater unit). In the practically one-man part, Spencer Tracy scored a personal success in the most demanding role of his 37 years of film-making. (*c*)

Oliver! √√ Spirited direction from Carol Reed in well-cast version of Lionel Bart's Dickens: Mark Lester, Ron Moody, Oliver Reed, Shani Wallis. All a bit harmless and cosy but OK if you're feeling indulgent; 1968. (*c*)

Oliver Twist √√ Strong 1948 adaptation of Dickens horror comic, with marvellous Fagin by Alec Guinness, Tony Newley as Artful Dodger, bloodthirsty Bill Sikes by Robert Newton, Kay Walsh as Nancy. Director David Lean. (*b/w*)

O Lucky Man! X O Pretentious Rubbish! The wilful confusion begins with the name of the character that Malcolm McDowell plays – Mick Travers, same as the one in the director, Lindsay Anderson's, *If . . .* But there is no other connection – this Mick is an aimless, smart young conformist, who has a series of rather tiresome adventures and keeps encountering the same actors (Rachel Roberts, Arthur Lowe, Ralph Richardson, Mona Washbourne) in various different parts. There is presumably a message, but it's hard to discern; 1973. (*c*)

Omar Khayyam X Did you know that the poet saved Persia from a gang of assassins? Well, that's what it says here. Cornel Wilde, Raymond Massey in fancy 1956 production, directed by William Dieterle. (*c*)

The Omega Man √ Remake in 1971 of *The Last Man on Earth* (1964), a version of Richard Matheson's novel, *I Am Legend.* This time, Charlton Heston takes the Vincent Price part and, instead of horror, we get fashionable ecology. He is a scientist, sought by zombies who have a plague due to a germ war, as sacrificial victim. Director Boris Sagal makes a dull job of it all. (*c*)

On a Clear Day You Can See Forever √√ Despite some shortcomings, this 1970 musical starring Barbra Streisand, Jack Nicholson, Bob Newhart and (one of the shortcomings) Yves Montand, soars above most of its genre. There is too much plot about reincarnation, but the principals sing, dance and act prettily. Director, Vincente Minnelli. (*c*)

On Approval √ Polished 1944 rendering of the Frederick Lonsdale play with Clive Brook directing himself, Beatrice Lillie, Roland Culver and Googie Withers in comedy of Edwardian fiancée-swapping. Desperately lacks colour. (*b/w*)

Once a Thief √ Meanwhile, back in San Francisco they are once more stealing, chasing, cheating and generally rushing up and down the over-filmed hills. This time (1965), Alain Delon is vainly trying to go straight with wife Ann-Margret; Jack Palance and Van Heflin in supporting roles. Director, flashy Ralph Nelson. (*b/w*)

Once Before I Die X John Derek directed, produced and appeared in this 1967 war film and so obviously cared about it that he almost managed to create an interesting film through sheer enthusiasm, despite such drawbacks as Ursula Andress slogging through the Philippine jungle without a hair out of place. The title comes from a request to Ursula from a soldier who has never been to bed with a woman asking her the favour before the next attack; it's that kind of film; 1967. (*c*)

Once is Not Enough X This was originally called *Jacqueline Susann's Once is Not Enough.* Alexis Smith, married to Kirk Douglas, is having a lesbian affair with Melina Mercouri, whose step-daughter is seduced by

George Hamilton but falls for David Janssen, who . . . and so on, in ever more boring vicious circles. Guy Green directed energetically; 1975. (c)

Once More With Feeling X Pretty dreadful piece about an orchestral conductor (excruciatingly played by Yul Brynner who hadn't mastered the necessary movements), saved by sparkling performance from Kay Kendall in her last film. Stanley Donen produced and directed; 1960. (c)

One Day in the Life of Ivan Denisovich X Worthy 1971 attempt to reproduce Solzhenitsyn's exposure of life in a Stalin camp which only showed how literary his approach was. Director Caspar Wrede failed to involve the audience, and left it gazing at Tom Courtenay, Alfred Burke and James Maxwell with more sympathy than understanding. (c)

One-Eyed Jacks √√ Marlon Brando's first essay in directing, in 1961. This successful western pivots on two superficially alike but actually contrasting ex-buddies, Karl Malden and himself. He plays a gunfighter who was betrayed by Malden and now seeks his revenge. The photography (by Charles Lang) is ravishing and the story (including the seduction of Malden's step-daughter) brilliantly realised. The strong supports include Katy Jurado, Ben Johnson, Elisha Cook. (c)

One Foot in Hell √ Alan Ladd plans a bitter revenge on the townspeople who let his wife die by their ineptitude. He becomes their deputy sheriff and plots a punishment for them. Unfortunately, director James B. Clark rather lets it slip out of his grasp into just another western; 1960. (c)

One For the Book √ Originally entitled *The Voice of the Turtle*, after the John Van Druten play it was taken from, this romance of a blind date between Ronald Reagan and Eleanor Parker is lightweight stuff. Director, Irving Rapper; 1947. (b/w)

One Is a Lonely Number √ Easy to dismiss this as a mere sob-story of a divorcee (Trish Van Devere), but with Janet Leigh as the President of the Divorcees of Marin County and Melvyn Douglas as a neighbour, there are some good moments and a satisfactory ending; Mel Stuart, 1972. (c)

One Man Mutiny XX This 1955 Otto Preminger-directed true-life account of military pioneer on trial for attacking US War Dept. as negligent provided Gary Cooper with strong central part and good ones for veterans Charles Bickford, Ralph Bellamy, Rod Steiger. Preminger blames producer Milton Sperling for its failure, but the critics pointed the finger at Otto himself, who failed to infuse his case with any zip. Coop was monumentally miscast as the fanatic with the light of justice in his burning eyes and the script didn't explain how he came to see himself as the Government's Nemesis. (c)

One Man's Way XX Inspirational biopic of Norman Vincent Peale, crime-reporter turned preacher, is unlikely to have much impact in Britain, where he has hardly been heard of – thank goodness. Defensive tone of this biopic is interesting, as it tries to protect its subject from common charge of 'easy religion'. You'll need a lot of patience. Don Murray plays the preacher under Denis Sanders' inspiration; 1964. (b/w)

One Million Years B.C. XX Those who remember a pin-up picture of Raquel Welch looking extremely sexy in a fur bikini have seen the best of this ponderous 1966 effort. The rest is inaccurate pre-history, grunts and groans and some unconvincing special effects. Don Chaffey directs without enthusiasm from a script that, if it isn't quite that old, is at least 26 years Before This – written in 1940 by Hal Roach and released under three titles at different times (one of those jolly tricks they used to get up to – *Man and His Mate* and *The Cave Dwellers* are the others – with Victor Mature, Carole Landis, Lon Chaney). Writer Michael Carreras tacked on another 24 minutes and Hammer added. (c)

One More Time XX When old-fashioned vaudevillains like Sammy Davis Jr. and Peter Lawford chant 'one more time' at the end of a routine, the heart sinks. To add to the enforced gaiety, there is Jerry Lewis directing and English character actors conforming to American stereotypes of Brits; 1969. (c)

One of Our Spies Is Missing XX If you happen to find Robert Vaughn and David McCallum still watchable as agents of that highly improbably near-omnipotent UNCLE you could give this 1966 actioner a whirl. It's about a rejuvenation process being used by arch-Women's Libber Vera Miles in furthering her wicked (?) idea that women should run the world. Its sympathies are out of date before it starts and the performances are, too. Director E. Darrell Hallenbeck. (c)

One Potato, Two Potato √√ Intelligent, sensitive and altogether worthy attempt to throw some light on black-white prejudice by means of a court custody case. Competently acted by unknowns, directed by Larry Peerce, this 1964 'sleeper' didn't arrive in Britain for another three years and wasn't widely shown then. It certainly deserved to be seen, and still does. (b/w)

One Spy Too Many XX One film too many, more like. Just a bad television actioner, one more episode – and rather a bad one – in the tired old UNCLE series, which was just about packing up when this film came out in 1965 and of which it was the third to be shown in the cinemas here. Dorothy Provine provides a flicker of interest as wife of the Man Who Wants to Rule the World (Rip Torn), chasing him for a bit of money; but Our Heroes, David McCallum and Robert Vaughn are hopelessly feeble. Joseph Sargent. (c)

The One That Got Away X In 1957 the British film industry was going through a strange attack of conscience about the last war, leading to glorification of Germans like Hardy Kruger, presented in Roy Baker's PoW chase as clever chap outwitting Britons. Alec McCowan has small part. (b/w)

One, Two, Three √√ Billy Wilder 1961 satire on Coca-Colonisation, capitalism and communism, with James Cagney peaking (and ending) his career with rattling performance as soft-drink salesman longing for transfer from Berlin to London but having hopes deflected by boss's daughter's marriage to Red. Wilder and Diamond took their plot from a one-act play by the schmaltzy Ferenc Molnar and turned it into a rapid-fire vehicle for Cagney's personality; he wasn't quite as fast as in previous days, however, and one scene took 52 takes (seven short of the world record, held by Marilyn Monroe on *Some Like It Hot*). If the story (not unlike *Ninotchka* in essentials) is weak, and Horst Buchholz's characterisation as the young firebrand unconvincing to the point of stupidity, at least the comedy is broad enough to carry it. (b/w)

One Way Pendulum √√ Peter Yates, due to go on to *Bullitt* and better things, directed this muted version of

the N. F. Simpson play in 1964. Eric Sykes, George Cole, Jonathan Miller, Julia Foster, Peggy Mount, Mona Washbourne – who could ask for more to provide that rarest of television pleasures, a loud laugh? (b/w)

One Way Street X Crooked doctor James Mason is on the run, chased by baddies William Conrad, Dan Duryea, Jack Elam. They catch up with him when his getaway plane is forced down near a Mexican village; director, Hugo Fregonese; 1950. (b/w)

On Friday at Eleven √ Taut caper movie with Rod Steiger, Ian Bannen, Peter Van Eyck and Jean Servais hijacking an armoured truck with wages for an American base in Germany. Alvin Rakoff directed sharply and excitingly; 1961. (b/w)

On Her Majesty's Secret Service X 1969 James Bond with inadequate George Lazenby trying to wear the hero's shoes. Despite spirited assistance from heroine Diana Rigg and villain Telly Savalas, the sheer weight of gadgetry, banality and routine direction by Peter Hunt keeps it all earthbound. (c)

Only Angels Have Wings √√ Group of fliers in South America battle to get the mail through. Cary Grant is airline captain, Jean Arthur a nice girl, Rita Hayworth a sexy one and Richard Barthelmess a coward. Howard Hawks turned it all into taut drama in 1939. (b/w)

The Only Game in Town √ Elizabeth Taylor as plump chorus girl (pushing it even in 1969) and Warren Beatty a compulsive gambler, living together in Las Vegas. Under George Stevens's old-fashioned direction, the she-loves-me-she-loves-me-not on-and-off action is boring, and Frank Gilroy's treatment of his own play showed just how much depended on the *deus ex machina* of the roulette wheel. (c)

Only the Valiant √ Nobody likes Gregory Peck until he fights off the Apaches; Gordon Douglas directs pliantly; 1951. (b/w)

Only Two Can Play √ Peter Sellers as Kingsley Amis librarian hero, strongly supported by Kenneth Griffith, Richard Attenborough. Sidney Gilliat directed; 1962. (b/w)

Only When I Larf √ Disappointing 1968 attempt at translating to the screen Len Deighton's amusing story of two con-men and their female accomplice. Director Basil Dearden pulls it back to an old-fashioned ambience while weak David Hemmings and Alexandra Stewart seem to plead for more contemporary handling. Only Richard Attenborough bridges the two styles, but he can't hold it together on his own. (c)

On Moonlight Bay √ Harmless musical based on Booth Tarkington characters; Doris Day and Gordon MacRae small-town sweethearts. Roy Del Ruth directed pleasantly; 1951. (c)

On the Avenue √ Irving Berlin ('I've Got My Love to Keep Me Warm', 'Let's Go Slumming') vehicle for Dick Powell at the height of his singing career, 1937. Madeleine Carroll is the richest girl in America lampooned by Alice Faye in sketch; she smacks co-star Powell's face, a sure sign they're going to fall in love in a Roy Del Ruth musical. (b/w)

On the Beach √ Australia in general; Gregory Peck, Ava Gardner in particular, under sentence of death by atomic radiation. Hailed in 1959 as an important contribution by director Stanley Kramer to world peace, it looks rather more commonplace today. (b/w)

On the Beat XX The usual awful Norman Wisdom comedy, here with the hard-working lad playing two parts. He's a co-opted policeman and a gang-leader, who loses his liberty and girlfriend to Wisdom-the-copper. You might not enjoy it much, but Wisdom obviously did: director Robert Asher allows him to prolong and laugh at his own jokes endlessly; 1963. (b/w)

On the Buses XXX Even worse than the dreadful TV series, this slab of unfunniness has women drivers causing upsets in the bus depot. Harry Booth directed the usual gang, headed by Reg Varney; 1971. (c)

On the Double √ Entertaining Danny Kaye vehicle made in 1961 when he was still funny. Resemblance to German officer makes him valuable Second World War spy, offers a chance for Walter Mittying. Director: Mel Shavelson. (c)

On the Fiddle √ There seemed to be some idea in Cyril Frankel's mind, in 1961, that he was directing a real war movie with a comedy twist. In fact, he came up with a farce on which real war awkwardly intruded. Alfred Lynch plays the universal skyver so familiar in British army comedies; with him are such familiars as Cecil Parker, Stanley Holloway, Eric Barker, Wilfrid Hyde White, John Le Mesurier and Kathleen Harrison. Less familiar in this carry-on is Sean Connery. (b/w)

On the Riviera XX One of those Danny Kaye movies that leaves one feeling patronised and dispirited; how could anyone have thought the silly plot about impersonating a French aviator (also played by the self-satisfied Mr Kaye) was amusing? Or that any of the complications about their women (Gene Tierney, Corinne Calvert) not knowing who was making love to them, were credible enough to entertain? Walter Lang; 1951 (c)

On the Town √√ Quite simply, the happiest musical ever, with Frank Sinatra, Gene Kelly, Ann Miller; marvellous music ('New York, New York, a Hell of a Town', bowdlerised to 'wonderful town'); stunning dancing; splendid direction (Kelly-plus-Stanley Donen); 1949. (c)

On the Waterfront √√ If you don't think about the political implications, which are suspiciously fascist-orientated, this is a devastatingly effective piece of film theatre, with at least two stunning performances – Brando's as the feather-bedded longshoreman who could have been a contender but has become a bully-boy (but, wait, there's nothing more regenerative than the love of a good woman, even such a pale, whiney one as Eva Marie Saint); Rod Steiger's as his elder brother, torn between his crooked union and family love. The scene in the back of the car is rightly regarded as one of the great movie moments of all time. For the rest, you can't really believe in Karl Malden's all-white priest or Lee J. Cobb's all-black union leader, but you happily suspend disbelief for the pleasure of watching Brando stagger (literally, at the end) through a plum of a part. 1954 Oscar winner for Best Picture, Best Actor; triple-nomination for Best Support – Cobb, Malden, Steiger; winner for Best Support, Saint; director Elia Kazan; writer Budd Schulberg; art-and-set Richard Day; editor Gene Milford; and photography Boris Kaufman. (b/w)

Ooh . . . You Are Awful √ Dick Emery manages better than most TV comedians on the big screen in this modest but assured story of con-men and the British Mafia, confidently directed by Cliff Owen; 1972. (c)

Operation Amsterdam XX As the Dutch diamond centre falls, a British major tries to bring the uncut stones to safety. Instead of concentrating on the human implications (why trust him? is he trustworthy?) director Michael McCarthy has co-written a script of wartime banality (with, incidentally, much too much gore). Peter Finch, Tony Britton, Eva Bartok are content to go through obvious heroics; 1959. (b/w)

Operation CIA XX The fighting in Vietnam had escalated to the point of real war by 1965, but you wouldn't know it from this routine cloak-and-dagger plot set in and around Saigon. Burt Reynolds plays the chief agent; director Christian Nyby must have been looking the other way. (b/w)

Operation Crossbow X Unconvincing attempt at convincing war film about blowing up V-2 sites in Germany. Michael Anderson manages to waste his talented cast (Sophia Loren, George Peppard, Tom Courtenay, Lilli Palmer are leads) though Jeremy Kemp fools him by giving a super performance that outshines all the clumsiness. From Madame Tussaud's, Patrick Wymark impersonates Churchill, Richard Johnson Duncan Sandys, Trevor Howard Professor Lindemann, John Mills MI6 chief; 1965. (c)

Operation Mad Ball X Not even Jack Lemmon can save this 1957 services comedy from disaster. It needed Phil Silvers in his Bilko role. Instead, Ernie Kovacs, Mickey Rooney, Kathryn Grant rave about wildly and unfunnily under Richard Quine's direction. (b/w)

Operation Petticoat √√ Slick, funny wartime comedy about a submarine that somehow gets painted pink and is hunted by both sides. As it's filled with various ladies and a crew headed by Cary Grant and Tony Curtis, it's all rather jolly in a navy lark sort of way. Blake Edwards was just the director to carry off such a carry on; 1960. (c)

Operation Snatch XX Boring 'comedy' about Terry-Thomas saving the British Empire by repopulating Gibraltar with apes – making a monkey of anyone who stays to watch. George Sanders, Lionel Jeffries, do their best with pale material. Directed by Robert Day; 1962. (b/w)

Operation Undercover √ Slick 1974 thriller from James Mills's novel, *Report to the Commissioner* (under which American title it may reach TV), in which an idealistic but fumbling police recruit bungles secret agent Susan Blakely's assignment. Milton Katselas directed competently and there is an effective shoot-out in Saks Fifth Avenue store. However, the casting of Michael Moriarty as the novice cop was unfortunate. (c)

The Opposite Sex XX Clare Boothe Luce wrote a witty, catty play called *The Women* that was made into a delicious 1939 comedy starring Norma Shearer, Rosalind Russell, Paulette Goddard and Joan Crawford, directed by George Cukor and containing only women in the cast. In 1956, MGM dusted the property off its shelves and gave it to David Miller to remake – with disastrous results. He broadened the plot to allow men in; he tarted it up with some musical numbers; and for the sharp clever ladies who glittered from the original he substituted June Allyson, Joan Collins, Dolores Gray and Ann Sheridan. It came out looking like a dated mish-mash of Society nonsense and you could no longer believe in the clutching and clawing for power, prestige and other people's husbands. A mess. (c)

The Optimists of Nine Elms √√ Refreshing use of children and dogs in a setting (the slums and equally forbidding tower blocks of a London suburb) which doesn't allow sentimentality – despite Peter Sellers's presence and his mooning over death of his dog. Anthony Simmonds's direction and co-scripting from his own novel steers away from the dangers, keeping a beady eye on the reality of working class life, circa 1973. (c)

Orchestra Wives √ Superior 1942 backstager built round Glenn Miller Orchestra, with Cesar Romero, Jackie Gleason, 'Serenade in Blue', 'Kalamazoo', 'Chattanooga Choo-Choo'. Pat Friday dubbed for Lynn Bari; Archie Mayo directed. (b/w)

Orders are Orders X Before Peter Sellers made it big with *The Lady-killers,* he had one or two small appearances in minor comedies, like this 1954 remake of the old 1932 army play. It nominally starred Tony Hancock and Sid James, with a raft of lesser comedy slapstickers. Directed by David Paltenghi, who as a director was a very good ballet dancer. (b/w)

Orders to Kill XX The weak Paul Massie as poorly-trained executioner in equally weak 1958 British Occupied France thriller with a few minutes of real tension towards the end when he prepares to kill a man he feels is innocent. Only Irene Worth, as French resistance worker, provides a touch of class. Anthony Asquith labours directorially. (b/w)

The Organization X Thriller featuring the black detective (Sidney Poitier) Mr Virgil Tibbs, first seen jousting with Rod Steiger (here sadly absent) during *In the Heat of the Night;* this is drugs and robberies in San Francisco; Don Medford, 1971. (c)

The Oscar XXX Tawdry attempt to cash in on glamour of Academy Awards night has stiff competition between actors Stephen Boyd, Tony Bennett and scriptwriters for Booby Prize. Even Eleanor Parker, Joseph Cotten, Ernest Borgnine (acting) and Bob Hope, Frank Sinatra (appearing as winner) can't begin to save it. Russell Rouse directed in 1966 a 'true movie rarity – a picture that attains a perfection of ineptitude' – *Life.* (c)

Oscar Wilde XX The worse (much worse) of the two Oscar Wilde films made in 1960 was this effort from Hollywood's Gregory Ratoff (as director), with Robert Morley sailing through the main part. The only marks it scored against Ken Hughes's *Trials of Oscar Wilde* were in Ralph Richardson's prosecuting counsel (over James Mason) and Phyllis Calvert as Mrs Wilde (over Yvonne Mitchell). For the rest, it's just a grubby Sunday poppaper's court transcript of the juicy bits. And it's in (b/w).

O.S.S. X Alan Ladd and Geraldine Fitzgerald parachute into France just before D-Day. It was made soon after in 1946, thus guaranteeing historical inaccuracy about the facts but correct details. Irving Pichel directed briskly. (b/w)

Othello √ A record of a very great stage performance from Laurence Olivier, but as a creative film of Shakespeare's great tragedy of jealousy it's a non-starter. Stuart Burge had the play photographed in little takes and joined them together unsatisfactorily in 1966. (c)

The Other X Produced by scriptwriter-novelist Thomas Tryon and directed by Robert Mulligan, this yarn involves curses, madness, twins, hallucination, murders and kidnappings. Uta Hagen, as a fairly sinister grandmother, is the only even moderately-known name in the cast; 1972. (c)

The Other Love XX Weep at it or for it, depending on taste – Barbara Stanwyck, dying of TB, has to choose between wild life on the Riviera with Richard Conte or the dedicated Dr David Niven. You guessed. Directed by André de Toth de absolute tosh; 1947. (b/w)

The Other Side of the Mountain
See *A Window to the Sky*

Otley √ Tom Courtenay gets mixed up in 1968 spy spoof by Dick Clement and Ian La Frenais, with direction by Clement. Some people found his involvements with Romy Schneider, Alan Badel, Leonard Rossiter, James Bolam funny. Maybe you will. (c)

Our Hearts Were Growing Up X Attempt to cash in on success of *Our Hearts Were Young and Gay,* in 1946, had same leads (Gail Russell, Diana Lynn) but their college days are a bore. William D. Russell directed. (b/w)

Our Hearts Were Young and Gay √ Cornelia Otis Skinner wrote a bestseller which told part of the story about a trip she and Emily Kimbrough made to Europe in the twenties. In this watering-down Gail Russell and Diana Lynn play the parts and it's hard to tell whether the old-fashioned quality of it all comes from deliberate recreation of the flapper period or the creaking 1944 direction of Lewis Allen. (b/w)

Our Man Flint √ Best of the James Bond rip-offs, this 1966 comedy-thriller has James Coburn marching starkly through, saving a few worlds. Daniel Mann directed briskly. (c)

Our Man in Havana √ Adaptation of Graham Greene novel was underrated at the time (1960), because Carol Reed chose to emphasise book's comedy. Now Noel Coward's performance as spy-recruiter stands out and Alec Guinness's vacuum-cleaner salesman gains solidity. Plus Ralph Richardson, Burl Ives, Ernie Kovacs, Maureen O'Hara, Paul Rogers. (b/w)

Our Man in Marrakesh XX One of the visitors to Morocco has two million dollars to be squeezed out of him. Which? If only one could care, but although the people are OK (Tony Randall, Herbert Lom, Wilfrid Hyde White, Terry-Thomas, John Le Mesurier) the writing, plot (Peter Yeldham), production (Harry Alan Towers), and direction (Don Sharp) aren't. A waste of everyone's time – let's hope not yours, too; 1966. (c)

Our Miss Fred XXX Director Bob Kellett has made an unappetising and embarrassing comedy of soldier

Danny La Rue in women's clothing escaping from the Germans. His TV-nightclub persona is a slyly observant camp male dressed in women's finery to make some comment about both sexes; but here he plays a man dressed up for the sake of the plot, and gets into dozens of scrapes as a result. The script is deplorable, the other 'acting' matches the star's; 1972. (c)

Our Mother's House √√ Brilliant, intriguing, macabre, but ultimately unsatisfying (because too many questions are left unanswered) cross between *Lord of the Flies* and *The Servant*. Seven children hide their mother's death, bury her in the garden, commune with her by séance, allow themselves to be invaded by Dirk Bogarde and Yootha Joyce – and there's plenty more (too much) plot to come. Producer-director Jack Clayton shied away from the whole hog, however, and this 1967 creepie only crawls. (c)

Our Relations √ Laurel and Hardy play their twin brothers in 1936 yoh, directed by Harry Lachman. (b/w)

Our Vines Have Tender Grapes √ Edward G. Robinson plays Margaret O'Brien's loving dad in awfully Sauterne yarn of Wisconsin family. Roy Rowland simply added sugar and mixed; 1945. (b/w)

The Outcast X John Derek fights for what's rightfully his. William Witney didn't turn this western into anything fancier; 1954. (c)

An Outcast of the Islands √√ Study of corruption in the South Seas, well-directed by Carol Reed, 1951. Trevor Howard plays Conrad's crooked clerk memorably, with support from Ralph Richardson, Robert Morley, Wendy Hiller. (b/w)

The Outcasts of Poker Flat √ Quite exciting western based on the Bret Harte story of four undesirables who are run out of a mining town and find themselves trapped together in a snowbound mountain cabin. But Joseph M. Newman didn't make the best of script or cast of Anne Baxter, Miriam Hopkins, Dale Robertson, Cameron Mitchell, in 1952. (b/w)

The Outfit √ Film of Donald E. Westlake's novel that was the sequel to the Lee Marvin-John Boorman thriller, *Point Blank*. Writer-director John Flynn imaginatively cast Robert Duvall as the professional who inadvertently crossed the Organisation. Set up by his girlfriend Karen Black,

he survives a series of attempts on his life, and counter-attacks. The result is a straightforward, if messy, actioner, with strong performances if precious few morals all round; 1973. (c)

The Outlaw X This is the famous western that Howard Hughes produced, directed and managed to publicise brilliantly through a spurious campaign suggesting that it was sexy. The famous busty still of Jane Russell spilling out of her blouse was the only erotic thing about it – and that wasn't even in the film, in itself a dull, mild encounter between Doc Holliday, Billy the Kid and Jane Russell. Thomas Mitchell, Jack Beutel, Walter Huston move anxiously about. Started in 1940, shown 1946. (b/w)

Outlaws of the Desert XX Hopalong Cassidy goes to Arabian desert to pick some horses, gets involved with villainous sheikh Duncan Renaldo (later to ride to fame himself as the Cisco Kid); director, Harold Bretherton; 1941. (b/w)

Out of Season √√ Absorbing triangle between mother (Vanessa Redgrave), daughter (Susan George), and mother's former suitor (Cliff Robertson) at an English seaside hotel. Neatly directed by Alan Bridges, it has a cop-out ending after a clever twist; 1975. (c)

The Out-of-Towners √√√ Wonderfully funny fable of two provincials, Jack Lemmon and Sandy Dennis, and their appalling experiences in the Big City. Director Arthur Hiller keeps up the pace, and Neil Simon's cracking script provides literally a laugh a minute; 1970. (c)

The Outrage √ Well, it isn't that bad, this re-setting of *Rashomon* in the Wild West. True, the acting is a bit dodgy, what with Paul Newman in a false nose and a black wig, Laurence Harvey with his usual supercilious myopia and Claire Bloom hamming it up in that very English dramatic way of hers. But Martin Ritt's direction is firm – until he collapses into broad comedy for the fourth and how-it-really-happened retelling of the anecdote. He has almost brought off the impossible feat of imposing a Japanese style on the conventional western. Unlike that other great remake, 'Seven Magnificent Samurai', this retains much of the spirit and feeling of the original. See *Rashomon* if you can, but this is a better-than-it-might-have-been substitute. Edward G. Robinson is among the storytellers who were sheltering from the rain in a temple in the original, in a railway station here. An unconvincing and sentimental postscript has been unnecessarily added; 1964. (b/w)

The Outsider √ (1) 1961 heart-breaker about Indian who was one of the men who raised the flag on Iwo Jima in famous photograph and became an outcast and drunk. Tony Curtis does well under Delbert Mann's direction. (b/w)

The Outsider X (2) 1967: Darren Mc-Gavin as ex-convict turned private eye investigates office frauds for Edmond O'Brien; Shirley Knight, Ann Sothern add to the mystery; so does director Michael Ritchie, not always intentionally. (c)

The Outsider √√ (3) 1967 version of Camus's book with Marcello Mastroianni hardly shown commercially in Britain. Director Luchino Visconti. (c)

The Overlanders √√ Powerful, authentic Australian western with Chips Rafferty driving cattle across desert; writer-director Harry Watt; 1946. (b/w)

Overlord √ Clever editing makes story of soldier (Brian Stirner) from call-up to D-Day almost convincing, as lashings of contemporary footage and newsreel are laced into acted scenes; Stuart Cooper; 1975. (b/w)

The Over-the-Hill Gang √ Four old Hollywood veterans make a nostalgic quartet – Pat O'Brien, Walter Brennan, Chill Wills, Edgar Buchanan – playing ex-Texas Rangers trying to run some young mobsters out of Boulder City. Other faces from the past who staggered over to play a part in this 1969 ride over Memory Prairie include Jack Elam, Andy Devine, Gypsy Rose Lee. (c)

Over the Moon X Might have been a charming comedy in 1939, but this romantic tale about Merle Oberon being exploited by fortune-hunters now seems stilted. Rex Harrison, Zena Dare, Ursula Jeans, Peter Haddon don't mitigate the theatricality of director Thornton Freeland. (c)

The Owl and the Pussycat √√ Funny bedroom farce about two pretentious people – Barbra Steisand as a whore who says she's a model and George Segal as a book-shop assistant who says he's a writer – shacking up together after various misunderstandings. Herbert Ross directed confidently from Buck Henry's adaptation of stage play; 1970. (c)

The Ox-Bow Incident √√ Flawed 1943 masterpiece (it suffered from *rigor artis*, according to James Agee), refused exhibition by the big circuits in Britain as too sombre. Henry Fonda is simple cowboy caught up in a lynching. William Wellman's best serious film. (b/w)

P

Pacific Destiny X Arthur Grimble's experiences as Colonial Service cadet in South Seas, dramatised – if that isn't too strong a word. Denholm Elliott, Michael Hordern. Directed by Wolf Rilla; 1956. (c)

Pack Up Your Troubles √ Jolly Laurel and Hardy army, half during First World War and half afterwards, tracing comrade's cute little daughter; directed by George Marshall and Raymond McCarey; 1932. (b/w)

The Pad – and How to Use It X Peter Shaffer wrote a funny short play called *The Private Ear*. Brian Hutton directed a dreadul film from it, this one. Brian Bedford, Julie Sommars reduce it to a silly chase; 1966. (c)

The Painted Hills X How Lassie avenges master's murder, playing the part of Shep in the Oregon gold rush. Director, Harold F. Kress; 1951. (c)

Paint Your Wagon √ Strictly for western and/or musical fanatics. The rest of you may find director Josh Logan's unimaginative transcription of the stage show to screen heavy going. Lee Marvin does his *Cat Ballou* drunk bit, Clint Eastwood wanders in and out, Jean Seberg is miscast as usual. The score is more than adequate – André Previn helping Lerner and Loewe; 1969. (c)

The Pajama Game √ This is the fast-paced 1957 movie version of George Abbott and Richard Bissell's show from Bissell's novel, 7½ *Cents*, which dealt rather more realistically with a wage demand at a pyjama factory, starring Doris Day; directed by Stanley Donen. (c)

The Paleface √ Entertaining Bob Hope western, let down by posturings of Jane Russell, who was all publicity and no talent. Bob was dentist; Jane was Calamity Jane in more ways than two. Director Norman Z. McLeod; 1948. (c)

Pal Joey √√ John O'Hara wrote a short story about a heel. He turned this into a musical play about the same character, who was still pretty nasty. Then this became a 1957 musical film and as they had Frank Sinatra for the part they couldn't make him too much of a bastard. The result is a sadly gooey plot, with the unpleasant little squitty social and business exploiter softened to a boyish charmer who can't be all bad since he loves his scene-stealing dog. Rita Hayworth is reduced by the change of emphasis, too; instead of the man-eating harridan who is prepared to be used by Joey if she can use him in turn, she's a petulant self-sacrificer. And Kim Novak, always sensual to look at if nothing else, is given a pretty-pretty part that any soppy ingenue could have fitted better and might have provided her own voice for. Nevertheless . . . Sinatra is Sinatra and the less ribald songs they have left in are outstandingly good ('Bewitched, Bothered and Bowdlerised', 'I Could Write a Book'). George Sidney. (c)

Palm Springs Weekend X One of those spurious teenage movies churned out around 1963 to snaffle the drive-in market in America, and put out as second features here. Norman Taurog, Elvis Presley's routine director, pushes a talent-scarce cast of Troy Donahue, Connie Stevens, Ty Hardin through various unbelievable low flings at Palm Springs. (c)

Pandora and the Flying Dutchman X Ava Gardner falls in love with mysterious Dutch dilettante James Mason. Pretentious and slightly risible in its romanticism, it nevertheless satisfied a lushness missing in British pictures of 1951. Albert Lewin came from the Hollywood of his *Moon and Sixpence* and *Dorian Gray* to write, produce and direct. (c)

Panic XX Second-feature about amnesiac second-guessing the police with a climax against the second-hand. Strictly second-rate. Writer-director John Gilling with cast who have paid us to leave their names out; 1965. (b/w)

Panic in the Streets √ Richard Widmark as doctor tracking down source of bubonic plague in Elia Kazan's exciting, location-aided 1950 thriller; Paul Douglas is sceptical police chief; Jack Palance, Barbara Bel Geddes, Zero Mostel are stops along the way. (b/w)

Panic in Year Zero √ Ray Milland directed as well as appearing in this last-family-left-alive sci-fi, in 1962. Jean Hagen good back-up. (b/w)

Papa's Delicate Condition √ Papa is Jackie Gleason and his delicate condition is alcoholism. It leads him into all sorts of trouble, like buying a drug store to get at the liquor and somehow a circus as well. Glynis Johns, Elisha Cook and Charlie Ruggles join in the rather dubious fun. George Marshall directed; 1963. (c)

Paperback Hero √ Keir Dullea is well cast as small-town ice hockey star who has himself made marshal on the strength of his popularity. When that goes sour, he goes crazy. Imaginative direction from Peter Pearson compensates for low budget; 1972. (c)

The Paper Chase √√ As those who saw the TV spin-off will know, the title refers to the chase for good grades in Harvard Law School: Timothy Bottoms contrives to shine in contracts class and win the Professor's daughter, too. Despite a totally unconvincing ending, director James Bridges brings off an intriguing, enjoyable movie; the outstanding ingredient is John Houseman's brilliant, Oscar-winning performance as the Professor; 1973. (c)

Paper Lion √ This dramatisation of journalist George Plimpton's account of participating with Detroit Lions football team depends on viewer's knowledge of and interest in American pro. football — and George Plimpton. Alan Alda plays him, under Alex March's direction; 1968. (c)

Paper Moon √√√ Delightful fable about Ryan O'Neal, a confidence trickster of recent widows. He only cons them out of a few dollars for a Bible he alleges their husbands ordered, so we can still like him. He is lumbered with Tatum O'Neal (real-life daughter) as *enfant terrible*. A finely-observed cameo by Madeleine Kahn almost succeeds in taking the honours away from Tatum. There is a beguiling soundtrack of thirties numbers and accomplished direction by Peter Bogdanovich; 1973. (b/w)

Paper Tiger XX Unfunny comedy which hedges its bets with kidnappings and assassination attempts. David Niven is given too great a responsibility by director Ken Annakin; 1974. (c)

Papillon √ Rather plodding account of supposedly true escapes from French penal colonies, including

Devil's Island, by Steve McQueen, sometimes aided by Dustin Hoffman. Writer Dalton Trumbo appears in a small part as the French Commandant. Franklin J. Schaffner directs, without undue imagination; 1973. (c)

The Paradine Case √ Hitchcock admits this one was full of mistakes, particularly in the casting over which he didn't have control (David Selznick did). Gregory Peck, he says, could never play an English QC – should have been Ronald Colman or Laurence Olivier. Louis Jourdan was 'worst flaw' as the groom who had been Alida Valli's lover – should have been Robert Newton or someone else who was 'manure-smelling'. Ann Todd's part wasn't satisfactory, either, as QC's wife fancied by Judge Charles Laughton. Above all, Hitch himself says that he was never quite sure how the murder was committed; 1947. (b/w)

Paradise, Hawaiian Style XX Elvis Presley's contribution to the art of 1966 was this tired old repetition of all his previous films, only this time he was a pilot. Ten songs, all out of context. A very slight nod in the direction of recent ideas about frozen frames from director Michael Moore in the course of one song. Otherwise, zero. (c)

The Parallax View √√√ Making the incredible seem possible is part of cinematic magic, and Alan J. Pakula marvellously plays on our neuroses about the Kennedy murder and the Nixon era's revelations of villainy in high places. Warren Beatty suspects an organisation at work training assassins, and nobody will believe him. The ending is clever, too; 1974. (c)

Paranoiac √ First of the many *Psycho*-inspired frighteners was this modestly exciting chiller directed with some skill by ex-cameraman Freddie Francis, in 1962. Janette Scott is the victim in a terrible plot to have her declared insane; Oliver Reed is brother, and Alexander Davion and Sheila Burrell back up in nicely-judged performances. Not a patch on Hitch, of course, but better than most of the field. (b/w)

Pardon My Sarong √ Abbott and Costello thwart Lionel Atwill's attempts to steal temple jewels; Erle C. Kenton directed; 1942. (b/w)

Pardon Us √ Laurel and Hardy in jail – it was actually called *Jail Birds* when first released. They are caught

making beer during prohibition. Director, James Parrott; 1931. (b/w)

Paris Blues X Would-be frothy location-shot story of jazzmen – Paul Newman and Sidney Poitier – pulling tourists Joanne Woodward and Diahann Carroll. This 1961 version of Harold Flender's novel doesn't come off – you simply can't care about the characters. The music's OK though; Martin Ritt; 1961. (b/w)

Paris Holiday XX By 1958, when this comedy was made, Bob Hope was going soft. He strolled through his movies with too insouciant an air, and you couldn't feel any of the necessary sense of involvement. To compound the faults, he produced this one himself from his own story-line (about international gangsters in Paris). Despite Gerd Oswald's directorial exertions, the result is a would-be chunk of hilariousness with a flaw right down the middle. Fernandel does provide a few moments of broad amusement, but the femme side is dull with Anita Ekberg and Martha Hyer. (c)

Paris When It Sizzles XXX Fizzles would have been better. There never was a more frizzled-up movie than this one in which Audrey Hepburn and William Holden are wilfully thrown away in an incredibly coy and silly story of an American writer dictating a plot (almost as bad as this film's and that's sure saying a lot) to a temporary secretary and, of course, falling for her. But the arrogant American's ideas of Gay Paree and the banality of Richard Quine's pictorialisation of a really rotten script are breathtaking. If television shows many pictures like this, people will start going out to the cinemas again, which were emptied in 1964 by films like this. (c)

Parrish XX So awful you might even enjoy Delmer Daves's 1961 drippy drama of robot-like Troy Donohue fighting to better his and mother Claudette Colbert's lot on tobacco (it should be corn) plantation. Amazing over-acting from Karl Malden. (c)

The Party XX Wretched attempt to provide one long laugh as Peter Sellers's Indian character wrecks a producer's party. Turns out to be one long groan as old gags fizzle out, Sellers is driven to further desperations and director-producer Blake Edwards throws in the sponge by wildly dragging in a painted elephant. Awful; 1969. (c)

Party Girl √ Standard Nicholas Ray (one of the more over-rated directors), made in 1958. He manages to reduce a promising script (gangsters and G-men in 1932) and some fine performers (Lee J. Cobb, Cyd Charisse) down to the level of the rest of the cast (Robert Taylor, Kent Smith, John Ireland). But there may still be enough excitement to pass a wet evening. (c)

The Party's Over XXX A real stinker of meretricious rubbish, with what are supposed to be Chelsea Bohemians hiding a girl from her fiancé and father. Oliver Reed glowers as leader of the bunch in a way that suggests he thought he was acting; the others lope about delivering explanatory lines, and the director, Guy Hamilton, must have popped out for a quick drink. It had censor trouble after it was made in 1962 and didn't get shown until 1965, when it was slaughtered by the critics. (b/w)

The Passionate Stranger XX Dreadful attempt to retell the Lady Chatterley story as a comedy, with an Italian chauffeur (Carlo Justini – weak) wooing Margaret Leighton (whose idea of acting here seems to be playing with her specs) while Ralph Richardson sits in his wheelchair. The central section (in colour) is the novel itself, as allegedly written by Leighton. Altogether tedious and typically Muriel Box; 1956. (mostly b/w)

Passionate Summer XXX One of the dregs of British film-making in 1958 was this perfectly awful romance about the three women in the life of a schoolmaster. Each of the women is worse played than the last one you saw on the screen, as if Virginia McKenna, Yvonne Mitchell and Ellen Barrie were engaged in some sort of gloomy contest to win the Wooden Oscar, female division (male division easily going to the hero Bill Travers). Rudolph Cartier faithfully responds to the mood of Joan Henry's turgid script and the technical credits are uniformly dreadful. (c)

Passport to Pimlico √ Sensational success in its day, but has dated much more than most 1948 comedies. About the London borough that found it could erect barriers between it and the rest of Britain. Henry Cornelius made it all very pleasant and chuckly as Stanley Holloway, fish-shop owner, unearths ancient treaty. (b/w)

Passport to Shame XXX A real stinker about French girl (Odile Versois) being white-slaved by Brenda de Banzie and Herbert Lom, while Eddie Constantine rounds up taxi-driving friends to release her from the House of Shame. Dreadful performances by Diana Dors and all others mentioned, due, partly, one can only think, to the sheer ineptitude of director Alvin Rakoff; 1959. (b/w)

The Password is Courage √ Andrew and Virginia Stone took the escapes of one Charles Coward during the war, when he was in German hands, as their 1962 excuse to show catastrophes and special effects. The bangs and crashes are fine. The casting is strictly mis- (Dirk Bogarde in a Kenneth More role; Reginald Beckwith as a very Camp Commandant). And the location shooting was mysteriously done around London instead of around Bremen – and it shows. (b/w)

Pat and Mike √√ The loving duo, Spencer Tracy (sports coach) and Katharine Hepburn (sports coached), make this slight anecdote delightful; George Cukor guided, 1952. Miss Hepburn shows what a good tennis-player, golfer, swimmer, hiker and basketball player she is. Garson Kanin and Ruth Gordon wrote a crackling script that won an Oscar nomination. (b/w)

A Patch of Blue √ Grossly sentimental Cinderella story about blind skivvy Elizabeth Hartman being rescued by Prince Charming Sidney Poitier – but, you see, she doesn't realise he's black – so what, in 1965? Shelley Winters overplays the wicked mother to the point of absurdity (winning Oscar in the process for Best Support) yet Hartman is so powerful under Guy Green's direction that you almost forgive the excesses of story and acting elsewhere. (b/w)

Pat Garrett and Billy the Kid √√ Wounded western – Sam Peckinpah publicly protested about how his film had been re-edited and that James Coburn's death at the hands of his own men had been omitted. The film would have carried more punch without pop stars Kris Kristofferson and Bob Dylan among the outlaw heroes. The lesson seems to be that there is no way out for violent men. Does that include director Peckinpah? 1973. (c)

Paths of Glory √√ Stanley Kubrick's 1957 revelation that war is not only hell, but political rascality. Kirk Douglas, Adolphe Menjou outstanding as French officers cynically slaughtering in the First World War for personal advancement. (b/w)

The Patsy √ Jerry Lewis, groomed for stardom by a syndicate consisting of Peter Lorre, Everett Sloane, Keenan Wynn, Phil Harris, John Carradine and Ina Balin sounds a promising idea. Trouble is, that although according to the script they make it, by the evidence of our eyes they don't. He can't blame the director – direction was his. 1964. (c)

Patterns of Power √√ Fielder Cook's first film as a director was this 1956 beady look at the ethics of big business executives, from Rod Serling's television play he produced. Van Heflin is the young (well, he was 46, but played younger) fellow whose lofty ideas are put through the mincer when Everett Sloane slaughters nice old Ed Begley's ideals and offers Heflin his chair. At least he doesn't do a Gary Cooper and renounce the corporate way of life for cutting down trees in God's country, but takes the chair muttering platitudes. (b/w)

Patton: Lust for Glory √√ Perhaps the most successful film about Second World War, because it takes a point of view (Patton's) and sticks to it, despite the distortion this inevitably gives to other characters and events. George C. Scott's vivid portrayal is totally impressive under Franklin J. Schaffner's confident realisation of Francis Ford Coppola's accomplished script. It may not be the war, but it is magnificent; 1969. (c)

The Pawnbroker √√√ Strong study in obsessive memory by Rod Steiger who earned an Academy Award nomination in 1965 for towering performance (absurdly beaten by Lee Marvin for *Cat Ballou*) as the Harlem uncle who lives within his consciousness of the concentration camp. Sidney Lumet didn't pander to popular stereotyping in his supporting characters either. (b/w)

Payday √√ Highly effective study of an ambitious country-and-western singer and his nasty habits, assuredly captured by Rip Torn under director Daryd Duke; 1971 (c)

Payment on Demand √√ 1951 weepie, directed by Curtis Bernhardt, which gives Bette Davis every chance to play centre-screen. She's a woman who is shocked to find that husband Barry Sullivan wants to divorce her after twenty years; afraid of winding up a middle-aged divorcée with nothing, she screws as big a settlement out of him as she can, but it's not the same as Love. The rest of the cast seems to have been chosen to prove, by contrast, what a great actress she is. (b/w)

Pay or Die √ Tough account of Mafia moving in on New York in 1906; made in 1960 by Richard Wilson, it has Ernest Borgnine as honest Italian cop. (b/w)

Payroll √ Ambitious 1961 British gangster thriller about wife of murdered armoured car driver seeking revenge, has strong cast (Michael Craig, Billie Whitelaw, Kenneth Griffith, Tom Bell, Stanley Meadows); direction from Stanley Hayers. (b/w)

Pay the Devil √√ Orson Welles is owner and tyrant of a huge ranch near the Mexican border. When he orders a mutinous peon killed, he doesn't expect the local sheriff, Jeff Chandler, to come poking his nose in. But he does. Jack Arnold succeeds in making this 1957 drama menacing and gripping, even if a little obvious. (b/w)

The Pearl of Death √ Basil Rathbone as Sherlock Holmes on the trail of six busts of Napoleon, one of which has the pearl in it. Miles Mander is in this 1944 effort, directed by Roy William Neill. (b/w)

Peeping Tom √√ Michael Powell's thriller about a sex-maniac who photographs the women he kills caused outcry when first shown in 1959 but has since become a cult film, ahead of its time in questioning just who the voyeur is – the killer or the viewer. Carl Boehm's hero-victim, Anna Massey's heroine, Powell himself as the sadistic father all notable; so is technical brilliance. (c)

Pendulum √ Duel between policeman evading arrest for murder and psychopath. George Peppard makes a lacklustre lead, but director George Schaefer kept the action going in 1969. (c)

Penelope XXX Dreadful comedy-thriller which is neither: Natalie Wood is neglected wife robbing her husband's bank to gain his attention. Embarrassed comedians Dick Shawn, Jonathan Winters fumble about under Arthur Hiller's 1966 direction. (c)

Penny Serenade √ Cary Grant and Irene Dunne find the strain of their marriage too much after the death of their adopted daughter. But romance, Hollywood and George Stevens, the director, make it all right again; 1941. (b/w)

The Penthouse X Terence Morgan, one of the weakest actors ever to grace an

English screen, and Suzy Kendall, pretty but not Bernhardt, are preparing to leave the show flat at the top of a new block when they are invaded by Tom, Dick and Harry (get the symbolism), three crooks high on pot, who tie them up, rape the girl and generally torture and torment in a totally gratuitous and nasty manner. Peter Collinson was roundly condemned in 1967 for directing a gloatingly sadistic romp. (c)

The People Against O'Hara X Disappointing 1951 Spencer Tracy vehicle about an unorthodox lawyer; wanting to help an old pal on the skids, he insisted that Pat O'Brien should be given a part. Irony was that O'Brien picked up good notices while Tracy got the back of the critics' hands. John Sturges couldn't make the plot about witness-bribery and extreme vindication convincing. (b/w)

People Will Talk √√ Cary Grant as unconventional doctor marrying pregnant patient Jeanne Crain in Joseph Mankiewicz-Darryl Zanuck thoughtful comedy. Ahead of its time in 1951. (b/w)

Pepe XXX Extraordinary goof with stars doing walk-ons, about Cantinflas following Dan Dailey to Hollywood because that's where his horse has gone. Only supportable as a Spot-the-Stars contest between those watching. Some tips: Maurice Chevalier, Bing Crosby, Greer Garson, Jack Lemmon, Kim Novak, Frank Sinatra, Zsa Zsa Gabor, Cesar Romero, Debbie Reynolds, Sammy Davis Jr. and Judy Garland's voice. Directed flaccidly by George Sidney; 1960. (c)

Perfect Friday XX Despite a posh director (Peter Hall) and a reputable cast (David Warner, Stanley Baker, Ursula Andress), this caper involving a rich couple and a bent bank manager lacks either tension or charm; 1970. (c)

Perfect Strangers √ Robert Donat and Deborah Kerr are dull couple with sparkle put back in eye by wartime romances. Rather daring in its genteel way for 1945 and unexpected from Alexander Korda. Support from Glynis Johns, Ann Todd, Roland Culver. (b/w)

Performance √√ Impressive failure by Nicholas Roeg and Donald Cammell: they explore the inter-changeability of identities, using gangster James Fox and retired pop star Mick Jagger. Despite much pretension and muddle, the film's strengths are considerable, and it is interesting as Roeg's first direction in 1968 (he was soon to make *Walkabout* and *Don't Look Now*). It was also Jagger's last attempt at becoming a film actor; 1970. (c)

The Perils of Pauline Silent serial was made into two camp movies: X (1) 1947. George Marshall directed Betty Hutton in what passed for biopic of Pearl White, who played original part. (c)

The Perils of Pauline √ (2) 1967. Herbert Leonard and Joshua Shelley made what they hoped was to have been pilot for TV series, but when they couldn't set it up this was released as cinema feature. Pat Boone seeking his long-lost sweetheart Pamela Austin, who is undergoing wild adventures. (c)

Period of Adjustment √ The troubles of just-marrieds Jane Fonda and Jim Hutton, contrasting with those of splitting Lois Nettleton and Tony Franciosa, are given an edge by their origins in a Tennessee Williams play and sharp, spare direction by George Roy Hill; 1962. (b/w)

Permission to Kill XX Granted. But start with director Cyril Frankel and anyone else who conned Dirk Bogarde into appearing in this rubbish about assassinating a politician returning to his country. The whole script should have been sold to the Saint for a last-minute intervention by him; 1975. (c)

Persecution XX Ridiculous little potboiler exploiting Lana Turner in 1974, aged 54. She plays a mad lady who cannot remember who pushed her downstairs. The whole sorry movie (listlessly directed by Don Chaffey) is a sensational, bloody working out of her lunacy that seems have touched every other member of the cast. That includes both hopeless newcomers and dazed stalwarts (Trevor Howard, Ralph Bates among them). (c)

Pete Kelly's Blues √ Fairly convincing re-creation of the jazz world in the jazz age, made in 1955. Director-star Jack Webb is a drag in both hats, but Peggy Lee (acting), Ella Fitzgerald (singing), Janet Leigh and Lee Marvin turn in performances above the line of duty. (c)

Pete 'n' Tillie √√ The first half is humorous, witty, with some of Walter Matthau's marvellous slow burns, spiritedly matched by Carol Burnett's own laconic style of humour. Then Martin Ritt's comedy-drama from a Peter de Vries story suddenly switches into tragedy. Confounding expectations in this way can be salutary, but in this case it almost defeats what started as a charming and memorable film; 1972. (c)

Petticoat Pirates XXX Laboured Charlie Drake comedy about mutinous Wrens being thwarted by the unlovely little chap. There's one sequence, where he plays several parts, that is passable; the rest you can pass by. David MacDonald directed; 1961. (c)

Petulia √ Julie Christie is married to Richard Chamberlain. Shirley Knight is divorced from Dr George C. Scott. Julie fancies George. Richard hits Julie. And so on. But director Dick Lester has jazzed it all up with such flashy pictures and clever cutting that you feel there must be less in it all than meets the eye. He has also made it cute and attempts to convince Miss Christie that she's kookie – maybe he thought he was directing Shirley MacLaine? Altogether, it's a dazzling mess. Somewhere in there: Joseph Cotten, Arthur Hill and the city of San Francisco; 1968. (c)

Peyton Place √ Mark Robson made a better film than the smutty, scratchy and ultimately unsexy model that Grace Metalious wrote badly enough for it to become a bestseller. Helped by some solid performances (Lloyd Nolan as a doctor, Arthur Kennedy as Lucas Cross, Diane Varsi and Lana Turner as Allison and her mother) he made, in 1958, a highly watchable film often let down by its dialogue and petty scandals, an imitation silk purse out of a sow's ear. (c)

Phantom Lady √√ Thriller by Robert Siodmak about Ella Raines trying to establish lover's innocence; good atmosphere of 1943 New York in menacing heatwave. Franchot Tone, Elisha Cook Jr. (b/w).

The Phantom of the Opera. Disfigured composer living in the sewers adopts young opera singer.

√ (1) 1943 version is remake of 1925 silent and keeps the action in the original Paris. Claude Raines hams his way through the Lon Chaney part; Arthur Lubin directs; winner of Oscars for art direction and photography. (c)

The Phantom of the Opera √ (2) 1962 Hammer version moves story to London with Herbert Lom as less grotesque Phantom; Terence Fisher directs in relatively restrained manner. (c)

Phantom of the Rue Morgue √ Remake of Poe's *Murders in the Rue Morgue* for 3D in 1954. Karl Malden makes an interesing change from Vincent Price's monopoly of such roles with Patricia Medina his fiancée and accomplice. Roy Del Ruth directed rather more cheerily than eerily. (c)

The Phantom Planet XXX One of those movies that are so bad that they almost take on a charm of their own as each effect outdoes the last in ineptitude, each line outdoes the last in triteness and each performance outdoes the last in inefficiency. Supposedly about a planet where the inhabitants are six inches high, including – amazingly – silent star Francis X. Bushman. William Marshall was responsible (fairly), in 1962. (b/w)

The Phantom Tollbooth √ Butch Patrick, a little boy in live action, drives in his toy car into cartoon world; director, David Monahan; 1970. (c)

The Phenix City Story √ Strong, lively actioner about the cleaning up of a sinful town, expertly directed by Phil Karlson in 1955. Unknown cast adds credibility. (b/w)

Phffft! √ Inspired teaming of Judy Holliday and Jack Lemmon insures that this comedy of divorce is squeezed to the full. Jack Carson and Kim Novak back up well. Mark Robson directed nattily; 1954. (b/w)

The Philadelphia Story √√√ Quite the best Hollywood comedy of its period, 1940 (and many believe ever), superbly played by Katharine Hepburn, James Stewart, Cary Grant and confidently directed by George Cukor from Philip Barry's crackling play. My, but it's yar. Six Oscar nominations, two awards (for the Stewarts). (b/w)

Phone Call from a Stanger √ Episodic, annoyingly jump-about story of various people in aeroplane crash, their survivors, and personal dramas. Director Jean Negulesco makes it all very easy to watch, but Gary Merrill isn't strong enough to carry the linking weight and Bette Davis is allowed to go overboard as paralytic wife of one of the passengers; 1952. (b/w)

Piccadilly Third Stop XXX Disastrous little mock-*Asphalt Jungle* set in a London there never was, with a parade of the weakest talent of 1960 (Terence Morgan, Yoko Tani, Mai Zetterling, William Hartnell); directed, if that is the word, by Wolf Rilla. (b/w)

Pickup on South Street √√ 'An analytical assault on the mental and physical strength and weakness of a professional pickpocket,' is how director Samuel Fuller describes his screenplay. Richard Widmark played crook caught in espionage web in this 1953 thriller, which betrays its period only in its obsession with anti-Communism. (b/w)

Pickwick Papers √ Rather plodding version, directed in 1952 by Noel Langley with James Hayter and second-league cast, of Dickens's picaresque novel that resists straight-jacket of a plot. (b/w)

Picnic √ Kim Novak was out of her depth as small-town girl awakening to life among accomplished players like William Holden, Rosalind Russell, Susan Strasberg, Cliff Robertson, Betty Field. Result is mixture of styles, but the old magic of the stranger who arrives and changes lives still works – and Kim was made a star. Joshua Logan directed, helped largely by James Wong Howe's camerawork and theme-music, 'Moonglow'; 1955. (c)

Picture Mommy Dead XX As unpleasant as its title, this is nonsense about Susan Gordon being possessed by her mother's spirit as she battles to win her rightful inheritance. Hammy cast includes Zsa Zsa Gabor, Don Ameche, Martha Hyer, Signe Hasso, all getting on a bit in 1966, indulged by director Bert I. Gordon. (c)

The Picture of Dorian Gray √ This was considered a huge success in 1945 for its pictorial elegance, winning the photography Oscar for Harry Stradling; but somehow its monochrome (except for flashes of the portrait), leaden script and George Sanders' tame (rather than Wilde) performance don't seem quite as brilliant now. Albert Lewin directed stylishly and deserves credit for the young Angela Lansbury's fine performance. (b/w)

The Pied Piper XX Weak, literal transcription of Browning's poem, with pop-folk singer Donovan ill at ease in the title role. Donald Pleasence, Michael Hordern, Roy Kinnear and other English character actors can do little to alleviate director Jacques Demy's flat fantasy; 1971. (c)

The Pigeon that Took Rome √ Charlton Heston sending messages behind the enemy lines in Italy makes a mildly amusing comedy under Mel Shavelson's tries-too-hard direction. Elsa Martinelli leads the locals; 1962. (b/w)

Pillow Talk √√ First film Doris Day and Rock Hudson made together (1959), it proved an irresistible com-

bination for all who aren't too stuffy to laugh at trivia; Tony Randall, Thelma Ritter add to the fun and the script won an Oscar. Michael Gordon's direction gets the best from I-love-you-I-hate-you misunderstandings. (c)

Pimpernel Smith √ Updating to 1941 and the Nazis of the Scarlet P. Directed by and starring Leslie Howard. Splendid fun. (b/w)

The Pink Panther √ One of those comedies that people swear by or at. Peter Sellers is bumbling French inspector after jewel thief; Robert Wagner, Claudia Cardinale, David Niven add distinction, but picture is stolen by cartoon panther in credits, later spun off to make own TV series. Blake Edwards directed; 1964. (c)

Pink String and Sealing Wax √ Robert Hamer directed this Victorian yarn in 1945 with youthful Gordon Jackson, Googie Withers; Mervyn Johns is heavy father. (b/w)

Pinky √ Elia Kazan's early (1949) taboo-breaking race-drama about black girl, passing for white, returning to the South to discover contrast with Northern ways. Since then, the US has woken up to the fact that the North isn't such a dandy place to be if you're black, either. Jeanne Crain vitiates theme by being white herself. Nina Mae McKinney, Ethels Barrymore and Waters, William Lundigan. (b/w)

The Pirate √ Rather corny 1948 musical with stagey plot worth idly watching for lavish costumes, Cole Porter songs, Judy Garland, Gene Kelly and director Vincente Minnelli's efforts to bind them all together. About lover posing as own rival. (c)

Pirates on Horseback XX Dull Hopalong Cassidy oater about an old-timer being murdered because he knows location of goldmine; director, Lesley Salander; 1941. (b/w)

The Pistolero of Red River √ Young Chad Everett tries to prove himself smarter than local marshal Glenn Ford; routine stuff but Jack Elam may save your night with one of his slimy-baddy parts, here blackmailing 'saloon-owner' Angie Dickinson; Richard Thorpe; 1966. (c)

The Pit and the Pendulum √ Director Roger Corman made it a fluid, exciting experience in 1961. Vincent Price and Barbara Steele go through their ritual roles, and it's satisfactorily creepy, although Poe's story is just tacked-on climax. (c)

Pit of Darkness XX One of those

amnesia plots, with William Franklyn as safe-designer with a lost memory; poor cast doesn't much help director Lance Comfort; 1956. (b/w)

A Place in the Sun √ Lumbering, slow-moving but convincing account of young man's dilemmas as he seeks to climb the social ladder, dragged down by pregnant girl-friend. This adaptation of Dreiser's *An American Tragedy* won 1951 Oscars for direction (George Stevens), script (Michael Wilson and Harry Brown), music (Franz Waxman), costumes (Edith Head), photography (William C. Mellor), editing (William Hornbeck). Star Montgomery Clift was nominated for Best Actor, draggy girl-friend Shelley Winters for Best Actress. One omission from the general prize-giving: Elizabeth Taylor. (b/w)

A Place to Go XX Attempt by Michael Relph and Basil Dearden to 'get with it', as the phrase was in 1964, by tranferring their normal boy-on-a-robbery theme to the sociologically interesting mileu of uprooted slum-dwellers living in new tower block. Bernard Lee is fine as a wayward dad, Rita Tushingham and Barbara Ferris make believable working-class girls, but Mike Sarne (formerly a weak pop-singer, later a weak film-director) is a weak actor in the main part. (b/w)

The Plague of the Zombies X Same old plot about the Voodoo cult in the remote English village, same old squire, same old graveyard, same old André Morell investigating, same old John Gilling directing, same old Hammer churning the films out and pulling the money in. Extraordinary it all still went on in 1965. (c)

The Plainsman √ Out-of-date 1967 remake of De Mille classic Gary Cooper-Jean Arthur 1937 Westerner, but since then the West has become a more complicated (and in the hands of better directors, a more interesting) place. Don Murray is no substitute for Coop and his attempts to bring some realism to the character just make him look dyspeptic. For the rest, director David Lowell Rich can't breathe any life into such worn characters as Buffalo Bill and Calamity Jane. There is, however, one black comedy moment when Mrs Abraham Lincoln chides her husband, 'Hurry up, Abraham, or we shall be late for the theatre.' (c)

Planet of the Apes √ First in line of surprisingly successful sci-flicks, with Charlton Heston as Man's representative in what easily could have been a jungler about savages, a western about Indians, but happens to be a planeter about actors with monkey masks. Franklin J. Schaffner directs efficiently but without much human or simian understanding; 1968. (c)

Play Dirty √ Straight pinch from *The Dirty Dozen* about ex-criminals now operating in the desert. Michael Caine is supposed to be in charge, but André de Toth's direction somehow subjugates his part to those of Nigel Davenport, Nigel Green and Harry Andrews – thus showing splendid taste in actors. Quite exciting; 1968. (c)

Play It Again Sam √ Woody Allen in adaptation of his own play about the Bogart-inspired shmuck is rarely as funny as he hoped. While the film passes the time adequately there is very little inspiration in his first (1972) on-screen collaboration with Diane Keaton. Director, Herbert Ross. (c)

Play it Cool XX Terrible little twist-era musical directed by Michael Winner in 1962 has an awkward Billy Fury and an equally inferior cast (excepting Dennis Price and Richard Wattis, both lost in the floss) in a fitful plot about a girl being saved from marriage to another pop-singer. (b/w)

Play Misty for Me √√ Really exciting thriller starring and directed by Clint Eastwood, about a psychotic fan (Jessica Walter) who gets busy with a sharp knife. Shot on Eastwood's home ground, near his estate at Carmel, south of San Francisco; 1971. (c)

Plaza Suite √√ Any movie with a script by Neil Simon and three performances by Walter Matthau can't be all bad, but director Arthur Miller made heavy weather of these three one-act plays all set in the same hotel. However, the opening dialogue between Matthau and Maureen Stapleton is delightful; 1970. (c)

Please Don't Eat the Daisies X David Niven is professor who becomes Clive Barnesish butcher-critic of Broadway. He pans a pal's production and gets his face slapped by Janis Paige. Meanwhile, at home, Doris Day is still singing 'Que Sera, Sera' from a film of hers made five years before 1960, when this disappointment, directed by usually reliable old Charles Walters, appeared. (c)

Please Sir! XX TV comedies rarely translate well to movie length, and this feeble working-over of the LWT series is no exception. The 'kids' look too old;

John Alderton and the other teachers appear stumped for a good idea or good lines; the 'characterisations' are the usual unpleasant stereotypes. Director, Mash Stuart; 1971. (c)

Please Turn Over XX That hoary old one about the girl who writes a novel which upsets family and friends by turning them into naughty-naughties. Awful little nothing from the Carry On team (director Gerald Thomas), with Ted Ray, Jean Kent, Leslie Phillips, Joan Sims, Julia Lockwood fulfilling all the expectations their very names conjure up; 1960. (b/w)

The Pleasure Girls √ Not quite the sexy cash-in it sounds, although there's a certain amount of jumping in and out of bed and a homosexual embrace or two. Surprisingly, Gerry O'Hara's script, which he directed himself, manages to catch quite a strong feeling of 1964 London, and Ian McShane, Francesca Annis, and Rosemary Nichols give some depth to characters who could so easily have been mere types. (b/w)

The Pleasure of His Company √ Taking a slice from The Philadelphia Story without its elegance and wit, but with at least some of its style, Samuel Taylor's 'rueful comedy', as he calls it, is about how a father (Fred Astaire) turns up for his daughter's wedding and proceeds to charm her (Debbie Reynolds) and her mother (Lilli Palmer). George Seaton directed, in 1961, with sure hand, and gets reliable supporting performances from Charlie Ruggles and Gary Merrill. But it's Astaire's picture and, without dancing a step, he dances away with it. (c)

The Pleasure Seekers X Or Three Coins in a Madrid Fountain. Jean Negulesco schmaltzily chronicles the exploits of Ann-Margret, Carol Lynley and Pamela Tiffin as they seek husbands in Spain. Candy-floss stuff; 1965. (c)

The Plunderers √ Four saddle-tramps invade a western town and terrorise it; how the town fights back is the theme of this unusual and interesting oater, particularly so because the producer-director, Joseph Pevney, usually sticks to safer subjects. Jeff Chandler, John Saxon, Dolores Hart star; 1960. (b/w)

Plymouth Adventure X Costume drama about Pilgrims Gene Tierney, Van Johnson, Leo Genn sailing to America under Captain Spencer Tracy. Dreadful script must have discouraged director Clarence Brown, who retired after this 1952 failure. (c)

Pocketful of Miracles XX Frank Capra's 1961 remake of his own Lady for a Day (1933), a solid slab of sentiment about an apple-selling Bette Davis (Shirley Booth turned him down) rescued from Skid Row by kindly gangster Glenn Ford (Sinatra turned him down) and pygmalioned as society hostess to impress daughter Ann-Margret and suitor. She finishes up with a proposal from alcoholic Judge Thomas Mitchell. This nonsense derives from a Damon Runyon tale of lovable hoodlums (Peter Falk), posh butlers (Edward Everett Horton) and molls (Hope Lange – Glenn Ford's 'young friend' of the moment). Capra and Glenn Ford were co-producers and got on very badly. In Capra's autobiography he writes: 'Pocketful of Miracles was shaped in the fires of discord and filmed in an atmosphere of pain, strain and loathing.' He had hoped it would be an antidote to permissive tide, but it was a huge box-office flop and 'there was dancing in the streets among the disciples of lewdness and violence'. (c)

Pocket Money √√ Paul Newman and Lee Marvin taken for suckers by some tough ranchers, who get them to drive 250 head of cattle and then short-change them. But, in place of fights or con-tricks, they shrug their shoulders the way most people would. A truer film than most about the West, director Stuart Rosenberg does well by Terence Malick's script; 1972. (c)

Point Blank √√ British director John Boorman's first American film was this 1967 exercise in gratuitous brutality, which nevertheless was well enough done to lift Lee Marvin out of the rut of baddies he had played for sixteen years. Absurdly constructed, with flashbacks crowding in on each other so that you never know where you are, the script ruined a perfectly straightforward and more exciting book, The Hunter by Richard Stark, and omitted much explanatory material (how, for instance, did our hero recover from two bullets in the gut and immediately swim from Alcatraz to San Francisco?). But, forced as the denouement and plot-twists are, Angie Dickinson and Keenan Wynn respond so well to Boorman's direction – as does Marvin – that the whole thriller, flashy editing and all, has a spurious compulsion at first viewing. But don't see it twice –

the holes are too obvious then. (c)

Pony Express √ Charlton Heston opening up the mail routes to the West, with help from Forrest Tucker, Rhonda Fleming, Jan Sterling and director Jerry Hopper in 1953. (c)

Pookie √√ Before subsiding into the role of Superstar, Liza Minelli made this acute and almost believable study of kookiness in 1969, subtly suggesting reasons as well as effects of her college drop-out's outspoken unconventionality and its effect on the boys in her life. Much of the credit must go to Alan J. Pakula, who went on to even more accomplished movies (*Klute*, *The Parallax View*, *All the President's Men*). (c)

Poor Cow √√ Kenneth Loach's debut on the big screen was with a small-screen subject and here it is back on the little one where it should have stayed (and not in the fancy colour Loach is so obviously unhappy with). In the cinema, the casual, surely-it-must-be-improvised manner distracted and there's every likelihood that it will look very 1968 and out of date by the time it gets on your home screen. Carol White moved confidently enough through the dramas in the life of a girl who's mixed up with villains, and Terence Stamp does all that's required of him, which isn't much. Incidentally, watch for the boy Billy. He's Malcolm McDowell who was later to make *If . . .* and *A Clockwork Orange*. (c)

Poor Little Rich Girl √ Shirley Temple wanders away from her nurse, who has an accident, so the 7-year-old (it was made in 1936) explores New York, having adventures, meeting up with Alice Faye and Jack Haley, a song and dance act. Result: song and dance. Director, Irving Cummings. (b/w)

Pope Joan X Poorly realised (by director Michael Anderson) apochryphal story of the 9th-century woman (Liv Ullman) who took monk's habit, became private secretary to a dying Pope and was named his successor. Despite obvious care not to give offence, this overlong bore manages to be sexy and pious in turn. In making her guilty about her sensuality Anderson has his meagre cake and forces us to eat it, too; 1972. (c)

Popi XX Tepid comedy which is meant to be terribly touching, about a Puerto Rican (Alan Arkin) who attempts to arrange a better life for his children by having them pose as Cuban refugees. Director Arthur Hiller does not convince; 1969. (c)

Poppy √ W. C. Fields stage play, a bit creaky in plot, about daughter Rochelle Hudson. Fun in places. Director, Edward Sutherland; 1936. (b/w)

The Poppy is Also a Flower XX The film is also a stinker. One of those do-gooding efforts with UN approval that turns out to be really awful despite presence of such luminaries as Yul Brynner, Trevor Howard, Angie Dickinson, E. G. Marshall, Rita Hayworth, Eli Wallach, Marcello Mastroianni. Blame rests partly on British director Terence Young; 1966. (c)

Porgy and Bess √ Whatever it may have been like when it was written in 1935 George Gershwin's 'folk opera' was downright insulting to black people by the time Otto Preminger filmed it in 1959. The inhabitants of Catfish Row are shown as indolent, lovable morons and the artificiality of the sets and acting positively cheeky. Not all of the cast sang for themselves (Sidney Poitier, Dorothy Dandridge, Ruth Attaway were all dubbed) and Uncle Tommy Davis Jr. scurried around unconvincingly. The music's fine of course, but the LP's better than the movie. (c)

Pork Chop Hill X Depressingly flag-waving celebration of the bravery of American troops in Korea, made in 1959 by Lewis Milestone, a director who knew how to shoot a battle scene. Unfortunately, he wasn't so strong on character, so Gregory Peck and his band of brave ethnics remain just caricatures. This actioner does contain one final irony, but by then it has written itself off as one more anti-Commie blast. (b/w)

Portrait in Black XX Right phoney load of codswallop with Lana Turner as wicked wife of Lloyd Nolan, conniving at his murder so that she and Anthony Quinn can find happiness, which of course they don't. Michael Gordon directs lushly, as if to take your mind off the inconsistencies and the dialogue; 1960. (c)

Portrait of Clare XX Margaret Johnston in weak effort about a grandma reminiscing, directed by Lance Comfort; 1949. (b/w)

Portrait of Jenny √ Lunatic plot about girl who grows much older every time Joseph Cotten meets her and is

233

finally found to have died before, in a storm. Despite this incredible storyline, William Dieterle managed to make Jennifer Jones more or less convincing, a genuine feat of direction; 1948. (b/w)

The Poseidon Adventure √√ Gene Hackman has to fight his and other passengers' way through an upturned liner with the water crashing in, in this 1972 disaster movie. Director Ronald Neame's limitations and the obviousness of the stories of the disparate bands thrown together in the usual way of these epics are minuses. (c)

Posse √√ Strong western with rare and welcome political overtones. The conventional pursuer-pursued storyline is strengthened by the fact that would-be US Senator, Kirk Douglas, is chasing Bruce Dern who is out to discredit him as well as to escape. Douglas directs himself, and comes up with a cut-above-the-average movie; 1975. (c)

Posse from Hell X Audie Murphy western about chase of four escaped convicts who killed the sheriff. Herbert Coleman; 1961. (c)

Possessed X Joan Crawford made two films of this name during her long career but it's not likely that the 1931 effort with her as a young factory worker who goes to the big city will get shown on TV. The 1947, more mature effort, has her doing her nut as a nurse who is obsessed with Van Heflin but marries employer Raymond Massey; typical Crawford larger-than-life stuff climaxing in a shooting scene, and she is indulged by director Curtis Bernhardt. (b/w)

The Possession of Joel Delaney X Elaborate hokum about Shirley MacLaine's brother, Perry King, being taken over by a spirit with decapitatory tendencies. Waris Hussein, too far from his own milieu in Puerto Rican Harlem, directed tentatively in 1971, and the result was a flop for Lord Grade's excursion into film-making. (c)

The Postman Always Rings Twice √√ Tough 1946 dramatisation of James M. Cain thriller about retribution catching up with Lana Turner who seduces John Garfield so that he'll murder her husband. Tay Garnett caught evil atmosphere of the roadside diner beautifully. (b/w)

Postman's Knock XX The manic Spike Milligan as an over-keen member of the GPO, with some lugubrious support from Wilfrid Lawson, Miles Malleson, Warren Mitchell. Director, Robert Lynn; 1961. (b/w)

The Pot Carriers √ Watered-down translation of Mike Watt's television play showing the inhumanity of British prison-life. This 1962 version, directed by Peter Graham Scott, introduces a wife and girlfriend shakily conceived and played. But Ronald Fraser's demoted trusty holds the picaresque action together. (b/w)

Powderkeg √ Actioner, set in 1914 Mexico, about a train hijack by Fernando Lamas. Rod Taylor sets out to fool him. Douglas Heyes directed; 1971. (c)

The Power X A kind of sci-fi whodunit posing the questions which of a group of super-scientists is the one from an alien planet (or somewhere like that)? and which is the goodie who's resisting him? If you manage to sort all this out, you are a candidate for superpower yourself. Director Byron Haskin tries to make it plausible and when that fails, uses his camera imaginatively for some clever effects. But George Hamilton, Suzanne Pleshette, Yvonne de Carlo, Nehemiah Persoff and Aldo Ray seem about as clued-up as the audience; 1968. (c)

The Power and the Glory √ Cramped little 1961 version of Graham Greene's novel, made for American television (but looking equally horrid there, with awkward continuity cuts to accommodate the frequent commercials and a murky print) by Marc Daniels. But the cast is magnificent: Laurence Olivier, Julie Harris, George C. Scott (as police lieutenant), Roddy McDowall, Keenan Wynn, Martin Gabel, Patty Duke, Cyril Cusack, Fritz Weaver, Mildred Dunnock, Frank Conroy. A pity that the adaptation (by Dale Wasserman) and production (by David Susskind) were so inferior. (b/w)

Precinct 45 – Los Angeles Police X What pretends to be an almost documentary account of life on and off the beat for two cops (George C. Scott, Stacy Keach) turns out to be a muddled and meretricious jumble of magazine fiction, liberally spiced with cliché situations. Director, Richard Fleischer; 1972. (c)

The Premature Burial √ Ray Milland is the man in the nightmare of being buried before he is dead. Roger Corman wrings out the shudders from the Poe story, with the help of superior photography and effects from cameraman Floyd Crosby; 1962. (c)

The President's Analyst √ Theodore J. Flicker has written and directed a satire on politics, medicine and spy movies, centred on James Coburn as the man who knows too many secrets. Which is an unfortunate piece of casting. For the rest, it's a pleasant enough diversion with some nice cameos and a couple of inventive plot-switches; 1967. (c)

The President's Lady √ Charlton Heston as Pres. Andrew Jackson defends his wife's bad name. Susan Hayward pulls out the stops a bit under Henry Levin's charge; 1953. (b/w)

Press for Time XX Norman Wisdom pathos (in more ways than one) in which the British Jerry Lewis (not meant as a compliment) plays a variety of parts and also takes it on himself to preach to us on how we should all live in harmony and forget party politics. Some funny gags that go on too long. Robert Asher indulges him directorially; 1966. (c)

Pressure Point √ Prison shrink Sidney Poitier sorts out American Nazi prison-patient Bobby Darin. Hubert Cornfield makes it quite interesting; 1962 – flashbacking to 1942. (b/w)

Pretty Boy Floyd √ Strong stuff from director Herbert J. Leder in this 1960 reconstruction of thirties outlaw. John Ericson, Barry Newman, Joan Harvey. (b/w)

Pretty Maids All in a Row X Rock Hudson is school seducer and counsellor in unpleasant 1971 American debut for director Roger Vadim. Angie Dickinson, Keenan Wynn and various nubilities do their best, but it's a long sad grind. (c)

Pretty Poison √√ The interplay between two seemingly-normal, actually unbalanced nice young people who egg each other on to arson and murder is frighteningly well-caught in this second directorial effort of Noel Black. His assurance is catching, and Tuesday Weld and Anthony Perkins are outstanding under his encouragement. Keep any junior pyromaniacs well away from the TV; 1969. (c)

Pretty Polly X Hayley Mills as a nice middle-class English girl who undergoes one of those old take-off-your-glasses, why-you're-beautiful transformations that never happen in real life. She then proceeds to knock out half the unsavoury characters of

Singapore – over-eating (and acting) Brenda de Banzie, gruff Trevor Howard, gigolo Shashi Kapoor, American-on-the-make Dick Patterson among them. Guy Green's obvious direction diminishes a pretty pale Noel Coward story still further; 1967. (c)

Pride and Prejudice √ Superb Olivier in Aldous Huxley co-adaptation of Austen delight. Robert Z. Leonard's direction in 1940 made a workmanlike job, far from a travesty, although Greer Garson is inadequate as Elizabeth. (b/w)

The Pride and the Passion √ 1957 spectacular with Frank Sinatra as simple Spaniard, Sophia Loren his girl, and Cary Grant as British officer, teaming up with peasantry to schlepp huge cannon to gates of French-occupied fort. One critic suggested that the gun almost out-acted the principals; another commented that the whirr of director Stanley Kramer's cameras seemed as loud as the thunderous cannonades; from C. S. Forester's *The Gun*. (c)

Prime Cut √√ Director Michael Ritchie makes a superior job of a white slave gang led by butcher Gene Hackman being busted by rival mobster Lee Marvin. There are some splendid moments, which rise above the sordidness of the subject; 1972. (c)

The Prime of Miss Jean Brodie √ Muriel Spark's penetrating novel of a schoolmistress who chooses her élite and is ultimately betrayed by one of them (which is the secondary but compelling whodunit element of the book) was ham-fistedly adapted for the stage by Jay Presson Allen. Ronald Neame has been content to film the play with a slightly opened-out script from the theatrical adapter. Maggie Smith, Robert Stephens and the four girls are creatures of the theatre, not the novel; Celia Johnson as the headmistress is the best bit of casting in the film. The result is a slighter drama, entertaining when it should have been disturbing; 1969. (c)

The Primitives X Slightly superior second-feature which doesn't take its own plot (about cabaret artistes who are really jewel thieves) too seriously. Jan Holden is leader of the gang; Alfred Travers directed with some flair; 1962. (b/w)

The Prince and the Pauper √ Fulfilled dream wish of every child: changing places with royalty. (1) Done with panache in William Keighley's

1937 version of Mark Twain's story, with Errol Flynn and Claude Rains. (b/w)

The Prince and the Pauper X (2) Well-produced, badly-acted (too many accents, including Australian) 1962 version was directed by Don Chaffey. Sean Scully, Guy Williams, Jane Asher. (c)

The Prince and the Showgirl √ Marilyn Monroe and Laurence Olivier together – the combination is irresistible, even if the film – a static reworking of Rattigan's *The Sleeping Prince* – turned out to be just too stiff for words. Olivier produced and directed as well as playing the Ruritanian royal who comes to London for coronation of George V and invites a chorus girl up for a quiet champagne supper. She gets involved with his local politics, acting as emissary between him and the young king, Jeremy Spenser. There's a definite anti-democratic tinge about the plot – but who cares? The great joy is to see two such wonderfully charismatic personalities clashing and blending; 1957. (c)

Prince of Foxes √ Tyrone Power v. Orson Welles in Renaissance drama, doughtily directed by Henry King in 1949. (b/w)

Prince of Players √ Curiosity value as Richard Burton impersonates 19th-century actor Edwin Booth, including chunks of *Hamlet*. Eva Le Gallienne's his Gertrude; Raymond Massey, Mae Marsh, Charles Bickford help put Philip Dunne's direction; 1955. (c)

Prince Valiant √ No wit or entertainment drawn from the fact that the main character is big comic hero. Instead, Henry Hathaway was content to direct James Mason, Janet Leigh, Robert Wagner in usual medieval movie blood-and-thunderer; 1954. (c)

The Prisoner √ Based on the true case of Cardinal Mindszenty in Hungary, this clash between Alec Guinness and Jack Hawkins is well and cerebrally directed by Peter Glenville; 1955. (b/w)

The Prisoner of Second Avenue √√ Jack Lemmon doing his familiar harrassed routine, with Neil Simon's lines. Here he is victim of gadgets that don't work and an inability to get a job, while his wife, Anne Jackson, has successful career. If Melvin Frank's direction is too broad, the production values he provides are useful; 1975. (c)

The Prisoner of Shark Island √

Tragic tale of the doctor imprisoned for innocently setting the broken leg of Lincoln's murderer. 'John Ford again shows his admiration for the hero who becomes so by fortitude and patient suffering, and Warner Baxter holds the film together with an intense depiction of indomitability and anguish' – programme note when this 1936 classic played at the NFT. (b/w)

The Prisoner of Zenda √ Scene-for-scene 1952 remake by Richard Thorpe of famous Ronald Colman 1937 version of Anthony Hope's royal impersonation swashbuckler; Stewart Granger, Deborah Kerr, Louis Calhern, James Mason. (c)

The Private Life of Sherlock Holmes √ Despite critical acclaim and a massive publicity campaign, Billy Wilder's attempt to breathe some fresh life into the Conan Doyle mythology flopped in 1970. Robert Stephens and Colin Blakely make an inferior Holmes and Watson, and the film works best when sticking to the well-worn Rathbone-Nigel Bruce track. It's as though Wilder intended a send-up but was defeated by the strength of the originals. (c)

The Private Lives of Elizabeth and Essex √√ Bette Davis as Queen Bess in star-crossed love with Errol Flynn as Earl of Essex; Olivia de Havilland, Vincent Price, Henry Daniell among Hollywoodiana pretending, none too successfully, to be Elizabethans; Michael Curtiz; 1939. (c)

Private Potter √√ Tom Courtenay magnificent as the soldier who claims to have seen God, but who has to be charged with a breach of discipline. Casper Wrede turned the television play into a deep and deeply funny film; 1962. (b/w)

Private Road √ Nice young girl (Susan Penhaligon) takes up with aspiring writer and junkie flat-mate. Barney Platts-Mills's second film (1971) after his acclaimed *Bronco Bullfrog* shows much of the same mastery of improvisation, but the result is more difficult to believe. (c)

A Private's Affair XX Flabby farce about a private soldier married to a lady general. There are also a few musical numbers and some rather silly jokes. Sal Mineo, Jim Backus, Jessie Royce Landis all miscast. Raoul Walsh obviously just looked on it as his 44th and quickly-forgotten movie; 1959. (c)

Private's Progress √ Ian Carmichael, Richard Attenborough,

Dennis Price, Terry-Thomas, William Hartnell in a sort of 1956 *Carry on Soldier* that did manage to criticise some of the weaknesses of the British army, and was first of Boulting Brothers's attacks on established institutions. *(b/w)*

Privilege √ Peter Watkins predicted a Britain in the near future (this was made in 1967) where people are so stupid and sheep-like that they accept a coalition government's attempts to manipulate them, with eager obedience. The main instrument in manipulation seems to be a thick pop singer, stolidly played by Paul Jones – but where's the Opposition? Where's the Press? To compound the unreality, Jean Shrimpton stumbles through her one (and understandably only) 'acting' role with a glazed expression. However, there is a moment at the start when Jones goes through a stage act of being beaten by 'police' while singing a song that is genuinely disturbing. *(c)*

The Prize X Comedy thriller about Paul Newman receiving the Nobel Prize and getting involved in Edward G. Robinson 'defecting'. Mark Robson makes it all implausibly slick; 1963. *(c)*

A Prize of Arms √ Straightforward caper about robbing an Army post office of £250,000; Stanley Baker, Tom Bell and Helmut Schmid are the thieves, and it's excitingly if gnomically developed. Cliff Owen did taut directing job; 1962. *(b/w)*

A Prize of Gold √ Richard Widmark leads a gold caper in Berlin, then decides to give it back. Mark Robson recruited weak supports to help even weaker plot from Max Catto novel. But he does have a way of keeping the action tight; 1955. *(c)*

The Prodigal XX What the Bible failed to mention happened to the Prodigal Son while he was off on his binge; he (Edmund Purdom) was falling for priestess (Lana Turner). Richard Thorpe directed; 1955. *(c)*

The Producers √√√ Brilliant black comedy about the staging of a play that must fail, *Springtime for Hitler*, but of course doesn't. Mel Brooks has drawn excruciatingly funny performances from Zero Mostel and Gene Wilder that, as *Time* rightly said in 1967, belong in the W. C. Fields and Marx Brothers league. The most under-rated comedy of the sixties. *(c)*

A Professional Gun √ Spaghetti western by Sergio Corbucci stars Jack Palance × Franco Nero fighting for possession of silver consignment on the way from Mexico to Texas; 1968. *(c)*

The Professionals √√ are a bunch of four men hired to do a job in Mexico. Thus far the comparison is with *The Magnificent Seven*, a similarity that is emphasised by the presence of the same actor playing village leader. But here the motivation is conflicting: the Seven are doing the job for peanuts because the bandit leader is a baddie. The Four go about this job of freeing a woman from bandits for money but come up against a problem: she's happy there, she's chosen to go out of love for the bandit-leader, and, anyway, they have an ideological sympathy with these bandits. But they are Professionals. So which is more important: their head and purse or their hearts? Burt Lancaster, Lee Marvin, Robert Ryan and Woody Strode make their dilemma believable. Jack Palance rouses himself out of his usual torpor to turn in an excellent performance as the bandit chief. Only Claudia Cardinale is deficient as the woman, but director Richard Brooks neatly covers up her inadequacies; 1966. *(c)*

The Projected Man XXX Rubbish about transmuted matter with Bryant Haliday as scientist. Among those impressed are Mary Peach, Derek Farr, Norman Wooland – that will give you some idea of the calibre. Director, Ian Curteis; 1967. *(c)*

The Projectionist √√ Not to be missed by movie buffs: director-producer-writer Harry Hurwitz weaves together clips and pastiches of a score of old movies, as they whizz through the head of fantasist Chuck McCann; 1970. *(c)*

The Promise XX Almost completely unfulfilled, alas. Instead of Judi Dench's intelligent heroine of the stage version, we are offered Susan Macready. Instead of feeling we are in war-devastated Leningrad, we are in a never-was never-land. Ian McKellen is out of his element; director Michael Hayes never enters into one; 1969. *(c)*

Promise at Dawn XX Melina Mercouri unwatchably histrionic as the actress mother of novelist Romain Gary (three actors at various ages). As usual, director-husband Jules Dassin permits her to over-act to an embarrassing degree; 1970. *(c)*

Promise Her Anything XX Awful attempt to make a movie about Greenwich Village without moving out of England. Warren Beatty is supposed to be blue film-maker looking after Leslie Caron's baby. Stifle the yawns in spotting Lionel Stander, Warren Mitchell; 1966. Arthur Hiller. (c)

The Proud and the Profane X You might have thought the main war going on in the Pacific in 1943 was between America and the Japanese. It was actually between Deborah Kerr, the proud (not to say snotty-nosed) widow of the title and William Holden as the profane (not to say sadistic) colonel who seduces her. There's an awful lot of plot (and a lot of awful plot) before the sentimental ending, and George Seaton cannot blame the script. He wrote it in 1956. (b/w)

The Proud Ones X Attempt to make a big western in 1956 failed from diffusion of story-line. It starts promisingly enough (if too reminiscent of *High Noon*), with a Marshal (Robert Ryan) who has to settle an old score before he can get married (to Virginia Mayo). Jeffrey Hunter comes to admire him in the course of the film, but it's difficult to share his awe. Robert D. Webb directed. (c)

The Proud Rebel √ With a mute boy and a dog and a rebel soldier wandering the South looking for a doctor to cure his son, Michael Curtiz must have thought he was on to such a box-office winner in 1958 that he didn't have to try too hard at anything except overdoing the sentiment. Unfortunately, Alan Ladd needed firmer handling than this, and the result was a decidely wooden performance, though his real-life son, David, does rather better. Olivia de Havilland, too, is over-sentimental as the lady who looks after them. As Lance the Dog, King is adequate. (c)

The Prowler √ Sam Spiegel to Joseph Losey in 1951: 'You're right for this, but you're not very experienced. I'll give you the best cameraman in Hollywood, the best technicians. I don't care what I pay, and you do it any way you want to'. The way he wanted was to pre-rehearse the actors like in the theatre but rarely for the movies. Result wasn't much tauter performances or deeper characterisation than seen in most bent-cop thrillers, but Van Heflin and Evelyn Keyes are acceptable. (b/w)

Prudence and the Pill X Dated in 1968, when it was made, this now looks ludicrous. It makes such a fuss about contraceptive pills and thinks it's so daring in the process as to be positively in need of the aspirins that people mistake for them. As it happens, it's based on completely false premises, as the way birth control pills are packed is quite different from the way vitamin pills and painkillers are. Still, Judy Geeson, David Niven, Deborah Kerr, Keith Michell, Michael Hordern and Vickery Turner (to name the best of a good cast) struggle on, sounding vaguely mid-Atlantic, thanks to American director Fielder Cook. (c)

Psyche 59 X 'Pretentious bosh' was the description that greeted this attempt at profundity – a slushy story about a husband (ill-at-ease Curt Jurgens) fancying his wife's (Pat Neal) sister (Samantha Eggar). Director Alexander Singer was attempting to make a French literary film in England, and that's something no red-blooded patriot would tolerate; 1964. (b/w)

Psycho √√√ Most people's favourite Hitchcock opened to poor notices in 1960: 'a fairground sideshow . . . *Emergency Ward 10* level of psychiatric mumbo-jumbo . . . the plot creaks . . . these violent, twisted trappings (a nauseating bathroom murder) are not the stuff that Hitch is blessed with the talent to give us', said one (it would be unfair to name the critic – he has almost certainly changed his mind by now). Gradually this thriller has come to be accepted as a major achievement in the way it pretends for the first reels to tell one story, then switches round again, to finish up with one of the most shocking denouements in the history of the cinema. If you haven't seen it before, make every effort to see it from the first shot (Hitchcock didn't allow latecomers into the cinema) and if you have, please, please don't give the ending away; as Hitch said at the time: 'It's the only thing we have.' A word of praise for all the acting: Janet Leigh just right in a difficult part; Anthony Perkins convincing twice over (once at the time, once looking back); Martin Balsam an impressive, doomed investigator. Altogether superb. (b/w)

Psychomania XX Codswallop of a high order: Nicky Henson commits suicide on his motorbike so that he can return from the grave and wreak havoc. His mum, Beryl Reid, has made a pact with the Devil; her butler is George Sanders. Robert Hardy, a detective, works hard to keep a straight face under Don Sharp's cynical direction; 1972. (c)

The Psychopath √ Director Freddie

Francis neatly handles who-is-it about a nutter who kills and leaves dolls behind. 1966 thriller has Patrick Wymark, Margaret Johnston, John Standing, Judy Huxtable among victims and suspects. (b/w)

PT 109 √ 1963 mythologising of John F. Kennedy as the naval hero. Cliff Robertson is Kennedy and Leslie H. Martinson directed action scenes with more reverence than the ruthlessness they undoubtedly demanded. (c)

Pulp √ Mildly amusing comedy-thriller about a hack writer (Michael Caine) embroiled by Lionel Stander into real gangster milieu with real bullets. Writer-director, Mike Hodges; Lizabeth Scott, Mickey Rooney and Dennis Price appear. Even if the nostalgic re-creation of the Chandler ambience does not come off, there is still enough to enjoy; 1972. (c)

The Pumpkin Eater √ The combined talents of director Jack Clayton, original novelist Penelope Mortimer, adapter Harold Pinter, leads Anne Bancroft, Peter Finch and James Mason should somehow have added up to a more convincing film than this. Perhaps the main fault is in Miss Bancroft's casting: she's a very fine American actress, but misses the essence of Englishness and Hampsteadness that should pervade the main character, who leaves one husband to marry Finch and is fecund to the point of neurosis. Nevertheless, the film deserves better treatment than when shown by LWT some years ago; they butchered it to squeeze it into a pre-ordained time-slot and all continuity and chunks of the plot were lost. Let us hope that future showings are in full – or not at all; 1964. (b/w)

The Punch and Judy Man XX Tony Hancock's 1963 attempt to do something other than his East Cheam character was doomed to popular failure and rightly so. It's self-indulgent and painfully slow. Nor are any of the rather obvious cast, Barbara Murray, Ronald Fraser, Hugh Lloyd, Hattie Jacques very happy under Jeremy Summers's direction. Sylvia Syms miscast (too posh) as wife. (b/w)

Punishment Park √ Depressing pseudo-documentary about Civil Rights protestors being put through an awful three-day ordeal, directed by Peter Watkins. (c)

The Pure Hell of St Trinian's √ Without Alastair Sim, St. T's isn't quite as funny, although this 1960 cash-in on previous successes does have Joyce Grenfell, Sid James, Dennis Price, George Cole, Cecil Parker as compensation. Girls burn down school, are propositioned for harem. Frank Launder directed. (b/w)

The Purple Gang X Teenage hoodlums in the twenties hunted by detective Barry Sullivan. Frank McDonald directed this rather unpleasant little piece in 1960. (b/w)

The Purple Mask X Swashbuckler in which Tony Curtis (in 1955 a dashing 30-year-old) plays a sort of Scarlet Pimpernel, saving aristocrats from Napoleon in 1803. Gene Barry, Angela Lansbury among those prancing through the balderdash served up by director Bruce Humberstone. (c)

The Purple Plain √ Gregory Peck discovers that crashing his plane in the jungle in the Second World War was the best thing for him. Robert Parrish directed emotional story in Burma, with British cast including Bernard Lee; 1955. (c)

Pursued √ Robert Mitchum seeking men who killed father in western that is far from conventional. Raoul Walsh made this 1947 thriller stand out with fine performances from Teresa Wright and Judith Anderson. (b/w)

The Pursuit of Happiness XX Botched 'youth pic' that was shot in 1970 but not released in Britain until 1974. Ambivalent story of a drop-out (Michael Sarrazin) who becomes mutely involved in two violent deaths. You can bet they tried a dozen endings before settling for this gratuitous one. What is puzzling and sad is that the director is Robert Mulligan, capable of *To Kill a Mockingbird* and *Summer of '42*. (c)

Pushover √ Fred MacMurray made a come-back in 1955 with first starring role for some years as a cop falling for Kim Novak, the gangster moll, in her first real part. Richard Quine. (b/w)

Putney Swope X This episodic reversal of white power – with a black accidentally taking over a big ad agency, running it to suit himself, and achieving success by default – had a cult success in New York, but was given a big raspberry here. Robert Downey's episodic collection of jokes might be redeemed by the presence of Mel Brooks in a walk-on part; 1969. (c and b/w)

Pygmalion √√√ Superb 1938 transcription of the play for Leslie Howard and Wendy Hiller, without the distraction of the *My Fair Lady* music and production numbers. Shaw changed the ending and wrote 14 extra scenes. Director was Anthony Asquith, who shared the credit with Leslie Howard for some reason. (*b/w*)

Q

Q Planes √ Alexander Korda saw a newspaper article about a plane that went permanently missing and commissioned a screenplay about one. He booked Olivier, Richardson and Valerie Hobson, and Tim Whelan as director; 1939. (*b/w*)

Quackser Fortune Has a Cousin in the Bronx X Although you wouldn't know it from the terrible title, this is a slight comedy about innocence in Dublin. The innocent is the remarkable Gene Wilder (still unknown enough in 1970 to have to make movies like this). The betrayer is Margot Kidder. Director, Waris Hussein. (*c*)

The Quare Fellow √ Patrick McGoohan as prison guard changing mind about capital punishment in 1962 Irish version of Brendan Behan play, faithfully and claustrophobically directed by Arthur Dreifuss. (*b/w*)

Quatermass II X Routine sci-fi about meteorites which, on contact, turn those who touch them into the zombies of a Superior Intelligence. Brian Donlevy had to be imported into Britain to make it safe for us British, because the year was 1957 and nobody dared make a movie without a washed-up American star to give it some sort of B-picture status over there. Val Guest directed, evidently hurriedly. (*b/w*)

Queen Bee X Joan Crawford in another of her tailored roles as an outwardly nice, inwardly horrid, lady who uses all about her for her own purposes. It's all tosh, of course, particularly when people start killing themselves at her revelations, but compelling for her vaster-than-life performance. Ranald MacDougall wrote and directed; 1955. (*b/w*)

Queen Christina √ How much of Garbo's magical appeal was due to her mid-sex qualities? Looking back on this 1933 blockbuster with our greater (we hope) sexual sophistication, you can't help feeling that her butch performance as the 17th-century Swedish queen dressed as a boy stirred equivocal passion – both in femme breasts and among males who would consider John Gilbert was having best of both worlds when the handsome lad he is forced to share an inn room with turns out to be a girl. Rouben Mamoulian ignored all the 'great actress' guff and had her move to a metronome and think about nothing in the famous final close-up. (*b/w*)

The Queen of Spades √ The slow English (1949) Thorold Dickinson version of the Pushkin story, filmed in Russia several times. Outstanding performance by Edith Evans as ageing countess who knows the secret of winning at faro; Anton Walbrook is the soldier who would sell his soul to learn. (*b/w*)

A Question of Adultery XX Sad little attempt at 'forthright' problem movie about artificial insemination in 1958 comes out looking tepid and fence-sitting. Don Chaffey's wooden direction isn't helped by matching teak performance from Anthony Steel as the husband. Julie London as the wife is a couple of shades better, but the whole thing's a stodge. (*b/w*)

The Quick and the Dead √ Superior war actioner in which cast of unknowns manage to convey something of what it must have been like to blow up an ammunition dump; it's not even spoiled by the entrance of two pretty sisters who lead them to Partisans. Credit must go to director Robert Totten; 1963. (*b/w*)

Quick Before It Melts √ Fitfully amusing comedy about Robert Morse and George Maharis covering life at the South Pole for Sage, 'the magazine that thinks for you'. Delbert Mann puts some zest into their picaresque adventures; 1965. (*c*)

The Quick Gun XX Audie Murphy returns as an outcast from serving short sentence for self-defence killing, but the townspeople love him again when he defeats a gang of outlaws. End of film. Don't bother. Sidney Salkow directed in 1964 – presumably in his sleep. (*c*)

The Quiet American X Michael Redgrave right as the narrator-character, Audie Murphy wrong as the Third Force-deluded American in Joseph L. Mankiewicz's 1958 screwing-up of Graham Greene's Vietnam novel. (*b/w*)

The Quiet Man √ Ireland was never like this rosy John Ford picture of it, but it's a darlin' place wherever it is. John Wayne goes back there and falls for Victor McLaglen's sister, Maureen O'Hara; but before the happy ending there's the longest, toughest bout of fisticuffs ever seen. Barry Fitzgerald, Jack McGowran and a bar-full of other Irish characters rally round; 1952. (c)

The Quiller Memorandum X Plusses in this espionage yarn are Pinter script, Berlin locations, George Segal, Alec Guinness. Minuses: Michael Anderson's pedestrian direction, Senta Berger's woeful inadequacy. Max von Sydow, as neo-Nazi heavy, veers between plus and minus; 1966. (c)

Quo Vadis? √ Spectacular third version in 1951 (the first two were Italian; 1912, 1924) of Henryk Sienkiewicz's novel of Romans' persecution of the Christians. Robert Taylor as Roman falls for Deborah Kerr as Christian; Peter Ustinov as Nero is extremely put out. To the lions with them all, we say. Mervyn Le Roy obliged with the lions but didn't give them enough to eat. (c)

R

The Rabbit Trap √ There's this little boy, and he's on holiday in the country with his Pa – that's Ernest Borgnine. And there's a rabbit alive in a trap they set. And Pa's like a rabbit in a trap, too, in his job. So when he's called back to the city and they forget the trap and the little boy is all cut up about leaving the rabbit to starve, should Pa stay in town and be a good little rabbit in a trap himself or should he risk his job and free the rabbit? United Artists brought British director Philip Leacock to America to direct this one because he had a reputation for directing kids. Unfortunately, he was so concerned not to be sentimental that this kid, Kevin Corcoran, never makes any impact. Which is sad; 1959. (b/w)

Race with the Devil √√ Effective thriller in which Peter Fonda and Warren Oates witness an 'Aztec' ritual at which a girl is sacrificed, and pay for being good citizens and reporting it. The chase of their motor-home is well done by director Jack Starrett; 1975. (c)

Rachel and the Stranger √ Loretta Young and William Holden are married. Robert Mitchum is the stranger in strong story of Northwest pioneers. Norman Foster directed; 1948. (b/w)

Rachel, Rachel √√ Drama of schoolteacher verging on middle age in small town. Joanne Woodward has never tried harder than under her husband, Paul Newman's debut as director-producer. Her anguish at fear of lesbianism; mistaking sex for love; and her phantom pregnancy might all be a bit hard to take, but it's clear that the Newmans cared - and sincerity is a rare virtue in the movies. 1968 winner of New York Critics' award for Best Director, Best Actress. (c)

The Rack √ Paul Newman in courtroom drama: was he a traitor during Korean war? Arnold Laven directed over-sentimental Rod Serling story in 1956, plus Lee Marvin, Edmond O'Brien, Anne Francis and Walter Pidgeon as Newman's father. (b/w)

Rage √√ George C. Scott directed and starred in this tale of vengeance for a son's death, in 1972. Richard Basehart, Martin Sheen take second and third fiddles. (c)

Rage in Heaven X Robert Montgomery plans his own murder, while Ingrid Bergman and George Sanders are implicated. Directed by W. S. Van Dyke from a James Hilton novel; 1941. (b/w)

A Rage to Live X Well, not exactly to live, more to go to bed with someone. This is the life of a nympho, folks, so roll up and see Suzanne Pleshette screwed and suffering. Walter Grauman directs it like a child playing traffic policeman with all the cars whizzing by non-stop; 1964. (c)

The Raging Moon √ Made in 1970 by Bryan Forbes and starring his wife Nanette Newman and Malcolm McDowell, this is a tight, interesting story of a wheelchair-bound couple's love affair. There are some unfortunate excursions into their backgrounds, which degenerate into caricature. The film never received proper cinema showing. (c)

The Raiders X More Buffalo Bill, Wild Bill Hickok and Calamity Jane adventures (they were a busy lot), this time extending the railroad to Texas, to help friends get their cattle there. Robert Culp was bushwacked by Herschel Daugherty; 1963. (c)

The Raiders of Leyte Gulf XXX Excruciating war film about the Philippines with poor technical credits, weaker acting abilities and, lowest of all, directorial skill from Eddie Romero; 1962. (b/w)

Raid on Rommel XXX Awful war film that, unbelievably, has Henry Hathaway as director: Richard Burton, no stranger to lousy films, is star. The little excitement there is comes from re-using bits of an old movie called *Tobruk;* 1971. (c)

The Railway Children √√ Highly enjoyable young persons' tale, nicely directed from a close adaptation of E. Nesbit's book by Lionel Jeffries. Jenny Agutter is personable as the elder sister of the family, and everyone will have a nice little weep and an afterglow of happiness; 1970. (c)

The Rainmaker √√ Joseph Anthony's 1956 retelling of *The Ugly Duckling,* notable for Katharine Hepburn's farmer's daughter, impressed, as everyone else is, by Burt Lancaster's poetic con-man who brings her rain and readiness for love. It won her and composer Alex North Oscar nominations. (c)

The Rain People √√ Francis Ford Coppola wrote and directed this downbeat yarn in 1969. Shirley Knight (Hopkins), frustrated housewife, jumps into her car, picks up ex-football hero James Caan. It ends abruptly. (c)

The Rains Came √ Suspend critical faculties and enjoy the slush – metaphorical and literal – of Louis Bromfield novel of love v. duty, directed by Clarence Brown in 1939 with monsoons, earthquakes, Myrna Loy, Tyrone Power, George Brent, Nigel Bruce. (b/w)

The Rains of Ranchipur √ 1955 remake of *The Rains Came* is wetter than ever, with Richard Burton, absurdly miscast as Indian doctor, Lana Turner and Fred MacMurray having to shout to be heard above that steady cats-and-dogs effect. They might as well have saved their breath; Jean Negulesco was evidently under orders to put the spectacle first, the human moisture second. (c)

Raintree County √√ You may have thought it had gone with the wind, but it was still there, in 1958. The proud Southern belle (Elizabeth Taylor), the young suitor (Montgomery Clift), the old father (Walter Abel) and the political and emotional rivals for her hand and honour (Lee Marvin and Rod Taylor). But it's really unfair to

put down Edward Dmytryk's big re-working of Ross Lockridge's novel, scripted by Millard Kaufman, because the people do come across as more real than those *GWTW* ciphers, even if the sweep isn't so vast. It certainly makes a satisfactory nearly-three-hours watching, but needs a box of chocolates in the lap for full effect. (c)

Raising a Riot XXX Kenneth More has to look after the children while wife Shelagh Fraser is away. That's funny? No, it isn't, despite director Wendy Toye's desperate efforts in 1955. (c)

Raising the Wind XX *Carry On* director Gerald Thomas rounded up a few of his regulars in 1961 to fit in an extra farce about music students. Leslie Phillips, Paul Massie, James Robertson Justice, Eric Barker are predictably wet; Sid James, Kenneth Williams raise a few weak smiles. (c)

A Raisin In The Sun √ Hailed in 1961 as true-life Negro drama, now looks suspiciously like trying-to-be-white-ism. Daniel Petrie directed Sidney Poitier and all-black cast in carbon-copy of Lorraine Hansberry play about ghetto family. (b/w)

Rally Round the Flag, Boys X Clumsy farce from Max Shulman's novel about New England commuters' community trying to stop the Army from building a rocket-launching site in its midst. Paul Newman and Joanne Woodward are unhappy in central roles as couple whose marriage is threatened by Joan Collins because Woodward is too busy being activist. Newman simply hasn't the comic touch and veteran producer-director Leo McCarey can't provide it; 1959. (c)

Rampage X Robert Mitchum, Elsa Martinelli and Jack Hawkins made an oddly-assorted triangle out in the jungle trapping half-tiger-half-leopard. When Mitchum also traps Martinelli, Hawkins does his nut. Director Phil Karlson keeps the pot boiling, however, and you don't notice the flaws at the time, you're too busy gasping; 1963. (c)

Ramsbottom Rides Again XXX Arthur Askey inherits Wild West ranch. Among those less than sparkling stars directed by John Baxter in 1957 were Shani Wallis, Sid James, Frankie Vaughan, Sabrina, Betty Marsden. (b/w)

Rancho Notorious X A poor cowboy's *Destry Rides Again,* with Marlene Dietrich in a faint echo of the earlier role. This 1952 oater mismatched a lot of fine talents including director Fritz Lang who was obviously unhappy on the prairie; Mel Ferrer, a laughable 'fastest gun in the West'; Arthur Kennedy as dogged Nemesis, chasing killer and ravisher of his sweetheart. He masquerades as an outlaw, penetrates desert hide-out and finally avenges his gal. Incidentally the key role of Kinch is played by Lloyd Gough, who – for some reason – doesn't get a credit. (c)

Random Harvest √ Get the tissues ready if you enjoy a weep, and Greer Garson. Harder hearts will yawn over this 1942 yarn about Ronald Colman losing his memory and finding love (and vice-versa). Mervyn Le Roy did slick director's job. (b/w)

Ransom! √ Glenn Ford, Donna Reed in kidnap yarn, rather well-directed by Alex Segal in 1955. Gives a vivid picture of parents under pressure. (b/w)

Ransom X Arid thriller about the kidnap of Britain's Norwegian ambassador (Robert Harris), with Ian McShane as villain, Sean Connery as head of National Security. Caspar Wrede fails to make you care enough; 1974. (c)

The Rare Breed X Maureen O'Hara introducing the Hereford bull to America with the help of James Stewart, but under Andrew McLaglen's direction the cattle act better than the humans, although visually it's fine; 1966. (c)

Rasputin – the Mad Monk XX Attempt at pre-revolutionary Russian shocker by Don Sharp, with Christopher Lee, Richard Pasco, Barbara Shelley, Francis Matthews, in descending order of credibility. This 1966 British effort was remake of the triple-Barrymore 1932 version. (c)

The Rat Race √ New York as seen through the jaundiced eyes of director Robert Mulligan, in his second film, 1960. It's a helluva town. Alone among its eight million, only innocents Tony Curtis and Debbie Reynolds aren't drunks, thieves, conmen, or other varieties of the dregs of humanity. (c)

The Rattle of a Simple Man XX Charles Dyer's golden-hearted-whore-meets-impotent-yob duologue was played for laughs in the theatre and just about worked due to the super performances of Sheila Hancock and Edward Woodward. Transferred to the screen in 1964, it sank like lead under Muriel Box's heavy-handed direction and feckless playing of Harry H. Corbett and Diane Cilento. (b/w)

The Raven √√ Horror director Roger Corman's 1963 spoof, biting the claw that fed him, aided and abattoired by three of the best – Vincent Price, Peter Lorre and Boris Karloff. Corman plucked Poe's plumage to feather his own gothic nest of plot about three 15th-century sorcerers on the rampage, hilarious and horrific by turns; and watch out for Jack Nicholson in a small part. (c)

Rawhide √ Should have been retitled to avoid confusion with TV series; this was original 1951 version, with Tyrone Power and Susan Hayward held prisoner by besieged outlaws. Director Henry Hathaway went thataway. (b/w)

Raw Wind in Eden X Society couple shipwrecked on strange island occupied by peasant, his daughter and mysterious American. Richard Wilson sorted something out of this hokum in 1958, despite Esther Williams, Jeff Chandler, Rossana Podesta. (c)

The Razor's Edge √ Maugham's soapy, philosophical novel gave Herbert Marshall his familiar role as the author, with Tyrone Power, Gene Tierney, John Payne and Clifton Webb as four of the characters he bumps into in posh Chicago in the twenties; the fifth was Anne Baxter as a dipsomaniac and it won her the 1946 Best Supporting Oscar. Edmund Goulding lushed it all up happily enough. (b/w)

Reach for Glory √ Philip Leacock, marvellous at handling child actors, manages again in this sorry story of prejudice among the evacuees at the start of the war. One of them is killed, à la *Lord of the Flies*. Harry Andrews and Kay Walsh stand out among the adults; 1961. (b/w)

Reach for the Sky √ Kenneth More convinces as legless ace Douglas Bader. Lewis Gilbert directed with polish in 1956 and it grips beyond routine war-picture heroism. (b/w)

Reap the Wild Wind √ Giant squid is real star of this spectacular about 19th-century salvagers, out-acting John Wayne, Ray Milland, Susan Hayward, Paulette Goddard, Raymond Massey. Which is probably what wily old director Cecil B. De Mille had in mind in 1942. (c)

Rear Window √√√ Delicious 1954 Hitchcock has James Stewart confined to wheelchair, passing the time by spying on the neighbours he overlooks.

He suspects a murder which, in fact, Hitch created from a combination of the Crippen and Mahon cases. All the separate stories he Tom-Peeps on are to do with love and reflect on his own conflict – does he love Grace Kelly or not? How the immobilised Stewart fights back when the murderer comes calling is a brilliant device. Certainly one of the finest Hitchcocks – here to be spotted winding a clock. (c)

Rebecca √√ Won the 1940 Oscar for the Best Picture but Hitchcock didn't get Director's Award – he has never won one although he has consistently been the best director over the last fifty-five years (his first film was in 1925). The Oscar went to producer David Selznick. Hitch sees this one as a fairy story – Cinderella with only one ugly sister – and set out to emphasise the Grimm aspects of the story. Daphne du Maurier's novelettish story could have been an ordinary movie melo but Hitch's love of mystery turned it into a thriller. Olivier as the well-meaning, self-blaming husband, Joan Fontaine as his timid new wife, Judith Anderson as the never-moving housekeeper were all superb. (b/w)

Rebecca of Sunnybrook Farm √ Strictly for lovers of cute little Shirley Temple (among whom Graham Greene, a film critic when this came out in 1938, was not numbered). She is singing star of cereal-sponsored radio show; with Randolph Scott, Jack Haley, under Allan Dwan's direction. (b/w)

The Rebel √ One of the many tragedies in Tony Hancock's life is that he never met up with a film director who could take his particular style of comedy and distil it for the cinema. In 1961, with a Simpson and Galton script that owed its inspiration to Gauguin's flight from respectability to Bohemia (Paris in this case), he could have been marvellously funny. As it was, he was funny all right, but round him was a film conceived in such banal terms (e.g. 'the beatniks' in Paris who are so impressed with his Infantile School obviously hadn't seen the King's Road, let alone the Left Bank) that its net effect was sadly flat. The fault lay squarely with director Robert Day. (c)

Rebel in Town √ J. Carrol Naish, who was the only worthwhile feature in so many actioners, got his chance to lead at last in 1956 with this study of a father driven to bank-robbing by the ostracism that Confederate soldiers felt on return from the Civil War. Alfred Werker did competent directorial job and Naish grabbed his opportunity. (b/w)

Rebel Without A Cause √ One of the two films that made James Dean a cult. Teenage victim of a world he didn't make and doesn't want, his charismatic performance is adequately complemented by Natalie Wood and Sal Mineo. Energetically directed by Nicholas Ray in 1955 it has, alas, lost its power with its contemporaneousness. (c)

The Reckless Moment X Max Ophüls brought his distinctive touch to this 1948 melo of Mama Joan Bennett being blackmailed by smoothie James Mason after she kills local womaniser who was trying to seduce daughter Geraldine Brooks. (b/w)

The Reckoning √ One of those return-to-Northern-roots plots, this time with Nicol Williamson as the successful businessman making a quick homecoming. Jack Gold's direction (1969), Nicol Williamson's bitter facetiousness, Rachel Roberts's typecast good-time matron don't develop much. (c)

The Red Badge of Courage √ This one has a special niche in the history of Hollywood as best-documented case of how studio bosses screw up creators. The *New Yorker's* Lillian Ross followed its making, and her piece anatomised John Huston's losing struggle to keep faithful to Stephen Crane's Civil War novel, against 1951 McCarthy-stamped MGM. But could Audie Murphy ever have made hero convincing? Some marvellous moments remain despite vain frantic re-editing to make it commercial. Ross's article was later published as a book, *Picture;* it's revelatory reading after you've seen the movie. (b/w)

The Red Baron X Curses, another flying war movie, not improved by Roger Corman's myth-serving. As Von Richthofen, John Philip Law only looks the haughty aristocrat. Hermann Goering is played by Barry Primus; 1971. (c)

The Red Beret XX Alan Ladd re-enlists as paratrooper when his friend is killed through his fault while an officer. Terence Young managed to squeeze a few thrills out of basically unconvincing script in 1952, but couldn't do much with stiff Leo Genn or soppy Susan Stephen. (b/w)

Red Garters √ 1953 attempt to move musicals on a bit by satire on standard western yarn and stylised sets and costumes (black baddies, white goodies, red naughties) didn't quite come off. But it's worth watching George Marshall try with help of Rosemary Clooney, Jack Carson, Reginald Owen. (c)

Red-Headed Woman X Banned by the British censor in 1932, this torrid tale of Jean Harlow making eyes at her married boss Chester Morris is pretty depressing. Una Merkel, Charles Boyer add some life, under Jack Conway's routine direction. (b/w)

Red Hell XXX Straightforward anti-communist tract in which torturer Basil Rathbone gives victim Mary Murphy a rabid lessson in the iniquities of the Reds, helped out by various selected bits of documentary footage. Hideous. William D. Faralla; 1962. (b/w)

Red Line 7000 √ Hallowed veteran Howard Hawks indulged himself in 1965 in making this episodic film in which drivers' love stories are interspersed with racing pictures. There's no real plot but plenty of action with James Caan, Laura Devon. (c)

Red Mountain √ Alan Ladd leads guerillas in Kansas and Missouri, sacking towns that are favourable to Union cause. Strong back-up cast includes Lizabeth Scott, John Ireland, Arthur Kennedy; and William Dieterle always turned in competent job; 1951. (c)

The Red Pony √ One of those boy-and-his-horse epics, where he relates more to the animal than the warring humans (Myrna Loy, Robert Mitchum, Louis Calhern among them) around him. Lewis Milestone kept it running wild, running free in 1949. (c)

Red River √√ Howard Hawks western about a cattle drive that John Wayne wants to take over the Chisholm Trail, past the Red River into Missouri, through which at that time – just after the Civil War – nobody had yet driven cattle. But foster-son Montgomery Clift wants to drive to Abilene and ship the cattle East by rail. They come to blows until Joanne Dru patches up the quarrel. Hawks gave the drive tremendous power and succeeded in lifting the film right out of the oater class into a classic statement of the generation-battle; 1948. (b/w)

The Red Shoes X Dreadful plot about impresario Anton Walbrook trying to force dancer Moira Shearer to renounce Love and Marius Goring, balanced by ballet sequences. Michael Powell and Emeric Pressburger managed to make ballet box office in 1948. (c)

Red Skies of Montana X Great fire sequences under Joseph M. Newman's direction save this otherwise routine yarn about US Forestry Service with Richards Widmark, Boone, Crenna; 1952. (c)

Red Sundown X Rory Calhoun as poacher-turned-gamekeeper in western setting, roughs up old villainous mates, woos sheriff's daughter Martha Hyer. Jack Arnold; 1956. (c)

Reflections in a Golden Eye √ A prize of a mint julep for anyone who understands what Marlon Brando is saying in the extraordinary Southern accent he has adopted here. Elizabeth Taylor is his wife who has to turn to other men because her husband's gay; Julie Harris is a nutter who uses a pair of garden shears somewhat painfully; so what he is saying may be better left a mystery. Based on a Carson McCullers novel, it's about how Brando gets obsessed with another soldier, who rides bareback and bare-bottom through the nearby woods. Director John Huston had the film bleached so that the colours all come out sepia except for scarlet that printed pink; but Warner Brothers – Seven Arts quickly had a 'glorious' full-colour print substituted after the first few showings in 1968. (c)

The Reivers √ Intermittently entertaining turn-of-the-century yarn, with Steve McQueen initiating young Mitch Vogel into the ways of the world, over the opposition of Will Geer. Mark Rydell directs without conviction; 1969. (c)

The Reluctant Astronaut XXX Don Knotts as misplaced hero. Terrifyingly unfunny. Director, Edward Montagne; 1967. (c)

The Reluctant Debutante XX Rex Harrison and his then (1958) wife Kay Kendall manage to make this old-fashioned stuff about will-daughter-marry-the-right-chap? watchable while they are on the screen. But Sandra Dee and John Saxon reduce this essentially British comedy into something more than faintly ludicrous. Being Italian-American, Vincente Minnelli probably thought he was being accurate enough, and, anyway, Hollywood companies of that period had little respect for British audiences. (c)

Reluctant Heroes XX Prime example of what used to be called pejoratively 'British pictures' in 1951, with the implicit boredom and (now) old familiar faces: Ronald Shiner, Brian Rix, Derek Farr. Green national servicemen muck up the manoeuvres but predictably end up as heroes. Jack Raymond directed. (*b/w*)

The Reluctant Saint XX Talk about the Flying Nun! This visible drama is about St Maximilian Schell who levitates when he prays; up he goes, in full sight of the tricky camera. Filmed in Italy, where it is supposed to have happened for real in the 17th century, this bit of religioso rubbish was apparently taken seriously by director-producer Edward Dmytryk; 1962. (*b/w*)

The Reluctant Widow XX 1950 costumer which was out of date when it was made, has Jean Kent as an English governess forced to marry drunkard in Napoleonic wars; director Bernard Knowles. (*b/w*)

The Remarkable Mr Pennypacker XX What makes him remarkable is that he has two families in separate towns totalling 17 children. As a Victorian bigamist, Clifton Webb doesn't seem happy in this 1958 comedy, possibly because his own personal inclinations made even one child unlikely. Henry Levin directed slowly and it's all a great big bore with an obvious ending it finally reaches. (*c*)

Remember the Day √ 1941 Henry King-directed weepie with Claudette Colbert back-flashing over her life as a teacher – and her lost love. (*b/w*)

The Reptile XXX Pathetic Hammer unhorror about a girl who turns into a snake. Jacqueline Pearce doesn't appear to have taken the trouble to watch any real snakes as her impression of one is inaccurate and ludicrous. And director John Gilling wasn't doing his job in not teaching her. In fact, he didn't seem to be doing much at all as this wearisome tale slithers on without any tension or fun; 1966. (*c*)

Repulsion √√√ Roman Polanski's powerful shocker of 1965 can be seen as just another horror picture, and a particularly good one as nothing supernatural provides the chills. Or it can be put into the context of Polanski's other works as a convincing study of disintegration, his pervasive theme. Catherine Deneuve – never called upon to portray more than the shell-shocked ingenue she always does best – slowly goes out of her mind. The everyday terrors of flies buzzing round a forgotten rabbit are even more frightening than the hands that clutch at her along the corridor. Polanski's skill shows in his handling of the lesser characters – Yvonne Furneaux as her sister, Patrick Wymark as lecherous landlord – who are so often just types in other low-budget British films. (*b/w*)

Requiem for a Gunfighter √ Rod Cameron is mistaken for judge and uses the time before he is recognised to prove that bully-boy is murderer in western town. Spencer G. Bennet didn't make it quite exciting enough in 1965. (*c*)

Requiem for a Heavyweight √ Famous TV play by Rod Serling makes a strong vehicle for Anthony Quinn as over-the-hill boxer. Jackie Gleason and Mickey Rooney are realistic as fight-game hangers-on under Ralph Nelson's 1962 direction; Julie Harris is self-kidding social worker. (*b/w*)

The Restless Breed X Agent's son sets out to avenge father's murder; Scott Brady plays single-minded lad in Western hamlet, Anne Bancroft intervening. Allan Dwan directed routinely; 1957. (*c*)

The Restless Years X Can dressmaker keep secret of illegitimacy from her teenage daughter? Dated (1957) small-town drama is given the works by Teresa Wright and Sandra Dee under Helmut Kautner. (*b/w*)

Return from the Ashes X Using the terrible plight of concentration camp returnees as the excuse for a thriller like this is a bit strong, even when it's tarted up with psychological and philosophical undertones. J. Lee Thompson must have known he was making over the old mother *v.* daughter (Ingrid Thulin *v.* Samantha Eggar) plot, both in love with the same man (Maximilian Schell), leading to a bathroom murder; 1965. (*b/w*)

The Return of Frank James √√ The film *Jesse James* had been such a big success in 1939 that Darryl Zanuck wheeled Henry Fonda out again the following year to play in a sequel. He's supposed to be avenging Jesse's (Tyrone Power) death in a totally unhistoric episode, and played opposite 'Miss' Gene Tierney (as they billed her) in her debut. But Fritz Lang was odd choice as director and Fonda and he were soon not on speaking terms. The result was a moody western, a cut above the ordinary. Jackie Cooper had grown up enough to play his younger brother; John Carradine led the baddies. (c)

Return of the Bad Men √ Randolph Scott wants to settle down with widow Anne Jeffreys but Robert Ryan comes riding into the Oklahoma land rush and holds up the proceedings, the nasty man. Ray Enright directs straightforwardly; 1948. (b/w)

Return of the Fly XX Sad little sequel to splendid horror movie, *The Fly*, of the previous year. This 1959 mini-budget effort puts the scientist's son (Vincent Price) through the same routine and he spends the rest of the picture literally buzzing about looking for the guy that did it to him. Writer-director Edward L. Bernds must have written it on flypaper. (b/w)

Return of the Gunfighter √ *The Gunfighter* was Gregory Peck in 1950. In this 1966 sequel a 55-year-old Robert Taylor plays a differently named character but with the same weariness for fighting and shooting, which doesn't stop him fighting and shooting. Here he avenges the deaths of Ana Martin's parents, helped by Chad Everett. James Neilson directs intelligently. (c)

The Return of the Pink Panther √√ Peter Sellers confirmed his movie niche at last with his Inspector Clouseau, when this Blake Edwards sequel to the earlier comedies came out in 1974. Slickly made, it glosses over the confusion about eponymity – here, the Pink Panther is a diamond. (c)

Return of the Seven X But not so magnificently and not the same ones. In fact, only one of the originals survives and he's the least attractive, Yul Brynner. The rest of the Second Eleven (to confuse the metaphor) aren't good enough to play even in the reserves. This sequel is how a crazy Mexican enslaves a village to build a monument to his dead sons – a pretty awful script by Larry Cohen matched by the direction of Burt Kennedy; 1967. (c)

Return to Macon County √√ One of those films where a cop chases two men and a girl across the state line. Richard Compton's version fortunately lacks pretension, and the hero is Nick Nolte (later to achieve fame when, like Lee Marvin, his former girlfriend sued him for a share of his earnings); 1975. (c)

Return to Paradise XX Taken from an episode in James Michener's book of the same name, this unfortunate South Sea Island film has Gary Cooper freeing a community from the tyranny of a preacher, Barry Jones; marrying a native girl (Roberta Haynes); then turning up again years later to save their daughter from a fate worse than death. Mark Robson struggled, as director, to put some life into a flat script from Charles Kaufman in 1953. (c)

Return to Peyton Place X Now let's sort this out nice and slowly. This Allison Mackenzie isn't Mia Farrow impersonated by Kathy Glass in the television series. This is Carol Lynley impersonating Diane Varsi who was the original movie Mackenzie. Here she is scandalising the old place with her book and living it up with her publisher (Jeff Chandler). Only Mary Astor as a selfish mother is worth watching. The rest is gossip. Director Jose Ferrer; 1961. (c)

Return to Treasure Island XX Dawn Addams as descendant of Jim Hawkins who goes back with his map; Porter Hall and baddies aim to steal it; Tab Hunter saves it. Terrible stuff, directed by E. A. Dupont; 1954. (c)

Return to Warbrow XX Western about three escaped convicts hunting for their buried loot. Phil Carey leads them; Ray Nazarro directs them; 1957. (c)

The Revenge of Frankstenstein XX Not very horrible Hammer horror, about Dr Frankenstein (not the monster) being nearly killed a couple of times and re-emerging with different identities. But he still keeps re-assembling bits of human bodies to make ever-more-terrifying patchwork people. Unfortunately, this can easily get ludicrous, and director Terence Fisher wasn't able to stop it doing so in 1958. Peter Cushing plays the Doc with his usual frenzied panache; apart from Lionel Jeffries the rest of the cast is strictly non-acting. (c)

The Revengers X Unprepossessing western in which William Holden hires a bunch of desperadoes from the local jail to revenge his wife's death. Daniel Mann directs with one and a half eyes on the box office that brought a fortune to the makers of *The Dirty Dozen; 1972.* (c)

Revolt at Fort Laramie √ Western with a nice idea: in a garrison besieged by Red Indians, the incumbents take sides as the Civil War breaks out. Red

Cloud exploits the situation. Director, Lesley Salander; 1957. (c)

The Revolt of Mamie Stover X Hawaii, 1941 (actually Hollywood, 1956). Jane Russell steals the affections of Richard Egan from posh Joan Leslie but as she. is a war-profiteering tart she is naturally unable to find True Happiness. Raoul Walsh lushes it all up; one small compensation is presence of Agnes Moorehead as dance-hall queen. (c)

The Revolutionary √ Jon Voight makes a convincing bourgeois caught up in becoming an activist on behalf of the workers in a time and country not clearly defined. Paul Williams manages to avoid many of the clichés of the genre, but there is no direct political message. Out of the rut; 1970. (c)

Rhapsody X Elizabeth Taylor, as rich girl, is spurned by violinist Vittorio Gassman, so marries pianist John Ericson among snippets of the popular classics. Charles Vidor conducts the proceedings; 1954. (c)

Rhapsody in Blue X The music's OK if you can stand that inferior orchestral banging-about that is the title-work, but Robert Alda's portrayal of George Gershwin is so far from the truth as to be farcical. His piano-playing is dubbed, as is Joan Leslie's voice. Irving Rapper must have thought he was on a winner when he started out in 1945; but the casting (Alexis Smith, Charles Coburn, Oscar Levant were in it, too) was against him. (b/w)

Rhino! XX Dull and rather rhino-less big game hunter *v.* ecologist drama shot in Africa or somewhere that looks vaguely like it. Robert Culp is the goodie, Harry Guardino the baddie. Shirley Eaton is baddie turned goodie (not her acting, though), and Ivan Tors' direction seems to consist of intercutting wild animal footage with tame human footage; 1964. (c)

Richard III √√ Olivier's 1956 triumph as the hunchback of history combining Shakespeare's flights of poetry with exciting pictures and filmic expertise. As producer-director, he also ensured great performances from Gielgud, Richardson, Alec Clunes, Cedric Hardwicke and, above all, himself. Claire Bloom was also in it. He was particularly successful in his use of soliloquies – straight to camera, without any voice-over or other worried film tricks, but didn't try for big battle sequences which might have been worth spending a bit on if he could have raised the extra money. (c)

The Ride Back √ Prisoner and lawman are forced to help each other in desperate ride through Apache country. Anthony Quinn, William Conrad. Director Allen H. Miner; 1957. (b/w)

Ride Beyond Vengeance √ Over-violent western in which a man is wrongly branded (literally) as a thief and rides on into town determined to pay his branders back in the same fashion. There are also a lot of bloody fights that Bernard McEveety directs only too well. Among the many old (some of them very, by 1966) friends present are Joan Blondell, Frank Gorshin, Michael Rennie, Gloria Grahame, Gary Merrill, Buddy Baer. In the main part, Chuck Connors fights a good fight. (c)

Ride 'Em Cowboy √ Harmless Abbott and Costello joke has Ella Fitzgerald and Douglass Dumbrille as added attractions. The lads are rodeo hot-dog sellers who get carried West; director Arthur Lubin, 1941. (b/w)

Ride Lonesome √ Randolph Scott captures young baddie, waits for brother to come and get him – because, many years before, Lee Van Cleef (the brother) hanged Scott's wife. Budd Boetticher's direction matches up to Burt Kennedy's interesting plot, which has James Coburn and Pernell Roberts also after the boy because amnesty has been declared on any outlaws who bring him in; 1959. (c)

Ride Out for Revenge X Rory Calhoun, Cavalry commander, challenges Chief's son Vince Edwards to single-handed combat, so as to avert all-out war. But there's gold in thar that reservation; director, Bernard Girard; 1957. (b/w)

Rider on the Rain √√ Effective thriller, nothing to do with the Wild West, but about rape and murder in Marseilles. Charles Bronson is arrogant investigator, Marlene Jobert is raped wife, accused of murder. Tautly directed by René Clement, late in his career; 1969. (c)

Ride the Pink Horse √ Robert Montgomery (directing himself in 1947) arrives in New Mexico town intent on blackmail and vengeance, but there's nothing like the love of a good woman like Wanda Hendrix. (b/w)

Ride the Wild Surf X Fabian, James Mitchum, Barbara Eden plus sundry other beach bums and gals in a surfing drama (i.e. not a comedy, except that there isn't much difference) shot mostly in Hawaii. Director Don Taylor; 1965. (c)

Ride, Vaquero X Ava Gardner switches from Howard Keel to his half-brother Robert Taylor, as they try to build ranch in area dominated by bandit Anthony Quinn. John Farrow's direction can't quite keep a grip on the action; 1953. (c)

Riding High X Undemanding Mark Hellinger race-track yarn has Bing Crosby as broke owner who has to rely on a horse called Broadway Bill (which was what the poor 1933 film was called) without much hope. Veteran director Frank Capra did this sentimental 1950 remake with Charles Bickford, James Gleason, and Oliver Hardy (sans Laurel). Some of the racetrack scenes were re-run from the original. Notable for the fact that all the songs were recorded direct – not lip-sung to pre-recordings. (b/w)

Right Cross X Boxing melo with Ricardo Montalban as boxer with the chip on his shoulder that he's Mexican and thus second-class citizen. Lionel Barrymore is his manager, Dick Powell a reporter who's in love with June Allyson. When she spurns him, he goes night-clubbing with some other birds – one of them, though not named on the credits, is Marilyn Monroe, still unknown in 1950. John Sturges directed. (b/w)

Ring of Bright Water X Documentary about otters, masquerading as a feature film. Bill Travers sees an otter in a pet-shop, takes it to his flat, finds the otter doesn't like it, takes it up to Scotland, where they meet up with Virginia McKenna. Man loses otter. Man gets otter. Fascinating for otters, not for humans. Jack Couffer directs like the graduate from the Disney wild-life school that he is. The otters are marginally worse actors than McKenna, marginally better than Travers; 1969. (c)

Ring of Fear X Mickey Spillane makes an appearance as private eye called in to stop seemingly accidental deaths in circus. Pat O'Brien strolls through, under James Grant's direction; 1954. (c)

Ring of Fire √ The first three-quarters of this actioner by Andrew L. Stone is an off-beat story of chase, escape, rape charges and mob violence. Then comes one of the best forest fires ever on the screen and the plot perishes in the flames, but by then you don't care. David Janssen, Joyce Taylor, Frank Gorshin; 1961. (c)

Ring of Spies XX Unconvincing partial plodding reconstruction of the Portland Spy Case, vitiated by its own admission that only the names have been kept to convict the guilty (although it doesn't quite put it that way). You don't know when you are watching what actually happened or what Frank Launder and Peter Barnes have dreamed up. This was made in 1964, and now that Houghton and Gee are out of jail it would be interesting to know what they make of Bernard Lee and Margaret Tyzack in their parts. Director Robert Tronson. (b/w)

Rio Bravo √√ Howard Hawks in 1959 got a great performance out of sheriff John Wayne helping drunken gunfighter Dean Martin regain moral stature in fight against outlaws. (c)

Rio Conchos √ Grand-scale 1964 actioner from Gordon Douglas with Richard Boone, whose family was massacred by Apaches, hunting out Edmond O'Brien who is selling guns to the Indians. Tough performances from Stuart Whitman, Tony Franciosa, Jim Brown. (c)

Rio Grande √ Fifteen years after the Civil War when John Wayne was forced to burn his wife's plantation, she (Maureen O'Hara) turns up at the HQ of his war against the Apaches, determined to rescue their son (Claude Jarman Jr.) from fighting. Plottier than most John Ford films, this 1950 actioner carries many of his splendid outdoor sweeps and his sympathy with martial tradition. (b/w)

Rio Lobo √ Violent, exciting, funny, familiar western: John Wayne hunts down a traitor and fights with small band of cronies against superior odds. Another veteran, Howard Hawks, directed this in 1970 with undiminished verve although it was to be his last film. (c)

Riot √ An old prison melo brought up to 1969 date with homosexuality and transvestism, shot by Buzz Kulik at Folsom Jail. Gene Hackman, just before making it at last with The French Connection, plays one of the convicts in a break-out. (c)

Riot in Cell Block 11 √√ Classic prison movie, directed by masterly Don Siegel in 1954, looking at the trouble from both sides. Neville Brand and Leo Gordon have real characters to play as the men's leaders. (b/w)

The Rise and Fall of Legs Diamond √√ Budd Boetticher's sharp direction distinguished this otherwise routine gangster film about the guy who thought he couldn't be killed (played by Ray Danton, with rare authority), in 1960. Incorporation of genuine newsreel material is neatly done. *(b/w)*

The Rise and Rise of Michael Rimmer XX Despite a phalanx of funny comedians (Peter Cook, John Cleese, Graham Chapman among both writers and performers) and a roll call of trustworthy supports (Denholm Elliott, Ronald Fraser, Harold Pinter, Dennis Price, Ronnie Corbett, Ann Beach), director Kevin Billington flopped with this string of sketches. As the ad. man who manipulates and murders to become Prime Minister, Cook is bland. Too many cooks, in fact; 1970. *(c)*

The Rising of the Moon √ John Ford put three short films together under one title in 1957. Two of them are blarney. The third, *1921*, is a moving, angry, exciting story about a condemned prisoner changing clothes with one of his last visitors, a 'nun', and escaping. It's worth turning on about an hour after the start for this episode. *(b/w)*

River Lady XX Nonsense about Yvonne de Carlo being a gambling-boat owner with eyes on lumber monopoly and Dan Duryea. Direction from George Sherman; 1948. *(c)*

River of No Return X Marilyn Monroe in the wild. She seems unhappy, more so than the plot demands. It's about the way she's torn between nasty husband Rory Calhoun and nice Robert Mitchum, saved by his ten-year-old son. Not one of Otto Preminger's masterpieces – if he made any; 1954. *(c)*

The River's Edge X Ray Milland is gangster on the run in this Allan Dwan-directed piece of phoney parable-prating. His only luggage is a million dollars in banknotes (should have thought it was heavier than it seems to be here) and he persuades simple farmer Anthony Quinn to help him across the border, down Mexico way. But their dangerous trek is meant to point out to the audience how superior the simple Quinn is to the hustler Milland, and the actor plays up to this, enjoying it much more than us. When they start burning the paper money for warmth, symbolism just goes too far, and when you see simple Quinn sacrificing his own few precious dollars first you know that they are really underestimating the audience; 1957. *(c)*

Road House X Lush melo about Ida Lupino at base of triangle involving flash Richard Widmark and ex-con Cornel Wilde. Jean Negulesco milks it for emotion; 1948. *(b/w)*

Road to Bali XX 1952 effort of Bing Crosby, Bob Hope and Dorothy Lamour. Hal Walker directed jokey yarn about evil princess and deep sea divers. *(c)*

Road to Hong Kong √ Has same trio but Lamour only pops in, as it's 1962 and she was 48 and retired for nine years. Instead, Joan Collins joins the two old men as they are involved in Oriental spy chase. Peter Sellers, Robert Morley beef up the laughs under Norman Panama's direction. *(b/w)*

Road to Morocco √ Made in 1942 when the laughs were still unforced. David Butler directed spontaneous-seeming jokery with Bob sold as slave for Dottie by Bing. Moonlight became them. *(b/w)*

Road to Rio √ 1947 effort, directed by Norman Z. McLeod; stowaways Bing and Bob rescue Dottie from grim Aunt Gale Sondergaard. *(b/w)*

Road to Singapore √ First one in 1940, in peaceful Saigon, where the lads meet up with saronged Dottie, under Victor Schertzinger's direction, and set the pattern of Bing outsmarting Bob for the lady. *(b/w)*

Road to Utopia √ Takes them to the Klondike in 1945, with a commentary by Robert Benchley and direction by Hal Walker. *(b/w)*

Road to Zanzibar √ 1941 search for diamond mine; Una Merkel and Eric Blore joined in, under Victor Schertzinger. *(b/w)*

The Roaring Twenties √√ Classic gangster movie, vintage 1939, with Bogart and Cagney face-to-face under Raoul Walsh's direction. *(b/w)*

Robbery √ Attempt to capture what planning, executing and detecting a crime like the Great Train Robbery must have been like, made four years after (1967) by Peter Yates, who made *Bullitt* as direct result of this modest British winner. Stanley Baker as chief crook, James Booth chief cop in uniformly competent cast. *(c)*

Robbery Under Arms XX Slight Australian-set 'western', showing that Jack Lee and the rest of his British crew hadn't got the hang of making oaters there in 1957 – and nobody in the outback has since. This was partly due to the purism in using only British or Australian actors like Peter Finch (as outlaw leader), David McCallum and Ronald Lewis (both weakly playing strong characters as his sons) and, above all, by such feeble females as Maureen Swanson and Jill Ireland for romantic relief. (c)

The Robe X First CinemaScope feature in 1953 won Richard Burton an Oscar nomination for his role of Roman in charge of Christ's execution, although Victor Mature gave surprisingly good performance as Demetrius (who fought the gladiators two years later). Henry Koster managed to avoid some of the usual Biblical pitfalls but still fell into the one of over-piety. (c)

Robin and the Seven Hoods √ Some like it lukewarm – even a lot of the gags are the same (gun-in-a-cake, for example), as is the setting (St Valentine's Day Massacre). But where *Some Like It Hot* piled agonising jokes upon each other without tumbling down, this 1964 indulgence for Frank Sinatra and his clan (Dean Martin, Sammy Davis Jr. are both in it) is merely tiresome. Gordon Douglas directs weakly, in order to give the boys as much elbow-room as possible; even this wouldn't have been too bad if David Schwartz's script about Prohibition gangsters had been strong. (c)

Robinson Crusoe on Mars X The panto Crusoe that is. Not for Byron Haskin the deeper implications of Defoe. His Crusoe is Paul Mantee, his Friday a work-party escapee from another colonised planet. Well gadgeted-up, though. Death Valley in Utah makes a marvellous facsimile of Mars for the *Destination Moon* producer; 1964. (c)

Rock-a-Bye Baby X Strictly for Jerry Lewis-lovers, this 1958 farce has him as a TV repairer doubling as baby-sitter for a film star's triplets. Reginald Gardner and James Gleason add their own touches of jokery. One of Frank Tashlin's script-directions. (c)

Rock Around the Clock XX Strictly museum piece of 1956 popular music, with Bill Haley and the Comets, the Platters, Alan Freed. Director Fred F. Sears. (b/w)

Rocket to the Moon XX What are supposed to be chuckly goings-on in Victorian scientific circles, based on Jules Verne's books, turn into a cheapie with big names in small parts (Hermione Gingold, for instance, couldn't have done more than two days' work) and medium-names (Burl Ives, Troy Donahue, Terry-Thomas, Lionel Jeffries, Graham Stark) poorly used. Don Sharp directs adequately, but it was a Harry Alan Towers production; 1967. (c)

The Rocking Horse Winner √√ Adaptation of D. H. Lawrence story about a boy with second sight. Anthony Pelissier got fine performances in 1949 from Valerie Hobson as the tragic mother, John Mills the father. John Howard Davies was the boy. (b/w)

Rocky Mountain X Errol Flynn's last western, 1950, had him recruiting outlaws for the Confederate army (as happened in California during Civil War) but neither the script nor William Keighley's direction had any ambitions beyond a routine oater. The girl they all heroically/stupidly die for in the end is Patrice Wymore, whom Flynn met on this location and eventually married. (b/w)

Rogue Cop √√ Robert Taylor as crooked policeman tracking down man who killed his brother. Classic cops-and-robbers, 1954 vintage, with George Raft as underworld boss, Janet Leigh, Anne Francis as dipso moll. Roy Rowland. (b/w)

Rogue's Gallery X Routine private eye thriller given a 1968 gloss by Leonard Horn. Roger Smith the detective, named Rogue. Old-timers Dennis Morgan, Edgar Bergen, Brian Donlevy, Farley Granger make appearances. (c)

Rollerball √√ Exciting if amoral (despite pretensions to be otherwise) sporting pic about a bloody game of the future which combines roller skating/hockey/rugby football. Masochist James Caan is forced to retire by big chief John Houseman and goes out in a blaze of what he thinks is glory. Norman Jewison directed this slick concoction in 1975. (c)

Roman Holiday X Audrey Hepburn got her first starring part in this mushy yarn of princess having a fling with Gregory Peck and it won her both the 1953 British and American Oscars. But William Wyler's fairy tale looks awfully coy and dated now. (b/w)

Romanoff and Juliet X Adaptation by Peter Ustinov (who produced, directed, starred) of his stage play about the Juliet and Romeoid children of Ruritanian country's American and Soviet ambassadors. If you like whimsy pleasantly served up, you'll enjoy this; 1961. (c)

The Roman Spring of Mrs Stone √ Vivien Leigh was ageing actress in 1961 version of Tennessee Williams novella, buying last fling from gigolo Warren Beatty. José Quintero directed with bravura. (c)

The Romantic Englishwoman √ Muddled (doubtless director Joseph Losey and writers Tom Stoppard, Tom Wiseman would say ambiguous) magazine story about Glenda Jackson (novelist Michael Caine's wife), who has an affair with drug-courier Helmut Berger. Kate Nelligan scores in a small role; 1975. (c)

Romeo and Juliet X (1) 1936 version by George Cukor had an elderly Leslie Howard and Norma Shearer (well, 43 and 36 respectively was a bit old for the teenage lovers). Irving Thalberg produced as a labour of love for his wife, Shearer, but it was an expensive flop – too Hollywooden. (b/w)

Romeo and Juliet XX (2) 1954 version by Renato Castellani in England was monumentally miscast, with Laurence Harvey and Susan Shentall laughable in the roles. The supports were equally risible: Mervyn Johns, Bill Travers, Norman Wooland. Only Flora Robson brought a breath of real presence to the muted shambles. (c)

Romeo and Juliet √√ (3) 1968 version by Franco Zeffirelli at least had the virtue of life, movement and panache, although neither Leonard Whiting nor Olivia Hussey could really carry the demanding parts. (c)

Room at the Top √√ 1959 adaptation of John Braine's novel shows nasty Joe Lampton (well-cast Laurence Harvey) clawing his way out of clerking and into riches via the rich man's daughter (Heather Sears), sacrificing mentor (Simone Signoret) en route. Jack Clayton directed. (b/w)

Room for One More √ Cary Grant and Betsy Drake, real-life wife (at the time, 1952) play doting married couple who can't say no to another and another and another adoptee. Norman Taurog directed sentimentally. (b/w)

Room Service √ A rare Marx Brothers in that it actually has a plot – about Groucho holding the wolves at bay while a play he is producing gets put on; Lucille Ball and Ann Miller provide the glam. Directed by William Sieter; 1937. (b/w)

Rooney XXX Not even Mickey, alas. Instead, John Gregson having a terrible difficulty with an Oirish accent in a ludicrous tale about Dublin dustmen and an inheritance. Barry Fitzgerald, the only authentic voice in the whole shenanigans, was a mistake from director George Pollock's point of view, because he shows up the rest as such dreadful performers and the general inauthenticity of the 1958 piece. (b/w)

The Roots of Heaven XX Attempt to make eco-film as early as 1958. It's elephants that Trevor Howard is fighting to keep from extinction. Sadly, John Huston indulged cast of Juliette Greco, Orson Welles and a dying, drunken, malarial Errol Flynn. It took an enormous effort to shoot the poor location sequences in Africa. Huston said afterwards: 'The pictures that turn out to be the most difficult to make, usually turn out to be the worst – like *The Roots of Heaven.*' (c)

Rope √√ Now dismissed by Hitchcock as a nonsensical stunt. He's referring to technical attempt to film in one continuous take (instead of the usual 600 – 1,400 short takes all joined together in the normal film). The only pauses were for reel changes when a character passed in front of the camera so that he could go to black, reload and start again with the same frame. But it stands up as a fairly exciting psychological thriller about two homosexual college boys (based by Patrick Hamilton on his play about real-life 'thrill killers' Leopold and Loeb) who do in a fellow-student for the fun of it. Cocky, they invite the boy's father and their professor round while his body is hidden in their apartment; Cedric Hardwicke and James Stewart handle the older men assuredly, but John Dall and Farley Granger could have done with a little help from conventional short takes. This was also Hitch's first colour picture and he was so dissatisfied with his cameraman's idea of a sunset that he reshot half the film; 1948. (c)

Rosebud XXX Otto Preminger's 1974 'thriller' is a plodding mishmash about the kidnapping of five wealthy girls by the Palestine Liberation Army, who threaten to kill them unless their films are shown on worldwide TV. Meekly giving in, the authorities arrange this, but when the demands escalate they allow *Newsweek* reporter Peter O'Toole to lead an Israeli commando force on villain Richard Attenborough's Corsican HQ. Almost the only point of note is that the first girl released is later French star Isabelle Huppert *(The Lacemaker, Violette Noziere)*. *(c)*

Rose Marie √ (1) 1936 version by W. S. Van Dyke with Jeanette Macdonald and Nelson Eddy was a remake of 1928 silent version with Joan Crawford. Quiz: what other superstar was in the cast of Macdonald-Eddy version? Answer: James Stewart, aged 24, in his second movie, as the brother Jeanette and Nelson are both hunting – she for family love, he to Get His Man. *(b/w)*

Rose Marie X (2) 1954 version by Mervyn Le Roy with Ann Blyth and Howard Keel was a mistake. Rudolf Friml tunes lose out to broad comedy from Bert Lahr and Marjorie Main. *(c)*

Rosemary's Baby √√√ The term 'woman's picture' is now taboo but women are incontrovertibly different from men in at least one respect: they can give birth. Thus it isn't sexism to call this a woman's picture, because it must have more power over the birth-givers than over those who can't know what it is like to feel life inside you . . . and fear, as here, that the baby may be a monster. This is the most terrifying aspect of this frightening film – it plays on the primeval fear of women and thus, sympathetically, on their men. Everything about this winner from Roman Polanski combines to scare; even the light touches are there only to provide chiaroscuro. The performance of Mia Farrow as the trusting girl who comes to perceive the ambiguities in her husband (well-played, if not quite in the same league as Miss Farrow, by John Cassavetes) is stunning. The climaxes are as terrifying as those in *Psycho*, with deeper reverberations. Astonishingly the only Oscar went to the weakest bit of the film, Ruth Gordon's comic witch-next-door. Mia Farrow didn't even get a nomination in the year that the unfunny girl Barbra Streisand won; 1968. *(c)*

The Rose Tattoo √ Daniel Mann turned this Tennessee Williams script, from his own play, into a vehicle for Anna Magnani. She plays widow of lorry-driver finding physical happiness from Burt Lancaster, whom she sees as reincarnation of dead husband – even down to a tattoo he has on him. OK if you like Italian histrionics; 1955. *(b/w)*

Rosie X Indulgence for Rosalind Russell on the part of director David Lowell Rich, resisting being put away by her children. Moderately funny; 1967. *(c)*

Rotten to the Core √ Anton Rodgers never really took off from this exceptionally promising start as a sort of surrogate Peter Sellers, but perhaps that's because this type of Rotten Comedy was dying the death by 1965, only the *Carry Ons* carrying on. He plays chief crook planning a caper. Eric Sykes and Thorley Walters are the deliciously incapable detectives. Directed by John Boulting; 1965. *(b/w)*

The Rough and the Smooth XX Somehow or other Robert Siodmak was persuaded to direct, and William Bendix to appear in this messy, silly yarn about a nymphomaniac German girl (Najda Tiller) and her involvement with various men, particularly Tony Britton and Tony Wright. You can't believe a word of it and don't want to; 1959. *(b/w)*

Rough Night in Jericho √ Sure is pretty rough when Dean Martin becomes a baddie and Jean Simmons a drunk. This makes the West look a bit too glossy, but it's certainly full of grown-up action, as the two of them square up for a show-down. Arnold Laven directed the fights well; 1967. *(c)*

The Rounders √√ An un-western western with hardly a shot fired and no-one you could really call a baddie. Instead, there are two nice cuddly goodies, Henry Fonda and Glenn Ford, always having to go back to work for a man they don't like because they're broke. How an untameable bronco brings their fortune is the plot of this pleasant affair, neatly written and directed by Burt Kennedy; 1965. *(c)*

Roustabout √ Elvis Presley's 1965 showcase was this slightly improved jollity about fairgrounds, with Barbara Stanwyck as the lady who runs the little one that the big'un is trying to muscle in on – but doesn't, of course, thanks to Elvis's singing, judo, motor-bike riding and sundry other talents. John Rich directed discreetly. *(c)*

Roxie Hart √√ Delicious 1942 spoof of libertarian twenties in America, when a showgirl on trial for murder could be sure to be let off and made a star. Ginger Rogers and Adolphe Menjou are perfectly-matched client and mouthpiece. Nunnally Johnson wrote the script, William Wellman directed it and the photographer's cry, 'The knees, Roxie, the knees!' could be emblazoned over every tabloid picture-editor's desk. (b/w)

Royal Flash √ Inexplicably dull period piece directed by Richard Lester in 1975, taking the bully Flashman from *Tom Brown's Schooldays* and following through his later, disreputable career. Malcolm McDowell's hero is too likeable. Support of varying usefulness comes from Alan Bates, Oliver Reed (negative), Lionel Jeffries, Michael Hordern, Alastair Sim (positive, if predictable). (c)

The Royal Hunt of the Sun √√ Peter Shaffer's noble play is somehow diminished on the screen, due to a combination of inadequate direction (Irving Lerner) and acting (Christopher Plummer as Inca chief disappoints more than Robert Shaw's Pizarro). But the theme is tremendous and the implication (man's need to join a band, the band's need to find an enemy) disturbing. Less than a fulfilment of the theatre-pageant, more than a routine adventure story; 1969. (c)

Ruby Gentry XX Jennifer Jones marries Karl Malden to spite Charlton Heston; King Vidor encouraged whole cast to overplay almost to the point of absurdity; 1952. (b/w)

The Ruling Class XX Peter O'Toole is unconvincing as the 14th Earl of Gurney who believes himself to be God and dresses as Jesus. Nor does director Peter Medak have the force to turn Peter Barnes's extravaganza into the glorious suspension of disbelief it should be, and this 1971 effort is no more than a string of variable character performances. (c)

Run for Cover X James Cagney was still playing westerns in 1955 and still getting the girl, in this case the insipid Viveca Lindfors. Nicholas Ray did his best to force some characterisation into tale of Cagney's sheriff v. former protégé John Derek, but there wasn't enough substance for him to work on. (c)

Run for the Sun XX Remake of the 1932 *Hounds of Zaroff* (from Richard Connell's *The Most Dangerous Game*) by Roy Boulting in 1956. The story has been lost in a tepid love affair, and neither Richard Widmark, Trevor Howard nor Jane Greer can save what should have been an exciting romp. (c)

Run Like a Thief X A little effort about stealing the diamonds that were stolen. And the bad girl joins Our Hero and there's a chase. You know the sort of thing. This particular rendering of the theme is made even worse by the presence of the stolid Kieron Moore, although Keenan Wynn does provide some small compensation, along with Victor Maddern. Bernard Glasser glassily directs and produces; 1967. (c)

The Running Man √ Husband Laurence Harvey fakes death in plane crash, disappears to Spain to meet up with wife Lee Remick, but insurance investigator Alan Bates follows. Carol Reed lifted this 1963 glossy into the Interesting class with neat direction of John Mortimer script. (c)

Running Scared √ Robert Powell lets a friend commit suicide because he considers that everyone is entitled to make their own decision. But the world is against him, in particular the man's sister, Gayle Hunnicutt. Alas, instead of this triggering off a complex of emotions and reactions, it becomes a commonplace love story with a banal ending in David Hemmings's first directorial (and co-script) effort; 1972. (c)

Run of the Arrow √√ This Rod Steiger-starring 1957 movie has an important place in the canon of Samuel Fuller, an increasingly honoured director. Steiger is the man who fired the last shot in the Civil War, and is rejected by the Sioux when he turns to them offering his services. Can be enjoyed as wry actioner or scanned by Fuller-buffs for deeper symbolism. (c)

Run Silent, Run Deep X 'Ran noisy, ran shallow' said *Time*. But Robert Wise did try to make more than run-of-the-Atlantic war film and included some cerebral rivalry between Clark Gable and Burt Lancaster in submarine; 1958. (b/w)

Run Wild, Run Free X A little boy who can't talk finds peace and speech with a wild white colt. If you like little boys on the screen and/or wild horses then you'll enjoy this rather simple-minded film. If not, then not all the sympathetic playing of John Mills and Sylvia Syms as parents, boy Mark Lester, and stalwarts Gordon Jackson and Bernard Miles will make it palatable. Director Richard C. Sarafian has caught some lyrical moments, but that might put you off, too; 1969. (c)

The Russians are Coming, the Russians are Coming √ Norman Jewison sees the funny side of a mistaken Soviet invasion of America in 1966. Alan Arkin shines as lieutenant, Theodore Bikel, Paul Ford, Carl Reiner almost match him. (c)

Ryan's Daughter X Grandiose yarn about a triangle (Sarah Miles, Christopher Jones, Robert Mitchum) amidst arms smuggling on the Irish coast in 1916. On the level of an old-fashioned women's magazine story it works adequately. Any greater pretension is ruined by David Lean's overblown ambitions for it, and miscasting all round, though John Mills won an Oscar for his portrayal of a crippled mute; 1970. (c)

S

Saadia XX Stunning Moroccan locations don't make up for messy plot about Dr Mel Ferrer and Sheikh Cornel Wilde both in love with Rita Gam. Albert Lewin; 1954. (c)

Sabaka X Boris Karloff, Reginald Denny, Victor Jory in old-timers' outing in Indian-set creepy about occult sect. Frank Ferrin; 1955. (c)

Saboteur X Famous for the climactic fight on the Statue of Liberty, this 1942 wartime chaser is not among Hitchcock's best. He blames the script for having too many ideas insufficiently worked out and the casting of Robert Cummings (wrong sort of face: even when he's anguished he looks amused) and Priscilla Lane (too ordinary, foisted on him by Universal). (b/w)

Saboteur – Code Name Morituri X Bernhard Wicki's 1965 film of Marlon Brando as anti-Nazi German who helps British capture cargo ship, has turgid script and Yul Brynner, Trevor Howard, Janet Margolin to keep it waterlogged. (b/w)

Sabre Jet X Routine Korean War story concentrates on wives waiting for Air Force husbands to return. Robert Stack, Coleen Gray, Julie Bishop led director Louis King's uninspired cast; 1953. (c)

Sabrina √√ Delicious Billy Wilder-directed version of Samuel Taylor's hit play has Audrey Hepburn as chauffeur's daughter, Humphrey Bogart and William Holden as wealthy brothers; 1954. (b/w)

Saddle the Wind √ Superior Robert Parrish-directed western about warring brothers has fine performances from Robert Taylor (law-abiding), John Cassavetes (trigger-happy), Julie London and some convincing dialogue; 1958. (c)

The Sad Horse X Low-budgeter about racehorse befriended by little David Ladd (little Alan's little boy). Patrice Wymore helps to spread out director James B. Clark's sentiment; 1959. (c)

The Sad Sack X Jerry Lewis as classic Army moron based on George Baker's cartoon character (who, when spying at a nudist camp through a knot-hole exclaimed 'Boy, I'd sure like to see that in a sweater!'), not making a very coherent story-line, although there's something about a lady major – Phyllis Kirk – being assigned to smarten him up. Suddenly the whole action is transported to North Africa, so that Peter Lorre can pop in as an Arab. George Marshall has saved it from absolute boredom for non-Lewis lovers; those who think he's funny will need no recommendation; 1957. (b/w)

Safari XX Mau-Mau for Red Indians, the Kenya Police for the US cavalry, and some jungle animals thrown in for added thrills. Now thoroughly out-of-date nonsense, with hunter Victor Mature guiding rich clients through the undergrowth; Janet Leigh, Roland Culver, John Justin. Spottily directed by Terence Young in far-off 1956. (c)

The Safe Cracker X One of those 1958 British quickies with an American star – Ray Milland here, who also directed – to make it saleable Stateside. he's a safe expert turned crook who goes on dangerous wartime mission. (b/w)

A Safe Place √ Considering the stars – Jack Nicholson, Orson Welles, Tuesday Weld – this mess is almost criminal, but the film was relegated to the vault from which no financial flop returns. If it does find its way on to the TV screen as part of a package, have a glance at how talent can be misapplied. There are a few moments of invention and pleasure; director Henry Jaglom; 1971. (c)

The Saga of Hemp Brown X Rory Calhoun as army lieutenant framed for payroll robbery; luckily, Beverly Garland believes in him. Richard Carlson directed in 1958. (c)

Sahara √ Humphrey Bogart lifts this desert war actioner about fight for oasis above routine Zoltan Korda direction.

J. Carroll Naish and Rex Ingram help. Made only two years after its setting in 1941 and adapted from Soviet film, *The Thirteen*. (b/w)

Sail A Crooked Ship X Even funny Ernie Kovacs, Frank Gorshin can't keep this silly comedy, about bank-robbers making getaway on boat, afloat. Robert Wagner, Dolores Hart, Frankie Avalon soon go down under Irving Brecher's direction; 1962. (b/w)

Sailor Beware X (1) 1952. American; beware of this one if you're not a Jerry Lewis-Dean Martin fan; this time they're in the navy, and director Hal Walker lets them get on with it. (b/w)

Sailor Beware XX (2) 1956. British; Peggy Mount buffaloing all over the screen in Gordon Parry's filming of famous farce about sailor (Ronald Lewis) who runs away from his wedding. Broad but not vulgar. (b/w)

The Sailor from Gibraltar XX Perhaps director Tony Richardson knew what this 1966 adaptation of a Marguerite Duras novel was all about. Unhappily, he did not let on to Jeanne Moreau, Ian Bannen, Vanessa Redgrave or Orson Welles, who gloomily wander through an obscure story of crossed love. (b/w)

Saint Joan XX Total disaster from Otto Preminger who failed, in 1957, to catch the spirit either of the historical period or of Shaw's play. Jean Seberg, whom he found after seeing 3,000 of the 18,000 unknown applicants, was visibly miscast (fey when she should have been tough, sweet when she should have been cerebral). The whole production was studio-bound and artificial, the selections from Shaw's play arbitrary and vulgarised, as if Graham Greene, who did the adaptation, wearied of the demands of the commercial Mr Preminger. Richard Widmark, as the Dauphin, wasn't quite as bizarre as he might have been, but to balance that, John Gielgud, Harry Andrews and Felix Aylmer stayed theatrical. Considering the money and talent available, Preminger's casting of the other parts was extraordinary: Richard Todd, Anton Walbrook, Barry Jones, Finlay Currie, Bernard Miles, Patrick Barr, Kenneth Haigh . . . it reads like a roster of the second-rate; 1957. (c)

Saintly Sinners X Don Beddoe as a priest who can see no evil, even in the wickedest parishioners. So he gets bounced from his church by the Monsignor, who understandably doesn't like to have him implicated in crookedness. But the crooks confess they were just conning the gullible old man and all ends happily. Director Jean Yarbrough manages to convey the small town ambience but not the characters; 1962. (b/w)

Saints and Sinners XX Kieron Moore returns home to Irish village to find his former girlfriend Sheila Manahan has given him the air while he has been in prison. Marie O'Neill and Michael Dolan believe in him, but it's blarney all the way; Leslie Arliss directed in 1949. (b/w)

Sally's Irish Rogue XX An oddity, with Julie Harris plonked in the middle of the Irish countryside surrounded by players from the Abbey Theatre, romping their way through a particularly tiresome tale of a young man's (Tim Seeley) rebellion. Miss Harris is the girl he was going to marry. George Pollock directs bemusedly, as if one of the little people was in the way; 1958. (b/w)

Salome X Director William Dieterle takes a long time getting to the Seven Veils bit, and Rita Hayworth disappoints when he does – well, it was only 1953. Charles Laughton, Stewart Granger, Alan Badel and a lot more. (c)

Salt and Pepper XX Flimsy farce has Sammy Davis Jr., Peter Lawford as Soho nightclub owners involved in murder and taking-over-the-Government type plot. Pity third Clan member Sinatra wasn't there to cheer it up. John Le Mesurier, Michael Bates remind us that this was British-made tedium; Richard Donner directs; 1968. (c)

Salty O'Rourke X Alan Ladd, having set up a crooked horse-race to win $20,000, is persuaded by schoolteacher Gail Russell to go back along the path of righteousness. Directed by Raoul Walsh; 1945. (b/w)

The Saltzburg Connection √ Entertaining thriller with Barry Newman picking his way through the myriad spies who inhabit the pretty town of the title; Lee H. Katzin; 1972. (c)

Samar √ Plenty of excitement as prison chief George Montgomery and his charges flee from the cruel Spanish in 19th-century Philippines. As if that weren't enough for any man, Montgomery co-wrote and directed too; 1962. (c)

Sammy Going South √√ A ten-year-old boy making a 4,500-mile trek across Africa to his aunt in Durban could have been a sloppy sentimental yarn tricked out to bring tears to the eyes of impressionable viewers. That it avoids this kind of false sob-stuff is director Sandy Mackendrick's most notable achievement in this unusual film. Edward G. Robinson is marvellously grizzled as the wily old diamond smuggler who is Sammy's only friend; the other people he meets – a Syrian pedlar (Zia Mohyeddin in a too-long episode), a rich American (Constance Cummings), a tribal chief (Orlando Martins) are interesting too. But ultimately it is in the character of Sammy (Fergus McClelland) that Mackendrick excels: he is shown as a nasty little tyke, who uses everyone more than they use him; 1962. (c)

Sam Whiskey √ Pleasant western comedy has Angie Dickinson hiring Burt Reynolds, Ossie Davis and Clint Walker to put back some gold bars her late husband happened to steal. Arnold Laven made it all harmless enough, in 1969. (c)

Sanctuary X Lee Remick, Yves Montand, Odetta, Bradford Dillman in lurid sex-and-murder melodrama set in Deep South, based on William Faulkner novel. Director Tony Richardson seemed unhappy in 1961 with this improbable plot of a maid who kills a baby to save the parents' happiness, and then resignedly trots off to the electric chair. (b/w)

The Sand Castle √ Pleasant little self-indulgence written, directed and produced by Jerome Hill about a day on the beach. Reminiscent of the Italian neo-realist masterpiece *A Sunday in August*, it ironically shows the many kinds of people (Barry and Laurie Cardwell, George Dunham) and groups who gather for a day in the sun. The centrepiece is a huge castle which the little boy who makes it dreams (in colour) has become real; 1962. (b/w)

San Demetrio London √ Dramatisation of evacuation of burning tanker, a true tale which happened in 1940; film was made in 1943 at Ealing Studios by Charles Frend. Walter Fitzgerald, Mervyn Johns, Ralph Michael, Robert Beatty make you proud. (b/w)

The Sand Pebbles X Far be it from us to countenance cuts made in movies by TV companies, let alone advocate them, but this turgid melodrama about a US ship raising the flag in 1926 China is very, very long (over three hours in the cinema) and could do with a few chops. That torture scene, for instance. Steve McQueen's crinkly eyes are no substitute for good dialogue, and Richard Attenborough and Candice Bergen are awfully draggy. Robert Wise produced and directed in 1966, so that's where the buck stops. (c)

The Sandpiper X Proof that smashing stars (Elizabeth Taylor, Richard Burton, Eva Marie Saint), respected writers (Dalton Trumbo, Michael Wilson), and experienced director (Vincente Minnelli) are no guarantee of a good film. This one is a farrago about straight headmaster chucking everything for wild affair with progressive mother (a pupil's, not his); 1965. (c)

Sands of Iwo Jima √ John Wayne as tough, rough sergeant is incredibly softened by night with Hawaiian whore and goes back to battle and his previously embittered troops a changed man. John Agar, who hated him before, recognises his greatness now. Allan Dwan manages to make all this tosh more or less convincing with a facsimile of the flag-raising ceremony as pay-off. Set in 1943, made in 1949. (b/w)

Sands of the Desert XXX Almost unwatchable Charlie Drake comedy about sabotage at a holiday camp. Not surprisingly, everyone but he seems embarrassed, but then he wrote the script, with director John Paddy Carstairs; 1961. (c)

Sands of the Kalahari √ The one about plane crash survivors stranded in the desert, saved only by strong casting – Stanley Baker, Susannah York, Harry Andrews, Nigel Davenport, Theodore Bikel. Cy Endfield wrote and directed; 1965. (c)

The Sandwich Man XX Strong cast in a weap episodic comedy, strung together by the device of Michael Bentine as a comic sandwich-man, somehow failing to get across in the script he wrote with director Robert Hartford-Davis the warmth of personality he usually manages in television variety shows. None of the standard British character-players and comedians (Dora Bryan, Harry H. Corbett, Diana Dors, Ian Hendry, Stanley Holloway, Ron Moody, Terry-Thomas, Wilfrid Hyde White, Norman Wisdom) are seen at their best; 1966. (c)

San Francisco √√ Although Clark Gable (as a gambler), Jeanette Mac-

Donald (his love), Spencer Tracy (this performance as priest turned him into star) were in 1936 Woody Van Dyke-directed soapy drama, it was reconstruction of 1906 earthquake at the end that was the hit of the show. It really is spectacular. Awful thing is, it's going to happen again, in real life, the experts say. (b/w)

The San Francisco Story X In spite of the pretentious title, it's just feeble Joel McCrea cleaning up the wicked city in the 1850s; and picking up Yvonne De Carlo while he's about it. Routine job by Robert Parrish in 1952. (b/w)

San Quentin √ New jail-yard captain Pat O'Brien trying to reform convict Humphrey Bogart in a 1937 Warner melo. Ann Sheridan, Barton MacLane are members of the team directed by Lloyd Bacon. (b/w)

Santa Fé X Randolph Scott and Peter Thompson are part of internecine-racked family after the Civil War. Irving Pichel's ordinary direction results in in-the-rut railroad banditry; 1951. (c)

Santa Fé Passage X John Payne hates Indians, fights against them, but falls in love with Faith Domergue, who's half one herself. William Witney can't get us caring; 1955. (c)

Santee √ Sentimental western with redeeming features – notably debut of director Gary Nelson and his assurance with characterisation and camera. 12-year-old Michael Burns first hates then admires bounty-hunter Glenn Ford, who devotes his life to wiping out gunmen. If the end is signalled too far ahead, there are some good moments on the way; 1972. (c)

Sapphire √ Michael Relph, Basil Dearden swallowed hard and made an almost convincing film about blacks and whites in Britain. But the year was only 1959 and a patronising sentimentality obtruded. Still, it was a good, taut thriller as well and can be enjoyed as such. Nigel Patrick is superior detective, plus sterling performances from Yvonne Mitchell, Michael Craig, Bernard Miles, Rupert Davies. (c)

Saps at Sea √√ Classic Laurel and Hardy comedy: they're on an ocean cruise with escaped convict Rychard Cramer. Support from Ben Turpin, director, Gordon Douglas; 1940. (b/w)

Saraband for Dead Lovers X Princess Joan Greenwood torn between her love for commoner Stewart Granger (who doesn't manage to look very common) and her Destiny. Get the tissues out (if you've got a cold). Basil Dearden; 1948. (c)

The Saracen Blade XX Dashing Ricardo Montalban had awful script and quickie-director William Castle to battle against, as well as Saracens, in pathetic 1954 Crusades costumer with Carolyn Jones. (c)

Saskatchewan X Insubstantial Raoul Walsh-directed western has Alan Ladd as Canadian Mountie, Shelley Winters, uprising Indians and some fine scenery; 1954. (c)

The Satan Bug √ Who is the mysterious millionaire who has stolen the deadly virus that could destroy all life on earth? You might not care, but you'll probably go on watching George Maharis, Richard Basehart, Dana Andrews, adequately directed by John Sturges from an Alistair Maclean thriller; 1965. (c)

Satan Never Sleeps XX Anti-Red hysteria this time takes the shape of two priests – William Holden, Clifton Webb – bravely defending their mission, and France Nuyen, against those nasty Chinese Communists. Was co-writer, director Leo McCarey being serious? 1962. (c)

Satellite in the Sky XX Poor little sci-fi produced by the Danzigers, those legendary churners-out of tripe in British studios. Here John Dickson has directed a tame tale of a spaceship with a superbomb attached, due to go off and kill its inhabitants. Donald Wolfit and Bryan Forbes were somehow in this one, along with the handsome but empty Kieron Moore and Lois Maxwell; 1956. (c)

Saturday Night and Sunday Morning √√√ In 1960 it was called 'the finest picture of the year' and 'the greatest English picture of all time', and it still stands as a valid, sympathetic, committed study of the limitations and frustrations of working-class life. This is how it was – and is – in Nottingham and a thousand other towns, and Albert Finney was how a hundred thousand young rebels-brought-to-heel were – and are. The triumph is, first, director Karel Reisz's; second, writer Alan Sillitoe's; third, a castful of people who lifted their characters into near-reality: Rachel Roberts, Hylda Baker, Norman Rossington, Bryan Pringle, Shirley Anne Field, Colin Blakely, and, above all, Finney. And it was funny, too. (b/w)

Saturday Night Out XX Episodic

British picture which tries for slices of life but finishes up with slivers of ham. Robert Hartford-Davis produced and directed without felicity or flair, and left it up to Heather Sears (as a way-out art student), Nigel Green (lush), Colin Campbell (nice fella who saves a girl from going on the streets), Bernard Lee (blackmailed via a two-way mirror), Patricia Hayes (on the bottle again), and that isn't the way to make a gripping movie; 1964. (b/w)

The Savage √ Question: whose side should Charlton Heston take – the Sioux, who brought him up as one of them, or the whites? Watch him make up his mind, under George Marshall's competent direction; 1953. (c)

The Savage Guns XX A 1962 experiment in making a Mexican-American western in Spain. It failed. The result was this third-grade oater directed sluggishly by Michael Carreras with stiff Richard Basehart playing that old gunfighter who can't lay down his guns and pacifist Don Taylor who realises at last that a Man Has to be a Man (i.e. a Killer). Sick stuff. (c)

The Savage Innocents X Fur-clad Anthony Quinn, Peter O'Toole, Yoko Tani in confusing Nicholas Ray-directed Eskimo drama that's likely to get a chilly reception; 1961. (c)

Savage Messiah X Ken Russell's 1972 betrayal of artist Gaudier-Brzeska and his unromantic liaison with the woman who shared his name. In these roles Scott Anthony and Dorothy Tutin have little chance, being overtaken by the director's ambitions, and left gasping behind as he flattens them and the rest of the cast (Helen Mirren, Lindsay Kemp, Peter Vaughan among them) with a parody of Edwardian London. (c)

Save the Tiger √√ Sympathetic Oscar-winning performance from Jack Lemmon as harassed, put-upon and ultimately cynical businessman, plagued by memories of war buddies as he agrees to resort to arson to solve his problems. A clever script (Steve Shagan) is well interpreted by director John G. Avildsen. Only some idyllic scenes with a complaisant hitch-hiker ring untrue; 1973. (c)

Say Hello to Yesterday XXX – or, better still, goodbye to tonight. Acutely embarrassing seduction yarn with Jean Simmons agreeing to spend the afternoon in bed with the nasty young man (Leonard Whiting) who has decided to seduce her for want of something better to do. Director Alvin Rakoff is to blame, since he helped with script and story, too; 1970. (c)

Sayonara √ Joshua Logan's heavy-handed adaptation of James Michener's novel about high-up American officer – Marlon Brando with a dreadful Southern accent – falling for Japanese showgirl which is even more ghastly than Irving Berlin's title song. On the other hand, if you loved that. . . . 1957 Oscars surprisingly went to supports Red Buttons and Miyoshi Umeki, and for art direction and sound recording. Ellsworth Fredericks deserved one for his pictures. (c)

Say One For Me X Save them for yourself, if you intend watching this one about Bing Crosby as priest of showbiz parish; Debbie Reynolds, Robert Wagner, Ray Walston among Frank Tashlin's 1959 congregation. (c)

The Scalphunters √ Episodic western has Burt Lancaster as dogged trapper, Ossie Davis as a bright runaway slave, an over-sexed Shelley Winters and some funny moments under Sydney Pollack's lively direction between the scalping, the cliff-falling and the thundering hooves; 1968. (c)

The Scamp √ Sickly title for not quite so sickly film about a little boy (Colin Petersen), whose father (Terence Morgan, with an unconvincing Cockney accent) is turning him into a delinquent. Solid, childless school-master Richard Attenborough takes an interest in him – but finds himself rejected after giving him a thrashing, the alternative to prosecution for burglary. Wolf Rilla wrote-directed slowly if dramatically, greatly helped by Freddie Francis's camerawork; 1957. (b/w)

Scandal At Scourie X Childless couple adopt illegitimate Catholic child in face of bitter local Protestant opposition. Greer Garson stars, Jean Negulesco directs – feel like a nice cry? 1953. (c)

Scandal Sheet X Unpleasant story of tabloid editor Broderick Crawford killing his wife and waiting for his own well-trained reporters to sniff out the story. Phil Karlson never hit the headlines with this one in 1952. (b/w)

The Scapegoat X English schoolteacher is conned into swapping places with his noble French 'double'. Alec Guinness – both of him – and Bette Davis make it just about watchable, but what a let-down from director Robert Hamer, working from a Gore Vidal adaptation of a Daphne du Maurier novel. Maybe it was written and directed by their doubles; 1959. (b/w)

Scaramouche X Colourful swashbuckler has Stewart Granger avenging brother's death in 18th-century France. Janet Leigh, Eleanor Parker, Mel Ferrer and vulgar George Sidney direction; 1952. (c)

Scarecrow √√ Interesting near-miss by director Jerry Schatzberg, exploring the friendship of Gene Hackman and Al Pacino, two former convicts who aim to set up in legitimate business together. Their searching for maturity and for other people in their past lives is deftly told: even if the whole film does not hang together closely enough, there is much to savour and enjoy; 1973. (c)

Scared Stiff X Bored stiff, more likely, by Dean Martin, Jerry Lewis, Lizabeth Scott and Carmen Miranda on haunted island. George Marshall; 1953. (b/w)

The Scarface Mob √ Two episodes of *The Untouchables* stitched together with a banal Walter Winchell commentary has Robert Stack bringing Al Capone (weakly played by Neville Brand against Rod Steiger's interpretation in the film biography) to justice. Phil Karlson, a director always best with violence, manages these capably; 1958. (b/w)

Scarlet Angel X Confused plot turns around Yvonne De Carlo posing as wealthy widow. Trouble is she fancies sailor Rock Hudson as much as she fancies the high life. Sidney Salkow; 1952. (c)

The Scarlet Blade XX Usual old Cavaliers v. Roundheads rubbish, with King's men the goodies and Cromwell's (Lionel Jeffries, Oliver Reed) a rotten lot. John Gilling doesn't convince with this one; 1963. (c)

The Scarlet Claw √ There's terror on the Quebec marshes in this Sherlock Holmes drama, improbably set in Canada. Rathbone-Bruce as Holmes-Watson; director is Roy William Neill; 1944. (b/w)

The Scarlet Coat X Who's giving away revolting American secrets to the British? Why, Benedict Arnold, of course. Cornel Wilde, George Sanders, Michael Wilding go through the history books under John Sturges; 1955. (c)

The Scarlet Hour X Thriller about an unhappy marriage is more fortunate in its minor players (E. G. Marshall, Elaine Stritch) than in leads Carol

Ohmart and Tom Tryon, neither of whom went on to bigger things after this inauspicious start under Michael Curtiz; 1956. (b/w)

The Scarlet Pimpernel. They filmed him here, they filmed him there . . .
√√ (1) In 1935, with Leslie Howard as the aristocrat who rescued members of his class from the French Revolution under the nose of Raymond Massey's Chauvelin. Director: Harold Young. (b/w)
XX (2) In 1938, when it was called *The Return of the Scarlet Pimpernel*, with Barry K. Barnes outwitting Francis Lister. Director: Hans Schwartz. (b/w)
XX (3) In 1950, as *The Elusive Pimpernel*, with David Niven as Sir Percy, directed by Michael Powell and Emeric Pressburger. Actually, it was Niven who was elusive; he was rowing with Goldwyn about his contract and insisted on holidays and other concessions before he would start work. The result reflects his unhappiness of the time. (c)

Scarlet Street √√ Edward G. Robinson murdering Joan Bennett and, for the first time ever in Hollywood, getting away with it. Carpet-puller Fritz Lang directed this epoch-maker in 1945, fourteen years after its original, *La Chienne*, had been made by Renoir in France. (b/w)

School for Scoundrels √ Lifemanship and Gamesmanship, Stephen Potter's clever and amusing way of cataloguing the Englishman's One-Upmanship . . . but how on earth to make a film about it? Director Robert Hamer (with, it is said, the help of Peter Ustinov) found the solution: put know-it-all Terry-Thomas against dude Ian Carmichael for the hand of Janette Scott, have the lovable goof enrol at Alastair Sim's College of Lifemanship, learn from him all the tricks of the trade and then defeat his rival on the tennis court, in bachelor flat, and so on. It all works surprisingly well, with the help of a dozen solid comic supports; 1960. (b/w)

Scorpio √ Slick spy thriller by Michael Winner with the usual double-crossings and counter-spy revelations. Burt Lancaster is a CIA man, who might be in KGB. Alain Delon is a killer, who might want Lancaster's job. Paul Scofield is a KGB man, who might be something else. Gayle Hunnicutt is Delon's girlfriend, who might be a spy in her own wrong. The violence may help to keep you awake; 1972. (c)

Scott of the Antarctic √ Sincere, worthwhile 1948 attempt to tell story of quixotic failure, always much admired by the British (but not the Americans, who wouldn't show it); made in Greenland, Norway, Antarctica and Ealing, with John Mills's finest performance. Charles Frend, director; Jack Cardiff, camera. (c)

Scream and Scream Again √ This nasty horror flick has become a cult classic, constantly being referred to as a standard for others of the genre. Although Vincent Price and Christopher Lee are given top billing, the producers couldn't afford them for many days' work. Christopher Matthews and Judi Bloom do most of the grind, as murderer Michael Gothard tears his handcuffed hand away at the wrist and hides in a vat of acid. Director, Gordon Hessler; 1969. (c)

Scrooge √ Musical adaptation of *A Christmas Carol,* with too many dead weights (Leslie Bricusse's musical numbers, obvious penny-pinching, elderly troupers) to offset Albert Finney's larger-than-life curmudgeon. Director, Ronald Neame; 1970. (c)

The Sea Chase √ Second World War adventure has John Wayne in (for him) unusual role of German sea captain. Lana Turner provides shipboard romance. John Farrow directs; 1955. (c)

Sea Devils X Napoleonic wars provided Raoul Walsh with background for routine smuggling yarn starring Yvonne De Carlo, Rock Hudson; 1953. (c)

Sea Fury X Victor McLaglen's last film was this rather turgid, rather predictable drama which has him lusting after Luciana Paluzzi in competition with First Mate Stanley Baker, with a bit of not-so-exciting salvage work thrown in. Cy Endfield (called C. Raker Endfield in 1958) directed briskly. (b/w)

The Sea Gull X Nobody could fault the cast, on paper: Vanessa Redgrave, James Mason, Simone Signoret, David Warner, Denholm Elliott, Alfred Lynch. However, director Sidney Lumet has not been able to fuse them into a coherent whole. This photographed 1968 stage play is likely to make you reach for your gun – or bed. (c)

The Sea Hawk √√ Splendid swashbuckler, directed by Michael Curtiz, with Errol Flynn flinging himself about like nobody since Douglas Fairbanks Sr. Plus Claude Rains, Donald Crisp, Henry Daniell, Flora Robson and other pirates; 1940. (b/w)

Seance on a Wet Afternoon √√ Genuinely chilling melo written and directed by Bryan Forbes in 1964 about a potty medium (methodical Kim Stanley) involving her timid husband (co-producer Richard Attenborough) in kidnapping. (b/w)

Sea of Sand X Routine war melo about the desert; solid performances from Richard Attenborough and Barry Foster, dreary ones from John Gregson and Michael Craig. Direction average, from Guy Green; 1958. (b/w)

The Search √ Montgomery Clift's 1948 debut as American soldier caring for orphan after Second World War won an Oscar for its story. Fred Zinnemann gave it a slightly sententious distinction. (b/w)

The Searchers √√√ 'If one could preserve a single John Ford film, it would perhaps be this Homeric western', wrote the National Film Theatre's programmer. For two hours and five years, John Wayne searches for the little girl who was taken away by the Indians, only to find that she has grown to womanhood as an Indian. Feeling that she has betrayed his family he attacks the village, intent on killing her. About Wayne's performance one contemporary (1956) critic wrote 'There's no kindness in his nature – he is crafty and arrogant and his eyes are cold as ice.' This goes pretty well for all his parts, but in this one his quality of cruelty is apposite The little girl was played by Natalie Wood's sister, Lana: Natalie played her grown up. (c)

The Search for Bridey Murphy X Teresa Wright more or less convincing in otherwise extremely doubtful account of housewife recalling a previous life under hypnosis, made in 1956 when a real-life case gave it relevance. Unfortunately, its specious use of hypnotism is not balanced by an interesting plot. Noel Langley wrote and directed. (b/w)

The Sea Shall Not Have Them X Michael Redgrave, Dirk Bogarde, Anthony Steele, Nigel Patrick, Bonar Colleano, Jack Watling in hollow tale of heroics about airmen awaiting rescue from raft. Made in 1954 by Lewis Gilbert. (b/w)

Sea Wife √ One of those life-raft dramas so popular around 1957. Floating about on this one are Richard Burton as an RAF officer, Joan Collins as a nun (but the others don't know that), Basil Sidney as a businessman, Cy Grant as a purser. Basically, it's a will-she-won't-she with the added titillation that she's supposed to be bound to celibacy. Unfortunately (fortunately?) Joan Collins could never be a nun. Director Bob McNaught. (c)

Sebastian √ Two of the best players in British pictures, Dirk Bogarde and Susannah York, spark off each other in this cryptic thriller about cryptographers breaking spy-codes. But everything else is so insouciant and tentative that director David Greene seems to be skating prettily along the top of the script rather than bringing out its meanings and subtleties (if any). Excellent names support: John Gielgud, Janet Munro, Nigel Davenport, Ronald Fraser, Lilli Palmer, Margaret Johnston; 1968. (c)

Second Chance √ Marvellous fight on stranded cable car between hunted Robert Mitchum and hood Jack Palance is climax to above-average 1953 thriller set in South America. Rudolf Maté got good performance from tragically-fated Linda Darnell. (c)

The Second Greatest Sex XX *Lysistrata* updated to western musical by George Marshall has Jeanne Crain, Mamie van Doren among women who barricade themselves in fort while men battle for safe containing crucial papers; 1955. (c)

Seconds √ Ageing businessman takes on new identity and Rock Hudson's face. Says director John Frankenheimer: 'It has a theme that fascinated me: the old American bullshit about having to be young, the whole myth that financial security is happiness.' Beginning and end are gripping, although orgy scene in the middle lets it down; 1966. (b/w)

The Second Time Around X Widow Debbie Reynolds running for Sheriff. Thelma Ritter, Juliet Prowse, Andy Griffith cheer up this 1961, Vincent Sherman-directed comedy. Too much corny clowning. (c)

The Secret Beyond the Door X Moody Fritz Lang thriller which gets stalled in half-baked psychology and miscasting of Michael Redgrave and Joan Bennett; 1948. (b/w)

Secret Ceremony √ What a disappointment this 1969 marriage of Elizabeth Taylor, Mia Farrow and Joseph Losey turned out to be. The fact that a story is totally incredible (motherless girl and daughterless mother accepting each other as mother and daughter) need not be an unscalable barrier to enchantment. But the way it's handled (and the casting of Robert Mitchum in a beard as bad-penny father) just leaves the viewer alienated. The set with its art nouveau extravagances is certainly worth a look, but you'll get more out of a visit to the appropriate gallery at the Victoria and Albert Museum. (c)

The Secret Fury √ Bride-to-be Claudette Colbert being driven round the bend: is it a plot to prevent her marrying Robert Ryan? Mel(-odramatic) Ferrer directs; 1950. (b/w)

The Secret Garden √ Fantasy has not-so-little Margaret O'Brien (it was made in 1949 when she was 12) befriending crippled Dean Stockwell and being admitted to his imagined hideaway. Fred M. Wilcox got some good junior performances and the usual up-market ones from Elsa Lanchester, Herbert Marshall, Gladys Cooper. (c)

The Secret Heart √ Will June Allyson follow father in throwing herself off a cliff? She doesn't like Claudette Colbert, her stepmother. Lionel Barrymore, Walter Pidgeon, Robert Sterling, Patricia Medina fuss around tiresomely under Robert Z. Leonard's atmospheric direction; 1946. (b/w)

The Secret Invasion √ Weak casting-Stewart Granger, Mickey Rooney, Raf Vallone – lets down otherwise gripping Second World War yarn about criminals on dangerous mission in Nazi-occupied Yugoslavia. Director, Roger Corman; 1964. (c)

The Secret Life of an American Wife √√ An under-rated comedy masterpiece, script-production-direction by George Axelrod. Anne Jackson is marvellous as the wife who realises that she must be losing her touch when the delivery boy doesn't even notice she's naked, and decides to do something about it. What she does is take the place of the 100-dollar-an-hour call-girl her expense-account husband (a well-observed study by Patrick O'Neal) is laying on for a film star (gorgeous Walter Matthau). What happens next is beautifully right and we won't spoil it for you; 1969. (c)

The Secret Life of Walter Mitty √√ Danny Kaye's best film (1947), derived from a James Thurber short story but embellished with Kay's own routines. Boris Karloff, Virginia Mayo, Fay Bainter make substantial contributions, but the praise belongs to Kaye and director Norman Z. McLeod, for a delicious film about daydreaming. (c)

The Secret of Convict Lake √ Strong on suspense, weak on cast (Glenn Ford, Zachary Scott, Gene Tierney), this is one of those thrillers about an escaped convict looking for the loot he stashed away. Complications arise after he is hidden by colony of women, whose husbands return. Director, Michael Gordon; 1951. (b/w)

The Secret of My Success XX Someone should have whispered it to director Andrew Stone before he embarked on this silly triple-barrelled nonsense about a naive policeman, James Booth, being taken in by scheming Honor Blackman (mad baroness breeding killer-spider), Stella Stevens (husband-killer), Shirley Jones (revolutionary); 1965. (c)

The Secret of Santa Vittoria X Director Stanley Kramer made this heavy-going yarn of Italian villagers, hiding a store of wine from the retreating Germans. He is not helped by the lugubrious performances of Anthony Quinn and Anna Magnani, while Hardy Kruger's attempts to make the German commander a likeable fellow become embarrassing. Music is intrusive, camerawork uninspired; 1969. (c)

Secret of the Incas X Charlton Heston, Robert Young, Nicole Maurey on treasure hunt. Spectacular backgrounds almost make up for routine plot and Jerry Hopper direction; 1954. (c)

The Secret Partner √ Modest but exciting thriller from Michael Relph and Basil Dearden in which only two people have the keys-and-combination of a strongroom but which keeps you guessing as to who stole them. Nice characterisation from Bernard Lee as the detective, and both Hugh Burden and Stewart Granger do better than their usual; 1961. (b/w)

The Secret Place X Competent diamond theft thriller which marked Clive Donner's debut as director, from a script by Linette Perry. Unfortunately, only George A. Cooper among the cast appears not to be a posh actor playing a Cockney: Belinda Lee, David McCallum, Ronald Lewis are doing us the favour of pretending; 1957. (b/w)

The Secret War of Harry Frigg X Paul Newman looks uncomfortable in this embarrassing Second World War farce about Allied generals imprisoned in Sylva Koscina's Italian villa – and well

he might. He's supposed to be escape-artist promoted to General so that he can give orders to the men he is sent to liberate. But he finds that being in prison is jollier than fighting the war. Jack Smight might have made something from all this with a genuine comedy actor in the lead. With Newman, he's dead; 1968. (c)

The Secret Ways X Routine escaping-to-the-West thriller has Richard Widmark in charge both of the escaping (he does it for money not patriotism, which is a nice change) and the production (but sensibly accepting Phil Karlson's highly competent direction). Set in Budapest, marred by poor supporting performances; 1961. (b/w)

The Seekers X Dull would-be adventure yarn of pioneers in New Zealand has Jack Hawkins, Glynis Johns heading plodding cast, with an out-of-place Kenneth Williams. Ken Annakin cynically directed; 1954. (c)

See You in Hell, Darling X Tawdry thriller derived distantly from Norman Mailer's *An American Dream*, retaining that rather impressive novel's plot-line, but throwing all its subtlety out of the window (which, as it happens, is what Stuart Whitman does to wife Eleanor Parker). Director Robert Gist missed the gist; 1966. (c)

The Sellout √ Crusading newspaper editor Walter Pidgeon fighting local corruption. Gerald Mayer directed; 1952. (b/w)

Seminole √ True-ish story of why the Seminole tribe never signed a peace treaty with the white man makes lively western directed by the excellent Bud Boetticher and strongly cast: Rock Hudson, Hugh O'Brian, Richard Carlson, Barbara Hale, Anthony Quinn; 1953. (c)

Seminole Uprising √ George Montgomery, now a cavalry officer, was brought up by Indians. He is ordered to bring in rampaging chief. His mind is made up when they capture his sweetheart, Karin Booth. Director Earl Bellamy doesn't make much of what could have been significant script; 1955. (c)

The Senator was Indiscreet √ And left a diary lying around. 1947 comedy directed by writer George S. Kaufman (his only try at the job) gains from William Powell's playing the main part. Ella Raines backs him up. (b/w)

Send Me No Flowers √ Must be seen in colour for full glossy effect of Doris Day being pushed into Clint Walker's arms because husband Rock Hudson and best friend Tony Randall mistakenly think he's dying. Director Norman Jewison has since (this was 1964) gone on to higher if not better things. (c)

Separate Tables √√ Rattigan double-bill about hotel, made into blockbuster by Delbert Mann, winning Oscars for Wendy Hiller, David Niven, and splendid performances from Burt Lancaster, Rita Hayworth; 1958. (b/w)

September Affair √ Believed dead when a plane crashed that they were supposed to be on, married Joseph Cotten and Joan Fontaine are free to continue their love affair. Not nearly as daring as it sounds – this is a 1951 William Dieterle-directed 'romance'. (b/w)

Serenade X Strictly for Mario Lanza fans. This time he's a sulky singer taken up by rich Joan Fontaine but finding true love with Sarita Montiel. Spectacular and spectacularly dull; Anthony Mann directed; 1956. (c)

The Sergeant √√ Unusual, thoughtful army drama about Sgt. Rod Steiger's desires for naïve Pte John Phillip Law. It has the inevitability of tragedy and director John Flynn made an impressive debut in this 1969 (set 1952) study of a hero in self-abasement. (c)

Sergeant Deadhead XX Silly Frankie Avalon vehicle wastes Buster Keaton – and your time. Norman Taurog; 1965. (c)

Sergeant Rutledge √ John Ford, whose career had been clouded by apparent colour prejudice, appears to have decided in 1960 to make some amends by this trial of a black soldier during the Civil War. Based on a real-life incident, it not only reminded a public that was by then more than ready to accept it, that blacks had fought in large numbers, but also that some of them had performed deeds of great gallantry. Woody Strode strode away with the acting honours and although the scene remains mostly in the court, there are enough action flashbacks to satisfy the eager western fan. (c)

Sergeant Ryker √ If this one looks like a TV film, that's because it was a pilot that never came off. Lee Marvin is Sergeant, accused of being a traitor to the Communist Chinese. But he says he was dispatched over the lines by a Colonel, now dead. As the series was to have been called 'Court Martial', rather a lot of the action takes place in an army courtroom; Buzz Kulik directed; 1965. (c)

Sergeants Three √ Comedy western indulging Sinatra's 1960 Rat Pack, with the man himself, Sammy Davis Jr., Dean Martin, Peter Lawford chasing marauding ghost riders. Saved by John Sturges' direction: after all, he did make *The Magnificent Seven*. (c)

Serious Charge XX Did Anthony Quayle touch up the choirboy – a hulking youth played by Andrew Ray who actually has lumbered a local girl? In the throes of this tortuous plot, the lad is trying to escape that responsibility by accusing the vicar of homosexual advances. Terence Young directed this nasty, meretricious little number, poorly played and conceived, in 1959. The only mystery is why, if the youth leader was at all that way, he wouldn't have chosen cuddly, curly Cliff Richard, in a supporting part, rather than butch yobbo Ray. (b/w)

Serpico √√ Strong honest-cop drama, with Al Pacino as a true-life stubborn hero, determined to clean up New York police dept. Well directed by Sidney Lumet in 1973. (c)

The Servant √√ Perhaps the most discussed film ever made in England, this 1963 collaboration of Joseph Losey and Harold Pinter from Robin Maugham's novel is about corruption: superficially that of a young master (James Fox) by a vicious servant (Dirk Bogarde), with the help of his girlfriend (Sarah Miles); but it is also about the whole class structure. Wendy Craig convinces as the fiancée who fights Bogarde's influence; look out for Pinter, Patrick Magee and Alun Owen in restaurant scene. (b/w)

Seven Angry Men √ Civil War drama about the ill-fated John Brown's fight to free the slaves, has a fine performance from Raymond Massey and some gripping moments under Charles Marquis Warren's direction; 1955. (b/w)

Seven Cities of Gold X Richard Egan, Anthony Quinn, Michael Rennie, Rita Moreno in run-of-the-mill costume drama about Spanish search for Indian gold in 18th-century California. Robert D. Webb directed; 1955. (c)

Seven Days in May √√ Military coup against the President of the USA (Fredric March) makes exciting story. John Frankenheimer in his heyday, 1964, got earnest, belief-suspendable performances with help of Rod Serling script. Burt Lancaster convinces as chief plotter, Kirk Douglas as his assistant who blows the plot; Edmond O'Brien, Martin Balsam, stand out among the supports. (b/w)

Seven Days to Noon √√ Efficient and exciting suspenser centred around atomic scientist's threat to blow up London if Government doesn't renounce atomic weapons within a week. Barry Jones makes him real, and the Boultings's inspiration to make his unwilling companion a sleazy prostitute (Olive Sloane) rather than a conventional heroine makes the whole plot seem more plausible. Ahead of its time (1950), both politically and in narrative technique. (b/w)

711 Ocean Drive √ Edmond O'Brien memorably outwitting syndicate boss Otto Kruger, with Joanne Dru as love interest in modest, Joseph H. Newman-directed bookmaking drama; 1950. (b/w)

The 7 Faces of Dr Lao √ All played by Tony Randall, seven little stories about the sideshows in his travelling entertainment, in which each of the film's main characters (among them: Barbara Eden, Noah Beery Jr.) learn something revelatory about themselves. Director-producer George Pal indulges himself in such tricks as a catfish that swells up to become a man-eating monster; 1965. (c)

Seven Hills of Rome XX Some pretty shots of the city and that's about all, unless you like Mario Lanza - in which case you may forgive slight plot about him following heiress to Italy. Roy Rowland directed; 1958. (c)

Seven Keys XX Weak little chase involving Alan Dobie dead-panning his way through a contrived and silly plot about blackmail and the recovery of a £20,000 cache. Jeannie Carson helps him, director Pat Jackson doesn't; 1962. (b/w)

The Seven Little Foys √ Bob Hope v. Jimmy Cagney dance sequence (Hope wins tap, Cagney soft-shoe shuffle) is best thing in Mel Shavelson-directed showbiz biography of comedian with large family; 1955. (c)

Seven Men from Now √ They rob the Wells Fargo office, kill Randolph Scott's wife, he vows vengeance. Lee Marvin leads the villains. Budd Boetticher as director guarantees distinction; 1956. (c)

The Seven Minutes X Irving Wallace's camp novel of Californian porn-busting is made even camper by Russ Meyer, who directs a largely unknown

cast in larger-than-life fun and murders. The quasi-statistical title refers to the time the average woman supposedly takes to achieve orgasm, and is as suspect as the rest of the nonsense; 1971. (c)

Seven Seas to Calais XX Costumer supposedly about Sir Francis Drake, with Rod Taylor a laughable Armada-sinker (the battle itself is staged by such obvious models that one almost wonders if it isn't supposed to be stylised), Irene Worth an apple-cheeked Queen Elizabeth, and an incoherent plotline. Rudolph Maté went to Italy to shoot this rubbish. He should have stayed at home; 1963. (c)

1776 XX While this debunking of famous figures of American history involved in the signing of the Declaration of Independence may have worked on the Broadway stage, it doesn't for British audiences. All that's left are indifferent musical numbers sung by people in wigs and bonnets; director, Peter H. Hunt; 1972. (c)

Seventh Cavalry √ Did Randolph Scott desert Custer at Little Big Horn? Barbara Hale believes in him and so do we. Joseph H. Lewis; 1956. (c)

The Seventh Cross √ Hollywood finally got around to making major anti-Nazi movies in a big way after America got into the war. This one, made in 1944, set in Germany 1936, miscasts Spencer Tracy as concentration camp escapee, but is reasonably exciting stuff, directed by Fred Zinnemann. (b/w)

The Seventh Dawn X It's all too much for rubber planter William Holden, what with the Communist uprising in Malaya and romantic dramas with Susannah York and Capucine. Obviously for director Lewis Gilbert, too, who can't do anything with Karl Tunberg's collection of clichés, optimistically called a script; 1964. (c)

Seven Thieves √ Sentimental caper movie with old-timer Edward G. Robinson determined to pull off the Big One at Monte Carlo casinos before he dies. Eli Wallach, Joan Collins are fellow rififis; Henry Hathaway; 1960. (b/w)

The Seventh Sin XX Risible remake of Maugham's *The Painted Veil* in Hollywood, with British director Ronald Neame and actor Bill Travers making unfortunate American debuts. Eleanor Parker's regeneration in a Chinese cholera epidemic is unbelievable, which goes for the whole picture.

George Sanders, Françoise Rosay and Jean-Pierre Aumont flounder around, embarrassed; 1957. (b/w)

Seven Thunders XX Dreadful mix-up of a film supposedly set in wartime Marseilles as Stephen Boyd and Tony Wright try to get back to England. There are the usual resistance heroes and German soldiers, and James Robertson Justice rolling his eyes as a murderer of rich refugees. Hugo Fregonese was obviously unhappy directing in England; 1957. (b/w)

The Seventh Veil √ Creaky tear-jerker that had enormous success in 1945, with Herbert Lom as psychiatrist helping concert pianist with burnt hands, Ann Todd, to decide which of three suitors to marry. James Mason is one of them, and director Compton Bennett encouraged him to go over the top with satisfactory results. (b/w)

The Seventh Voyage of Sinbad √ How Sinbad (Kerwin Matthews) helps princess (Kathryn Grant) who has been reduced to thumb-size. Torin Thatcher is the dirty dog of a magician what did it. Ray Harryhausen's effects are ingenious; Nathan Juran directed; 1958. (c)

The Seven-Ups √√ French Connection producer Philip D'Antoni is director of this carbon copy, using Roy Scheider again as tough detective. Car chases, ransoms and impersonations all play a part, but it is difficult to complain about copy-catting when it is all so well done; 1973. (c)

Seven Waves Away √ Which-should-be-saved? drama about overturned lifeboat with Tyrone having Power of life or death over neatly-assorted bunch of stock characters. If his choice were on acting ability it would include Lloyd Nolan, Noel Willman, Gordon Jackson, Victor Maddern, David Langton; but Mai Zetterling, Stephen Boyd, Moira Lister, James Hayter are swimming, too. Writer-director Richard Sale keeps it afloat; 1957. (b/w)

Seven Ways from Sundown X Barry Sullivan chased by Texas ranger Audie Murphy. Harry Keller's direction does not enliven obvious plot; 1960. (c)

Seven Women √ John Ford's last completed film, 1966, is set in 1935 China, where Margaret Leighton runs a five-woman mission in grip of warlord. 'Marvellous Anne Bancroft's doctor makes a sacrifice far beyond the textbook Christian ethics of her companions', as the NFT programmer delicately put it. (c)

Seven Women from Hell X Patricia Owens and six other American ladies outwit Japanese captors. Set in New Guinea, 1942; made 1961. Cesar Romero, John Kerr also in Robert D. Webb's cast. (b/w)

The Seven Year Itch √√ Marilyn Monroe's subtle dumb blonde act is matched by Tom Ewell's archetypal husband on the loose in the apartment downstairs. While Marilyn was making this in 1955 she was going through the divorce from Joe Di Maggio, but Billy Wilder steered her through and came up with a delicious movie, the name of which, at least, has entered the language. (c)

A Severed Head X Casting sabotages this film of the play of Iris Murdoch's novel. Claire Bloom, Richard Attenborough, Lee Remick, Ian Holm, Jennie Linden are all pretty hopeless in the parts thrust on them: Dick Clement, working on a script from Frederic Raphael, pushed everyone up the social scale, for some reason. 1970. (c)

Sex and the Single Girl √ Helen Gurley Brown's factual best-seller ignored, and this glossy 1964 romantic comedy sold under its title. Magazine editor Tony Curtis chases psychologist Natalie Wood, with Henry Fonda, Lauren Bacall, Mel Ferrer. Edward Everett Horton helping fun along, under Richard Quine's direction. (c)

Shack Out on 101 √ Posing as half-wit dishwasher, spy works at café near secret electronics laboratory. Lee Marvin, Keenan Wynn stand out in Edward Dein's capable cast; 1955. (b/w)

Shadow in the Sky X Discharged from hospital, a disturbed ex-serviceman goes to live with his sister and her husband. Starts well, but director Fred M. Wilcox lets it all get out of hand. Jean Hagen and little-known cast do their best; 1951. (b/w)

Shadow of a Doubt √√ Teresa Wright gradually realising that her beloved uncle is on the run from the police, and what happens to her then. Joseph Cotten outstanding as the heavy, under Hitchcock's persuasive direction in 1943. Thornton Wilder's collaboration on the script ensured an authentic feeling of a small American town. (b/w)

Shadow of Fear XX Poor little thriller about girl (Mona Freeman) who feels herself threatened by step-mother Jean Kent, whom she suspects of already polishing off her Dad. Albert S.Rogell couldn't breathe any life into poor script in 1956. (*b/w*)

Shadow of the Thin Man √ William Powell and Myrna Loy solve jockey's murder, in 1941. W. S. Van Dyke directed crisply and expertly; Donna Reed, Sam Levene support. (*b/w*)

Shadows √√ The first underground movie to break the commercial barrier was this 16mm effort of John Cassavetes and the alumni of his acting school, shot on location in New York, with scenes grabbed whenever they could. It took three years to shoot and edit this story of sophisticated blacks and their problems and it was shown in 1959. Some of it is jejune, but gets nearer to real people than anything seen up to then on the screen. If it looks a bit dated today it is more because of the story with its 'shocks' about passing-for-white (a conventional preoccupation of the cinema then) than the technique which has been absorbed into both the feature and documentary streams. Lelia Goldoni, who had the fattest part, came to England as an American actress in poor British television plays. (*b/w*)

Shaft √ Predictable mindless gangster melo, the only novelty being that director Gordon Parks and all the cast are black. Richard Roundtree plays the randy private eye with aplomb; 1971. (*c*)

Shaft in Africa X This undercover sex thriller imitates the worst in white decadence. Richard Roundtree's black private eye has become more explicitly porny, and is here showing his equipment to white nymphos and Emir's daughters alike. Frank Finlay is the heavy in this yarn about the black slave traffic; director, John Guillermann; 1973. (*c*)

Shaft's Big Score √ Another black detective opus, with Richard Roundtree directed by Gordon Parks, in 1972. This one is about a missing quarter-of-a-million dollars from the numbers racket. (*c*)

Shakedown √ Photographer Howard Duff resorts to blackmail to claw his way up the ladder; among those present in this 1950 thriller are established, pencil-moustached Brian Donlevy and up-and-coming Rock Hudson in a tiny part; director, Joe Pevney; 1950. (*b/w*)

The Shakedown XXX If anyone is shaken down by this piffle it's the audience. Supposedly about a blackmailing gang, it makes a hero of one gang-leader, who is slightly less nauseating than his rival. Donald Pleasence earned a crust by appearing in it, but otherwise it's an awful tatty affair. The director John Lemont co-scripted it (with Leigh Vance), so he has no excuses; 1960. (*b/w*)

Shake Hands With The Devil X Producer-director Michael Anderson chose his cast well – James Cagney, Michael Redgrave, Don Murray, Glynis Johns, Sybil Thorndike, Cyril Cusack – for this tale of Irish Rebellion, 1921 vintage, when the Black and Tans were in repressive command. Cagney finds himself forced to fight for Irish freedom. The emphasis, however, is on excitement not morality and the accents are at wild variance with each other; 1959. (*b/w*)

The Shakiest Gun in the West X Comedy-western has Don Knotts as a timid dentist who becomes a hero by mistake. Director Alan Rafkin manages a few laughs in 1968 remake of Bob Hope's *The Paleface*. (*c*)

Shalako √ Routine western dressed up as a European aristocratic hunting-party in eighties New Mexico. Plenty of stars – Sean Connery, Brigitte Bardot, Stephen Boyd, Jack Hawkins, Honor Blackman, Eric Sykes - but nothing very distinguished in plot, dialogue or Edward Dmytrk's direction. It's rather long and you may find yourself glancing too often at the clock; 1968. (*c*)

Shall We Dance? √√ Vintage Astaire-Rogers musical from 1937. Songs include 'Let's Call the Whole Thing Off', 'They Can't Take That Away from Me'. Eric Blore; Edward Everett Horton support. Mark Sandrich put them through their paces as ballet dancer falls for musical comedy star. (*b/w*)

Shampoo √√ Amusing comedy of sexual manners, with Warren Beatty splendid as an all-conquering hairdresser. If the political ambience (made in 1975, it is set during the 1968 Presidential elections) is intrusive, it does give an underpinning of reality to an otherwise amoral never-never-land. Julie Christie, Goldie Hawn, Lee Grant shine as girlfriends. Director Hal Ashby is felicitous. (*c*)

Shamus √ Just another private eye excitement with an involved, gory plot, and Burt Reynolds in the main part. The characters' names (Colonel Hardcore, Springy and Shamus) seem to point to an in-joke – intended, but not realised; Buzz Kulik; 1972. (c)

Shane √√ Among the great westerns of all time, this story of the mysterious stranger (Alan Ladd) who helps the homesteaders (Van Heflin, Jean Arthur) beat the baddies, led by Jack Palance. George Stevens took classic ingredients in 1953 and made them fresh and unforgettable. Unfortunately, it has now been copied by so many other film-makers that it has lost much of its magic. Loyal Griggs won an Oscar for his photography. (c)

Shanghai Express √√ Remarkable culmination of star-director relationship between Marlene Dietrich and Josef von Sternberg, in 1932. On the surface, a thriller about a train hold-up in China, it takes on all kinds of mysterious overtones, as destroyer (Clive Brook) faces the woman he discarded and who became the notorious 'white flower of China'. The explanation of the even monotone all the actors speak in – Sternberg told them 'This is the Shanghai Express. Everybody must talk like a train'. (b/w)

Shark! √ Routine *Jaws*-stuff under tough director Samuel Fuller: Burt Reynolds escapes from soldiers by signing on for suspect under-sea mission. A stunt-man was actually killed by a shark during the shooting; 1967. (c)

Shark's Treasure √ One of Cornel Wilde's adventure homilies about ecology. There aren't many sharks in it, but the producer-writer-director-star must have thought he had more chance if he cashed in on the *Jaws* boom in 1975. (c)

She XX Arsula Undress is the 2000-year-old ever-youthful Queen who waits in Mountains of the Moon for her virile young discoverer; but this Hammer production, far from hitting the nail on the head, gives all concerned a painful thumb. In 1965, the production looked almost as out-of-date as the Queen, with its tatty scenery and gear. Director Robert Day allows Peter Cushing, Christopher Lee, André Morell and the rest of the Hammer mob to look as lost all the time as they are supposed to in the desert. And Bernard Cribbins' Cockney valet is plain embarrassing. They even did a sequel, *The Vengeance of She*, three years later. (c)

She Didn't Say No XX Ghastly attempt to turn illegitimacy into a saucy, funny subject. Eileen Herlie has had babies by five different fathers. Oddly enough somebody paid director Cyril Frankel to concentrate on it, only he doesn't appear to have given it enough attention; 1958. (c)

She Done Him Wrong √√ 'I'm the finest woman who ever walked the streets', announces Mae West in her own play, directed for the screen in 1933 by Lowell Sherman. Then she meets a 29-year-old Cary Grant, posing as a Salvation Army Captain. Legend has it she says to him 'Come up and see me some time'. In fact in this film she says, 'Why don't you come sometime and see me? I'm home every evening. Come up. I'll tell your fortune.' For what happens next, tune in. (b/w)

The Sheepman √ Director George Marshall let Glenn Ford, Shirley MacLaine play this 1958 western mainly for laughs. He's a stranger who comes to town to raise sheep. The cattle people are angry. It's typical of this woolly plot that at the end he pulls the rug from under their feet. (c)

Shenandoah √ Big, sentimental Civil War drama has James Stewart perfectly cast as head of Southern family reluctantly drawn into the conflict. Director Andrew McLaglen; 1965. (c)

She Played with Fire X Arlene Dahl came all the way to England in 1957 to make this arsonous little drama with Jack Hawkins. Sidney Gilliat directed; 1958. (b/w)

The Sheriff of Fractured Jaw XX Nominally British western made in Spain in 1958. Director Raoul Walsh, co-star Jayne Mansfield and heavy Bruce Cabot just manage to convince that location is Wild West, and Kenneth More is a possible comic sheriff. (c)

Sherlock Holmes in Washington √ Disappearing documents and agents as Rathbone and Bruce scrutinise Marjorie Lord, Henry Daniell, George Zucco, under Roy William Neill's 1943 direction. (b/w)

She's Working Her Way Through College X Virginia Mayo, Gene Nelson, Ronald Reagan in adequate musical about song-and-dance star wanting a college education. H. Bruce Humberstone directed this 1952 version of *The Male Animal*. (c)

She Wore a Yellow Ribbon √√ An elegiac western from the master, John Ford, about the failure of the ageing cavalry officer to hold off the Indians; superb photography (Winton C. Hoch won 1949 Oscar); John Wayne in his favourite western, and Victor McLaglen. (c)

Ship of Fools √ Symbolic drama about shipful of assorted types going back to Germany (from South America) in thirties, starting with little Michael Dunn. Then we meet divorcée Vivien Leigh, anti-semite Jose Ferrer, Heinz Ruehmann ('There are a million Jews in Germany – what are they going to do, kill us all?'), soak Lee Marvin, trite young couple Elizabeth Ashley and George Segal, intense (and most convincing of all the motley crew and passengers) late-flowering lovers Simone Signoret and Oskar Werner. When he can forget that he is directing a Film of Significance, Stanley Kramer makes it quite gripping; 1965. (b/w)

The Shiralee X Unpleasant roustabout story of Australian bully looking for work encumbered by 5-year-old daughter. Peter Finch makes main character more sympathetic than it deserves and the morality is made over-simple by having his erring wife a real cow (a miscast Elizabeth Sellars). Nor has director Leslie Norman managed to make the smaller parts particularly convincing, and there's a hang-dog air about the whole enterprise that confirms the worst suspicions that outsiders have (doubtless unfairly) about Australia; 1957. (b/w)

Shock Corridor √ Journalist gets himself committed to mental hospital in order to expose a murder. Peter Breck, Constance Towers. Samuel Fuller wrote and directed with style in 1963. (c)

Shock Treatment X Director Denis Sanders gives us far too much of it in this lurid melo about Stuart Whitman pretending to be mad in order to wheedle secret of hidden money out of fellow-mental patient Roddy McDowall. Lauren Bacall is psychiatrist; 1964. (b/w)

The Shoes of the Fisherman XX 'Behind closed Vatican doors', with Anthony Quinn as Pope. Olivier demonstrates his inability to turn down money however rotten the part, the script and the director (Michael Anderson). It ends with the Church selling up to give all to the poor. Truly unbelievable; adapted in 1970 from Morris West's best-seller. (c)

Shootout X Half-hearted revenge western adventure, as Gregory Peck (lumbered with a 10-year-old girl) tracks James Gregory. Henry Hath-

away was clearly ill at ease directing this in 1971, and the result was a lack of conviction all round. (c)

The Shop Around the Corner √ Schmaltzy 1940 Ernst Lubitsch whimsy that somehow works; plot about love by correspondence is pretty foolproof (it spawned another film, *In the Good Old Summertime*, and a musical, *She Loves Me*) and the actors enjoy themselves – James Stewart, Margaret Sullavan, Frank Morgan and the MGM rep. (b/w)

Shopworn Angel √ Margaret Sullavan is flattered when James Stewart, unsophisticated First World War soldier, falls in love with her without realising about her Past. Walter Pidgeon, Hattie McDaniel cluck around under H. C. Potter's 1938 direction. (b/w)

Short Cut to Hell √ James Cagney's only attempt at directing was this fairly exciting small-scale remake of Graham Greene's *This Gun For Hire*, with unknowns who stayed that way. Georgann Johnson was cop's girlfriend kidnapped by killer Robert Ivers; 1957. (b/w)

Shotgun X Sheriff Sterling Hayden catches up with outlaw Zachary Scott in Indian village and saves half-breed Yvonne de Carlo's life. Leslie Selander couldn't make it more than routine in 1955. (c)

Shot in the Dark √ Sequel to *The Pink Panther*. Peter Sellers as the bumbling and tiresome French Inspector Clouseau was over-indulged by director Blake Edwards in 1964. The best jokes are broad and visual. With Elke Sommer, Herbert Lom, George Sanders. (c)

Show Boat √ George Sidney's 1951 remake of Jerome Kern-Oscar Hammerstein musical ('Ol' Man River', 'Can't Help Lovin' That Man') has Howard Keel, Kathryn Grayson and a dubbed Ava Gardner paddling down the Mississippi with the best of intentions, if not of results. Earlier versions are Harry Pollard's in 1929 and James Whale's, 1936. (c)

Showdown √ Adequate western about friends on opposite sides of the law. Sheriff Rock Hudson finds that he has to hunt outlaw Dean Martin. Veteran director, George Seaton; 1972. (c)

Showdown at Abilene X Gun-shy sheriff (Jock Mahony) returns from the wars to find his ex-girlfriend engaged to nasty cattle king. David Janssen, Martha Hyer, go through the motions under director Charles Haas; 1956. (c)

Showdown at Boot Hill √ Charles Bronson kills outlaw for the reward but can't collect because townsfolk won't identify the body. Gene Fowler Jr. made this 1958 western above average. (b/w)

The Shrike √ Director Jose Ferrer saddled with miscast June Allyson as nagging wife who almost destroys her husband (Ferrer showing off again). Not quite the chiller it was on stage; 1955. (b/w)

Side Street √ Farley Granger, working in the post office, steals a package; he thinks it contains only a small sum but it's a whacking $30,000. Director Anthony Mann makes the subsequent drama exciting enough, with plenty of locations of 1950 New York. Cathy O'Donnell, Paul Kelly, Jean Hagen strong supports. (b/w)

The Siege at Red River X Routine western has Van Johnson as Confederate spy romancing Yankee nurse Joanne Dru. Rudolph Maté directed; 1954. (c)

The Siege of Pinchgut X Unconvincing yarn about two brothers on Sydney Harbour island after one of them has escaped from jail. Mixed American (Aldo Ray), British (Victor Maddern, Barbara Mullen), Australian (small parts) casting is particularly cumbersome, and Harry Watt's last feature film a disappointment; 1959. (b/w)

The Siege of Sidney Street XX Played for excitement rather than exploring the murky political undertones of the 1911 anarchist movement which led to the famous siege, with Winston Churchill stationing himself in the front line (or round the corner, anyway). Donald Sinden, Kieron Moore, Peter Wyngarde make passable revolutionaries, but it's guesswork not history. Robert S. Baker and Monty Berman share the producing-directing credits, and a gloomy love of violence for its own (or its commercial) sake; 1960. (b/w)

Siege of the Saxons XX 'Robin Hood Meets King Arthur' would be a better name for this rubbish. Ronald Lewis is the Hoodlike Robert Marshall, Mark Dignam the Richardlike King Arthur, Ronald Howard the villain, Janette Scott the love interest. Nathan Juran directed; 1963. (c)

Sierra √ Wanda Hendrix stumbles across hideout of father and son running from the law and helps them establish Dad's innocence of murder after scrap with rustlers. Alfred E. Green had a stalwart cast going for him in 1950: Tony Curtis, Burl Ives, Audie Murphy, Dean Jagger, Sara Allgood, James Arness. (c)

Sierra Baron X Land baron hires gunman to kill Mexican land-owner so that he can grab land for himself. James B. Clark only had Rita Gam for a name; Brian Keith, Rick Jason can't hold the interest as well as the scenery does; 1958. (c)

Sign Of The Pagan X Over-ambitious Douglas Sirk-directed spectacle has Jeff Chandler as Roman and Jack Palance overacting like mad as Attila the Hun; 1954. (c)

Signpost to Murder XX Joanne Woodward and Stuart Whitman are two players with some justifiable pretensions, and it's extraordinary how they allowed themselves to be trapped into such a non-thriller as this creaking escaped - lunatic - threatens - lonely - woman routine. But perhaps George Englund had more persuasive charm than directorial ability; 1965. (b/w)

The Silencers X One of those insouciant thrillers that not even those concerned can take seriously; puts more emphasis on mild sexy larks than getting on with the plot. Dean Martin as Matt Helm and various plastic beauties. Phil Karlson; 1966. (c)

The Silent Enemy X Underwater war between frogmen in Gibraltar harbour. Allegedly biographical of Commander Crabb, the admirably named Royal Navy skin-diver, he never comes to life in Laurence Harvey's cheerful vacuity. William Fairchild wrote and directed, but the technical honours must go to underwater cameraman Egil Woxholt. Fairly obvious casting for his mates: Michael Craig, John Clements, Sid James, Alec McCowen, Nigel Stock. Harvey is aptly if not eptly partnered by the primping Dawn Addams; 1958. (b/w)

The Silent Playground √ Unpretentious little British thriller about some children in possession of dangerous drug. Too obviously rushed, the direction (by writer Stanley Goulder) shows some nice touches. Roland Curram, Bernard Archard, Jean Anderson, John Ronane pull their weight; 1964. (b/w)

Silent Running √ Bruce Dern desperately trying to save the Earth in a sci-flick set in 2001, which now doesn't look quite so far away as it did when Douglas Trumbull directed this well-meaning fable in 1972. There are some endearing scenes with little robots he programmes to replace humans. (c)

The Silken Affair X Little British comedy about accountant David Niven fleeing his wife (Dorothy Alison), whose chief fault seems to be that she prefers doing crosswords. He has a fling with Genevieve Page, but it's all so harmless and 1956 that it floats away on a cloud of non-sequiturs. Roy Kellino. (b/w)

Silk Stockings X Lacklustre Rouben Mamoulian-directed musical based on *Ninotchka* has Fred Astaire thawing out Cyd Charisse in Garbo-part of icy Russian, and a disappointing Cole Porter score; 1957. (c)

The Silver Chalice XXX 'The worst motion picture filmed during the fifties', says its star Paul Newman. He should know. When it was shown on American TV he took an ad in a local newspaper disclaiming all responsibility. And who can blame him? About a young Greek sculptor who designs the cup used in the Last Supper, it's memorable only as Newman's first film. Victor Saville directed – if that's the word – in 1954. (c)

Silver City √ Edmond O'Brien, Richard Arlen as rival miners. Ambushes, dynamitings, mob attacks and plain bare fists keep action going under Byron Haskin's spirited direction, 1951. Among those present and fighting: Edmond O'Brien, Yvonne De Carlo, Richard Arlen, Gladys George, Barry Fitzgerald. (c)

Silver Lode X That old one about a man clearing himself of murder charge while running away from the law – has it ever happened in real life, one wonders? In this 1954 Allan Dwan effort, disaster strikes on his wedding day. John Payne, Dan Duryea, Lizabeth Scott, Dolores Moran go through the usual motions. (c)

Simba XX Dirk Bogarde arrives in Kenya to find brother murdered by Mau-Mau. He stays on, with Virginia McKenna, to work for peace. Out of date stuff, not even particularly relevant in 1955. Under Brian Desmond Hurst's direction, Basil Sydney, Donald Sinden droop. (c)

Simon and Laura √ Pleasantly dated comedy, made in 1955 when everything to do with television was new and glamorous; about Mr and Mrs Television, the ideal couple, at least on screen. Peter Finch and lamented Kay Kendall splendidly matched. (c)

Sinbad the Sailor X Douglas Fairbanks Jr. was the dashing lead in this 1947 fairy-tale. Maureen O'Hara is Anthony Quinn's slave-girl; Richard Wallace directed; 1947. (c)

Sincerely Yours XXX Simply awful 1955 Liberace vehicle about a kindly deaf pianist who has the power to read people's lips and does so with his binoculars. Then he pokes his pretty little nose into their affairs and sets them all to rights. Such stalwarts as Joanne Dru, Dorothy Malone, William Demarest and Lurene Tuttle had to put up with all this, and Gordon Douglas sat benignly in the director's chair. They all got paid for it – you aren't. (c)

Since You Went Away X Claudette Colbert and family (Shirley Temple, Jennifer Jones) suffering on the home front during Second World War. Long drawn-out, treacly stuff, enlivened for those on the set by the switch during production of Jennifer Jones's favours from her husband Robert Walker (playing opposite her) to producer David Selznick. She found herself unable to act the necessary love-scenes with Walker and they were divorced immediately afterwards. John Cromwell had the directorial headaches, and the difficult Monty Woolley, Nazimova and Lionel Barrymore to contend with besides; 1944. (b/w)

Sinful Davey XX Unsuccessful attempt in 1969 by John Huston to make a cross between *Tom Jones* and *Dick Turpin*. John Hurt is no Albert Finney nor Errol Flynn, and despite some usually reliable names (Nigel Davenport, Robert Morley) in an otherwise poor cast the result is rowdy, boring, enervating; 1969. (c)

Sing As We Go √ There'll be many a nostalgic tear in Lancashire over this flagwaving (literally, as Gracie Fields leads the workers back to the factory), 1934 comedy. Basil Dean directed. (b/w)

Sing, Boy, Sing √ Tommy Sands in a surprisingly interesting little attempt to put a story into the breaks between the singing. He plays an exploited pop-singer who isn't even allowed to know that his grandfather is dying by owner-manager Edmond O'Brien. When he finds out he rushes to the bedside and nearly gives up his career to stay home. But not quite. Henry Ephron at least tried to direct-produce a teenage American movie that isn't absolute dross; 1958. (b/w)

The Singer Not the Song √ As a Mexican bandit, Dirk Bogarde gave an accomplished and convincing performance in this 1960 adaptation by Nigel Balchin of someone else's highly-coloured novel. But as the priest he is in constant conflict with, John Mills is poorly cast and clearly unhappy; a fault compounded by the casting of the strident Mylene Demongeot as a girl he improbably gets caught up with. Producer-director Roy Baker permits the melodramatic elements to get out of hand, but is saved time and again by Bogarde's quality acting. (c)

The Singing Nun XXX Debbie Reynolds called it her favourite part, but let's hope you've got more taste. Based on the real-life nun who had a record in the hit parade, it must be a strong contender for title of sickliest film ever made. A lot of the blame must go to director Henry Koster; 1966. (c)

Singin' In The Rain √√√ One of the great musicals of all time. Apart from that most-seen title number with Gene Kelly and the lamppost, it has 'All I Do is Dream of You'; 'Make 'Em Laugh' (superb Donald O'Connor); 'You Are My Lucky Star'; lovely Cyd Charisse, peppy Debbie Reynolds, funny Jean Hagen. Directed by Gene Kelly and Stanley Donen, it didn't win one 1952 Oscar. (c)

Sink the Bismarck! √ – the pride of Hitler's Navy. Naval officer Kenneth More has orders to dispose of it. Lewis Gilbert liberally used special effects in 1960 documentary reconstruction of 1941 yarn, not always convincingly. Everyone is a type (stiff British officers, lovable Cockney lower-deckies, super-efficient Germans), and it will confirm stereotyped ideas about the last war in general and the Navy in particular. (b/w)

The Sins of Rachel Cade √ If anyone is unclear as to the crucial role of the director in motion pictures, let him sit through this drama of a nurse at a Belgian mission in the Congo. Given a great or even good director, Angie Dickinson, who has proved since this 1960 effort that she is a more than capable actress, could surely have turned in a performance of some power. As it is, Gordon Douglas, whose idea of drama is to cut to a close-up, lets this episodic series of survived blows (a doctor's death, prejudice, witch-doctors, appendix-operations, air-crashes, love, seduction, and conflicts of faith) trickle away into nothingness. Peter Finch is a good enough actor to go his own way (as the local administrator) but Roger Moore remains wooden. And a bit more of the title-sinning would have been welcome. (c)

Sirocco √ Without Humphrey Bogart this might be only routine Pépé-le-

Moking, but Curtis Bernhardt surrounded Bogie with splendid sinister Algerians and Frenchmen including Lee J. Cobb, Everett Sloane, Zero Mostel. Set 1925, shot 1951. (b/w)

Sitting Bull X Standing, lying down and jumping up and down bull, too. Dale Robertson, J. Carrol Naish in poor western about Custer's Last Stand that doesn't even bother to get its facts right. Sidney Salkow directed; 1954. (c)

Sitting Pretty √ (1) 1933 musical with Jack Oakie and Jack Haley hitch-hiking to Hollywood, meeting up with nice girl Ginger Rogers and nasty girl Thelma Todd. Director: Harry Joe Brown. (b/w)

Sitting Pretty √ (2) First of the Mr Belvedere series, with Clifton Webb as a camp but effective baby-sitter, some very funny scenes (kid's punishment for cereal-scattering), game support from Robert Young, Maureen O'Hara, Louise Allbritton, Ed Begley, and happy direction from Walter Lang; 1948. (b/w)

Sitting Target XX Any thriller that ends with Oliver Reed embracing the wife (Jill St. John) he has spent the movie trying to kill, just before the car they are sitting in blows up, does not deserve much of your attention. Ian McShane and Freddie Jones are villains who have broken out of jail with him; Douglas Hickox directed garishly in 1972 from a script by Alex Jacobs, who wrote *Point Blank* five years before. (c)

Situation Hopeless but Not Serious X An odd metamorphosis for Robert Shaw's claustrophobic novel and play about two soldiers hiding in a German cellar long after the war has ended because the man who is hiding them enjoys the power it gives him and won't tell them it's all over. Gottfried Reinhardt turned it into a comedy, casting Alec Guinness as the captor, Robert Redford and Michael Connors as the captives. Paramount took a long look at it and decided that it was costing more to distribute than it would take at the box office and promptly hid it in as deep and inaccessible a place as the characters in the film. Somebody rethought the decision and issued it in 1969 – only to prove the earlier thinking to have been right. There are some genuinely funny moments, and the twist when they do manage to get away is ingenious. But it's never more than a smile. (b/w)

Six Black Horses XX Dan Duryea, Audie Murphy, Joan O'Brien limping across the prairie. Don't bother: director Harry Keller didn't seem to in 1962. (c)

Six Bridges to Cross √ Minutiae of

famous robbery in Boston – $2,500,000 from Brinks' store – told as a caper planned by Tony Curtis (who was to return to the city 13 years after this was made in 1955 as another local character, the Boston Strangler). George Nader is a detective with a love-hate relationship with Curtis; Julie Adams, his wife; Sal Mineo. Director, Joseph Pevney wasn't able to dissociate himself from the dozens of B-pictures he had previously made and so prevented this promising thriller from developing into much more. (b/w)

633 Squadron X Flying extravaganza with all the usual dramas, set in a never-never-land kind of war with terrible dialogue, some half-hearted direction by Walter E. Grauman and tongue-in-cheek and helmet-on-head acting from Cliff Robertson, George Chakiris, Harry Andrews and Donald Houston; 1964. (c)

Sixty Glorious Years X Plummy slices of history with Anna Neagle and the make-up artists failing to convince as Queen Victoria. Anton Walbrook is her Consort, C. Aubrey Smith the Duke of Wellington; Herbert Wilcox directed; 1938. (c)

Skidoo X Desperate attempt from Otto Preminger in 1968 to extract some fun from a confrontation of old-style gangsters (Jackie Gleason, Carol Channing, Mickey Rooney, Frankie Avalon, Groucho Marx, Frank Gorshin) with hippies (John Phillip Law and friends). The humour is forced, the jokes stillborn and the ambience out-of-date. (c)

Skin Game √ This con-man movie with a twist is directed by Paul Bogart; James Garner keeps selling slave Lou Gossett, and then rescuing him. This could have been the starting-point for a novel exploration of black-and-white relationships and slavery in general. Instead, it becomes black comedy and a variation on the buddy-buddy theme made popular by *Easy Rider* and *Butch Cassidy and the Sundance Kid;* 1971. (c)

Skirts Ahoy! X Harmless musical about three lady sailors; hard-working cast includes Vivian Blaine, Esther Williams, Barry Sullivan. Sidney Lanfield directed; 1952. (c)

The Skull XX Belongs to the Marquis de Sade (deceased) and is supposed to have magical powers. Unfortunately, its baleful influence extended to director Freddie Francis and caused him to turn in sub-standard horror pic in 1965, despite presence of Peter Cushing, Patrick Wymark, Nigel Green, Jill Bennett, Michael Gough, George Coulouris, Patrick Magee. (c)

Skyjacked X Tepid thriller with stock characters (brave pilot, disgruntled veteran, pregnant woman, amorous teenagers, etc., etc.). They are put through their motions by director John Guillermin, as a Boeing 707 is forced to Alaska then Moscow by James Brolin. Naturally, Charlton Heston manages to fly everyone through safely; 1972. (c)

Sky West and Crooked √ John Mills took the easy way out for his first try as director (in 1965). He cast his reliable daughter Hayley as a mentally-retarded teenager obsessed with death. When she gets involved with violent goings-on and a kindly gypsy youth (Ian McShane) she ensures there isn't a dry eye in the house. Good back-up artists (Annette Crosbie, Norman Bird, Geoffrey Bayldon) made his task even easier. But that's not to begrudge his success in bringing home (his wife is co-writer, too) the bacon. (c)

Slander X Van Johnson, Steve Cochran, Ann Blyth in mechanical drama about TV star blackmailed, and almost destroyed, by muckraking magazine. You can understand Hollywood wanting to get back at smear-magazines but it could have been done with more panache. Director, Roy Rowland; 1957. (b/w)

Slattery's Hurricane √ Richard Widmark as pilot fighting way through super-storm flashes back over his aimless life and the two girls in it, Linda Darnell and Veronica Lake. Directed by André de Toth; 1949. (b/w)

Slaughterhouse-Five √√ American prisoner-of-war who survived the bombing of Dresden loses his marbles and tells the story of his life (part true, part imagined – like a trip to another planet). Kurt Vonnegut's best-seller provided George Roy Hill with something like a sequel to his *Butch Cassidy and the Sundance Kid,* but the strength of the author's vision and Billy Pilgrim's performance as the dazed ex-soldier carry the audience; 1972. (c)

Slaughter On Tenth Avenue √ Richard Egan as Assistant DA investigating crime on New York waterfront; Walter Matthau is a plus, but director Arnold Laven can't quite sustain the excitement; 1957. (b/w)

Slaughter Trail X Brian Donlevy, Virginia Grey, Gig Young, Andy Devine are on it. Three Indians and an army fort commander strew it. Irving Allen directed it; 1951. (c)

Slave Girl X She's Yvonne de Carlo

helping to free ten American seamen from clutches of cruel Pasha. George Brent, Broderick Crawford, Albert Dekker, Andy Devine provide more laughs than thrills for director Charles Lamont; 1947. (c)

Slave Girls XXX Nonsense about brunettes enslaving blondes in the secret jungle, and a white hunter being trapped there. Carol White and Martine Beswick are among those present, Michael Carreras the director; 1966. (c)

Slaves of Babylon X Nebuchadnezzar builds the Hanging Gardens of Babylon for Linda Christian and Julie Newmar under orders from director William Castle. Richard Conte; 1953. (c)

Sleeper √ Woody Allen's body has been frozen and he is transported to the future. He and Diane Keaton lark around with bits of science fiction (robots, cell reconstruction, world totalitarianism), but it doesn't really add up to a satisfying comedy; he is director and co-writer, too; 1973. (c)

The Sleeping City √ Richard Conte as detective trying to smash drug ring. Conventional George Sherman-directed thriller is set in large New York hospital; 1950. (b/w)

The Sleeping Tiger √ Directed in 1954 by political refugee Joseph Losey under the pseudonym Victor Hanbury, it's a tense yarn about a teddy boy (Dirk Bogarde, would you believe?) adopted by a psychiatrist to prove his theories of reform. Now Losey looks back on it uneasily, liking only the love scenes between Bogarde and Alexis Smith as the doctor's wife. Losey buffs will see foreshadowings of *The Servant* in the Bogarde character. (b/w)

The Slender Thread √ Anne Bancroft takes an overdose, then phones Samaritan-type Crisis Clinic; volunteer Sidney Poitier tries to keep her on the line, while police trace the call. Director Sydney Pollack spins it out with flashbacks. Good performances from Bancroft and Poitier are best thing in otherwise rather contrived drama; 1965. (b/w)

Sleuth √ Anthony Schaffer's brilliant stage play converted to a mediocre film, with cracks showing in the clever and convoluted plot. Olivier gives a memorable performance; Michael Caine is inadequate. If the makers were serious about bamboozling the audience with the cast list, they should have found a more convincing name for those who remember *All About Eve* than Margo Channing; 1972. (c)

A Slight Case of Murder XX Terribly unfunny comedy about gangsters going straight after Prohibition. Edward G. Robinson barks, Ruth Donnelly dithers, Allen Jenkins and Ed Brophy mug, all to nil effect; Lloyd Bacon failed to bring it home in 1938. (b/w)

The Slime People X Prehistoric dwellers awakened from their slumber by atomic explosions. Robert Hutton directed them – and himself – in 1963. (b/w)

Slither √ If this amusing thriller runs out of steam too long before the anticlimactic end, there is still some fun to be had from the presence of Peter Boyle, Allen Garfield and Sally Kellerman in Howard Zieff's directorial debut. James Caan as the main protagonist is less endearing, being chased round the countryside by sinister mobile homes and generally scratching his head as events take strange turns; 1973. (c)

The Small Back Room √ Jack Hawkins is best thing about this adaptation of Nigel Balchin best-seller made over by Powell-and-Pressburger. It's a study of broken army scientist and his struggle to find self again. Nominal leads David Farrar and Kathleen Byron below par; 1949. (b/w)

The Smallest Show on Earth √ Virginia McKenna and Bill Travers inherit fleapit cinema to find eccentrics Peter Sellers, Margaret Rutherford and Bernard Miles still scratching away in there. Basil Dearden directed cheerfully in 1957. (b/w)

Small Town Girl X That's Jane Powell, with Farley Granger as Big City type passing through the small town in question, in Leslie Kardos-directed musical that won't give offence (or much pleasure) to anyone; 1953. (c)

The Small Voice √ Surprisingly gripping variant on killers-hold-innocents-hostage, with Valerie Hobson, James Donald mistakenly giving a lift to Howard Keel, escaped convict; 1948. (b/w)

The Small World of Sammy Lee √ Originally this was a television play with just one character, Sammy, stranded in his Soho room, desperately trying to raise enough money to pay his gambling debts before the heavy mob arrives. In this 1963 film Ken Hughes opened out his own script with a vengeance, taking in the whole of Soho. The love-me-please character of Anthony Newley is matched by fine performances from Julia Foster, as his girlfriend, who becomes a stripper in an effort to help him; Miriam Karlin as his cow of a sister-in-law and a whole gallery of cameo players. (b/w)

Smashing Time ✓ But times have changed, and this knock-about comedy of two innocent country girls – Rita Tushingham, Lynn Redgrave – in the Swinging London of 1967 looks awfully dated now. Still, that's not director Desmond Davis' fault. (c)

Smile ✓✓✓ Immense fun with a Young Miss America contest, zestfully produced and directed by Michael Ritchie. He skilfully makes us aware of the girls as individuals, while in the background there is a ghastly but fascinating family row between pageant financier Bruce Dern, his wife Barbara Feldon and Peeping Tom son. Michael Kidd scores as choreographer, the only professional around, who makes a gesture towards humanity by reducing his fee so that a proper ramp can be built; 1975. (c)

Smiley ✓ Australian boy wants a smile but becomes involved with smugglers in getting it (he can't want it as much as he pretends; he's lost it in sequel, below). Ralph Richardson strengthens down-under cast, where film-making in 1957 meant Chips Rafferty with everything. Anthony Kimmins. (c)

Smiley Gets a Gun ✓ 1958 attempt by Anthony Kimmins to repeat success of original *Smiley* has a new Smiley in Keith Calvert, but the same Dad (no longer a drunk) and the same kindly cop (Chips Rafferty). Instead of Ralph Richardson giving a bit of class to the proceedings, this time there's Sybil Thorndike as Granny McKinley, a bit of a witch. OK if you pine for the outback – either having never been there or having escaped from it. (c)

Smilin' Through X (1) 1932 tearjerker with Norma Shearer, Leslie Howard, Fredric March. Orphaned girl falls for murderer. Director: Sidney Franklin. (b/w)

Smilin' Through X (2) 1941 remake had Jeanette Macdonald, Brian Aherne, Gene Raymond and was even more sentimental and mushy. Director: Frank Borzage. (c)

The Snake Pit ✓✓ Slightly glib and suspect exploiting of insanity this may have been, but it did open eyes to plight of mental patients in 1948. Olivia de Havilland excellent in Anatole Litvak's best-directed movie. (b/w)

The Snake Woman XX People are dying of snake bites all round the village but it doesn't occur to anyone that there might be a venomous snake about; instead, this being one of these gloomy English low-budget horrors, they go on about The Curse. The girl with The Curse turns out to be a pretty dire actress named Susan Travers, whose father injected her mother with snake-venom before she was born. The only possible interest in all this malarkey is that the director was Sidney J. Furie in his cornier (1960) days. (b/w)

The Sniper ✓ Arthur Franz is unbalanced gunman who picks on women as victims; Edward Dmytryk would have had a better picture if he'd given us a few reasons, as well as an exciting, but conventional, manhunt; 1952. (b/w)

Snowbound XX Dennis Price was the young lead in this 1949 mystery, being led into danger by phoney film director Robert Newton; 1949. (b/w)

The Snows of Kilimanjaro ✓ 1953 movie of Hemingway's story which, as usual, retains the melodrama but loses the flavour. Gregory Peck does his best with the total-recalling hunter and you can see why Ava Gardner was so big. Henry King. (c)

So Big ✓ Jane Wyman as self-sacrificing mother in 1953 Robert Wise version of Edna Ferber's prizewinning sob-story; with Sterling Hayden, Nancy Olson, Steve Forrest. (b/w)

Soft Beds, Hard Battles X Peter Sellers playing six parts, none of them convincingly, in silly story of brothel in Occupied France; Roy Boulting; 1973. (c)

Soldier Blue X Nasty concoction of gore and sadism, strung together with a love affair between the two survivors of an orgy of violence that starts the film, leading to another that infamously ends it. As the loving couple, Candice Bergen and Peter Strauss are unmemorable; what stays in the mind is director Ralph Nelson's gratuitous use of violence to shock and his specious excuse (it really happened) for wallowing in it; 1970. (c)

Soldier in the Rain ✓ Steve McQueen as dopey soldier who hero-worships his sergeant (Jackie Gleason) in what they call a comedy-drama (meaning the director – in this case Ralph Nelson – can't make up his mind what he wants, and ends up with neither). It's all very gay, however; 1963. (b/w)

Soldier of Fortune ✓ Clark Gable hired by Susan Hayward to free husband captured by Reds in Hong Kong. Edward Dmytryk turned out slick, empty thriller with solid performances from Michael Rennie and Gene Barry; Anna Sten, much-promoted star of thirties, made this penultimate pic in 1955. (c)

Soldiers Three X Dates (and that's the

275

right word) from Hollywood's Empire-saluting period around 1951, and has Stewart Granger, Robert Newton, Cyril Cusack as troublemakers who put aside their hell-raising inside the army to teach rebellious tribesmen a few lessons. Least embarrassing feature is David Niven who covers up for the privates. Tay Garnett directed lustily a long way from Rudyard Kipling. (*b/w*)

The Solid Gold Cadillac √ Imitative comedy about small shareholder disrupting giant company moved easily from Broadway to the screen, under the able direction of Richard Quine. Judy Holliday made it sparkle as small shareholder who asks awkward questions at annual general meeting. Paul Douglas, Fred Clark splendid members of the board. But the title's a bit misleading; 1956. (*b/w*)

Solomon and Sheba XX Vulgar Hollywood version of Biblical episode stars Yul Brynner and Gina Lollobrigida. Brynner took over from Tyrone Power who died of a heart attack after one of the fight scenes. 'A simply marvellous picture', King Vidor says it would have been if Power had lived to complete the role; as it is, it turned out to be 'an unimportant, nothing sort of picture'. Well, if the director says so, who are we to argue? 1959. (*c*)

So Long at the Fair √ When her brother mysteriously disappears from their hotel during the 1889 Paris Exhibition, and everyone denies his existence, Jean Simmons is understandably frantic. Luckily nice Dirk Bogarde is standing by to help. It's an old plot, attractively reworked by Terence Fisher and Anthony Darnborough in this 1950 version, and if you haven't come across it before it should keep you guessing until the end. (*b/w*)

Somebody Up There Likes Me √ True – well, quite true – story of prizefighter Rocky Graziano, with strong performance from Paul Newman (it was to turn him overnight into a star) as Graziano, the tough New York slum kid who became a world champ. Everett Sloane, Pier Angeli and competent Robert Wise direction; 1956. (*b/w*)

Some Came Running √ James Jones novel about soldier returning home, which in 1959 switched Frank Sinatra's screen career mostly to 'serious' acting. Banal sob-stuff directed by Vincente Minnelli, who got appropriate performances from Shirley MacLaine and Dean Martin, playing a dying character who never takes his hat off – except at a

lady's funeral (and that's supposed to be touching, not funny – it's that kind of picture). (*c*)

Some Girls Do XX And some films don't; this one, for instance. Supposedly a spy comedy-thriller in the tradition of James Bond, it has the doleful Richard Johnson in the Sean Connery part, a tentative James Villiers as the villain, and some rather unattractive girls pushing their bodies at them and us. The plot is so infantile, the dialogue so banal, the acting so incompetent and the direction (by Ralph Thomas) so slapdash that it even outdoes those Matt Helm travesties. And this is meant to be a 1969 Bulldog Drummond. (*c*)

Some Like It Hot √√√ Wildest Wilder comedy is this 1959 classic of Tony Curtis and Jack Lemmon fleeing gangsters after 1929 St. Valentine's Day Massacre, dressing up as girls while wooing Marilyn Monroe (and Joe E. Brown). If you don't laugh out loud during the sleeping car sequence, Curtis's send-up of Cary Grant and the chase scenes, consult a psychiatrist, as director Billy Wilder had to do during the making, so impossible was Monroe. She was bitter that the film was not in colour to show her off best, was invariably late and fluffed her lines so that one scene took 59 takes. 'She has breasts like granite and a brain like Swiss cheese', he said about her. It's Wilder's genius that none of the tension showed. (*b/w*)

Some People √ Clive Donner speeds some capable young players (Ray Brooks, Annika Wills, Angela Douglas, David Hemmings) along in a plot about teenage boredom and the alternatives offered by the Duke of Edinburgh Award scheme. Kenneth More helps to disguise the do-gooding plugs, but it's all too firmly set in 1962 for much contemporary interest. (*c*)

Something Big X Jokey 1971 western: Dean Martin kidnaps a Colonel's wife (Honor Blackman) by mistake, and she intercedes with husband to let him carry out a piece of swashbuckling. Adequate time-passer, with director Andrew McLaglen over-indulging his cast. (*c*)

Something of Value X Sidney Poitier and Rock Hudson as friends forced to take opposite sides by Mau-Mau uprisings in Kenya. Richard Brooks directed uninspiringly, though Wendy Hiller turns in good cameo; 1957. (*b/w*)

Something to Hide XX Director Alastair Reid should have hidden this misbegotten thriller which has Peter Finch going crazy, Shelley Winters in a drunken fury, Linda Hayden pregnant, John Stride as a ludicrous policeman and the audience in a fitful slumber; 1971. (c)

Something to Live For X Ray Milland, having dried out after *The Lost Weekend*, tries to help Joan Fontaine through the same affliction, but this 1952 bender is off the wagon. Not even George Stevens' direction helps. (b/w)

Something Wild √ Carroll Baker's husband, Jack Garfein, directed her in 1960 in this hysterical but compelling story of degradation, that foreshadowed *The Collector* in its plot about a girl held captive. (b/w)

Somewhere I'll Find You √ Clark Gable's last film before he joined army in 1942 has him as war correspondent following another, Lana Turner, to Pacific. Wesley Ruggles did better with love stuff than war stuff. (b/w)

The Song of Bernadette X Jennifer Jones's wide-eyed all-American saint was greatly aided by the monumental joke of Linda Darnell as the Virgin Mary. So much so that she actually won the 1943 Academy Award for it. Henry King delivered the soupy religiosity required by William Perlberg, but Charles Bickford, Vincent Price, Lee J. Cobb and Gladys Cooper seemed about as French as Phyllis Isley, as Jennifer Jones was called before this film. (b/w)

Song of Norway XXX Poor attempt at Grieg's life-story has splendid Norwegian locations but awful transcriptions of his melodies into pop songs. Director Andrew Stone, whose successes have been with big stunts, tries to work a few of them in but the composer's life is pretty dull – and so is the picture. Uninspired casting, although Robert Morley and Edward G. Robinson do their best; 1970. (c)

Song of the Thin Man √√ Last of the Nick Charles sagas has William Powell-Myrna Loy cracking a killing on a gambling ship. Keenan Wynn as jazz clarinetist holds the key. Dean Stockwell as their son is threatened, but justice triumphs in time. Eddie Buzzell directed; 1947. (b/w)

A Song to Remember XX Cornel Wilde would disagree; he has spent the years since 1945 trying to forget this awful biopic with him as a ludicrous Chopin, Merle Oberon as an even more ludicrous George Sand, and Paul Muni, George Coulouris, Nina Foch

camping it up under Charles Vidor's baleful direction. (c)

Song Without End X George Cukor took over after director Charles Vidor died in the middle of making this pretty but over-dramatic picture about Franz Liszt, 'and the first thing I did was to take out all those lines like "Hiya Mendelssohn",' he said. Dirk Bogarde not too out-of-tune as the composer, considering what he was up against - co-star Capucine, for one thing; 1960. (c)

Son of Ali Baba XX Silly costume adventure with Tony Curtis, Piper Laurie; Kurt Neumann directed; 1952. (c)

Son of Dracula √ Count Alucard (try it backwards) comes to stay in America. Robert Siodmak directed this follow-up in 1943 with Lon Chaney Jr. and Louise Allbritton. Should get your blood tingling if not sucking. (b/w)

Son of Frankenstein √√ One of the best of the early horror pix (1939), with Basil Rathbone chipping off the old Karloff block with the help of Bela Lugosi; Rowland V. Lee directed. (b/w)

Son of Lassie √ 1945 sequel to *Lassie Come Home* has the canine sex-problem following his/her master on wartime bombing. Sylvan Simon directed Peter Lawford, Donald Crisp and a girl called Helen Koford whose resemblance to Terry Moore is explicable because she later changed her name. (c)

The Son of Monte Cristo √ Louis Hayward doesn't count for as much as Robert Donat, sadly missed from this 1940 sequel, but Rowland Lee is the same director. It's less campy than might have been expected with George Sanders the villain and Joan Bennett the lady. (b/w)

Son of Paleface √ Follow-up to *The Paleface*, and made four years later in 1952 by Frank Tashlin. More successful than most sequels, it's about Bob Hope tangling with Jane Russell again. Roy Rogers and Douglas Dumbrille help recreate that Saturday morning western feeling. (c)

Son of Robin Hood XX Winner of the most misleading title award. It isn't a son, it's a daughter. And it isn't Joan Collins, who turned the part down, but June Laverick with equally undistinguished cast making it look more like Sherbert Forest. Or Sherman Forest, as director George is responsible; 1959. (c)

Son of Sinbad √ Caliph Ian McDonald captures Dale Robertson, forces him to bring the secret of Greek Fire. Vincent Price is his pal. Hard to care one way or the other. Ted Tetzlaff; 1955. (c)

Sons and Lovers √ Game, if ultimately unsuccessful, try at the D. H. Lawrence novel about the Notting-hamshire coalfields before the First War. The young, lightly disguised Lawrence, played as acceptably as any American could manage by Dean Stockwell, is helped by mother Wendy Hiller to escape from bully of a father, Trevor Howard. Mary Ure won a 1960 Oscar nomination for her supporting role. Jack Cardiff and Freddie Francis, director and cameraman, neatly observe the minutiae of Edwardian working-class life. (b/w)

The Sons of Katie Elder XX If she'd lived, she would have been proud of them. John Wayne, Dean Martin, Michael Anderson Jr., Earl Holliman as tearaway sons avenging parents' deaths in slow, disappointing Henry Hathaway western; 1965. (c)

The Sorcerers √ Competently directed (by Michael Reeves at 23) low-budgeter with Boris Karloff as a gentle scientist whose discovery of long-distance manipulation by hypnosis is perverted by wife Catherine Lacey; 1967. (c)

Sorry, Wrong Number √ Barbara Stanwyck as bedridden hypochondriac who overhears plan to kill her on crossed line and has to sit waiting to be murdered when no-one will believe her. Director, Anatole Litvak; 1948. (b/w)

S.O.S. Pacific X Seaplane-full of usual assorted cinema-types (crook, captor, girl, scientist, etc.) stranded on Pacific isle with H-Bomb about to explode. Can the scientist defuse the bomb in time? Answer depends on which version of the film they show on television – there was more than one. Guy Green directed stale stuff with as much panache as he could summon in 1959 – which wasn't much. Richard Attenborough, Eddie Constantine, Pier Angeli, John Gregson, Eva Bartok make it all rather more boring than it might have been with more charismatic players. (b/w)

So This is Love X Kathryn Grayson as real-life opera star, Grace Moore, doesn't convince; nor does anything else in this inadequate biopic. Gordon Douglas directed; 1953. (c)

So This Is Paris √ Who are they kidding? But this Hollywood-bound musical about three sailors on leave in Paris has Tony Curtis, Gene Nelson, Gloria De Haven and relaxed Richard Quine direction; 1955. (c)

The Sound and the Fury X Martin Ritt's uninspired 1959 film of young Joanne Woodward seeking freedom from strict Southern background with no-good carnival charmer. Margaret Leighton, Stuart Whitman help lift it just above soap-opera level; Yul Brynner is brooding step-uncle. Supposedly adapted from William Faulkner novel, but too many other familiar influences are discernible. (c)

The Sound Barrier X Despite suffocating upper-class ethos, accents and Terence Rattigan script, this David Lean-directed portrait of a man obsessed has some exciting moments. Ralph Richardson convinces as the aircraft maker; the rest are just too, too stiff-upper-lip to carry this 1952 effort. (b/w)

Sounder √ Slightly woolly account of black sharecroppers during the Depression, with Cicely Tyson doing her 'indominatable' bit as mother of family that gets into trouble when the young son steals some meat. The lad is eventually persuaded to go to school. Sounder is his dog's name; dogged direction by Martin Ritt; 1972. (c)

Sound Off X Mickey Rooney drafted into the Army; you have to be a fan. Richard Quine directed; 1952. (c)

The Sound of Music √√ How can you knock everybody's favourite piece of schmaltz? Would it be fair to say that Julie Andrews acts like a superannuated fairy on the Christmas tree? Could one dare whisper that if one were saddled with the Singing Trapps for a family, one would leave home? What wrath would be incurred by the remark that Christopher Plummer would be better employed as a plumber? That the songs are hummable kitsch? The settings as authentic as nylon? That Eleanor Parker is a latter-day Zsa Zsa Gabor and just as gaboring? You can't – and anyway what good would it do – the BBC paid so much money for it that it's there on our Christmas screens for the next ten years or so with monotonous (that's the word) regularity. Director, Robert Wise; 1965. (c)

The Southerner √√ Jean Renoir managed his usual lyrical job on this 1945 Texan assignment, but was let down by his ignorance of American types; 'most of the people were screechingly, unbearably wrong . . . to the point of unintentional insult', wrote James Agee. They don't seem to do much work, either, for what is supposed to be a faithful portrayal of a year in the life of cotton tenant farmers. But, having said all that, he does coax some uncommonly fine performances from Zachary Scott, Betty Field and Beulah Bondi, as they struggle against the odds and the superbly photographed land. (b/w)

The Southern Star √ Stick around for Orson Welles's appearance about two-thirds of the way through as a sacked policeman in the jungle. Otherwise this chase after a huge diamond is pretty routine stuff, distinguished by some swift direction from Sidney Hayers and a particularly strong cast of George Segal, Ian Hendry, Harry Andrews and Johnny Seka. Also appearing: Ursula Andress; 1969. (c)

South Pacific √ Considering the immense success this musical achieved at the box office, it isn't such a great film. In his history of musicals John Kobal talks of Josh Logan's 'disastrously self-indulgent direction, with every number lost in the blue of camera lenses diffused out of focus, while the action slowly succumbed to death from diabetes'. Casting was poor, too, with Mitzi Gaynor taking the part Doris Day wanted; Rossano Brazzi conceitedly smirking while another man's voice (Giorgio Tozzi's) issued from his lips; France Nuyen and John Kerr (also dubbed) simply inadequate. Only Rodgers and Hammerstein save the show: 'Nothing Like a Dame', 'Some Enchanted Evening', 'I'm in Love with a Wonderful Guy', etc. It's simply a couple of love stories, in essence, blown up to immense Todd-AO proportions, which unfortunately are minimised on your home screen; 1958. (c–very)

South Sea Woman X Knockabout stuff with Burt Lancaster, Chuck Connors as wild Marines in Second World War Pacific; Virginia Mayo plays stranded showgirl. Arthur Lubin directs; 1953. (b/w)

Southwest Passage X Bank robber and girl join experimental camel train on its way West; except for camels, nothing new about this Ray Nazarro-directed oater. Rod Cameron, Joanne Dru, John Ireland; 1954. (c)

Southwest to Sonora √√ This is Marlon Brando and John Saxon fightin' and feudin' over a horse. Sidney J. Furie shot it (in 1966) with all sorts of moody compositions, but it keeps cantering along, as Brando tracks down Saxon the Mexican and his stolen horse. Set in the 1870s. (c)

Soylent Green √ A curiosity: murder in the 21st century over a new process for the chemical food most people live on. A strong cast (Charlton Heston, Edward G. Robinson, Joseph Cotten) cannot quite carry a weak story and scrappy direction by Richard Fleischer; 1973. (c)

Spaceflight IC-1 XX Cut-price sci-flick about spaceship searching for planet to colonise. Few names, unless you count Donald Churchill, Norma West, Linda Marlowe. Director Bernard Knowles isn't one of the best known, either; 1965. (b/w)

The Spanish Gardener √ Disappointing adaptation of A. J. Cronin's novel about a father desperately trying to reach the heart of his young teenage son. Philip Leacock has turned it into a vehicle for Dirk Bogarde as the gardener who can touch the boy, and changed the fate of this character from the book's. Michael Hordern never gives an all-round impression of the father, but Cyril Cusack, as another jealous servant, is splendid, as is Bogarde; 1956. (c)

Spare the Rod X This sincere 1961 effort to show the awfulness of the average English state school suffers from two central flaws. One is the rewriting of the script under threat of censorship so that the master who was to get a kick out of beating kids (Geoffrey Keen) is no longer seen to do so. The other is Max Bygraves as a timid new teacher who believes you can get through to children with kindness; he can't act and lets down the whole film. Otherwise, director Leslie Norman and ambivalent headmaster Donald Pleasence manage to save what could have been a disaster, given the central casting, and even turn it into a sympathetic and realistic piece of social comment whenever Norman can manage to shoot round his 'star'. (b/w)

Sparrows Can't Sing √ Lively attempt by Joan Littlewood to transfer her ensemble hit to the screen in 1963, with James Booth, Barbara Windsor, Victor Spinetti, Roy Kinnear. It should have been a sad comedy of infidelity amid changing social and architectural backgrounds, but it's not much more than a lark and a sing-song. (b/w)

Spartacus √√ Probably the best 'epic' ever made (which isn't saying much), with Stanley Kubrick (who took over as director from Anthony Mann after two weeks) marshalling vast crowds and big stars (Kirk Douglas as the slave-revolution leader; Laurence Olivier, Charles Laughton, Jean Simmons, Peter Ustinov, Tony Curtis) into a cohesive whole. He is greatly aided by Dalton Trumbo's unusually literate script and the involvement any libertarian must feel with the under-dogs. The hand-to-hand battles are particularly well-composed and edited (by Robert Lawrence); 1960. (c)

Speedway XX Tiresome Elvis Presley 1968 vehicle (joke) has him as racing driver who can't pay his income tax because he has kindly given away his money. But who's the income tax inspector? Nancy Sinatra. And they fall in love, so that's all right. What a bore; Norman Taurog. (c)

Spellbound X In 1945 Alfred Hitchcock decided to make the first picture about psychoanalysis and opened up a Pandora's Box for the cinema. Although it contains some of his most famous scenes (particularly in Dali's dream and memory sequences) it's a poor script, as he now admits, and there were some terrible longueurs like the schmaltzy music. Gregory Peck was never bright enough for a Hitchcock hero and Ingrid Bergman compounded her usual faults. (b/w)

Spencer's Mountain √ Sentimental stuff about Simple Mountain Folk in Wyoming wastes Henry Fonda, Maureen O'Hara, James MacArthur, but writer-director Delmer Daves pops in some nice touches of humour; 1963. (c)

The Spider's Web XX There is only one way to stage Agatha Christie and this isn't it. To make her special world of golf, bridge, country house murder and red-herrings live it has to be done straight – which is why *The Mousetrap* ran and ran and ran and ran and ran. In 1960, Godfrey Grayson went in for farce, with a cast of competent but determinedly lightweight players (Glynis Johns, Jack Hulbert, Cicely Courtneidge, Ronald Howard, David Nixon). The result is inconsequential. (c)

The Spikes Gang √ Lee Marvin in 1974 western in which he plays Fagin to a group of three young would-be gunmen. There are some good moments, but the whole is hardly edifying; Richard Fleischer directed. (c)

Spinout XX Elvis Presley vehicle about singer who prefers racing cars to girls. Spun out. Norman Taurog directed; 1966. (c)

Spinster XXX Don't watch this one if you are easily embarrassed by bad films, bad acting and bad directing. On the other hand, connoisseurs of the awful will revel in Shirley MacLaine's unbelievable schoolteacher (so warm and understanding to the children, so cold and uptight to her suitors), Laurence Harvey's callow, sex-mad war hero who rips open her blouse shouting 'Open Sesame' in public, over-acting to the point of absurdity. Only Jack Hawkins, who finally tumbles the walls of her Jericho manages to approximate a real performance, but even here veteran director Charles Walters turns him into a smug mug. It's set in New Zealand; 1961. (c)

The Spiral Road X Rock Hudson and Burl Ives play Dr Kildaring parts of young turkey and wise older doctor in adaptation of Jan de Hartog novel about leprosy in the Java jungle. Robert (*Summer of '42*) Mulligan directed, in summer of '62. Unfortunately, it's all a bit of a bore. (c)

The Spiral Staircase √√ (1) 1946. Genuinely thrilling, directed in 1946 by Robert Siodmak, with Dorothy McGuire making a convincing deaf mute in an institute where a mad killer is on the loose. (b/w)

The Spiral Staircase X (2) 1975. Clumsy remake by Peter Collinson with a worse script and pretty but inadequate actress Jacqueline Bisset. (c)

The Spirit is Willing √ Amusing second-feature based on Nathaniel Benchley's *The Visitors*, about the old haunted house situation, tricked up with 1969 generation-gap and nymphomaniac ghosts. John Astin scores as a psychiatrist bent on finding rational explanations for the son's behaviour, and Sid Caesar accepts William Castle's direction with good grace. (c)

The Spirit of St. Louis X Uneven Billy Wilder-directed drama about Lindbergh's transatlantic flight, with an excellent, if too old (47 playing 25), James Stewart. 1957 flashback misses presenting seeds of the personality faults which later led Lindbergh into apologising for Hitler. It cost $6,000,000 and flopped. 'I have never been able to figure out why', wrote producer Jack L. Warner. Wilder's own explanation: 'A bad decision. I succeeded in a couple of moments, but I missed creating the character.' (c)

Splendour in the Grass √ It may be sentimental, over-directed by Elia Kazan, and sub-Tennessee Williams, but this 1961 William Inge drama of adolescence is absorbing for Natalie Wood and Warren Beatty's promising performances, later fulfilled. Premature permissiveness interesting too; moral is sleep with him or be sorry. (c)

The Split √√ Robbery caper on a crowded football stadium gets its interest from the people involved, and they are certainly an intriguing bunch: Jim Brown, Diahann Carroll, Julie Harris, Ernest Borgnine, Gene Hackman, Jack Klugman, Donald Sutherland. Director Gordon Flemyng orchestrates them well and holds the interest through the recruitment, planning, operation and aftermath. Fine of its kind; 1968. (c)

The Spoilers √ There must be something about a novel that has been made into movies five times; in this case it's a tremendous fight between the two leading men. (1) William Farnum and Tom Santschi in 1914; (2) Milton Sills and Noah Beery in 1922; (3) Gary Cooper and William Boyd in 1930; (4) John Wayne and Randolph Scott in 1942; (5) Rory Calhoun and Jeff Chandler in 1955. Only the last two are likely ever to reach your screen: Marlene Dietrich is in the 1942 version, directed by Ray Enright; Anne Baxter in the 1955 one directed by Jesse Hibbs. It's all about gold mines in the Yukon and who owns a disputed one; 1942 and before (b/w); 1955 (c)

Spring and Port Wine XX Despite a sterling cast – James Mason, Diana Coupland, Rodney Bewes, Hannah Gordon, Adrienne Posta, Frank Windsor, Arthur Lowe, Susan George – director Peter Hammond has made the worst of Bill Naughton's family play. You can't believe in the characters or their situations. Reminiscent of *The Family Way*, also set in Bolton, but without that adaptation's sparkle; 1970. (c)

Springfield Rifle X Gary Cooper as spy investigating arms thefts; unexciting stuff under André de Toth's direction; 1952. (c)

Spring in Park Lane X Harmless Anna Neagle-Michael Wilding nonsense about an earl pretending to be a footman. Herbert Wilcox was at home in the tasteless decor and general putting-about of the nice, rich life; 1947. (b/w)

Spring Reunion X Get-togethers of Old Boys and Girls can be pretty depressing affairs, even if you were at school with them. For the outsider – in this case the audience – they are almost bound to be boring, too. Betty Hutton and Dana Andrews can't stop this one from being both and Robert Pirosh's direction only underlines the tedium. One flash of interest for older viewers with long memories is the appearance of silent star Laura La Plante as Betty's Ma; 1957. (b/w)

The Spy in the Green Hat XX Last of the lamentable *Man from U.N.C.L.E.* movies opts for farce, which is one way of getting through a tedious plot. Eduardo Cianelli, Jack la Rue, Joan Blondell, Elisha Cook, Maxie Rosenbloom and Jack Palance were wheeled out of the geriatric ward in 1967 to provide some guying of their former screen personae. Janet Leigh and Leo G. Carroll are on hand. And Robert Vaughn and David McCallum look as if they can't wait to take the money and run. Directed by Joseph Sargent. (c)

S*P*Y*S XX Wearisome attempt to re-unite the M*A*S*H partnership of Elliott Gould and Donald Sutherland showed only how dreary they could be with poor material. A strained, coincidence-packed, silly script was compounded by director Irvin Kershner's ineptitude ; 1974. (c)

The Spy Who Came in from the Cold √√ John Le Carré's thriller used by Martin Ritt as 1966 vehicle for Richard Burton. Cast of character actors scores; Cyril Cusack and Sam Wanamaker shine, even if film is disappointing measured against book. (b/w)

The Spy With a Cold Nose XX Weak comedy about bulldog that has mike hidden in it, given to Soviet leader. Lionel Jeffries, Eric Sykes OK; Laurence Harvey, Daliah Lavi, yawnful. Galton-Simpson script disappoints or maybe it's Daniel Petrie's direction; 1965. (c)

The Spy with My Face X Tedious 1966 espionager with Robert Vaughn in one of those unbelievable 'double' roles. The rest of the men from U.N.C.L.E. go through their paces with understandable lack of enthusiasm in this 1966 spin-off; director, John Newland. (c)

The Square Jungle X Under-privileged grocery boy becomes boxing champ. One big cliché with Tony Curtis, Ernest Borgnine, Pat Crowley, Jim Backus and uninspired Jerry Hopper direction; 1955. (b/w)

The Square Peg XXX The ghastly Norman Wisdom, parachuted into Occupied France by mistake. The first person he meets is a beautiful English agent (Honor Blackman). Then he finds that the local German general is his double. So he changes places. And so on. And so on. Hattie Jacques provides a moment or two of fun, and that's about it. That master of the banal, John Paddy Carstairs, directed; 1959. (b/w)

The Squeaker X Squeaky, creaky Edgar Wallace thriller had slight charm in this 1937 version with Edmund Lowe, Robert Newton, Alastair Sim, Ann Todd. Who is the mysterious jewel fence? William K. Howard directed. (b/w)

Stagecoach √√√ (1) The most famous western ever made, it set standards in plot (five passengers – can they survive the journey?), photography, direction (John Ford surpassing himself), characterisation (outlaw, whore, drunken doctor, expectant mother, gambler), acting (respectively John Wayne, Claire Trevor, Thomas Mitchell, Louise Platt, John Carradine) that have never been bettered; 1939. (b/w)

Stagecoach XX (2) Draggy remake (1966) has Bing Crosby, Ann-Margret, Van Heflin, Keenan Wynn, and Alex Cord in John Wayne part; Gordon Douglas shows what a great director John Ford was. (c)

Stagecoach War X Hopalong Cassidy oater in which he helps an old man regain his Wells Fargo pony express contract; William Boyd hops along under director Lesley Salander; 1940. (b/w)

Stage Fright √ Hitchcock foolishly believed thriller reviewers who suggested that this novel would make a good Hitchcock movie. Jane Wyman refused to be made up as dowdily as she should have been and he regretted choice of Alastair Sim as her father. Marlene Dietrich stole the picture in a showy actress role, and he broke the rule that flashbacks must always tell the truth. Nevertheless, bad Hitchcock is better than no Hitchcock, and Richard Todd put in surprisingly fine performance as chief suspect; 1950. (b/w)

Stage Struck X Small-town girl becomes Broadway star after sleeping with producer. Susan Strasberg is no substitute for Katharine Hepburn in this 1958 remake of *Morning Glory*, and weakens otherwise reliable cast (Henry Fonda, Joan Greenwood, Herbert Marshall). Some vivid on-location photography and sharp Sidney Lumet direction weren't enough. (c)

Stage to Thunder Rock √ Not-quite-straightforward western with Barry Sullivan as a sheriff who has to turn on the family who brought him up. Sullivan doesn't get much shade of character, but Keenan Wynn makes

rather more of the father. Somehow director William F. Claxton didn't put quite enough push into it all; 1964. (c)

Staircase X A slight case of over-casting. Richard Burton and Rex Harrison simply don't fit the pair of ageing queens who seemed so real and right in the theatre (helped by Patrick Magee's massive performance there) and so false and wrong here. Partly it's the result of a miscast director, too: producer Stanley Donen would have done better to employ one with flair for dramatic and human foibles. Instead, he chose himself; 1969. (c)

Stakeout on Dope Street √√ Remarkable little B-picture made with unknowns by director Irving Kershner, tells excitingly of the finding of a tin of heroin by a gang of teenagers and their moral dilemma of whether to sell it for big money – and thus increase the general misery dope brings. The morality isn't overdone, and the chase and hunt scenes are particularly well developed; 1957. (b/w)

Stalag 17 √√ Definitive PoW drama directed by Billy Wilder in 1953, won Academy Award for William Holden as cynical sergeant who may be spy. Otto Preminger acts – as a (very) camp commandant. (b/w)

The Stalking Moon √√ Stunning climax between Gregory Peck as kindly army scout and the Indian intent on revenge for his white squaw's (Eva Marie Saint) escape is worth the wait while Robert Mulligan piles on the suspense; 1969. (c)

Stampeded √ Routine post-Civil War oater with Alan Ladd riding into town again; this time to help a worried Virginia Mayo and Edmond O'Brien as reforming drunk. Actually, the plot, such as it is, is merely an excuse for one of those big stampedes which Gordon Douglas appears to have supplemented with clips from previous filmed cattle-panics; 1957. (c)

Stanley and Livingstone √ Spencer Tracy as reporter who searches for long-lost Dr (Sir Cedric Hardwicke) and finally delivers what is presumably most-quoted line ever spoken in Africa. Forgive the imperialism for the authenticity. Henry King; 1939. (b/w)

The Star √√ 1953 tour de force by Bette Davis, never off the screen, as washed-up ex-movie queen. She's fighting to make comeback to earn enough to have her 12-year-old daughter (young Natalie Wood) with her. Stuart Heisler. (b/w)

Star! X Julie Andrews is Julie Andrews. Gertrude Lawrence was Gertrude Lawrence. Both considerable artists in their own way, but it's not the same way and they don't meet here. Robert Wise tries to convince by using the device (from the *Citizen Kane* he edited?) of a film-within-the-film with a documentary reality. But Julie can't carry it, and Daniel Massey is not Noel Coward. No wonder it was a flop in 1968 and after. (c)

Stardust √ Unpleasant pop star fable, cashing in on public interest in drug-ridden singers; cast with comparatively elderly pop stars David Essex, Adam Faith, Marty Wilde, Keith Moon. Director Michael Apted toned down scriptwriter Ray Connolly's worst excesses, but the pastiche of the Beatles's story (of course, everyone concerned in 1974 disingenuously denied it was) gave a sense of secondhand familiarity. (c)

A Star is Born √√ (1) 1937. Lovely performances from Janet Gaynor and Fredric March as she goes up and he comes down in the star stakes; William Wellman directed, and, surprisingly – considering the date – it's (c)

A Star is Born √√ (2) 1954. The quintessential Judy Garland movie; love her, you'll love it; think she's an over-indulgent, over-indulged creation of show-biz mythology, you'll find this grossly dramatic slice of Hollywood life a supercilious phoney. When her role as band-singer married to drunken star (James Mason) and eclipsing him, failed to win her Oscar, Groucho Marx called it the biggest robbery since Brink's. Bravura speech in clownish make-up, pitying self and husband, is highspot; George Cukor. (c)

Star of India XX Cornel Wilde in weak yarn about French nobleman trying to get his estates back; there's some boring complication about Dutch jewels. Herbert Lom lurks, Jean Wallace smirks. Arthur Lubin directed, sort of; 1953. (c)

Stars And Stripes Forever X Some rousing tunes in otherwise dull biog. of American brass-bandsman John Philip Sousa, with Clifton Webb, Robert Wagner, Debra Paget. Henry Koster conducted; 1952. (c)

The Stars Are Singing XX Silly plot about singer (Rosemary Clooney) sheltering escaped refugee, Anna Maria Alberghetti, only to find *she* can sing too, is the poor excuse for this 1953 Norman Taurog-directed musi-cal. Lauritz Melchior sings along, Fred Clark does his bumbling bit. (c)

Stars in my Crown X Conflict between a doctor and a minister who preaches with his gun in a 19th-century western town. Directed by Jacques Tourneur in 1950, with Joel McCrea, Ellen Drew, Dean Stockwell. (b/w)

Star Spangled Girl √ Never released to the cinemas in Britain, this Neil Simon comedy is about Olympic swimmer Sandy Duncan crossing paths with hippies (this is 1971) Tony Roberts and Todd Susmann; director, Jerry Paris. (c)

Start the Revolution Without Me √ Gene Wilder and Donald Sutherland, both in twin roles, save this comedy from oblivion, despite Bud Yorkin's anything-for-a-laugh direction. The historical setting is merely there to be sent up; 1969. (c)

State Fair XX Jose Ferrer made the great mistake in 1962 of remaking Walter Lang's 1944 glowing version of Rodgers and Hammerstein's engaging musical, with a cast of Pat Boone, Bobby Darin, Ann-Margret, Alice Faye (as a Mum), Pamela Tiffin. Only Tom Ewell stands out under Ferrer's ill-judged direction. He had no feeling for music, no feeling for lightness, and should have stuck to those heavy-handed dramas which suited his deadpan style. (c)

State Secret √ Thriller with comedy touch about surgeon tricked into helping head of state. Glynis Johns, Jack Hawkins, Douglas Fairbanks Jr. Directed in 1950 by Sidney Gilliat. (b/w)

Station Six Sahara X Cheap melo has Carroll Baker disrupting sex-starved men on desert oil station. Seth Holt directed; 1962. (b/w)

Stay Away Joe XX And what better advice could one possibly give? This is a sad boring effort to make Elvis Presley into a comedian with an unfunny script and the unpleasant idea that Indians (what used to be called Red ones) have to prove themselves to be fit members of society. This particular example is ludicrously portrayed by Burgess Meredith, Katy Jurado, L. Q. Jones and Elvis, whose usual immunity from direction (supposedly by Peter Tewksbury) has been extended to the rest of the cast, with disastrous results; 1969. (c)

Steamboat Round the Bend √ Essentially a vehicle (a paddle steamer, in fact) for homespun philosopher Will

Rogers, this 1935 John Ford features a routine but exciting race down the Mississippi reminiscent of Buster Keaton's *The General*. Beware wincing appearance by Stepin Fetchit. (*b/w*)

The Steel Bayonet XX Leo Genn, Kieron Moore, Michael Medwin (what a ghastly lot of officers for any platoon to have, only here two of them are supposed to be heroes) hold out in a Tunisian farmhouse. Director Michael Carreras must have thought that a war story of this kind was commercial in 1957; there isn't any other explanation. (*b/w*)

The Steel Claw X It's on the hand of brave marine corps captain about to be discharged from Manila. Instead, he ducks underground and organises local guerrillas, who must have been grateful. As he directed it as well as starring, George Montgomery made sure they were; 1961. (*c*)

Steel Town X John Lund and Howard Duff scrapping over Ann Sheridan in mill. Spectacular molten shots atone for obvious storyline; director, George Sherman; 1951. (*c*)

Steelyard Blues √ Some excellent scenes don't add up to the anarchic celebration of zany individualism that director Alan Myerson must have been hoping for in 1972. Donald Sutherland's shaggy dog optimism grows wearisome in its monotony; Jane Fonda in a sub-*Klute* part is never stretched; and only Peter Boyle adds an extra dimension of character as the would-be lovable conspirators assemble an aeroplane from stolen parts. (*c*)

Step Down to Terror X You remake Hitchcock at your peril, as Harry Keller found in 1959 when he tried a regrind of *Shadow of a Doubt*. Charles Drake took the Joseph Cotten part of returning murderer. He should have stayed away. (*b/w*)

Step Lively √ In 1944 during Frank Sinatra's swoony-croony period, RKO brushed up the Marx Brothers failure, *Room Service*, added some songs and gave it to Tim Whelan to direct. Gloria de Haven is chief swooner. (*b/w*)

Steptoe and Son √ As viewable as an average-to-good episode in the TV series, this would have been acceptable in 1972, when it was made, but isn't now. The posturing of Wilfrid Brambell looks spiteful, Harold's ice-thin insouciance familiar, and the comparative luxury of this opening-out unnecessary. Carolyn Seymour does not convince as a bride for Harry H.

Corbett's rag-and-bone man, and the complications about babies are just silly. (*c*)

Steptoe and Son Ride Again X Closer to *Carry On Ragman* than the original, often finely-drawn, TV series, this second movie exploitation of Corbett and Brambell is based on a knockabout insurance fraud; director, Peter Sykes; 1973. (*c*)

The Sting √ √ √ Delightful compendium of con-tricks, played by Paul Newman and Robert Redford (among their victims: Robert Shaw), working up to a wonderfully orchestrated heist. Scott Joplin's piano rags on the soundtrack inaugurated a whole musical craze in 1973; director, George Roy Hill. (*c*)

Sting of Death XXX 'Numbingly bad' was one reviewer's verdict on this horrible horror pic in 1966. It's about half-man, half-jellyfish in the Florida swamps, and isn't even funnily awful. Neil Sedaka sings a couple of songs but otherwise the cast is sunk in swamps of anonymity; director was William Grefé. (*c*)

A Stitch in Time XXX Rather an unpleasant Norman Wisdom comedy set in a hospital exploiting illness (and spastics) for laughs, in 1964. Robert Asher indulges his star's mock-innocence, which all too often comes out as malice. (*b/w*)

St. Louis Blues X Why do all biopics of musicians and composers have to have exactly the same story? Papa says no music – girl singer says stick at it – leaves home to seek fortune in New York (or Paris or Vienna) – setbacks, acceptance, fame – and Papa comes round, proud of his boy. Here it is again, in black. The subject is 'Father of the Blues' W. C. Handy and he is played by Nat King Cole, with Pearl Bailey, Eartha Kitt, Mahalia Jackson and Ella Fitzgerald thrown in for value. All perfectly acceptable, and directed by Allen Reisner in a dull, plodding way. Sad that the real W. C. Handy's story was an exciting, better one; 1958. (*b/w*)

Stolen Assignment XXX One of those stinkers churned out around 1955 which had a mysterious murder, a detective and a so-called surprise ending. They usually featured people like John Bentley, Hy Hazell, Eddie Byrne, Patrick Holt, all of whom were in this one, directed by Terence Fisher. (*b/w*)

Stolen Hours X Poor 1963 remake of *Dark Victory*, transferred to England, in which Susan Hayward takes a long time a-dying and a-proving that Bette Davis, the original doomed socialite, was a more compelling actress. Nor is director Daniel Petrie a patch on 1939's Edmund Goulding for coaxing tears out of the audience. (c)

Stolen Life √ Two Bette Davises for the price of one; she's twin sisters competing for the same man: result is murder. Glenn Ford and Dane Clark out-dazzled by double Davis. Curtis Bernhardt directed; 1946. (b/w)

The Stone Killer √ Charles Bronson is one of those cops who are more brutal than the crooks in this Michael Winner-directed, American-set amalgam of Mafia, conspiracy and carchase movies. Plot-line is obscure, but it holds the interest as long as it's on the screen; it is instantly forgettable afterwards. Martin Balsam makes a rather Jewish Italian Godfather; 1973. (c)

The Stooge X Big-headed singer (Dean Martin) discovers he's a flop without his partner (Jerry Lewis). And with him, for our money. Norman Taurog; 1951. (b/w)

Stop-Over Forever XX Mistaken identity 1964 thriller with Ann Bell wondering who would want to bump her off: Anthony Bate? Bruce Boa? Director Frederic Goode? (b/w)

Stork Talk XXX As awful as its title, this ill-conceived item has a tepid Tony Britton trying to be funny as a doctor whose wife (Anne Heywood) and girlfriend (Nicole Perrault) are both having babies at the same time. Or perhaps he isn't really the father in both cases – it's hard to tell or to care. Anyway, they both have twins so his plan to have both babies put down to his wife doesn't work. But as he's supposed to be a gynaecologist, surely he knew . . . oh, don't bother. Michael Forlong compounds the general grisliness with appropriate direction; 1962. (b/w)

Storm Boy √ Pleasant Australian adventure, with children in mind, about a boy and pet pelican. Henri Safran directed his white, aboriginal and bird cast more than adequately; 1976. (c)

Storm Centre √ Small-town librarian Bette Davis causes a rumpus when she refuses to remove 'subversive' book from her shelves. Important theme – the dangers of political censorship – is trivialised by melodramatic plot and direction (Daniel Taradash was re-sponsible for both in 1956). (b/w)

Storm Fear √ Dan Duryea, Lee Grant, and producer-director Cornel Wilde take refuge from the law in mountain shack; they meet Dennis Weaver, Jean Wallace. Adequate thrills; 1955. (b/w)

Storm Over the Nile X Poor remake of *The Four Feathers* unsympathetically cast with Laurence Harvey, James Robertson Justice, Anthony Steel, Mary Ure; directed without flair by Zoltan Korda and Terence Young in 1955. Steel has to prove he isn't a coward in the Sudan. (c)

Storm Warning √ Some odd casting has Doris Day and Ginger Rogers, as sisters, with Ronald Reagan and Steve Cochran in otherwise predictable 1951 Ku Klux Klan melo, directed by Stuart Heisler. (b/w)

The Story of Esther Costello √ Shocker about a blind, deaf and dumb girl who is first exploited and then raped by Rossano Brazzi. Meanwhile, Joan Crawford, who's married to Brazzi and has made a protégée of the girl (nicely played by Heather Sears – 19 in 1957), is doing her nut. Producer-director David Miller has calculatedly ignored the social and medical implications to make a sensational picture. He has succeeded, and it's rather unpleasant. (b/w)

The Story of GI Joe √ Actually it's the story of Ernie Pyle, war correspondent, well played by Burgess Meredith. Slightly interesting for marking Robert Mitchum's major debut, as soldier. William Wellman; 1945. (b/w)

The Story of Mankind XXX Candidate for the worst film ever made is this unbelievable charade supposedly taken from Hendrik van Loon's popular history. You won't believe it, but here it is: Cedric Hardwicke sits in the clouds deciding whether Mankind should live or die by H-bomb; prosecutor is Vincent Price in morning coat, defender is Ronald Colman in grey suit (sadly anticipating his own visit to Heaven by one year; this was made in 1957, he died in 1958). As evidence, they call up some of humanity's better-known events – Moses (Francis X. Bushman) receiving the Ten Commandments; Helen of Troy (Dani Crayne) breaking them; Nero (Peter Lorre) fiddling; Hippocrates (Charles Coburn) giving his oath; Cleopatra (Virginia Mayo) killing her brother; Joan of Arc (Hedy Lamarr); Elizabeth I (Agnes Moorehead) with Sir Walter Raleigh (Edward

Everett Horton) and Shakespeare (Reginald Gardiner). Most of this is supposed to be serious, but advanced lunacy sets in with the appearance of Peter Minuit buying Manhattan from the Indians (Groucho); the monk who doubted Columbus (Chico); and Sir Isaac Newton (Harpo). Producer-director of this pageant is Irwin Allen. (c)

The Story of Ruth XX You're lucky. You aren't committed to go where this film goeth; you can turn it off and go for a walk, or do the washing-up. But do try to catch a few minutes to see just how low Hollywood can stoop when taste is replaced by box-office greed; the acting (Stuart Whitman, Tom Tryon, Viveca Lindfors) is terrible and that's better than the direction (Henry Koster) which is better than the sets that are better than the script – which sadly, is by Norman Corwin, who used to write marvellous radio dramas; 1960. (c)

The Story of Three Loves √ Triple-decker directed by Vincente Minnelli and Gottfried Reinhardt about ballet-dancer finding, losing love; governess in love with her charge; trapeze boy meeting trapeze girl. Strong cast includes Ethel Barrymore, Farley Granger, James Mason, Agnes Moorehead. Also present: Pier Angeli, Zsa Zsa Gabor, Leslie Caron, Moira Shearer, Kirk Douglas; 1953. (c)

The Story of Will Rogers √ Affectionate memoir of the homespun philosopher has Will Rogers Jr. playing his father, Jane Wyman and competent Michael Curtiz direction; 1952. (c)

The Story on Page One X Clifford Odets's final film, which he both wrote and directed, is sad memorial to the man who wrote *Waiting for Lefty*, *Golden Boy* and *The Big Knife*. A cheaply-made courtroom drama, it has an ill-cast Gig Young as falsely-accused murderer of his mistress's (Rita Hayworth) husband, with Tony Franciosa a gnomic defence lawyer; 1960. (b/w)

Stowaway √ Shirley Temple gets lost again. In 1936, it was on board ship and in Shanghai, where she encountered Robert Young, Alice Faye, Eugene Pallette, Arthur Treacher and other Chinese; director, William A. Seiter. (b/w)

Straight on Till Morning XX One of Peter Collinson's hysterical thrillers, with ugly duckling Rita Tushingham

falling for psychotic killer. She, Tom Bell and James Bolam deserved better in 1972. (c)

Strait-Jacket X Joan Crawford was incarcerated in asylum for 20 years after killing her adulterous husband and his girl with an axe. Shortly after her release – and reunion with daughter – there's a series of axe murders in the district and she becomes chief suspect. Biggest mystery is why Crawford ever agreed to appear in such an extravagant piece of rubbish. William Castle directed; 1964. (b/w)

The Strange Affair √√ Det. Sgt. Jeremy Kemp uses PC Michael York to plant drugs on a criminal family he's out to get. Apart from some conventional love stuff between the PC and Susan George (kinkily photographed through a two-way mirror) and the unforgivable pun on the PC character's name in the title, this was a refreshing entry in 1968 and makes the usual TV detective story seem old-fashioned. David Greene directs with strength and simplicity. (c)

Strange Bedfellows √ Oil executive Rock Hudson is afraid that scatty wife, Gina Lollobrigida, is bad for his image – she's not, but this movie is. Gig Young, Terry-Thomas and lots of unconvincing slapstick in mild Melvin Frank comedy; 1965. (c)

Strange Cargo X Strange, indeed, with Ian Hunter as Christ-like figure converting Clark Gable, Peter Lorre, Eduardo Ciannelli, Paul Lukas and J. Edward Bromberg as they escape with Joan Crawford from Devil's Island. Frank Borzage's direction suffered from his usual romanticism; 1940. (b/w)

The Strange Door X Charles Laughton and Boris Karloff overacting like mad in this absurd adaptation of Robert Louis Stevenson creepie. But perhaps director Joseph Pevney meant it to be funny? 1951. (b/w)

Strange Lady in Town √ Greer Garson as Santa Fé's very busy new lady doctor. Grand Mervyn Le Roy western with Dana Andrews, Cameron Mitchell; 1955. (c)

The Strange One √√ This portrait of a sadistic cadet, superbly realised by Ben Gazzara, provides prophetic explanation for My Lai and behaviour of US troops in Vietnam. Jack Garfein; 1957. (b/w)

The Stranger √√ (1) 'Much more graceful, intelligent and enjoyable than most other movies', wrote James Agee in 1946, defending Orson Welles against the knockers of first film he had directed (all of) and starred in after *Citizen Kane*. He played escaped war criminal, disguised as professor, tracked down by Edward G. Robinson (in part intended for Agnes Moorehead, would you believe?). Loretta Young is unsuspecting wife. (b/w)

The Stranger √√ (2) Roger Corman ('the Orson Welles of the B picture') used the same title in 1961 for his first 'serious' drama, made with his own money in Southern towns that kept moving his unit on when they discovered that he had come to expose their racialism. The central character (William Shatner) is a rabble-rousing fascist and if the film is flawed, it is because Corman becomes more interested in the man than the political and social roots that made him. (b/w)

The Stranger √√ (3) Visconti's brilliant 1967 version of Camus's novel, with Marcello Mastroianni and Anna Karina, must surely be shown on television sometime; it was given a limited cinema showing here. (c)

Stranger in My Arms √ Mary Astor dominates daughter-in-law June Allyson and this three-handkerchief weepie. Helmut Kautner squeezed last drop of sentiment from Jeff Chandler's involvement with widow; 1959. (b/w)

Stranger in the House XX Small disaster in the Home Counties, detonated by Pierre Rouve, trying his hand at directing, as well as mis-adapting a Simenon novel and transplanting it to England. James Mason is the only watchable figure on the screen, and then solely for his siliconised shedding of the excesses of script and direction. Geraldine Chaplin (as his daughter in whose room a body is found), Bobby Darin as the corpse, Ian Ogilvy and the rest of the rather untalented British cast, give poor accounts of themselves. A mess; 1967. (c)

Stranger on Horseback √ Strong stuff well directed by Jacques Tourneur, about Judge Joel McCrea, who is so determined to bring miscreant to justice that he kills in order to extricate him from the town that's sheltering him. Kevin McCarthy, Nancy Gates, John Carradine back up strongly; 1955. (c)

Strangers on a Train √√√ One of Hitchcock's very best, with taut writing from Raymond Chandler, adapting Patricia Highsmith's novel of proposed exchange of murders. Robert Walker a consummate villain; Farley Granger a convincing tennis champion, although Hitchcock would have preferred someone like William Holden. It came at an opportune time in 1951, after Hitch had made two failures *(Under Capricorn, Stage Fright)* and his career needed a boost. If you've seen it more than twice before, see if you can spot the tricks: slowing-up the film when the dog licks intruder Granger's hand, and the use of a model blown up (in both senses of the phrase) in the climactic scene. (b/w)

Strangers When We Meet X Kirk Douglas and Kim Novak cheating on their spouses in Middle America. Richard Quine tries to keep them in the centre of the picture, but Walter Matthau does his usual scene-stealing. Unfortunately, the story (by Evan Hunter) fails to make the characters believable or alive; 1960. (c)

The Stranger Wore a Gun √ Randolph Scott joins in hold-up as tribute to bandits who saved his life. Claire Trevor, Ernest Borgnine, Lee Marvin provided director André de Toth with easy task in 1953. (c)

The Strangler √ The other film about the Boston Strangler, with Victor Buono, who does the ladies in because of his possessive invalid mother. Burt Topper directed in 1964. (b/w)

The Stranglers of Bombay XX Nasty wallow in Indian thugeeism, 1959, giving Terence Fisher the chance to show eyes being burned out by tongs, tongues being cut and communal graves being filled with murdered natives. Perhaps Guy Rolfe, Allan Cuthbertson, and Andrew Cruickshank were just a bit ashamed when they saw what kind of a film they were involved in. (b/w)

Strategic Air Command X Even James Stewart can't get this one about baseball player recalled to flying duty airborne. Director Anthony Mann seemed to care more about the planes than rather humdrum story; 1955. (c)

The Strawberry Statement √ Boy meets girl among the student rioters. This rather opportunist 1970 movie has Kim Darby, Bud Cort, Bruce Davison as main characters, although James Coco in a small part is worth spotting. Some splendid contemporary pop is on the track, but the film itself is off it. Director, Stuart Hagmann. (c)

Straw Dogs √ Infamous Sam Peckinpah thriller about nasty British yokels terrorising Dustin Hoffman and Susan

George first with teasing, then with rape and finally a murderous siege. A victim of the familiar paradox that the better it's done, the worse it is, morally and stomach-turningly; 1971. (c)

A Streetcar Named Desire √√ The film that catapulted Marlon Brando to superstardom, just as Tennessee Williams's original play, in which he played the same part on Broadway, had made him the most talked-about stage actor of the decade. Elia Kazan guided the hysterics and home truths of Vivien Leigh's faded Blanche, Karl Malden's good guy and the rest of the talented cast, through steamy New Orleans atmosphere; 1951. (b/w)

Street Corner XX Stories of Chelsea women police that probably looked out-of-date when this film was made in 1953, as Peggy Cummins, Terence Morgan, Anne Crawford were very much of the charm school, and Muriel Box, who directed and co-wrote, was no innovator. (b/w)

The Streetfighter X Depression-time boxing-booth fighter Charles Bronson rises in his tough profession, but so morosely that one doesn't care. As his manager, James Coburn is a bit livelier, Jill Ireland just about there; dour direction from Walter Hill; 1975. (c)

Streets of Laredo √ Remake of 1936 *The Texas Rangers* in 1949 had William Holden, Macdonald Carey, William Bendix as mates who split when one stays crooked. Leslie Fenton did routine western director's job, but the film is better than most oaters. (c)

Strictly Dishonourable X Vehicle for Italian opera star Enzio Pinza has him saving Janet Leigh's reputation by marrying her, and singing an aria or two. Melvin Frank, Norman Panama wrote and directed; 1951. (b/w)

Strictly for the Birds XX - or at least the uncritical. Tony Tanner just couldn't carry this supposedly wry account of a day in the life of a Soho wide boy, 1964 model, whose easy-come cash easy-goes. Some nice little cameos from Joan Sims as his sister, Graham Stark as a street musician, and Toni Palmer, Carol Cleveland and Christine Hargreaves, but Vernon Sewell can't either make you believe in his London or forget the real one. (b/w)

Strike Up the Band √ One of several musicals Judy Garland made with Mickey Rooney around 1940. This is the one where Rooney is leading his school band in a radio contest and she sings 'Our Love Affair'. Busby Berkeley directed with nary an overhead camera. (b/w)

The Stripper X William Inge's play *A Loss of Roses* provided Franklin Schaffner with his first feature, in 1963. Unfortunately, the vulgarisation of the title extended to the casting - Joanne Woodward in a blonde wig as Older Woman, Richard Beymer in a permanent sulk as budding boy - and treatment of this very French theme. Claire Trevor, Carole Lynley, Robert Webber offer what help they can. (b/w)

The Student Prince X Edmund Purdom mouthing to Mario Lanza recordings in lush operetta about prince falling for barmaid (Ann Blyth) in Heidelberg. Director Richard Thorpe made it strictly for the coach trade in 1954. (c)

Studs Lonigan √ Could have been a great film except for casting of Christopher Knight as the hero of J. T. Farrell's novel of growing up in the Chicago twenties. Director Irving Lerner made it vivid cinematically, but it ran to 2¼ hours and was only fitfully seen here drastically cut after showing at the 1960 London film festival. Frank Gorshin and Jack Nicholson outstanding in lesser parts. (c)

A Study in Terror √ Oddly light-hearted Sherlock Holmes having a go at Jack the Ripper murders. Excellent cast (John Neville, Anthony Quayle, Robert Morley, Barbara Windsor, Frank Finlay, Georgia Brown), cursorily treated by script and director James Hill; 1965. (c)

The St. Valentine's Day Massacre √√ In 1967 this was dismissed as too violent and over-dramatic; but, since, director Roger Corman has become cult figure and we've had *The Godfather*. Now it's regarded as superior urban jungle reportage, with Jason Robards's Al Capone and George Segal's Cagney figure as merely part of one of the best gangster movies since the thirties. (c)

The Subject Was Roses √ Talky version of the Frank D. Gilroy play about Mom and Dad poisoning the return of their soldier son with their own bitterness. Ulu Grosbard directed stolidly, but Patricia Neal takes off as the mother and Jack Albertson won the Best Supporting Actor Oscar for 1969. Never shown commercially in Britain for some reason best known to the potty cinema industry. (c)

Submarine Command X Navy drama

with William Holden as guilt-ridden officer starts well, but director John Farrow lets it go over the top; 1951. (b/w)

Submarine X-1 X Poorly-written and directed (William Graham) war-film about three mini-subs whose mission is to plant explosives under a German battleship; two are lost. American James Caan is somehow in charge of a British submarine and Rupert Davies is an admiral. Otherwise, the only remote surprise is when this dispirited actioner was made – 1967, at least ten years after all the other bravy-navy epics. (c)

The Subterraneans XX Leslie Caron, George Peppard, Roddy McDowall, Janice Rule among early (1960) hippies in California. Cheap adaptation of Jack Kerouac novel poorly directed by Ranald MacDougall. The ending is particularly banal. (c)

Subway in the Sky X Competent thriller about Van Johnson on the run in West Berlin from military police and in a clinch with Hildegarde Neff. Muriel Box directs a cast of minor British supports adequately, but there isn't much feeling of Berlin; 1959. (b/w)

Such Good Friends √ A pseudonymous script from Elaine May and game performances by Dyan Cannon, James Coco, Burgess Meredith almost survive Otto Preminger's heavy hand. There are some very funny lines and scenes in the grimly comic hospital, but Preminger suddenly changes the mood to tragedy and has a final exit into the sunset on a theme song; 1971. (c)

Sudden Fear √ Wealthy Joan Crawford realises husband Jack Palance is planning to kill her for her money. Director David Miller kept up the suspense in 1952. (b/w)

Suddenly √ Frank Sinatra as killer hired for half-a-million to snipe and kill President in small town. Lewis Allen made this in 1954, with James Gleason, Sterling Hayden, and drew such a vicious performance from the recent crooning idol that there were protests from the bobbysoxers. He and his cronies hold family prisoner as they await the President's train. The name of the town is Suddenly. (b/w)

Suddenly Last Summer √√ Cannibalism rears its unexpected head in elongation of Tennessee Williams one-acter. Super superstars Elizabeth Taylor, Katharine Hepburn, Mont-gomery Clift play out the grisly, baroque horror story of the girl who is to be given a lobotomy to keep her quiet about what went on that summer. It's to be arranged by her aunt who offers a million dollars to the local hospital if Dr Clift will perform the operation. All reached great heights of melodrama in Gore Vidal's treatment and Joseph L. Mankiewicz charmed something even more from Liz Taylor. Amazingly, it was all filmed in England, in 1959. (b/w)

Sugarland Express √ Strident odyssey, with Goldie Hawn and William Atherton escaping from prison to collect their baby. The press turns them into heroes, to the chagrin of police captain Ben Johnson. Director Steven Spielberg makes it all seem more significant than it is; 1974. (c)

Sullivan's Empire XX Search for crashed father in Amazon jungle takes three sons on an epic journey. Or that was the idea. The actual film is rather more pedestrian. Martin Milner. Directors, Thomas Carr, Harvey Hart; 1967. (c)

Sullivan's Travels √√ Wry comedy made in 1941 by Preston Sturges about Joel McCrea as film director, searching the country for significant theme, coming to the conclusion that they want to laugh. Punctuated by some brilliant episodes, with Veronica Lake, William Demarest, Franklin Pangborn, Porter Hall. (b/w)

Summer Holiday √ (1) The egregious Mickey Rooney in 1947 adaptation of Eugene O'Neill's *Ah! Wilderness*. It's the turn of the century; a young man is about to be initiated into the wonders and terrors of life. Agnes Moorehead, Walter Huston add some distinction to Rouben Mamoulian's direction. (c)

Summer Holiday √ (2) Sweet unpretentious Cliff Richard vehicle (double-decked) about group of clean-living kids who dance and prance their way across Europe. Notable as the film that brought director Peter Yates to Hollywood's attention in 1962; he went on to *Bullitt*. (c)

Summer Love X Simple-minded stuff about teenagers at summer camp, with John Saxon, Jill St. John, Rod McKuen and minimal direction from Charles Haas; 1958. (b/w)

Summer Madness √ The irresistible combination of Katharine Hepburn and Venice gives a distinction to this bitter-sweet, David Lean-directed brief encounter between lonely American spinster and Romantic Italian (Rossano Brazzi, as always: weren't there any other actors?); 1955. (c)

Summer of '42 √√ Movies about 15-year-old boys becoming sexually experienced tend to be embarrassing, but this New England idyll of war widow Jennifer O'Neill and Gary Grimes is mostly an exception. Robert Mulligan directed in 1971 from Herman Raucher's autobiographical script. (c)

Summer of the Seventeenth Doll √ Life down under among the sugar-cane workers and their summer-only girlfriends well characterised by Ernest Borgnine, John Mills, Angela Lansbury and Anne Baxter, coming to grief when the plot starts involving them in marriage lines. Leslie Norman produced-directed more than competently from John Dighton's making-over of Ray Lawler's theatre play; 1960. (b/w)

A Summer Place X Peyton Place, that surely is. During family holiday at gorgeous summer resort, unhappily married (to other people) Dorothy McGuire and Richard Egan resume an old affair, while their teenage children – Troy Donahue, Sandra Dee – embark on new one with each other. Messy soaper was written and directed by Delmer Daves in 1959. (c)

Summer Stock √ Judy Garland gets the show biz bug when Gene Kelly and his theatrical company come to stay on her family's farm. Phil Silvers, Gloria de Haven add to the fun provided by director Charles Walters in 1950. (c)

Summer Wishes, Winter Dreams X Joanne Woodward experiencing menopausal crisis, brought on by her dying mother, homosexual son, quarrelling daughter and her own frigidity. Director Gilbert Cates overdid the whole breakdown in 1973, and her recovery as she appreciates husband Martin Balsam's problems is forced. (c)

Sumuru XXX Shirley Eaton leads the beautiful Roman Amazons who intend world domination through enslavement of world's leaders. Hokum, to put it mildly, directed by Lindsay Shonteff, with George Nader as the investigator who blows their cover; 1967. (c)

The Sun Also Rises X Errol Flynn, as Mike Campbell, drunken fortune-hunter, took fourth billing, behind Tyrone Power as the impotent Jake Barnes, Ava Gardner as the nymphie Lady Brett Ashley and Mel Ferrer as Robert Cohn, in this dreadful attempt by Darryl F. Zanuck to turn Hemingway's spare prose into a lush spectacular. All were much too old for the parts (except possibly Gardner) and Henry King directed with stolid lack of imagination. Only Flynn came out of it at all well, but by 1957 he was too drunk, too dissolute and too beat-up to capitalise on his success. He made two more features and died. (c)

The Sun Comes Up X Sodden with sentimentality, a Richard Thorpe 1949 soaper about tragedy-struck singer Jeanette MacDonald hiding from world, with Lassie and a little boy bringing her something to live for. (c)

Sunday, Bloody Sunday √ Overpraised view of Swinging London, 1971, with Murray Head vacillating between two lovers, Glenda Jackson and Peter Finch, who also share a telephone answering service. The spurious air of calm reasonableness misled many critics of the time to acclaim John Schlesinger's direction of Penelope Gilliatt's script, but later viewings have shown up the many weaknesses, not least Murray Head's inability to portray a convincing fulcrum to the seesaw of his two affairs. (c)

Sunday Dinner for a Soldier X 'Their eyes met! Their lips questioned! Their arms answered!' ran an ad for this hokum in 1944. 'They' were Anne Baxter and John Hodiak; the movie is as mawkish as the publicity. Grandpa Charles Winninger has invited soldier Hodiak to lunch. Lloyd Bacon. (b/w)

Sunday in New York √ Jane Fonda quite unlike her later self in this 1964 Doris Day-type comedy in which novice director Peter Tewksbury gets smooth performances from Rod Taylor and Cliff Robertson. Her big problem is should-she-before-marriage? No, you read the date right – it was playwright Norman Krasna who didn't. (c)

The Sundowners √ (1) 1950: standard western about brothers fighting against outlaw who is really a third brother. George Templeton's neat direction gets best from Robert Preston, Robert Sterling, John Barrymore Jr., Jack Elam. (c)

The Sundowners √ (2) 1960: Australian adventure falls uneasily between intimate conflict of a travelling man – who always wants to keep moving, with his wife who wants to stay in one place, and a spectacle lightened with comedy touches. Fred Zinnemann never appears to know quite which of the two films he was making; Robert Mitchum and Deborah Kerr give him more than adequate performances as the wandering couple, but Peter Ustinov and Glynis Johns are allowed to broaden their comedy into a riot. The landscape sequences are refreshing to start with, but quickly pall; and they do go on. (c)

Sunflower X Italian, dubbed (as all Italian pictures are, even Italian-language ones), romantic drama about Marcello Mastroianni's wartime adventures and Sophia Loren's odyssey to find him after the war. Henry Mancini's lush score beats relentlessly out. Sophia over-acts, Marcello under-acts and all the vast cast react to Vittoria de Sica's wild direction; 1970. (c)

Sunrise at Campobello √ Reverential treatment of F. D. Roosevelt's pre-presidential retirement from politics when first stricken with polio. Dore Schary, who wrote and produced, obviously idolised the man but that didn't help the drama. Ralph Bellamy gives a surprisingly fine performance in the central role, but Greer Garson reduces his wife Eleanor, substituting mimicry for acting. The bigger failure, however, is director Vincent J. Donahue's; what should have been inspiring ends up dull. The final tottering up to the lectern for FDR's political comeback comes too late; 1960. (c)

Sunset Boulevard √√√ Superb 1950 vision of decaying Hollywood, through Billy Wilder's mordant directorial eye; 'full of exactness, cleverness, mastery, pleasure', wrote James Agee, 'microscopically right in casting, direction and performance. Miss Gloria Swanson, required to play a 100 per cent grotesque, plays it not just to the hilt but right up to the armpit.' William Holden is corrupt writer enmeshed in her fantasy. Erich von Stroheim outplays them all as ex-husband-cum-nursemaid but never liked the role, often referring to it as 'that lousy butler part'. (b/w)

The Sun Shines Bright √ In the early thirties John Ford made a comedy about Irving Cobb's Judge Priest. In 1953, he came back to the character, now played by Charles Winninger, and a more sombre tale of a prostitute's return to her Southern home. Unfortunately, it is marred by some nasty ideas about black people. (b/w)

Sun Valley Serenade √ Time-passing

1941 musical with chubby Sonja Henie, mostly notable for frequent numbers by Glenn Miller, including 'In The Mood'. Director: Bruce Humberstone. (b/w)

Superfly √ 'Superfly' is what cocaine is called in the black ghettos. Ron O'Neal has made a fortune from it. The white cops are bent. There is much plottery about these two pressuring each other for money, but it's slow and, given the subject's possibilities, remarkably uninteresting, though the film was a huge success in America. Gordon Parks directed in 1972. (c)

Support Your Local Gunfighter √ Pleasant, jokey western, with James Garner conning the inhabitants of the town of Purgatory; being found out; discovering gold. Director Burt Kennedy does well by the humour, despite allowing some of the cast to mug it up. Nice to see Joan Blondell, in 1971, as a Madame. (c)

Support Your Local Sheriff √√ *High Noon* played for laughs, with James Garner as lawman in a jail that hasn't got its bars yet. After a lifetime of heavy westerning, Walter Brennan, Harry Morgan and Jack Elam obviously enjoy the opportunity given to them by director Burt Kennedy to play around a bit. You should too; 1969. (c)

Suppose They Gave a War and Nobody Came √ Muddled comedy about army base and nearby town comes over as both naïve and satirical, like the title. Sgt. Tony Curtis, playing about the last of his juvenile leads (at 44 in 1969), is arrested for spending the night with the property (Suzanne Pleshette) of the Sheriff (Ernest Borgnine), as a rehearsal for the Third World War breaks out; director, Hy Averback. (c)

Surprise Package X No surprises in this misnamed comedy-caper about exiled ex-monarchs: former King of the Gangsters is Yul Brynner; Noel Coward is former real King. They meet on a Greek isle. Mitzi Gaynor is moll. Director Stanley Donen wasn't the right chap for this unrisen soufflé; 1960. (b/w)

Susan Slade X Connie Stevens as hapless teenage heroine having one piece of bad luck after another (including illegitimate baby, which mother Dorothy McGuire pretends is hers). Bound to turn out OK in the end, though, with Troy Donahue around as faithful friend and the soft-centred Delmer

Daves writing and directing in 1961. (c)

Susan Slept Here X Dick Powell as scriptwriter hoping feckless teenager Debbie Reynolds (actually 22 in 1954) will provide him with material. If we tell you it's a Frank Tashlin-directed romantic-comedy, you won't have to actually watch it to find out what happens. (c)

The Suspect √ Strong stuff with Charles Laughton echoing the Crippen case, with Ella Raines as his Ethel Le Neve, plus a calculating Henry Daniell. Robert Siodmak guaranteed the thrills in 1945. (b/w)

Suspicion √√ The novel by Francis Iles that Hitchcock adapted this very English thriller from was about a woman who married a murderer and was so much in love with him that she allowed herself to be killed rather than leave him. But Hitch changed the plot for Joan Fontaine and Cary Grant. Just how, you must find out for yourself if you haven't already seen it. Sadly, the present end doesn't convince anyone, including the director. Made a long way from England, in Hollywood; 1941. (b/w)

Svengali XX Ill-cast version of the Trilby story by Noel Langley, with Donald Wolfit clomping about as the man Du Maurier drew as thin and diabolic, and Hildegarde Neff much too sophisticated for the sweet innocent he controls into an opera star. Terence Morgan, Noel Purcell, Alfie Bass complete a dull team; 1955. (c)

Swallows and Amazons X Old-fashioned children's story may please an uncritical young audience with six of themselves against unsympathetic adults, and plenty of fights and fun, but it makes a dispiriting movie for parents forced to watch. Perhaps middle-class children were as prissy and naughty-nice as this in 1929, when Arthur Ransome's novel was set. But adults (Ronald Fraser, Virginia McKenna) never were. Claude Whatham directed, in 1974. (c)

Swamp Women XX Roger Corman swiftie about Marie Windsor, Beverly Garland, Carole Matthews, Susan Cummings as escaped convicts searching for hidden loot in swamp. Has two other titles: *Swamp Diamonds; Cruel Swamp*. You'll get that sinking feeling, whatever the name; 1955. (c)

The Swan √ Ruritanian romance has attractive cast of Grace Kelly, Alec Guinness, Louis Jourdan in Royal triangle. After making this charming soufflé for Charles Vidor in 1956, Kelly left films to marry her real-life prince. What you might call a swan song. (c)

Sweet Bird of Youth √√ Richard Brooks' cleaned-up 1962 film of raw Tennessee Williams' drama. Paul Newman returns home from unsuccessful Hollywood gigoloing in wake of Geraldine Page, terrific as ageing, drunken movie queen. Ed Begley splendid as local boss who goes after Newman for ruining his daughter, Shirley Knight. In the play the girl got syphilis; here it's an abortion. In the play, the boy got castrated; here it's a thump on the face, otherwise, a highly satisfactory baroque experience. (c)

Sweet Charity √√ Boisterous and beguiling musical imaginatively directed by Bob Fosse in 1968, one of the last of the big spenders. Shirley MacLaine manages well in the part Giulietta Masina did rather better in the original *Nights of Cabiria*, from which Neil Simon took his stage musical. Sammy Davis Jr. is seen briefly, but the music's fine ('Where Am I Going?' 'If My Friends Could See Me Now') and Fosse's choreography is as inventive as his direction. The story of the put-upon girl with the too-big-heart is always good for a few tears. (c)

Sweethearts X MGM's first (1938) all-talking, all-singing, all-in-colour extravaganza, with the ghastly Nelson Eddy and ugly Jeannette MacDonald trilling along. They go to Hollywood, where they encounter Mischa Auer, Ray Bolger and other comic characters of the period. W. S. Van Dyke directed. (c)

Sweet November X Sandy Dennis plays a promiscuous girl who doesn't have long to live (that's why she's promiscuous, you see) . . . But her policy of a new man every month is threatened when one of the men (Anthony Newley) falls in love with her – and she with him. Only masochists will be able to sit through such a dismally silly plot *and* a couple of hours of more or less undiluted Newley and Dennis out-cutesying each other. Director Robert Ellis Miller must have had a strong stomach in 1968. (c)

Sweet Smell of Success √√√ Overwhelming stench of perversity, money and bitch-goddess worship comes up from this melodramatic slice of Broadway life, astonishingly well directed by

Alexander Mackendrick, and precisely photographed by James Wong Howe, 1957. Burt Lancaster icily chilling as columnist, Tony Curtis blusteringly sycophantic as feed in strong Clifford Odets, Ernest Lehman script. (b/w)

The Swimmer √√ Remarkable, out-of-the-ordinary and haunting saga of Burt Lancaster, eight miles from home and clad only in his swimming-trunks, who announces that he will walk and swim (through his rich neighbours' and public pools) whenever possible, home to his own gracious house. But this is no larking college boy – he's a 50-year-old man just beginning to run to fat. The John Cheever short story Frank and Eleanor Perry have adapted this sharply-etched movie from made the symbolism of the self-imposed marathon acceptable. Lancaster has never been better, and Frank Perry's cast matches his fine direction – Janice Rule, Cornelia Otis Skinner, Marge Champion among them; 1968. (c)

The Swinger X Trashy tale of nice girl Ann-Margret pretending she's depraved so that sex-obsessed Robert Coote and Tony Franciosa will publish her stories in their nasty little girlie magazine. George Sidney directed without taste in 1966. (c)

Swingin' Along XXX For exactly three minutes of its otherwise tedious length, this stupid little film about a songwriting contest cheers up; that is when Ray Charles is inserted singing 'What'd I Say', with utter irrelevance. Barbara Eden is the only person with anything remotely resembling stardom in this mess, which was directed by Charles Barton in 1962. (c)

Swing Time √ One of the lesser Astaire-Rogers, with Fred as compulsive gambler, late for his wedding to Betty Furness. Rather fortunate, as Ginger is waiting in the wings. George Stevens directed; 1936. (b/w)

The Switch XX Gormless kidnap drama with wooden Anthony Steel and Zena Marshall; director Peter Maxwell; 1964. (b/w)

The Sword of Ali Baba XX Crafty 1965 remake of 1940 *Ali Baba and the Forty Thieves*, using some of the original actors (e.g. Frank Puglia) and miles of the original footage as a way of bringing in a cheap cheapie. It's about how Ali Baba and his thieves liberate their country and his sweetheart. Director: Virgil Vogel. (c)

Sword of Sherwood Forest X Richard Greene, Richard Greene riding through the glen. Terence Fisher turned out a long episode from the old tele-series in this obvious tale about plotting the death of the Archbishop of Canterbury; 1960. (c)

Sylvia X Private eye George Maharis is hired to investigate murky past of bad-girl-turned-good Carroll Baker by her rich fiancé. Such inadequate casting of the main part couldn't have made director Gordon Douglas' job any easier. Nor does the presence of Joanne Dru, Peter Lawford, Viveca Lindfors, Nancy Kovack as mostly flashback characters inspire, although Ann Sothern and Edmond O'Brien do turn in a couple of neat cameos. What he turns up clears the way for a new romance – 'twixt detective and detected; 1965. (b/w)

The System X Unpleasant early (1964) example of permissive (i.e. cashing-in on sex and sadism) British cinema, directed by Michael Winner. Oliver Reed is girl-chasing, seaside photographer; Jane Merrow, Barbara Ferris, Julia Foster his prey. (b/w)

T

Taggart √ Dan Duryea rides away with western from R. G. Springsteen about Tony Young seeking revenge on his father's murderers. He finds himself the object of a search by nasty gunslingers; 1965. (c)

The Take X Impossible to tell the goodies from the baddies in this dense yarn of the syndicate and bent cops in New Mexico. However, there is a certain amount of fun to be had watching Robert Hartford-Davis's slick direction of Eddie Albert, Frankie Avalon, heavies Vic Morrow and Albert Salmi, and black anti-hero (Billy Dee Williams); 1974. (c)

Take a Giant Step √ Honourable failure from British director of children, Philip Leacock, to dramatise the pressures of an American black child growing up in a white world. Modestly ambitious and stout without name players, it's all too middle-class and muted to make the impact it could have done if set lower in the social scale. Here, it is the family maid who helps the teenager win through and take the title step. And how many families have maids? 1958. (b/w)

Take a Girl Like You XX Sad to have to report that Jonathan Miller (director) and George Melly (script) failed to breathe any life into Kingsley Amis's old-fashioned plot of virginity and seduction. They are not helped by principals Hayley Mills, Oliver Reed and Noel Harrison; 1970. (c)

Take Care of My Little Girl X Over-dramatic 1951 college yarn with Jeanne Crain, Mitzi Gaynor, Jean Peters among the gals, Dale Robertson, Jeffrey Hunter among the beaux. All about how the fraternity system of clubs for freshmen is so dangerous; but why should you care? Jean Negulesco attempts to wring out your handkerchief. (c)

Take Her, She's Mine X Tired generation-gap comedy, desperately trying to get with 1964 but out-of-date before it begins. If James Stewart weren't such a big star with the possibility of choosing his own scripts (Nunnally Johnson from a play by P. & H. Ephron) and director (Henry Koster, who also produces), one would be sorry to see him floundering as Sandra Dee's worried father. Robert Morley is also in it, but has no real part to play. A mess. (c)

Take Me High XX Cliff Richard as a merchant banker? Who did director David Askey think he was kidding in 1973? Hugh Griffith, George Cole, Richard Wattis couldn't save this 'comedy'. Not surprising when the main plot device is a wonderful Birmingham hamburger, the 'Brumburger'. (c)

Take Me Out to the Ball Game √ Gene Kelly and Frank Sinatra not only play the most popular turn-of-the-century song-and-dance team, but they are also the star sportsmen in a baseball side that Edward Arnold is trying to wreck. You can see how Kelly wins the pennant and the girl (Esther Williams), while Frankie has to make do with the comedy support, Betty Garrett and six so-so songs. Busby Berkeley directed; 1949. (c)

Take Me to Town X Ann Sheridan, a naughty crook on the run, lands up at a logging camp where she falls for preacher Sterling Hayden and his three lovable (?) moppets. Douglas Sirk did as competent as possible job with this unpromising material in 1953. (c)

Take My Life XX Ronald Neame's first directorial effort (1947): a mystery about Greta Gynt found murdered after a tiff with husband Hugh Williams. Francis L. Sullivan's prosecuting counsel was played with his usual style, but not much else is worth looking at. (b/w)

Take the High Ground X If you happen to like films about tough recruiting sergeants, filmed on location at a real military training establishment, you may enjoy this. For the rest of us, the sight of Richard Widmark and Karl Malden being tamed by the love of a good woman (Elaine Stewart) and director Richard Brooks is less appealing; 1953. (c)

Take the Money and Run √√ Woody Allen's reputation has gone up and up since this 1969 effort, directing himself as a habitual criminal. Judged in the context of his later, more overtly philosophical, work, it has resonances not apparent at the time, and seems even funnier. (c)

Taking Off √ Rapturously received in 1971, this first American feature by accomplished Czech emigré Milos Forman can now be seen to have benefited more by his reputation than his skill. The plot, about parents of runaway teenagers, is woolly; the observation (particularly in the celebrated scene where middle-class parents try pot) askew; the acting mechanical. However, as a curiosity, it retains a certain interest. (c)

The Taking of Pelham 123 √√ Exciting hijack thriller in which the vehicle is an underground train; Robert Shaw, Martin Balsam among the hijackers. With sharp direction by Joseph Sargent and Walter Matthau cast as the detective in charge, there is much to recommend it; 1974. (c)

A Tale of Two Cities √√ (1) A far, far better film than has ever been made since of this Dickens novel. Ronald Colman splendidly directed by Jack Conway in 1935 drama of moral necessity. (b/w)

A Tale of Two Cities √ (2) Muted but adequate British 1957 remake of Dickens's honourable tale. T. E. B. Clarke script balances Ralph Thomas direction. Dirk Bogarde's Carton excited a generation of schoolgirls; solid support from Dorothy Tutin, Cecil Parker, Athene Seyler. (b/w)

Tales of Beatrix Potter √√ Known as 'Dancing Animals' in our house, where it was one of the most-viewed cassettes by our 3-year-old daughter, this balletic adaptation of Squirrel Nutkin (Wayne Sleep) and friends is resolutely stage-bound but very beguiling; Reginald Mills; 1971. (c)

The Tales of Hoffmann XX Michael Powell and Emeric Pressburger's attempt to repeat the earlier success of their *Red Shoes* floundered in 1951. Without a strong story, the combination of ballet and opera seemed a heavy slog. Robert Helpmann, Moira Shearer, Bruce Dargavel, Monica Sinclair, Robert Rounseville. (c)

Tales of Manhattan √ Can we hope to see the W. C. Fields episode restored to this collection of short stories? It was cut out of the 1942 release because it made an already long film overlength. Julien Duvivier had smashing cast: Henry Fonda, Rita Hayworth, Ginger Rogers, Charles Boyer, Edward G. Robinson, Charles Laughton (great as a conductor) among others. They carry some weak anecdotes. (b/w)

Tales of Terror √√ Three baroque exercises from Edgar Allan Poe put together by Roger Corman and his team of creepie-crawlers. Vincent Price stars in all three; in *Morella* he's a hermit who's haunted; in *The Black Cat* he is walled-up while still alive by Peter Lorre; and in *The Case of Mr Valdemar* he's a ghost who haunts Basil Rathbone. Splendid stuff, gorgeously done; 1963. (c)

Tall Man Riding X The man is Randolph Scott, concerned at seeing fair play for Dorothy Malone and others when crooked ranchers manoeuvre to get more than their fair share of the land being granted to Montana settlers. Lesley Selander's direction doesn't rise above routine western; 1955. (c)

The Tall Men √ Strong cast: Clark Gable, Cameron Mitchell as brothers who come to rob but stay to make more money legally as cattle runners, plus Mae Marsh and Jane Russell. But it's a weak plot and Raoul Walsh never seems happy with this 1955 effort. (c)

Tall Story X Notable only as Jane Fonda's film debut, this 1960 college comedy paired her with Anthony Perkins as earnest biology students who finally get to put it all in practice, strictly legitimately, of course. Director Joshua Logan was her godfather and that's how she got the part and her start; sweet are the uses of nepotism. (b/w)

The Tall Stranger √ It's Joel McCrea, who helps the wagon-train that rescues

him from difficulties to get through Colorado in 1865, winning the heart of Virginia Mayo on the way. Thomas Carr does it all very well; 1957. (c)

The Tall T √ Expert western director Budd Boetticher makes more of routine Randolph Scott battling with Richard Boone and hold-up gang than you would have thought possible with the material. Maureen O'Sullivan the gal in the stage-coach; 1957. (c)

The Tall Target √ .... is President Lincoln, whom Dick Powell prevents from being assassinated between election and taking office in 1850s. Anthony Mann made this suspenser-on-a-train (going to Baltimore) adequately exciting stuff in 1951. Adolphe Menjou, Will Geer, Paula Raymond make splendid back-ups. (b/w)

Tamahine XX Effort about Polynesian girl in English public school. Dennis Price manages the part of the headmaster by remaining aloof from the script, which has Nancy Kwan being both outrageous and decorous at the same time. Philip Leacock seems unhappy with the comedy and never gets a chance to develop his strength, the direction of children; 1963. (c)

The Tamarind Seed X British Government employee Julie Andrews falls for Russian military attaché, to the dismay of both their bosses. The fact that the liaison is innocent could have made a genuinely interesting boy-loses-girl plot. But director Blake Edwards has reduced it to conventional spy stuff, and his very ordinary direction vitiates the suspense; 1974. (c)

The Taming of the Shrew √√ Who's Afraid of William Shakespeare? Not Franco Zeffirelli, to judge from this cheerful making-over of the Shakespeare story and some of the text. Liz Taylor and Richard Burton play it like an amalgam of the Albee play combined with *Kiss Me Kate*. Rest of the performances (Cyril Cusack, Michael Hordern, Alfred Lynch, Victor Spinetti, Alan Webb, Natasha Pyne, Michael York) are watered down rep. Nevertheless there's an engaging vitality about it all, which is very Italian, and the crowding of every inch of screen with gesticulating extras is hypnotic; 1967. (c)

Tammy ... XX Cutie-pants country-gal teenager who gets into all sorts of romantic scrapes:

... and the Bachelor: 1957, played by Debbie Reynolds who nurses pilot Leslie Nielsen back to health; King

Kong's playmate Fay Wray is in the cast. Joseph Pevney directed. (c)

... and the Doctor: 1963, played by Sandra Dee. Dr Peter Fonda woos her in the big city. Harry Keller directed. (c)

... and the Millionaire: 1967, played by Debbie Watson. Inspirational stuff worked up from an unsuccessful TV pilot. Sidney Miller directed. (c)

... Tell Me True: 1961, played by Sandra Dee. She goes to college, and is ever so helpful to old folk and the Dean. Tiresome stuff. Harry Keller directed. (c)

Tap Roots X Civil War drama in Mississippi about Van Heflin and Susan Hayward's tempestuous – or at least that was the idea – love story, played against a background of battles for states-rights. Unfortunately, George Marshall couldn't get it going, partly due to miscasting of Boris Karloff and Julie London; 1948. (c)

Tarantula √ If you're one of those people who get scared at the very idea of a spider being in the room, give this horror-pic about a giant, indestructible species that escapes from a lab a miss. Jack Arnold squeezes the last drop of chills from shivery story, and Leo G. Carroll, John Agar, Mara Corday abet him happily; 1955. (b/w)

Taras Bulba XX Mish-mash of epic proportion about Poles and Cossacks in the 16th century that should have thundered home with swords flying, but sinks in an ever-increasing apathy of plot and spectacle for spectacle's sake. Yul Brynner makes a singularly unsympathetic Taras, and Tony Curtis less than convincing Andrei Bulba, with his wife (of the moment – 1962) Christine Kaufmann apparently included as part of his contract. It has its moments (like the Polish horsemen tricked into toppling over a cliff) but it never convinces, never grips, never really entertains. Culprit: director J. Lee Thompson. (c)

Target Earth XX One of those mechanical movies about robots invading. Director Sherman Rose and the acting of Virginia Grey and Richard Denning make it difficult to tell which of the cast are supposed to be playing automata; 1954. (b/w)

Targets √√ Startlingly good debut by Peter Bogdanovich in 1968 who not only wrote, produced and directed, but actually appears as the cinéaste director who convinces Boris Karloff to make a personal appearance. Mean-while, an innocent-looking madman is stalking the city with a rifle, picking off passers-by haphazardly. How the two meet up at a drive-in movie is compelling and exciting. Bogdanovich went on to direct the Oscar-winning *The Last Picture Show.* (c)

Target Unknown √ Wartime drama of escaping bomber crew inside France with vital information. Inventive George Sherman had some competent players in Gig Young, Mark Stevens, Alex Nichol; 1951. (b/w)

The Tarnished Angels √ Respectable 1957 adaptation of William Faulkner's *Pylon,* telling the story of a First World War flyer who comes back to do stunts to thrill the crowds and has to choose between crashing into a lake or risking the crowd that has swarmed on to a landing field. Douglas Sirk has made the flying scenes exciting and has managed as well by the more intimate scenes – between flyer Robert Stack, wife Dorothy Malone and reporter Rock Hudson – as the range of these limited actors permits. (b/w)

Tarzan √ Edgar Rice Burroughs's English lord who grew up in the jungle with the apes had already been the hero of eight silent pictures by the time Johnny Weissmuller swung on to the scene. At least 15 actors have played the part, and there's no point in assessing all the movies, which are as alike as monkeys in a cage.

Here are the titles, years, directors, Tarzans and (where applicable) Janes:
Tarzan the Ape Man, 1932; W. S. Van Dyke, Johnny Weissmuller, Maureen O'Sullivan. (b/w)
Tarzan the Fearless, 1933; Robert Hill, Buster Crabbe. (b/w)
Tarzan and his Mate, 1934; Cedric Gibbons, Johnny Weissmuller, Maureen O'Sullivan. (b/w)
New Adventures of Tarzan, 1935; Edward Kull and W. F. McGough, Herman Brix. (b/w)
Tarzan Escapes, 1936; Richard Thorpe, Johnny Weissmuller, Maureen O'Sullivan. (b/w)
Tarzan and the Green Goddess, 1938; Edward Kull, Herman Brix. (b/w)
Tarzan's Revenge, 1938; D. Ross Lederman, Glenn Morris. (b/w)
Tarzan Finds a Son!, 1939; Richard Thorpe, Johnny Weissmuller, Maureen O'Sullivan. (b/w)
Tarzan's Secret Treasure, 1941; Richard Thorpe, Johnny Weissmuller, Maureen O'Sullivan. (b/w)

Tarzan's New York Adventure, 1942; Richard Thorpe, Johnny Weissmuller, Maureen O'Sullivan. (*b/w*)

Tarzan Triumphs, 1943; William Thiele, Johnny Weissmuller. (*b/w*)

Tarzan's Desert Mystery, 1943; William Thiele, Johnny Weissmuller. (*b/w*)

Tarzan and the Amazons, 1945; Kurt Neumann, Johnny Weissmuller, Brenda Joyce. (*b/w*)

Tarzan and the Leopard Woman, 1946; Kurt Neumann, Johnny Weissmuller, Brenda Joyce. (*b/w*)

Tarzan and the Huntress, 1946; Kurt Neumann, Johnny Weissmuller, Brenda Joyce. (*b/w*)

Tarzan and the Mermaids, 1948; Robert Florey, Johnny Weissmuller, Brenda Joyce. (*b/w*)

Tarzan's Magic Fountain, 1949; Lee Sholem, Lex Barker, Brenda Joyce. (*b/w*)

Tarzan and the Slave Girl, 1950; Lee Sholem, Lex Barker, Vanessa Brown. (*b/w*)

Tarzan's Peril, 1951; Byron Haskin, Lex Barker, Viginia Huston. (*b/w*)

Tarzan's Savage Fury, 1952; Cy Endfield, Lex Barker, Dorothy Hart. (*b/w*)

Tarzan and the She-Devil, 1953; Kurt Neumann, Lex Barker, Joyce MacKenzie. (*b/w*)

Tarzan's Hidden Jungle, 1955; Harold Schuster, Gordon Scott. (*b/w*)

Tarzan and the Lost Safari, 1957; H. Bruce Humberstone, Gordon Scott. (*c*)

Tarzan's Fight for Life, 1958; H. Bruce Humberstone, Gordon Scott, Eva Brent. (*c*)

Tarzan, the Ape Man, 1959; Joseph Newman, Dennis Miller, Joanna Barnes. (*c*)

Tarzan's Greatest Adventure, 1959; John Guillermin, Gordon Scott. (*c*)

Tarzan the Magnificent, 1960; Robert Day, Gordon Scott. (*c*)

Tarzan Goes to India, 1962; John Guillermin, Jock Mahoney. (*c*)

Tarzan's Three Challenges, 1963; Robert Day, Jock Mahoney. (*c*)

Tarzan and the Valley of Gold, 1966; Robert Day, Mike Henry. (*c*)

Tarzan and the Great River, 1967; Robert Day, Mike Henry. (*c*)

Tarzan and the Jungle Boy, 1968; Robert Gordon, Mike Henry. (*c*)

Tarzan's Deadly Silence, 1970; Robert L. Friend and Laurence Dobkin, Ron Ely. (*c*)

Tarzan's Jungle Rebellion, 1970; William Witney, Ron Ely. (*c*)

A Taste of Excitement X You know that old plot about the girl who saw a murder and is now lined up as the next victim, but nobody will believe her except an apparently nice young man? You do? Then don't bother to watch it again. Eva Renzi's the girl, David Buck the bloke. Even Peter Vaughan can't do much with the detective director Don Sharp has him play. 1968. (*c*)

Taste of Fear √ Susan Strasberg was the American 'star' dragged over from the US to make this 1961 Hammer mystery acceptable to American audiences, but her performance was so poor that her presence reduced an already weak concept to practically nothing. Ann Todd does her spirited best as one who may or may not be in a plot to disinherit heiress Strasberg but neither her nor director Seth Holt's occasionally brilliant efforts could save a basically silly and unsurprising script (from Jimmy Sangster) from the hole in the central performance. (*b/w*)

A Taste of Honey √√ Triumphant 1961 translation of Shelagh Delaney's successful play into a strong and moving film, distinguished by outstanding performances from Rita Tushingham as the independent, pregnant girl; Murray Melvin as the homosexual who adores and helps her; Dora Bryan as her cow of a mother. Tony Richardson has done more than open out the play; he has taken the cast to locations (none of it is studio-shot) and let them live the story. (*b/w*)

Tawny Pipit √ Comfortable, very British mini-drama about rare bird threatened by army tanks and egg-collectors. Bernard Miles directed himself in 1944 premature environmental plea. (*b/w*)

Tea and Sympathy √ Vincente Minnelli's 1956 version of the schoolmaster's wife who touchingly thinks she has cured a lad of the fear of homosexuality by sleeping with him. Trouble is everyone else connected with the film and the play seemed to think so too. Ah well, 1956 was a long time ago. The Kerrs – Deborah and John (no kin) - do a sturdy job of acting. (*c*)

Teacher's Pet √√ Clark Gable, tough editor, accidentally becomes journalism-teacher Doris Day's evening class pupil, which leads to complications with her unsteady steady Gig Young.

George Seaton made it zing; 1958. (b/w)

Tea for Two √ No, No Nanette updated to 1950 for Doris Day and Gordon MacRae is stronger on the songs ('I Only Have Eyes for You' is added) and comedy (S. Z. Sakall, Billy de Wolfe, Eve Arden) than on soppy plot about heiress who can't back show because she has been cheated of her money. David Butler directed cheerfully. (c)

Teahouse of the August Moon √√ Beguiling and often oddly touching comedy of East meets West with conquering Americans on a rehabilitation scheme for a village in Okinawa. Thanks to Marlon Brando's beautifully-realised interpreter, the project to build a school becomes a teahouse (which serves more than tea) and the not-so-simple peasants run rings round their masters. Glenn Ford diminishes his part, but Eddie Albert as an Army psychoanalyst sent to investigate and seduced by the charms of the local geisha girl (Rashomon's Machiko Kyo) is delightful. Altogether a 1956 success for director Daniel Mann. (c)

Teenage Rebel X Dated mother-daughter drama with divorcée Ginger Rogers as Mum the only point of interest; everything else (plot, background, assumptions, Edmund Goulding's direction) is machine-tooled and unengaging; 1956. (b/w)

Tell Me That You Love Me, Junie Moon X Pretty tasteless stuff from Otto Preminger, with scar-faced Liza Minelli setting up house with two other misfits. Spiced with jokes, it tries desperately to be compassionate and understanding but is too clumsy; 1969. (c)

Tell Them Willie Boy is Here √√ Outstanding western written and directed by Abraham Polonsky in 1969, in which a fugitive Indian seeks the identity refused him by the white man; Robert Blake, and Katharine Ross as his girlfriend, do splendidly as fugitives; Robert Redford, Barry Sullivan, Susan Clark make the whites seem real. (c)

The Ten Commandments √ Like nothing so much as those huge Victorian bibles with an engraving per page, Cecil B. De Mille remade his 33-year-old silent classic into a vast, sprawling epic with such modern conveniences as colour, wide-screen, plagues inflicted by a green hand from the sky, tablets engraved by neon magic and a cast-list containing the most obvious and unsuitable stars in the 1956 firmament – Yul Brynner as the Pharaoh, Anne Baxter, Edward G. Robinson, Yvonne de Carlo, Vincent Price, John Carradine (as Aaron!), Douglas Dumbrille, Debra Paget and Charlton Heston as a handsome Moses. The result has little to do with religion and a great deal to do with worshipping the golden calf. As for the pictures themselves, full as they are with people, they look uncannily like those Victorian plates: those costumes come out of De Mille's memory of childhood, oleographs, not the period when it was lived. (c)

Tender is the Night XX 1962 travesty of F. Scott Fizgerald's 1934 novel, with Jennifer Jones woefully inadequate as tragic Zelda-figure. Jason Robards as psychiatrist who marries her and Joan Fontaine as sister slog their way through turgid script (Fitzgerald had done one himself that nobody wanted) and Henry King's direction. Authentic Riviera and Zurich locations aren't nearly enough. (c)

The Tender Trap √ Bachelor Frank Sinatra thinks there's nothing wrong, then Snap! he's caught in Debbie Reynolds' t.t. Impeccable support from Celeste Holm, Lola Albright, David Wayne and director Charles Walters; 1955. (c)

Ten Gentlemen from West Point √ George Montgomery as downtrodden goodie and Laird Cregar as Commanding Officer in story about early days at the famous US military academy. Henry Hathaway, who directed in 1942, can't salute the flag with the same nostalgic devotion as John Ford, but his skill gets him by. (b/w)

Ten Little Indians √ Who invited the ten people to the lonely castle on the Austrian mountain-top and is killing them off, one-by-one? Answer is the great surprise twist in this game of ten green bottles falling off the wall – dead. (The other question – why on earth should they go in response to an invitation from someone they don't know? – isn't even asked, let alone answered.) Agatha Christie's splendid whodunit – which used to be called Ten Little Niggers, but is surely almost as offensive under its new name – is cheerfully acted by Leo Genn, Wilfrid Hyde White, Dennis Price, among others. George Pollock doesn't try to impose any directional style – or, alas, speed; 1966. (b/w)

Ten North Frederick X Conventional weeper adapted from John O'Hara's novel about man supposedly too old for love that he finds when visiting his daughter in New York. Gary Cooper's the man, Suzy Parker the girl, and Geraldine Fitzgerald his pushing wife. He's so decent it hurts, as does Philip Dunne's puffing script and direction; 1958. (b/w)

10 Rillington Place √ John Hurt's marvellous portrayal of the dupe Evans fails to redeem Richard Attenborough's false, fat Christie and Richard Fleischer's over-dramatic 1970 direction. However, the film's heart is in the right place and should make pro-hangers rethink. (c)

Ten Seconds to Hell √ Pretentious, poorly-cast (imagine anyone thinking that Jeff Chandler and Jack Palance could stand for the two conflicting sides of Man's nature) thriller about bomb-disposal men in Berlin at war's end. Robert Aldrich is always good for a few cataclysmic excitements, but this one tried just too hard with inferior material; 1959. (b/w)

Ten Tall Men √ Foreign legion jollification, not to be taken seriously, with Burt Lancaster beau-gesting his way through desert adventures. George Tobias, Gilbert Roland support; Jody Lawrance is a princess; director, Willis Goldbeck; 1951. (c)

Ten Thousand Bedrooms XX Dean Martin choosing between two boring sisters (Eva Bartok, Anna Maria Alberghetti) in Rome is tiresome, obvious stuff that even the background can't lift. Richard Thorpe came up with a yawny in this 1957 would-be romantic comedy. (c)

Ten Wanted Men X Randolph Scott *v.* Richard Boone again. This time they are older generation involved in scrap over whether Jocelyn Brando, Boone's daughter, should be allowed to marry Scott's nephew, Skip Homeir. H. Bruce Humberstone makes it all very ho-hum; 1955. (c)

Teresa √ GI John Ericson brings back war-bride Pier Angeli to the States. Future star Rod Steiger was in the lower reaches of Fred Zinnemann's undistinguished cast list in 1951. (b/w)

Term of Trial √√ 15-year-old girl gets a crush on teacher, tries to seduce him and when scorned (or at least gently repulsed) cries Rape. On this firm outline – with a couple of deliberate twists of the knife and the plot – Peter Glenville has built a strong drama,

never less than compelling. His cast could almost have carried the film by themselves: Olivier as a schoolmaster perfect down to his shoelaces; Sarah Miles, at 19 (in 1962) already accomplished sex-pot enough for the part; Simone Signoret as the teacher's affectionate, exasperated wife. (b/w)

A Terrible Beauty √ Well, pretty terrible, anyway. Robert Mitchum is an IRA man who is first seen raiding Ulster and shooting British soldiers up and then reneging on the IRA after they won't rescue buddy-buddy Richard Harris. So he escapes to England and Anne Heywood instead. This having-it-both-ways drama comes out as a British gangster movie under Tay Garnett's direction. Incidentally, the period is at the height of the Second World War and Mitchum's exploits are timed to coincide with a Nazi invasion, though it was made in 1960. (b/w)

The Terror √ Roger Corman certainly was, in 1964. The publicity for this horror-quickie claimed that it was written on a wet Sunday afternoon (pity the weather cleared up in the evening, they might have tied up loose ends of the plot) and shot in three days. There are a few stock shots (from *The Fall of the House of Usher*) and the sets have all been used before too (the graveyard in *The Premature Burial*, the hall in *The Raven*, the torture chamber in *The Pit and the Pendulum*) but there are several new and imaginative scenes. Unfortunately, the actors seem to have been hurried through without any time to grasp their characters or their lines, and Jack Nicholson gives a non-performance as the hero. Boris Karloff seems bemused. (c)

Tess of the Storm Country √ Diane Baker plays Grace Miller White's heroine in Pennsylvania Dutch America from Scotland and is involved in local quarrels. If you like unpretentious, rather solid costume drama, you might enjoy it, despite uninspired direction from Paul Guilfoyle; 1960. (c)

Test Pilot √ Clark Gable versus Spencer Tracy (on and off the set) made this 1938 flying drama more tense than director Victor Fleming had reckoned. Myrna Loy is the girl they meet. (b/w)

Texas Across the River X Dressy western played for laughs has the too-charming Alain Delon as a Spanish nobleman fleeing to Texas after being accused of killing his sweetheart's fiancé. Dean Martin, a gunrunner, pals up with him, leaving most of the jokes for Joey Bishop, playing his deadpan Red Indian mate. Michael Gordon tried hard, perhaps too hard; 1966. (c)

Texas Carnival X Waterlogged musical with Esther Williams, Howard Keel, Ann Miller, sunk by forgettable songs and soggy plot. Directed 1951 by Charles Walters. (c)

Texas Lady X That's no Texan, that's Claudette Colbert. She gambles to pay back her father's debts and takes over a newspaper in the process. Then she starts crusading. It's not really the chic Parisienne's glass of vermouth, though. Tim Whelan directs straightforwardly and Barry Sullivan is the man in her life; 1955. (c)

The Texas Rangers √ (1) 1936 King Vidor-directed big western about Lloyd Nolan turning on old chums Fred MacMurray, Jack Oakie. (b/w)

The Texas Rangers X (2) 1951 effort – not a remake – with director Phil Karlson doing usual competent job with Texas outlaws forming a gun-slingers' co-op to oppose George Montgomery and mates. An uphill ride. (c)

That Certain Feeling XX Of heart-sinking when faced with yet another Bob Hope session of wisecracks, misunderstanding, double-takes, all coming right in the end. In 1956 he was a cartoonist who got together with ex-wife Eva Marie Saint. George Sanders gives a certain life to his scenes; Pearl Bailey is on hand to sing the title-song and know her place as a coloured maid. Panama and Frank. (c)

That Funny Feeling √ Mistaken identity boy-meets-girl comedy with a certain plastic glossiness which makes it an entertaining if forgettable watch. Richard Thorpe swiftly whistles Sandra Dee and Bobby Darin through a thin-ice plot, while Lary Storch and Donald O'Connor keep it going amusingly enough; 1965. (c)

That Kind of Woman √ Keenan Wynn walks away with this one as the pimp-cum-personal assistant of George Sanders, keeping an eye on his two mistresses, Sophia Loren and Barbara Nichols. What could have been a sharp look at the morals of rich businessmen becomes a trite sailors-on-leave comedy when Tab Hunter and Jack Warden arrive, but Wynn keeps bringing it back to what Sidney Lumet perhaps first conceived but couldn't

deliver because of Walter Bernstein's weak 1958 script and the wishes of producers Carlo Ponti and Marcello Girosi. (b/w)

That Lady X Costumer set at the Spanish court of 1570 with proud Olivia de Havilland's love having to be sacrificed. Paul Scofield gamely plays a small part, managing to hide – almost – what he must have thought of the script based on Kate O'Brien novel. Gilbert Roland, on the other hand, seems to be enjoying himself. Terence Young fumbled along directionally in 1954. (c)

That'll Be the Day √ Pretentious pop vehicle (script: Ray Connolly, direction: Claude Whatham) for 1973 Keith Moon, in holiday-camp band. Ringo Starr, his mate; Billy Fury and Keith Moon, in holiday camp band. The songs are OK. (c)

That Man in Istanbul X Just another spy melo, played partly for laughs, as lady FBI agent (Sylvia Koscina) posing as unemployed stripper, searches for kidnapped scientist. Anthony Isasi manages cloak-and-dagger location shooting adequately, but Horst Buchholz and Koscina quickly grow tiresome; 1966. (c)

That Night √ Neo-realism in New York, 1957, in which John Beal decides that a heart-attack is nature's way of telling him to get out of the rat race. Scene in subway when he's taken ill among callous commuters is well done, but then it becomes a bit over-sentimental. John Newland brings a certain force and freshness to the direction. (b/w)

That Riviera Touch X That rib-tickling touch, so gloriously present in their television programmes, has so far escaped Morecambe and Wise when they've made movies. Yet this second of their three attempts, made in 1966, used their then regular script-writers, Sid Green and Dick Hills, and a more than competent director, Cliff Owen. What went wrong, then, with this escapade about jewel thieves in the South of France? Well, partly there's no audience for them to play against, and partly all concerned have been seduced by the idea of having a plot. (c)

That's Entertainment √ You wouldn't think that Jack Haley Jr. could have gone wrong with all the MGM musicals to cannibalise, but despite some absolutely marvellous moments – mostly much seen elsewhere on the telly – the whole enterprise seems portentous and poorly orchestrated. The device of having each bit introduced by stars who are in other chunks becomes as sickly as one of those televised industry award affairs; 1974. (c)

That's My Boy √ Jerry Lewis as timid hypochondriac, bullied by athletic father (frighteningly well played by Eddie Mayehoff) to get into the college football team. Although you can spot the ending a stadium-length away, this 1951 Lewis-and-Martin comedy is sufficiently in director Hal Walker's control to make it fitfully funny. (b/w)

That Touch of Mink √√ Delicious Doris Day comedy from Delbert Mann, with Cary Grant only getting her to bed when the wedding ring's firmly through his nose (it's 1962, remember). John Astin almost walks away with it all with a dreadfully true portrait of a wolf who has nothing to offer but his imaginary idea of himself; and Gig Young and Audrey Meadows do some pretty nifty scene-stealing of their own. (c)

That Woman Opposite XX Little whodunit written and directed by Compton Bennett from John Dickson Carr's novel, *The Emperor's Snuffbox*. One of those British quickies which was supposed to invade the American market, in 1957, this one had Phyllis Kirk and Dan O'Herlihy backed up by Petula Clark, Wilfrid Hyde White and Jack Watling. Clumsy. (b/w)

Theatre of Blood √ Vincent Price plays a sensitive star, understandably hurt by his bad notices. He decides to murder the critics, one by one, in ways that parody episodes in Shakespeare's plays. Douglas Hickox has great fun directing luminaries Diana Rigg, Robert Morley, Dennis Price, Harry Andrews, Ian Hendry, Michael Hordern, Jack Hawkins; 1973. (c)

Their Secret Affair √ Warner Brothers bought J. P. Marquand's novel *Melville Goodwin USA* for Humphrey Bogart and Lauren Bacall. But when Bogart fell ill (he died just as this picture was released in 1957) they gave it to Kirk Douglas and Susan Hayward, at the same time changing the plot so much that only the characters were left. Douglas is a general, Hayward a *Time*-like magazine publisher out to discredit him. In scenes palely reminiscent of *The Philadelphia Story*, she tries to compromise him at her fancy Long Island home, with concealed photographers. After she

falls for him but discovers he's not keen on marriage, she publishes such a virulent piece about him that a Congressional Committee has to investigate. Sadly, it lacks the very light touch that director H. C. Potter might have been expected to bring to it, and remains only an exercise in satirical comedy. Paul Stewart her editor and Jim Backus as the Army PRO have a few amusing moments. (b/w)

Them! √ Effective and occasionally genuinely frightening piece of sci-fi about giant ants threatening the world. Gordon Douglas makes a highly professional job of directing both ants and hum-ants, including old reliable Edmund Gwenn as entomologist, Joan Weldon as his daughter and stolid James Arness. Nominated for special effects Oscar in 1954. (b/w)

Then Came Bronson √ – but not Charles. The star of this easy riding sentimentality is Michael Parks, who takes off from San Francisco across the country on his motorbike. On his picaresque, picturesque journey he meets up with all kinds of fascinating (?) characters, including Bonnie Bedelia, Akim Tamiroff, Sheree North, Martin Sheen. Director, William A. Graham; 1970. (c)

There's a Girl in My Soup XX Roy Boulting's adaptation of Terence Frisby's mildly funny farce goes off the top and ends in vulgarity. Peter Sellers is allowed to camp it up; Goldie Hawn makes an over-simple target for him. The gadgets are particularly boring; 1970. (c)

There's Always Tomorrow √ Superior soap-opera with Barbara Stanwyck making a Sacrifice, Fred MacMurray making Barbara Stanwyck, and Joan Bennett making the beds. Douglas Sirk ground it all out competently, but Stanwyck and MacMurray must have looked back with regret to their earlier partnership with Billy Wilder in *Double Indemnity*; 1956. (b/w)

There's No Business Like Show Business X 1954 quasiography of Irving Berlin: loud, religioso, stodgily directed by Walter Lang, stridently acted by Ethel Merman, Mitzi Gaynor, Donald O'Connor, plunged into bathos by Johnny Ray, occasionally lit by budding Marilyn Monroe. (c)

There was a Crooked Man X (1) 1960. Old-fashioned (even in 1960) comedy with Norman Widsom whose trousers don't actually fall down for a change.

Susannah York is a pleasant passenger, and Andrew Cruickshank's a villain. There's a nice send-up of a safe caper, suggesting that Stuart Burge was too good a director for this kind of film, and he didn't make any more of the genre. (b/w)

There was a Crooked Man √√ (2) 1970. Kirk Douglas v. Henry Fonda in an exciting tale of bad v. good in 1883 Arizona. Joseph L. Mankiewicz, in the last picture he directed, rallied some impressive support for baddie Douglas, including Hume Cronyn, Warren Oates, Burgess Meredith, Alan Hale. The result is an exciting yarn of treachery and come-uppance. (c)

These Dangerous Years XXX Appalling little Herbert Wilcox cheapie supposedly about Liverpool youngsters made in 1957 before Liverpool got on the map as teenage centre. George Baker, Thora Hird, John Le Mesurier lost in a morass that better suited the talents of co-stars Frankie Vaughan, Carole Lesley and Jackie Lane. (b/w)

These Thousand Hills X Ponderous western in which Don Murray has to choose between his posh friends and the whore (Lee Remick) who first put him on the road to his fortune. Richard Fleischer seems to have got out of breath climbing all those hills; 1959. (c)

These Wilder Years X Hard executive James Cagney seeks for the son he allowed to be adopted, learns humanity under tutelage of guardian angel Barbara Stanwyck and helps unmarried mother who reminds him of the girl he got into trouble all those years ago. Slushy stuff, directed by Roy Rowland in uninspired fashion. Was originally meant as vehicle for Debbie Reynolds to be called *All Our Tomorrows*; 1956. (b/w)

They Call Me Mister Tibbs X Unsequential sequel to *In the Heat of the Night* has Sidney Poitier in a routine 1970 TV-type urban thriller from uninspired director Gordon Douglas. In the hacking that must have gone on at the script or post-production stage, somebody cut out an explanation of the clumsy title. Martin Landau looks stricken as a suspected murderer of whore. There are some nauseous domestic scenes of the Tibbs family and the plot is worked out painfully slowly. (c)

They Came to Cordura XX This was such a disaster critically and at the box office in 1959 that Robert Rossen, the director, tried to salvage something of his reputation by buying up the film and re-editing it the way he wanted. But the plan came to nothing, Rossen died, and this grim memorial is left of his errors. One of them was casting veteran Gary Cooper, who at 58 was much too old for the part of commander of a small group of war heroes in Pancho Villa country. His physical listlessness seemed to have communicated itself to Van Heflin, Tab Hunter, Richard Conte and everyone around except old trooper Rita Hayworth who was still relatively peppy as prisoner suspected of collaborating. (c)

They Died with Their Boots On √ Custer's Last Stand, with Errol Flynn as far-from-cowardly Custer. Done big by Raoul Walsh, in 1941, with Olivia de Havilland, Charley Grapewin, Gene Lockhart, Anthony Quinn, Sydney Greenstreet and a lot of extras. (b/w)

They Drive By Night √√ Splendid 1940 drama of truck-driving brothers Humphrey Bogart, George Raft tackling crooked bosses, with Raoul Walsh coaxing the best out of Ida Lupino, Ann Sheridan, Alan Hale. (b/w)

They Live By Night √√ Cleaning-up of Edward Anderson's novel *Thieves Like Us*: the new title doesn't divulge that star-crossed lovers Farley Granger and Cathy O'Donnell are not all good. Directed by Nicholas Ray (1948), they emerge as sympathetic figures. Remade in 1973 by Robert Altman, under the book's original title. (b/w)

They Might Be Giants √√ An attractive curiosity: George C. Scott as a lawyer with the delusion he is Sherlock Holmes, and Joanne Woodward a psychiatrist named Dr Watson, tracking a villain through modern New York. Director Anthony Harvey steers a path between whimsy and literalness, emerging with a thriller that is almost touching and certainly inventive; 1972. (c)

They Only Kill Their Masters √ Whodunit with James Garner as detective in a small community having to decide which of a cast of old-time favourites (Hal Holbrook, June Allyson, Tom Ewell, Peter Lawford, Edmond O'Brien, Ann Rutherford) is involved in a woman's death. Stronger on atmosphere than plot, this 1972 effort by director James Goldstone will pass a comfortable 100 minutes;

unfortunately, Katharine Ross is the romantic interest. (c)

They Rode West √ Phil Karlson made this into a better than average western, concentrating on the dilemma of a young army doctor who wants to go and save Indian tribe hit by malaria but is called back by his commander. Robert Francis, Phil Carey do well; Donna Reed is plucky gal; 1954. (c)

They Shoot Horses, Don't They √√ Evocative and full of suspense, this study of a 1932 dance marathon has some marvellous cameos, even if it finally lacks the excitement of Horace McCoy's novel. Sydney Pollack wrings some memorable performances out of his talented cast, notably Jane Fonda, Gig Young, Bruce Dern and Bonnie Bedelia; 1969. (c)

They Were Expendable √√ John Ford's classic about Robert Montgomery, John Wayne, Jack Holt, Ward Bond and other he-men involved in running untried motor torpedo boats in the Philippines at the time of Pearl Harbour; 1945. (b/w)

They Were Not Divided X Terence Young wrote and directed this 1951 war yarn, mostly about friendship between a Briton and American serving together in Europe. With Edward Underdown, Michael Trubshawe and real RSM Ronald Brittain. (b/w)

They Who Dare √ Effective war drama, with Dirk Bogarde and Denholm Elliott blowing up Nazi airfields in Rhodes, directed by Lewis Milestone in 1953. (c)

The Thief √ Back to the silent days. Ray Milland as Red spy steals atomic secrets without saying a word. In fact, nobody does. The only sound is music and effects. Russell Rouse sustains the gimmick for longer than one would have thought possible, but it does grow wearisome; 1952. (b/w)

Thief of Damascus X Over-generous *Arabian Nights* fantasy with Sinbad, Aladdin and Ali Baba all thrown in. Will Jason seemingly couldn't bear to leave anything out, and Paul Henreid, Lon Chaney and the rest look uncomfortable; but perhaps their sandals were hurting? 1952. (c)

The Thief Who Came to Dinner √ Flat crime comedy, with Ryan O'Neal as a nice diamond thief, crossing swords with cop Warren Oates. Ned Beatty is his fence, Jacqueline Bisset his girlfriend. Director Bud Yorkin; 1973. (c)

Thieves Highway √ Exciting American film by *Rififi*'s Jules Dassin, which introduced Valentina Cortese, plus Lee J. Cobb, in trucking drama; 1949. (b/w)

Thieves Like Us √√ Effective remake of Nicholas Ray's *They Live By Night*, by Robert Altman in 1973, using the novel's original title. This time Keith Carradine and Shelley Duval are the fugitives, but instead of being an innocent (as Farley Granger made him in the earlier thriller), this young man is a convicted killer who goes on using his gun, to die, *Bonnie and Clyde*-wise, by the gun. (c)

The Thing from Another World √ Arctic scientist finds space man (James Arness) and rumour says Howard Hawks may have directed, although, as producer, he gave Christian Nyby the credit. The Thing was an eight-foot vegetable with a superhuman brain. They can't kill it until someone comes up with a culinary solution; 1951. (b/w)

The Thing That Couldn't Die X Girl with power to find what is buried uncovers 400-year-old hidden casket; in it is severed head that forces her to find the rest of itself (singing I ain't got no body?). William Reynolds; Andra Martin. Will Cowan must have had his tongue in that ancient cheek in 1958. (b/w)

The Thin Man √√ Who played the part of the Thin Man in this 1934 movie? is a great movie quiz question. The answer is not William Powell; it's Edward Ellis, the first victim of the murderer. Yet somehow the title stuck to the detective, Nick Charles (William Powell), who wasn't even particularly thin, and he made five sequels, with Myrna Loy as his wisecracking wife. W. S. Van Dyke directed from a Dashiell Hammett story, which, like all the successors, gathered the suspects together for denouement. (b/w)

The Thin Man Goes Home √ William Powell, Myrna Loy in penultimate (1945) thriller of the series, in which a young man is shot on their hometown doorstep. Mild stuff, directed by Richard Thorpe. (b/w)

The Thin Red Line X James Jones's novel of feud between sadistic sergeant and young soldier taunted for stealing pistol. The private battle lasts through the Guadalcanal campaign but you may not. Ray Daley is even duller than Keir Dullea, and Andrew Marton, the director, is dullest; 1964. (b/w)

The Third Day X Car crashes into a

river, man escapes leaving girl in car. OK thriller directed in 1965 by Jack Smight, with George Peppard and brief appearance by sexy Sally Kellerman. (c)

The Third Man ✓✓✓ The only film written directly for the screen by Graham Greene, it is famous for all kinds of disparate gems: the chase in the Vienna sewers; that insistent zither music; Orson Welles' oil-drippingly sinister performance as a drug trafficker; his encounter with his disillusioned friend, Joseph Cotten, in the fairground ferris wheel; the cinema's most highly-polished aphorism (about Swiss cuckoo clocks); Carol Reed's vivid direction; and Robert Krasker's crystalline photography. A great treat, however many times you may have seen it since 1949, and an enviable one for anybody who hasn't yet seen it. (b/w)

Third Man on the Mountain X Mildly exciting mountaineering movie about assault on the Matterhorn by Michael Rennie and novice James MacArthur; 1959. (c)

The Third Secret XX A psychiatrist commits suicide except that he didn't; so which of his patients did him in? Or was it someone else? Stephen Boyd, as an unbelievable American reporter, plods round London interviewing his daughter Pamela Franklin and half-a-dozen patients, which gives a bunch of character actors (Richard Attenborough, Diane Cilento, Jack Hawkins, Alan Webb, Peter Sallis among them) a chance to do a couple of days' work in cameo parts. The answer to the puzzle is so silly as not to have been worth bothering with in the first place. Charles Crichton directed in 1964 as well as producer Robert L. Joseph's rotten script allowed. (b/w)

The Third Voice ✓ Edmond O'Brien and Laraine Day gang up to murder financier, impersonate him, and attempt to extricate his money. Unfortunately, after this neat start and adventure with Julie London, Hubert Cornfield let the whole plot peter out when it needed a slambang ending; 1960. (b/w)

13 Ghosts X You may be forgiven for thinking that the witch from *The Wizard of Oz* is haunting this old house; it's Margaret Hamilton, who played the part in the MGM classic, made up by director William Castle for the housekeeper here as close to her original part as he could get away with

without sacrificing all disbelief. It's that kind of movie, stopping just this side of spoof to stay spooky. A professor moves into this old place and it's got ghosts and treasure. How his family discover both is plot; 1960. (c)

13 Rue Madeleine ✓✓ Strong wartime thriller with James Cagney winkling out spy among the spies under director Henry Hathaway. Annabella, Richard Conte, Everett (sic) G. Marshall among supports; 1946. (b/w)

The 13th Letter ✓ A close remake of Clouzot's *Le Corbeau*, set in Canada, by Otto Preminger in 1951. Linda Darnell, Charles Boyer, Michael Rennie, Francoise Rosay are among those whose lives are affected by poison pen letter. Effective moments and some strong red herrings before who-wrote-it – and why – is revealed. But it has the feeling of a carbon-copy. (b/w)

13 West Street ✓ Alan Ladd's penultimate film had him, under Philip Leacock's direction, as electronics engineer out to revenge himself on gang of well-dressed hoodlums that beat him up. Strong stuff, with Rod Steiger as patient police sergeant and Michael Callan contributing convincing cameos; 1962. (b/w)

–30– X Jack Webb does his actor-bit on a newspaper instead of his usual draggy *Dragnet.* William Conrad among the toilers putting out a Los Angeles daily paper; 1959. (b/w)

30 Foot Bride of Candy Rock X Lou Costello (without Bud Abbott for the only time) plays amateur scientist who literally enlarges girlfriend Dorothy Provine. Sidney Miller couldn't make it sparkle; 1959. (b/w)

30 is a Dangerous Age, Cynthia ✓ There's nobody called Cynthia in this comedy, which is doubtless a very square observation to make, but a valid one. If we are expected to expend an hour and more of our valuable time on Dudley Moore's private home movies (he's the star, composer and co-author) we are entitled to some consideration, but this is one of those films that was doubtless hugely amusing to all concerned in the production, but left the paying public out in the cold. The story, such as it is, places a 29-year-old composer in the predicament of having to marry and write a musical within six weeks if he is to fulfil his self-imposed target. How he manages is told in a multitude of fantasies in which director Joe McGrath does his nut.

Whether you will even begin to do yours is quite another matter, though there are some rewarding moments, particularly when Suzy Kendall and Patricia Routledge are on the screen; 1968. (c)

36 Hours √ The Nazis kidnap army officer, con him that war is ended to extract secrets from him. George Seaton almost succeeded in 1964 in getting Rod Taylor, Eva Marie Saint, James Garner to make this fascinating but phoney premise believable. (b/w)

The Thirty-Nine Steps √√ (1) 1935 Hitchcock original with Robert Donat and Madeleine Carroll handcuffed as they flee over Scottish moors. Both before and after that climactic chase John Buchan's story of murder and spying has been treated with scant respect by Hitch, who added imaginatively to the increasing tension and action. The railway journey is particularly nerve-wracking and the denouement, where Datas the Memory Man (here called Mr Memory) is forced by his professional impulse to blurt out the right answer to Donat's question 'What are the Thirty-Nine Steps?', one of the great moments in exciting cinema. (b/w)

The Thirty-Nine Steps X (2) 1959 version lost most of the tension. Truffaut in his book-length dialogue with Hitchcock says: 'I went to see the remake that was done by Ralph Thomas, with Kenneth More. It was poorly directed and rather ridiculous, but the story is so fascinating that the audience was interested anyway. At times the breakdown followed your own very closely, but even these parts were inferior. And wherever there were changes, they were mostly all wrong.' A failure in all departments, casting (Taina Elg for Madeleine Carroll!) too. (c)

This Above All X 1942 propaganda picture uses sentiment as patriotic drum-roll; deserter (Tyrone Power) finds strength to fight again through love of posh girl (Joan Fontaine) and rector (Alexander Knox). Characteristic Anatole Litvak schmaltzy direction. (b/w)

This Angry Age X Odd international starrer set in Indo-China, with Jo Van Fleet as matriarch who tries to force Anthony Perkins and Silvana Mangano to carry on the family rice-field cultivation. Alida Valli, Nehemiah Persoff, Richard Conte don't mix well under veteran French director René Clement; 1958. (c)

This Could Be the Night X But isn't, alas. You can't overcome the disbelief that starts clanging the moment prim schoolteacher Jean Simmons takes a part-time job as secretary to Paul Douglas, who runs a nightclub. Why doesn't she leave as soon as she finds out he's a gangster? Because then there'd be no film, that's why. Which might have been preferable. As it is, Joan Blondell, Zasu Pitts, J. Carrol Naish and other faces from the past (this was made in 1957) try desperately to make it work, but director Robert Wise couldn't do it. Tony Franciosa makes the young hood who romances our nice Miss Simmons seem odd, if not actually perverse. (b/w)

This Earth is Mine! X Jean Simmons again (see previous entry), this time as the grand-daughter of a California wine-grower falling for a distant relative, Rock Hudson, who gets most of the action and the few good lines, as well as a crippling car accident and Dorothy McGuire's jealous love. Claude Rains is in there, to give extra value, and Henry King pulls out the stops with some abandon; 1959. (c)

This Gun For Hire √ Not much was left of Graham Greene's entertainment, A Gun For Sale, when Frank Tuttle directed it in 1942, not even the title. But, transposed as it was to America, it still gripped, thanks to a taut script in its own right from Albert Maltz and W. R. Burnett. Alan Ladd well fitted emotionless killer who, aided by Veronica Lake, is out to shoot man who hired him to kill and then betrayed him, a memorable performance by Laird Cregar, fat and decadent. (b/w)

This Happy Breed √ Noel Coward's chronicle of lower middle-class life through several generations has some neat observation from director David Lean and solid acting from Robert Newton, Celia Johnson, Kay Walsh, John Mills, Stanley Holloway; 1944. (c)

This Happy Feeling X Can't be brought on by the film in question. This is a dull, corny comedy of teenager Debbie Reynolds being attracted to aged (well, quite old, like 43 in 1958) Curt Jurgens who is thus considered shockingly unsuitable. Luckily young, rich, handsome John Saxon is around. Before the happy ending every member of the cast manages to fall off a horse or into a pond or something similar, and Estelle Winwood has got away with a couple of mildly funny lines. In fact, a fairly typical script-direction job by Blake Edwards. (c)

This Island Earth √ Splendid sci-fi, about an Earthly scientist (not all that convincingly played by Rex Reason) being recruited by a warring planet. Joseph M. Newman starts the action off cunningly in familiar surroundings, only gradually letting the special effects department take over. Gadget-lovers will relish it, the politically-conscious will discern a message; 1955. (c)

This is My Love X Dan Duryea is competed over, for some reason, by two sisters, Linda Darnell and Faith Domergue. As one of them is married to an invalid, it seems unnecessarily loaded against a happy ending. Stuart Heisler did his usual superior soap-operatics; 1954. (c)

This is My Street √ Wife June Ritchie has an affair with mother's lodger Ian Hendry; Battersea location. Director, Sidney Hayers; 1963. (b/w)

This Property is Condemned √ Or *A Pullman Car Named Alva* – because we're back in Tennessee Williams-land here, with Natalie Wood as the girl dreaming about a palace of a train with her name, which Robert Redford forces her to realise is just a beat-up old wagon. How she used to grant favours to the railroad men to attract them to her mother's boarding house and how Mom used this to threaten her Real Love is the plot. Director Sydney Pollack made the most of it in 1966. (c)

This Rebel Breed X Two undercover young police graduates are assigned to break up high school dope gangs. Rita Moreno, Mark Damon and Dyan Cannon (she was called Diane then, in 1960) come off best under Richard L. Bare's direction. (b/w)

This Rugged Land X Rancher Richard Egan puts justice above his living when he defends and continues to employ suspect murderer Charles Bronson. Arthur Hiller directed hurriedly; 1962. (b/w)

This Sporting Life √√ 1963 realisation by Lindsay Anderson of David Storey's novel about a rugby player and his uptight affair with his landlady has served as a model for countless films and television plays since; Richard Harris has never been nearly as good as this brute of a man who hides his realisation of the future. He was matched by a splendid performance from Rachel Roberts as the widow forced into 'respectability' by the neighbours, and excellent supporting playing (Alan Badel, William Hartnell, Colin Blakely, Vanda Godsell, Anne Cunningham, Leonard Rossiter) that extended them all past previous performances, thus indicating how much the director gave to them. The rugby games themselves remain as the best sporting photography (Denys Coop) and editing (Peter Taylor) ever seen – though both director Anderson and producer Karel Reisz must have had guiding hands in both these departments. (b/w)

This Woman is Dangerous X Joan Crawford's troubles include a serious operation, renouncing the gangster she loved for her doctor (Dennis Morgan), and then throwing him over so that her old boyfriend won't shoot him. Felix Feist directed all this stuff in 1952 with the camera instead unblinkingly on his heroine. As critic Bosley Crowther said at the time: 'For people of mild discrimination, her suffering will be matched by their own.' (b/w)

The Thomas Crown Affair √√ Urbane thriller with the unfortunate handicap that the central premise is totally unacceptable: that Steve McQueen's rich and successful businessman is so bored as to set up a bank robbery. Only slightly less credible is that Faye Dunaway is an insurance investigator. And then, of course, they fall for each other. However, if you can accept all this (and Michel Legrand's haunting but inappropriate 'Windmills of My Mind' endlessly going round and round), you will doubtless applaud director Norman Jewison's handling of Haskell Wexler's superior camera work. Warning: only those with large screens will be able to see all the action, because of Jewison's penchant for splitting it into tiny compartments and showing them all simultaneously; 1968. (c)

Thoroughly Modern Millie X Disappointing twenties lark with Julie Andrews and Mary Tyler Moore primly avoiding the clutches of Madame Beatrice Lillie. George Roy Hill just isn't the man to make *The Boy Friend*'s girlfriend appealing enough, and it doesn't get any better as it goes on and on. And on; 1967. (c)

Those Calloways √ Why have films about wild animals (or, in this case, birds) got to be so goddam cutesy?

Here we have Brian Keith, Vera Miles and Sonny Brandon de Wilde battling thru' to build a sanctuary for wild geese. Director Norman Tokar takes us on quite a chase for them, only slightly more worth going on than the proverbial one; 1965. (c)

Those Magnificent Men in Their Flying Machines X Don Sharp's second-unit directing is the best thing in this rather clumsy but sporadically amusing yarn about early flying. His are the aerial shots and they show up the rather leaden entertainment on the ground (Stuart Whitman, James Fox, Terry-Thomas and assorted comics vying for Robert Morley's early flying prize) directed by Ken Annakin; 1965. (c)

Those Redheads from Seattle X Odd mixture of music and murder of crusading newspaper owner in Alaskan gold-rush. Agnes Moorehead, Rhonda Fleming, Gene Barry seem a bit mixed-up, too, under Lewis R. Foster's direction; 1953. (c)

A Thousand Clowns √√ Funny, witty and enjoyable 1965 comedy about a TV writer who throws it all up to mooch round New York with his 12-year-old nephew. It could have been silly and whimsical (one shudders to think what some British comedians would have done with the situation), but it triumphantly sustains a cracking level and even manages to say something useful about compromise and selling-out. If director-producer Fred Coe has a fault it is not to have allowed his talented cast of Jason Robards, Barry Gordon, Barbara Harris, William Daniels, Martin Balsam and Gene Saks (as the ghastly comedian Robards writes for) quite enough rein. But it's a joy, nevertheless. (b/w)

The Thousand Plane Raid XX Unconvincing bombing war pic, with weak Christopher George leading armada to saturate factory target. Boris Sagal directed in 1968. (c)

Thousands Cheer X – but millions were disappointed in this overblown variety bill in 1943, where anyone around was jammed in to do their bit. Gene Kelly, Kathryn Grayson, Mary Astor are in central 'plot' involving putting on all-star show at army base. Among those appearing: Mickey Rooney, Judy Garland, Ann Sothern, Lucille Ball, Lena Horne, June Allyson, Red Skelton; director, George Sidney. (c)

Three Bad Sisters X Maria English, Kathleen Hughes, Sara Shane (if you've ever heard of 'em) fight each other for even greater fortunes after they inherit estate. Hard to care about their plots and violent dramas, when directed by Gilbert L. Kay; 1956. (b/w)

Three Bites of the Apple XX If it's Wednesday, this must be Italy. Dull travelogue about a courier, David McCallum, who wins a fortune at the Casino but loses his job when Tammy Grimes reports him (in revenge for not sleeping with her). You wouldn't guess it was meant to be a comedy except for the pauses that director-producer Alvin Ganzer puts in for laughs that are unlikely to come; 1967. (c)

Three Blondes in His Life XX Insurance agent is discovered to have had affairs with sexy clients and helped them swindle the company. Strictly ho-hum, under Leon Chooluck's 1960 direction. Jack Mahoney is only semi-name in it. (b/w)

Three Brave Men √ By 1957, Hollywood was trying to work its passage back from the rabid anti-Communism that characterised both its films and its local politics (e.g. the Hollywood Ten banned from working) of the previous decade. This little effort traces the story of one clerk in the Navy Department (Ernest Borgnine), wrongly smeared as a security risk. Ray Milland is a lawyer who rallies to his defence. Writer-director Philip Dunne has done well in showing how the individual can fight back in one case, but you may get a nagging feeling that there were plenty of others unjustly smeared who didn't have Ray Milland pitching for them. And how about those who did once give a dollar to a communist-front organisation and thus, by the ethics of the time, were guilty? (b/w)

Three Came Home √√ Claudette Colbert as Agnes Newton Keith, who wrote a book about her prison experiences under the Japanese. Jean Negulesco wrung equally fine performances from her and Sessue Hayakawa as camp commandant. Harrowing, heart-warming stuff; 1950. (b/w)

Three Coins in the Fountain X First of the wide-screen travelogue-injected love stories, used the Trevi Fountain in Rome as link between three romantic yarns. Jean Negulesco's sentimental style was only too well-suited to the sweetness of the stories, with Clifton Webb and Dorothy

McGuire coming out best; 1954. (c)

Three Comrades √ After the First World War, Robert Taylor, Franchot Tone and Robert Young all seek the favours of Margaret Sullavan, Bobby's girl. F. Scott Fitzgerald worked on the script from Erich Maria Remarque's novel. Frank Borzage directed in 1938. (b/w)

Three Days of the Condor √√ Ambitious CIA thriller from director Sydney Pollack and writer Lorenzo Semple: Robert Redford plays that familiar figure, the nice guy in the organisation who suddenly finds he can trust nobody. Among the ambiguous agents are Cliff Robertson, Max von Sydow, John Houseman. Forcing Faye Dunaway to give him shelter, Redford naturally becomes involved with her; 1975. (c)

The Three Faces of Eve √ Supposedly true case history, Alistair Cooke narrating. Sure, there may have been a girl like the one played by Joanne Woodward - it won her a 1957 Oscar - with three conflicting personalities, but you can bet it was a lot more complex than Nunnally Johnson's movie made out; 1957. (b/w)

Three for Bedroom C X For her first appearance after *Sunset Boulevard* come-back, Gloria Swanson was again playing a movie star in this 1952 cross-America railroad comedy about a romance between her and scientist on a train going to Los Angeles. Fred Clark, Margaret Dumont, Steve Brodie make it all seem like a ride down Memory Lane. Milton Bren directed. (c)

Three for Jamie Dawn √ What happens when the heavy mob puts the pressure on three members of a murder jury. Thomas Carr made it moderately compulsive, with help of Ricardo Montalban, Richard Carlson, June Havoc, Laraine Day; 1956. (b/w)

Three for the Show X Betty Grable, Jack Lemmon, Marge and Gower Champion in weak remake of *Too Many Husbands* (Jean Arthur - Fred MacMurray) which in turn was remake of Maugham play *Home and Beauty*. All about a husband, missing believed dead, who turns up to find his wife married again. H. C. Potter directed this one diligently but unconvincingly; 1955. (c)

Three Godfathers √ John Ford-John Wayne western about outlaws finding abandoned baby. Ignore banal attempts to parallel Bethlehem journey and concentrate on the superb photography. With Pedro Armendariz and Harry Carey Jr.; 1948. (c)

Three Guns for Texas X Strictly for lovers of *Laredo*, this is, in fact, three episodes of TV series strung together. Best of the trio is about Linda Little Trees, a far from beautiful Indian squaw (Shelley Morrison) who pursues Texas Ranger Bill Smith. David Lowell Rich; 1968. (c)

Three Guys Named Mike X Fly Jane Wyman to Miami: you might click if your name is Mike. That's about the plot of this nonsense about an air stewardess who is romanced by pilot Howard Keel, scientist Van Johnson, ad-man Barry Sullivan. Would you believe that they are all named Mike? Charles Walters wasn't taking the mickey - he just had to fly this one to a safe and happy landing; 1951. (b/w)

Three Hats for Lisa XXX Dreary little British musical about docker Joe Brown commandeering famous Italian film star Sophie Hardy (who?) and taking her round London in Sid James's taxi to look for hats. The acting, music, invention, dancing and direction (by Sidney Hayers) about the same level as the plot; 1965. (c)

Three Hours to Kill √ Dana Andrews, stagecoach driver, has just three hours to uncover real murderer of his girl's (Donna Reed) brother. Alfred L. Werker makes this 1954 western a cut above average for tension. (c)

The 300 Spartans X Richard Egan, Ralph Richardson, David Farrar, Donald Houston dress up as Greeks and Persians and fight out the Battle of Thermopylae with 300 extras. Rudolph Maté makes it a standard epic, no more; 1962. (c)

Three in the Attic X Sexploiter to titillate male fantasy of being locked up with three lovely, raping girls. Christopher Jones plays the happy (at first) victim. Director, Richard Wilson; 1968. (c)

Three into Two Won't Go √√ Judy Geeson as predatory hitch-hiker screwing up an already wobbly marriage between Rod Steiger and Claire Bloom (who were married in real life in 1969 and afterwards unscrewed themselves, too). Closely observed, it makes a convincing slice of life, neatly brought to the screen by Peter Hall from Edna O'Brien's screenplay from Andrea Newman's novel. Peggy Ashcroft makes a realistic bitchy mother for Claire Bloom; they really do look and feel like mother and daughter.

Whether a girl would really go barging into a man's home on the strength of a night in a hotel with him is another matter; but you believe it while you are watching. (c)

Three Little Girls in Blue X That old *How to Marry a Millionaire* plot (a remake, in fact, of *Three Blind Mice* and *Moon Over Miami*) about three smart girls looking for millionaires. This time round they are June Haver, Vivian Blaine and Vera-Ellen; but Celeste Holm, in her first film, outshone them all. H. Bruce Humberstone had some good songs going for him, though, notably 'You Make Me Feel So Young'; 1946. (c)

Three Little Words X Minor musical about minor song-writers Bert Kalmar (Fred Astaire), Harry Ruby (Red Skelton) was given standard MGM treatment by Richard Thorpe in 1950. Singing voices issuing from mouths of Vera-Ellen, Debbie Reynolds don't belong to them; 1950. (c)

Three Men in a Boat XX Jerome K. Jerome's gentle, charming, funny account of a trip along the Thames becomes a coarse, heavy-handed series of obvious farcical situations under Ken Annakin's fumbling direction. Jimmy Edwards and Laurence Harvey are utterly wrong for their characters, and David Tomlinson has been encouraged to overplay his. Read the book instead; 1956. (c)

The Three Musketeers XX (1) 1935 version by Rowland V. Lee of Dumas swashbuckler made the least of the possibilities. Walter Abel, Paul Lukas, Ian Keith didn't deserve the feather in their caps. (b/w)

The Three Musketeers √ (2) 1939 saw a very jolly and funny musical version, with the Ritz Brothers standing in for the all-for-one-one-for-allers, leaders Don Ameche, Lionel Atwill, John Carradine, Joseph Shildkraut gave splendidly spirited performances under Allan Dwan's direction. (b/w)

The Three Musketeers X (3) 1948 spoofy version with Gene Kelly as an athletic D'Artagnan suffered from an unimaginative script, but Lana Turner, Van Heflin, Frank Morgan, Vincent Price, Gig Young, Keenan Wynn kept it going, under George Sidney's expert hand. (c)

The Three Musketeers – The Queen's Diamonds √√ The first part of Richard Lester's double-sized 1974 version of the Dumas swashbuckler, scripted by George MacDonald Fraser, is a send-up of traditional romance. While the sword fights are mostly straight, his musketeers (Oliver Reed, Frank Finlay, Richard Chamberlain, with Michael York as D'Artagnan) then engage in elegant horseplay with Raquel Welch, Geraldine Chaplin, and such refugees from Lester's TV days as Spike Milligan and Roy Kinnear. Charlton Heston and Christopher Lee try to remain aloof from the larks, without much success. (c)

Three on a Couch XX Dreadful Jerry Lewis attempt at sophisticated comedy in 1966 about (you won't believe it but it's true) how he poses as three different men and a girl to cure his psychiatrist-fiancée's three man-hating girl patients so that she'll be happy to leave for a vacation with him. Jerry Lewis can't blame the producer or director; they were both him (or at least him posing as them). (c)

Three on a Spree XX *Brewster's Millions* – Jack Watling must spend a million in two months if he is to inherit eight million – brought up to 1961 with disastrous results. Sidney J. Furie was the wrong director for this one and his cast of Carole Lesley, Renée Houston, John Slater couldn't find it in themselves to give adequate performances. (b/w)

Three Ring Circus XX Dean Martin and Jerry Lewis dragged even further down by Zsa Zsa Gabor, Joanne Dru, and Joseph Pevney's unenthusiastic direction; 1954. (c)

Three Sailors and a Girl XX On leave on the town, Gordon MacRae and chums are conned into investing the ship's back pay in a Broadway show starring Jane Powell. You can guess the rest. It's extremely silly, the music is undistinguished and the direction (Roy Del Ruth) is downright dull; 1953. (c)

Three Secrets √ Whose child survived air-crash? Eleanor Parker's? Ruth Roman's? Patricia Neal's? Robert Wise keeps up the suspense; 1950. (b/w)

Three Sisters √ Film of Olivier's production, with the master himself playing the Doctor; Lady O. (Joan Plowright) doing Masha; and Derek Jacobi as Andrei. You can't fault it, but you can't cheer very loud, either; 1970. (c)

Three Strangers √√ John Huston co-wrote but Jean Negulesco directed this yarn about three complete strangers who share a winning sweepstake ticket with disastrous results. Cast of Peter Lorre, Sydney Greenstreet, Geraldine Fitzgerald made this one stand out in 1946. (b/w)

Three Stripes in the Sun √ They are on Aldo Ray's arm, somewhere near the chip he carries on his shoulder about the Japs. Surprise for him, then, when he finds himself falling for Japanese Mitsuko Kimura. Based on a real-life story reported in the New Yorker, it's fairly believably directed by Richard Murphy; 1955. (b/w)

3.10 to Yuma √√ Tense 1957 western about Van Heflin as impecunious farmer trying to keep killer Glenn Ford under lock and key until the title train arrives. Delmer Daves made it a nailbiter. (b/w)

Three Violent People √ Anne Baxter is unfaithful wife in lush post-Civil War actioner, with Charlton Heston and a ranchful of solid supports: Gilbert Roland, Forrest Tucker, Elaine Stritch. But Rudolph Maté's direction is as slow as the Texan drawl; 1957. (c)

The Three Worlds of Gulliver X Well, two, actually. The voyages to Lilliput and Brobdingnag, lightly acted by an unstarry cast (June Thorburn, Lee Patterson, Kerwin Mathews) helped out with some over-ambitious special effects. Clearly meant by director Jack Sher for the child market, there's just enough of Swift's attitudes left to make it more than a picture-panto; 1960. (c)

Three Young Texans X Why is Jeffrey Hunter robbing that train? Not to get at the gold but to stop his dad from doing the job. He plans to put the money back, and Mitzi Gaynor is cheering him on. Henry Levin attempts to make this 1954 western half-way credible, but can't quite manage. (c)

The Thrill of it All √ Funny send-up of TV commercials with Doris Day, James Garner, Reginald Owen, with particularly good cameo from Carl Reiner. Norman Jewison gave it gloss; 1963. (c)

Thunderball √√ This 1965 James Bond was the one where Sean Connery had to find out who was holding the world to ransom with two hijacked H-bombs. The climax is underwater fighting and hydrofoil athletics. Terence Young directed energetically. (c)

Thunder Bay √ The old reliable about two sets of workers brawling in opposition; this time it's shrimp fishermen and oil-drillers off the coast of Louisiana, with James Stewart, Dan Duryea among the brawlers, Joanne Dru on the sidelines. Director Anthony Mann can't save the pay-off from being obvious; 1953. (c)

Thunderbird 6 X Just a long episode of the *Thunderbird* TV series, with efficient puppetry, about hijacking a new airliner. Ho-hum. Director: David Lane; 1968. (c)

Thunderbolt and Lightfoot √ Caper thriller that starts as comedy and ends as tragedy, with visibly shuddering gear-changes along the way. Clint Eastwood's immobile face doesn't change, though. He is chased by George Kennedy, befriended by Jeff Bridges and gets away with a lot of money, thanks to a questionable coincidence. Director Michael Cimino was making his debut in 1974. (c)

Thunder in the Sun X Basques going to California in the 1840s to start new vineyards is setting for triangle between Susan Hayward, Jeff Chandler and Jacques Bergerac. Climax is attack by hostile Indians (of course). Russel Rouse routine direction; 1959. (c)

A Thunder of Drums √ Veteran Richard Boone gets a chance (which he takes with both hands) to show what a fine actor has been jogging along on the saddle all these years. In this 1961 western Joseph Newman has used James Warner Bellah's fine script to probe beneath the surface of characters who would ordinarily remain ciphers. Boone is commander of a garrison in conflict with an over-conscientious young lieutenant (a disappointing George Hamilton) whose father has just denied Boone's promotion. Hamilton, in trying to win back his girl from another officer, is responsible for the massacre of a patrol. Can be enjoyed as a routine blood-and-thunderer but has a bit more to offer. (c)

Thunder on the Hill √ This mystery drama tells how Claudette Colbert, a nun, can't believe that Ann Blyth, a convicted murderess who happens to be taking shelter in her convent, really did it. In uncovering real murderer, she runs into danger. Gladys Cooper is superior Mother Superior, and Douglas Sirk manages to pull it up this side of melodrama; 1951. (b/w)

Thunder Over Arizona X Silver mine is object of corrupt mayor's envy. Wallace Ford comes out best under

Joseph Kane's direction; 1956. (c)

Thunder Over the Plains X Randolph Scott protecting Phyllis Kirk and the people of Texas from carpetbaggers. Elisha Cook, Henry Hull, Lex Barker among the crowd directed by André de Toth; 1953. (c)

Thunder Road X Robert Mitchum comes back from Korea to join in bootlegging in the South. But the law and the lawless gang up on him and his record delivery run. Arthur Ripley managed to keep it going cheerfully enough; Gene Barry, Keely Smith weak supports; 1958. (b/w)

Thunder Rock √√ Michael Redgrave outstanding as lighthouse-hermit visited by the ghosts of a wrecked ship, urging him to engage himself in the world's affairs. James Mason, Barbara Mullen are strong aides. The Boultings; 1942. (b/w)

Tiara Tahiti X Quite a hit in its day (1962), tells story of urbane battle between James Mason and John Mills for possession of desert isle for a hotel. Should still pass undemanding couple of hours. Director: Ted Kotcheff. (c)

A Ticket to Tomahawk X The second girl on the left in the number 'Oh What a Forward Girl You Are!' is Marilyn Monroe. Otherwise there is little of interest in this 1950 western about the battle to get a train to its destination in time to win the right to operate in the nineties, and thus knock out the villainous stage-coach owner, who hires Rory Calhoun to sabotage it. Anne Baxter manages to get it there, with help from salesman Dan Dailey, driver Walter Brennan, and somehow, the song-and-dance troupe of which Marilyn is a member. Director-co-writer Richard Sale didn't realise he was using the future hottest property in movies. (c)

Tickle Me XX Deadly Elvis Presley 1965 vehicle, with him as cowboy who works on a health farm and is much pursued by the inmates. Finally he marries the richest and prettiest one. Big deal. He also sings rather a lot. Norman Taurog. (c)

A Ticklish Affair X There's a quarter of an hour towards the end of this largely tedious comedy when a child cuts the tethering-ropes of some helium balloons and goes floating away, rather like the little boy in *The Red Balloon*, that's great fun. Thanks to superior process work and some sleight-of-hand direction from George Sidney it's possible to suspend one's disbelief and to enjoy the sight of Red Buttons shooting the air out of the balloons and Gig Young inching his way to the rescue. Otherwise it's a silly story about widow Shirley Jones rebuffing the advances of Gig because he's in the Navy and she has buried one naval husband already; 1963. (c)

Tick . . . tick . . . tick √ One of those now-familiar yarns about how a black sheriff finally wins out against white prejudice. Jim Brown plays the lawman, Fredric March (in his penultimate role; he was 72 when this was made in 1969) is the Mayor. Ralph Nelson directs adequately. (c)

Tiger Bay √ J. Lee Thompson's taut 1959 thriller which launched 12-year-old Hayley Mills upon us. As a pinched and plain dockland waif she spies on Horst Buchholz committing murder and then protects him. John Mills, as the law, sees justice done. (b/w)

Tiger By the Tail X Routine adventure-whodunit with weak Christopher George as put-upon hero, colourless Tippi Hedren the object of his affections (and suspicions), Dean Jagger as capitalist. By the end you don't care, and an amazing denouement goes for nothing; R. G. Springsteen; 1968. (c)

Tiger in the Smoke √ Thriller with religious undertones, emphasised by making a clergyman (Laurence Naismith) and daughter (Muriel Pavlov) the objects of the evil Tony Wright's terrorising. He is searching for a treasure he thinks is priceless but which turns out to be beyond price (spiritually). Donald Sinden spends most of the film tied up. Roy Baker's opening sequence in the fog is justly celebrated as a small tour-de-force; but it sags a bit from then on; 1956. (b/w)

The Tiger Makes Out √ From Murray Schisgal's play that he adapted for this weakened comedy. When Eli Wallach and his wife Anne Jackson toured it, there were two parts; now there are forty more speaking roles, including some amusing little cameos. But Arthur Hiller directs it unsurely. Wallach is now a postman who grabs typist Jackson and together they make a bid for freedom from urban anonymity; 1968. (c)

Tight Spot √√ Ginger Rogers is in it. She's a gangster's moll who is threatening to blow the gaff and all sorts of people are out to get her, including boss Lorne Greene. Mostly shot in a hotel room, where she is being guarded, thus betraying its theatre origins, it nevertheless builds up a pretty strong feeling of suspense, as Edward G. Robinson helps to guard her – or is he the one who's waiting his chance to do her in? Phil Karlson directs surely and tautly; 1955. (b/w)

Till Death Us Do Part √ The 1969 extended flashback into how Alf Garnett and family got that way, adequately directed by Norman Cohen. The usual family, plus Liam Redmond, Bill Maynard, Brian Blessed, Sam Kydd, starts at 1939 and tells the Garnett Saga. (c)

Tillie's Punctured Romance √√ Charlie Chaplin's early two-reelers are far superior to later, more pretentious full-lengths. Marie Dressler, Mabel Normand add lustre to this 1914 fortune-hunting saga. (b/w)

Till the Clouds Roll By X Marvellous songs in otherwise tepid biography of Jerome Kern with a pregnant (with Liza) Judy Garland hiding the fact behind a pile of pots and pans in the late-shot 'Look for the Silver Lining'. Lena Horne, singing *Show Boat* songs, was cut out for Deep South cinemas because whites joined in with her. Frank Sinatra singing 'You And Me We Sweat And Strain' is wildly unconvincing in his immaculate white suit. Richard Whorf directed this 1946 mish-mash; musical numbers directed by Judy Garland's husband Vincente Minnelli; 1946. (c)

Timberjack √ Sterling Hayden fights the lumber crooks who may have killed his father. Joseph Kane directed cheerfully in 1955, with the confidence that having Adolphe Menjou and Hoagy Carmichael in the cast gave him. (c)

Timbuktu XX Slow, weak Second World War drama with Sudanese and French plots and counter-plots. Jacques Tourneur could do little with soft script and casting of Victor Mature, Yvonne de Carlo; 1959. (b/w)

Time Limit √√ Karl Malden's first and only attempt at directing turned out so well that it's surprising he hasn't repeated the experiment. This taut courtroom story of an army colonel accused of collaborating with the Communists while a PoW in Korea holds the attention all through; the dramatic moments are well-defined; the characters (Richard Basehart as the accused, Richard Widmark as the accuser, Martin Balsam as a sergeant

providing some light relief) convincing; the denouement surprising enough. Unfortunately, Henry Denker's script makes some assumptions about the self-evident evils of Communism that look naïve today, but as a product of its time, 1957, it's acceptable. (b/w)

Time Lock √ Quite exciting little thriller set in a Canadian bank where a child has got trapped in a large safe; can they get it open before he suffocates? Gerald Thomas directed this one in 1957, before he started Carrying On. His only known star in the cast was Robert Beatty, but down at the very bottom of the credits there's '2nd welder, Sean Connery'. (b/w)

The Time Machine √ George Pal took the first section of H. G. Wells' visionary novel and reduced it to Hollywood proportions in 1960. What remains is acceptable sci-fi, however, with beautifully-designed sets and special effects that won an Oscar. Rod Taylor, Yvette Mimieux. (c)

Time of Indifference X Afraid it is; you won't be able to get very involved in this heavy yarn of Rod Steiger involved with mother Paulette Goddard (making a failed attempt at comeback in 1963) and daughter Claudia Cardinale. Director Francesco Maselli hasn't been able to convey the essence of Moravia's novel; supports Shelley Winters, Tomas Milian don't help. (b/w)

The Time of Their Lives √ Abbott and Costello as ghosts come back to haunt modern (1946) inhabitants of country house, including Abbott, Binnie Barnes, Gale Sondergaard; director, Charles Barton; 1946. (b/w)

The Time of Your Life √ William Saroyan's talky-talky philosophising in a San Francisco bar lacked the dramatic backbone to make a gripping film, but it has its moments. Very much a Cagney affair, James took the main part, sister Jeanne the whore he freeloads off, brother William produced it. What chance had director H. C. Potter? 1948. (b/w)

A Time to Love and a Time to Die √ Pretentious yarn about Germany during the Second World War written by *All Quiet*'s Erich Maria Remarque (who plays the sympathetic part of a professor in it himself). John Gavin and Lilo Pulver are debut-leads. Douglas Sirk directed a blown-up, heavy-handed adaptation (of a novel) which drags on and on in seemingly unending (133 minutes of cinema time) boredom, detailing the fighting and leaves of one German soldier from the Russian front. The final indignity is that we are supposed to sympathise with this fighter for fascism and not the Russian guerrilla who finally does for him; 1958. (c)

The Time Travellers √ Marooned in the horrible future, a small band of explorers, led by Preston Foster, battle their way through mutants, robots, guerrilla survivors, and sundry clichés. Director-writer Ib Melchoir manages to make it look fairly fresh; 1965. (c)

Time Without Pity √ Flashy public resumption of Joseph Losey's career in 1957 (he had been under a Red ban in America and had to make films under pseudonyms until given this chance) is conventional tale of will-the-real-murderer - be - revealed - before - the - innocent - man - is - hanged? Michael Redgrave is Dad, desperately trying to prove innocence of son Alec McCowen (marvellous). Real killer is absurdly over-acting Leo McKern (this is no giveaway - the film has a prologue spoiling its own plot). Small parts well cast: Renée Houston, George Devine, Joan Plowright, Peter Cushing among those present. (b/w)

The Tingler √ Incredible but frightening theory is there's an insect at the bottom of your spine that fright activates, only to be assuaged by screaming; so deaf-and-dumb girl is perfect guinea pig. Then insect gets loose. Seats at film's 1959 premiere were wired with electric shocks to add to screaming. Vincent Price; director William Castle. (b/w)

Tin Pan Alley X Naïve song-and-dancer set pre-First World War. Alice Faye, Betty Grable, Jack Oakie. Directed by Walter Lang; 1940. (b/w)

The Tin Star √√ Made in 1957 by Anthony Mann, who helped bring westerns out of the Saturday morning cinema, it's in the classic law and order mould. Henry Fonda, a cool, laconic cowboy, is bounty-hunter asked for help by freshman sheriff Anthony Perkins. Reminiscent of *Shane* (the lone stranger ridin' in from the prairie) and *High Noon* (the reluctant sheriff), it doesn't denigrate these elements, and its characterisation is of a high order. (b/w)

Tip on a Dead Jockey √ Irwin Shaw story provides Robert Taylor with unusually animated vehicle for his somewhat stiff talents; he's a retired flyer in Madrid who decides that smuggling might be a useful money-bringer; Gia Scala and Martin Gabel stand out; Richard Thorpe; 1957. (b/w)

Titanic √ Not as impressive as *A Night to Remember*, on the same subject, but this 1953 American effort to do a *Bridge of San Luis Rey* on the sinking of the liner passes muster. Clifton Webb, Barbara Stanwyck, Robert Wagner, Audrey Dalton are among the passengers, and Jean Negulesco does better with their personal dramas than the epic special effects. (b/w)

The Titfield Thunderbolt √ One of those eccentric English comedies making a hero out of a piece of machinery, this time a local train. The usual jolly jokers (Stanley Holloway, Hugh Griffith, Naunton Wayne) rescue an antique locomotive and keep their Bluebell Line running, despite underhand goings-on. Mildly amusing. Charles Crichton; 1953. (b/w)

The Toast of New Orleans X A bit burnt round the edges. Director Norman Taurog, who later made a career out of pushing Elvis Presley through a series of unmemorable motion pictures, had Mario Lanza and Kathryn Grayson to humanise in 1950. Their singing's fine, but when they start trying to act, he quickly turns the camera towards David Niven, J. Carrol Naish and James Mitchell - not always soon enough. It's a long way to the *Madame Butterfly* finale when the young fisherman at the turn-of-the-century is finally launched into a successful career as an opera star. (c)

Tobacco Road √ Made in 1941, the year after his *Grapes of Wrath*, this superficially similar effort by John Ford is derived from Erskine Caldwell's novel about poor whites in the Deep South via a Broadway theatre adaptation. It lost its vitality (to be polite) under the censor's scissors; Charley Grapewin and Marjorie Rambeau grimace; Gene Tierney was miscast under Darryl Zanuck's orders; 1941. (b/w)

To Be or Not to Be √√ Delightful Ernst Lubitsch comedy about actors outwitting the Nazis as Poland falls. This was Carole Lombard's last film (1942) and is fitting memorial to her gaiety and witty way with a line. Jack Benny, Sig Ruman, Lionel Atwill all super. (b/w)

Tobruk X Unbelievable war story made unbelievably in 1967, by which time you would have thought the time for cheap heroics about the Second World War was over. Director Arthur Hiller doesn't seem to think so and we get the old only-man-who-can-save-the-war stuff from Rock Hudson, stiff-upper-lip fanatic George Peppard, martinet Nigel Green, Cockney sparrer Norman Rossington and so on. The only ingenious bit is the opening when German frogmen capture Hudson: they turn out to be German Jewish frogmen – on our side. (c)

To Catch a Thief √ Lightweight Hitchcock set in a Riviera that came out looking disappointingly phoney. In fact, the whole plot's awfully cheaty, with Cary Grant an unconvincing catburglar who has to catch the 'Cat' so that he will cease to be under suspicion himself. Grace Kelly (with what Hitch called her 'indirect sex appeal') is the girl who surprises Grant (and, intentionally, the audience) with her forwardness; 1955. (c)

To Have and Have Not √ Humphrey Bogart and Lauren Bacall and the basic plot of fishermen involved in hanky-panky reset in the Second World War (it was made in 1944) didn't improve Hemingway's story, although it made an above-routine romantic thriller, directed by Howard Hawks. Since then, it has twice been refilmed, but not under its own name. In 1951, it became *The Breaking Point* with John Garfield and in 1958 *The Gun Runners* with Audie Murphy. (b/w)

To Hell and Back √ And on to Hollywood. Audie Murphy's best-selling autobiography of how a poor boy became America's most-decorated war hero, made a perfectly acceptable vehicle for actor Audie Murphy, who had already made five pictures by the time he got round to this one, in 1955. Most of it doesn't convince – due to a poor script and unimaginative direction by Jesse Hibbs – but the battle scenes take on a special sort of excitement from Murphy's presence. (c)

To Kill a Mockingbird √ Superficially a fine, even great, sermon on racial tensions, involving the defence (by Gregory Peck) of a black (Brock Peters) unjustly accused of murder, all seen from a child's viewpoint. Robert Mulligan's direction was hailed as 'sensitive' and 'daring' at the time (1963) but Horton Foote's adaptation of Harper Lee's novel has a very hollow centre. Can you believe in the morally

whitewashed black, the Southern court and the handy ending? Peck did, and it won him an Oscar. (b/w)

Tokyo Joe X Sad to see Humphrey Bogart in the middle of all this stupid carrying-on about blackmail and counter-threats in post-War Tokyo, compounded by heroics over a 'sweet' little girl of 7. Under Stuart Heisler, it lacks sharpness or the necessary sardonic quality; 1949. (b/w)

Tomahawk √ Van Heflin, friend of the Indians, versus Alex Nicol, Indian killer. More interesting for its premature pro-Indian sentiment (it was made in 1951) and some of the supports director George Sherman managed to work in: Preston Foster, Jack Oakie, Yvonne de Carlo from the veterans; Rock Hudson, Tom Tully among the up-and-comers. (c)

The Tomahawk and the Cross X Originally called *Pillars of the Sky* in 1956, this western directed by George Marshall has Jeff Chandler as army officer fighting Indians, while courting Dorothy Malone. Lee Marvin plays a small part. (c)

The Tomb of Ligeia √ √ Poe's favourite story and Poe's great film-interpreter Roger Corman's best work of this genre. How Vincent Price came to free himself of his dead wife's hypnotic will and how she takes revenge on him from the grave; 1965. (c)

Tomboy and the Champ XX Sickly confection of child (the repulsive Candy Moore) and animal (an Angus bull named Champy) she grooms to win the Chicago Prize. Only then does she realise that he will be sold for steak; she collapses and is only saved from death or something by the appearance of Champy by her hospital bed. There's a ghastly Parson Dan (Jess Kirkpatrick) wandering through the film pointing up heavenly morals as fast as he can. What was John Ford's Ben Johnson (as Uncle Jim) doing in a mess like this? The director was Francis D. Lyon; 1962. (c)

Tom Brown's Schooldays XX (1) 1939 version had Cedric Hardwicke as Dr Arnold, Freddie Bartholomew, and a cast of absurd Americans as the other inmates of Rugby. Robert Stevenson. (b/w)

Tom Brown's Schooldays X (2) 1951 version had Robert Newton as a less than satisfactory Arnold, John Howard Davies as a wispy Tom, but some solid support from James Hayter, Michael Hordern, Diana Wynyard. Gordon

Parry directed from a just-competent Noel Langley script under Brian Desmond Hurst as producer. (b/w)

Tom Jones √√ Rollicking, bawdy, hugely enjoyable free adaptation of Fielding's novel by John Osborne and Tony Richardson, in 1963. Albert Finney's foundling-to-gallows-via-a-thousand-beds hero is nicely done, and matched by the creations he comes up against: the delicious Susannah York, his final reward; Hugh Griffith's bellowing squire; Edith Evans, outrageous among the cows; Joyce Redman's succulent dining companion; Diane Cilento's slut; the list could go on and on. Walter Lassally's camerawork is particularly brilliant, never letting down the fun, often adding to it. Oscars won for best film, best direction (Richardson) and John Addison's music. (c)

Tommy √ At last in 1975 Ken Russell lets himself loose on material that was so base that it didn't matter how much he vulgarised it. Pete Townshend's 'rock opera' lent itself well to Russell's mixture of pretentiousness and flashiness. Roger Daltrey did what was asked of him as the traumatised lad, cured by being pushed through a mirror by his mother (Ann-Margret). Some pop stars had their egos flattered by joining in (Elton John, Eric Clapton, Keith Moon). Some good actors (Jack Nicholson, Robert Powell) got lost. (c)

Tom Sawyer √ Pleasant musical version of the classic American children's story, with Johnnie Whittaker as Tom, plus Celeste Holm, Jodie Foster, Warren Oates; directed in real locations (Arrow Rock, Missouri and state park) by Don Taylor, the former actor; 1973. (c)

Tom Thumb √ Russ Tamblyn (youngest boy in *Seven Brides for Seven Brothers*) makes a more than adequate Tom in this mixed live-and-cartoon-and-special-effects children's film, and Terry-Thomas and Peter Sellers make a splendid pair of robbers. George Pal produced and directed in 1958 with a happy command of technical tricks. Rotten choreography. (c)

Tonight and Every Night XX Terrible reconstruction of what the Windmill Theatre wasn't like during the war, with the worst backcloths of searchlights you ever did see. Victor Saville (who was in Hollywood in 1945) put Rita Hayworth, Janet Blair through their staid paces. (c)

Tonight We Sing X The music's all right but the story is terrible. One of those biopics that bear almost no relation to the way it must really have happened. The mythical figure being biographed here is Sol Hurok the impresario. David Wayne made a ludicrous Hurok – for anyone who knows what the real one was like. Anne Bancroft does her best with silly lines and plots. Even the artistes aren't really very gripping – Enzio Pinza, Roberta Peters, Tamara Toumanova, Isaac Stern. Director Mitchell Leisen was saddled with an impossible task; 1953. (c)

Tons of Trouble XXX The awful Mr Pastry (Richard Hearne) dithers his way through a quasi-romantic story as caretaker of block of flats. Leslie Hiscott wrote and directed in 1955. (b/w)

Tony Draws a Horse XX Pathetic little British comedy about rows between psychologist and wife over correct attitude towards their graffiti-oriented little boy. Cecil Parker, Anne Crawford, Derek Bond, Barbara Murray make it rather heavy going under John Paddy Carstairs' uninspired direction; 1951. (b/w)

Tony Rome √√ The first time in his long career that Frank Sinatra played a private detective was in this 1967 thriller which, besides Sinatra, managed to show a lot of Miami and Jill St. John. Suspiciously like Chandler's *The Big Sleep*, it provoked comparisons with Bogart's portrayal of Philip Marlowe in that; and while nobody could match Bogie, Sinatra does better than anyone else ever has since. The plot's to do with a wayward heiress (Sue Lyon), stepmother (Gena Rowlands) and some jewels, real and fake. Director: Gordon Douglas. (c)

Too Hot to Handle √ (1) Delightful 1938 typical pre-war crackling comedy with Clark Gable and Walter Pidgeon scrapping over Myrna Loy; they are newsreel photographers, with Gable not too scrupulous. Jack Conway. (b/w)

Too Hot to Handle XXX (2) Really awful melo about Soho crooks, involving Jayne Mansfield as night-club singer and some unbelievable stuff about a club-owner (Leo Genn, manager Christopher Lee) she fancies. Terence Young directed with as much flair as the script by Herbert Kretzmer allowed: none; 1960. (c)

Too Late Blues √ John Cassavetes's first attempt at a commercial film, after

Shadows, in 1959, two years before. Bobby Darin, Stella Stevens go through quasi-improvised motions under his aegis, about a jazz musician pinching a blonde from his mate. (*b/w*)

Too Late the Hero √ Members of patrol sent by Gen. Henry Fonda to blow up Jap radio site are Cliff Robertson, Michael Caine. Robert Aldrich produced, directed and co-wrote in 1970. (*c*)

Too Many Crooks √ Mario Zampi directed, 1958, this tale of bungling kidnappers using undertakers as cover, and laid on a few surreal touches with help of Terry-Thomas, George Cole, Sid James. Point of the plot is that wife Brenda de Banzie is upset to find that hubby Terry-Thomas is only too glad to have her snaffled, so in revenge takes over gang-leadership and collects the cash for herself. There's a soft ending, of course, it being a British comedy. Fascinatingly, this same plot was used nine years later for *The Happening* but becomes a tragedy. (*b/w*)

Too Many Thieves √ Agreeable caper with Peter Falk as attorney helping to recover the Viktor Emblem, a priceless diamond stolen in Macedonia. Nehemiah Persoff employs him, Britt Ekland slows him (and the film) up. Director Abner Biberman; 1965. (*c*)

Too Much, Too Soon XX Sub-title: 'The Daring Story of Diana Barrymore'. John's daughter romanced a lot, drank a lot and married three times. Dorothy Malone had the impossible task of playing her while she was still alive. The only interest in this rotten film, poorly directed by Art Napoleon in 1958, was that it was one of the last Errol Flynn (playing his old drinking companion John Barrymore) was to make. Jack L. Warner later wrote: 'I could not bear to watch him struggle through take after take ... He was playing the part of a drunken actor and he didn't need any method system to get him in the mood. He *was* drunk. "Too much too soon". The words should have been carved on a tombstone at the time for he was one of the living dead.' (*b/w*)

Too Young to Kiss X Minor comedy (reminiscent of *The Major and the Minor,* in fact) with pouting June Allyson dressing up as 13-year-old so that she can be discovered by Van Johnson as child prodigy pianist. Gig Young, her fiancé, is naturally upset, even more so when she falls in love with Johnson. Billy Wilder would have

turned it into satire on *Lolita;* but Robert Z. Leonard settles for the obvious; 1951. (*b/w*)

Too Young to Love XXX Woefully out of date when it was made in 1960, this making-over of Elsa Shelley's always unbelievable, sensational play *Pick-Up Girl,* seems like one of those warnings against promiscuity that well-meaning but ineffective VD campaigns used to put over. Direction (by Muriel Box), acting (gruff Thomas Mitchell as a kindly judge, strident Joan Miller as Mum, unconvincing Pauline Hahn as the 15-year-old wayward lass), script (Muriel and Sydney Box) all outdo each other in awfulness. (*b/w*)

To Paris with Love XX Alec Guinness starring, Robert Hamer directing should have produced a more engaging comedy than this one of a widower taking his son to the Wicked City to learn the facts of life. Desperately dated; 1955. (*b/w*)

Topaz X Hitchcock's least favourite among his own films is this 1969 lulu about the 1962 Cuban missile crisis. Abandoning his usual intimate style, Hitch follows Leon Uris's novel round the world and allows outrageous coincidence to play too large a part. There are few typically interesting touches. Non-stars Frederick Stafford, Dany Robin, John Forsythe serve him adequately. (*c*)

Top Gun X Sterling Hayden is found Not Guilty on murder charge and gets elected marshal instead. Rod Taylor has a small part. Ray Nazarro made this into routine western; 1955. (*b/w*)

Top Hat √√ Cherishable Astaire-Rogers, vintage 1935, in which they do 'Cheek to Cheek' (with feathers) and 'Isn't This a Lovely Day' in the park bandstand. Edward Everett Horton, Helen Broderick, Eric Blore join in, under Mark Sandrich's direction. (*b/w*)

Topkapi √√ Director Jules Dassin repeated his *Rififi* caper in spades (or at least in colour and with comedy) in 1964 with theft of jewel-encrusted dagger from museum in excitingly-photographed Istanbul. Joy to watch Peter Ustinov, Robert Morley, Akim Tamiroff, Melina Mercouri upstaging each other. (*c*)

To Please a Lady √ Clark Gable as unpopular racing driver and Barbara Stanwyck as tough columnist are nominal stars of this rather obvious yarn, but the car and the Indianapolis track are the real standout feature.

Strictly for small boys; director Clarence Brown; 1950. (b/w)

Top of the Form XX Pretty awful remake (in 1952) of the classic Will Hay comedy, *Good Morning Boys*. Ronald Shiner, never a very sympathetic player, is tipster disguised as professor, who takes charge of a bizarrely overgrown form including Anthony Newley, Alfie Bass, Harry Fowler, Gerald Campion and 22-year-old Ronnie Corbett as the tich of the class; John Paddy Carstairs directed. (b/w)

Top of the World X Triangle stuff between Evelyn Keyes, ex-husband Dale Robertson, boyfriend Frank Lovejoy. Dale's a jet pilot who is assigned to find them, lost in the wilds of Alaska. Lewis R. Foster keeps it from getting frozen right up; 1955. (b/w)

Tora! Tora! Tora! √ Interminably long (144 minutes plus commercials, if it's on that channel) reconstruction of both sides' initiation into the Japanese-American flare-up in 1941, seen from 1970. It's really three separate films by different directors: Richard Fleischer did the American bits, Ray Kellog the Pearl Harbor attack, Toshio Masuda and Kinji Fukasaku the Japanese. What should have been taut and revelatory all through (parts certainly are) becomes merely tedious. (c)

Torch Song √ It's burning bright for Joan Crawford, though the rest of the cast (Michael Wilding as a blind pianist; Gig Young as a Broadway parasite; Mom, Marjorie Rambeau) don't get much of a look in. Centre-stage the whole time (she could rely on 'her' director, Charles Walters), she struts about, throwing tantrums, doing a bit of a dance, moving her lips (while India Adam's voice issues forth in song) and gradually realising True Love; 1953. (b/w)

Tormented XX Richard Carlson unconvincing as haunted (literally) jazz pianist, worried that he shouldn't marry. Bert I. Gordon can't make this nonsense work; 1960. (b/w)

Torn Curtain XX One of Alfred Hitchcock's less successful thrillers, it suffered from a poor script (Brian Moore) and unfortunate performances from Julie Andrews (never the greatest actress in the world nor the most docile to direct) and Paul Newman (he found it hard to get on with Hitch, who wanted him to play it like Cary Grant). Main trouble was the ambience of Iron Curtain spying which by 1966 had gone into the cold. (c)

Torpedo Alley X Lew Landers' direction makes this routine Korea plot about grounded flier becoming submariner a bit more acceptable than otherwise. Dorothy Malone brings Mark Stevens romance in hospital; 1953. (b/w)

Torpedo Run XX Glenn Ford, his cute little face in tormented grimace, vows revenge for his wife and child who were on a boat he sank when the wicked Japs were using it to screen their aircraft carrier. He dogs the carrier, with Ernest Borgnine as fellow-officer. Director Joseph Pevney isn't helped by the script; 1958. (c)

Torture Garden √ Four short horror films, directed somewhat obviously by Freddie Francis, strung together by Burgess Meredith foretelling the future of a disparate group of characters – for the sole purpose of fitting in the stories. Michael Bryant is faced with a man-eating domestic cat; John Standing with a spooky piano; and Peter Cushing with Jack Palance; 1968. (c)

To Sir, With Love X Sidney Poitier as black teacher in an East End school taming wild about-to-be-leavers, doesn't convince. It makes for a cosy tract on kindliness being better than brutality. As pupils, Judy Geeson and Lulu do better than the direction, by James Clavell, has any right to expect. This was a big success in America, where they don't know what British schools are really like; 1967. (c)

To the Ends of the Earth √ Dick Powell as US agent tracking drug ring all over the place. Has twist ending. Robert Stevenson; 1948. (c)

To Trap a Spy X Early UNCLE rip-off has Robert Vaughn, David McCallum repeating their then-fresh, now-tired double act. Don Medford; 1966. (c)

The Touch X Not one of Ingmar Bergman's great moments, this English-language effort in which Bibi Andersson leaves Dr Max von Sydow for 'an English archaeologist', who turns out to be American Elliott Gould; 1970. (c)

Touch and Go XX It's touch and go whether you'll stay awake through this old-fashioned (vintage 1955, but it seems earlier) comedy about why Jack Hawkins and family (Margaret Johnston, June Thorburn) can't get their emigration to Australia under way. Director Michael Truman. (c)

A Touch of Class √ Successful

coupling of Glenda Jackson and George Segal in 1973. Mel Shavelson extracts heavy-handed fun from a naughty weekend in Spain. (c)

Touch of Evil √√ Orson Welles was writer, director and heavily disguised actor in this absorbing movie about corruption down Mexico way, although Charlton Heston and Janet Leigh don't seem much at home in the steamy, dark border country between Mexico and the USA and between death and degradation. All sorts of players rallied round in 1958 to give old Orson a hand: Marlene Dietrich as a brothel-keeper; Joseph Calleia and Akim Tamiroff, matching him in seediness; Joseph Cotten and Ray Collins from *Citizen Kane;* a highly sinister Mercedes McCambridge. You may find it overdrawn and outrageous but many cinéastes include it among their favourite films. (b/w)

A Touch of Larceny √ Comedy-thriller combining a multitude of talents with slightly disappointing results: James Mason, George Sanders, Peter Barkworth, Harry Andrews, John Le Mesurier; scriptwriter Roger MacDougall, director Guy Hamilton and producer Ivan Foxwell; even an assistant director was Peter Yates. James Mason carries the fun along, not always succeeding in his involved schemes for making money but coming out OK in the end – if not quite morally; 1959. (b/w)

A Touch of Love √ Old-fashioned (for 1969) weepie about pregnant Sandy Dennis spurning father-of-the-child Ian McKellen, a TV newsreader (so that she and we can continually see him on her little screen). She's not a Bad Girl, though; it was her first time – which seems a bit retarded of her at 32. She's also nicely playing around with Michael Coles and John Standing. Director Waris Hussein seems overawed at having Hollywood star Dennis in his first feature film. He has let her get away with hogging the screen from a cross-section of solid Armchair Theatre supports, which is of course easy enough when a script comes from one of Margaret Drabble's woman-centred novels. (c)

The Toughest Gun in Tombstone X George Montgomery poses as a villain in order to winkle out Johnny Ringo's gang. Beverly Tyler as girl in the way. Earl Bellamy as director in the way of this becoming more than routine western; 1958. (b/w)

The Toughest Man Alive X Same plot as previous entry, only this time it's Dane Clark pretending to be villain, in order to round up gun-smuggling gang in South America. Sidney Salkow; 1955. (b/w)

The Toughest Man in Arizona √ Vaughn Monroe falls for Joan Leslie, gets deeper into crusade against crime on the frontier than he intended. R. G. Springsteen kept up the excitement moderately well in 1952. (c)

Toward the Unknown √ Superior test-pilot stuff, involving rocket-planes and William Holden's fight to inspire confidence despite past mistakes. Mervyn Le Roy produced and directed; 1956. (c)

The Towering Inferno √ Occasionally exciting 1974 disaster movie about a skyscraper on fire. Among those trapped by the fire or by John Guillermin's relentless direction are Steve McQueen, Paul Newman, William Holden, Faye Dunaway, Fred Astaire, Richard Chamberlain, Jennifer Jones, Robert Vaughn, Robert Wagner. (c)

Tower of London √ Vincent Price in a Poe-faced telling of the Tragedy of Richard III by Roger Corman in 1962. A remake of the 1939 version by Rowland V. Lee, with Basil Rathbone as Richard. Vincent Price was in that one, too — as Clarence. (b/w)

A Town Called Bastard X Unpleasant, disquieting western with a total of 22 killings. Telly Savalas plays a sadistic bandit commander in the Mexican rebellion of 1905. Up turns Stella Stevens in a hearse driven by Dudley Sutton, with a coffin ready to take away her husband's killer. Among others in the way of the guns: Robert Shaw, Michael Craig, Fernando Rey, Martin Landau. Alas, director Robert Parrish failed to make the best of this company in 1971. (c)

A Town Like Alice √ This is Virginia McKenna and friends having a rough time of it after the Japs invade. Stalwart Peter Finch and director Jack Lee defeated in attempt at documentary realism by poor studio sets. Altogether too episodic and sadistically loaded with suffering for its own sake; 1956. (b/w)

Town on Trial √ Patchily interesting whodunit about the wild girl at the tennis club getting done in, with John Mills as class-conscious detective. Alec McCowen, Elizabeth Seal, Maureen Connell fine; Charles Coburn, Barbara

Bates out of place in Home Counties. Director John Guillermin was obviously striving to make more than just a routine thriller, and nearly succeeds; 1956. (b/w)

Town Without Pity √ Defending four GIs accused of rape, Kirk Douglas has to discredit the victim. Hating himself for his task, he nevertheless goes on with it. Gottfried Reinhardt manages well enough with the German actors (notably Christine Kaufmann as the girl) but is too concerned at getting over a woolly message about justice and humanity to make the film incisive; 1961. (b/w)

Toys in the Attic √ Wendy Hiller and Geraldine Page make this 1963 adaptation of Lillian Hellman play worth watching despite Dean Martin and Yvette Mimieux as timid husband and child-wife. George Roy Hill directed with panache. (b/w)

Toy Tiger X Jeff Chandler, ad-man, finds himself adopted as pseudo-big-game hunter by little boy at school, and has to oblige. Pretty soft stuff, with Laraine Day as Mom. Director: Jerry Hopper; 1956. (c)

Track of the Cat √ Robert Mitchum and Teresa Wright are nominal stars of 1954 cougar hunt, but William Wellman's experiment in cinephotography is main interest. As snow covers the ground, he is able to try filming a black-and-white subject with colour film. The startling dramatic intrusion of colour every now and again is highly effective. (c)

Track of Thunder XX Stock-car 'thriller' with Tom Kirk and Ray Stricklyn having rivalry thrust on them by gambling syndicate. Joseph Kane directed, routinely, in 1968. (c)

Track the Man Down X If this murder-at-the-dog-track drama seems out of true, it's because an American director was imported to shoot it. R. G. Springsteen, veteran of so many westerns, was ill-at-ease with such British character players as Renée Houston, Pet Clark, George Rose; although his lead, Kent Taylor, arrived with him. Still, that's the kind of loopy compromise they made in 1953 when all that mattered was showing the films in America. (b/w)

The Train √√ Stunning action sequences as fanatical Paul Scofield tries to get train-load of French masterpieces to his masters in Germany while French Resistance leader Burt Lancaster tries to stop him. If only John Frankenheimer had given as much attention to the over-simplified characters and their philosophies as he did to the spectacular train-ride this really would be a three-tick pic. Michel Simon, Jeanne Moreau among your actual French; 1964. (b/w)

The Train Robbers √ Double-crossing western, with John Wayne doing his gentlemanly gunman act on behalf of Ann-Margret, who hires him to find some gold in an abandoned train. Hard to care when romance and reward both go sour. Writer-director is Burt Kennedy; 1973. (c)

The Traitor √ A double whodunit: who was the traitor in the German underground movement that betrayed them and is thus on the spot at their reunion? And who killed the messenger with the evidence that would have done for him? Donald Wolfit, Rupert Davies, Anton Diffring are among those present. Writer-director Michael McCarthy kept his camera too much in the house where they were reuniting – but perhaps that was the fault of the budget? 1956. (b/w)

The Traitors XX Uninspired spy-chase round London, with Patrick Allen and James Maxwell as chasers. Robert Tronson; 1962. (b/w)

Traitor's Gate XX Churned-out Edgar Wallace thriller about two brothers in plot to steal the Crown Jewels. Gary Raymond, Albert Lieven; director Freddie Francis in a hurry; 1955. (b/w)

The Trap √ (1) 1959 thriller with Lee J. Cobb as head of a crime syndicate on the run; Richard Widmark determined to catch him. But the gangster's pals move in to rescue him. Norman Panama who directed and produced with partner Mel Frank are better known for their comedies, but managed well in 1959. (c)

The Trap X (2) 1967 co-Canadian effort with Oliver Reed buying mute Rita Tushingham to be his trapper-wife. She has to amputate his leg and finds that she loves him. As corny as it sounds, it's almost saved by Tush's winning performance and the scenery. Sidney Hayers; 1966. (c)

Trapeze √ The daring young man is Burt Lancaster playing a cripple who can't walk without a stick but is still capable of performing great feats of partner-catching on the trapeze. The whole film's a bit like that, lame on the ground in its trite and familiar story of the two swingers (Tony Curtis is the other one) both in love with the lady in the act, Gina Lollobrigida. But in the air the doubling is neatly done and Carol Reed's camera does some dizzy work; 1956. (c)

Trauma X One of those long-way-after-*Psycho* thrillers churned out in the years following that 1960 masterpiece. This one, 1962, is about a shocked girl, who is married for her money and set up for murder. John Conte, Lynn Bari, Lorrie Richards can't do much under Robert Malcolm Young's direction. (b/w)

Travels with My Aunt XX Devotees of Graham Greene's charming novel should stay away from George Cukor's misbegotten attempt to improve it. Besides changing the characterisation (Alec McCowen in the narrator's role has become a confidence trickster) he had the misfortune of losing Katharine Hepburn in 1972 and had to make do with a caricature of a performance from Maggie Smith instead. (c)

Tread Softly Stranger XXX This candidate for Stinker of 1958 (and the next decade) is about two brothers who get involved with thieving and killing because one of them is infatuated with good-time girl Diana Dors. George Baker and Terence Morgan compete for the accolade of Worst Performance, but have some handy opposition in Patrick Allen and Miss Dors, who doubtless blame the awful script and the direction of Gordon Parry. (b/w)

Treasure Island √√ 1934, classic Wallace Beery-Jackie Cooper version; Victor Fleming directed. More yo-ho-ho, less bottle of rum than Robert Newton's later, 1950 effort with Byron Haskin. (b/w)

The Treasure of Lost Canyon X One of those money-can't-buy-happiness movies (you wonder why the producers were so keen to make money on them), this time about a small boy uncovering some treasure and almost ruining the lives of his family with their new-found wealth. William Powell brings some distinction as an old prospector, but otherwise Ted Tetzlaff's direction doesn't manage to add credibility; 1952. (c)

The Treasure of Monte Cristo X (1) 1949: directed by William Berke. Adele Jergens marries Glenn Langan for his money; then she truly falls in love with him. (b/w)

The Treasure of Monte Cristo X (2) 1960: one more rip-off of Dumas, with Rory Calhoun imported into Britain by Monty Berman and Roy S. Baker to help Patricia Bredin dig up treasure. (c)

The Treasure of Pancho Villa √ Mercenary Rory Calhoun hijacking train in 1915 Mexico on behalf of revolutionary Villa. He and Shelley Winters, as his blowsy girlfriend, are acted off the screen by veterans Gilbert Roland and Joseph Calleia. Director George Sherman keeps it moving and doesn't waste time with the script's pretensions; 1955. (c)

Treasure of Ruby Hills X Some useful westerners – Zachary Scott, Barton MacLane, Lola Albright, Dick Foran – in tiredly directed (Frank McDonald), rather obvious story of land-raiders; 1955. (b/w)

Treasure of the Golden Condor X Director Delmer Daves camps up this yarn about Cornel Wilde, cheated out of his rightful inheritance in France, seeking his fortune in 18th-century Guatemala. Fay Wray a welcome addition to 1953 cast. (c)

The Treasure of the Sierra Madre √√√ Stunning adventure story that has been copied so many times since that it may seem over-familiar, but John Huston (seen as tourist near start) rightly won both writing and directing Oscars in 1948 and his father Walter Huston ('All I had to tell Dad was talk fast') the Award for best support. B. Traven himself probably acted as technical adviser, although the author of the original novel hid under identity of 'old friend and translator, Hal Croves'. Humphrey Bogart never surpassed his dramatic acting as the vulnerable, greedy Dobbs, and Tim Holt keeps his end up as third of trio of gold-searchers. (b/w)

Trent's Last Case X E. C. Bentley's classic 1913 detective story is almost proof against even Herbert Wilcox's heavy directorial hand in this 1952 version. Orson Welles gives a touch of distinction to straightforward casting of the flowers (albeit a little faded) of the British screen: Michael Wilding, Margaret Lockwood, Hugh McDermott. Where was Anna Neagle? (b/w)

Trial √ Murder trial of Mexican boy exploited by fellow-travelling organisation; belongs in Hollywood's 1955 Red-baiting era, but Mark Robson does adequate directorial job. Arthur Kennedy, as double-dealing lawyer, steals it from Glenn Ford and Dorothy McGuire. (b/w)

The Trials of Oscar Wilde √ Although it reached the cinema five days after the rival Robert Morley *Oscar Wilde* in

1960, this won the critical battle. Peter Finch was moving as Wilde, Lionel Jeffries frightening as the Marquess of Queensberry, James Mason splendid as prosecutor Carson. Ken Hughes wrote and directed. (c)

Tribute to a Bad Man X Well, not really bad, only ruthless. James Cagney plays a cattle baron who makes his own laws; despite this, he has a heart of gold and is loved by Irene Papas. Role was originally intended for Spencer Tracy, who was fired for arguing about the script; he was well out of it – apart from lovely pictures, Robert Wise didn't make much of a job of it in 1956. (c)

Trick Baby √ Black con-man, passing for white, gets into trouble when he finds his victim was a Mafia fence; Kiel Martin, Mel Stewart move sharply along under Larry Yust's direction. (Alternative title, *The Double Con*.) 1973. (c)

Trio √ Three good Maugham stories directed rather stiffly by Ken Annakin and Harold French; the ones about the illiterate, rich man (James Hayter); the ship-board bore with rather more to him (Nigel Patrick); and romance in a sanitorium (Jean Simmons, Michael Rennie); 1950. (b/w)

Triple Cross XX *The Eddie Chapman Story* was a book that claimed that a former safe-cracker was a wartime double agent. Whether the story was true or not, this James Bond-type film about him, directed by James Bond director Terence Young, makes one believe that it was all nonsense. Everything about this melodrama – from Chapman's easy acceptance by the Germans to his literally incredible expertise with their language, Morse Code and guns – stinks of fiction. Nor are any of the cast convincing – Christopher Plummer makes a self-satisfied Chapman, and Yul Brynner as a German Baron, Romy Schneider as a bedroom lady and Trevor Howard as a British intelligence man are all from stock; 1967. (c)

Triple Deception X Guy Green's French location filming helps this incredible yarn about an imposter and a murder ring. Michael Craig plays the con-man, but Brenda de Banzie helps out splendidly; 1956. (c)

The Triple Echo √√ Glenda Jackson convinces deserter Brian Deacon to dress as a girl and move in with her. Oliver Reed was, at last, well cast as a coarse and brutal sergeant in Michael Apted's well-directed version of an H.

E. Bates story (script: Robin Chapman). The climax, where he discovers the charade, is powerful; 1972. (c)

Trip to Kill √ Exciting actioner with Telly Savalas as an even nastier Kojak-type narcotics cop, using Vietnam hero Tom Stern in his battle to catch dope boss Robert Vaughn; Tom Stern directed himself with the help of Lane Slate; 1971. (c)

Trog XX Whatever happened to Joan Crawford by 1970 that she agreed to take part in this nasty sci-flick about her finding the Missing Link and training him? Freddie Francis. (c)

The Trojan Women X Katharine Hepburn and Vanessa Redgrave, poorly served by Michael Cacoyannis in this over-elegant version of Euripides. Only Irene Papas comes out well, if over-strong. The rest is muted, cold, performing. 1971. (c)

Trooper Hook √ Summarily dismissed at the time (1957) as being just another western, this story of Barbara Stanwyck scorned for having co-habited with Apache and borne him a child, was forerunner of a new line in socially-conscious oaters. Joel McCrea gave authority to the part of the soldier who marries her despite the prejudice; Earl Holliman and Susan Kohner add sympathetic performances. Director Charles Marquis Warren deserves a hand for trying. (b/w)

Trouble Along the Way XX A right sickly mess, mixing football and religion with custody of children and falling in love with a social worker. Central figure is wooden John Wayne as coach on the skids, saved by God, the grid-iron and Donna Reed. Michael Curtiz directs professionally enough to disguise the worst moments, but it's an awful lot to take; 1953. (b/w)

Trouble Brewing √ Ghastly enough to be almost enjoyable – George Formby trying to become private eye in 1939. Anthony Kimmins keeps fun going with Googie Withers, Ronald Shiner, Martita Hunt. (b/w)

Troubled Waters XX Tab Hunter, as a loony, in a rather mad British thriller, in which he may be about to drown his son; Stanley Goulder directed; 1964. (b/w)

Trouble in Paradise √√√ Delicious comedy of manners. The most famous Lubitsch movie, 1932. Miriam Hopkins and Herbert Marshall are crooks who both get jobs in Kay Francis's household; Edward Everett Horton gorgeously spends whole film trying to remember where he has seen Miriam before. Starts with Venetian gondolier singing 'O Sole Mio' from what is revealed as a garbage boat – and never lets up. (b/w)

Trouble in Store XX Strictly for Norman Wisdom fans, if any, this has him working in a department store. Margaret Rutherford gives it temporary moments, but John Paddy Carstairs's direction is awfully clumsy; 1953. (b/w)

Trouble in the Glen XX Orson Welles must have been down on his uppers in 1955 to appear in this dreadful Herbert Wilcox rip-off from *The Quiet Man* (same authors) about an American visitor caught by local feud, in Scotland this time. Forrest Tucker is the Yank, Margaret Lockwood the girl he falls for, Orson a local laird. Victor McLaglen is trundled in and out as another lure for American distribution, but the result is an embarrassment all round. (c)

The Troublemaker √ Spotty but at times wildly amusing broad satire. Country - mouse - come - to -town formula allows co-writer and director Theodore J. Flicker (who also appears) and friends from the stage company, The Premise, to send up Greenwich Village and a whole shooting gallery-full of targets. Among the company: Buck Henry (co-writer) and Godfrey Cambridge; among the film references: *Citizen Kane, Brute Force, The Third Man, The Victors*. Can you spot them? (b/w)

The Trouble With Angels √ Tears (from Rosalind Russell) and coy jokes (from Hayley Mills) at the convent, as a Mother Superior learns not to be so superior, and a novice learns not to be such a nuisance. Ida Lupino; 1966. (c)

The Trouble with Girls √ Elvis Presley appeared to have wandered into this twenties yarn about a travelling fair by mistake. As the manager coping with union maid Marlyn Mason he seems vague, to say the least. Some nice cameos from old-timers John Carradine, Vincent Price, Sheree North can't save Peter Tewkesbury's desperate direction; 1969. (c)

The Trouble With Harry √ A black comedy in the sunshine – a corpse is found and buried and exhumed three times over. Several people think they killed the man and so stow away the evidence. Under Hitchcock's touch the worst longueurs of Jack Trevor Story's novel were avoided, and he gave

Shirley MacLaine her first screen break here. One strains to appreciate it because of Hitch's imprimatur, but it's hard going; 1955. (c)

True as a Turtle XX Weak little British comedy of 1957 about an old sailing ship. Cecil Parker captains her amateurishly, and a crew of minor actors (John Gregson, June Thorburn, Keith Michell, Elvi Hale) get involved in a plan to swindle casinos with forged plastic chips. Wendy Toye directed cheerfully but weakly. (c)

True Grit √ At 62 (in 1969), John Wayne was still riding tall with the best of the lawmen, here hired to get the man (Jeff Corey) who killed Kim Darby's father; if Wayne was bitter, cursory and unpleasant, he wasn't meant to be all that sympathetic. Henry Hathaway – at 71, no chicken himself – directed with the strength of experience. Reportedly, this is one of ex-President Nixon's favourite movies and he runs it every now and then to remind himself of some of the great American virtues. (c)

The True Story of Jesse James √ Robert Wagner is 1956 Jesse in this not-really-very-true story (among other film Jesses: Ty Power, Lawrence Tierney, Macdonald Carey, Audie Murphy, Willard Parker), strongly supported by Nicholas Ray's cast – Agnes Moorehead, Alan Hale, John Carradine, Hope Lange. A superior job all round. (c)

The Trunk XX Elaborate plan to cheat lawyer and new bride backfires. So does the movie. Donovan Winter gathered a cast of weak players (Phil Carey, Julia Arnall, Dermot Walsh, Vera Day) to match his story; 1960. (b/w)

The Truth About Spring X John and Hayley Mills in yarn about a captain passing his daughter off as a starving boy – it's to cadge supplies from richer Caribbean boats. But he's found out by millionaire's son, James MacArthur, who helps him dish would-be treasure map thieves Harry Andrews and Lionel Jeffries. Director Richard Thorpe seemed to be taking a pleasant West Indian holiday in 1965, some way away from the crew who were filming this comedy of his. (c)

The Truth About Women XX Laurence Harvey flashbacking over his past with his five loves: feminist Diane Cilento, slave girl Jackie Lane, Parisienne Eva Gabor, American Julie Harris, Swedish Mai Zetterling. This

British costumer was put on the circuits in 1958, without a West End showing. No wonder. Directed by Muriel Box. (c)

The Trygon Factor XX Susan Hampshire, Robert Morley, Stewart Granger in a farrago about smuggling nuns and a stately home where everyone is mad. Just doesn't work. Director, Cyril Frankel; 1967. (c)

Tumbleweed X Did Audie Murphy desert the wagon train when the Indians attacked? No, he was just saving the ladies by seeking a truce. Nathan Juran does what he can with suspicious townsfolk; 1953. (c)

Tunes of Glory √√ Splendidly acted drama of character differences between rough, tough, hard-drinking Lt.-Col. Alec Guinness, successful wartime leader of Highland regiment, and his correct, by-the-book peacetime CO, John Mills. The clash results in tragedy. Other plusses are Susannah York's first appearance and Ronald Neame's immaculate direction; 1960. (c)

The Tunnel of Love √ Peter de Vries novel was turned into a Doris Day vehicle, directed by Gene Kelly as musical without music. Richard Widmark, Gig Young, Gia Scala aid and abet adoption comedy. But it's soft-centred; 1958. (b/w)

Turkey Time √ Strictly a museum piece, this 1933 Aldwych farce gives students of comedy an opportunity to see Tom Walls, Ralph Lynn and Robertson Hare getting into awkward situations with Mary Brough and Norma Varden. Ben Travers wrote the script, about Walls and Lynn raising the ready to help Dorothy Hyson; Walls directed, too. (b/w)

The Turning Point √ Stuff about crime commission and how a reporter discovers that his chairman is sabotaging the good work. Edmond O'Brien is chief investigator, William Holden the reporter, but Ed Begley steals this one as he did so many of his movies. William Dieterle directs safely. 1952. (b/w)

Turn the Key Softly X How prison affected lives of three women. Overwrought acting by Yvonne Mitchell, Joan Collins, Terence Morgan seems to have been encouraged by director Jack Lee in 1953. Kathleen Harrison and Thora Hird back up gamely. (b/w)

Twelve Angry Men √√ 1957 classic of one juror (Henry Fonda) holding out. Sidney Lumet directed this, his first classic, so tautly and cleverly that you are never conscious of the constrictions of the jury room. All the cast is brilliant – to identify them, start with foreman Martin Balsam and clockwise round the table they are: John Fielder, Lee J. Cobb, E. G. Marshall, Jack Klugman, Edward Binns, Jack Warden, Henry Fonda, Joseph Sweeney, Ed Begley, George Voskovec, Robert Webber. (b/w)

The Twelve Chairs √√ Made in 1970, but not released in Britain until Mel Brooks had established himself with *Blazing Saddles*, this familiar yarn of a Russian who has to find treasure hidden in one of twelve identical chairs works pretty well. If Ron Moody was a mistake as the hero, Dom de Luise as a greedy priest is constantly hilarious. (c)

Twelve Hours to Kill √ Suspenser about newly-arrived Greek immigrant being chased round New York by murderers, as he was only witness to killing. Sadly Edward L. Cahn failed to extract maximum from locations or cast (Nico Minardos, Barbara Eden, Art Baker); 1960. (b/w)

Twelve O'Clock High √ Gregory Peck getting too involved with his airmen on British base during Second World War. Highly efficient direction from Henry King helped Dean Jagger to win Oscar as Best Support; 1949. (b/w)

24 Hours to Kill X Unoriginal title (see *Twelve . . .*, *Three . . .*) labels unoriginal suspenser about airline pilot Mickey Rooney being threatened by smuggling gang led by Walter Slezak when forced to land in Beirut. Director Peter Bezencenet failed to convince; 1965. (c)

20 Million Miles to Earth √ Zoologist and granddaughter open sealed container from wrecked rocket ship in Italy. The jelly-like mass inside becomes a clawed monster that soon doubles in size. Director Nathan Juran didn't add much to the genre, but Ray Harryhausen's stunning special effects include the Venusian monster to end all monsters. William Hopper, Frank Puglia, Joan Taylor haven't much to do; 1957. (b/w)

The 27th Day √ Five people, in different parts of the earth, are each given capsule with which they can destroy a continent. Behaving more intelligently than in most sci-fi movies, they realise that this will just let in the Alien Civilisation who handed them the power, despite pleas by their respective countries' leaders to use it against enemies. So they hide out, Gene Barry on a racecourse. Based on John Mantley's novel, it has the fault of a pat denouement, but William Asher makes it an unusually gripping tale of its type; 1957. (b/w)

23 Paces to Baker Street √ Modern detective story with deliberate echoes of Sherlock Holmes has Van Johnson as an amateur detective who's blind and Cecil Parker as his Watson-Jeeves. Henry Hathaway shot a lot of London locations, but it's basically a Hollywood mystery; 1956. (c)

Twice Round the Daffodils X *Carry On Nursing* would have been a more appropriate title, as *Carry On* director-producer Gerald Thomas-Peter Rogers let loose a *Carry On* cast (Juliet Mills, Donald Sinden, Donald Houston, Lance Percival, Joan Sims, Kenneth Williams) in a TB ward. Presumably the sentimental intrusions would have been out of place if it had been called that; 1962. (b/w)

Twice-Told Tales √ Nathaniel Hawthorne's stories don't make obvious screen adaptations so it's to Sidney Salkow's great credit that they work so well, particularly as his 1963 cast of Vincent Price, Sebastian Cabot, Mari Blanchard are hardly distinguished actors. (c)

Twilight for the Gods X On a broken-down sailing boat sail a 'ship of fools', running away from the South Seas to Mexico. Among them: Rock Hudson, Cyd Charisse, Arthur Kennedy. Joseph Pevney makes it seem like a very slow journey; 1958. (c)

Twilight of Honour √ Richard Chamberlain stopped being a young doctor to become a young lawyer for this 1963 courtroom drama. The actual case is a bit steamy, concerning a whore, an aged adulterer and a dopey tramp. Claude Rains, Nick Adams, Joey (she's a girl – and a sexy one) Heatherton do well enough, as does director Boris Sagal. (b/w)

Twisted Nerve √ Rather a crude attempt by Roy Boulting at a psychological thriller manages to create a few exciting moments and a few bits of comic relief but is bogged down by over-emphasis – of script, of direction and of acting by Hywel Bennett as the crafty killer, Hayley Mills as the girl who's taken in, Billie Whitelaw as her mother, Phyllis Calvert as his; 1969. (c)

Twist of Sand XX That old story about buried loot being sought by cell-mate. Richard Johnson, Roy Dotrice, Jeremy Kemp, Honor Blackman make this pretty dull going, and director Don Chaffey can't galvanise them. Only Peter Vaughan as survivor of wartime massacre brings the film alive but isn't allowed to outshine the dull principals; 1969. (c)

Two and Two Make Six XX Ah, for the innocent days of 1961 – this is a feeble comedy of Janette Scott and Jackie Lane getting on the wrong motorbikes and finding themselves drawn to their new drivers, George Chakiris and Alfred Lynch. Freddie Francis couldn't make the improbable plot work. (b/w)

The Two Faces of Dr Jekyll XX How could Stevenson's story of split personality ever be boring? If you want to know, watch this. Paul Massie's unimaginative characterisations of both parts is matched for stiffness by Christopher Lee, and the lesser parts (Dawn Addams, David Kossoff, and a host of other undistinguished supports) are nowhere more than competent and frequently less. Mind you, Terence Fisher's direction is handicapped by Wolf Mankowitz's uninspired script and all the violence, blood and sundry mayhem which looks as though it has been casually thrown in for effect; 1960. (c)

Two for the Road √ Contrived exercise from director-producer Stanley Donen, from an ingenious but empty script by Frederic Raphael about Audrey Hepburn and Albert Finney driving through France. Their regular trips through their courtship and marriage are jumbled up in a series of flashbacks that should perhaps be called flashybacks. Some gorgeous photography from Christopher Challis, but ultimately a disappointing effort; 1967. (c)

Two for the Seesaw √ The play by William Gibson from which this was taken in 1962 was a wry Feiffer-like look at the meeting and parting of two bruised New Yorkers. It's hard to know whether to place the fault of the adaptation on writer Isobel Lennart, director Robert Wise, or leads Robert Mitchum (on the run from a broken marriage) and Shirley MacLaine (a supposedly lovable, over-generous kook). Certainly the split-screen, so you can see both being lonely at once, was a mistake. (b/w)

Two Guns and a Badge X Owing to a mistake, Wayne Morris, just out of jail, is made assistant sheriff. Will he let the badge down? Unfortunately for predictability, no. Lewis D. Collins must have been tempted to make a switch of plot, but sadly refrained; 1954. (b/w)

The Two-Headed Spy √ Routine spy melo which purports to tell the true story of General Schottland, who was close to Hitler but a British agent as well. It's all rather poorly done, which suggests that the weakness lay with director André de Toth and writer James O'Donnell, because Jack Hawkins, Gia Scala, Alexander Knox and Erik Schumann were all capable players. By the way, if he was so anti-Hitler and so close to him, why didn't General Hero get in a quick shot one dark night? 1958. (b/w)

Two-Lane Blacktop √√ Remarkable and unusual odyssey across America, partly an intermittent race between two souped-up cars, partly a philosophical comment on the aimlessness of contemporary (1971) America. Monte Hellman extracted convincing performances from Warren Oates, James Taylor, Dennis Wilson and the cars. (c)

Two Left Feet XX Dispiriting shuffle through the mods-and-rockers phenomenon of the mid-sixties, providing Michael Crawford, Julia Foster, David Hemmings and Dilys Watling inadequate range for their talents. Roy Baker directed without inspiration. For some reason it got an X certificate at the time; 1963. (b/w)

Two Letter Alibi XX Poor little nonsense about husband accused of wife's murder. Peter Williams 'starred'; Ursula Howells, Stratford Johns backed up under Robert Lynn's vapid direction, in 1962. (b/w)

The Two Mrs Carrolls X A stinker for Humphrey Bogart was this nonsense about him as artist painting his wives as Angel of Death and then doing them in. He is getting ready to dispatch Barbara Stanwyck when the chemist he has been buying the poison from starts blackmailing him. From then on, it's all go. Alexis Smith plays the putative third Mrs Carroll and there are some sickly scenes with a little daughter. Incidentally, it's all supposed to be happening in England (the presence of Nigel Bruce is the proof of that), a place where director Peter Godfrey came from many years before this was made in 1946, and seemed to have forgotten. (b/w)

Two Mules for Sister Sara √ Shirley MacLaine as a nun who isn't all she

seems and Clint Eastwood as her protector make a delightful pair to lead Don Siegel's 1969 survival western over some arid patches. (c)

Two of a Kind X Plan to foist boy on old folks as long-lost son goes wrong. Edmond O'Brien, Lizabeth Scott, Terry Moore star in rather unpleasant yarn, directed in 1951 by Henry Levin. (b/w)

Two on a Guillotine X If Connie Gilchrist is to inherit $300,000 she must spend seven nights in haunted house. Cesar Romero is her (presumably) dead father and her mother died guillotined in his stage act that went wrong. Director William Conrad manages to turn the screw here and there; 1965. (b/w)

Two Rode Together √ Producer Harry Cohn asked John Ford for a quick, profitable western in 1961, so James Stewart and Richard Widmark were hustled into this can't-fail conflict between, respectively, a not-too-honest sheriff and an uptight cavalryman tracking down some white prisoners held by the Comanches. If it reminds you of *The Searchers*, that's where Ford found it. (c)

2,000 Women XX A veritable Who's Who of 1944 British film actress are interned in a German camp: Phyllis Calvert, Flora Robson, Patricia Roc, Renée Houston, Anne Crawford, Jean Kent, Thora Hird, Dulcie Gray. They hide three airmen who bale out into camp grounds. Director, Frank Launder. (b/w)

Two-Way Stretch √√ Classic Peter Sellers about prisoners breaking out to do a job and getting back again. Wilfrid Hyde White, Bernard Cribbins, Lionel Jeffries, Irene Handl. Robert Day directed, 1960, which, looking back, Sellers may feel was the peak of his career. After this, he became a major international star and the fun seemed to go out of his films. (b/w)

Two Weeks in Another Town X Fascinating example of how good acting (Edward G. Robinson, Kirk Douglas) can almost overcome direction (Vincente Minnelli) and script (Charles Schnee from a far tougher Irwin Shaw novel) about hysterical film-making in Rome. They run large chunks of *The Bad and the Beautiful* as the model of a great film. Oddly enough it was made by the same team as this 1962 effort. (c)

Two Weeks with Love XX Mild, early (1950) generation gap comedy with

Debbie Reynolds and Ricardo Montalban in a resort in the Catskill Mountains; director Roy Rowland had some help from Busby Berkeley with the dances. (c)

U

The Ugly American XX Naïve political statement about Vietnam and neutrality, presented in 1963 as though it was the last word in political maturity. Even then it looked hollow. Today it seems pretentiously absurd. Marlon Brando was ill-cast as American ambassador, forced to reject wartime buddy-buddy, a local leader, in order to avert that most dreaded of all fates – a Communist take-over. Producer-director George Englund's un-named Indo-chinese country looks awfully studio-bound and phoney, too. (c)

Ulysses XX (1) Homer, Ben Hecht and Irwin Shaw, who all had a hand in the script, should have done better with this 1955 parade of shaky spectacle and crude muscle. Kirk Douglas, Anthony Quinn, Silvana Mangano look and feel out of place; clearly director Mario Camerini found the whole international co-production just too much to handle. (c)

Ulysses √√ (2) James Joyce's stream of consciousness was the subject of a brilliant attempt by Joseph Strick in 1967. Milo O'Shea wasn't really solid enough as the hero and Barbara Jefford not earthy enough as his wife. But some extracts from the text came over marvellously, and the atmosphere of Dublin was faithfully retained despite a forced up-dating. Only in the Fellini-and-water brothel scenes does it sag. (b/w)

Ulzana's Raid √ 1972 western which has no truck with current ideas about Red Indians: they are baddies and that's that. But taking the equally old-fashioned battle between ageing Burt Lancaster and brash youngster Bruce Davison as a universal theme, Robert Aldrich used the genre to make some thoughtful statements. (c)

Unchained XX Prison-without-bars melo with Chester Morris; main point of interest is the song, 'Unchained Melody'. Director: Hall Bartlett; 1955. (b/w)

The Unconquered X SEE . . . Paulette Goddard at the stake and in the bath! . . . Gary Cooper organising to throw the British out!! . . . Boris Karloff dressed up as an Indian chief!!! . . . Cecil B. DeMille's cast of thousands!!!! . . . and don't believe a word of it; 1947. (c)

The Undefeated X Three thousand stampeding horses go some way to make up for an otherwise dull western, but director Andrew McLaglen doesn't get the best out of his human actors. John Wayne and Rock Hudson meet up after the Civil War, feud a bit, then get drunk together. It all goes on for rather a long time; 1969. (c)

Under Capricorn XX Every great director must be allowed some disasters and this 1949 costumer set in Australia turned out to be Hitchcock's biggest one. He only did it because pretentious Ingrid Bergman (then reigning queen of moviedom) consented to play the lead – at a cripplingly large salary – then chose the wrong scriptwriters (Hume Cronyn, James Bridie) and male lead (Joseph Cotten – too posh; Burt Lancaster would have been better, Hitch says, looking back). Bergman was supposed to be English aristo drinking herself to death over a guilty secret and being poisoned by a *Rebecca*-type housekeeper (Margaret Leighton) at the same time. It was a huge financial and critical flop and Hitchcock had some harsh words to say about the preening afterwards. (c)

Undercover Girl X Gladys George walks away with this one under nominal star Alexis Smith's nose. It's one of those crime dramas where a girl joins the police to root out her father's murderer and gets trapped by dope-running gang. Joseph Pevney could have directed in his sleep, in 1950 – and maybe did. (b/w)

Undercover Man √ The neutral Glenn Ford in semi-documentary attempt to show how Capone-type gangster is nailed on tax-evasion charge, as Al was. Nina Foch is female interest. Director Joseph H. Lewis made it a cut above the average in 1949. (b/w)

Undercurrent √ Katharine Hepburn marries Robert Taylor but is bothered by mysterious reticence about his brother; when Robert Mitchum finally turns up, she is scared that he is a psychopathic murderer – or could it be that his brother, her husband, is the nut? Vincente Minnelli keeps you guessing; 1946. (b/w)

Under Fire XX Are these soldiers deserters? It's hard to care under James B. Clark's lack-lustre direction, in 1957. Rex Reason, Steve Brodie, Henry Morgan among those present. (b/w)

Under Milk Wood X Illustrated version of the Dylan Thomas poem, with Richard Burton intoning and revisiting the mythical town. A galaxy of stars (Liz Taylor, Peter O'Toole, Glynis Johns, Vivien Merchant, etc.) are not well served by director Andrew Sinclair's literalness; 1971. (c)

Under My Skin √ Bent jockey tries to go straight for the sake of his son. Director Jean Negulesco helped to soften – and weaken – original Hemingway story. With John Garfield, Luther Adler; 1950. (b/w)

Under Ten Flags √ Van Heflin as captain of enterprising German warship pursued by British (namely Charles Laughton) in Second World War. Duilio Coletti directed; 1960. (b/w)

Under the Clock √ Judy Garland was kept tightly under control by second husband Vincente Minnelli in 1945; she plays an office worker in New York who bumps into soldier-on-leave Robert Walker. They spend the day and night (delivering milk) together. James Gleason, Keenan Wynn make outstanding supports. (b/w)

Under the Gun √ Jail drama of breaks and pardons, with Richard Conte, Sam Jaffe, Audrey Totter. Director: Ted Tetzlaff; 1950. (b/w)

Under the Yum Yum Tree √ Irresistible Jack Lemmon makes rather old-fashioned (1963) comedy about sex-obsessed landlord more than just watchable. Carol Lynley is the highly fanciable, but virtuous, tenant he leches after; David Swift directs. (c)

Underwater! X Silly plot about sunken treasure in the Caribbean can only have been an excuse to see Jane Russell in a diving suit. John Sturges directed in 1955. (c)

Underwater Warrior √ Dan Dailey as America's Commander Crabbe, Commander Francis D. Fane, shot, documentary style, in the Philippines. Director Andrew Marton keeps the suspense going down among the so-easily-dead men; 1958. (b/w)

The Underworld Story √ Dan Duryea buys an interest in a small newspaper,

finds himself threatened when he starts uncovering corruption. Herbert Marshall and Gale Storm help to make it all rather more believable than usual under Cy Endfield's brisk direction; 1950. (b/w)

Underworld USA √√ 'Give Blood Now' proclaims a poster under which one of the many victims of this cold-blooded but brilliant gangster-thriller dies. One of the most explicitly violent and corrupt works by writer-producer-director Samuel Fuller, it manages to be moralistic at the same time. Cliff Robertson is Nemesis for his father's murderers; but then he falls in love with an ex-whore, Dolores Dorn, which makes him vulnerable to a Nemesis of his own. In 1961, it looked like the end of the gangster cycle. Today, it seems the beginning of the sado-masochistic one. (b/w)

The Unearthly XX John Carradine as mad scientist hooked on human experiments. Not very distinguished in any department, particularly direction – Brook L. Peters; 1957. (b/w)

Unearthly Stranger X Flashbacking 1963 sci-fi has scientist John Neville discovering he is married to Alien Being (Gabriela Licudi) sent to destroy him; with Jean Marsh, Warren Mitchell, Patrick Newell. Director John Krish. (b/w)

Uneasy Terms XX Rubbishy Peter Cheyney 'thriller' about stupid wills and soppy murderesses. Vernon Sewell churned it out with the help of Michael Rennie, Moira Lister and Joy Shelton in 1948. (b/w)

Unfaithfully Yours √ Rex Harrison plotting revenge for wife's infidelity during a concert — murder while the Rossini plays, renunciation during the Wagner, doing himself in during Tchaikovsky. Preston Sturges directed with style and wit. Linda Darnell plays the wife; 1948. (b/w)

The Unfinished Dance XX 1947 American remake of *La Mort du Cygne* has B+ dancing, B— acting. Recommended only for ballet-mad little girls. 10-year-old Margaret O'Brien played one; Cyd Charisse was prima ballerina. Director, Henry Koster. (c)

The Unforgiven √ John Huston epic, 1960, about cowboys and Indians fighting over Audrey Hepburn's parentage; exciting climax. Audie Murphy, Lillian Gish, Burt Lancaster, Charles Bickford. (c)

The Unguarded Moment XX Esther Williams stays out of the swimming pool and in the classroom as teacher whose life is upset by sexy notes from one of her class. Esther should have stuck to swimming; Rosalind Russell, who helped write it, to acting. And director Harry Keller to better pictures; 1956. (c)

The Unholy Wife X One of Diana Dors's American disasters; she's Rod Steiger's wife and in attempting to do him in, kills another chap. John Farrow failed to make you care; 1957. (c)

Union Station √ Director Rudolph Maté keeps us in some suspense while police hunt for blind girl and her kidnapper; with William Holden, Barry Fitzgerald, Nancy Olson; 1950. (b/w)

Universal Soldier X Oddity in which George Lazenby plays a mercenary who sees the error of his ways, thanks to Germaine Greer (playing someone very like herself). There follows a chase by an African leader who was employing him. Director Cy Endfield appears as a landlord, and delivers some apparently improvised lines; 1971. (c)

The Unknown Man √ Lawyer Walter Pidgeon discovering to his horror that the client he so ably got off a murder charge was guilty after all – and what he does about it. Richard Thorpe holds the interest; 1951. (b/w)

The Unknown Terror X Creeper about molecular monsters, whatever they are, in South America. The usual mad scientist guff. John Howard, Mala Powers; director Charles Marquis Warren, who may have been consumed by abnormal fungus creatures shortly after the start of the picture; 1957. (b/w)

Unman, Wittering and Zigo X Unpleasant, rather inept version of Giles Cooper's radio drama that became a TV play. A class of murderous public schoolboys terrorise their teacher (David Hemmings), set out to rape his wife (Carolyn Seymour), and behave generally nastily. Director, John MacKenzie; 1971. (c)

The Unsinkable Molly Brown X More's the pity. Noisy musical has a boisterous Debbie Reynolds as social-climbing heroine, a hardly-adequate Harve Presnell and indulgent Charles Walters direction; 1964. (c)

The Unsuspected √ Suave, smiling villain Claude Rains intends to murder niece Joan Caulfield. Will Hurd Hatfield stop him? Director, Michael Curtiz; 1947. (b/w)

Untamed X Boer pioneers as heroes doing to the Zulus what the wagon trains did to the Indians: with He-man Tyrone Power. Director Henry King has some excuse in that it was made in less aware 1955; (c)

Untamed Frontier X Ranchers versus homesteaders plot, with Diana Cotten on the side of the little people, cheered on by Shelley Winters. Hugo Fregonese must have found an old script lying around somewhere in 1952. (c)

Until They Sail √ Paul Newman falling for one of four sisters while serving in US Army in New Zealand. Widow Jean Simmons is the one who dispels his cynicism (if not ours); the others are Joan Fontaine, grim spinster softened by Charles Drake; Piper Laurie, who sleeps around; Sandra Dee, who waits for her soldier-boy to come home. Robert Wise didn't try to push it further than the outer limits of soap opera; 1957. (b/w)

Up From the Beach X Routine Second World War adventure has Cliff Robertson, Broderick Crawford trying to liberate French village and director Robert Parrish trying to hold our interest; 1965. (b/w)

Up in the World XX 1957 Norman Wisdom farce has an English stately home setting and John Paddy Carstairs direction; with Maureen Swanson, Jerry Desmonde, Ambrosine Phillpotts. (b/w)

Up Jumped a Swagman XXX Gimmicky attempt by Christopher Miles, making his first full-lengther, to project singer Frank Ifield as an actor. It fails miserably on about every possible count. Suzy Kendall, Richard Wattis seem desperately wrong in stock parts, and while Annette André looks pretty, she doesn't look happy; 1966. (c)

Up Periscope X James Garner and Edmond O'Brien as naval officers on submarine fighting each other as well as the Japs in unexceptional Gordon Douglas-directed Second World War picture; 1959. (c)

Up Pompeii X Opening-out of Frankie Howerd's leering TV series, made in 1971, strengthened with some useful additions: Michael Hordern, Adrienne Posta, Russell Hunter, Roy Hudd, but still basically boring. Director, Bob Kellett; 1971. (c)

Upstairs and Downstairs XX Snobbish British comedy about the absolutely ghastly problems poor Michael Craig and Anne Heywood have with their servants, my dears; Joan Sims, Claudia Cardinale, Mylène Demongeot are three of a feckless succession. It must have been offensively out-of-date even in 1959, when Ralph Thomas directed. James Robertson Justice, Sid James, Daniel Massey also appear. (c)

Up the Chastity Belt XXX Fans of Frankie Howerd may find an occasional snigger in this medieval romp, but the rest of the population will yawn and go to bed – not aroused, alas, despite much coupling and (because it's a twin-brother plot) tripling. Bob Kellett attempts to marshal a large cast of varying talents (Anna Quayle, Eartha Kitt, Godfrey Winn, Billy Walker among them), but his efforts resemble a shortsighted groom flogging a dead horse; 1971. (c)

Up the Creek √ 1958 British slapstick with David Tomlinson trying to curb Peter Sellers, Lionel Jeffries and other lower-deckies. Good fun from Val Guest. (b/w)

Up the Down Staircase √ Sandy Dennis unconvincing as pie-eyed teacher in *The Blackboard Jungle* territory. Unfortunately, Robert Mulligan, the director, seems as impressed as she is with the superiority of letters over life and thus neither he, she, nor the film comes as closely to terms with the reality of slum existence as the unblinking location camera held by Joseph Coffey; 1967. (c)

Up the Front XX Tasteless Frankie Howerd vehicle. He has the German's master plan to win the First World War tattooed on his bottom; director, Bob Kellett; 1972. (c)

Up the Junction X Ruination of raw yet sensitive television play by director Peter Collinson in 1967, who reduced the factually-based story of upper-class girl in Cockney-land to caricature. Suzy Kendall is the posh girl; Dennis Waterman her working-class boyfriend; Adrienne Posta, Liz Fraser, Hylda Baker, Maureen Lipman, Susan George some of the sketchy people she encounters. (c)

Up the Sandbox √ – or 'The Secret Life of Barbra Mitty', as La Streisand wanders about fantasising, having discovered she is pregnant again. Women's Lib and its derivatives occupy most of her thoughts, but there are saving graces in her ingratiating performance and director Irvin Kershner's objectivity about the character; 1972. (c)

Up Tight X *The Informer* remade as a 1969 black power movie by Jules Dassin. Uses newsreel footage to give a documentary gloss, but this just shows up the phoniness of the rest. And when a fancy director, however distinguished, attempts to tell it like it is, baby, in the ghetto, it simply doesn't work. Raymond St. Jacques, Frank Silvera, Ruby Dee. (c)

Up to His Neck XX Weak 1954 British comedy about skyving sailor Ronald Shiner, occasionally cheered up by glimpses of Harry Fowler, Brian Rix, Bryan Forbes, Anthony Newley, Hattie Jacques. John Paddy Carstairs sort of directed. (b/w)

Uptown Saturday Night √ A raft of black stars – Sidney Poitier, Bill Cosby, Flip Wilson, Richard Pryor, Harry Belafonte – enjoy themselves in a comedy about a missing lottery ticket and gangsters; Poitier directed it all in 1974 with both eyes on the newly profitable black audience. (c)

Uranium Boom XX Hard to care about Dennis Morgan and William Talman scrapping over love for Patricia Medina. There's a fortune in uranium under their feet. William Castle churn-out; 1956. (b/w)

Utah Blaine X Rory Calhoun and Susan Cummings inherit range and have to fight renegades to stop them from taking it away. Dull stuff from Fred F. Sears; 1957. (b/w)

V

The Vagabond King XX Kathryn Grayson warbles through hygienic Hollywood 1956 remake of Friml's operetta of 15th-century Paris rabble and their poet-champion, played by the awful Oreste. Michael Curtiz directed. (c)

Valdez is Coming √√ Superior 1970 western, with Burt Lancaster as a determined if muddled idealist lawman, taking on villain Jon Cypher and hirelings singlehanded. Director Edwin Sherrin's first film effort; he brought some thoughtful actors with him from the theatre and there are appreciably greater characterisation and undercurrents of real conflict than usual. (c)

Valentino XX This biography of Rudolph could have been a winner if it had stuck to the facts. Instead, like nearly all show-biz biopics, it reduces its subject by fictitious clichés. Anthony Dexter, Eleanor Parker, with Lewis Allen the guilty director; 1951. (c)

Valerie X Courtroom drama with multi-flashbacks about Sterling Hayden, Anita Ekberg, Anthony Steel – dour performers, every one. Nor does Gerd Oswald's 1957 direction exactly shine. (b/w)

The Valiant X Italian prisoners-of-war won't talk, so is Captain John Mills justified in refusing them medical aid? Subordinates Robert Shaw, Liam Redmond think not, but director Roy Baker didn't take sides in this disappointing 1961 naval yarn. (b/w)

The Valley of Decision √ Sticky stuff about an Irish servant girl (Greer Garson, would you believe?) and involvement with son of the family she serves (Gregory Peck). Efficient Tay Garnett 1945 heart-string-puller with lovable old Donald Crisp, crusty old Lionel Barrymore and sweet little Dean Stockwell. (b/w)

Valley of Eagles X Scientist's assistant steals his research and his wife; the chase is on. Terence Young keeps it going, although cast of Jack Warner, Nadia Gray and Christopher Lee (in a small part) wasn't the sprightliest, even in 1951. (b/w)

The Valley of Gwangi √ Little circus in need of a new attraction discovers valley where prehistoric monsters live. They capture one. It escapes, causes havoc. Sadly, James O'Connolly's direction of the humans involved (James Franciscus, Gila Golan, Laurence Naismith) makes them less convincing than producer Ray Harryhausen's special effects; 1969. (c)

Valley of Mystery X Characters you've all seen before struggle against the Bolivian jungle and plodding screenplay after plane is forced down. Richard Egan is 'star' of this strictly B-picture. Director, Joseph Leytes; 1967. (c)

Valley of the Dolls X Hard to know which is the nastier – Jacqueline Susann's original, or this 1967 Mark Robson adaptation of trashy best-seller about three hopefuls (Barbara Parkins, Sharon Tate, Patty Duke) in the wicked world of showbiz. (c)

Valley of the Kings √ Robert Taylor, Eleanor Parker, on archaeological dig in routine adventure yarn set against stunning Egyptian background. Robert Pirosh directed; 1954. (c)

Value for Money XX Mild little comedy about John Gregson coming into money and Diana Dors. Ken Annakin; 1955. (c)

Vampire Circus XXX Weak 1971 Hammer horror with the second eleven batting on a sticky wicket. Laurence Payne is a tepid hunter, gypsy Adrienne Corri fails to chill, and Robert Tayman is a blunt fang-bearer. Robert Young directed; 1971. (c)

The Vampire Lovers X Ingrid Pitt as lesbian Dracula in rather desperate 1970 version of the old fang-bearer. She charms her way into Peter Cushing's household, after Douglas Wilmer forgets to drive a stake through her heart. Among the ladies she eyes are Madeleine Smith, Dawn Addams, Kate O'Mara, while Jon Finch fancies her. Roy Ward Baker directed with tongue in hollowed cheek. (c)

Vanishing Point √ One long car chase from Colorado to California, with some excitement. Barry Newman, Dean Jagger, directed by Richard Sarafian in 1971. (c)

The Vanquished X John Payne returns to town after the Civil War to spy out who's responsible for corruption. Edward Ludwig didn't make the most of it; 1953. (c)

The Veils of Baghdad XX Victor Mature joins Arabian ruler's palace guard. Strictly for pipe-dreamers. James Arness, Virginia Field. George Sherman directed slavishly; 1953. (c)

The Venetian Affair X Despite the Venice exteriors, this is a Bonding of the old Bulldog Drummond with the Man from UNCLE. Indeed, here is the man himself, Robert Vaughn, looking the worse for wear after being bounced from the CIA because his wife turned out to be Red agent. They meet up again, with predictable results. Helen MacInnes's novel gets drowned somewhere between the Rialto and the Bridge of Sighs by director Jerry Thorpe and co-producer-scripter E. Jack Neuman; 1967. (c)

Vengeance X Sci-fi thriller about scientist being taken over by kept-alive brain, and uncovering a murder; with Peter Van Eyck, Anne Heywood, Bernard Lee, Cecil Parker. Director Freddie Francis; 1963. (b/w)

The Vengeance of She XX Shoddy 1968 follow-up to *She*, with John Richardson, Edward Judd, Colin Blakely, Olinka Berova. Director: Cliff Owen. (c)

Vengeance Valley √ Noble Burt Lancaster takes the blame for his womanising younger brother Robert Walker in actionful western. Director Richard Thorpe did a fine job of work in 1951. (c)

Vera Cruz √ Gunmen Gary Cooper, Burt Lancaster mixed up in Mexican revolution and lots of Robert Aldrich-directed, location-shot action. They can't decide which side to fight on and finally fall out over some gold. Big box-office success; disliked by the critics; 1954. (c)

Verboten! X James Best uncovers neo-Nazi German youth plot in Berlin, under Samuel Fuller's gutsy direction; 1959. (b/w)

Vertigo √√ 1958 Hitchcock has so much going for it (James Stewart, Kim Novak's carnality, trick photography, our vertigo) that you forgive pre-posterous story, plot flaw, Hitch's hostility towards Novak. (c)

The Very Edge X Anne Heywood is raped by Jeremy Brett. Husband Richard Todd is naturally most upset. Then the rapist reappears. Elizabeth Jane Howard wrote the screenplay, adequately directed by Cyril Frankel in 1963. (b/w)

Very Important Person X British comedy has pompous James Robertson Justice taken prisoner-of-war by Germans, and old faithfuls like Leslie Phillips, Eric Sykes, Stanley Baxter, Richard Wattis to keep you smiling. Ken Annakin directed; 1961. (b/w)

A Very Special Favour XX If you don't find the thought of father (Charles Boyer) asking womaniser (Rock Hudson) to seduce career-girl daughter (Leslie Caron) because he's afraid she's growing frigid funny, nothing else in this smutty 1965 sex-comedy will make you laugh. Director Michael Gordon couldn't make it watchable. (c)

Vice Squad √ Edward G. Robinson lifts this day-in-the-life-of-a-cop drama above the triteness of its title. Arnold Laven directed; 1953. (b/w)

Vicki X Richard Boone is bull-like cop determined to prove Elliott Reid killed his sweetheart, singer Jean Peters. Heavy 1953 remake by Harry Horner of H. Bruce Humberstone's 1941 *I Wake Up Screaming (Hot Spot).* (b/w)

Victim √√ Ahead of its time (1962)

treatment of homosexuality as mainspring of detective story. Michael Relph, Basil Dearden directing, Otto Heller photographing, Dirk Bogarde giving tremendous performance in exacting role. (b/w)

The Victors √ Director Carl Foreman follows squad of American soldiers through Second World War Europe (a nastier bunch you never met), and takes a long time about it. Large starry cast of this 1963 episodic drama includes George Peppard, George Hamilton, Eli Wallach, Jeanne Moreau, Melina Mercouri, Romy Schneider, Albert Finney. (b/w)

The View From Pompey's Head √ Cinematic equivalent of a good long read adapted in 1955 from Hamilton Basso best-seller about return to Southern town by successful New York publisher. Lightweight cast (Richard Egan, Dana Wynter) and director, Philip Dunne. (c)

A View From the Bridge √ Sidney Lumet version of Arthur Miller's powerful play about Italian stevedore's obsessive lust for his niece was rather let down by the casting of Raf Vallone, Carol Lawrence in central roles; 1962. (b/w)

The Viking Queen XX Can you spot the wrist-watch on the arm of one of the characters in this junk set in the times of Boadicea? It's about the only entertainment you'll get in Don Chaffey's violent cut-price epic with Don Murray and a large weak British cast; 1967. (c)

The Vikings X Tony Curtis, Kirk Douglas, Ernest Borgnine, Janet Leigh in energetic costumer about Nordic invasion; Richard Fleischer directed the Norse-play; 1958. (c)

Villa √ One more ride round the life of Pancho Villa, this time with Brian Keith as American who joins his band, Cesar Romero. Directed by James B. Clark in 1958. Rodolfo Hoyos is Villa, the only Mexican actor to essay the part. (c)

Village of Daughters XXX Eric Sykes judging Italian beauty contest, with Carol White among the many unconvincing Italians. Director, George Pollock; 1961. (b/w)

Village of the Damned √ Wolf Rilla chilla about creepy look-alike kids taking over village; based on John Wyndham's *The Midwich Cuckoos.* George Sanders, Barbara Shelley, Michael Gwynn; 1960. (b/w)

Village of the Giants X Uninspired

adaptation of H. G. Wells's *Food of the Gods*, with teenagers discovering that if they eat grub invented by 12-year-old they will grow to great height and be able to terrorise rest of the village. Bert I. Gordon directed cast of unknowns; 1965. (c)

Villain √ Gangster thriller set, unusually, in England, with Richard Burton making one of his better appearances in this 1971 effort. TV director Michael Tuchner did well by an unfunny script from Dick Clement and Ian La Frenais. There are some nasty moments of sadism and the film often looks like a rip-off of the James Cagney thriller, *White Heat*. Involved are Joss Ackland, T. P. McKenna, Donald Sinden, Nigel Davenport, and Cathleen Nesbitt as the mother with whom cowardly gangster Burton is fixated. (c)

Villa Rides! X Long, disappointing account of Mexican revolutionary, Pancho Villa, with Yul Brynner, Robert Mitchum, Charles Bronson, Herbert Lom. Buzz Kulik directed; 1968. (c)

The Vintage XX Made in France by Jeffrey Hayden with Mel Ferrer and John Kerr as two Italian brothers on the run, in the wine country. They meet up with Michèle Morgan and Pier Angeli but it's all awfully nebulous; 1957. (c)

The Violent Enemy √ Tom Bell, Susan Hampshire in ambivalent attempt to discuss the use of violence for such causes as the IRA, and at the same time exploit it as basis of a thriller. He is IRA hero sprung from Dartmoor by crooks who want to use his expertise to break into electronics factory. Ed Begley turns in fine performance as old guard freedom fighter. But Don Sharp's direction tends to blur the argument; 1969. (c)

The Violent Men √ Glenn Ford, ex-Civil War officer, against cattle king Edward G. Robinson and nasty wife, Barbara Stanwyck. Superior oater, directed by Rudolph Maté; 1956. (c)

The Violent Ones √ Mexican girl is raped. Before she dies she says her attacker was an American. But which of the three in the district is it? Fernando Lamas, as both deputy and director, takes them on a trek to the next town to escape the lynch-mob. On the way the murderer is revealed; 1967. (c)

Violent Playground X Something of an early (1957) *Z-Cars*, even down to John Slater as sergeant. Stanley Baker

is chief cop and do-gooder; David McCallum (later a Man from UNCLE) is a tough lad, Anne Heywood his nicely spoken (i.e. sympathetic) sister. Basil Dearden directed. (b/w)

Violent Road X A kind of remake of *The Wages of Fear*, with Efrem Zimbalist Jr., Dick Foran among the drivers with the dynamite on board. Howard W. Koch directed; 1958. (b/w)

Violent Saturday √ Strong cast – Lee Marvin, Ernest Borgnine, Victor Mature – in 1955 thriller about effect of bank robbery caper on small town. Richard Fleischer brings series of individual stories into focus as action progresses. (c)

The VIPs √ Splendid people (Elizabeth Taylor, Richard Burton, Margaret Rutherford, Orson Welles) all hanging about in London Airport lounge and not done complete justice to in multi-plotted mish-mash directed by Anthony Asquith, 1963. Watch David Frost walk through. (c)

The Virgin and the Gypsy √ Honourable attempt by Christopher Miles in 1970 to bring to life D. H. Lawrence's novella about the girl from the rectory and 'the natural man' is sabotaged by unsympathetic casting (Joanna Shimkus, Franco Nero) and a string of 'rep' actors (Maurice Denham, Fay Compton, Kay Walsh, Norman Bird) in smaller parts. Another mistake was to give all too solid flesh to the girl's fantasies. (c)

Virginia City XX Even lovers of Humphrey Bogart will find it hard to watch him faltering through a Spanish accent in a big-budget, small-brained Civil War western, directed by Michael Curtiz in 1940. Others to pity are Errol Flynn, Miriam Hopkins, Randolph Scott. (b/w)

The Virginian √ 1946 remake by Stuart Gilmore of the famous 1929 Gary Cooper starrer, this time with Joel McCrea as the good guy, Brian Donlevy as the bad. Main drama comes when hero has to hang his friend as a rustler, and there's a climactic shoot-out. (c)

Virgin Island X Modest 1958 British comedy about young writer and his bride setting up home on tiny Caribbean island; with John Cassavetes, Virginia Maskell, Sidney Poitier. Pat Jackson directed. (c)

The Virgin Queen √ Bette Davis as Elizabeth 1st – or, in this case

Elizabeth 2nd, as she first played the part back in 1939 in *The Private Lives of Elizabeth and Essex*, with Errol Flynn. It was Elizabeth and Raleigh in 1955, with Richard Todd and obsequious Henry Koster direction. (*c*)

The Virgin Soldiers √ Leslie Thomas's best-seller about national servicemen in Singapore comes over well in 1969 version by John Hopkins, adapted by John McGrath, added to by Ian La Frenais (how's that for TV influence?). Hywel Bennett as Chief Male Virgin meeting up with Chief Female Virgin Lynn Redgrave (weakest performance in a strongly-cast film) is convincing, as is the climactic regimental dance. Nigel Davenport, Jack Shepherd, Rachel Kempson stand out; and while there's a lot of talk about sex, there isn't much on the screen. Incidentally it makes a powerful argument against conscription. John Dexter. (*c*)

The Visit X Frederic Dürrenmatt's rather unpleasant play about richest woman in the world trying to get her first seducer sentenced legitmately to death by bribed town. Made even more unsympathetic by casting of two of the most self-regarding stars in the business in the main parts: Ingrid Bergman and Anthony Quinn. They are directed sycophantically by Bernhard Wicki; 1964. (*b/w*)

Visit to a Small Planet √ Jerry Lewis as visitor from Outer Space, sent to observe us earthlings. OK knockabout stuff for fans, but what happened to the wit of Gore Vidal's original Broadway satire? Norman Taurog; 1960. (*b/w*)

Viva Max! X Mexican bandit comedy with schmaltzy characterisation and lack of tension. Everything depends on your appreciation of Peter Ustinov's coy general, who too often seems more Jewish than Mexican. Jerry Paris; 1970. (*c*)

Viva Zapata! √√ Today it seems several shades too simplistic, but in 1952, Elia Kazan's clear-eyed interpretation of John Steinbeck's tidy script about a hero of the Mexican revolution moved, inspired, and excited. Owing more to the paintings of Diego Rivera and Orozco than the photographs of the time, it makes a beautiful set of pictures. Over it all, towers Marlon Brando's tragic interpretation of an idealist. Whether Emiliano Zapata was anything like that is, of course, another matter. Anthony Quinn won Support Oscar as his younger brother, but by far the better performance was Joseph Wiseman's agent provocateur. (*b/w*)

Voice in the Mirror √ Richard Egan flashbacking his way through addiction to drink and out the other side, thanks to his wife Julie London. Harry Keller directs neatly; 1958. (*b/w*)

Von Ryan's Express √√ American PoW 'von' Sinatra leading escape in Mark Robson's fast-moving Second World War chase drama. Trevor Howard gives outstanding support; 1965. (*c*)

Voodoo Island X Boris Karloff as exposer of hoaxes, goes to tropical isle at the request of businessmen who plan to develop it, to discover cause of strange goings-on there. Elisha Cook's presence does something to redeem poor script and direction by Reginald le Borg; 1957. (*b/w*)

Vote for Huggett XXX Terrible old (1949) British comedy with Jack Warner and Kathleen Harrison heading unbelievable Cockney family. This time he is standing as councillor, planning to build a war memorial. Director, Ken Annakin. (*b/w*)

Voyage to the Bottom of the Sea √ Captain Walter Pidgeon ordering Joan Fontaine, Peter Lorre and others around in his super-submarine. Irwin Allen made it all very jolly in 1961. (*c*)

W

W X Twiggy's short-lived Hollywood career consisted entirely of this unpleasant little thriller in which she plays an unsympathetic spoiled wife (or wasn't she meant to be off-putting?) who is threatened by convict-husband (allowed out on visits), Eugene Roche. Richard Quine directed, failing to ensure that the audience interest is focussed on any of the characters; 1973. (*c*)

Wabash Avenue √ 1950 Henry Koster remake of *Coney Island* switches turn-of-the-century location to Chicago; provides Betty Grable with some boisterous song-and-dance routines and leading man Victor Mature. (*c*)

The Wackiest Ship in the Army √ Second World War comedy-drama has Jack Lemmon in charge of tacky old boat and useless crew. Richard Murphy directed; 1961. (c)

Wagonmaster √√ Almost a documentary as John Ford shows a Mormon trek hounded by Indians and outlaws. It rambles magnificently on through some superb Ford landscapes to the inevitable showdown; Ben Johnson, Ward Bond, Joanne Dru, James Arness; 1950. (b/w)

The Wagons Roll at Night √ Humphrey Bogart is circus manager, Sylvia Sidney's his star, Eddie Albert is local hero turned lion-tamer. A version of *Kid Galahad*, directed by Ray Enright in 1941. (b/w)

Wait Until Dark √ Saccharine-sweet blind Audrey Hepburn trapped by thug Alan Arkin and friends in a Greenwich Village basement. They are looking for a doll filled with heroin and are prepared to kill to get it. She turns out the lights, but . . . The climax is fine, and Terence Young extracts the most from it, but the build-up takes for ever; 1967. (c)

Wake Me When It's Over X Depressingly apt title for 1960 Mervyn Le Roy-directed, over-acted comedy about Bilko-like soldier on desert isle. Ernie Kovacs, Dick Shawn. (c)

Walkabout √√ Remarkable, unusual journey across Australian desert by 14-year-old girl (Jenny Agutter), her 6-year-old brother and an aborigine makes the centrepiece of a haunting film by Nicholas Roeg; 1970. (c)

Walk Don't Run X Cary Grant lifts this otherwise fluffy 1966 remake by Charles Walters of *The More the Merrier* with Samantha Eggar in Jean Arthur part. She shares apartment with athlete Jim Hutton and Cary during Tokyo Olympics. Nicely, naturally. (c)

The Walking Dead √ 1936 horror with Boris Karloff, brought back from execution in the electric chair, taking his vengeance; Edmund Gwenn, Ricardo Cortez among those present; director, Michael Curtiz. (b/w)

Walking My Baby Back Home X Uninspired jazz musical has Donald O'Connor as band leader, Janet Leigh for love-interest and flat Lloyd Bacon direction; 1954. (c)

Walking Tall √ Honest-Sheriff-Brings-Law'n'Order-to-Corrupt-Town thriller is supposed to be eighty per cent true. Based on the life of Buford Pusser, played by Joe Don Baker, he is shown using every kind of violence in the interests of Good. Is that good?

Phil Karlson directed expertly in 1973. (c)

A Walk in the Spring Rain XXX Unfortunately, they got wet. Ingrid Bergman is fractionally more watchable than Anthony Quinn, if only because his Zorba-like character wooing her suburban housewife in the wilds has degenerated completely into a collection of mannerisms by 1969. The yarn belongs in one of those women's magazines that have gone out of business; and Guy Green is just the director to deliver the sententious coup de grâce. (c)

A Walk in the Sun √√ Lewis Milestone's famous 1945 exposition of the human side of war, as American infantry battalion advances in Italy. Richard Conte, John Ireland stand out. (b/w)

Walk into Hell XX Australian effort, filmed in New Guinea, about lady explorer winning undying love of savages by curing their sick child. Chips Rafferty's in it, of course. Lee Robinson directed; 1957. (c)

Walk Like a Dragon √ Jack Lord saves Nobu McCarthy, a Chinese slave-girl, from life of prostitution; takes her to his home town, where he has to overcome prejudice, and her former boyfriend. Director James Clavell made it watchable; 1960. (b/w)

Walk on the Wild Side √ If the rest of the film doesn't live up to the credits sequence, it still isn't as bad as some critics have said. Nelson Algren's bestseller made adequate 1962 setting for strong performances from Jane Fonda and butch Barbara Stanwyck in New Orleans brothel, even if leads Laurence Harvey and lost love Capucine were dreadful. Edward Dmytryk did his directorial best. (b/w)

Walk Tall X Disappointing western about chase after rapists, with Willard Parker, Kent Taylor; director, Maury Dexter; 1960. (c)

Walk the Proud Land √ Audie Murphy in what's claimed to be true story of the Indian agent who captured Geronimo and brought peace between Apaches and whites. Anne Bancroft, Charles Drake; director, Jesse Hibbs; 1956. (c)

Wall of Noise √ Routine soaper – handsome Ty Hardin involved with Dorothy Provine and married Suzanne Pleshette – given a racetrack setting, and Richard Wilson as director in 1963. (c)

The Walls of Jericho X Soapy yarn of

small-town lawyer Cornel Wilde, married to common, alcoholic Ann Dvorak, lusted after by wife (Linda Darnell) of best friend Kirk Douglas, but loving pure assistant, Anne Baxter. There are courtroom and boudoir battles before the final clinch, and director John M. Stahl makes it pretty heavy going; 1948. (b/w)

Waltz of the Toreadors X Disappointing adaptation of Jean Anouilh's featherweight farce into a heavy-footed clomp round the ballroom floor. Peter Sellers does one of his mimicries as old soldier that might have been funny for a few lines but rapidly bores; Margaret Leighton tries hard but is defeated by the script; and a handful of useful character-actors are whizzed through their paces by director John Guillermin, who seemed, in 1962, to be getting into speed practice for his later flying movie, *The Blue Max*. The plot, such as it is, involves Sellers's life of love. (c)

Wanda √√ Roughly made in 16mm, this story of a woman who wanders (the choice of name must be more than random) from pick-up to pick-up, involving herself in crime on the way, has real power. Barbara Loden both directed and acted the main part, and it deserves to be seen, with sympathy, as an early attempt (1970) to make a Women's Lib movie. (b/w)

War and Peace √ American style. Audrey Hepburn a natural Natasha, Henry Fonda miscast as Pierre, Mel Ferrer a laughable Andrei; heavily directed by King Vidor in 1956, who managed the battle scenes well enough but not the more intimate ones. Fonda said later, 'I knew I was physically all wrong, but they didn't want a Pierre who looked like Pierre. One who looked like Rock Hudson was closer to what they had in mind.' He wasn't allowed to wear padding and producer Dino De Laurentiis was against eyeglasses, too; he was only able to wear them when the producer wasn't around. Despite this, *Time* magazine's critic said that he seemed to be the only one around that had read the book. (c)

War Arrow X Supposedly the true story of Major Howell Brady who trained the Seminoles to defeat the Kiowa Hordes. Jeff Chandler plays him, Maureen O'Hara's the object of his affection. George Sherman directed modestly; 1953. (c)

The War Between Men and Women X Unfortunate rifling of James Thurber's life and work for the soppier bits, thoughtlessly compiled. Jack Lemmon has Thurber's blindness and profession, but not his happy marriage. He 'draws' sentimental stuff like The Last Flower, but not the biting cartoons. Director and co-writer Mel Shavelson did a soft-centred job in 1972. (c)

War Drums X Goldminers provoke Apaches during Civil War. Lex Barker, Ben Johnson, Stuart Whitman in violent western, directed by Reginald Le Borg; 1957. (c)

War Hunt √ Effective low-budget Korean war drama stars John Saxon as soldier psychopath and the then – 1962 – unknown Robert Redford. Denis Sanders directed. (b/w)

War is Hell X . . . Just in case you didn't know. That's about the only message this mechanically well-made actioner has got to offer from Korea. Burt Topper directed himself; 1964. (b/w)

Warlock √ Brighter-than-average western about lawman cleaning up town, then challenged by the man who helped him. Made in 1959 by Edward Dmytryk, it was early adult oater with Henry Fonda as clean-cut cultured sheriff; Anthony Quinn as unnaturally close, adoring friend; Richard Widmark, Dorothy Malone. (c)

The War Lord X Charlton Heston demanding another man's bride as feudal right. Franklin Schaffner made a real effort in 1965 to create a medieval epic that wasn't just a comic strip but a genuine drama, but it didn't work out that way; 11th-century Normandy was never like this. (c)

The War Lover X Steve McQueen, Robert Wagner as pilots in love with same girl (Shirley Anne Field). Strictly for war-lovers and those who enjoy Second World War dramas. Philip Leacock; 1963. (b/w)

A Warm December X Sidney Poitier mooning round England after dying Esther Anderson, who rejects his offer of marriage to help her emerging African nation. Codswallop with a black face, directed by its star, who should have stayed in front of the camera; 1972. (c)

Warning Shot √ 1967 police thriller has David Janssen clearing himself of a charge of murdering an innocent man while on duty; Ed Begley gives strong support, and Eleanor Parker, Lillian Gish, Joan Collins, George Sanders manfully back up director Buzz Kulik. Drugs are the clue. (c)

War of the Satellites √ One of Roger Corman's jolly low-budget sci-fis, rather dragged out, with its yarn about scientist's mind being controlled by alien planet. Dick Miller, Susan Cabot; 1958. (b/w)

War of the Worlds √ Weak transfer of H. G. Wells's early sci-fi novel to present day (well, 1953) and California, and given an unfortunate religious undertone the author would surely have found unacceptable. Byron Haskin does what he can with a cynical script by Barré Lyndon and stolid performances by Gene Barry and Jack Kruschen. Special effects are ingenious, however, and there are quite a lot of laughs, some of them intentional. (c)

War Paint √ Will the peace treaty get to the Indians? Or will murdering fanatic stop it? Lesley Selander manages to keep the suspense more or less going. Robert Stack, Joan Taylor humour him; 1953. (c)

Warpath √ Edmond O'Brien doing the Nemesis bit in western, after his woman has been killed. Dean Jagger and Forrest Tucker give a familiar look to the old prairie under Byron Haskin's direction; 1951. (c)

The Warriors X Attractive, but not awfully convincing, casting has Errol Flynn as the Black Prince, Joanne Dru his highborn damsel-in-distress and Peter Finch as villainous French nobleman in this colourful, English-shot costume lark. Director Henry Levin used the same castle set as the *Ivanhoe* made at Elstree three years before this 1955 effort. Flynn agreed with critics that, at 46, he was a bit old for the dashing young hero stuff. (c)

The War Wagon √√ Lively, often funny, Burt Kennedy-directed western has John Wayne planning to rob $250,000 gold shipment from armoured coach. His helpers are gunslinger Kirk Douglas, Red Indian Howard Keel, dynamite whizz Robert Walker, old thief Keenan Wynn and his young bride Valora Noland; 1967. (c)

Washington Story X Muck-raking reporter Patricia Neal can't get the dirt on Congressman Van Johnson, because there isn't any. Writer-director Robert Pirosh couldn't make it believable in 1952. (b/w)

Watch It, Sailor √ Brisk farce with Dennis Price, Liz Fraser, Irene Handl, Marjorie Rhodes in great complications about a wedding and an official telegram cancelling it. Wolf Rilla keeps it going; 1962. (b/w)

Watch the Birdie X Silly stuff about Red Skelton as photographer that doesn't do even his small talent justice. Arlene Dahl, Ann Miller and frantic Jack Donohue direction; 1950. (b/w)

Watch Your Stern X Could have been called *Carry On Up Your Torpedo*, as it was made by the *Carry On* team and their director Gerald Thomas, and contains same blend of blue slapstick. Supposedly about Kenneth Connor losing plans and substituting fridge blueprint. Eric Barker, Leslie Phillips, Joan Sims, Hattie Jacques, Sid James; 1960. (b/w)

Waterhole 3 X Self-satisfied western caper with James Coburn, Joan Blondell and treasure buried in the desert; William Graham directed in 1967. (c)

Waterloo Road XX Stewart Granger as wartime spiv (remember spivs?) who makes a pass at Joy Shelton and gets beaten up by John Mills, unconvincing in a Cockney role. Directed in 1945 by Sidney Gilliat. (b/w)

Watermelon Man √ Idea of a white man waking up to find himself black is full of possibilities, but disappointing director Melvin Van Peebles took little advantage of them. Godfrey Cambridge did his best in the rather dated 1970 role, but Estelle Parsons as his wife and the rest of the cast were encouraged to play for laughs – any laughs. (c)

Watusi! XX Cynical remake of *King Solomon's Mines*, made nine years later to use up the footage left over from the 1950 version. Kurt Neumann was in charge of the cobbling; lesser stars David Farrar, George Montgomery, Taina Elg, Rex Ingram caper about discovering long-lost kingdom (and library film). (c)

The Way Ahead √ Propaganda film, scripted by Eric Ambler and Peter Ustinov in 1944, showing how a group of civilians were transmogrified into a close-knit fighting unit in North Africa. David Niven, Raymond Huntley, William Hartnell, Stanley Holloway did so well under Carol Reed's direction that the film was commercially released. (b/w)

Way of a Goucho X Run-of-the-Pampas melo has Rory Calhoun, Gene Tierney, Richard Boone lovin' and killin' in rugged last-century Argentina. Jacques Tourneur; 1952. (c)

The Way Out XX But not very far.

Creaky chase story with Gene Nelson imported in 1956 to star with Sidney Tafler, Michael Goodliffe, John Bentley. Director, Montgomery Tully. (b/w)

The Way to the Gold X Wooden Jeffrey Hunter on the trail of buried treasure; Robert D. Webb directed; 1957. (b/w)

The Wayward Bus X Watering-down of John Steinbeck best-seller has Joan Collins, Jayne Mansfield, Dan Dailey among passengers stranded when bus breaks down on the way to Mexico. Victor Vicas; 1957. (b/w)

The Wayward Girl XX Mother and stepdaughter both fancy same chap. Mother kills him, blames daughter. Lesley Selander directed Marcia Henderson in this tripe; 1957. (b/w)

Way . . . Way Out X Jerry Lewis on the moon, with Connie Stevens as astronaut wife. They're supposed to be manning US weather station. Gordon Douglas; 1966. (c)

The Way West √ Made in 1967, it's on a big scale ($5,000,000) and it has got big stars (Kirk Douglas, Robert Mitchum, Richard Widmark) but it suffers from telling too many stories. Director Andrew McLaglen, son of Victor, just can't seem to deliver more than spectacle in his big oaters. As a travelogue, though, it has its moments. (c)

The Way We Were √√ Surprisingly persuasive and watchable evocation of the radical years between 1937 and early fifties by hard-working Barbra Streisand, under Sydney Pollack's direction. Robert Redford makes a convincing WASP, all too keen to compromise; 1973. (c)

The Weak and the Wicked X Inside a British women's prison with J. Lee Thompson. Glynis Johns, Diana Dors, Jane Hylton and what happens to them; 1953. (b/w)

The Weapon X Little boy finds gun; accidentally shoots his friend; runs away in horror. George Cole, Steve Cochran are just two of the many after him in this 1956 Val Guest attempt at suspense. (b/w)

The Webster Boy X Undistinguished melo, directed in 1962 by Don Chaffey, that takes itself far too seriously. Elizabeth Sellars's ex-lover, John Cassavetes, turns up on the scene after 14 years and makes problems for his already-difficult illegitimate son. (b/w)

Wedding Breakfast √ Sentimental family comedy about hard-up Bronx

cab driver and wife wanting to splash out on fancy wedding for their daughter; she wants a quick, quiet one. Youngsters Debbie Reynolds and Rod Taylor (this was 1956) appear more insipid than usual beside Bette Davis and Ernest Borgnine's larger-than-life performances as self-sacrificing parents. Richard Brooks directed from Paddy Chayefsky play. (b/w)

Weekend at the Waldorf X Portmanteau of dubious plots on the pattern of *Grand Hotel*. This 1945 update of the 1933 hotel drama had Ginger Rogers, Lana Turner, Walter Pidgeon, Van Johnson, Edward Arnold, Keenan Wynn, Robert Benchley among guests and staff; but director Robert Z. Leonard made it all hard, and rather dull, going. (b/w)

Weekend with Father √ Patricia Neal, widow, falls for Van Heflin, widower, but their children object. Douglas Sirk makes it entertaining enough; 1951. (b/w)

Wee Willie Winkie √ Shirley Temple saves the British Army on the Northwest Frontier, aided by Victor McLaglen. Made in 1937 and about worth the ninepence it cost then. Although the Hollywood pre-war system compelled John Ford to direct such rubbish as this, he still manages to work in marvellous moments, like his child's-eye view of the terrain. C. Aubrey Smith, Constance Collier, Cesar Romero do their usual lovable bits. (b/w)

We Joined the Navy X Cheerful, undemanding romp has Kenneth More as blundering naval officer, Lloyd Nolan, Mischa Auer, John Le Mesurier, Kenneth Griffith, Derek Fowlds; Wendy Toye directed; 1962. (c)

Welcome To Hard Times √√ Evil Aldo Ray terrorises small town, and mayor Henry Fonda is inclined to let him get on with it until accusations of cowardice force him into showdown. Janice Rule is chief spur. Written and directed by Burt Kennedy as an erotic, violent parable; 1967. (c)

The Well √ Prejudice goes when a black child is trapped in a well. Leo Popkin used his cast of little-knowns (Henry Morgan is only near-name) effectively in 1951. (b/w)

We're no Angels √ Soft-centred story of escapees from Devil's Island saving kindly family from clutches of Basil Rathbone. What Michael Curtiz would have done without Humphrey Bogart and Peter Ustinov must have caused him sleepless nights in 1955. The other non-angel was Aldo Ray. (c)

We're Not Married √ Five couples discover their marriages are not legal; Marilyn Monroe, Ginger Rogers, Mitzi Gaynor, Fred Allen, Paul Douglas among the unwed. Pity that writer Nunnally Johnson couldn't quite keep up the fun through all five episodes. Light Edmund Goulding direction; 1952. (b/w)

The Werewolf XX Unscrupulous scientists seeking serum against radiation turn man into a blood-sucker. Director Fred F. Sears fails to chill; Steven Rich, Joyce Holden; 1956. (b/w)

Werewolf of London √√ 1935 classic horror movie directed by Stuart Walker about botanist (Henry Hull) bitten by Tibetan werewolf (Warner Oland of Charlie Chan fame), turning into London rampager. Lycanphobic Valerie Hobson and Spring Byington support. (b/w)

Westbound √ Strong Randolph Scott-Budd Boetticher team job about bringing in gold from California during the Civil War to help the Yankees, through Confederate opposition. Karen Steele appears to pack a strong punch as she looks after crippled husband. Virginia Mayo is Scott's girl; 1959. (c)

West 11 XX Seedy British drama about young layabout (Alfred Lynch) agreeing to murder Eric Portman's rich aunt for a share of the money; with Diana Dors, Kathleen Harrison. Michael Winner directed; 1963. (b/w)

Western Approaches √√ Wartime (1944) tribute to merchant seamen tells story of lifeboat full of real-life sailors and their encounter with a U-boat. Pat Jackson directed; Jack Cardiff photographed; greatest strength is use of sound and real-life casting. (c)

The Westerner √ Highly praised in 1940, this William Wyler-directed oater had Gary Cooper v. Walter Brennan in a land-grab dispute. (b/w)

Western Union √ Big-budget western about the laying of wires to bring the message, directed by Fritz Lang. Randolph Scott, Robert Young, John Carradine, Barton MacLane head workaday cast; 1941. (c)

West of Montana √ Buddy Ebsen promises dying friend to look after ranch, but has to involve a mail order bride to do so. A lightweight, directed by Burt Kennedy, 1963. Keir Dullea, Lois Nettleton. (c)

West of Zanzibar XX Anthony Steel looking tough but acting weakly in his tracking-down of ivory-poaching gang. Sheila Sim precise match for his milk-and-water heroics. Harry Watt's message seemed to be that the simple African folk were better off under the paternalistic British administrators; a comforting fiction in 1954. (c)

West Side Story √√ It was either the greatest musical ever filmed or a pretentious piece of gimcrack, according to which side of the barricade you were on when it came out in 1961. Either way it killed the old-style *Singin' in the Rain, No, No, Nanette* type of musical, both on stage and screen (except for camp revivals), with its harsh Bernstein rhythms, Stephen Sondheim lyrics and easy adaptation of modern ballet techniques from Jerome Robbins (who was also directing the movie until They tired of his 'perfectionism' and replaced him with Robert Wise). True, the dialogue is embarrassing; true, the nerveless borrowing from *Romeo and Juliet* is half-hearted; true, Richard Beymer's acting is laughable and Natalie Wood doll-like. Rita Moreno, George Chakiris are fine, however; the social significance isn't all cop-out, and those ten Academy Awards were not entirely undeserved. (c)

Westward the Women √ Paramount wouldn't let out-of-favour Frank Capra make his own story of 200 women trekking across America to meet blind-date husbands in California, with Gary Cooper. So in 1951 he sold it to MGM for his close friend William Wellman to make with Robert Taylor. It turned out a successful and off-beat western. (b/w)

Westworld √√ Genuinely frightening sci-flick, cleverly combining robots with the western myth. Richard Benjamin (convincing) and James Brolin (wooden) go for an expensive holiday in a future entertainment-camp which will realise your fantasies for you. But the robots who can usually be killed and humiliated are in revolt. One of them, 'Gunslinger' Yul Brynner, chases them for real and is unstoppable even by acid. Writer-director Michael Crichton is better at ideas than execution, which tends to be messy and incomplete. But there is enough to scare you; 1973. (c)

Wetbacks √ Are what Mexicans smuggled North of the Border to work in USA are called. Hank McCune got a strong chase yarn out of this human drama, with Lloyd Bridges, Barton MacLane, Nancy Gates, in 1956. (c)

What A Crazy World XX Dated pop musical about out-of-work East End kid writing hit song, with then (1963) pop stars Joe Brown (and his Bruvvers), Marty Wilde, Susan Maugham, Freddie and the Dreamers. Harry H. Corbett, Avis Bunnage (as Joe's dogs-and-Bingo-mad mum and dad) are good for a different kind of giggle today. Michael Carreras. (b/w)

What A Way To Go XX Thin 1964 comedy doesn't support top-heavy talent and production; oft-widowed Shirley MacLaine is pursued by undaunted suitors. With Paul Newman, Dean Martin, Robert Mitchum, Gene Kelly (who hits highest spot), Bob Cummings, Dick Van Dyke. J. Lee Thompson directed and got roasted by the critics for the film's lack of style, grace and wit. (c)

What Did You Do in the War, Daddy? X Blake Edwards's Second World War farce has James Coburn, Dick Shawn, Harry Morgan clowning in a very unwarlike Sicily; 1966. (c)

Whatever Happened to Aunt Alice √ She got used in a meretricious title, that's what. This would-be chiller was produced in 1969 by Robert Aldrich, the man who had made *Whatever Happened to Baby Jane?* seven years before, but that's all they have to do with one another. This one is about Geraldine Page who manages to get some well-lined ladies to come and keep house for her out there in the Arizona desert. Then she does them in. The current one is Ruth Gordon, the witch from *Rosemary's Baby*, which should have been warning enough. It may give you a few mild thrills, but not many sleepless nights; 1969. (c)

Whatever Happened to Baby Jane? √√ Bette Davis *v.* Joan Crawford in 1962 contest to out-overact the other in Robert Aldrich's *grand guignol* pic. Not as horrifying as it sets out to be, the story is ingenious and not without surprises, and there are several moments of genuine tension. The best bits are the two-women scenes outfreaking each other in grotesque makeup. (b/w)

What Price Glory √ John Ford remake of silent comedy classic about two brawling soldiers (James Cagney and Dan Dailey in this 1952 version) in First World War France. (c)

What's Good for the Goose XXX This 1969 comedy was claimed as changing Norman Wisdom's image. All that meant was the only time his pants came off was when he took them down to go to bed with Sally Geeson. Otherwise, it's the same old boring Norman, rather worse-directed than usual by Israeli Menahem Golan. (c)

What's New, Pussycat? √ Desperately painful attempt at sustained comedy had a big success in 1965, when the idea that sex could be (a) explicit, and (b) an object of fun, was novel. But Clive Donner couldn't make a monumentally boring cast (Peter Sellers, Peter O'Toole, Romy Schneider, Capucine, Woody Allen, Ursula Andress) do more than preen themselves and dare us not to share their high opinion of themselves. Woody Allen's script contains flashes of genuine humour, but it's an awfully forced exercise. (c)

What's So Bad About Feeling Good? X Tropical bird spreads happiness bug over New York. George Peppard and Mary Tyler Moore are Village dropouts infected by it. Well, director George Seaton must have thought it was a cute idea in 1968. (c)

What's the Matter with Helen? √ The answer is that she has been trapped in an even cruder version of the excesses of *Whatever Happened to Baby Jane?* by the same author, Henry Farrell; director, Curtis Harrington. This time, Debbie Reynolds and Shelley Winters (Helen) play out their nostalgic and camp horror moves, with Dennis Weaver and Michael MacLiammoir sucked in; 1971. (c)

What's Up, Doc? √ Fitfully amusing but comprehensively dispiriting attempt, in 1972, to generate the goofiness of a thirties crazy comedy, by Peter Bogdanovich. Unfortunately, everyone is trying so hard to be cute that the strain shows, the very opposite of the effortless ease which the real masters of the genre used to achieve. Barbra Streisand is gauche where Katharine Hepburn was wide-eyed; Ryan O'Neal dull against Cary Grant's memory, but support Kenneth Mars as O'Neal's rival for a music prize achieves the true Mischa Auer panache and Madeleine Kahn makes an entertaining shrew who gets hers. The main plot, about identical suitcases, is just silly. (c)

What's Up, Tiger Lily? XX Spy send-up – the plot to steal recipe for the best egg-salad in the world – leadenly re-edited by Woody Allen from a poor Japanese original. Occasional commentary and appearances by Allen are far from helpful or amusing; 1966. (c)

The Wheeler Dealers √ Slick Arthur Hiller comedy has James Garner as oil man come to New York to raise money; Lee Remick's presence ensures that that's not all he goes back to Texas with; 1963. (c)

When Eight Bells Toll √ Anthony Hopkins, Robert Morley, Jack Hawkins in routine actioner from Alistair Maclean novel. Lots of boats and gold bullion in pretty Scottish scenery. Director, Etienne Périer; 1971. (c)

When Gangland Strikes X Should county prosecutor pull his punches when gang threatens to expose his daughter? Veteran R. G. Springsteen doesn't seem to care as much as he should, and result is a rather inconsequential movie. Raymond Greenleaf, Marjie Millar, Anthony Caruso; 1956. (b/w)

When Hell Broke Loose X Charles Bronson, serving in the army, was once a racketeer. But he gives it up for the sake of German girl, and stops a Nazi assassination attempt on General Eisenhower into the bargain. Kenneth Crane doesn't convince; 1958. (b/w)

When in Rome X Con man Paul Douglas disguises himself as priest when he's on the run from police in Rome; finds himself being converted by real-life priest Van Johnson. Director Clarence Brown tried to make it funny in 1952. (b/w)

When the Boys Meet the Girls X 1966 remake of *Girl Crazy* provided work for uncharismatic Harve Presnell and Connie Francis and an excuse for reworking of old Gershwin score ('I Got Rhythm', 'Embraceable You', etc.). Louis Armstrong, Herman's Hermits, Liberace looked in but didn't help director Alvin Ganzer any. (c)

When the Legends Die √√ Impressive essay of what happens when a proud Indian boy finds himself trapped in a reservation and then learns the 'new ways' of the white man which mostly consist of drunkenness and chicanery. Frederic Forrest makes an impressive Indian, whose skill at bronco-riding provides a temporary escape from poverty; Richard Widmark has one of the best roles in his career as the white promoter who exploits him. Director, Stuart Miller; 1972. (c)

When the Redskins Rode XX Beautiful French spy tries to con the Indians to fight for France in the New World. Jon Hall resists. Lew Landers directed; 1951. (c)

When Willie Comes Marching Home X What happens to small-town boy Dan Dailey when he joins the Army. Corinne Calvet's just one of many adventures in this soft-centred Second World War comedy that even John Ford fanatics admit to be a failure; 1950. (b/w)

When Worlds Collide √ Earth is about to be destroyed by star hurtling towards it, and there's a race on to build a spaceship to carry off would-be survivors; they include Richard Derr, Barbara Rush. Special effects won 1951 Oscar, but nothing else about this routine sci-fi was much of a winner. Rudolph Maté directed. (c)

Where Angels Go, Trouble Follows X Someone, somewhere, must have enjoyed Mother Superior Rosalind Russell in *Trouble With Angels*, because they went and made a sequel for her in 1968. So whoever you are out there, this one – with Stella Stevens as 'progressive' young nun – is for you. James Neilson directed. (c)

Where Danger Lives X Dr Robert Mitchum, infatuated with the near-crazy Faith Domergue, is afraid he might have killed husband Claude Rains so he hops it, silly man. Difficult to know which is the more unbelievable – the plot or Miss D.'s performance. John Farrow directed; 1950. (b/w)

Where Does It Hurt? XXX Everywhere, but mostly in Peter Sellers's already shredded reputation in 1971, as he wearily goes through what are supposed to be zany motions in a hopeless hospital. Director Rod Amateau is amateur. (c)

Where Eagles Dare X Parachuters into Germany again, this time with a woman, Mary Ure, among them. Richard Burton, Clint Eastwood, Patrick Wymark, Peter Barkworth in an orgy of blood-letting which may have satisfied director Brian G. Hutton but which disgusted most reviewers; 1969. (c)

Where Love Has Gone X A Harold Robbins not-about novel (not about Lana Turner) with Susan Hayward's daughter killing her mother's latest lover and Bette Davis as domineering grandma. Edward Dmytryk evidently just let it happen; 1964. (c)

Where's Charley? √ 1952 musical remake of the farcical *Charley's Aunt* has reliable vaudevillain Ray Bolger dragging-up and lively Frank Loesser score. David Butler directed. (c)

Where's Jack? √ Romp through the not very smelly stews of London with Tommy Steele as honest Jack Sheppard, turned villain by nasty Stanley Baker, loved by simple Fiona Lewis, and, a bit later, patronised by posh Sue Lloyd, which gives director James Clavell the chance of a bit of cleavage. Although it has its eye on the U-cert. audience, it's acceptably enjoyable by the slightly more sophisticated, as well; 1969. (c)

Where's Poppa? √√ Funny black comedy about George Segal trying to get rid of his ghastly mother, Ruth Gordon. Outrageous sub-plot concerns his brother, Ron Leibman, who goes walking in Central Park because he likes getting mugged. The wonderfully funny Carl Reiner directed in 1970. (c)

Where the Boys Are XX And the laughs aren't. Henry Levin has been stuck with a dreary, dry-cleaned script (by George Wells) about Fort Lauderdale, notorious American resort where college girls and boys go lemming off to spend their vacations. But the film isn't sexy, made as it was in pre-permissive 1960, where getting pregnant meant that you had to be knocked down by a car to prove that God punished wrongdoers. George Hamilton, Dolores Hart, Yvette Mimieux, Paula Prentiss, Connie Francis move around energetically instead of acting. (c)

Where the Bullets Fly XX Poor spy stuff with Dawn Addams saving the world by stopping secret substance falling into enemy hands. The rest of the cast seemed to have been carefully chosen by director John Gilling not to show up the lack of ability in his star – about the only bit of his job he managed adequately; 1966. (c)

Where There's A Will XX George Cole, Kathleen Harrison in pathetic British comedy. If you're forced at gunpoint to watch this rubbish about city lads inheriting farm, see if you can spot Edward Woodward's film debut; he was 24 in 1954. Vernon Sewell directed. (b/w)

Where the Sidewalk Ends √ Vicious cop Dana Andrews kills murder suspect, hopes to pin it on mobster; but falling in love with victim's widow, Gene Tierney, upsets his plans. Otto Preminger kept our interest, even if dull leads couldn't; 1950. (b/w)

Where the Spies Are √ Bright spy thriller, from a novel by James Leasor, laced with dry comedy from David Niven as Dr Jason Love, reluctant agent. Support from John Le Mesurier, Cyril Cusack, Françoise Dorléac, Nigel Davenport; directed, 1965, by Val Guest. (c)

Where Were You When the Lights Went Out? √ Doris Day's wholesome presence ensured that this Hy Averback-directed comedy about the 1965 New York blackout was just good clean fun – well, clean, anyway. Robert Morse, Terry-Thomas, Patrick O'Neal, Lola Albright involved in the unlikely goings-on. 1968. (c)

While the City Sleeps √ Ambitious newspapermen compete in hunting down dangerous killer. As so often, director Fritz Lang was let down by uncharismatic cast: Dana Andrews, Rhonda Fleming, Vincent Price, George Sanders, Ida Lupino; 1956. (b/w)

Whiplash X Dane Clark, artist, is transformed into prize-fighter with murderous instincts; Alexis Smith and Zachary Scott add unconvincing dramatics. Forties archetype Eve Arden is the other woman. Director, Lewis Seiler; 1948. (b/w)

Whirlpool √ (1) Moody, ingenious hokum directed by Otto Preminger about Svengaloid Jose Ferrer using Gene Tierney to further nefarious schemes; 1949. (b/w)

Whirlpool XX (2) Ex-Left Bank cellar girl Juliette Greco sings and looks sultry in Lewis Allen's 1959 dull and undemanding mystery, with Marius Goring and O. W. Fischer. (b/w)

Whisky Galore √√ If Sandy Mackendrick's funny about shipwreck of liquor-laden boat off Hebridean isle seems a bit genteel now, remember that as well as creasing us all in 1948, it changed a nation's (France's) drinking habits, and even named a style of dancing (go-go, from *Whisky A-Gogo*, the film's French title, adopted for name of first discothèques). It had Joan Greenwood, Catherine Lacey, Gordon Jackson prominent among the islanders. (b/w)

The Whisperers √√ Remarkable *tour de force* by Dame Edith Evans (winning her 1967 British Oscar) as neglected old woman haunted by voices in her head. Bryan Forbes's script and direction eschewed commercial considerations (except in tangential sub-plots) and the film made no impact at the box-office. Strong support from Gerald Sim as assistance man, Nanette Newman as aggravated girl upstairs, Eric Portman as the old woman's indifferent husband. (*b/w*)

Whispering Smith v. Scotland Yard XX Famous detective proves 'suicide' is murder. But it's all so old-fashioned and creaky, you're hardly likely to care. Director Francis Searle reduced Greta Gynt (not difficult to do), Herbert Lom, Dora Bryan to ciphers; 1952. (*b/w*)

The Whistle at Eaton Falls √ Unusual drama centres round problems of union leader who becomes manager of a factory and is faced with sacking the workers. Robert Siodmak directs documentarily, and has strong cast in Ernest Borgnine, Dorothy Gish, Anne Francis, Lloyd Bridges; 1951. (*b/w*)

Whistle Down the Wind √√ When Hayley Mills (actually 15 when it was made in 1961, but playing younger) finds murderer Alan Bates in the barn and mistakes him for Christ, the stage could have been set for pathos. Under Bryan Forbes's skilful direction, it never succumbs, although the religious parallels – three-fold betrayal, 'crucifix' shot – are a bit forced. Touching when it could have been trite. (*b/w*)

White Christmas √ 1954 version of *Holiday Inn* has Bing Crosby, Danny Kaye involved with Rosemary Clooney, Vera-Ellen, at winter resort owned by their old army officer, Dean Jagger. It's in trouble and they save it. Only the title song is good enough; the rest of Irving Berlin's score reveals how patchy this over-rated composer was. Michael Curtiz, 1954. (*c*)

The White Cliffs of Dover X Watch it only if you are feeling very sentimental or want a good laugh at the expense of those who fought and suffered at home; Hollywood's idea of Britain at war in 1914-18 (director, Clarence Brown, 1944) is unrecognisable to anyone who was there. Irene Dunne, Van Johnson, C. Aubrey Smith, Peter Lawford. (*b/w*)

White Corridors XX Googie Withers loves James Donald over the operating tables of a Midlands hospital. Made in 1951, before *Emergency Ward 10* and the rest had introduced a measure of realism into this kind of studio stuff; director, Pat Jackson. (*b/w*)

White Feather X Cowboys *v*. Indians with Robert Wagner trying to get Cheyenne tribe, led by Jeffrey Hunter and Debra Paget suitably blacked up, to move to reservation. Robert D.

Webb's 1955 actioner a long time out of date. (*c*)

White Heat √√ In 1949, Jame Cagney had escaped from gangster movies for ten years, but it was a bad patch for him and he had to accept another such part – as an Oedipus-complexed gunman in what turned out to be classic Raoul Walsh thriller. Critics agree that only a dirctor as tough as Walsh could have got away with Cagney sitting on his mother's lap. Virginia Mayo plays the girl he puts second to his Mom. (*b/w*)

White Lightning √ Burt Reynolds ingratiates his way through moonshine thriller, as he attempts to trap Sheriff Ned Beatty for the FBI. Car chases are well done and there are some fresh characterisations, but director Joseph Sargent can't hold the interest tightly enough; 1973. (*c*)

White Line Fever X Lacklustre trucking drama in which Jan-Michael Vincent stands out against corruption in freight hauling, so incensing the freeloaders that they go to enormous lengths to frame and/or kill him. But he's a hero in the end. Ho hum. Jonathan Kaplan directed, without conviction, in 1975. (*c*)

The White Squaw X When a white rancher is told to give his land back to the Indians because he didn't file legal claim he goes berserk. But director Ray Nazarro fails to make much of what could have been fascinating situation. William Bishop, Nancy Hale; 1956. (*b/w*)

The White Tower √ Hard work for mountaineering doubles as six people tackle virtually unclimbable Alp. But director Ted Tetzlaff makes you suspend disbelief pretty effectively and you'll find yourself involved in the struggles and past lives of Glenn Ford, Claude Rains, Alida Valli, Oscar Homolka and Cedric Hardwicke. 1950. (*c*)

White Witch Doctor X The witch doctor's a lady – dedicated nurse Susan Hayward, wanting to share the marvels of modern medicine with those poor ignorant savages in Darkest Africa. Travelling companions Robert Mitchum, Walter Slezak don't go along with her missionary zeal – they're just after hidden treasure. Not one of Henry Hathaway's best; 1953. (*c*)

Who Goes There? XX Peggy Cummins falls in love with Buckingham Palace sentry. Valerie Hobson, Nigel Patrick, George Cole, A. E. Matthews chased around in circles under Anthony

Kimmins's limp direction, in 1952. (b/w)

Who Is Harry Kellerman and Why Is He Saying Those Terrible Things About Me? X Anyone who has read more than one story about psychopaths could tell you the answer – it's his Hyde hiding. More to the point is Who Is Dustin Hoffman and Why Does He Take Part in Terrible Films Like This One? Director, Ulu Grosbard; 1971. (c)

Who Killed Mary Whats'ername? √ Stylish little thriller from director Ernie Pintoff, with Red Buttons tracking down a whore's killer; Sylvia Miles is another hooker; 1971. (c)

Who Killed Teddy Bear? X Juliet Prowse is getting obscene phone calls, Jan Murray is the detective, but is he also the caller? Sal Mineo, Elaine Stritch are too good for this rubbish; director Joseph Cates; 1965. (b/w)

The Whole Truth X Did producer Stewart Granger, filming in the South of France, murder starlet? The police think so – but would he really have endangered his investment that way? John Guillermin skims over the surface, 1958. Donna Reed, George Sanders weigh in professionally enough. (b/w)

Who's Afraid of Virginia Woolf? √ √ √ Stunning performances by Elizabeth Taylor (Oscar) and Richard Burton made this already compulsive drama by Edward Albee of in-fighting between academic husband and wife, involving another couple, played by mannered Sandy Dennis (Oscar) and George Segal, into something really special. Mike Nicholas's direction has been criticised as dull, but he managed to convey a total effect of marital desolation that few films have ever done. More Academy Awards were won by Haskell Wexler's photography, art direction, costumes; 1966. (b/w)

Who's Been Sleeping In My Bed? X 1963 farce with Dean Martin as hero of TV medical series bothered by women patients; Elizabeth Montgomery tries to push him altarwards, Carol Burnett jolly as his psychiatrist's nurse. Daniel Mann. (c)

Who's Got the Action? X Careful wife tries to keep compulsive gambler hubby's money in the family by turning bookie. Lana Turner and Dean Martin are shown up by Walter Matthau, the only laugh in this strained Daniel Mann attempt; 1962. (c)

Who Slew Auntie Roo? X The 1971 edition of director Curtis Harrington's *Baby Jane* cycle starred Shelley Winters as a strange lady whom two children are convinced is a witch. Could have been terrifying. Isn't. (c)

Who's Minding the Mint? √ Good-natured romp with Mint employee who destroys $50,000 by mistake, trying to forge replacements. Milton Berle, Joey Bishop, Dorothy Provine, Jim Hutton; director, Howard Morris; 1967. (c)

Who's Minding the Store? X Jerry Lewis as incompetent assistant in big department store. Jill St. John, as boss's daughter, provides the romance; Agnes Moorehead and Ray Walston, a touch of class; and Jerry, the inevitable fooling. But who provides the laughs? Not director Frank Tashlin; 1963. (c)

Who Was That Lady? √ Professor Tony Curtis enlists help of old pal Dean Martin in cooking up unlikely explanation when wife Janet Leigh (real-life wife in 1960) catches him kissing one of his students. The whole thing gets out of hand when they – and director George Sidney – bring the FBI into it. (b/w)

Why Must I Die? X Sombre stuff about night-club singer, daughter of a crook, being executed for murder she didn't commit. Terry Moore is poor substitute for *I Want to Live*'s Susan Hayward, and Roy Del Ruth makes it merely histrionic; 1960. (b/w)

Wichita √ The year is 1874 (actually, it's 1955) and Wyatt Earp (Joel McCrea) takes over as sheriff. Lloyd Bridges and Wallace Ford provide the excitement, and Vera Miles the clinches. As Jacques Tourneur is the director, it's all rather stylish. (c)

Wicked As They Come X Unappetising melo in spite of Arlene Dahl as man-eating executive; Ken Hughes directed; 1956. (b/w)

The Wicked Lady X Margaret Lockwood in famous highwaywoman part that was lapped up by a spectacle-hungry wartime (1946) audience. It all looks distinctly creaky today, though there are a few moments of fun from James Mason, Martita Hunt, Patricia Roc. Director, Leslie Arliss. (b/w)

Wicked Women X Waitress entices boss to leave his wife, but then along comes a sailor. Russell Rouse doesn't convince, despite spirited attempts by his cast, Richard Egan, Beverly Michaels, who just haven't got the weight; 1954. (b/w)

The Wicker Man √ Clever tosh, written by Anthony Shaffer, directed by Robin Hardy and acted by a game lot of players (including Edward Woodward, Diane Cilento, Christopher Lee) who seduce you into believing one plot, then reveal that the truth is quite different. Luckily it doesn't bear two minutes' examination, so shouldn't keep you awake, after chilling you at the time; 1973. (c)

The Wilby Conspiracy √ His heart may be in the right place, but Ralph Nelson makes a mess of this thriller which combines a run-of-the-mill pursuer - pursued, double - crossing, diamond-stealing plot with condemnation of apartheid. Sidney Poitier and Michael Caine are hardly representative samples of their races; Nicol Williamson as an out-and-out fascist who is chasing them on behalf of the South African Government comes off better; 1974. (c)

The Wild Affair XX One of those pretentious trifles in which the star is given two parts to play - separate sides of her personality. For this 1965 effort Nancy Kwan was imported into England to be nice Marjorie and naughty Sandra, who takes over disastrously at the office party. It must have been intended as a comedy because the sprinkler system breaks down at the end and floods Terry-Thomas, Victor Spinetti *et al*. They are supposed to be too drunk to care; it might be more tolerable if you were, too. John Krish. (b/w)

The Wild and the Innocent √ Trapper Audie Murphy meets mountain girl Joanne Dru running away from home. Before it's all over he has to put his peaceful principles aside to protect her. Jack Sher had Jim Backus and Sandra Dee to stop it from getting too serious; 1959. (c)

The Wild and the Willing X Pretentious university drama has Ian McShane as a rather churlish student having it away with his professor's wife, Virginia Maskell; also Paul Rogers and newcomers - in 1962 - Samantha Eggar and John Hurt. Ralph Thomas directed. (b/w)

Wild and Wonderful XX Mild and middling more like. Tony Curtis outacted by dog star in fight for Christine Kauffmann's affection. In real life he married her, then was divorced. Michael Anderson did tepid job of direction; 1964. (c)

The Wild Angels √√ If this movie ever gets scheduled for TV there is bound to be a bit of an outcry, as there was in 1966 when it was banned for public showing in British cinemas (it did get club showings in 1969). However, it is a fascinating, authentic, disturbing and well-made film – the American entry at Venice – showing just how amoral the Hell's Angels motorcycle gangs were (are?). There is no plot, only a series of ever-more-violent incidents: rumbles, goading police, rapes, the shooting and capture of an Angel, his funeral. But it's made by the master of thrill, Roger Corman, and Peter Fonda plays the main role – hero would be the wrong term. Only Nancy Sinatra is out of place; Michael J. Pollard and the rest look real – and a lot of them are. (c)

The Wild Bunch √√ Outstanding western by Sam Peckinpah about the last battles of a group of gunslingers – William Holden, Robert Ryan, Ernest Borgnine – brilliantly made, with an authority and intelligence unmatched by other western directors. Unfortunately, it's also gratuitously violent, particularly at the end; 1969. (c)

The Wild Heart X Romantics may warm to this farrago of wide-eyed Jennifer Jones courted by courtly David Farrar and Cyril Cusack, but only caring deeply about a fox-cub. Powell-Pressburger directed and wrote; 1951. (c)

Wild Heritage X Teenage western about two families making it to the Rockies. But oldsters Maureen O'Sullivan, Rod McKuen come off best under Charles Haas's direction; 1958. (c)

Wild in the Country √ Elvis Presley's metamorphosis from no-good country hick to industrious college boy; and all because that nice social worker, Hope Lange, discovered he could write. Oh dear. Philip Dunne directed; 1961. (c)

Wild in the Sky √ Black comedy about skyjacking of air force plane. Meanwhile Keenan Wynn as misappropriating general is imprisoning blackmailer. The action grows steadily wilder and soon goes over the top, but there are some funny moments. William T. Naud; 1971. (c)

Wild in the Streets √ How a pop idol becomes President of America. A bit slapdash, it nevertheless manages to generate a sort of spurious conviction, thanks partly to Shelley Winters's bravura performance as his ghastly mother and Barry Shear's lively direction. In the main part, Christopher Jones is just about adequate; 1968. (c)

Wild Is The Wind X Turgid drama of Nevada sheep farmer Anthony Quinn marrying dead wife's sister Anna Magnani and getting a bit confused. Tony Franciosa. Directed by George Cukor, it isn't one of his best, but still managed to win Oscar nominations for his two stars; 1957. (b/w)

The Wild North X Wendell Corey as Mountie, Stewart Granger the man he's out to get – but is he such a bad 'un after all? Cyd Charisse is obligatory inamorata; Andrew Marton the director; 1952. (c)

The Wild One √√ Marlon Brando as head of motorcycle gang terrorising small town; Laslo Benedek directed brilliantly, and his gang of tough motor-bike Angels has entered the mythology of our times. Banned at the time, 1953, it looks milk-and-water against *The Wild Angels*, and was later permitted to be shown. Lee Marvin contributed a memorably evil role. (b/w)

The Wild Party √ (1) Unusual actioner with Anthony Quinn as skidding football star freaking out in roadside cafe and holding young couple to ransom. Jay Robinson, Kathryn Grant come off well under Harry Horner's naturalistic direction; 1956. (b/w)

The Wild Party √ (2) Suggested by the 1921 Fatty Arbuckle scandal about a young girl's death at a party (the suggestion was that he squashed the life out of her). James Ivory's sensational transposition was to a 1929 shooting. Neither James Coco nor Raquel Welch as his straying girlfriend were well cast, but Ivory managed considerable atmosphere and observation; 1974. (c)

Wild River √√ Absorbing account of TVA official Montgomery Clift trying to get old lady to relinquish her house and land, a genuine conflict between pride and progress; Elia Kazan obviously cared. Set in thirties, meticulously made in 1960, with Lee Remick caught in the middle. Jo Van Fleet, 37, plays an 80-year-old. (c)

Wild Rovers √ Chase western, with William Holden and Ryan O'Neal as quarry for Karl Malden's revenge. Conventional director Blake Edwards does well and introduces one or two distinctive touches; 1971. (c)

The Wild Seed √ Celia Kaye runs away from New York to seek parent in California. Meets up with freight-train

rider Michael Parks and goes with him. Brian Hutton directs imaginatively and quite touchingly; 1965. (b/w)

Wild Stallion X Lieutenant flashbacks through his military academy days remembering kindly officer and pet colt. Martha Hyer, Edgar Buchanan, Ben Johnson. Director Lewis D. Collins made it pretty sticky; 1952. (c)

The Wild Westerners X Duane Eddy and Guy Mitchell pop up in this routine 1963 western about newly-wed marshal investigating series of gold robberies. James Philbrook, Nancy Kovack. Oscar Rudolph directed. (b/w)

Willard √ You might think that a movie about a young man who trains rats to do his thieving and killing for him would be gruesome, but under Daniel Mann's mild direction the rats gradually become furry friends. Bruce Davison does well as the rat trainer (a real one, Moe de Sesso, gets a credit); Elsa Lanchester, Ernest Borgnine, Sondra Locke back him up; 1971. (c)

Will Penny √√ The best western for years, with Charlton Heston as a thoroughly believable, dirty, illiterate line rider (isolated for the winter looking after the prairie cattle); Joan Hackett, the young wife he gets involved with, is equally de-glamourised. Writer-director Tom Gries has allowed Donald Pleasence to go a bit mad as the villainous Preacher Quint, but everything else conveys for once what the West must really have been like; 1967. (c)

Will Success Spoil Rock Hunter? √ Historically interesting as belonging to Hollywood's Hate-TV period of 1957. In Frank Tashlin's neat direction of George Axelrod satire on commercials, Tony Randall and Joan Blondell make Jayne Mansfield look positively gawky. (c)

Willy Wonka and the Chocolate Factory √√ Stylish and imaginative realisation of Roald Dahl's children's book *Charlie and the Chocolate Factory*. The new title shows the switch of emphasis, towards the dapper magician who owns the magical factory – a role clearly enjoyed and, if anything, under-played by the extremely talented Gene Wilder. Director, Mel Stuart; 1971. (c)

Wilson √ Well-meaning, grandiose attempt by Darryl Zanuck to bring the message of internationalism to 1944 audiences; instead they stayed away in droves and it was a $3½ million flop. In name part Alexander Knox was worthy but uncharismatic; director Henry King couldn't rise to the occasion. And it's very long. (c)

Winchester 73 √√ (1) Superior western with James Stewart trailing Dan Duryea to settle grudge. This 1950 version by Anthony Mann had Shelley Winters, Tony Curtis, Rock Hudson in cast. (b/w)

Winchester 73 XX (2) Apart from Dan Duryea, again, weak 1967 remake by Herschel Daugherty has inferior players (Tom Tryon, John Saxon) and would be a total write-off if it weren't for Joan Blondell's cameo as floozie. (c)

Wind Across the Everglades √ Poorly cast by Nicholas Ray, this lyrical attempt to tell conservationist story of Florida at the turn of the century suffers from Christopher Plummer in the hero's role, Burl Ives as the heavy. Gypsy Rose Lee, clown Emmett Kelly and author MacKinlay Kantor take smaller parts more imaginatively; 1958. (c)

The Wind and the Lion X Quasi-historical charade in which *The King and I* meets 'The Sheik of Araby': Moroccan rebel kidnaps American lady and provokes an international incident. Meanwhile, she is educating him and he teaches her his primitive ways. Those who can stand smiling Sean Connery (a Scottish African?) and smug Candice Bergen will doubtless enjoy John Milius's direction; 1975. (c)

The Wind Cannot Read √ 1958 weepie with Dirk Bogarde as RAF officer married to Japanese Yoko Tani during Second World War and escaping from PoW camp to see her; Ralph Thomas directed. (c)

Windom's Way √ Predictable story of Dr Peter Finch running hospital on troubled Far East island, getting unwittingly involved with his estranged wife Mary Ure and local politics. With Natasha Parry, Michael Hordern. Directed in 1958 by Ronald Neame. (c)

A Window to the Sky XX True story of Jill Kinmont (Marilyn Hassett), a once-likely Olympic runner who broke her back and now teaches from a wheelchair. But surely nobody really talks like that; nobody responds so breathlessly to jejune pep-talks; nobody turns down marriage because they may be a drag, then relents, then accepts Fate's killing a fiancé (Beau Bridges) with such uplift. All in all,

Larry Peerce directed a pretty spurious piece of exploitation in 1975. May play under original US title, *The Other Side of the Mountain*. (c)

Wings of Chance X Crashed pilot puts faith in wild bird to get him help. Jim Brown, Frances Rafferty; director, Edward Dew; 1959. (c)

The Wings of Eagles √ John Ford tribute to old friend and air hero Frank 'Spig' Wead, with John Wayne, Dan Dailey, Maureen O'Hara. A peacetime trail-blazer, he fights paralysis to help after Pearl Harbor. But his marriage goes wrong; 1957. (c)

Wings of Fire X Suzanne Pleshette as flyer who has to win air race to save the air freight service her father runs. Juliet Mills turns up in small part; Ralph Bellamy. Director David Lowell Rich; 1967. (c)

Wings of the Hawk X Van Heflin, Julia Adams down Mexico way, involved in revolution; doubtful if you'll get equally involved, despite director – Budd Boetticher; 1953. (c)

Winning √ Fine as long as Paul Newman is driving his racing car, but not when he and wife (true-life as well as fictional) Joanne Woodward mouth a dull script about her (fictional) infidelity with Robert Wagner (excellent as rival driver). Director James Goldstone unblushingly includes real crash footage from Indianapolis; 1969. (c)

The Winning Team X Supposedly the story of real-life American baseball star, Grover Cleveland Alexander; that's Ronald Reagan, and Doris Day is his plucky wife. Lewis Seiler directed; 1952. (b/w)

The Winslow Boy √ Terence Rattigan's theatrical treatment of the famous case in which a 12-year-old naval cadet was unjustly accused of theft, was opened out by him and producer Anatole de Grunwald into a less convincing screen treatment. Gone is the relationship of father and son, in its place a conventional court scene, with Robert Donat saving the day as his defending counsel. Anthony Asquith directed, in 1948, with his rather stuffy elegance. (b/w)

Winter Meeting XX Interminable talk-talk-talk about falling in love, being afraid, becoming a priest. Should be bought up and burnt by Society for the Protection of Bette Davis who was made to go through humiliation of appearing as sexless spinster in 1948. Bretaigne Windust is said to have directed. (b/w)

The Witches XX Cast (Joan Fontaine, Kay Walsh, Alec McCowen, Ann Bell, Gwen Ffrangcon-Davies, Leonard Rossiter) much too good for this dreary yarn about witchcraft in an incredible English village, even though Nigel Kneale did the script. Maybe Cyril Frankel wasn't quite the right director? 1967. (c)

Witchfinder General √√ Remarkable effort by young director Michael Reeves who died soon after it was completed in 1968. Vincent Price makes a genuinely scary witch-hunter in Cromwell's England; Ian Ogilvy and Hilary Dwyer more than adequate young lovers. Rather a lot of gore, but most of it is justified. (c)

With A Song In My Heart √ 1952 tearjerker based on the dramatic – not to say melodramatic – life of singer Jane Froman, crippled in plane crash. An inadequate Susan Hayward mimes to Froman's voice on Alfred Newman's Oscar-winning soundtrack. Thelma Ritter, Robert Wagner, Rory Calhoun give her much-needed support; director Walter Lang tries hard. (c)

With Six You Get Eggroll XX Widow with three sons, Doris Day, marries widower with one daughter, Brian Keith. That's when the fun begins – or so director Howard Morris hoped anyway. In fact, this 1968 attempt at a 'happy' film (there are no bad guys, promised the publicity) is sickening enough without the promised eggroll. (c)

Witness for the Prosecution √√ Billy Wilder's fancywork with Marlene Dietrich being indulged, Charles Laughton licking his chops with contentment, plus Tyrone Power, Elsa Lanchester enjoying themselves in Agatha Christie courtroom hokum; 1957. (b/w)

Witness to Murder √ Barbara Stanwyck sees a murder but no one will believe her. Roy Rowland's direction makes this 1954 cliff-hanger a bit more than run-of-the-thrill. (b/w)

Wives and Lovers X Success looks like spoiling writer Van Johnson and his marriage to Janet Leigh; agent Martha Hyer, divorcée Shelley Winters, Ray Walston add to their problems. Director John Rich just couldn't make their dramas add up to the sophisticated fun he must have hoped for in 1963. (b/w)

The Wizard of Baghdad XX Unsuccessful genie is given one more chance. George Sherman attempted send-up

of *Arabian Nights* genre without conspicuous success. Dick Shawn, Vaughn Taylor try too hard. 1960. (c)

Wolf Dog XX Paroled ex-marine runs up against land-grabbing neighbour when he settles in the wild Canadian north. Jim Davis, Tony Brown. Director Sam Newfield; 1958. (b/w)

Wolf Larsen √ Jack London's *Sea Wolf* done over to give Barry Sullivan the chance to enjoy himself as tyrannical sea captain. Director Harmon Jones; 1958. (b/w)

The Wolf Man √√√ Contender for title of the best-ever American horror movie, with Lon Chaney undergoing a lycanthropic metamorphosis before your eyes (it took three hours, little bits of make-up being added and then bits more filmed). Claude Rains plays his unknowing father; Bela Lugosi a gypsy; Ralph Bellamy an investigator. Director George Waggner made it engrossing in 1941, despite the plot, and it is still riveting. (b/w)

The Woman and the Hunter XX Ann Sheridan's last picture, made in 1957, ten years before her death, was a weak triangle story set on safari, with David Farrar and John Loder competing for bad-actor-of-the-year award. Director, George Breakston; 1957. (b/w)

Womaneater XX It's a long slide from Walter P. Thatcher in *Citizen Kane* to mad scientist in this tedious little so-called horror picture, but George Coulouris made it. It's about a tree of life that needs to eat young ladies to flourish. You can guess the rest. The guilty director was Charles Saunders; 1957. (b/w)

A Woman for Charlie XX Originally called 'The Cockeyed Cowboys of Calico County', this vehicle for the small talents of large Dan Blocker, given a starring role as a result of his *Bonanza* appearances, was understandably never released in British cinemas. He books himself a mail-order bride, but she gets lost in the mail. Director Tony Leader had a splendid cast: Jim Backus, Wally Cox, Jack Elam, Mickey Rooney, Stubby Kaye, Marge Champion, Noah Beery Jr., but it wasn't enough; 1969. (c)

Woman in a Dressing Gown X 'The *Brief Encounter* of the council houses', cracked one critic. Anthony Quayle is the husband, driven by slapdash wife Yvonne Mitchell into arms of secretary Sylvia Syms. J. Lee Thompson directed Ted Willis's would-be Chayefskyan script, which did well in

1957 but looks pretty unconvincing now. (b/w)

The Woman in Green √ Sherlock Holmes mystery from the 1945 Rathbone-Bruce days. Moriarty is suspected of a wave of murders. Henry Daniell plays the villain, under Roy William Neill's direction. (b/w)

The Woman in Question √ Dirk Bogarde, Hermione Baddeley, Charles Victor, John McCallum, all recall murdered Jean Kent differently; pity detective Duncan Macrae, who has to sort their stories out. Director Anthony Asquith did a neat job in 1950. (b/w)

The Woman in the Window √√ Edward G. Robinson as weak, unfulfilled professor entangled with Joan Bennett and murder in 1944. Fritz Lang conjured up dark streets and overfurnished rooms, and Dan Duryea's menacing whine is one of the great movie memories. (b/w)

Woman Obsessed X Wilds of Canada are setting for this mushy Henry Hathaway-directed melo about widow Susan Hayward's stormy second marriage to Stephen Boyd; her young son is just one of their many problems; 1959. (c)

A Woman of Distinction √ But a film of not very much. 1950 Edward Buzzell-directed farce, about headmistress of girls' school getting involved with visiting academic, has a lot of energetic clowning from Rosalind Russell and Ray Milland but few laughs. (b/w)

Woman of Straw X The one about wicked nephew (Sean Connery) and sexy nurse (Gina Lollobrigida) plotting to do away with wealthy old gent (Ralph Richardson) and inherit fortune. Basil Dearden directed; 1964. (c)

Woman of the North Country X Mining tycoon Rod Cameron fights treachery for control of the ore. Gale Storm, Ruth Hussey, J. Carrol Naish support. Director, Joseph Kane; 1952. (c)

Woman on the Run √ Can Ann Sheridan find her husband before mobsters do? He was the only witness to murder. Dennis O'Keefe, Frank Jenks. Director, Norman Foster; 1950. (b/w)

A Woman's Devotion X Ralph Meeker goes potty in Mexico; Janice Rule stands by him. Paul Henreid directs and appears, too; 1956. (c)

A Woman's Face √√ Exciting archetypal Joan Crawford yarn in which she undergoes plastic surgery by Melvyn Douglas to remove scar. This makes her want to give up crime; but Conrad Veidt has other ideas. George Cukor directed with bravura; 1941. (b/w)

Woman's World √ Three out-of-town executives and their wives are summoned to New York so that auto company boss Clifton Webb can observe them more closely before deciding which of them he gives important promotion to. Lauren Bacall, Fred MacMurray, Van Heflin, Arlene Dahl, June Allyson, Cornel Wilde are hopefuls, and director Jean Negulesco gave it a (tooth and nail) polish in 1954. (c)

Woman They Almost Lynched √ Because she was premature women's-libber in being quicker than all the men in town on the draw. As she was an outlaw, you can understand why the townsfolk were upset. Joan Leslie metamorphoses from nice young lady to gunslinger. Allan Dwan had been directing films for 39 years when he turned this one out, so it's got to have a professional gloss. Audrey Totter, Brian Donlevy, John Lund among townsfolk; 1953. (b/w)

Woman Times Seven X Vittorio de Sica directed seven different stories about seven different women giving Shirley MacLaine (who played them all) too great an opportunity to indulge herself in 1967. Whether you'll enjoy yourself as much, watching her, is another matter. The necessarily large cast includes Michael Caine, Peter Sellers, Rossano Brazzi, Alan Arkin, Anita Ekberg, Patrick Wymark, Robert Morley. (c)

Woman Without a Face √ James Garner has lost his memory. Who is he? All kinds of nice characters try to help him find out: Jean Simmons, Suzanne Pleshette, Katharine Ross, George Voskovec among them. Evan Hunter didn't make the adaptation from his own book, *Buddwing;* for some reason Dale Wasserman did. Delbert Mann directs as if he had some idea that he was creating an allegory of all men finding themselves; 1968. (b/w)

The Women √√ Clare Boothe Luce's all-female play, bitchily transposed to the screen, directed by George Cukor in 1939. Norma Shearer, Joan Crawford, Rosalind Russell, Mary Boland, Paulette Goddard, Joan

Fontaine, Marjorie Main, Virginia Grey, Ruth Hussey, Hedda Hopper, Cora Witherspoon . . . what else do you want? Truth, insight or satisfactory plotting not available. (b/w)

Women in Love √√ Comparatively sane for a Ken Russell movie, this faintly vulgar version of D. H. Lawrence's novel had the advantage of fine performances from Alan Bates as a school inspector, Jennie Linden as a teacher and Glenda Jackson as her sister. It also had Oliver Reed, Eleanor Bron and Christopher Gable; 1969. (c)

Women's Prison X Ida Lupino is sadistic superintendent, responsible for awful conditions; the inevitable revolt by prisoners leads to clean-up, so we can all switch off at the end with an easy mind. Director Lewis Seiler was obviously sincere in 1955, if wildly over-optimistic about penal reform. (b/w)

The Wonderful Country √ Robert Mitchum, gun-running between Mexico and Texas, finds time to make love to Julie London in this 1959 timepasser. Aged fans will welcome sight of Jack Oakie. Director, Robert Parrish. (c)

Wonderful Life X Must have been if you had Cliff Richard under contract and uncritical teenagers would go and see him, whatever old rubbish he was in. This 1964 effort, with Susan Hampshire, Una Stubbs, Derek Bond was about Cliff and his mates trying to make a movie. Did director Sidney Furie let them practise on this one? (c)

The Wonderful World of the Brothers Grimm XX The grim world of the Brothers Wonderful would suit this slice of sentimentality better. Laurence Harvey and Karl Boehm as the story-tellers, with Terry-Thomas, Oscar Homolka, Walter Slezak and Claire Bloom adding to the goo; director, Henry Levin; 1962. (c)

Wonder Man √ Nothing to do with Wonder Woman, but frantic Danny Kaye as twin brothers, with the serious one forced to take the entertainer's place. Virginia Mayo, Vera-Ellen make insipid bits of glamour; H. Bruce Humberstone directed; 1945. (c)

The Wonders of Aladdin X Retelling of the old panto story, with Donald O'Connor and a nine-foot genie. Vittorio de Sica among Henry Levin's cast; 1961. (c)

Wonderwall XX Right load of codswallop about a voyeur with fantasies. Jack MacGowran did his best in the circumstance of acute miscasting. Jane Birkin is appealing as the object of his desires; Irene Handl, Richard Wattis, Beatrix Lehmann go through their usual paces. Over Iain Quarrier's performance as Jane's boyfriend let a veil be drawn. Also over Joe Massot's direction; 1969. (c)

The Wooden Horse √ Best-known Second World War real-life escape story, 1950, using vaulting horse as cover for getting away from Stalag Luft PoW camp. Good performances from Leo Genn, David Tomlinson, Anthony Steel and Bryan Forbes. Tight, tense direction from Jack Lee. (b/w)

Words and Music √ Not strong in the production department, but Rodgers and Hart songs ('Thou Swell, Blue Moon', 'I Wish I Were In Love Again', 'Manhattan' et al.) are marvellous and cast (Mickey Rooney, Judy Garland, Lena Horne, Ann Sothern, Perry Como) not bad. Same can't be said for Norman Taurog's direction; 1948. (c)

World for Ransom X Dan Duryea tries to prevent kidnapping of nuclear scientist – rather harder than director Robert Aldrich, who was new at the game in 1954. (b/w)

The World in His Arms X Old-fashioned (and we're not just referring to the 19th-century San Francisco setting) romance has Gregory Peck as dashing sea captain, Ann Blyth as lovely Russian countess he loves and fights for, and lush Raoul Walsh direction; 1952. (c)

World in My Corner X Audie Murphy, on his way to championship, nearly throws away a fight and his good name for money. But, with Barbara Rush standing by, he's gonna be OK. Yes, you've seen it before, though maybe not with these particular actors or Jesse Hibbs's directing; 1956. (b/w)

The World of Henry Orient √ Occasionally funny comedy from director George Roy Hill in 1964 has Peter Sellers well-cast in role of narcissistic, womanising pianist and appealing performances from Tippy Walker and Merrie Spaeth as the adoring teenage fans who chase him round New York; plus Angela Lansbury, Paula Prentiss. (c)

The World of Suzie Wong XX Richard Quine's brilliant direction of the Hong Kong background to this East-meets-West yarn is by far the best thing in this otherwise hokey melodrama. You can't

349

believe in William Holden's American painter and even less in Nancy Kwan's 'hostess' (in 1960 they couldn't say whore) or the gooey relationship between them. Sylvia Syms and Michael Wilding are a real couple of pills. (c)

The World Ten Times Over X Bleak little drama about two disillusioned nightclub hostesses; competent British cast is led by June Ritchie, Sylvia Syms, Edward Judd, William Hartnell. Wolf Rilla directed; 1963. (b/w)

The World, the Flesh and the Devil X Is Harry Belafonte the only one left alive on earth after nuclear holocaust? No, it turns out that Inger Stevens and Mel Ferrer survived too, and they all meet up in an eerily deserted New York – very handy, as far as the future of mankind is concerned. Director Ranald MacDougall begged a lot of questions in 1959. (b/w)

The World Was His Jury X Was the captain to blame for sinking of his ship with the loss of 162 lives? In Fred F. Sears' dull courtroom drama the truth comes out; Edmond O'Brien is lawyer; 1958. (b/w)

World Without End √ Hugh Marlow, Rod Taylor, Nancy Gates, Nelson Leigh are scientists landing on strange planet and finding that they have broken time barrier and are on Earth in the year 2508. Edward Bernds makes it lively sci-fi; 1956. (c)

The Wrath of God XX One of director Ralph Nelson's nasty chunks of sado-masochism, with Robert Mitchum at both ends of the dubious pleasures. Rita Hayworth, in what seems to have been her last role, in 1972, stands by, obviously not taking the whole farrago seriously. (c)

The Wrecking Crew XX This Matt Helm-Bond-like adventure was clearly ground out in desperation in 1969. Few of the players seem to care – Dean Martin, Elke Sommer, Nancy Kwan are all deadly, as is Phil Karlson's surprisingly lackadaisical direction. A melancholy fact is that it features Sharon Tate and Nigel Green, both of whom were to die shortly afterwards in garish circumstances. (c)

The Wreck of the Mary Deare √ Sea-yarn of English Channel shipwreck was Gary Cooper's penultimate picture (1960). Strong story, strong special effects, strong supports (Charlton Heston, Michael Redgrave, Emlyn Williams, Richard Harris); let down by Michael Anderson's weak direction. (c)

Written on the Wind √ Well, it goes something like this: Rock Hudson is in love with Lauren Bacall who is married to Robert Stack whose nympho sister, Dorothy Malone, is in love with Rock Hudson, who, you may recall . . . Like all good magazine stories, it works out happily in the end – for two of them, at least – and Dorothy Malone won 1956 Academy Award for Best Supporting Actress. Douglas Sirk. (c)

The Wrong Arm of the Law √ Farce, with Peter Sellers switching accents, about rival gangs. The Law, in the person of Lionel Jeffries, is continually made a monkey of – first by one gang dressing up as policemen, then with the other suspending activities to help catch them. Bernard Cribbins adds to the fun. Cliff Owen directed; 1963. (b/w)

The Wrong Box X Bryan Forbes directed and produced this adaptation of Robert Louis Stevenson story in 1966. John Mills and Ralph Richardson were the two brothers, murderously out to inherit a fortune from each other, and gave credence to camp, which is sometimes pitched at wrong level. Peter Cook and Dudley Moore make uninspired appearances; Tony Hancock and Peter Sellers do OK; Nanette Newman beautiful and inevitable. (c)

The Wrong Man X Unusual, highly documentary direction in 1957 from Hitchcock of this true but somehow dull story about New York musician wrongly accused of murder. Fine performances from Henry Fonda as helpless accused, and Vera Miles his wife, going mad under the strain. But Hitch himself files it 'among the indifferent Hitchcocks', feeling that he was too true to life. (b/w)

W.U.S.A. √√ Powerful drama of personalities (drunken Paul Newman, anguished Joanne Woodward, liberal Anthony Perkins, ruthless Pat Hingle) caught in a web of right-wing manipulation through a radio station. Stuart Rosenberg directed adeptly in 1970. (c)

Wuthering Heights √√√ (1) 1939. Despite Merle Oberon's miscasting as Cathy, William Wyler directed a melodramatically convincing adaptation of Emily Brontë. Laurence Olivier stands out in what is perhaps his best-ever screen performance as Heathcliff. (b/w)

Wuthering Heights XX (2) 1970. Awful botch-up, directed by Robert Fuest, turns a complex Gothic story into soap opera that refuses to lather. Timothy Dalton is a weak Heathcliff, Anna Calder-Marshall a tame Cathy. (c)

W.W. and the Dixie Dancekings √ By the time you have deciphered the meaning of the title, the flimsy fun is well on its way: W.W. is Burt Reynolds who doubles as gas station hold-up man and band-manager. Dixie is Conny Van Dyke, a girl he fancies who leads a band, the Dixie Dancekings. After various picaresque adventures round Georgia and Tennessee, he is hunted by Art Carney. Director John G. Avildsen makes it all quite ingratiating, in 1975. (c)

Wyoming Mail √ Stephen McNally, joining gang as part of his job as undercover agent, discovers that Alexis Smith is part of it. Reginald Le Borg's lively direction of postal robbery scenes is helped by support from Ed Begley, Richard Egan, James Arness; 1950. (c)

Wyoming Renegades X Phil Carey comes out of jail, determined to go straight, but townspeople are sceptical. Martha Hyer believes in him and helps him prove his worth. Fred F. Sears made it pretty conventional; 1955. (c)

X

X-15 X Charles Bronson, Mary Tyler Moore, David McLean, Patricia Owens among scientists and wives who suffer at a Californian missile base. Richard Donner directs, James Stewart narrates; 1961. (c)

X – The Unknown XX Sci-fi set in Scotland, about Something Nasty from earth's centre trying to take us us – or, at least, Dean Jagger, Leo McKern, William Lucas, Edward Chapman – over. Leslie Norman directed; 1956. (b/w)

Y

The Yakuza √ Robert Mitchum in Japan, seeking Brian Keith's kidnapped daughter. Attempt to bring the qualities of indigenous action on to Western screens runs into stylistic problems. Director Sydney Pollack only solves them by abandoning oriental values for Hollywood action; 1975. (c)

Yangtze Incident X Michael Anderson's tepid 1957 account of crippled HMS Amethyst's 140-mile escape from Red Chinese in 1949. Richard Todd plays Lt.-Commander John Kerans, with William Hartnell, Robert Urquhart, Donald Houston as crewmembers; Akim Tamiroff as a heavy heavy. Actually, it wasn't quite so heroic because the Chinese deliberately refrained from firing on them and even fed them, so as to win a diplomatic victory. (b/w)

Yankee Buccaneer X American pirates v. international pirates, Jeff Chandler flying the skull-and-crossbones for Uncle Sam. David Janssen among those up in the rigging, shouted at by director Frederick de Cordova (a good name for a pirate); 1952. (c)

Yankee Doodle Dandy √ James Cagney winning an Oscar as early showman George M. Cohan in classic musical biopic that defies criticism; Walter Huston, Joan Leslie. Michael Curtiz; 1942. (b/w)

Yankee Pasha X Unlikely costume yarn has Jeff Chandler going to the rescue of girlfriend Rhonda Fleming who's been kidnapped and shipped to Morocco. Joseph Pevney directed; 1954. (c)

A Yank in the RAF X Henry King's wartime (1941) time-passer about Tyrone Power's involvement with chorus-girl Betty Grable. With John Sutton, Reginald Gardiner. (b/w)

The Yearling √√ Entrancing story of a young boy's love for a pet fawn which his father must destroy. Remarkably unsentimental, Clarence Brown's 1946 direction delicately explores complex emotions. Beautifully photographed, with splendid performances from Gregory Peck, Jane Wyman and Claude Jarman Jr., it won two Academy Awards. (c)

The Yellow Balloon √ Andrew Ray in his child-actor days – 1952 – shocked by chum's death and used by crook. Kenneth More, Bernard Lee, directed by J. Lee Thompson. (b/w)

The Yellow Cab Man √ Red Skelton invents unbreakable glass; gets job as cab driver to test it. OK for fans, if any. Edward Arnold, Walter Slezak. Jack Donahue directed; 1950. (b/w)

The Yellow Canary X (1) 1944 British spy drama has Anna Neagle pretending to be Nazi sympathiser; Margaret Rutherford, Richard Greene and director Herbert Wilcox. (b/w)

The Yellow Canary √ (2) 1963 melodrama has singer Pat Boone hunting down baby son's kidnappers; Jack Klugman, Barbara Eden, Steve Forrest and director Buzz Kulik. (b/w)

Yellow Dog XX Fashion photographer Terence Donovan made an expensive mistake in producing and directing this extravagant 1973 spy thriller. Bogged down by the Japanese ambience, he allowed a large cast too much latitude; some of them, notably Robert Hardy and Joseph O'Conor, appear to realise it. (c)

Yellow Mountain XX There's gold in them thar hills, and gals, and guns. Lex Barker, Howard Duff, William Demarest are fightin' for 'em. Jesse Hibbs is directin'; 1954. (c)

The Yellow Rolls-Royce √ Anthony Asquith's experienced direction keeps this episodic 1965 movie about the title car's various owners running smoothly. Despite bumper cast – Rex Harrison, Shirley MacLaine, Ingrid Bergman, Jeanne Moreau, George C. Scott, Omar Sharif, Alain Delon – it's only occasionally entertaining. (c)

Yellow Sky √√ Bizarre but fascinating 1948 attempt by William Wellman to retell The Tempest as a western. Anne Baxter is Miranda-called-Mike, with Gregory Peck against Richard Widmark for prize of stolen gold. Super photography by Joe MacDonald. (b/w)

Yellowstone Kelly X Nothing much new about this western, with Clint Walker warring with Sioux over Indian girl. Gordon Douglas directed; 1959. (c)

Yellow Submarine √√ Inventive, over-long, sporadically brilliant period (1968) piece, when the Beatles were in their infant-regression Sgt. Pepper stage. George Dunning's direction of the animation is remarkably successful and it stands as a lasting monument to the end of an era. (c)

The Yellow Teddybears XXX Silly little attempt to cash in on spurious 1963 news-story that some schoolgirls had taken to wearing Robertson's free-gift golliwogs to show they were no longer virgins. Inferior in almost every department, the blame must go mostly to Robert Hartford-Davis as director and producer. (b/w)

The Yellow Tomahawk X Rory Calhoun browned-up as Indian guide and browned-off with his mates when he learns they intend to attack whites, Noah Beery, Peggie Castle. All a bit Uncle Tomahawkish. Lesley Selander; 1954. (c)

Yesterday's Enemy X Second World War drama has Captain Stanley Baker and what's left of his men under threat from nearby Japanese in Burmese jungle; Val Guest directs equivocally – seeming uncertain whether to approve or disapprove of their cruelties ('Come on Dad, over here,' says Sgt. Gordon Jackson, gently leading an old bewildered Burmese to the firing squad) or to take a neutral moral stance. Is the final shot of a war memorial ironic or not? Take your choice; 1959. (b/w)

Yield To the Night √ Grim prison drama about condemned girl awaiting execution. Under J. Lee Thompson's didactic direction, Diana Dors made the switch from pin-up (this was 1956) to drab dramatic actress without causing too much embarrassment; Yvonne Mitchell, Athene Seyler, Michael Craig. (b/w)

Yolanda and the Thief XX Fred Astaire plans to con heiress Lucille Bremer out of her fortune. Fred, Frank Morgan and Mildred Natwick can't save this Mexican-set musical from disaster; director, Vincente Minnelli; 1945. (c)

You Can't Run Away From It XX Ghastly 1956 musical remake of It Happened One Night has June Allyson as runaway heiress, Jack Lemmon as the newspaperman she falls for. Director Dick Powell had a heavy-handed touch in 1956, and it's all a shameful shadow of the original. (c)

You Can't Sleep Here √ Cary Grant, in drag, makes this comedy of a Frenchman pretending to be an American lady soldier so as to accompany wife Ann Sheridan back to the US, funnier than it sounds.

Howard Hawks did a jovial job in 1949. (b/w)

You Can't Win 'em All XXX Or, in this case, any of 'em. Charles Bronson and Tony Curtis start this farrago adrift in a boat. They reach Turkey and get involved in stealing a casket of jewels, but the film remains adrift. Howard Hawks was to have directed, in 1970, but Peter Collinson took over, with predictably dire results. (c)

You Don't Need Pajamas at Rosie's XX The prettiest walking robot on the screen, Jacqueline Bisset, helps three teenagers learn some of the facts of life in this lifeless comedy directed by James Neilson in 1969. (c)

You For Me X What Jane Greer has got that makes millionaires and doctors flip so madly over her as a nurse isn't explained by director Don Weis in this light entertainment, but Gig Young and Peter Lawford go happily along; 1952. (b/w)

You Know What Sailors Are X Only surprise in this 1953 British farce, directed cheerfully but ineptly by Ken Annakin, about repercussions following naval officer's spoof about secret weapon is appearance of marvellously-cured ham, Akim Tamiroff. For the rest it's Donald Sinden, Naunton Wayne and a cast of wet *Carry-On* types; 1953. (c)

You'll Like My Mother √√ Unpretentious but remarkably effective thriller in familiar territory – helpless girl trapped in cut-off house with loony murderer. But Patty Duke (in a part that must have been written for Mia Farrow) manages the implausibilities of the plot (she gives birth, her baby is hidden in the attic yet survives) with skill, and director Lamont Johnson keeps us on the edges of our seats; 1972. (c)

You Must Be Joking X Collection of mostly weak comics (Terry-Thomas, Bernard Cribbins, Clive Dunn, Norman Vaughan, Leslie Phillips, Irene Handl, Lionel Jeffries) in tentative yarn about army initiative tests. Made by Michael Winner in 1965, before he discovered his forte as director of crude thrillers. (b/w)

You Never Can Tell X No, not Shaw's nineties comedy, but a pretty dire farce about a German sheepdog who's murdered and returns to Earth as human private detective to track down his killer; with Dick Powell, Charles Drake, directed by Lou Breslow; 1951. (b/w)

Young and Dangerous X The one about the teenage Lothario who bets he can make nice girl fall in love with him; he does, she does, then he does, then she finds out . . . yawn, yawn. Mark Damon's the boy; Lili Gentle. Director, William Claxton; 1957. (b/w)

The Young and the Guilty XXX Awfully dated Ted Willis drama has Andrew Ray and Janet Munro as gauche teenage lovers – this was 1958. Edward Chapman plays girl's heavy father; Phyllis Calvert, her mum. Peter Cotes. (b/w)

Young and Wild X Tough yarn about three lads in a stolen car and the havoc they wreak – mostly on the viewer. Scott Marlowe, Gene Evans, Robert Arthur, directed by William Witney; 1958. (b/w)

Young At Heart √ 1955 musical remake of John Garfield tearjerker, *Four Daughters*, has Doris Day running off with hard-bitten musician Frank Sinatra; some nice songs ('Someone To Watch Over Me', 'Just One of Those Things', 'One For My Baby'); and a happy ending. Gordon Douglas directed; 1954. (c)

Young Bess √ Historical romance that's more romance than history, has Jean Simmons as future Queen Elizabeth, Stewart Granger as love interest, Thomas Seymour; Charles Laughton plays Henry VIII again. George Sidney; 1953. (c)

Young Billy Young √ Marshal Robert Mitchum has jailed the chief heavy's son which makes for the excitement in this otherwise routine Burt Kennedy western. Angie Dickinson is the saloon gal, Robert Walker plays the title-role. Perfectly acceptable stuff; 1969. (c)

Youngblood Hawke √ How fame and fortune change young writer's life; although neither Delmer Daves's direction – nor adaptation from Herman Wouk's real-life best-seller – nor wooden performances from James Franciscus, Genevieve Page, Suzanne Pleshette make you care much, it does have a compulsion. Mary Astor shines momentarily as Broadway actress; 1964. (c)

Young Cassidy XX Rod Taylor monumentally miscast as the young Sean O'Casey, with Julie Christie, Maggie Smith as his young ladies and Flora Robson as his mother. John Ford directed some of it, Jack Cardiff rather more, and between them they failed to give either a coherent or a convincing picture of the man or the period in Ireland; 1965. (c)

Young Dillinger X Casting of colourless Nick Adams as real-life thirties gangster, John Dillinger, robs this 1965 biopic of credibility; not that director Terry O. Morse had given it much. (b/w)

The Young Doctors √ Ben Gazzara and Fredric March give shots in the arm to otherwise conventional hospital drama about young, progressive doctor clashing with old, directed by a tired Phil Karlson; 1961. (b/w)

The Young Don't Cry X Sal Mineo platonically involved with escaped convict and refusing to tell on him. James Whitmore, J. Carrol Naish; directed by Alfred L. Werker; 1957. (b/w)

The Younger Brothers √ Not younger as opposed to older, but Younger was their name; waiting for a pardon, they hear that their younger (sorry) brother has been forced to kill a man, so off they go on their lawless lives once more. Wayne Morris, Robert Hutton, Alan Hale, Fred Clark, Janis Paige head a strong cast; 1949. (c)

Young Frankenstein √√ Mel Brooks has a monster time with Gene Wilder as the mad scientist, Peter Boyle as his handiwork, Madeleine Kahn, Gene Hackman, Cloris Leachman; apart from Marty Feldman's strained mugging, it all goes swimmingly. Unfortunately, the film goes over the top as usual and is reduced to an occasional belly-laugh instead of sustained rich humour; 1974. (b/w)

The Young Guns X Teenage western with Russ Tamblyn trying to live down town's memory of gunslinger father; Albert Band; 1956. (b/w)

Young Guns of Texas √ Has some curiosity in casting of Robert Mitchum's son James, Joel McCrea's Jody, Alan Ladd's daughter Alana, as searchers for stolen Army gold, and searched for by Chill Wills. Then Apaches strike. Maury Dexter; 1962. (c)

Young Jesse James XX How famous outlaw – played here by Ray Stricklyn – got to be that way, but don't believe a word of it. William Claxton; 1960. (b/w)

The Young Land √ Before 1848, any American who killed a Mexican in California could be sure to get away with it. This interesting western tells what happens when the first one was put on trial. Pat Wayne, Dan O'Herlihy, Dennis Hopper score in Ted Tetzlaff's unusual try; 1959. (c)

The Young Lions √ Worth sitting through interwoven wartime stories of two Americans (Montgomery Clift, Dean Martin) and one enemy for Marlon Brando's correct, precise German, changed at his insistence from Irwin Shaw's original brutalised Nazi to sensitive soul. Edward Dmytryk; 1958. (b/w)

The Young Lovers XX Weak college drama has unmarried students Peter Fonda and Sharon Hugueny in a tizzy about unwanted pregnancy. Samuel Goldwyn Jr. couldn't make us care in 1965. (b/w)

Young Man of Music √ Supposedly based (via Dorothy Baker's novel) on life of Bix Beiderbecke – but *he* died at 28. Kirk Douglas as jazz trumpeter (miming to Harry James); Doris Day and Lauren Bacall as the good and bad women in his life – no prizes for guessing which one is which. Michael Curtiz; 1950. (b/w)

Young Man With Ideas √ Harmless comedy about lawyer Glenn Ford and family trying to make a home for themselves in California. Mitchell Leisen; 1952. (b/w)

Young Mr Lincoln √ Not particularly true to life, but always dramatic, occasionally over-sentimental, account of Abraham Lincoln's early days. The make-up man gave supersincere Henry Fonda a new nose, but he didn't need the famous beard – Lincoln grew it later. John Ford directed, in 1939, with worship for the future president. (b/w)

The Young Ones X This naïve but lively musical about Cliff Richard and mates trying to save their local youth club from property developers (Robert Morley) seems embarrassingly out-of-date today; it was too goody-goody even by 1961 standards, when Sidney Furie directed. (c)

Young People XX Shirley Temple was pretty well over the top in 1940 aged 12. She plays the vaudeville star adoptee of Jack Oakie and Charlotte Greenwood, and finds it difficult to settle down when her new parents want to retire to the country. Director, Allan Dwan. (b/w)

The Young Philadelphians √ Long, glossy fable about ambitious young lawyer-on-the-make in Philadelphian society, based on Richard Powell's best-seller. Compelling performance from Paul Newman as the heel who reforms. Strong support from Robert Vaughn, Otto Kruger, Barbara Rush and Alexis Smith gave this slick Vincent Sherman-directed soaper a distinction it didn't really deserve in 1959. (b/w)

The Young Racers X Ex-racing driver plans to expose racing champ in book he's writing, changes his mind. They used to call director Roger Corman King of the B-pictures, and you can see why in this one. Mark Damon, Patrick Magee; 1963. (c)

The Young Savages √ Burt Lancaster as assistant district attorney v. juvenile street murder gang; John Frankenheimer's second film, 1961. Sharp and socially conscious. Shelley Winters, Telly Savalas. (b/w)

The Young Stranger √ Well-intentioned little domestic drama about teenage boy reacting against busy father's neglect. James MacArthur, James Daly, Kim Hunter made a believable family in John Frankenheimer's modest 1956 directorial debut. (b/w)

The Young Warriors X James Drury is tough sergeant in charge of inexperienced platoon in this low-budget (and it shows) Second World War drama. John Peyser; 1966. (c)

Young Winston √ Costume drama about the early years of Winston Churchill, with Simon Ward playing him in the Sudan and the Boer War. A galaxy of British stars, including Robert Shaw, Jack Hawkins, Ian Holm, Edward Woodward, Robert Hardy, contribute reasonably well-rounded characters, but the movie isn't much more than a lifeless biography. To put all the blame on either Carl Foreman's script or Richard Attenborough's direction is unfair; the subject doesn't live up to its promise; 1972. (c)

Young Wives' Tale XX Terribly British comedy about couples sharing to beat the housing shortage – how quaint. Spot Audrey Hepburn in tiny part if you can keep awake amidst posturing of Joan Greenwood, Nigel Patrick, Derek Farr, Helen Cherry. Director, Henry Cass; 1951. (b/w)

You Only Live Once √√ Classic convict-on-the-run thriller with Henry Fonda and Sylvia Sidney. Fritz Lang's first major American film (1937) with William Gargan, Barton MacLane, Jerome Cowan. (b/w)

You Only Live Twice √ Routine Bond thriller, with £500,000 set of Donald Pleasence's headquarters inside a volcano. Among the hardware: a working monorail, a heliport, a space-rocket that really fires, one-seat autogiro, helicopter with electro-magnet. 007 was still Sean Connery in 1967; director, Lewis Gilbert. (c)

Your Cheatin' Heart X Biopic of country singer Hank Williams who died from drink at the early age of 29, homogenised to make just another movie with songs. Maybe the presence of his widow as 'technical adviser' and his son as George Hamilton's singing voice had something to do with feeling of unreality. Gene Nelson directed; 1966. (b/w)

You're a Big Boy Now √√ If you can find the sexual awakening and education of young lad in New York screamingly funny then you'll probably fall about over this one directed by Francis Ford Coppola (in 1967, before he hit the big time). Gimmickly directed, using the locations to the full (and more) and borrowing from a dozen influential movies, it has a zany sophistication. But it's strictly Fantasyland, even down to calling the characters names like Miss Thing (Julie Harris as his landlady). Peter Kastner's naïveté becomes wearing, though perky cameos by Geraldine Page (Mom), Rip Torn (Pa), Michael Dunn and Elizabeth Hartman (boy-eater) stop boredom. Karen Black is his saviour, if not ours; 1967. (c)

You're in the Navy Now √ Innocent Second World War fun has an inexperienced Captain Gary Cooper trying to run experimental ship and dopey crew – Eddie Albert, Lee Marvin, Jack Webb. Grown-ups may prefer a slightly more sophisticated brand of humour than they'll find in this 1951 lark from Henry Hathaway. Originally called USS Teakettle, from the steam engine that plays major role. Cooper was never more lovable, but the film's a bit strained. (b/w)

You're Never Too Young X Dean Martin-Jerry Lewis romp, with Jerry dressing up as child to hide from criminals. Norman Taurog; 1955. (c)

You're Only Young Twice XXX Tepid farce about riotous goings-on at Scottish university. Diane Hart's presence is supposed to drive the inmates mad. Director Terry Bishop adds to the embarrassment of the script he helped to write in 1952. (b/w)

Your Money Or Your Wife XX Donald Sinden and Peggy Cummins must divorce so as to inherit fortune. Ho hum. 1959 effort of Anthony Simmons, who later directed the off-beat *Four in the Morning*. (b/w)

Yours, Mine and Ours X Director Melville Shavelson must have thought he could rely on old pros Henry Fonda and Lucille Ball to save this noisy farce about widow with eight children marrying widower with ten. But at 62 and 56, respectively, in 1968, they were too creaky and the movie was just too old-fashioned. (c)

You Were Never Lovelier √ Rita Hayworth makes an inadequate substitute dancing partner for Fred Astaire in 1942 musical, with Adolphe Menjou as match-making father; William A. Seiter directed routinely. (b/w)

Z

Zabriskie Point √ Always intriguing if never completely satisfactory, Antonioni's 1969 excursion into California stands as a milestone in the career of an important director. While never completely mastering the speech, ethos or *zeitgeist* of contemporary young America, he supplies an intriguing outsider's view of them. Ostensibly the story of two individual members of the new generation, it is really the director playing guessing games with the audience. If he cheats (e.g. how and why does the house explode?), you cannot really expect Antonioni to play fair. Of a cast that was largely unknown when it was made (and have stayed that way since), only Rod Taylor, a peculiar choice for a role that needs some acting ability, is familiar. (c)

Zarak X Northwest Frontier adventure has Michael Wilding as British officer after outlaw leader Victor Mature, Anita Ekberg. Terence Young directed; 1957. (c)

Zardoz √ Fascinating failure written-produced-directed by John Boorman in 1973, telling a sophisticated, ultimately bewildering metaphysical story in territory (the future, when

Man has both progressed and retarded) usually reserved purely for adventure. Sean Connery, the last of the macho men, is trapped by an elitist group, but escapes with the help of Charlotte Rampling. Easy to dismiss as the load of codswallop it is, there is a haunting element that should keep you watching. (c)

Zebra in the Kitchen √ Little boy lets animals out of the zoo because he can't bear his pet mountain lion under lock and key. Pleasant enough stuff, directed by Ivan Tors. Andy Devine, Joyce Meadows; 1965. (c)

Zee and Co. XX Elizabeth Taylor screaming and shouting all over the place as a betrayed wife; Michael Caine as the betrayer; Susannah York as sincere mistress, all swing together in what must have been out of date in 1971 and looks antediluvian now. Director Brian Hutton manages no characterisation – surely scriptwriter Edna O'Brien supplied him with some? – only forced lyricism which looks like a reject for a commercial. (c)

Zeppelin XX Stiff Michael York as a spy on our side, trying to steal German plans for a lethal balloon ship in First World War. The hopeless Elke Sommer is an unconvincing flyer, and a cast of character actors drift around, untethered by the direction of Etienne Périer; 1970. (c)

Zero Hour X Predictable tale of guilt-ridden wartime pilot Dana Andrews who lost entire squadron, forced to take over airliner (with wife Linda Darnell and son aboard) when crew falls sick. Directed, 1957, by Hall Bartlett. (b/w)

Ziegfeld Follies √ Example of rare kind of movie, the musical revue. William Powell makes brief opening appearances as the impresario, but it's just a string of numbers, mostly worth watching. Outstanding are Fred Astaire with Gene Kelly, Lena Horne, Judy Garland burlesqueing a film-star interview, Victor Moore and Edward Arnold in comedy sketch. Main director Vincente Minnelli; 1946. (c)

Ziegfeld Girl √ Memorable for three Busby Berkeley dance numbers, particularly 'You Stepped Out Of A Dream'; Judy Garland singing 'I'm Always Chasing Rainbows'; Lana Turner as Bad Girl. Robert Z. Leonard; 1941. (b/w)

Zombies of Mora-Tau XX Soppy stuff about wife becoming one of the walking dead when she is killed by one of them guarding her husband's diamond mine. Gregg Palmer; director Edward L. Cahn; 1957. (b/w)

Zorba the Greek √ A great success in 1964, this long indulgence of Anthony Quinn as a life-loving, illiterate Greek who persuades Alan Bates to employ him, is a bit of a bore unless you want to be taken in by Michael Cacoyannis's beguiling way with a camera; particularly when held by Walter Lassally. The music helps, of course. Lila Kedrova won Academy Award support as dying whore. (b/w)

Zotz! X Stuff about professor finding magic coin that makes people move in slow motion; with Tom Poston, Jim Backus, Julia Meade. William Castle directed; 1962. (b/w)

Zulu √√ Considering the flag-waving jingoistic ghastliness that the theme of Empah-building has so often received in movies – both British and American – from *Four Feathers* to *The Lives of a Bengal Lancer,* the temptations in Cy Endfield's way must have been very great. That he resisted them, and made a film in 1963 that treated the 'other side' with respect was a major feat. Bloodthirsty and B.O.P. – exciting it still was, but the performances of co-producer Stanley Baker, Jack Hawkins, Ulla Jacobsson, James Booth, Michael Caine, Nigel Green and Patrick Magee in and around the Battle of Rorke's Drift were of a very high standard. More than an epic, a real film. (c)

ALTERNATIVE TITLES

Sometimes a film is made under one title and released under another, to avoid confusion with a similarly-named movie or because British distributors think a reference to an American phrase or institution too obscure. When they are shown on television, they often revert to the original title – usually because the print comes direct from America – and a confusion arises.

To help overcome this, here is a list of alternative titles: the left-hand one is the title that has been substituted after the film was made but may still be attached to the print used. The right-hand one is the more usual title and the one we have used when listing the film in the main body of this book.

By way of a small digression, if the makers of *The Parallax View* and *The China Syndrome* had had as good a judgement in naming their films as in making them, they would almost certainly have been twice as commercially successful.

Abandon Ship	Seven Waves Away
Abbott and Costello Meet the Ghosts	Abbott and Costello Meet Frankenstein
The Abominable Snowman	The Abominable Snowman of the Himalayas
Adventure at Rugby	Tom Brown's Schooldays
The Adventurers	I See a Dark Stranger
African Fury	Cry, the Beloved Country
Agent 008¾	Hot Enough for June
Alias Bulldog Drummond	Bulldog Jack
All At Sea	Barnacle Bill
All This and Money Too	Love is a Ball
America, America	The Anatolian Smile
Angel Street	Gaslight
Anzio	The Battle for Anzio
The Appaloosa	Southwest to Sonora
Arrivederci Baby	Drop Dead Darling
Bachelor Girl Apartment	Any Wednesday
The Baited Trap	The Trap
The Bank Detective	The Bank Dick
Battle Hell	Yangtze Incident
The Beasts of Marseilles	Seven Thunders
Bengal Brigade	Bengal Rifles
Beyond the River	Bottom of the Bottle
The Big Carnival	Ace in the Hole
Big Hand for a Little Lady	Big Deal At Dodge City
The Big Heart	Miracle on 34th Street
The Big Land	Stampeded
Big Time Operators	The Smallest Show on Earth
Blonde Sinner	Yield to the Night
Blood Money	Requiem for a Heavyweight
Blood on My Hands	Kiss the Blood Off My Hands

Rookies	Buck Pirates
Rough Company	The Violent Men
A Run on Gold	Midas Run
Savage Wilderness	The Last Frontier
Season of Passion	Summer of the Seventeenth Doll
Secret Interlude	The View from Pompey's Head
See No Evil	Blind Terror
Separate Beds	The Wheeler Dealers
Sherlock Holmes and the Secret Code	Dressed to Kill
The Silent Stranger	Step Down To Terror
Sol Madrid	The Heroin Gang
Something For Everyone	Black Flowers for the Bride
Sometimes A Great Notion	Never Give an Inch
Sons of the Desert	Fraternally Yours
Sons of the Musketeers	At Sword's Point
Spin of a Coin	The George Raft Story
Spitfire	The First of the Few
Spylarks	The Intelligence Men
The Sterile Cuckoo	Pookie
Strange Incident	The Ox-Bow Incident
Suicide Squadron	Dangerous Moonlight
Summertime	Summer Madness
Sword of Lancelot	Lancelot and Guinevere
Synanon	Get Off My Back
Target For Scandal	Washington Story
Tarzan and the Jungle Queen	Tarzan's Peril
Teenage Bad Girl	My Teenage Daughter
Ten Little Niggers	And Then There Were None
Thank You All Very Much	A Touch of Love
That Forsyte Woman	The Forsyte Saga
These Are the Damned	The Damned
They All Died Laughing	A Jolly Bad Fellow
The Third Key	The Long Arm
This Is My Affair	I Can Get It For You Wholesale
Those Daring Young Men in their Jaunty Jalopies	Monte Carlo or Bust
Thundercloud	Colt 45
Thunder In the Dust	The Sundowners (1950)
Tiger In the Sky	The McConnell Story
Tight Little Island	Whisky Galore
A Time For Killing	The Long Ride Home
Time Lost and Time Remembered	I was Happy Here
Top Secret Affair	Their Secret Affair
Tops Is the Limit	Anything Goes
Toward the Unknown	Brink of Hell
Trial and Error	The Dock Brief
Twenty Plus Two	It Started In Tokyo
Two Loves	Spinster
Unconventional Linda	Holiday
Unseen Heroes	Battle of the V1
Vacation from Marriage	Perfect Strangers
Valley of Fury	Chief Crazy Horse
Venetian Bird	The Assassin
Vessel of Wrath	The Beachcomber
Viva Las Vegas	Love in Las Vegas or Meet Me in Las Vegas
The Voice of the Turtle	One For the Book
Walk in the Shadow	Life For Ruth

General Editor:
Shelford Bidwell

WORLD WAR 3

Within five years the events in this book could be a horrifying reality. World War 3 – total devastation – may have already begun . . .

With more and more countries in possession of nuclear weapons the prospect of worldwide conflict is terrifying.

The facts are ominous. The Soviet bloc has built up a massive superiority in conventional weapons – while cuts in Western defence spending constantly increase NATO'S reliance on the nuclear deterrent.

One day the deterrent might not be enough.

World War 3 looks at the rivals and their weapons. It describes the way in which the third – and maybe the last – world war could develop. As tensions mount in North West Europe, nuclear attack ceases to be merely a possibility . . . All too soon it could be history.

NON-FICTION

GENERAL

☐ Guide to the Channel Islands — J. Anderson & E. Swinglehurst — 90p
☐ The Complete Traveller — Joan Bakewell — £1.95
☐ Time Out London Shopping Guide — Lindsey Bareham — £1.50
☐ World War 3 — Edited by Shelford Bidwell — £1.25
☐ The Black Angels — Rupert Butler — £1.35
☐ Hand of Steel — Rupert Butler — £1.35
☐ A Walk Around the Lakes — Hunter Davies — £1.50
☐ Truly Murderous — John Dunning — 95p
☐ In Praise of Younger Men — Sandy Fawkes — 85p
☐ Hitler's Secret Life — Glenn B. Infield — £1.50
☐ Wing Leader — Johnnie Johnson — £1.25
☐ Me, to Name but a Few — Spike Mullins — £1.00
☐ Our Future: Dr. Magnus Pyke Predicts — — 95p
☐ The Devil's Bedside Book — Leonard Rossiter — 85p
☐ Barbara Windsor's Book of Boobs — Barbara Windsor — £1.50

BIOGRAPHY/AUTOBIOGRAPHY

☐ Go-Boy — Roger Caron — £1.25
☐ The Queen Mother Herself — Helen Cathcart — £1.25
☐ George Stephenson — Hunter Davies — £1.50
☐ The Queen's Children — Donald Edgar — £1.25
☐ Prince Regent — Harry Edgington — 95p
☐ All of Me — Rose Neighbour — £1.00
☐ Tell Me Who I Am Before I Die — C. Peters with T. Schwarz — £1.00
☐ Boney M — J. Shearlaw and D. Brown — 90p
☐ Kiss — John Swenson — 90p

HEALTH/SELF-HELP/POCKET HEALTH GUIDES

☐ Pulling Your Own Strings — Dr. Wayne W. Dyer — 95p
☐ The Pick of Woman's Own Diets — Jo Foley — 95p
☐ Woman X Two — Mary Kenny — 90p
☐ Cystitis: A Complete Self-help Guide — Angela Kilmartin — £1.00
☐ The Stress Factor — Donald Norfolk — 90p
☐ Fat is a Feminist Issue — Susie Orbach — 85p
☐ Related to Sex — Claire Rayner — £1.25
☐ The Working Woman's Body Book — L. Rowen with B. Winkler — 95p
☐ Woman's Own Birth Control — Dr. Michael Smith — £1.25
☐ Allergies — Robert Eagle — 65p
☐ Arthritis and Rheumatism — Dr. Luke Fernandes — 65p
☐ Back Pain — Dr. Paul Dudley — 65p
☐ Pre-Menstrual Tension — June Clark — 65p
☐ Migraine — Dr. Finlay Campbell — 65p
☐ Skin Troubles — Deanna Wilson — 65p

REFERENCE

☐ What's Wrong with your Pet? — Hugo Kerr — 95p
☐ You *Can* Train Your Cat — Jo and Paul Loeb — £1.50
☐ Caring for Cats and Kittens — John Montgomery — 95p
☐ The Oscar Movies from A-Z — Roy Pickard — £1.25
☐ Questions of Law — Bill Thomas — 95p
☐ The Hamlyn Book of Amazing Information — — 80p
☐ The Hamlyn Family Medical Dictionary — — £2.50

GAMES & PASTIMES

☐ The Hamlyn Book of Brainteasers and Mindbenders — Ben Hamilton — 85p
☐ The Hamlyn Book of Crosswords Books 1, 2, 3, and 4 — — 60p
☐ The Hamlyn Book of Crosswords 5 — — 70p
☐ The Hamlyn Book of Wordways 1 — — 75p
☐ The Hamlyn Family Quiz Book — — 85p

FICTION

GENERAL

☐ Stand on It	Stroker Ace	95p
☐ Chains	Justin Adams	£1.25
☐ The Master Mechanic	I. G. Broat	£1.50
☐ Wyndward Passion	Norman Daniels	£1.35
☐ Abingdon's	Michael French	£1.25
☐ The Moviola Man	Bill and Colleen Mahan	£1.25
☐ Running Scared	Gregory Mcdonald	85p
☐ Gossip	Marc Olden	£1.25
☐ The Sounds of Silence	Judith Richards	£1.00
☐ Summer Lightning	Judith Richards	£1.00
☐ The Hamptons	Charles Rigdon	£1.35
☐ The Affair of Nina B.	Simmel	95p
☐ The Berlin Connection	Simmel	£1.50
☐ The Cain Conspiracy	Simmel	£1.20
☐ Double Agent—Triple Cross	Simmel	£1.35
☐ Celestial Navigation	Anne Tyler	£1.00
☐ Earthly Possessions	Anne Tyler	95p
☐ Searching for Caleb	Anne Tyler	£1.00

WESTERN BLADE SERIES

☐ No. 1 The Indian Incident	Matt Chisholm	75p
☐ No. 2 The Tucson Conspiracy	Matt Chisholm	75p
☐ No. 3 The Laredo Assignment	Matt Chisholm	75p
☐ No. 4 The Pecos Manhunt	Matt Chisholm	75p
☐ No. 5 The Colorado Virgins	Matt Chisholm	85p
☐ No. 6 The Mexican Proposition	Matt Chisholm	75p
☐ No. 7 The Arizona Climax	Matt Chisholm	85p
☐ No. 8 The Nevada Mustang	Matt Chisholm	85p

WAR

☐ Jenny's War	Jack Stoneley	£1.25
☐ The Killing-Ground	Elleston Trevor	£1.10

NAVAL HISTORICAL

☐ The Sea of the Dragon	R. T. Aundrews	95p
☐ Ty-Shan Bay	R. T. Aundrews	95p
☐ HMS Bounty	John Maxwell	£1.00
☐ The Baltic Convoy	Showell Styles	95p
☐ Mr. Fitton's Commission	Showell Styles	85p

FILM/TV TIE-IN

☐ American Gigolo	Timothy Harris	95p
☐ Meteor	E. H. North and F. Coen	95p
☐ Driver	Clyde B. Phillips	80p

SCIENCE FICTION

☐ The Mind Thing	Fredric Brown	90p
☐ Strangers	Gardner Dozois	95p
☐ Project Barrier	Daniel F. Galouye	80p
☐ Beyond the Barrier	Damon Knight	80p
☐ Clash by Night	Henry Kuttner	95p
☐ Fury	Henry Kuttner	80p
☐ Mutant	Henry Kuttner	90p
☐ Drinking Sapphire Wine	Tanith Lee	£1.25
☐ Journey	Marta Randall	£1.00
☐ The Lion Game	James H. Schmitz	70p
☐ The Seed of Earth	Robert Silverberg	80p
☐ The Silent Invaders	Robert Silverberg	80p
☐ City of the Sun	Brian M. Stableford	85p
☐ Critical Threshold	Brian M. Stableford	75p
☐ The Florians	Brian M. Stableford	80p
☐ Wildeblood's Empire	Brian M. Stableford	80p
☐ A Touch of Strange	Theodore Sturgeon	85p

NON-FICTION

GENERAL COOKERY
☐ The Best of Dial-a-Recipe   Audrey Ellis   80p
☐ Hints for Modern Cooks   Audrey Ellis   £1.00
☐ Comprehensive Guide to Deep Freezing   50p
☐ Cooking For Your Freezer   80p
☐ Home Made Country Wines   50p
☐ Salads the Year Round   Joy Larkcom   £1.25

KITCHEN LIBRARY SERIES
☐ Know Your Onions   Kate Hastrop   95p
☐ Home Preserving and Bottling   Gladys Mann   80p
☐ Home Baked Breads and Cakes   Mary Norwak   75p
☐ Easy Icing   Marguerite Patten   85p
☐ Wine Making At Home   Francis Pinnegar   80p
☐ Mixer and Blender Cookbook   Myra Street   80p
☐ Pasta Cookbook   Myra Street   75p
☐ The Hamlyn Pressure Cookbook   Jane Todd   85p

GARDENING/HOBBIES
☐ Restoring Old Junk   Michèle Brown   75p
☐ A Vegetable Plot for Two–or More   D. B. Clay Jones   £1.00
☐ The Sunday Telegraph Patio Gardening
    Book   Robert Pearson   80p
☐ 'Jock' Davidson's House Plant Book   £1.25

NAME ....

ADDRESS...

....

Write to Hamlyn Paperbacks Cash Sales, PO Box 11, Falmouth, Cornwall TR10 9EN.

Please indicate order and enclose remittance to the value of the cover price plus:

U.K.: 30p for the first book, 15p for the second book and 12p for each additional book ordered to a maximum charge of £1.29.

B.F.P.O. & EIRE: 30p for the first book, 15p for the second book plus 12p per copy for the next 7 books, thereafter 6p per book.

OVERSEAS: 50p for the first book plus 15p per copy for each additional book.

Whilst every effort is made to keep prices low it is sometimes necessary to increase cover prices and also postage and packing rates at short notice. Hamlyn Paperbacks reserve the right to show new retail prices on covers which may differ from those previously advertised in the text or elsewhere.